Machine Learning and Data Analytics for Cyber Security

Machine Learning and Data Analytics for Cyber Security

Collection Editors

Phil Legg
Giorgio Giacinto

 Basel • Beijing • Wuhan • Barcelona • Belgrade • Novi Sad • Cluj • Manchester

Collection Editors

Phil Legg
School of Computing and
Creative Technologies
University of the West of England
Bristol
United Kingdom

Giorgio Giacinto
Department of Electrical and
Electronic Engineering
University of Cagliari
Cagliari
Italy

Editorial Office
MDPI AG
Grosspeteranlage 5
4052 Basel, Switzerland

This is a reprint of the Topical Collection, published open access by the journal *Journal of Cybersecurity and Privacy* (ISSN 2624-800X), freely accessible at: https://www.mdpi.com/journal/jcp/topical_collections/MachineLearning_Cybersecurity.

For citation purposes, cite each article independently as indicated on the article page online and as indicated below:

Lastname, A.A.; Lastname, B.B. Article Title. *Journal Name* **Year**, *Volume Number*, Page Range.

ISBN 978-3-7258-3359-7 (Hbk)
ISBN 978-3-7258-3360-3 (PDF)
https://doi.org/10.3390/books978-3-7258-3360-3

Contents

About the Editors vii

Preface ix

Mohamed Ali Kazi
Detecting Malware C&C Communication Traffic Using Artificial Intelligence Techniques
Reprinted from: *J. Cybersecur. Priv.* **2025**, 5, 4, https://doi.org/10.3390/jcp5010004 1

Filippo Sobrero, Beatrice Clavarezza, Daniele Ucci and Federica Bisio
Towards a Near-Real-Time Protocol Tunneling Detector Based on Machine Learning Techniques
Reprinted from: *J. Cybersecur. Priv.* **2023**, 3, 35, https://doi.org/10.3390/jcp3040035 32

Andey Robins, Stone Olguin, Jarek Brown, Clay Carper and Mike Borowczak
Power-Based Side-Channel Attacks on Program Control Flow with Machine Learning Models
Reprinted from: *J. Cybersecur. Priv.* **2023**, 3, 18, https://doi.org/10.3390/jcp3030018 46

Raghvinder S Sangwan, Youakim Badr and Satish M Srinivasan
Cybersecurity for AI Systems: A Survey
Reprinted from: *J. Cybersecur. Priv.* **2023**, 3, 10, https://doi.org/10.3390/jcp3020010 59

Laurens D'hooge, Miel Verkerken, Tim Wauters, Filip De Turck, Bruno Volckaert
Characterizing the Impact of Data-Damaged Models on Generalization Strength in Intrusion
Detection
Reprinted from: *J. Cybersecur. Priv.* **2023**, 3, 8, https://doi.org/10.3390/jcp3020008 84

Shadi Sadeghpour and Natalija Vlajic
ReMouse Dataset: On the Efficacy of Measuring the Similarity of Human-Generated Trajectories
for the Detection of Session-Replay Bots
Reprinted from: *J. Cybersecur. Priv.* **2023**, 3, 7, https://doi.org/10.3390/jcp3010007 111

Maha Alghawazi, Daniyal Alghazzawi and Suaad Alarifi
Detection of SQL Injection Attack Using Machine Learning Techniques: A Systematic Literature
Review
Reprinted from: *J. Cybersecur. Priv.* **2022**, 2, 39, https://doi.org/10.3390/jcp2040039 134

A M Mahmud Chowdhury and Masudul Haider Imtiaz
Contactless Fingerprint Recognition Using Deep Learning—A Systematic Review
Reprinted from: *J. Cybersecur. Priv.* **2022**, 2, 36, https://doi.org/10.3390/jcp2030036 148

Griffith Russell McRee
Improved Detection and Response via Optimized Alerts: Usability Study
Reprinted from: *J. Cybersecur. Priv.* **2022**, 2, 20, https://doi.org/10.3390/jcp2020020 165

Emmanuel Aboah Boateng and J. W. Bruce
Unsupervised Machine Learning Techniques for Detecting PLC Process Control Anomalies
Reprinted from: *J. Cybersecur. Priv.* **2022**, 2, 12, https://doi.org/10.3390/jcp2020012 188

Laura Genga, Luca Allodi and Nicola Zannone
Association Rule Mining Meets Regression Analysis: An Automated Approach to Unveil
Systematic Biases in Decision-Making Processes
Reprinted from: *J. Cybersecur. Priv.* **2022**, 2, 11, https://doi.org/10.3390/jcp2010011 213

Andrew McCarthy, Essam Ghadafi, Panagiotis Andriotis and Phil Legg
Functionality-Preserving Adversarial Machine Learning for Robust Classification in Cybersecurity and Intrusion Detection Domains: A Survey
Reprinted from: *J. Cybersecur. Priv.* **2022**, *2*, 10, https://doi.org/10.3390/jcp2010010 . . . . **242**

Maryam Taeb and Hongmei Chi
Comparison of Deepfake Detection Techniques through Deep Learning
Reprinted from: *J. Cybersecur. Priv.* **2022**, *2*, 7, https://doi.org/10.3390/jcp2010007 . . . . **279**

Kimia Ameri, Michael Hempel, Hamid Sharif, Juan Lopez Jr. and Kalyan Perumalla
CyBERT: Cybersecurity Claim Classification by Fine-Tuning the BERT Language Model
Reprinted from: *J. Cybersecur. Priv.* **2021**, *1*, 31, https://doi.org/10.3390/jcp1040031 . . . . **297**

Pooria Madani and Natalija Vlajic
RSSI-Based MAC-Layer Spoofing Detection: Deep Learning Approach
Reprinted from: *J. Cybersecur. Priv.* **2022**, *1*, 23, https://doi.org/10.3390/jcp1030023 . . . . **320**

Paul M. Simon, Scott Graham, Christopher Talbot and Micah Hayden
Model for Quantifying the Quality of Secure Service
Reprinted from: *J. Cybersecur. Priv.* **2021**, *1*, 16, https://doi.org/10.3390/jcp1020016 . . . . **337**

About the Editors

Phil Legg

Phil Legg is a Professor of Cyber Security at the University of the West of England (UWE Bristol), UK. His research interests span across cyber security, machine learning, visualization, and human–computer interactions to better understand the detection and mitigation of security threats. He has led various research activities related to cyber security, including insider threat detection, adversarial attacks on ML systems, software security testing, and privacy-based learning, supported by DSTL, NCSC, UKRI, CCAV, CPNI, along with industry and academic collaborators. He has published over 60 academic journal and conference papers across his research interests, with successful research funding of over GBP 2.2M. He is Co-Director of the NCSC-supported Academic Centre of Excellence in Cyber Security Education, and the Cyber Security research theme lead within the Computer Science Research Centre, with previous roles including Programme Leader of the NCSC-certified MSc Cyber Security at UWE. Before joining UWE in 2015, his previous academic posts were held at the University of Oxford, Swansea University, and Cardiff University. He holds a Ph.D. in computer science (2010) and a B.Sc. in computer science (2006), both from Cardiff University, Wales, UK.

Giorgio Giacinto

Giorgio Giacinto is a Full Professor of Computer Engineering at the University of Cagliari, Italy, and a Guest Professor at Luleå University of Technology, Sweden. He is the Co-Director of the cybersecurity research area within the sAIfer Lab, a joint initiative between the University of Genoa and the University of Cagliari. In 1995, he joined the Pattern Recognition and Applications Lab at the Dept. of Electrical and Electronic Engineering, University of Cagliari, Italy; in 2000, he was appointed a permanent faculty position as an Assistant Professor from 2000 to 2004, and as an Associate Professor from 2005 to 2017. He obtained a Ph.D. in information engineering in 1999 from the University of Salerno, Italy.

Preface

Cyber security is primarily concerned with the protection of digital systems and their respective data. Therefore, how we analyze and monitor such systems are continual challenges that require innovation to keep pace with the modern technological world and ensure that systems are continually protected. Machine learning, as a form of artificial intelligence and data analysis, has been utilized in various ways within the field of cyber security, due to its ability to process and analyze vast volumes of information, therefore creating actionable intelligence for security analysts. This Topical Collection on "Machine Learning and Data Analytics for Cyber Security" invited papers that address the topics of machine learning and data analytics, as well as their applications in emerging challenges in cyber security. We are pleased to have welcomed a range of papers since the Collection first began in 2021, covering topics such as large language models for cybersecurity claim classification, adversarial machine learning attacks against intrusion detection systems, the detection of PLC process control anomalies, identifying session-replay bots compared to human users, and mitigating against side-channel attacks. In this Special Issue, we present 16 papers that have been published in the Topical Collection between 2021 and 2025.

Phil Legg and Giorgio Giacinto
Collection Editors

Journal of
Cybersecurity and Privacy

Article

Detecting Malware C&C Communication Traffic Using Artificial Intelligence Techniques

Mohamed Ali Kazi

Department of Computer Science, School of Computing and Communications, Faculty of Science, Technology, Engineering & Mathematics, The Open University, Walton Hall, Milton Keynes MK7 6AA, UK; m.a.kazi@open.ac.uk

Abstract: Banking malware poses a significant threat to users by infecting their computers and then attempting to perform malicious activities such as surreptitiously stealing confidential information from them. Banking malware variants are also continuing to evolve and have been increasing in numbers for many years. Amongst these, the banking malware Zeus and its variants are the most prevalent and widespread banking malware variants discovered. This prevalence was expedited by the fact that the Zeus source code was inadvertently released to the public in 2004, allowing malware developers to reproduce the Zeus banking malware and develop variants of this malware. Examples of these include Ramnit, Citadel, and Zeus Panda. Tools such as anti-malware programs do exist and are able to detect banking malware variants, however, they have limitations. Their reliance on regular updates to incorporate new malware signatures or patterns means that they can only identify known banking malware variants. This constraint inherently restricts their capability to detect novel, previously unseen malware variants. Adding to this challenge is the growing ingenuity of malicious actors who craft malware specifically developed to bypass signature-based anti-malware systems. This paper presents an overview of the Zeus, Zeus Panda, and Ramnit banking malware variants and discusses their communication architecture. Subsequently, a methodology is proposed for detecting banking malware C&C communication traffic, and this methodology is tested using several feature selection algorithms to determine which feature selection algorithm performs the best. These feature selection algorithms are also compared with a manual feature selection approach to determine whether a manual, automated, or hybrid feature selection approach would be more suitable for this type of problem.

Keywords: banking malware; Zeus malware variants; machine learning; binary classification algorithms; automated feature selection; manual feature selection

Academic Editors: Phil Legg and Giorgio Giacinto

Received: 26 November 2024
Revised: 10 January 2025
Accepted: 14 January 2025
Published: 18 January 2025

Citation: Kazi, M.A. Detecting Malware C&C Communication Traffic Using Artificial Intelligence Techniques. *J. Cybersecur. Priv.* **2025**, *5*, 4. https://doi.org/10.3390/jcp5010004

1. Introduction

Cybercrime poses a serious danger to cybersecurity [1], and according to [2], the cost of cybercrime reached USD 8 trillion in 2023, with malware such as banking malware accounting for a large proportion of this total cost. In recent years, banking malware has emerged as a major concern, because malicious actors can make huge profits from these types of malware variants [3], and the cost to businesses is high. For instance, Emotet banking malware infections can cost up to USD 1 million per incident to remediate [4]. Banking malware attacks are continuing to rise [5], and the discovery of new banking malware variants is also continuing to increase. For example, over a thousand variants of the banking malware Godfather were discovered in 2023 alone [6].

The Zeus banking malware has emerged as one of the most notorious banking malware variants ever developed [7], and since the release of the Zeus source code, many additional variants of Zeus have been developed and have emerged, including Ramnit, Zeus Panda, and Ramnit [8].

1.1. Need for Detecting Banking Malware

New malware variants are always being discovered and are becoming more sophisticated in the way that they attack systems [9], and they will continue to increase [10]. Banking malware follows the same trajectory, and, in this category, Zeus and its variants are still the most prevalent and widespread of all the banking malware variants discovered. For example, Figure 1 shows that Zeus and Ramnit were amongst the top ten banking malware variants discovered in Q3 of 2022 [11]. Figure 2 depicts the number of banking malware attacks that were detected during the same time, and an upward trend is clearly visible [11].

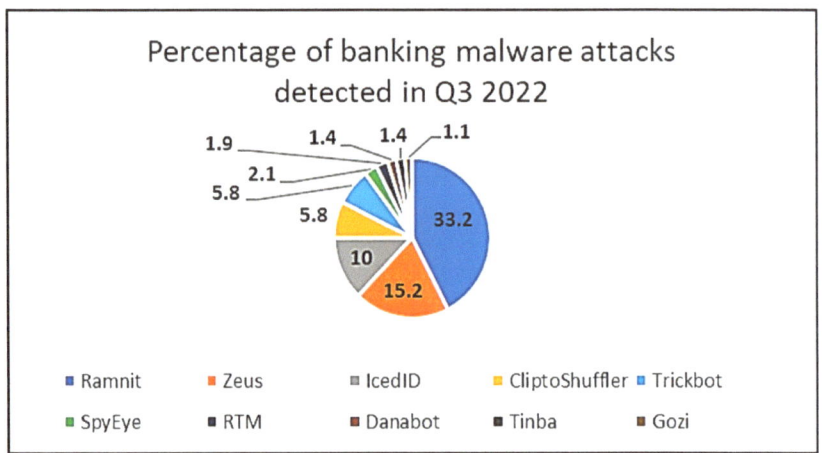

Figure 1. Top ten malware discovered in Q3 of 2022. This is the proportion of distinct users who experienced this malware family relative to the total number of users targeted by financial malware.

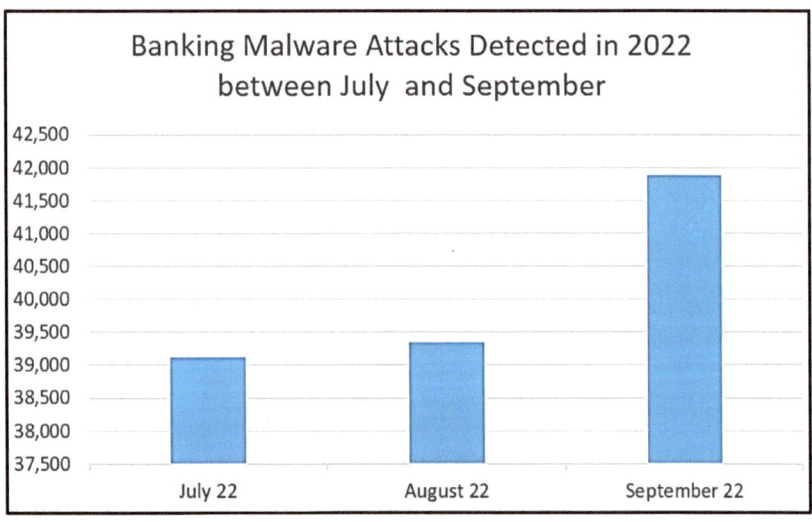

Figure 2. Banking malware attacks detected in Q3 of 2022.

Banking malware have also diversified their tactics, expanded their capabilities, and, over time, evolved into more sophisticated software tools that leverage several attack vectors to cause financial loss. The fact that threat actors can use Malware-as-a-service (MaaS) providers to target victims has also led to their increased prevalence, and some of these MaaS providers can charge up to USD 4000 per month for their services [12].

Many strategies exist to detect banking malware, and these include signature-based, anomaly-based, behavior-based, and heuristic-based approaches [13], but these do have limitations [14]. These approaches and limitations are explored further over the next few sections, however, some of these limitations include the following:

- The need to update signature-based malware systems.
- The inability of these systems to detect newer malware variants.
- The inability to detect malware that uses sophisticated obfuscation techniques.
- The inability to detect zero-day malware.

This research paper is broken down into the following sections. Firstly, a review is conducted of the Zeus, Zeus Panda, and Ramnit banking malware variants and then a banking malware family tree is proposed. The purpose of this review is to understand the similarities and differences between these various banking malware variants. Next, a literature review of related research is provided, followed by a problem statement. Finally, this paper proposes a machine learning approach for detecting banking malware and also proposes a feature section approach that supports the proposed machine learning approach.

1.2. Paper Contribution and Rational

The main objectives of this paper are to develop a methodology and approach for detecting several banking malware variants' Command and Control (C&C) communication network traffic and to distinguish this from benign network traffic using binary classification machine learning (ML) algorithms. For this research, machine learning algorithms are used rather than deep learning algorithms or neural networks. The rationale for this is that, firstly, machine learning algorithms are preferred for smaller datasets. This is because machine learning algorithms can perform well even with limited data. Deep learning algorithms require large amounts of data to perform effectively and have many parameters that need to be tuned. Machine learning algorithms also require fewer computational resources and can be deployed quickly, which could help to identify malware more rapidly and effectively [15,16]. Ref. [17] also conducted extensive research in this area and compared several binary classification and deep learning algorithms, using these to detect banking malware C&C communication traffic. The paper demonstrated that machine learning algorithms are more than capable of detecting banking malware, and in fact, in many cases, machine learning algorithms performed much better than deep learning algorithms. The authors also discovered that developing and tuning deep learning algorithms can be complex, time consuming, and increases the training time.

Many other researchers have used machine learning algorithms in their research, and some of these are discussed in Section 2. It is clear from these research findings that machine learning algorithms are effective at detecting many different types of malware variants, including several banking malware variants.

Three ML algorithms and an ensemble approach are all examined, analyzed, and compared in this paper, and these include the decision tree (DT), random forest (RF), and K-Nearest Neighbors (KNN) ML algorithms. The ensemble approach combines all three of the above algorithms, and the rationale for selecting these three algorithms is that, in [17], many common machine learning algorithms were tested, and it was determined that the random forest, decision tree, and KNN machine learning algorithms performed the best when used for detecting malware C&C communication traffic. Ref. [17] also demonstrated that these ML algorithms performed better than or similar to several deep learning approaches. Ref. [18] also concluded in their research that, out of over 179 ML algorithms tested, the KNN, SVM, random forest, and decision tree algorithms performed the best.

This paper aims to develop a machine learning approach that will detect the Zeus banking malware and its variants. It will then test and compare the detection results of several binary ML classification algorithms to determine which one provides the best detection results when used to detect the Zeus banking malware's C&C communication traffic. It will also examine, test, and compare the detection results of other banking malware C&C communication traffic to understand whether the methodology proposed in this paper works. This research also identifies the minimal number of features that could be used to identify these banking malware variants. This paper aims to achieve the following:

- From all the ML algorithms being analyzed, identify which one performs the best.
- Establish whether the features used to detect the Zeus banking malware can also be used to detect the other banking malware variants.
- Determine a minimum set of features that could be used for detecting Zeus.
- Determine a minimum set of features that could be used for detecting other variants of the Zeus malware.
- Compare the performance results of all the ML algorithms.
- Compare the classification results with other research examined in Section 2.

1.3. Overview of the Zeus Banking Malware

Zeus, also known as Zbot, is a notorious banking malware designed to steal financial information such as online banking credentials through methods like keylogging, screen capturing, and the real-time manipulation of web sessions (man-in-the-browser attacks). It spreads via phishing emails, malicious downloads, and software vulnerabilities. Once installed, Zeus establishes persistence, evades detection using rootkits and encrypted communication, and connects to a remote Command and Control (C&C) server to send stolen data and receive instructions [19]. Known for its modular architecture, Zeus can be customized for specific targets and often forms botnets for large-scale cybercrime operations. Its source code leak in 2011 led to numerous variants, making it one of the most impactful and studied banking malware families in cybersecurity history.

Once the Zeus malware gets onto a device, it needs to perform several actions to infect the device. The Zeus bot inserts malicious code into the winlogin.exe process after copying itself to the system 32 directory, and this is achieved by escalating its privileges and manipulating the winlogin.exe and svchost processes. Two files are created, local.ds, which is used to download the configuration file, and user.ds, which is used to transmit stolen data back to the threat actors' C&C servers. The additional code injected into the svchost process is used by the Zeus bot for communication purposes, and Zeus communicates using a Command and Control (C&C) channel which can either use a centralized or P2P architecture. In the centralized architecture, the IP address of the C&C server is hardcoded into the bot's binary file, which leaves the bot vulnerable, because if the C&C channel is discovered and blocked, the Zeus bot becomes inactive and is unable to recover [20]. Modern-day variants of the Zeus malware use a P2P architecture, as this is more resilient to disconnections and is much harder to detect and block [21]. One reason is simply because the IP address is not hardcoded into the bot binary and because, in the P2P network, multiple bots can act as C&C servers. This architecture also allows stolen data to be routed through the bot network via these intermediary C&C bots and, crucially, allows bots to recover from failures [22]. This recovery is possible, because each peer C&C bot can essentially provide support to a failed bot, for example, by sending the failed bot an updated IP address to help it resume malicious communications.

1.4. Overview of the Zeus Panda Banking Malware

Zeus Panda, a variant of the original Zeus malware, is a sophisticated banking malware designed to steal sensitive financial data through techniques such as keylogging, web form data theft, and man-in-the-browser (MITB) attacks. It primarily propagates via phishing emails, malicious attachments, and compromised websites, often targeting financial institutions and systems in specific regions [19]. Panda communicates with remote Command and Control (C&C) servers to exfiltrate data and receive instructions, using encrypted communication and Domain Generation Algorithms (DGAs) for resilience. Its modular design allows it to adapt to various targets, and it employs advanced evasion techniques like anti-debugging and polymorphism to avoid detection, making it a significant threat in the cybersecurity landscape.

The Zeus Panda banking malware portrays similar characteristics to the Zeus banking malware. Research shows that it infects devices using spam emails and exploit kits, and it has been known to spread like a virus [19]. Zeus Panda's communication architecture is similar to the Zeus banking malware architecture, and its communication is generally encrypted using RC4 or AES [19]. Zeus Panda's authors have also enhanced the code to allow it to detect and evade security protection tools such as anti-virus software and firewalls [23]. Zeus Panda is intelligent enough to detect that it is running in a virtual environment, and upon sensing such an environment, it can disable itself to ensure that researchers are unable to detect communication patterns [23]. The Zeus Panda malware is difficult to detect and can persist on a device for a long time, and researchers have concluded that Zeus Panda is a sophisticated variant of the Zeus malware [23].

1.5. Overview of the Ramnit Banking Malware

Ramnit is a versatile and persistent malware that evolved from a worm in 2010 into a sophisticated banking Trojan targeting financial institutions and sensitive data. It spreads through phishing emails, malicious attachments, exploit kits, and infected files, using techniques like man-in-the-browser (MITB) attacks and web injections to steal online banking credentials and other personal information. Ramnit communicates with Command and Control (C&C) servers via encrypted channels, enabling data exfiltration and command execution. Its modular architecture allows for adaptability, while advanced evasion techniques, such as polymorphism and rootkits, make it difficult to detect. Despite law enforcement disruptions, Ramnit has resurfaced over the years with enhanced capabilities, posing a significant threat to global cybersecurity.

Ramnit is an enhanced version of the Zeus malware and incorporates code from the Zeus banking malware [24]. The C&C communication channel is encrypted, and this is usually achieved using custom encryption techniques [25]. Ramnit can also use HTTPS to obfuscate the communication channel and hide any data that are transmitted between systems. Ramnit is sophisticated enough to detect and evade security tools, and once it infects a device, it can persist on the device for a long time [25]. Ramnit can also use evasion techniques to avoid detection, and some of these include the use of anti-debugging techniques, polymorphism, and encryption [26].

1.6. Banking Malware Communication (C&C) Architecture

Zeus, Zeus Panda, and Ramnit are all sophisticated malware families targeting financial institutions, employing similar techniques like phishing-based propagation, Command and Control (C&C) communication, a modular architecture, and advanced evasion methods such as polymorphism and MITB attacks to steal banking credentials and personal data. While Zeus is the foundational banking Trojan known for its widespread botnet use, Zeus Panda enhances targeting with tailored regional attacks and advanced MITB capabilities. Ramnit, evolving from a worm, extends its reach with broader infection methods, including USB and executable file propagation, exhibiting a stronger persistence through polymorphic techniques and rootkit functionality. Despite their similarities, each malware family has unique traits that make it distinct in its evolution and attack strategies.

Banking malware use C&C communication channels to communicate between the infected device and malicious entity, and the focus of this study is to identify these communication patterns. Once a device becomes infected, outgoing communication is hard to detect, as it can very easily obfuscate itself with the normal traffic flows of the network, thus making the malware hard to detect.

Banking malware variants are made up of bots that communicate with the C&C server and, initially, these communication channels are centralized, because each bot will communicate with the C&C server directly. These bots are also controlled directly by the C&C server, and this architecture uses a push model for communication purposes. Instructions and malicious commands are all pushed from the C&C server to the bot [27]. The C&C channel always remains active in the 'connect mode', as the bot needs to be ready to receive commands [27]. This communication uses the HTTP/HTTPS protocol and can also use other protocols such as DNS tunneling, which makes the malware more difficult to detect. The bots also reach out to the C&C server at predefined intervals, and this ensures that the C&C server maintains communication with these bots. The centralized C&C architecture has limitations, and the key one is that, if the C&C server becomes inactive, all the bots fail, and the bot network becomes inactive.

The centralized architecture evolved into a peer to peer (P2P) architecture in which the bots build a decentralized network of bots. This means that the bots can receive commands from other bots, and there is no longer a reliance on a centralized C&C server. This P2P network is more difficult to detect and take down [28], and makes the botnet more resilient. If a bot in a botnet loses communication, it can automatically try other bots or domains to resume communication. Also, this bot failure does not affect the botnet, as the botnet remains active and other bots are still able to communicate with each other. There are some weaknesses inherent in this type of network, and one of them is that updates can take longer to propagate across the network, as these updates have to be routed through many other bots. Also, stolen data that need to be routed back to the malicious attacker can also face similar challenges.

Machine learning (ML) is critical for detecting the C&C communicating traffic used by malware due to its ability to overcome the limitations of traditional detection methods. Unlike signature-based approaches, which struggle in detecting zero-day malware, polymorphic threats, or encrypted traffic, ML focuses on patterns, behaviors, and anomalies in network communications. By analyzing network features such as packet sizes, traffic flow, and timing intervals, ML models can identify malicious communications even when the data are obfuscated. Furthermore, machine learning enables real-time detection capabilities and can efficiently scale to handle vast amounts of network traffic. It can also adapt to evolving threats, as ML models can be retrained on new data. It is particularly effective against decentralized P2P C&C architectures, like the Zeus banking malware, as it can model peer relationships and detect botnet traffic. Supervised algorithms such as random forest and unsupervised methods like clustering can help to optimize feature selection, improving detection accuracy while reducing computational overhead. By leveraging behavioral analysis, ML provides a robust and dynamic solution for identifying and mitigating sophisticated malware C&C activities.

1.7. Proposed Banking Malware Tree

This section examines and discusses the relationships between the three banking malware variants that were discussed above and establishes a timescale of when they emerged. Figure 3 shows that Zeus was discovered in 2006 [29], Ramnit was discovered in 2010, and Zeus Panda was discovered in 2016 [30], and research indicates that they all share similar code and perform similar actions. Based on this research [30–36], this paper proposes that all banking malware variants belong to a specific family of banking malware, and this proposed family tree can be seen in Figure 4. A historical timeline of a selection of banking malware variants can be seen in Figure 3, which suggests that all banking malware variants can be traced back to one of the parent banking malware variants, Zeus, Snifula, and Gozi, as shown in Figure 4.

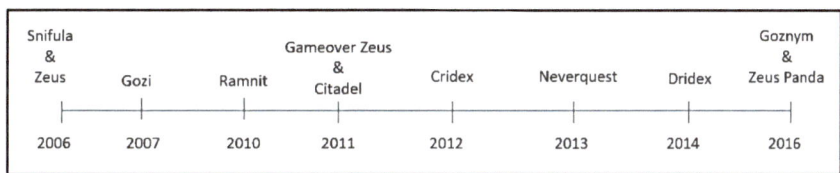

Figure 3. Banking malware timeline.

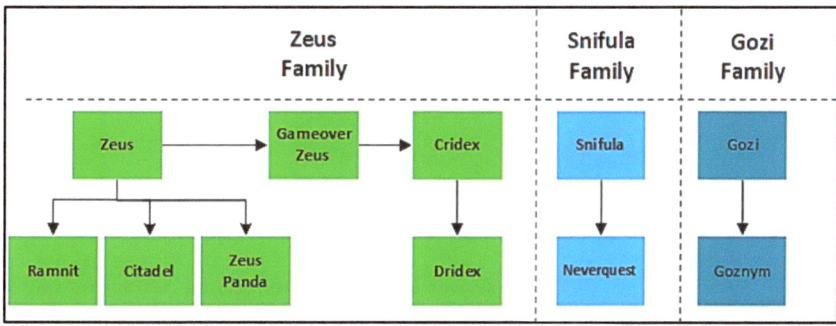

Figure 4. Banking malware tree.

The key conclusions from this research reveal that most banking malware variants belong to one of the three primary families identified in Figure 4. These variants frequently borrow code from one another, with newer malware still sharing similarities in code and behavior with those outlined in Figure 4. Despite these overlaps, banking malware continues to evolve, becoming increasingly sophisticated and more effective at targeting victims.

The rest of the paper is organized as follows: Section 2 discusses some of the key research that has been conducted in this field. In Section 3, a problem statement is presented. Section 4 proposes a framework to detect the banking malware variants discussed in Sections 1.2–1.4, Section 5 analyzes and compares the research findings, and Section 6 concludes with a summary and conclusion.

2. Related Studies

Malware detection approaches can be categorized using several methods. However, the method discussed by [37] is used in this paper, which is that malware detection can either be signature-based, heuristic-based, or behavioral-based. Also, malware detection tools can either be host-based or network-based [38], and this research examines a network-based approach, as it focuses on C&C network communication traffic.

The authors in [39] used the SVM machine learning algorithm to develop an intrusion detection system which uses the NSL-KDD dataset to classify network traffic. To select appropriate features, ref. [39] used a hybrid feature selection approach which ranks features using a feature selection approach called Information Gain Ratio (IGR) and then refined this further by using the k-means classifier. They achieved an accuracy of 99.32 and 99.37 when used with 23 and 30 features.

A simple yet effective method was developed by [40], which involved extracting statical features called 'function call frequency' and 'opcode frequency' from Windows PE files. These features were extracted from both the executable files' header and from the executables' payload, and the features were extracted from a total of 1230 executable files. The dataset contained 800 malware and 430 non-malware executable files, and the experimental work was conducted using a tool called WEKA. Several classifiers were experimented with, and the results of these experiments can be seen in Table 1.

Table 1. Test results from [40] when using the SVM ML algorithm.

Classifier	FP	FN	Accuracy
Kstar	0.275	0.026	88.69
J48	0.156	0.026	92.84
DT	0.14	0.031	97.47

Research was carried out by [41], who used an unsupervised machine learning algorithm to detect botnet communication traffic. They used datasets obtained from the University of Georgia which contained botnet traffic from both the Zeus and Waledac malware variants. Features were extracted from the dataset by using a tool called Netmate, which extracts traffic as flows and then analyzes each flow to calculate their statistical features. The datasets were analyzed using WEKA and all the experimental analyses were also conducted using this tool. The experimental results can be seen in Table 2.

Table 2. Test results from [41] when using an unsupervised ML algorithm.

Malware Variant	FP	TN	FP	FN	Accuracy
Zeus 1	14,678	4352	969	1	0.9515
Zeus 2	14,663	4341	991	5	0.9502
Waledac 1	14,536	4500	963	1	0.9518
Waledac 2	14,521	4525	963	1	0.9523
Storm 1	10,139	4499	501	1386	0.8858
Storm 2	2300	503	247	3	0.9181

BotOnus is a tool developed by [42] which can extract a set of flow specific features and then, by using an online fixed-width clustering algorithm, can arrange these features into unique clusters. These clusters are examined and analyzed for suspicious behaviors. Suspicious botnet clusters are defined as flow clusters that have at least two members that have been identified as potentially suspicious. This is determined using an intra-cluster similarity score which is set to a predefined threshold. BotOnus is an online detection technique that makes use of unsupervised machine learning algorithms and can identify unknown botnets. Table 3 shows the experimental results obtained by BotOnus.

RCC Detector (RCC3) is a tool developed by [43] that uses a multi-layer perceptron (MLP) and a temporal persistence (TP) classifier to analyze the traffic flows from a host, and the aim is to identify malware communication traffic. The botnet detection system was trained and tested using the DETER testbed and two datasets were used, the DARPA and LBNL datasets. The authors aimed to predict Zeus, Blackenergy, and normal traffic, and the key to this paper was that RCC examined traffic generated from a host. The tool achieved a detection rate of 97.7%.

Table 3. Test results from [42] when using an unsupervised ML algorithm.

Botnet	Average Detection Rate	Average False Alarm Rate
HTTP-based	0.95	0.041
IRC-based	0.96	0.033
P2P-based	0.91	0.037

Classification of Network Information Flow Analysis (CONIFA) is a tool developed by [44] which was used to identify and detect the Zeus banking malware. For the experimental analysis, ref. [44] used a standard framework, a cost-sensitive, and a cost-insensitive version of the C4.5 machine learning algorithm. For the cost-sensitive experimental analysis, the following parameters were used.

- Lenient version with cost settings of 10, 20, and 30
- Strict version with a cost setting of 10, 20, and 30

Two Zeus datasets were used for training and testing, and these comprised 432 samples of the Zeus v1 malware and 144 samples of the Zeus v2 malware. The prediction results of the tests conducted using the standard framework can be seen in Table 4, and the test results of using the cost-sensitive and cost-insensitive versions of C4.5 can be seen in Table 5. Table 5 demonstrates an improvement in the recall score and shows that the cost-sensitive and cost-insensitive versions of C4.5 performed better than the standard framework at predicting the Zeus malware.

Table 4. Test results of using the standard framework.

Algorithm	Recall Score	Precision Score	F-Measure Score
Standard	0.556	0.964	0.705

Table 5. Test results of CONIFA using the cost-sensitive and -insensitive versions of C4.5.

Botnet	Recall Score	Precision Score	F-Measure Score
Lenient with cost 10	0.556	0.964	0.705
Lenient with cost 20	0.667	0676	0671
Lenient with cost 30	0.667	0.686	0.676
Strict with cost 10	0.667	0.952	0.787
Strict with cost 20	0.611	0.989	0.755
Strict with cost 30	0.611	0.989	0.755

Table 4 demonstrates that, when the standard framework was evaluated against the Zeus v2 dataset after being trained on the Zeus v1 dataset, the detection results decreased. About half of the Zeus flows were incorrectly identified, with a recall rate of approximately 56%. As seen in Table 5, CONIFA showed improvement during the same experiment, with the recall rate rising to almost 67%.

The authors in [45] used the Symbiotic Bod-Based (SBB) and C4.5 machine learning algorithms to create a framework for detecting malware communication traffic. Features were extracted from the communication (C&C) channels of various malware variants, which included the C&C communication traffic of the Zeus banking malware. The samples were obtained by generating C&C communication traffic to known malware domains. Additional malware samples were obtained from various sources, including NETRESEC and Zeustracker, and these were used in the experimental analysis. Table 6 shows the datasets that were used for the experimental analysis.

Table 6. Information about the datasets used by [45].

Dataset	Benign Samples Used for Training	Benign Samples Used for Testing	Malware Samples Used for Training	Benign Samples Used for Testing
Zeus-1	6099	6099	2614	2614
Zeus-2	611	611	262	262
Zeus (NETRESEC)	252	252	108	108,100
Zeus (Snort)	100	100	43	43
Conficker	28,951	28,951	12,386	12,416
Torpig	1864	1856	794	800

After the data were collected, a program called Softflowd was used to extract the features that were used during the experimental analysis. Two feature sets were used, and these are depicted in Figure 5.

Softflowd set.1 & 2	Softflowd set.2 only
Duration	Flag-A
Total number of packets (Pkts)	Flag-P
Total number of bytes (Byts)	Flag-R
Flows	Flag-S
Type of Service (TOS)	Flag-F
Bits per second (bps)	Flag-U
Packets per second (pps)	
Bytes per packet (Bpp)	

Figure 5. The two feature sets used by [45] during their experimental analysis.

The results obtained during the experimental analysis can be seen in Tables 7 and 8. Table 7 shows the classification results when the ML algorithms were trained and tested using the features in feature set 1 and 2. Table 8 shows the results obtained when the ML algorithms were trained and tested using the features in feature set 1 only. For brevity, only the results for the Zeus malware are shown. The results depicted in both Tables 7 and 8 show good prediction results across all the datasets. The highest true positive rate was achieved when the algorithms were trained and tested using the features from the Softflowd set.1 and 2 feature set, and was obtained by both the C4.5 and SBB machine learning algorithms. The true positive scores obtained were 99% and 98%, respectively. Table 8 shows that the highest true positive rate achieved was 100%, and this was achieved by the SBB machine learning algorithm.

Auto-mal is a product developed by [46] which analyzes binary codes and identifies a set of features that are used to identify malware such as the Zeus banking malware. These features are then used to automatically classify the malware samples into malware families, and this is performed by using several machine learning algorithms. These algorithms include the Support Vector Classification (SVM), logistic regression (RG), Classification Tree (CT), and K-Nearest Neighbor (KNN) machine learning algorithms. Auto-mal captures and categorizes network traffic by using information such as the IP address, port numbers, and protocol types, and during this experimental analysis, 1.980 Zeus malware samples were analyzed. The Zeus samples were split into two datasets, one of which was used for training and the other was used for testing. For testing, 979 samples of Zeus and 1000 normal samples were used, and the testing results showed that the SVM algorithm performed the best and was able to correctly identify 95% of the Zeus malware samples. The decision tree algorithm produced a high false negative result, and from this, ref. [46] concluded that the decision tree algorithm was limited in its usefulness.

Table 7. Classification results when used with Softflowd set.1 and 2.

Dataset and Algorithm	Benign TPR	Benign FPR	Malware TPR	Malware FPR
Zeus-1—C4.5	86	17	83	14
Zeus-2—C4.5	96	1	99	4
Zeus (NETRESEC)—C4.5	97	3	97	3
Zeus (Snort)—C4.5	98	12	88	2
Zeus-1—SBB	80	27	73	20
Zeus-2—SBB	96	1	99	4
Zeus (NETRESEC)—SBB	93	13	87	7
Zeus (Snort)—SBB	98	2	98	2

Table 8. Classification results when used with Softflowd set.2.

Dataset and Algorithm	Benign TPR	Benign FPR	Malware TPR	Malware FPR
Zeus-1—C4.5	90	16	84	10
Zeus-2—C4.5	97	3	97	3
Zeus (NETRESEC)—C4.5	97	6	94	3
Zeus (Snort)—C4.5	97	1	99	3
Zeus-1—SBB	73	18	82	27
Zeus-2—SBB	94	0	100	6
Zeus (NETRESEC)—SBB	87	7	93	13
Zeus (Snort)—SBB	100	0	100	0

An XAI-driven antivirus software was developed by [47], which essentially uses Explainable Artificial Intelligence (XAI) to create AI models. This XAI-driven antivirus software was designed to identify the Citadel banking malware, which is a variant of the Zeus banking malware. Ref. [47] highlights the limitations of traditional antivirus programs and argues that an AI-driven approach is more robust, accurate, and proactive in detecting new and evolving malware variants of the Citadel banking malware. XAI uses multiple Extreme Learning Models (mELMs) to detect the Citadel banking malware, and mELM is a morphological technique used for digital image processing. Ref. [47] adopted this in their software program to detect Citadel and concluded that mELM is a viable technique that can be used to detect malware. The software achieved an accuracy of 98% and was also quick at training and learning. One of the key characteristics of XAI is that the authors provided some insights into how the algorithm works, and these insights can help other researchers in their research projects.

The authors in [48] used a Convolutional Neural Network (CNN) to classify malware samples which included the banking malware variant Ramnit. The authors transformed the malware binary files into grayscale images, which then enabled the CNN to detect patterns that could be used to classify the malware. Ref. [48] built a CNN network which consisted of a convolutional layer, pooling layer, and fully connected layer. Features were generated by analyzing the executable files, and although many techniques exist to perform this, ref. [48] used the following methodology. First, 1600 unique opcodes were created, which then allowed [48] to use the opcode frequency as the discriminatory feature for the experimental work. To select the optimal number of features for the experimental work, ref. [48] used different dimensionality reduction techniques, which included the variance threshold approach, a single layer auto-encoder, and a three-layer stacked auto encoder.

The authors in [49] used both machine learning and deep learning algorithms to build several models to train, test, and classify malware. The machine learning algorithm used was the random forest algorithm, and three deep learning models were used. The three deep learning models were architected using two hidden layers (DNN-2L), four hidden layers (DNN-4L), and seven hidden layers (DNN-7L). Ref. [48] used several criteria to measure the performance of the algorithms and models used, and these included accuracy, recall (true positive rate (TPR)), true negative rate (TNR), and precision (positive predictive value (PPV)). The experimental analysis produced good results. The lowest score was a precision score of 87.97%, achieved by the DNN-7L model, and the highest score was achieved by the RF model, with a PPV/precision score of 100.

Fingerprinting Windows API system function calls is an approach developed by [49], in which the frequency of Windows API system function calls are captured and analyzed to identify malicious patterns. This approach also allows for various malware variants to be categorized based on their relationships. The relationship is determined by understanding and grouping common behaviors and patterns that are identified during the analysis stage. Around 65,000 malware samples were analyzed, and this was conducted using the Cuckoo Malware Sandbox, which allowed [49] to identify the name of the API calls being called and the number of times each API call was made. Ref. [49] used several machine learning algorithms to train and test samples, and these included KNN, logistic regression, and the decision tree ML algorithm. The detection results obtained were good, and for the Ramnit.gen!A malware, an accuracy of 79.495% was achieved, and for the Ramnit.gen!C malware, an accuracy of 95.473% was achieved.

Similar research was conducted by [50], who created a machine learning model that was able to classify and identify malware and also able to group malware variants based on their relationships. These included several variants of the banking malware Ramnit. Ref. [50] extracted features from the malware samples using an approach called static analysis. This approach enabled them to extract features without having to execute or run the malware executable. The authors claimed that this approach allowed them to achieve a better performance with a low computational risk. Using the static approach, features could be extracted from two files within the executable, the hex file or the byte code file. During their research, ref. [50] extracted the features from the byte code files. This was performed using the n-gram feature extraction approach, which analyzed the byte sequence or opcode patterns within the malware executable files and then represented these patterns as words, in this case using the hex format. Ref. [50] used the K-Nearest Neighbor, logistic regression, random forest, and XGboost machine learning algorithms to train, test, and classify the malware, and for the evaluation, accuracy and log-loss were used to measure the performance of the machine learning algorithms. Table 9 shows the classification results obtained when classifying the malware using the byte file features. Table 9 shows that the

XGBoost and decision tree ML algorithms performed the best, achieving an accuracy of 98.76 and 97.98, respectively.

Table 9. Experimental results of the algorithms when classified using byte file features.

Algorithm	Test Log-Loss (%)	Misclassification Rate	Accuracy
KNN	0.24	4.5	95.5
Logistic regression	0.528	12.32	77.68
Random forest	0.085	2.02	97.98
XGBoost	0.078	1.24	98.76

3. Problem Statement

The goal of this study is to develop a methodology and create a framework for predicting banking malware using machine learning approaches. Many malware detection approaches already exist and have been researched and used by researchers. Some of these include signature-based approaches [51,52] and anomaly-based detection approaches [53,54], however, these do have limitations [55]. Some of these limitations include the following.

- Signature-based systems are unable to detect zero-day malware or unknown malware variants.
- Signature-based systems must be updated frequently to accommodate newly emerging malware variants.
- Malware uses various obfuscation techniques to evade detection.
- There can be a time delay between discovering new malware and creating a signature to identify the malware.
- Signature databases can consume significant system resources and have a slow performance.
- Modern malware can dynamically change its structure (polymorphic malware) or rewrite its code (metamorphic malware) to avoid signature-based malware systems.
- As the malware landscape evolves, maintaining and updating the signature database becomes increasingly complex.
- Effective and continuous tuning is required to reduce false positives.
- The network has to be baselined, and normal communication traffic needs to be identified.
- Network traffic must be constantly monitored.
- Malware can hide within the normal traffic flows, making these malware types difficult to detect.

Machine learning has been used to resolve these issues, and while researchers have used machine learning algorithms to detect banking malware [35,44–47], there has been minimal research aimed at detecting a wide range of banking malware variants using a model trained exclusively on one dataset containing a single banking malware variant. This study seeks to address this gap by developing a machine learning model trained on a single dataset representing one variant of banking malware. The primary objectives of this research are as follows:

- Cross-Variant Detection: To apply the trained model to identify other banking malware variants and evaluate its generalizability.
- Algorithm Performance Evaluation: To compare the detection performances of various machine learning algorithms in this context.

- Feature Optimization: To determine the minimum set of features required to achieve satisfactory prediction results, thereby optimizing computational efficiency and simplifying the detection process.

This approach aims to advance the understanding of cross-variant malware detection and provide insights into the effectiveness of machine learning algorithms and feature selection when used to detect diverse banking malware threats.

4. Research Methodology

This research paper aims to classify C&C network traffic flows as belonging to Zeus, which indicates that the C&C network traffic is malicious. The high-level activities include the following steps:

- Obtain pcap samples of the Zeus banking malware and benign traffic.
- Extract features from the pcap samples.
- Train and test the algorithms with the data.
- Compare and discuss the results.

Bot samples are collected as pcap files, and these pcap files are made up of network flows. A flow is defined as a sequence of packets flowing between a source and a destination host. Each flow is referred to as an ML sample, and the features are extracted from these samples. For this research, supervised ML algorithms are chosen, as these algorithms are well-suited for solving predication and classification problems such as the one being researched in this paper [56]. This paper analyzes three supervised ML algorithms, which are the decision tree (DT), random forest (RF) and K-Nearest Neighbor (KNN) ML algorithms, and examines an ensemble approach. The approach and methodology are explained in the next few sections.

4.1. Machine Learning Algorithms

Artificial intelligence (AI) is made up of several fields, which include deep learning, neural networks, and machine learning. Figure 6 depicts the various fields of AI [57].

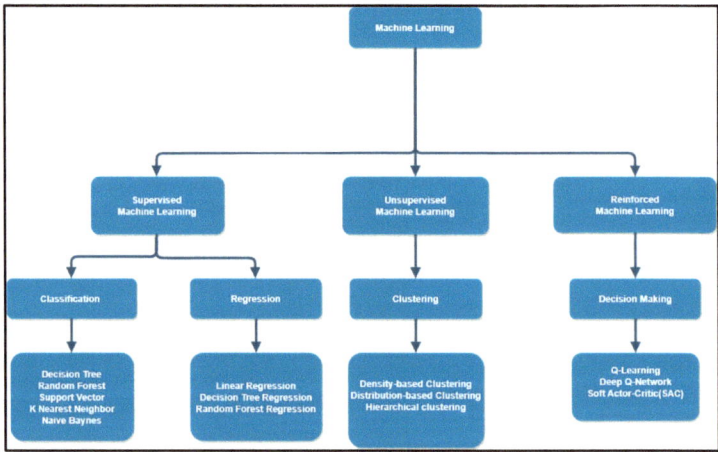

Figure 6. Machine learning approaches with example algorithms.

The most widely used approaches in machine learning are supervised, unsupervised, and reinforced learning, and Figure 7 illustrates the various types of machine learning approaches [58] that can be used. For this paper, supervised ML approaches are used.

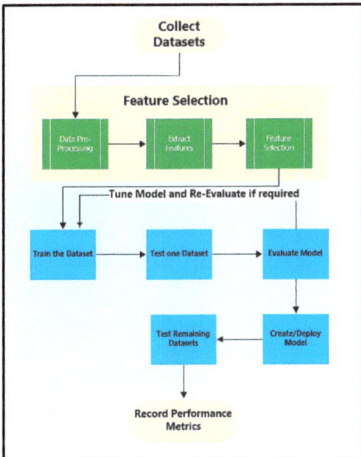

Figure 7. System architecture.

There are several types of supervised ML approaches that could be considered for the problem being researched in this paper, and these are as follows [58]:

- Binary classification—Two possible classifications can be predicted, for example, an email can either be spam or not spam. The two possible classes are usually either normal or abnormal.
- Multi-Class classification—Multiple classes are involved, and each data point is classified into one of the available class options.
- Multi-Label classification—Multiple classes can be predicted for each data point. For example, a house could be present in multiple photos.

For this research, the binary classification approach was selected, as this has been used by many researchers to solve similar problems, as discussed in Sections 1 and 2. For the supervised ML algorithms used in this research, a brief description of these is provided below.

One of the most effective and noteworthy machine learning methods for predictive modeling is the decision tree (DT) algorithm, which performs exceptionally well when dealing with binary classification problems [59]. The decision tree algorithm operates by splitting data into subsets based on the value of the input features. This results in a treelike structure, where each node represents a feature, each branch represents a decision rule, and each leaf node represents an outcome. This hierarchical structure facilitates a straightforward interpretation and visualization of decision-making processes. Traditionally, the decision tree algorithm did not produce optimum results, however, recent advances utilize techniques to construct optimal decision trees and are able to balance the accuracy and complexity of the trees built and used [60]. Since this research aims to ascertain whether the network flow is malicious (banking malware traffic) or benign, the decision tree technique is a good fit for this prediction problem. Additionally, the decision tree algorithm learns and makes predictions extremely quickly [59].

In comparison to the decision tree algorithm, the random forest (RF) algorithm can be more effective, can produce better prediction results, and can lessen the likelihood of overfitting [61]. The random forest algorithm is a robust ensemble learning method that enhances the performances of decision trees by constructing a multitude of trees and then aggregating these results. This approach mitigates the overfitting commonly associated with individual decision trees and improves predictive accuracy. The ensemble approach used by RF reduces variance and enhances model stability. Each tree is trained on a different sample of the dataset, and RF randomly selects the features for training, which promotes diversity among the trees [62]. When utilizing the RF method, it is crucial to adjust the parameters of the algorithm in order to improve the prediction accuracy. It can be challenging to foresee the ideal values in advance, and the parameters are chosen by experimentation. One of these parameters is the quantity of the trees constructed during the training and testing phases, and research shows that constructing more than 128 trees can raise the cost of training and testing while offering no appreciable improvement in accuracy [63]. Constructing between 64 and 128 trees has been shown to be the ideal number of trees that should be used, so, the experimental analysis for this research also used between 64 and 128 trees [63].

The K-Nearest Neighbors (KNN) algorithm is a supervised learning algorithm that can be utilized for both classification and regression tasks. It operates on the principle that data points with similar features are likely to belong to the same class or share similar output values. For a given input, KNN computes the distance between this input and all other instances in the training dataset, which enables KNN to make predictions [64]. KNN is a non-parametric method [65], meaning that it makes no assumptions about the underlying data. Following the computation of the distance between each new data point and every other training data point, the algorithm can classify the new data point in relation to the trained data points [66]. KNN is a simple and adaptable ML algorithm that can solve various predication problems such as multi-class and binary classification problems, like the one being researched in this paper. However, research shows that KNN can be computationally complex to run, and the distance between points can become less meaningful in high-dimensional spaces [67].

An ensemble approach [68] is also used in this research, and for this, the random forest, decision tree, and the K-Nearest Neighbor ML algorithms are all used together in the ensemble approach. A voting classifier was used to combine the results of all the models, and for this research, a soft vote [69] was used for predicting the malware. The soft voting approach is useful, because it can select the average probability of each class [70].

4.2. System Architecture and Methodology

The system architecture shown in Figure 8 depicts the steps that are completed for the experimental work conducted during this research. These include the following:

- The datasets are identified and collected.
- Features are extracted from these datasets.
- The extracted features are transferred to a CSV file and prepared.
- The features are selected for training and testing.
- The algorithm is trained and tested, and a model is created. Only one dataset is used for the training.
- The model is tuned, trained, and tested again if required.
- The model is used to test and evaluate the remaining datasets.
- The final model is deployed, all the data samples are tested, and a report highlighting the evaluation metrics is created.

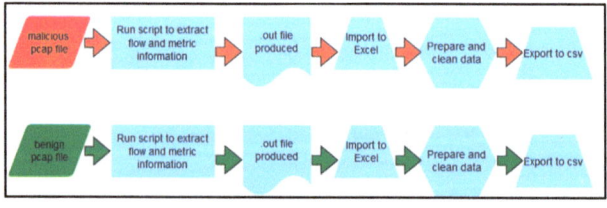

Figure 8. Process for extracting and computing flow statistics.

4.3. Data Samples

In this study, a variety of datasets were collected, and these datasets represent real-world activity that was captured by various reputable organizations. These datasets are represented as pcap files. Six datasets were used for this research, and these were collected from Zeustracker [71], Stratosphere [72], Abuse.ch [73], and Dalhousie University [74]. Abuse.ch correlates samples from commercial and open-source platforms such as VirusTotal, ClamAV, Karspersky, and Avast [73]. Dalhousie University's botnet samples are part of the NIMS botnet research project and have been widely utilized by many researchers [74]. Table 10 defines all the data sets that were used during this research and provides some information around the banking malware variants collected and used during this research. Table 10 also specifies the year that the samples were detected and categorized by the antivirus vendor and depicts the number of flows extracted from these samples.

Each pcap file is made up of network flows, and for this research, the network characteristics for each flow were extracted from these pcap files. A flow is a sequence of packets flowing between a source and a destination (IP and port combination) during a certain period of time. Figure 9 shows the process used to extract the characteristics from each flow, and the first step was to set up and configure Netmate-flowcal on a virtual machine, which allowed the pcap files to be input into the Netmate-flowcal tool. Netmate-flowcal then calculated the key statistics of each flow within each pcap file and output these into an .out file, which had to be converted to a text file and cleaned. The text file was then converted into an excel file, and the data were prepared, cleaned, and then converted into a CSV file, which prepared the file for the machine learning algorithm. As there were thousands of pcap files, a script was developed to automate this process.

Each sample in the CSV files was labeled, and this identified whether the sample was benign or malware. A label of '0' was applied to the benign traffic samples and a label of '1' was applied to the Zeus malware traffic samples. The Pandas library was used to create and manipulate the data frame and prepare the data for the machine learning tasks.

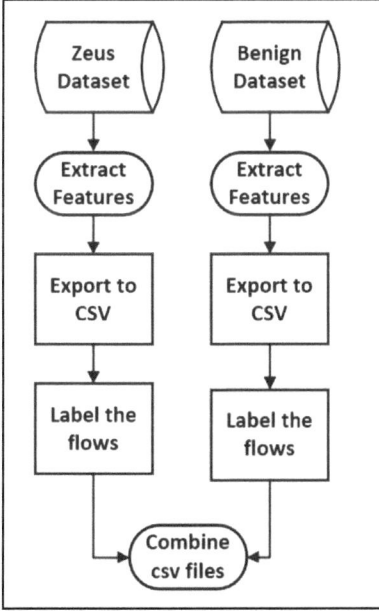

Figure 9. Feature rankings calculated by SelectKBest.

Table 10. Datasets used in this research.

Dataset Type	Malware Name/Year	Number of Flows	Name of Dataset for This Paper
Malware	Zeus/2019	66,009	Dataset1
Benign	N/A	66,009	
Malware	Zeus/2019	38,282	Dataset2
Benign	N/A	38,282	
Malware	Zeus/2022	272,425	Dataset3
Benign	N/A	272,425	
Malware	ZeusPanda/2022	11,864	Dataset4
Benign	N/A	11,864	
Malware	Ramnit/2022	10,204	Dataset5
Benign	N/A	10,204	
Malware	Dridex/2018	134,998	Dataset6
Benign	N/A	134,998	

4.4. Feature Selection

The statistical features were extracted and exported into a CSV file, and these were used as the features. A total of 44 features were extracted, however, not all the features were used. It is important to select the appropriate and best features, as this helps to reduce overfitting and computational cost and helps the ML algorithm to learn faster [75,76]. Several approaches can be used to identify the appropriate features, and the three predominant approaches are the following [77]:

- Filter method—Feature selection is independent of the ML algorithm.
- Wrapper method—Features are selectively used to train the ML algorithm, and through continual experimental analysis, the best features are selected for the final model. This method can be very time-consuming.
- Hybrid—A fusion of the filter and wrapper approaches.

For this research, the features were analyzed using the filter-based approach, and three automated feature selection algorithms were used for this analysis, including the ANOVA [78], CFS [79], and SelectKBest [80] feature selection algorithms.

SelectKBest is a feature selection approach which selects the top K features from all the features available. This is based on a scoring function based on how well each feature correlates with the target variable, and for this research, f_classif was used for the scoring mechanism, which scores each feature and then ranks these based on the score. The score assigned to the feature measures the relationship between the feature and the target variable, in this case, malware or benign, and then selects the top K features. The formula for calculating the f_classif is shown in Equation (1) [81]. K is the number of classes (distinct target labels), n_i is the number of samples in class i, N is the total number of samples in the dataset, $\bar{x}_i$ is the mean of feature values for class i, $\bar{x}$ is the overall mean of the feature across all samples, and x_{ij} is the value of the feature for sample j in class i.

$$F = \frac{\frac{1}{k}\sum_{i=1}^{k} n_i(\bar{x}_i - \bar{x})^2}{\frac{1}{N-k}\sum_{i=1}^{k}\sum_{j=1}^{n_i}(x_{ij} - \bar{x}_i)^2} \tag{1}$$

SelectKBest compares the mean values of different groups. The two groups considered are the 'between-group variances' and 'within-group variances'. A larger value assigned to a feature means that the feature is a good candidate for predicting the malware, whereas a smaller value means that the feature is unlikely to help predict the malware. The top

10 features calculated by SelectKBest were selected for this research, and this was performed by setting the K Value to 10. This was based on experimental analysis, and increasing the K value further did not influence the prediction results. Figure 10 shows the feature rankings calculated using SelectKBest.

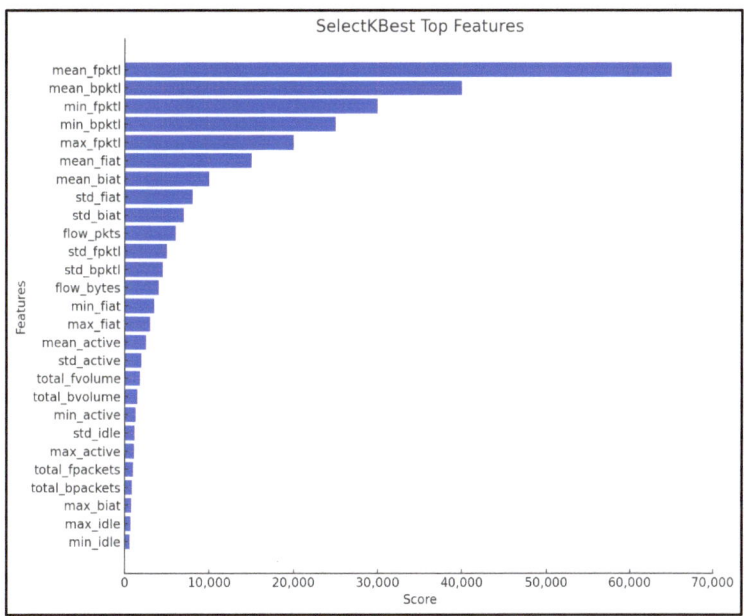

Figure 10. Feature rankings calculated by SelectKBest.

CFS works by considering the correlation between each feature and the target variable and the correlations between the features themselves. CFS then selects the features that maximize and minimize the correlation between the features. A subset of these features is evaluated further, and this is based on the average correlations with the target variable and the inverse of the correlation between the features themselves. The formula for calculating the CFS is shown in Equation (2) [82]. S is the subset of selected features, r_{cf} is the correlation between the selected features and the target variable, r_{ff} is the correlation between the features themselves, k is the number of features in the subset S, and m is the total number of features in the dataset.

$$CFS(S) = \frac{r_{cf}}{\sqrt{r_{ff} + \frac{k(k-1)}{m}}} \tag{2}$$

The features with the highest combined score are selected. Figure 11 shows the feature ranking scores calculated by CFS.

ANOVA is another feature selection approach that was used during this research. In ANOVA, the data are split into groups, and these groups represent the different categories being compared. The groups are compared to the target variable, and the differences between these groups are calculated. Several calculations are performed by ANOVA, and these can be seen in Equation (3) [83]. The first is SSB, which is the Sum of Squares Between groups, calculated as follows: k is the number of groups, n_i is the number of observations in group i, $\bar{x}_i$ is the mean of group i, and $\bar{x}$ is the overall mean. The second calculation is SSW, which is the Sum of Squares within Groups and is calculated as follows: $\bar{x}_{ij}$ is the value of the observation in group I and $\bar{x}_i$ is the mean of group i. The final calculation is F, which is the F-statistics, and in this formula, *MSB* is the Mean Square Between, *MSW* is the Mean Square Within, *k* is the number of groups, and *N* is the total number of observations.

$$SSB = \sum_{i=1}^{k} n_i (\overline{x}_i - \overline{x})^2$$
$$SSW = \sum_{i=1}^{k} * \sum_{j=1}^{n_i} (\overline{x}_{ij} - \overline{x}_i)^2 \quad (3)$$
$$f = \frac{MSB}{MSW} = \frac{SSB/(k-1)}{SSW/(N-k)}$$

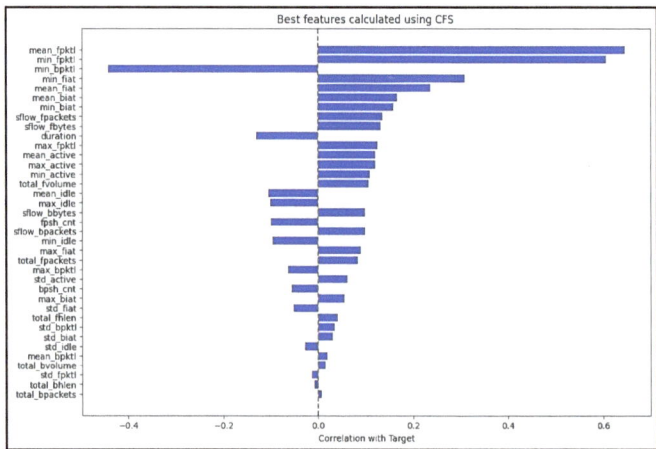

Figure 11. Feature rankings calculated by CFS.

A large value suggests that the groups are different and can be considered as a suitable feature to use for the experimental work, and a small number suggests that the feature might not be suitable. Figure 12 illustrates the scores calculated by ANOVA, and the scores are ranked from the highest to the lowest.

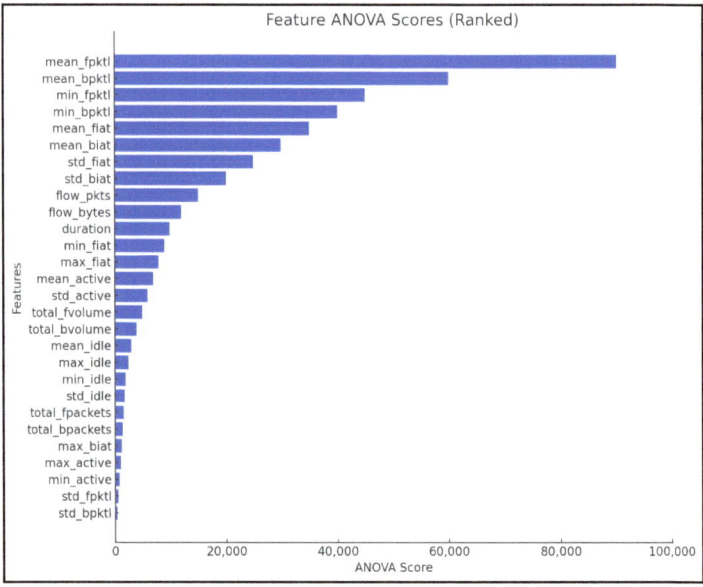

Figure 12. Feature rankings calculated by ANOVA.

Several experiments were conducted using different features, and it was determined that the following ten features would be the most appropriate and minimum number of features required for predicting the different malware variants: mean_fpktl; min_fpktl; min_bpktl; min_fiat; mean_fiat; mean_biat; min_biat; sflow_fpackets; sflow_fbytes; and Duration.

Increasing the number of features does not help to improve the prediction results and using a lower number of features reduces the efficiency of ML algorithms. The above ten features were used in the training and testing of the machine learning algorithms, and the results of the experimental analysis can be viewed in Section 5.

4.5. Evaluation Approach of the Experimental Analysis

The evaluation metrics of precision, recall, and F1-score were used for the experimental analysis conducted for this research. Precision is the percentage of correctly identified positive cases from the whole data sample [84], and recall is the percentage of correctly identified positive cases from the positive samples only [85]. The formulas used are as follows:

$$Precision = \frac{TP}{TP + FP} \tag{4}$$

$$Recall = \frac{TP}{TP + FN} \tag{5}$$

The F1-score considers both the positive and negative cases combined, and the formula used to calculate the F1-score is set out as follows [86]:

$$F1 - Score = \frac{2 * (Precision * Recall)}{Precision + Recall} \tag{6}$$

A confusion matrix [87], as shown in Table 11, will also be generated for each experiment that is conducted. The confusion matrix calculates the true positive (TP), true negative (TN), false positive (FP), and false negative (FN) scores for each dataset.

Table 11. Confusion matrix that will be used to measure the detection accuracy.

	Predicted Benign	**Predicted Zeus**
Actual Benign (Total)	TN	FP
Actual Zeus (Total)	FN	TP

5. Results

This section presents the training and testing results for all the ML algorithms and compares the prediction results for each of the datasets. For each ML algorithm, two tables are presented. The first table shows the precision, recall, and F1-score results and the second table depicts the following information: the number of samples tested; the number of samples correctly classified (true positives); and the number of samples misclassified (false negatives). The table also depicts the prediction results of the benign C&C network samples.

5.1. Training and Testing the Decision Tree Machine Learning Algorithms

The DT ML algorithm was trained using the features defined in Section 4.4 and for the training, 3 folds were used. A training accuracy of 0.974 was achieved, and Table 12 shows the testing results and Table 13 depicts a confusion matrix for each of the datasets tested. By examining the key metric, which is the recall score for the malware, most of the recall scores were above 95. The lowest recall rate was 66 for dataset 6, and the highest recall score was 99 achieved by both datasets 3 and 4.

Table 12. Testing results when using the decision tree ML algorithm.

Dataset Name	Malware Precision Score	Malware Recall Score	Malware F1-Score	Benign Precision Score	Benign Recall Score	Benign F1-Score
Dataset 1	1.00	0.95	0.97	0.95	1.00	0.97
Dataset 2	1.00	0.95	0.97	0.96	1.00	0.98
Dataset 3	1.00	0.99	0.99	0.99	1.00	0.99
Dataset 4	1.00	0.99	0.99	0.99	1.00	0.99
Dataset 5	0.87	0.97	0.92	0.97	0.86	0.91
Dataset 6	0.78	0.66	0.71	0.70	0.82	0.76

Table 13. Confusion matrices depicting the testing results of the decision tree ML algorithm.

Dataset Name	Malware Total Samples Tested	Malware Samples Classified Correctly	Malware Samples Classified Incorrectly	Total Benign Samples Tested	Benign Samples Classified Correctly	Benign Samples Classified Incorrectly
Dataset 1	66,009	62,906	3103	66,009	65,722	287
Dataset 2	38,282	36,519	1763	38,282	38,152	130
Dataset 3	272,425	270,328	2097	272,425	271,439	986
Dataset 4	11,864	11,728	136	11,864	11,820	44
Dataset 5	10,204	9941	263	10,204	8759	1445
Dataset 6	134,998	88,500	46,498	134,998	110,167	24,831

5.2. Training and Testing the Random Forest (RF) Machine Learning Algorithm

The results of testing the RF ML algorithm can be seen in Tables 14 and 15. A training accuracy of 0.997 was achieved, and by examining the key metric, which is the recall score for the malware, most of the recall results were above 95. The lowest recall score was for dataset 6, which was 66, and the highest recall score was obtained by datasets 3 and 4, which 99.

Table 14. Testing results when using the random forest ML algorithm.

Dataset Name	Malware Precision Score	Malware Recall Score	Malware F1-Score	Benign Precision Score	Benign Recall Score	Benign F1-Score
Dataset 1	1.00	0.95	0.97	0.95	1.00	0.97
Dataset 2	1.00	0.95	0.97	0.96	1.00	0.98
Dataset 3	1.00	0.99	0.99	0.99	1.00	0.99
Dataset 4	1.00	0.99	0.99	0.99	1.00	0.99
Dataset 5	0.87	0.97	0.92	0.97	0.86	0.91
Dataset 6	0.78	0.66	0.71	0.70	0.82	0.76

Table 15. Confusion matrices depicting the testing results of the random forest ML algorithm.

Dataset Name	Total Malware Samples Tested	Malware Samples Classified Correctly	Malware Samples Classified Incorrectly	Total Benign Samples Tested	Benign Samples Classified Correctly	Benign Samples Classified Incorrectly
Dataset 1	66,009	65,051	958	66,009	66,003	6
Dataset 2	38,282	37,737	545	38,282	38,278	4
Dataset 3	272,425	272,276	149	272,425	272,401	24
Dataset 4	11,864	11,758	106	11,864	11,863	1
Dataset 5	10,204	9990	214	10,204	8852	1352
Dataset 6	134,998	88,586	46,412	134,998	111,428	23,570

5.3. Training and Testing the K-Nearest Neighbor (KNN) Machine Learning Algorithm

The KNN testing results can be seen in Tables 16 and 17. A training accuracy of 0.950 was achieved, and by examining the key metric, which is the recall score for the malware traffic, most of the malware recall results were above 90. The lowest malware recall rate was 50, which was achieved by dataset t6, and the highest malware recall score was 100, achieved by dataset 3.

Table 16. Testing results when using the K-Nearest Neighbor (KNN) ML algorithm.

Dataset Name	Malware Precision Score	Malware Recall Score	Malware F1-Score	Benign Precision Score	Benign Recall Score	Benign F1-Score
Dataset 1	1.00	0.90	0.95	0.91	1.00	0.95
Dataset 2	1.00	0.91	0.95	0.91	1.00	0.95
Dataset 3	1.00	1.00	1.00	1.00	1.00	1.00
Dataset 4	1.00	0.99	0.99	0.99	1.00	0.99
Dataset 5	0.92	0.97	0.95	0.97	0.92	0.95
Dataset 6	0.85	0.50	0.63	0.65	0.91	0.76

Table 17. Confusion matrices depicting the testing results of the K Nearest Neighbor (KNN) ML algorithm.

Dataset Name	Total Malware Samples Tested	Malware Samples Classified Correctly	Malware Samples Classified Incorrectly	Total Benign Samples Tested	Benign Samples Classified Correctly	Benign Samples Classified Incorrectly
Dataset 1	66,009	59,476	6533	66,009	66,003	6
Dataset 2	38,282	34,659	3623	38,282	38,278	4
Dataset 3	272,425	272,423	2	272,425	272,401	24
Dataset 4	11,864	11,719	145	11,864	11,863	1
Dataset 5	10,204	9939	265	10,204	9397	807
Dataset 6	134,998	68,156	66,842	134,998	123,232	11,766

5.4. Training and Testing Using the Ensemble Machine Learning Approach

An ensemble approach was used to train and test all the datasets, and the results of this can be seen in Tables 18 and 19. Again, focusing on the malware recall score for each dataset, the highest malware recall score was achieved with both datasets 3 and 4, with a score of 99. The lowest malware recall score achieved was for dataset 6, which was 66.

Table 18. Testing results when using the ensemble machine learning approach.

Dataset Name	Malware Precision Score	Malware Recall Score	Malware F1-Score	Benign Precision Score	Benign Recall Score	Benign F1-Score
Dataset 1	1.00	0.95	0.97	0.95	1.00	0.97
Dataset 2	1.00	0.95	0.97	0.96	1.00	0.98
Dataset 3	1.00	0.99	0.99	0.99	1.00	0.99
Dataset 4	1.00	0.99	0.99	0.99	1.00	0.99
Dataset 5	0.87	0.97	0.92	0.97	0.86	0.91
Dataset 6	0.78	0.66	0.71	0.70	0.82	0.76

Table 19. Confusion matrices depicting the testing results of the ensemble ML approach.

Dataset Name	Total Malware Samples Tested	Malware Samples Classified Correctly	Malware Samples Classified Incorrectly	Total Benign Samples Tested	Benign Samples Classified Correctly	Benign Samples Classified Incorrectly
Dataset 1	66,009	65,051	958	66,009	66,003	6
Dataset 2	38,282	37,737	545	38,282	38,278	4
Dataset 3	272,425	272,276	149	272,425	272,401	24
Dataset 4	11,864	11,758	106	11,864	11,863	1
Dataset 5	10,204	9990	214	10,204	8852	1352
Dataset 6	134,998	88,586	46,412	134,998	111,428	23,570

5.5. Comparing the Predication Results of all the Algorithms Tested

The results obtained from testing all the algorithms are compared in this section. Figure 13 shows the malware recall results of all the algorithms when tested against all the datasets and Figure 14 shows the benign traffic recall scores. An expanded view of the results can be seen in Figures 15 and 16, which show both the recall and precision scores for both the malware and benign traffic samples.

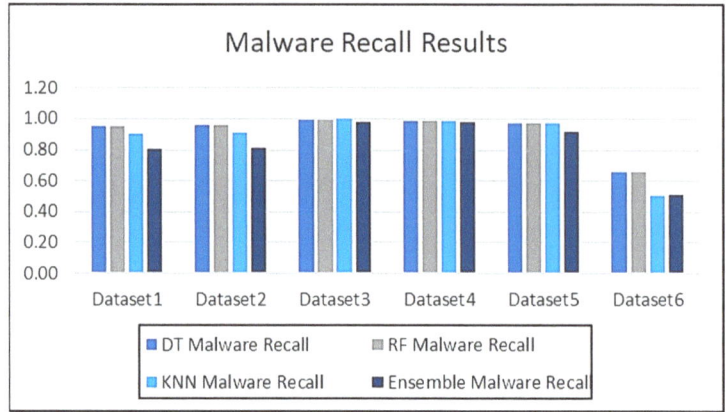

Figure 13. Comparison of the prediction results for all three ML algorithms.

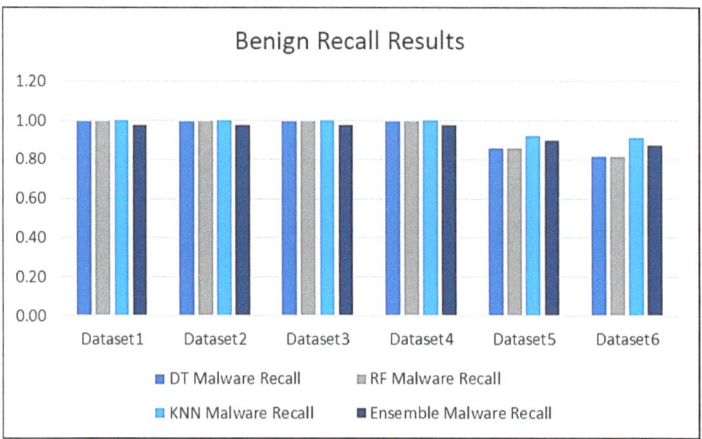

Figure 14. Comparison of the prediction results for all three ML algorithms.

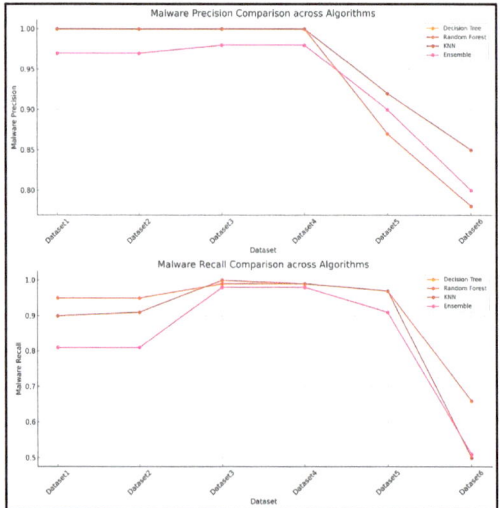

Figure 15. Malware precision and recall scores.

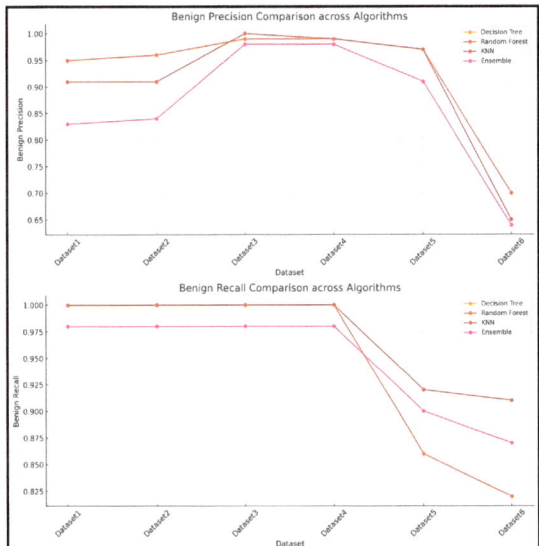

Figure 16. Benign precision and recall scores.

The results obtained during the testing phase indicate that the decision tree algorithm performed consistently well across all the datasets, with high accuracy scores for datasets 1–4. The performance for dataset 6 did decrease slightly, which seems to indicate that the decision tree algorithm faced some challenges when used for testing on a large dataset. Similar results were obtained for both the random forest and KNN algorithms. The results demonstrate that the random forest algorithm performed the best and is the most suited for this type of problem.

All the results are compared in Figure 17, and the experimental results and the patterns observed suggest that the random forest and decision tree models were more robust and consistent across all the datasets, while the K-Nearest Neighbor and ensemble models may face some difficulties with larger or more complex data. Dataset 6 seems particularly challenging, reducing performance across all the datasets.

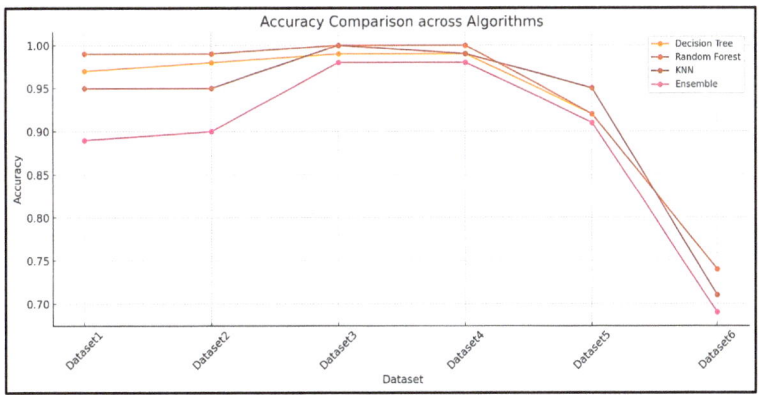

Figure 17. Accuracy comparison across all the algorithms.

This paper has demonstrated an approach that can be used to detect banking malware and some its variants, and has demonstrated that the methodology does work across multiple datasets and other variants of the Zeus malware. The research also allows key inferences to be made, because one dataset was used for training and to create an ML model. This model was tested to evaluate its generalization and ability to classify other various banking malware variants. Metrics such as precision, recall, F1-score, and accuracy were used to assess the performance across these datasets. The model performed exceptionally well on datasets 2–4, achieving a high accuracy (≥97%) and balanced F1-scores, indicating that these datasets share similar feature distributions with dataset 1. However, its performance declined on datasets 5 and 6, with its accuracy dropping to 92% and 74%, respectively. The decline in the precision and recall scores suggests that there were some behavioral differences between the malware samples. This underscores the importance of using diverse training data and robust ensemble methods to improve generalization across malware variants.

5.6. Comparing the Predication Results with Previous Research

This section compares the results obtained in this research with the previous research identified and discussed in Section 2. Several experimental results are compared, and the first comparison is performed with the research conducted by [44]. The model developed in this paper is referred to as 'User Model'. Figure 18 compares the performance of the user model with that of the models developed by [44].

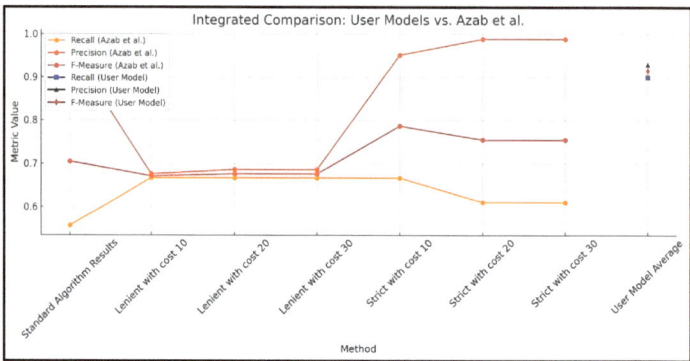

Figure 18. Results of [44] compared to the results of this research.

The comparison between the results of this research and the results presented by [44] reveals several key insights. This research demonstrated a well-balanced performance and achieves a recall of approximately 0.90, significantly outperforming all the configurations from [44], where the highest recall was 0.667. This highlights that the model developed in this research has a greater ability to correctly identify malware patterns. In terms of precision, the strict configurations from [44] (cost 20 and 30) achieved slightly higher values (0.989) compared to the precision of 0.93 of this research. However, the trade-off for this higher precision is a lower recall, resulting in a less balanced performance. The F-measure, which balances precision and recall, was notably greater in this research (~0.914), exceeding all configurations from [44], except for the strict configuration with cost 10 (0.787). These results indicate that the model developed for this research is highly effective and achieves a balance between detecting true positives and minimizing false positives, making it more robust for practical implementations.

The results obtained by [45] are also compared with the user model, and Figure 19 compares these results. The comparison reveals that the model developed in this research had a TPR of 90%, which is competitive with or exceeds most methods tested by [45], except for the "Zeus (Snort)—SBB" and "Zeus (Snort)—C4.5", which both achieved a TPR of 98%. However, the model developed in this research minimized the false positive rate (FPR), maintaining a consistent FPR of 5%, significantly outperforming methods like "Zeus-1—SBB" (27%) and "Zeus-1—C4.5" (17%). This highlights the robustness of the user model in accurately identifying true positives while reducing false alarms, making it highly effective in real-world scenarios. Overall, the user model provides a balanced approach with a strong performance in both detection and minimizing errors, positioning it as a reliable alternative to [45].

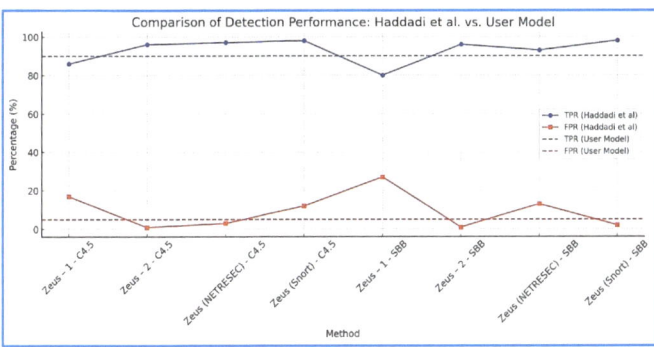

Figure 19. Results of [45] compared to the results of this research.

6. Conclusions

The framework's ability to identify banking malware and its variants were demonstrated by the empirical analysis conducted during this research. The research showed that the methodology and framework used for this study can identify both older and newer versions of the Zeus banking malware. It is possible that this approach can be used to detect a large number of banking malware variants without having to examine each one in order to understand its characteristics. This is because the framework and technique developed during this research identified key features that could be used and may also predict other banking malware variants. Also, this research showed that a reduced set of features can be used for detecting banking malware, and this should help to increase the performance and time required for training and testing machine learning or deep learning algorithms, especially for large datasets. This research will also benefit other researchers, as they should be able to adopt this approach in their own research and will have a good base to begin conducting experiments of a similar nature.

It may be possible to advance this research in the future by improving the methodology to include more banking malware variants, especially variants belonging to a different banking malware family. Additionally, more research may be conducted to identify other malware types and increase the prediction accuracy of these predictions. The results of this study may also be utilized by researchers to develop an intrusion detection system (IDS) that can identify a variety of malware, and by anti-virus manufacturers to support their development of malware detection tools. Once an infection has been identified, action can also be taken against malicious communications. Researchers can improve their work by using the results of this study to create their own malware prediction systems.

Funding: This research received no external funding.

Data Availability Statement: Data are contained within the article.

Conflicts of Interest: The author declares no conflicts of interest.

References

1. Wadhwa, A.; Arora, N. A Review on Cyber Crime: Major Threats and Solutions. *Int. J. Adv. Res. Comput. Sci.* **2017**, *8*, 2217–2221.
2. Morgan, S. Cybercrime to Cost the World 8 Trillion Annually in 2023. Cybercrime Magazine. 17 October 2022. Available online: https://cybersecurityventures.com/cybercrime-to-cost-the-world-8-trillion-annually-in-2023/ (accessed on 7 December 2024).
3. Banking Malware Threats Surging as Mobile Banking Increases—Nokia Threat Intelligence Report. n.d. Nokia. Available online: https://www.nokia.com/about-us/news/releases/2021/11/08/banking-malware-threats-surging-as-mobile-banking-increases-nokia-threat-intelligence-report/ (accessed on 7 December 2024).
4. Kuraku, S.; Kalla, D. Emotet malware—A banking credentials stealer. *IOSR J. Comput. Eng.* **2020**, *22*, 31–41.
5. Etaher, N.; Weir, G.R.S.; Alazab, M. From zeus to zitmo: Trends in banking malware. In Proceedings of the 2015 IEEE Trustcom/BigDataSE/ISPA, Helsinki, Finland, 20–22 August 2015; Volume 1, pp. 1386–1391.
6. Godfather Banking Trojan Spawns 1.2K Samples across 57 Countries. Darkreading.com. 2024. Available online: https://www.darkreading.com/endpoint-security/godfather-banking-trojan-spawns-1k-samples-57-countries (accessed on 16 January 2025).
7. Nilupul, S.A. Evolution and Impact of Malware: A Comprehensive Analysis from the First Known Malware to Modern-Day Cyber Threats. *Cyber Secur.* **2024**. [CrossRef]
8. Mishra, R.; Butakov, S.; Jaafar, F.; Memon, N. Behavioral Study of Malware Affecting Financial Institutions and Clients. In Proceedings of the 2020 IEEE Intl Conf on Dependable, Autonomic and Secure Computing, Intl Conf on Pervasive Intelligence and Computing, Intl Conf on Cloud and Big Data Computing, Intl Conf on Cyber Science and Technology Congress (DASC/PiCom/CBDCom/CyberSciTech), Calgary, AB, Canada, 17–22 August 2020; pp. 79–86.
9. Owen, H.; Zarrin, J.; Pour, S.M. A survey on botnets, issues, threats, methods, detection and prevention. *J. Cybersecur. Priv.* **2022**, *2*, 74–88. [CrossRef]
10. Boukherouaa, E.B.; Shabsigh, M.G.; AlAjmi, K.; Deodoro, J.; Farias, A.; Iskender, E.S.; Mirestean, M.A.T.; Ravikumar, R. *Powering the Digital Economy: Opportunities and Risks of Artificial Intelligence in Finance*; International Monetary Fund: Washington, DC, USA, 2021.
11. AMR. IT Threat Evolution in Q3 2022. Non-Mobile Statistics. Securelist.com. Kaspersky. 18 November 2022. Available online: https://securelist.com/it-threat-evolution-in-q3-2022-non-mobile-statistics/107963/ (accessed on 16 January 2025).
12. Kazi, M.A.; Woodhead, S.; Gan, D. Comparing the performance of supervised machine learning algorithms when used with a manual feature selection process to detect Zeus malware. *Int. J. Grid Util. Comput.* **2022**, *13*, 495–504. [CrossRef]
13. Punyasiri, D.L.S. Signature & Behavior Based Malware Detection. Bachelor's Thesis, Sri Lanka Institute of Information Technology, Malabe, Sri Lanka, 2023.
14. Gopinath, M.; Sethuraman, S.C. A comprehensive survey on deep learning based malware detection techniques. *Comput. Sci. Rev.* **2023**, *47*, 100529.
15. Alaskar, H.; Saba, T. Machine learning and deep learning: A comparative review. In *Proceedings of Integrated Intelligence Enable Networks and Computing: IIENC 2020*; Springer: Singapore, 2021; pp. 143–150.
16. Madanan, M.; Gunasekaran, S.S.; Mahmoud, M.A. A Comparative Analysis of Machine Learning and Deep Learning Algorithms for Image Classification. In Proceedings of the 2023 6th International Conference on Contemporary Computing and Informatics (IC3I), Gautam Buddha Nagar, India, 14–16 September 2023; Volume 6, pp. 2436–2439.
17. Kazi, M.A.; Woodhead, S.; Gan, D. Comparing and analysing binary classification algorithms when used to detect the Zeus malware. In *2019 Sixth HCT Information Technology Trends (ITT)*; IEEE: Piscataway, NJ, USA, 2019; pp. 6–11.
18. Bansal, M.; Goyal, A.; Choudhary, A. A comparative analysis of K-nearest neighbor, genetic, support vector machine, decision tree, and long short term memory algorithms in machine learning. *Decis. Anal. J.* **2022**, *3*, 100071. [CrossRef]
19. Kazi, M.; Woodhead, S.; Gan, D. A contempory Taxonomy of Banking Malware. In Proceedings of the First International Conference on Secure Cyber Computing and Communications, Jalandhar, India, 15–17 December 2018.
20. Falliere, N.; Chien, E. Zeus: King of the Bots. 2009. Available online: https://www.google.co.uk/url?sa=t&source=web&rct=j&opi=89978449&url=https://pure.port.ac.uk/ws/portalfiles/portal/42722286/Understanding_and_Mitigating_Banking_Trojans.pdf&ved=2ahUKEwizroXLwZqJAxU-VUEAHdgzKqEQFnoECDMQAQ&usg=AOvVaw1St11bbRwbhYj9IB4VdQv4 (accessed on 19 October 2024).
21. Lelli, A. Zeusbot/Spyeye P2P Updated, Fortifying the Botnet. Available online: https://www.symantec.com/connect/blogs/zeusbotspyeye-p2p-updated-fortifying-botnet (accessed on 5 November 2019).
22. Cluley, G. GameOver Zeus Malware Returns from the Dead. Graham Cluley. 14 July 2014. Available online: https://grahamcluley.com/gameover-zeus-malware/ (accessed on 16 January 2025).
23. Brumaghin, E. Poisoning the Well: Banking Trojan Targets Google Search Results. [online] Cisco Talos Blog. 2017. Available online: https://blog.talosintelligence.com/zeus-panda-campaign/#More (accessed on 16 January 2025).
24. Lamb, C. *Advanced Malware and Nuclear Power: Past Present and Future*; No. SAND2019-14527C; Sandia National Lab. (SNL-NM): Albuquerque, NM, USA, 2019.

25. De Carli, L.; Torres, R.; Modelo-Howard, G.; Tongaonkar, A.; Jha, S. Botnet protocol inference in the presence of encrypted traffic. In Proceedings of the IEEE INFOCOM 2017-IEEE Conference on Computer Communications, Atlanta, GA, USA, 1–4 May 2017; pp. 1–9.

26. Lioy, A.; Atzeni, A.; Romano, F. Machine Learning for Malware Characterization and Identification. Master's Thesis, Politecnico di Torino, Turin, Italy, 2023.

27. Paganini, P. HTTP-Botnets: The Dark Side of a Standard Protocol! Security Affairs. 22 April 2013. Available online: http://securityaffairs.co/wordpress/13747/cyber-crime/http-botnets-the-dark-side-of-an- (accessed on 16 January 2025).

28. Sood, A.K.; Zeadally, S.; Enbody, R.J. An empirical study of HTTP-based financial botnets. *IEEE Trans. Dependable Secur. Comput.* **2014**, *13*, 236–251. [CrossRef]

29. Niu, Z.; Xue, J.; Qu, D.; Wang, Y.; Zheng, J.; Zhu, H. A novel approach based on adaptive online analysis of encrypted traffic for identifying Malware in IIoT. *Inf. Sci.* **2022**, *601*, 162–174. [CrossRef]

30. Black, P.; Gondal, I.; Layton, R. A Survey of Similarities in Banking Malware Behaviours. *Comput. Secur.* **2018**, *77*, 756–772. [CrossRef]

31. Pilania, S.; Kunwar, R.S. Zeus: In-Depth Malware Analysis of Banking Trojan Malware. In *Advanced Techniques and Applications of Cybersecurity and Forensics*; Chapman and Hall/CRC: Boca Raton, FL, USA, 2024; pp. 167–195.

32. CLULEY, Graham. Russian Creator of NeverQuest Banking Trojan Pleads Guilty in American Court. Hot for Security. 2019. Available online: https://www.bitdefender.com/en-us/blog/hotforsecurity/russian-creator-of-neverquest-banking-trojan-pleads-guilty-in-american-court/ (accessed on 16 January 2025).

33. Fisher, D. Cridex Malware Takes Lesson from GameOver Zeus. Threatpost.com. Threatpost. 15 August 2014. Available online: https://threatpost.com/cridex-malware-takes-lesson-from-gameover-zeus/107785/ (accessed on 16 January 2025).

34. Ilascu, I. Softpedia. 16 August 2014. Available online: https://news.softpedia.com/news/Cridex-Banking-Malware-Variant-Uses-Gameover-Zeus-Thieving-Technique-455193.shtml (accessed on 16 January 2025).

35. Andriesse, D.; Rossow, C.; Stone-Gross, B.; Plohmann, D.; Bos, H. Highly resilient peer-to-peer botnets are here: An analysis of gameover zeus. In Proceedings of the 2013 8th International Conference on Malicious and Unwanted Software: "The Americas" (MALWARE), Fajardo, PR, USA, 22–24 October 2013; pp. 116–123.

36. Sarojini, S.; Asha, S. Botnet detection on the analysis of Zeus panda financial botnet. *Int. J. Eng. Adv. Technol.* **2019**, *8*, 1972–1976. [CrossRef]

37. Aboaoja, F.A.; Zainal, A.; Ghaleb, F.A.; Al-Rimy, B.A.S.; Eisa, T.A.E.; Elnour, A.A.H. Malware detection issues, challenges, and future directions: A survey. *Appl. Sci.* **2022**, *12*, 8482. [CrossRef]

38. Chen, R.; Niu, W.; Zhang, X.; Zhuo, Z.; Lv, F. An effective conversation-based botnet detection method. *Math. Probl. Eng.* **2017**, *2017*, 4934082. [CrossRef]

39. Jha, J.; Ragha, L. Intrusion detection system using support vector machine. *Int. J. Appl. Inf. Syst. (IJAIS)* **2013**, *3*, 25–30.

40. Singla, S.; Gandotra, E.; Bansal, D.; Sofat, S. A novel approach to malware detection using static classification. *Int. J. Comput. Sci. Inf. Secur.* **2015**, *13*, 1–5.

41. Wu, W.; Alvarez, J.; Liu, C.; Sun, H.M. Bot detection using unsupervised machine learning. *Microsyst. Technol.* **2018**, *24*, 209–217. [CrossRef]

42. Yahyazadeh, M.; Abadi, M. BotOnus: An Online Unsupervised Method for Botnet Detection. *ISeCure* **2012**, *4*, 51–62.

43. Soniya, B.; Wilscy, M. Detection of randomized bot command and control traffic on an end-point host. *Alex. Eng. J.* **2016**, *55*, 2771–2781. [CrossRef]

44. Azab, A. The effectiveness of cost sensitive machine learning algorithms in classifying Zeus flows. *Int. J. Inf. Comput. Secur.* **2022**, *17*, 332–350. [CrossRef]

45. Haddadi, F.; Runkel, D.; Zincir-Heywood, A.N.; Heywood, M.I. On botnet behaviour analysis using GP and C4. 5. In Proceedings of the Companion Publication of the 2014 Annual Conference on Genetic and Evolutionary Computation, Vancouver, BC, Canada, 12–16 July 2014; pp. 1253–1260.

46. Mohaisen, A.; Alrawi, O. Unveiling zeus: Automated classification of malware samples. In Proceedings of the 22nd International Conference on World Wide Web, Rio de Janeiro, Brazil, 13–17 May 2013; pp. 829–832.

47. Wang, J.; Yang, Q.; Ren, D. An intrusion detection algorithm based on decision tree technology. In Proceedings of the 2009 Asia-Pacific Conference on Information Processing, Shenzhen, China, 18–19 July 2009; Volume 2, pp. 333–335.

48. Sajjad, S.; Jiana, B. The use of Convolutional Neural Network for Malware Classification. In Proceedings of the 2020 IEEE 9th Data Driven Control and Learning Systems Conference (DDCLS), Liuzhou, China, 20–22 November 2020; pp. 1136–1140.

49. Walker, A.; Sengupta, S. Malware family fingerprinting through behavioral analysis. In Proceedings of the 2020 IEEE International Conference on Intelligence and Security Informatics (ISI), Arlington, VA, USA, 9–10 November 2020; pp. 1–5.

50. Ramakrishna, M.; Rama Satish, A.; Siva Krishna, P.S.S. Design and development of an efficient malware detection Using ML. In *Proceedings of International Conference on Computational Intelligence and Data Engineering: ICCIDE 2020*; Springer: Singapore, 2021; pp. 423–433.

51. Ghafir, I.; Prenosil, V.; Hammoudeh, M.; Baker, T.; Jabbar, S.; Khalid, S.; Jaf, S. BotDet: A System for Real Time Botnet Command and Control Traffic Detection. *IEEE Access* **2018**, *6*, 38947–38958. [CrossRef]

52. Agarwal, P.; Satapathy, S. Implementation of signature-based detection system using snort in windows. *Int. J. Comput. Appl. Inf. Technol.* **2014**, *3*, 3–93. [CrossRef]

53. He, S.; Zhu, J.; He, P.; Lyu, M.R. Experience report: System log analysis for anomaly detection. In Proceedings of the 2016 IEEE 27th International Symposium on Software Reliability Engineering (ISSRE), Ottawa, ON, Canada, 23–27 October 2016; pp. 207–218.

54. Zhou, J.; Qian, Y.; Zou, Q.; Liu, P.; Xiang, J. DeepSyslog: Deep Anomaly Detection on Syslog Using Sentence Embedding and Metadata. *IEEE Trans. Inf. Forensics Secur.* **2022**, *17*, 3051–3061. [CrossRef]

55. Khraisat, A.; Gondal, I.; Vamplew, P.; Kamruzzaman, J. Survey of intrusion detection systems: Techniques, datasets and challenges. *Cybersecurity* **2019**, *2*, 20. [CrossRef]

56. Sharma, P.; Said, Z.; Memon, S.; Elavarasan, R.M.; Khalid, M.; Nguyen, X.P.; Arıcı, M.; Hoang, A.T.; Nguyen, L.H. Comparative evaluation of AI-based intelligent GEP and ANFIS models in prediction of thermophysical properties of Fe_3O_4-coated MWCNT hybrid nanofluids for potential application in energy systems. *Int. J. Energy Res.* **2022**, *46*, 19242–19257. [CrossRef]

57. Choi, R.Y.; Coyner, A.S.; Kalpathy-Cramer, J.; Chiang, M.F.; Campbell, J.P. Introduction to machine learning, neural networks, and deep learning. *Transl. Vis. Sci. Technol.* **2020**, *9*, 14. [PubMed]

58. Ahsan, M.; Nygard, K.E.; Gomes, R.; Chowdhury, M.M.; Rifat, N.; Connolly, J.F. Cybersecurity Threats and Their Mitigation Approaches Using Machine Learning—A Review. *J. Cybersecur. Priv.* **2022**, *2*, 527–555. [CrossRef]

59. Elmachtoub, A.N.; Liang, J.C.N.; McNellis, R. Decision trees for decision-making under the predict-then-optimize framework. In Proceedings of the International Conference on Machine Learning, Virtual, 12–18 July 2020; pp. 2858–2867.

60. Liberman, N. Decision Trees and Random Forests. Towards Data Science. 27 January 2017. Available online: https://towardsdatascience.com/decision-trees-and-random-forests-df0c3123f991 (accessed on 16 January 2025).

61. Demirović, E.; Lukina, A.; Hebrard, E.; Chan, J.; Bailey, J.; Leckie, C.; Ramamohanarao, K.; Stuckey, P.J. Murtree: Optimal decision trees via dynamic programming and search. *J. Mach. Learn. Res.* **2022**, *23*, 1–47.

62. Schonlau, M.; Zou, R.Y. The random forest algorithm for statistical learning. *Stata J.* **2020**, *20*, 3–29. [CrossRef]

63. Oshiro, T.M.; Perez, P.S.; Baranauskas, J.A. How many trees in a random forest? In *Machine Learning and Data Mining in Pattern Recognition, Proceedings of the 8th International Conference, MLDM 2012, Berlin, Germany, 13–20 July 2012*; Proceedings 8; Springer: Berlin/Heidelberg, Germany, 2012; pp. 154–168.

64. Halder, R.K.; Uddin, M.N.; Uddin, M.A.; Aryal, S.; Khraisat, A. Enhancing K-nearest neighbor algorithm: A comprehensive review and performance analysis of modifications. *J. Big Data* **2024**, *11*, 113. [CrossRef]

65. Suyal, M.; Goyal, P. A review on analysis of k-nearest neighbor classification machine learning algorithms based on supervised learning. *Int. J. Eng. Trends Technol.* **2022**, *70*, 43–48. [CrossRef]

66. Aggarwal, C.C. (Ed.) *Data Classification*; Springer International Publishing: New York, NY, USA, 2015.

67. Kazi, M.A.; Woodhead, S.; Gan, D. Detecting Zeus Malware Network Traffic Using the Random Forest Algorithm with Both a Manual and Automated Feature Selection Process. In *IOT with Smart Systems: Proceedings of ICTIS 2022, Volume 2*; Springer Nature Singapore: Singapore, 2022; pp. 547–557.

68. Chung, J.; Teo, J. Single classifier vs. ensemble machine learning approaches for mental health prediction. *Brain Inform.* **2023**, *10*, 1. [CrossRef] [PubMed]

69. Salur, M.U.; Aydın, İ. A soft voting ensemble learning-based approach for multimodal sentiment analysis. *Neural Comput. Appl.* **2022**, *34*, 18391–18406. [CrossRef]

70. Jabbar, H.G. Advanced Threat Detection Using Soft and Hard Voting Techniques in Ensemble Learning. *J. Robot. Control (JRC)* **2024**, *5*, 1104–1116.

71. Shomiron. Zeustracker. Available online: https://github.com/dnif-archive/enrich-zeustracker (accessed on 25 July 2022).

72. Stratosphere. Stratosphere Laboratory Datasets. Available online: https://www.stratosphereips.org/datasets-overviewRetrieved (accessed on 20 September 2024).

73. Abuse.ch. Fighting Malware and Botnets. Available online: https://abuse.ch/ (accessed on 13 May 2022).

74. Haddadi, F.; Zincir-Heywood, A.N. Benchmarking the effect of flow exporters and protocol filters on botnet traffic classification. *IEEE Syst. J.* **2014**, *10*, 1390–1401. [CrossRef]

75. Kasongo, S.M.; Sun, Y. A deep learning method with filter based feature engineering for wireless intrusion detection system. *IEEE Access* **2019**, *7*, 38597–38607. [CrossRef]

76. Miller, S.; Curran, K.; Lunney, T. Multilayer perceptron neural network for detection of encrypted VPN network traffic. In Proceedings of the 2018 International Conference on Cyber Situational Awareness, Data Analytics and Assessment (Cyber SA), Glasgow, UK, 11–12 June 2018; pp. 1–8.

77. Kazi, M.A.; Woodhead, S.; Gan, D. An Investigation to Detect Banking Malware Network Communication Traffic Using Machine Learning Techniques. *J. Cybersecur. Priv.* **2023**, *3*, 1–23. [CrossRef]

78. Nasiri, H.; Alavi, S.A. A Novel Framework Based on Deep Learning and ANOVA Feature Selection Method for Diagnosis of COVID-19 Cases from Chest X-Ray Images. *Comput. Intell. Neurosci.* **2022**, *2022*, 4694567. [CrossRef] [PubMed]
79. Alshanbari, H.M.; Mehmood, T.; Sami, W.; Alturaiki, W.; Hamza, M.A.; Alosaimi, B. Prediction and classification of COVID-19 admissions to intensive care units (ICU) using weighted radial kernel SVM coupled with recursive feature elimination (RFE). *Life* **2022**, *12*, 1100. [CrossRef] [PubMed]
80. Kavya, D. Optimizing Performance: SelectKBest for Efficient Feature Selection in Machine Learning. Medium. 16 February 2023. Available online: https://medium.com/@Kavya2099/optimizing-performance-selectkbest-for-efficient-feature-selection-in-machine-learning-3b635905ed48 (accessed on 16 January 2025).
81. dos Santos, C.H.M.; de Lima, S.M.L. XAI-driven antivirus in pattern identification of citadel malware. *J. Comput. Sci.* **2024**, *82*, 102389. [CrossRef]
82. Liu, Z.; Wang, C.; Li, G. Feature Selection Algorithm Based on CFS Algorithm Emphasizing Data Discrimination. *preprint* **2023**. [CrossRef]
83. St, L.; Wold, S. Analysis of variance (ANOVA). *Chemom. Intell. Lab. Syst.* **1989**, *6*, 259–272.
84. Luan, H.; Tsai, C.C. A review of using machine learning approaches for precision education. *Educ. Technol. Soc.* **2021**, *24*, 250–266.
85. Davis, J.; Goadrich, M. The relationship between Precision-Recall and ROC curves. In Proceedings of the 23rd International Conference on Machine Learning, Pittsburgh, PA, USA, 25–29 June 2006; pp. 233–240.
86. Fourure, D.; Javaid, M.U.; Posocco, N.; Tihon, S. Anomaly detection: How to artificially increase your f1-score with a biased evaluation protocol. In *Joint European Conference on Machine Learning and Knowledge Discovery in Databases*; Springer International Publishing: Cham, Switzerland, 2021; pp. 3–18.
87. Visa, S.; Ramsay, B.; Ralescu, A.L.; Van Der Knaap, E. Confusion matrix-based feature selection. *Maics* **2011**, *710*, 120–127.

Journal of
Cybersecurity and Privacy

MDPI

Article

Towards a Near-Real-Time Protocol Tunneling Detector Based on Machine Learning Techniques †

Filippo Sobrero *, Beatrice Clavarezza , Daniele Ucci * and Federica Bisio

aizoOn Technology Consulting, 10146 Turin, Italy; beatrice.clavarezza@aizoongroup.com (B.C.); federica.bisio@aizoongroup.com (F.B.)

* Correspondence: filippo.sobrero@aizoongroup.com (F.S.); daniele.ucci@aizoongroup.com (D.U.)

† This paper is an extension of our paper published in IEEE Symposium Series on Computational Intelligence, Orlando, FL, USA, 5–7 December 2021.

Abstract: In the very recent years, cybersecurity attacks have increased at an unprecedented pace, becoming ever more sophisticated and costly. Their impact has involved both private/public companies and critical infrastructures. At the same time, due to the COVID-19 pandemic, the security perimeters of many organizations expanded, causing an increase in the attack surface exploitable by threat actors through malware and phishing attacks. Given these factors, it is of primary importance to monitor the security perimeter and the events occurring in the monitored network, according to a tested security strategy of detection and response. In this paper, we present a protocol tunneling detector prototype which inspects, in near real-time, a company's network traffic using machine learning techniques. Indeed, tunneling attacks allow malicious actors to maximize the time in which their activity remains undetected. The detector monitors unencrypted network flows and extracts features to detect possible occurring attacks and anomalies by combining machine learning and deep learning. The proposed module can be embedded in any network security monitoring platform able to provide network flow information along with its metadata. The detection capabilities of the implemented prototype have been tested both on benign and malicious datasets. Results show an overall accuracy of 97.1% and an F1-score equal to 95.6%.

Keywords: passive network analysis; DNS tunneling; anomaly detection; machine learning; deep learning

Citation: Sobrero, F.; Clavarezza, B.; Ucci, D.; Bisio, F. Towards a Near-Real-Time Protocol Tunneling Detector Based on Machine Learning Techniques. *J. Cybersecur. Priv.* **2023**, *3*, 794–807. https://doi.org/10.3390/jcp3040035

Academic Editor: Marina L. Gavrilova

Received: 29 August 2023
Revised: 17 October 2023
Accepted: 24 October 2023
Published: 6 November 2023

1. Introduction

Cybersecurity attacks keep increasing year over year at an unprecedented pace, becoming ever more sophisticated and costly [1,2]. The growth between 2021 and 2022 has resulted in a rise of attacks' volume and impact on both private/public companies and critical infrastructures. Companies comprise digital service providers, public administrations, and governments and include businesses operating in the finance and health sectors. In particular, service providers have experienced a raise of more than 15% in intrusions (infamous is the case of Solarwinds [3]) compared to 2021 [1], a trend destined to grow in the next years [4]. At the same time, due to the COVID-19 pandemic, the security perimeters of many organizations expanded to cope with the new needs of remote working, causing an increase in the attack surface exploitable by attackers [4]. The European Union Agency for Cybersecurity estimates that more than 10 terabytes of data are stolen monthly from target assets that are made unavailable, until a ransom is payed [1], while IBM calculates that the average cost of these attacks is USD 4.54 M, increasing up to USD 5.12 M [2]. On the other hand, malware attacks are still on the rise after the pause recorded during the pandemic, and phishing continues to be the common attack vector for initial access [1].

Given these factors, it is of primary importance to monitor the security perimeter and the events occurring in the network, according to a tested security strategy of detection and response. According to Gartner [4], newly proposed solutions should be automated as much as possible, since human errors continue to play a crucial role in most security breaches. In this context, machine learning turned out to be a natural choice for automated analyses and prevention of this kind of threats [5]. The strength of machine learning lies in its ability to identify hidden patterns and correlations in large volumes of raw data and leverage such features to recognize previously unseen attacks. In this paper, we present a protocol tunneling detector prototype which inspects—in near real-time—a company's network traffic using machine learning. Tunneling techniques allow attackers to create a tunnel through a network by encapsulating traffic inside another protocol [6]; hence, it can be used to let infected machines contact their corresponding command-and-control centers. Thus, by abusing legitimate network traffic protocols, like DNS [7], the attacker maximizes the time in which the infection remains undetected. In this work, we rely on a commercial network security monitoring platform for detecting and investigating potentially malicious or anomalous activities [8–11], but the proposed solution can be easily integrated into any network security monitoring platform able to provide network flow information along with its metadata. The platform we employ is responsible for collecting, processing network flows, and dispatching them to one or more advanced cybersecurity analytics (ACAs) which are able to recognize the signals of possible occurring attacks and anomalies. In this scenario, the detector monitors only clear-text protocols, but it works jointly with an ACA responsible for analyzing encrypted traffic [11]. Indeed, while some clear-text protocols are extensively used (i.e., DNS), nowadays, the vast majority of Internet traffic is encrypted [12–16]: this enabled threat actors to perform malware campaigns relying on HTTPS for delivering malware and contacting command-and-control centers [17]. Just in 2020, 67% of malware has been delivered via encrypted HTTPS connections [18]. Along with malware delivery, malicious secure communications are used to exfiltrate data and steal sensitive information from private and public companies [19–21]. While the analytics dealing with encrypted traffic has been extensively described in [11], we extend this previous work by backing up secure connection analysis to the monitoring of clear-text protocols. As mentioned before, the latter can be used to discover the abuse of such protocols and signal network packets' contents which are not usually observed in the monitored network. The module presented in this paper extracts a sequence of N bytes from each single network packet and computes features associated to the collected stream of bytes. Through the combination of deep learning and machine learning, each network packet is assigned to a specific network protocol; if a connection exhibits anomalies (e.g., an interleaving of different protocols), a security analyst is notified about the discovered inconsistency. More specifically:

- we implement a protocol tunneling detector prototype which analyzes, in near real-time, a byte sequence of the packets flowing in the monitored network.
- the proposed prototype combines
  - an artificial neural network (ANN), based on [22], that accurately classifies clear-text protocols and identifies possible anomalies in network connections;
  - a support vector machine that is able to detect compressed/encrypted traffic within unencrypted connections.
- we design and implement an input sanitization module, which automatically removes inconsistent data from models' training sets to significantly increase the models' performance.

With respect to [22], we changed both the input byte sequences we provide to the ANN and their sizes in bytes (as detailed in Sections 4.1 and 5). The performance of the proposed approach has been evaluated on different datasets that either contain legitimate traffic or simulate DNS tunneling attacks, which are the most common [7]. The obtained overall accuracy of the proposed prototype is 97.1%, along with an F1-score equal to 95.6%. It is worth noting that, being the prototype trained with only legitimate traffic, it is potentially able to identify zero-day attacks that deviate from the usual traffic observed in the network.

The rest of the paper is organized as follows: Section 2 discusses related work, while Section 3 introduces basic notions that will be later used to detail the proposed approach (Section 4). The experimental evaluation is reported in Section 5, followed by Section 6, where we discuss the strengths of our prototype and some key design choices we made. Finally, Section 7 concludes the paper.

2. Related Work

Tunneling attacks are a specific typology of network attacks in which an attacker creates a tunnel through a network by encapsulating traffic inside another protocol [6]. This allows the attacker to bypass traditional network security controls and potentially exfiltrate sensitive information. Therefore, as discussed in Section 1, using clear-text network protocols may pose a significant risk when these are abused by malicious actors. In this context, DNS tunneling represents one of the most common techniques employed for covertly exfiltrating data from a network, by encoding the data in DNS queries and responses. Since this method is becoming increasingly prevalent, a growing body of research aims at detecting and mitigating DNS tunneling attacks. In [23], the authors review detection technologies from a perspective of rule-based and model-based methods with descriptions and analyses of DNS-based tools and their corresponding features, covering detection approaches developed from 2006 to 2020 by means of a comparative analysis.

Latest works in the area of DNS tunneling detection mainly cover three main categories, i.e., detection approaches via machine learning, real-time detection approaches, and detection of DNS tunneling variants (e.g., fast flux [9] and domain generation algorithms (DGAs) [8]).

Regarding the first group, researchers have recently proposed both machine and deep learning algorithms for detecting DNS tunneling traffic, such as support vector machines (SVMs), random forests and Convolutional Neural Networks (CNNs) and Recurrent Neural Networks (RNNs), respectively. Do et al. have proposed an SVM to identify DNS tunneling attacks within mobile networks, by using features such as time, traffic source and destination, and length of DNS queries [24]. Other researchers have proposed a random forest classifier to detect this kind of attack [25]. They included in their features the number of answers provided by a DNS response and the time between two consecutive packets and responses for a specific domain. Random forests are also employed in hybrid solutions like the one proposed in [26], where a 100-trees random forest is paired with a CNN; they achieved good performance on their dataset, and it is worth noting that, during their experiments on traffic collected from a real network, they were able to identify a domain associated to a command-and-control center. In [27], the authors developed a novel DNS tunneling detection method employing a Convolutional Neural Network (CNN) to analyze DNS queries and responses and identify DNS tunneling activities. The proposed approach is evaluated using a dataset of real-world DNS traffic and shows promising results in detecting DNS tunneling attacks with high accuracy. The work of [28] applies both Convolutional Neural Networks (CNNs) and Recurrent Neural Networks (RNNs) for detecting DNS tunneling traffic. The authors have shown that these algorithms can effectively spot and identify malicious patterns.

The second group of studies has focused on developing real-time detection systems for DNS tunneling. These systems use a combination of several detection techniques to timely identify malicious DNS traffic [29]. In [30], the authors presented an overview of principal countermeasures for DNS tunneling attacks.

Regarding the state of the art of approaches that analyze encrypted communications, it has already been presented in [11].

The approach we present and evaluate in the next sections passively extracts both sequential and statistical features from network flows to detect tunneling attacks in clear-text protocols. As sequential features, we refer to those characteristics obtained from raw flow sequences. Most works rely on similar features, like domain-based features [23,29,30], including the domain name itself [27,28] and payload and volumetric features [23,30]. These can only be obtained when the entire packet has been reconstructed by a network analyzer. Differently, for each packet, we directly examine a specific sequence of bytes without requiring to compute and store any packet-related metadata. In addition, we use artificial neural networks, which are simpler deep learning models and, hence, require less computing resources to be trained.

3. Background

3.1. DNS Tunneling

Protocol tunneling is an attack technique commonly used to maximize the time in which the infection remains undetected in a targeted network. In this context, the DNS protocol is usually abused in order to bypass security gateways and, then, to tunnel malware and other data through a client–server model [7]. Figure 1 depicts a typical DNS tunneling scenario: firstly, an attacker registers a malicious domain (e.g., attacker.com, accessed on 17 October 2023) on a C&C center managed by her; at that point, assuming that the attacker has already taken control over a machine inside the targeted network and violated its security perimeter, the infected computer sends a query to the malicious domain. Since DNS requests are typically allowed to move in and out of the network, the query through the DNS resolver reaches the attacker's C&C center, where the tunneling program is installed. This established tunnel can be used either to exfiltrate data and sensitive information or for other malicious purposes.

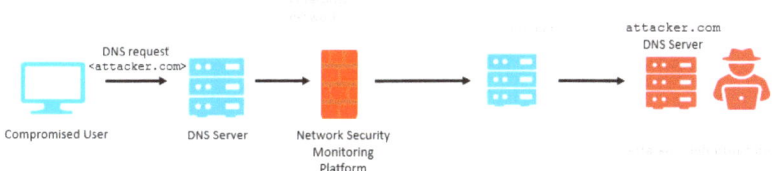

Figure 1. A DNS tunneling example.

3.2. Support Vector Machines

The original formulation of support vector machines [31] (SVMs) is related to the resolution of supervised tasks with the objective of finding a maximum margin hyperplane that separates two or more classes of observations. In the last years, one-class SVMs have also been shown to represent a suitable choice in the context of anomaly and outlier detection [32]. It is defined as a boundary-based anomaly detection method, which modifies the original SVM approach by extending it in order to deal with unlabeled data. Like traditional SVMs, one-class SVMs can also benefit from the so called kernel trick when extended to non-linearly transformed spaces, by defining an appropriate scalar product in the feature space.

3.3. Artificial Neural Networks

Artificial neural networks (ANNs) are deep learning models that have been successfully applied to a vast number of knowledge fields ranging from computing science to arts [33]. They are internally constituted by groups of multiple neurons, which can be thought of as mathematical functions that take one or more inputs. In ANNs, inputs are only processed forward and are multiplied by weights within each neuron and summed up to be then passed to an activation function, which becomes the neuron's output. In general, artificial neural networks consist of three different layers: input, hidden, and output; the first layer accepts inputs, while the hidden layers process them to learn the optimum weights. Finally, the output layer produces the result.

4. Protocol Tunneling Detector

The proposed architecture splits the burden of processing the traffic of a monitored network into two different sub-modules: the first mainly deals with secure connections, while the second inspects unencrypted traffic. As previously discussed, the former analytics has been detailed in [11]. At a glance, it detects possible anomalies occurring during an SSL/TLS handshake between a client, located inside the network monitored by the software platform outlined in Section 1, and an external server. The SSL/TLS detection analytics examines information contained in X.509, SSL, and TLS exchanged protocol messages. Instead, the second module looks for anomalies in unencrypted traffic regarding the abuse of specific protocols (i.e., tunneling attack techniques). To provide these detection capabilities, this prototype collects a sequence of bytes from each network packet and inspects its content. The content, along with its features, is fed to a testing module, which detects possible anomalies that are signaled to security analysts.

4.1. General Approach

Figure 2 reports the general structure of the proposed anomaly detection methodology, which runs in near-real-time fashion. Indeed, a delay is introduced both by data processing and anomaly evaluations that are not performed on the single packet but, rather, on the entire connection, meaning that the approach has to wait to have enough information to make a decision. Hence, for each packet observed in the live network traffic, the prototype collects a sequence of N bytes belonging to the highest network protocol used in the communication. As an example, in a secure connection which relies on HTTPS, the bytes returned by the extraction process are the ones related to HTTPS, and not to the other lower-layer protocols (e.g., TCP).

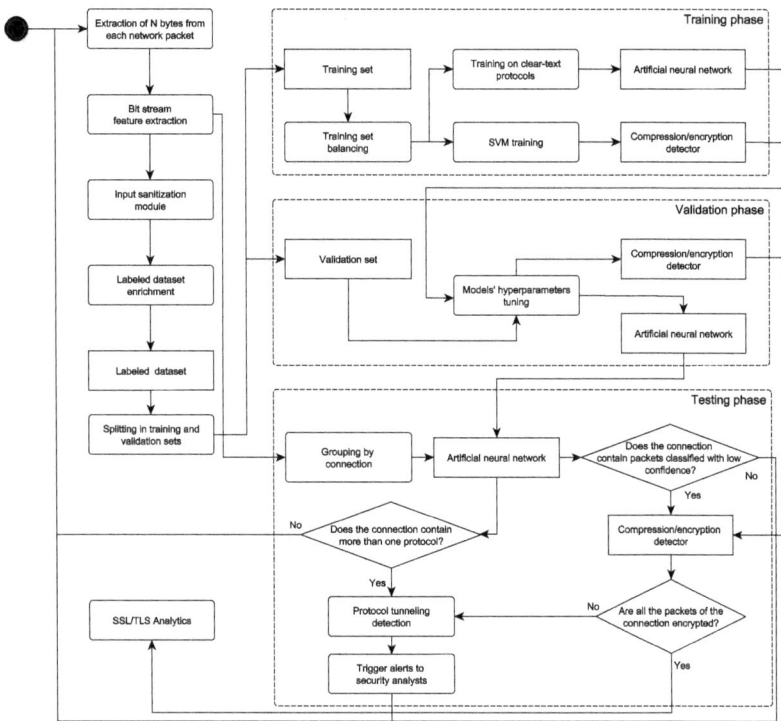

Figure 2. Protocol tunneling detector prototype overview.

From the obtained bit stream, we extract the following sequential features (i.e., those features obtained from raw flow sequences):

- binary representation of collected bytes

- bit-stream entropy and *p*-values obtained from statistical tests for random and pseudorandom number generators for cryptographic applications [34]
- statistical properties of the bit-stream hexadecimal representation

and we keep the protocol label associated to the bit stream itself. While the binary representation of the N bytes is meant to label the protocol of each packet under analysis, the sequential features allow to understand if the packet content is either compressed or encrypted.

After feature extraction, the raw dataset constituted by streams of bits and their corresponding labels is properly sanitized. Indeed, it is easily possible to lightly label the network packets belonging to a connection by simply looking either at the ports or at the connection metadata. However, this labeling may be prone to errors since it either does not take into account potential custom configurations of services (e.g., SMB protocol operating on a port different from 445) or intentional misuse of specific protocols by attackers (as in the case of tunneling). Moreover, clear-text protocols may transfer packets containing compressed data, whose presence could compromise the identification of the correct network protocol. Hence, it is paramount to have a refined and clean dataset to let models perform at their best. During our experimental evaluations, we have found out that the accuracy of the trained models, after refining the raw dataset, has significantly increased: 7% for the ANN and 20% for the compression/encryption detector.

To achieve this performance boost, we have specially implemented an input sanitization module, shown in Figure 3. In this module, we combine unsupervised and supervised support vector machines (SVMs) to clean the raw dataset: first, for each network protocol, we train a one-class SVM both on clear-text and encrypted protocols in order to filter out outliers from the raw dataset. As an example, in protocols like HTTP and SMB, requests and responses may contain either the content of (compressed) files or other types of information that are not strictly correlated with the specific protocol communication patterns. Thus, in order to exclude these outliers, we build one-class SVMs, one for each different protocol, whose hyperparameters are properly tuned on the raw labeled dataset. Trained models are then applied to identify outliers and remove them from the raw dataset. This refined dataset is then used to train an SVM by applying a one-vs-all classification for detecting packets which are either compressed or encrypted. This single classifier is applied to remove both compressed and encrypted packets from clear-text protocols. It is worth mentioning that, in proxied environments, encrypted packets may be present in connections labeled as HTTP: indeed, in these scenarios, secure communications also pass through the proxy, even if these connections are erroneously labeled as HTTP. As already outlined in Section 3, one-class SVMs are successful in identifying outliers; for this reason, we have extensively used them to sanitize our training sets with remarkable results.

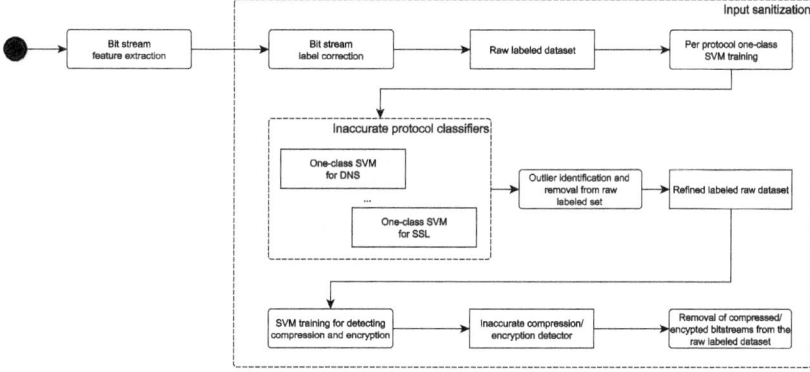

Figure 3. Input sanitization module.

This sanitized dataset is then split into training and validation sets to essentially build two different models: (i) an artificial neural network (ANN) able to classify cleartext protocols (e.g., DNS) and (ii) an SVM that is a compression/encryption detector for identifying, respectively, compressed and encrypted packets. As later shown in Section 5, after construction, the training set is considerably unbalanced towards secure protocols. For this reason, we apply the SMOTE data augmentation technique [35] to increase the samples of those protocols belonging to minority classes. During the test phase, performed light labeling based on connection's destination port is not taken into account, and the resulting bit streams are grouped by connection. Each packet is given in input to a trained ANN (whose training process is detailed in Section 4.3) and the analytics both verifies if, in the connection, there are some packets that have been classified with low confidence and more than one protocol is present. While in this latter case, the co-presence of multiple protocols might signal a possible tunneling attack, when the ANN classifies packets with low confidence, then, the connection could contain either compressed/encrypted packets or packets whose byte sequences differ from the ones usually observed in the network. To distinguish between these two cases, a more in depth verification is carried out: if the connection is not entirely encrypted, meaning that it is a not a secure communication, the prototype checks if the packets signaled as anomalous (i.e., with low confidence) by the ANN are either encrypted or belongs to another protocol. If either encryption or compression is detected, the anomaly is notified to security analysts. On the other hand, if the entire connection is encrypted, it is collected and stored in a database, periodically accessed in order to retrieve data and metadata about X.509, SSL, and TLS exchanged protocol messages in order to be analyzed by the analytics described in [11]. As outlined earlier, all the compression/encryption tests are performed using an SVM, capable of correctly classifying network packets, but the proposed classifier could be substituted with other valid alternatives, such as random forest models.

4.2. Feature Extraction

As discussed in Section 4.1, sequential features allow us to understand if the content of a network packet is either compressed or encrypted. We rely on a statistical package developed by the Information Technology Laboratory at the National Institute of Standards and Technology, containing a set of 15 tests that measure the randomness of a binary sequence [34]. These tests have been designed to provide a first step towards the decision whether or not a generated binary sequence can be used in cryptographic applications, namely if the sequence appears to be randomly generated. In other words, each new bit of the sequence should be unpredictable. From a statistical point of view, each test verifies if the sequence being under analysis is random. This null hypothesis can be either rejected or accepted depending on the statistic value on the data exceeding or not a specific value—called critical value—that is typically far in the tails of a distribution of reference. Test reference distributions used in the NIST tests are the standard normal and the χ^2 distributions. Even if the statistical package contains 15 tests, we use only 5 of them, because the length N of the binary sequence we test does not meet the corresponding input size recommendation in [34]. To each sequence, we apply the following tests: frequency within a block, longest-run-of-ones in a block, serial test, approximate entropy, and cumulative sums. In addition, in our experimental evaluations, we extract some statistical properties and compute the Shannon entropy metrics [36] that, combined with the previously mentioned tests, have shown to improve the overall accuracy of the classification. As statistical properties, the following features are extracted from the corresponding hexadecimal representation h of a bit stream of N bytes:

- number of different alphanumeric characters in h normalized over h length;
- number of different letters in h normalized over h length;
- longest consecutive sequence of the same character in h normalized over h length.

4.3. Input Sanitization

For accurately training machine learning models, the training set should be as much "clean" as possible. In Section 4.1 we have already discussed how labeling based on connection metadata could be error prone either due to potential custom configurations of services, intentional misuse of specific protocols by attackers, or network protocols encapsulating compressed data. In addition, during our experimental evaluations, we have observed that in some cases the employed traffic analyzer can assign an empty label or multiple labels to a single network packet. While in the first case bit streams with empty labels can be easily discarded for the training phase, in the presence of multi-labels, it is possible to assign a unique correct label if a protocol that is monitored by the prototype itself exists among the labels. As an example, if the assigned labels are NTLM, GSSAPI, SMB, and DCE_RPC, the resulting label is SMB. For these reasons the very first step of the sanitization module is to correct the multi-labels associated to bit streams and discard the empty ones. Then, we train an ensemble of one-class SVMs, one for each protocol (see Figure 3): each different classifier is properly tuned to filter out outliers from the raw dataset. As stated in Section 4.1, HTTP and SMB requests or responses may contain either the content of (compressed) files or other types of information that are not strictly correlated with the specific protocol communication patterns. Trained models are then applied to identify these kinds of network packets, and they are removed from the raw dataset. This preprocessed dataset is used to train a supervised support vector machine, called compression/encryption detector, by applying a one-vs-all classification for detecting packets which are either compressed or encrypted. It is worth noting that all these models are still inaccurate because they are trained on a "dirty" dataset. Hence, to further increase the quality of the labels and obtain the final training set, the compression/encryption detector is fed with clear-text bit streams to remove possible compressed/encrypted packets from clear-text protocols, as in the case of proxied environments. The result of this sanitization process is a dataset which allows to train and validate two accurate models: an artificial neural network for clear-text protocols and an SVM for compressed and encrypted traffic.

4.4. Anomaly Detection

During the test phase (see Figure 2), bit streams are analyzed by the trained ANN. In turn, the ANN flags three different cases as potential tunneling attacks and alerts security analysts when these cases occur: (i) the high confidence detection of more than one protocol in the same connection, (ii) the low confidence detection of one protocol for all the packets in the same connection, and (iii) the labeling, both with high and low confidence, of one or more protocols for the packets belonging to the same connection (as in the case of secure protocols over DNS). As later specified in Section 5, in the ANN, the high/low confidence threshold c can be dynamically set. In any case, the detection of encrypted packets into a clear-text connection generates alert notifications enriched with the information about the presence of encrypted protocol messages. Possibly, notified alerts can be filtered whitelisting source and/or destination IPs to reduce the false positives caused by well-known machines.

Hence, if some packets of the connection are classified with low confidence, the corresponding bit stream's sequential features (refer to Section 4.2) are given in input to the compression/encryption detector. If all the packets contained in the connection are encrypted, then the connection and its corresponding metadata are given in input to the SSL/TLS analytics for further scrutiny [11]. On the contrary, if the connection contains some compressed/encrypted packets or none of them, depending on the protocol, the connection is considered anomalous. Indeed, it is worth noting that the combination of two different protocols is not always a signal of an occurring attack: as already discussed, SMB and HTTP connections can contain protocol-specific messages along with compressed data; however, DNS messages interleaved with other protocols are highly suspicious. Finally, since each single module of the proposed prototype has been trained only with legitimate traffic, it is potentially able to spot zero-day attacks having features which are different from the ones usually observed in the network.

5. Experimental Evaluation

The proposed prototype and the experimental evaluations have been, respectively, implemented and performed in Python. The size N we have chosen for the byte sequences, extracted from network packets, is 52 bytes. More in detail, we retrieve the first 64 bytes of the payload of each TCP/UDP packet, from which we remove the first 12 B: indeed, a preliminary evaluation has shown that these first bytes had a very low variance in their binary representation among different packets of the same protocol. The specific selection of the byte sequence to extract has improved the accuracy of the trained neural network, increasing its anomaly detection capabilities.

For the experimental evaluation of the proposed prototype, we collected both benign and malicious datasets. The benign communication dataset contains a subset of legitimate traffic observed in a real corporate network during a period of about 2 days. From this initial dataset, we sample connections to start building the models training sets and the dataset that will be used for testing. Figure 4 summarizes general statistics about the collected training set in terms of packets, before and after sanitization, while Table 1 reports how the test set of legitimate network traffic is characterized. The sanitization process makes the training set, which is obviously unbalanced towards encrypted protocols, balanced: indeed, after sanitization, the number of packets belonging to, respectively, clear-text and secure protocols is almost even. It is worth noting that the balanced training set for the ANN, containing DHCP, DNS, NTP, HTTP, and SMB packets, also comprises data belonging to the KRB network protocol (i.e., encrypted): our experimental evaluations have shown that during the test phase, the neural network performs better when it is also trained with encrypted byte sequences. As an ANN, we use a Keras sequential model with three hidden layers. The input layer accepts 416 bits (i.e., 52 B) and the output layer consists of six neurons, one for each clear-text protocol and KRB. Regarding SVMs, we rely on the open-source library scikit-learn. For completeness, we report in Table 2 the hyperparameters we have used to train the different SVMs in the sanitization module; in addition, we also report the hyperparameters we obtained by tuning the compression/encryption detector in the validation phase. It is worth mentioning that the parameter t, in Table 2, is used for each protocol one-class SVM as a threshold to filter only those outliers which have a Shannon entropy greater than t.

The intuition behind this filtering is that byte sequences having high entropy do not specifically belong to clear-text protocol communications; thus, they have to be discarded from the training set.

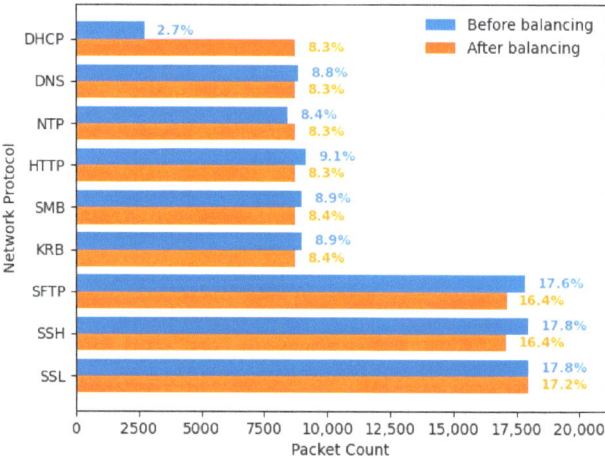

Figure 4. Packet distribution for each network protocol, before and after balancing.

Table 1. Benign test set composition.

Statistics	Count [(%)]
DNS packets	30,669 (1.10%)
SMB packets	65,944 (2.35%)
HTTP packets	262 (0.01%)
NTP packets	46 (0.002%)
DHCP packets	20 (0.001%)
KRB packets	741 (0.03%)
SFTP packets	69,158 (2.46%)
Not labeled packets	61,552 (2.20%)
SSL packets	2,571,608 (91.84%)
Distinct connections	51,459
Distinct source machines	758
Distinct dest. machines	1566

On the other hand, malicious datasets are constituted by packet captures (PCAPs) shared by [37–39]. The former dataset contains three different types of DNS tunnels generated in a controlled environment, whose sizes are approximately 750 MB each. Tunneled data contain, respectively, SFTP, SSH, and Telnet malicious protocol messages. Each sample is made up of one single connection containing millions of DNS packets. It is reasonable to note that such connections would either easily stand out to security analysts or be simply detectable through well-known statistical approaches (e.g., outlier detection). Subsequently, as stated in Section 4.1, our approach groups data by connection; therefore, a single malicious packet is enough to flag the entire connection as anomalous. For the above reasons, we have decided to split each sample in n different connections, composed by approximately 5000 DNS packets each. The size of the split, reported in Table 3, has been chosen according to the size of the connections monitored in the controlled environment. The second malicious dataset, instead, was born by the collaboration between the Bell Canada company's Cyber Threat Intelligence group and the Canadian Institute for Cybersecurity.

Table 2. Support vector machine hyperparameter settings.

Model	Kernel	γ	ν	t	C
DHCP one-class SVM	RBF	0.7	0.03	0.77	–
DNS one-class SVM	RBF	0.7	0.03	0.77	–
NTP one-class SVM	RBF	0.03	0.1	0.92	–
HTTP one-class SVM	RBF	0.08	0.07	0.91	–
SMB one-class SVM	RBF	0.06	0.08	0.77	–
KRB one-class SVM	RBF	0.04	0.05	0.97	–
SFTP one-class SVM	RBF	0.7	0.05	0.97	–
SSH one-class SVM	RBF	0.7	0.05	0.97	–
SSL one-class SVM	RBF	0.0001	0.0028	0.97	–
Compression/encryption detector	RBF	0.01	–	–	100

In this dataset, we only take into account DNS packets that, in their payloads, contain exfiltrations of various types of files and we discard legitimate traffic. Moreover, it is worth mentioning that all the packets contained in [38] have been truncated at capture time to 96 B; this has required a slightly different approach to test these samples that will be discussed later in this Section. Finally, [39] is a single packet capture to test detection and alerting capabilities of Packetbeat, Elastic's network packet analyzer. Malicious packet captures have been injected into the network security platform in order to be processed and analyzed as ordinary traffic. Table 3 reports a summary of the malicious assembled datasets: for each PCAP, we list the number of packets in the capture and which of these packets have been successfully processed by the platform's network analyzer (i.e., those packets whose size is greater or equal than 64 B); in addition, Table 3 depicts the number of connections in the PCAP and the number of them that have been identified as protocol tunneling attacks (i.e., true positives TP). Finally, the true positive rate TPR of the proposed detector is reported for each packet capture. Analogously, Table 4 reports the same information contained in Table 3, but with reference to the test set described in Table 1. Being legitimate traffic, the last two columns report the connections mistakenly classified as tunnels (i.e., false positives FP) and the false positive rate FPR. The results of the evaluation, reported in Tables 3 and 4, show a false positive rate and a true positive rate, respectively, equal to 5.8% and 96.6%. The overall accuracy of the proposed prototype is 97.1%, while the resulting F1-score is 95.6%.

We conclude this section by discussing how we slightly modified the proposed approach, used in the other datasets, to be compliant with [38]. Indeed, the DNS packets contained in this dataset have been truncated during traffic acquisition, resulting in byte sequences that do not have the same length. In order to solve this dataset generation problem, we reduced all the DNS packets to a common length of 44 B, discarding the shorter byte sequences and trimming the longer ones. The result of the filtering operation is clearly shown in Table 3, where the number of processed PCAP packets is more than 54% less than the ones received in input by the traffic analyzer.

Since the bit-stream lengths are different from the datasets [37,39], we retrained our ANN to be fed with 44 B sequences. On the contrary, for this evaluation, we maintained the same hyperparameters for the different SVMs, reported in Table 2, and the same threshold c, used in the other experiments. In particular, for all our experimental evaluations, we set c to 0.999999 in order to maximize the algorithm sensitivity and to compensate for the lesser information provided by the processing of [38]. This explains why, in the experimental evaluations, we were not able to achieve a very low false positive rate, as shown in Table 4.

Table 3. Malicious test set summary.

Tunnel Type	No. of PCAP Packets	No. of Processed PCAP Packets	No. of Connections	TP	TPR(%)
Telnet over DNS tunnel [37]	2.4 M	2.2 M	457	457	100%
SFTP over DNS tunnel [37]	2 M	1 M	209	209	100%
SSH over DNS tunnel [37]	2.8 M	2.7 M	545	545	100%
Light file exfiltration [38]	187,500	102,000	7617	7361	96.6%
Heavy file exfiltration [38]	1.34 M	765,000	43,964	42,441	96.5%
Data exfiltration over Iodine DNS tunnel [39]	438	247	1	1	100%

Table 4. Benign test set summary.

Dataset	No. of PCAP Packets	No. of Processed PCAP Packets	No. of Connections	FP	FPR(%)
Legitimate traffic	5.4 M	2.8 M	51,459	2966	5.8%

However, in context where a high number of false positives could be detrimental, c can be tuned to obtain a 0.5% false positive rate or lesser without losing accuracy on protocol tunneling attacks.

6. Discussion

One of the most relevant challenges in cybersecurity is the detection of zero-day attacks, which can easily evade all the products based on signature or pattern detection. The proposed approach leverages various characteristics that are known to perform well when facing zero-day threats [40] like, for example, the absence of malicious samples in the training set, the training set sanitization process, and the absence of signature-based features and filters.

On the other hand, in Section 4.4, we suggested the usage of whitelists as a way of reducing false positives. While in the experimental evaluation of Section 5, we intentionally used them as little as possible (i.e., only 11 of the 758 machines in the benign test set were actually whitelisted), a security analyst could customize such whitelists in order to filter out machines that do not require monitoring. Adding domain knowledge to machine learning algorithms in the form of data (in our context, machines) that should not be modeled or monitored can not only reduce the amount of alerts that an analyst has to evaluate, but also increase model performance. In conjunction with the integration of whitelists, the number of false positives generated by our approach can be tuned in two other ways. The first one is represented by the threshold c which, as already described in Section 5, controls the sensitivity of the ANN; in turn, it impacts the false positive rate because the lower the minimum value of the ANN output confidence considered as "high", the harder to match the conditions we have defined for the connection to be an anomaly (see Section 4.4). The second way of reducing false positives is a periodic retraining of proposed models. As briefly described in Section 7, once the prototype will be included in a streaming architecture, the training phase will be performed periodically. Real networks changes over time, so keeping the models updated is the key to maintain an accurate modeling of what is the current state of the network.

Finally, as already pointed out in Section 3, differently from other approaches, we extract features directly from the raw traffic without relying on network analyzers that reconstruct network traffic metadata. This allows to save computing resources and to speed up the analyses. Furthermore, the use of bit-stream representation is independent from protocol specific fields (e.g., DNS query field), making the prototype also able to detect tunneling attacks on different clear-text protocols.

7. Conclusions

In this paper, we proposed a software prototype for detecting protocol tunneling attacks in a monitored network. Relying on a combination of machine learning and deep learning techniques, the proposed solution identifies anomalous connections that deviate from the ones usually established in the network. Since machine learning models are only built based on legitimate traffic, the proposed solution is therefore able to deal with zero-day attacks, because malicious traffic is not required for the learning phase. The prototype has been evaluated both on malicious and benign datasets: results show a very high accuracy in detecting malicious samples and a low false positive rate on legitimate traffic.

As future work, we plan to optimize the algorithm through a deeper analysis on how the choice of byte-stream length affects the computational time, in order to find a value which guarantees the best trade-off between efficiency and accuracy. Indeed, in this work, we mainly focused on accuracy. Secondly, we envision that the engineered prototype will be integrated into a streaming architecture, where new data will be analyzed by the proposed prototype as soon as they are collected to provide the fastest possible response. In parallel, the models of the protocol tunneling detector are periodically retrained to keep them up-to-date with possible deviations from the usual behaviour of the monitored network. It is important to mention that the envisioned streaming architecture can always count on a trained model to process incoming traffic during possible retrainings; old models will be available until the new ones are ready. Finally, in Section 6, we discussed the benefits of IP whitelisting filters. Once in production, the prototype can be easily extended with other SOC-defined whitelists (e.g., whitelists regarding domains and/or autonomous systems), allowing security analysts to enrich the proposed detector with their domain-specific knowledge, further reducing possible false positives and improving the overall performance.

Author Contributions: Conceptualization, F.S., D.U. and F.B.; methodology, F.S. and D.U.; software, F.S. and B.C.; validation, F.S., B.C., D.U. and F.B.; formal analysis, F.S. and B.C.; investigation, F.S. and B.C.; resources, D.U. and F.B.; data curation, F.S. and B.C.; writing—original draft preparation, F.S., B.C, D.U. and F.B.; writing—review and editing, F.S., B.C. and D.U.; supervision, D.U. and F.B. All authors have read and agreed to the published version of the manuscript.

Funding: This research received no external funding.

Data Availability Statement: Datasets containing DNS tunneling attacks can be found here: https://s3.eu-central-1.wasabisys.com/dns-tunneling/dns_tunnel_sftp.pcapng, https://s3.eu-central-1.wasabisys.com/dns-tunneling/dns_tunnel_ssh.pcapng, https://s3.eu-central-1.wasabisys.com/dns-tunneling/dns_tunnel_telnet.pcapng, https://www.unb.ca/cic/datasets/dns-exf-2021.html, and https://github.com/elastic/examples/blob/master/Security%20Analytics/dns_tunnel_detection/dns-tunnel-iodine.pcap, all accessed on 17 October 2023. Regarding the dataset containing the legitimate communications observed in a real corporate network, it is owned by aizoOn Technology Consulting and cannot be made available due to company policies.

Conflicts of Interest: The authors declare no conflict of interest, given that aizoOn Technology Consulting has not interfered with their ability to analyze and interpret data. Moreover, for this research, authors have not received any additional grant or funding.

References

1. ENISA Threat Landscape 2022. Available online: https://www.enisa.europa.eu/publications/enisa-threat-landscape-2022 (accessed on 6 February 2023).
2. Cost of a Data Breach. A Million-Dollar Race to Detect and Respond. 2022. Available online: https://www.ibm.com/reports/data-breach (accessed on 6 February 2023).
3. The SolarWinds Cyber-Attack: What You Need to Know. Available online: https://www.cisecurity.org/solarwinds (accessed on 6 February 2023).
4. 7 Top Trends in Cybersecurity for 2022. Available online: https://www.gartner.com/en/articles/7-top-trends-in-cybersecurity-for-2022 (accessed on 6 February 2023).
5. Ucci, D.; Aniello, L.; Baldoni, R. Survey of machine learning techniques for malware analysis. *Comput. Secur.* **2019**, *81*, 123–147. [CrossRef]
6. Protocol Tunneling. Available online: https://attack.mitre.org/techniques/T1572/ (accessed on 6 February 2023).
7. Encrypted Traffic Analysis. Available online: https://www.enisa.europa.eu/publications/encrypted-traffic-analysis (accessed on 6 February 2023).
8. Bisio, F.; Saeli, S.; Lombardo, P.; Bernardi, D.; Perotti, A.; Massa, D. Real-time behavioral DGA detection through machine learning. In Proceedings of the International Carnahan Conference on Security Technology (ICCST), Madrid, Spain, 23–26 October 2017; pp. 1–6. [CrossRef]
9. Lombardo, P.; Saeli, S.; Bisio, F.; Bernardi, D.; Massa, D. Fast Flux Service Network Detection via Data Mining on Passive DNS Traffic. In Proceedings of the International Conference on Information Security, Guildford, UK, 9–12 September 2018; pp. 463–480. [CrossRef]
10. Saeli, S.; Bisio, F.; Lombardo, P.; Massa, D. DNS Covert Channel Detection via Behavioral Analysis: A Machine Learning Approach. In Proceedings of the International Conference on Malicious and Unwanted Software (MALWARE), Nantucket, MA, USA, 22–24 October 2019; pp. 46–55.
11. Ucci, D.; Sobrero, F.; Bisio, F.; Zorzino, M. Near-real-time Anomaly Detection in Encrypted Traffic using Machine Learning Techniques. In Proceedings of the IEEE Symposium Series on Computational Intelligence, SSCI 2021, Orlando, FL, USA, 5–7 December 2021; pp. 1–8. [CrossRef]
12. Felt, A.P.; Barnes, R.; King, A.; Palmer, C.; Bentzel, C.; Tabriz, P. Measuring HTTPS Adoption on the Web. In Proceedings of the 26th USENIX Conference on Security Symposium, Vancouver, BC, Canada, 16–18 August 2017; pp. 1323–1338.
13. The Relevance of Network Security in an Encrypted World. Available online: https://blogs.vmware.com/networkvirtualization/2020/09/network-security-encrypted.html/ (accessed on 6 February 2023).
14. Encryption, Privacy in the Internet Trends Report. Available online: https://duo.com/decipher/encryption-privacy-in-the-internet-trends-report (accessed on 6 February 2023).
15. Keeping Up with the Performance Demands of Encrypted Web Traffic. Available online: https://www.fortinet.com/blog/industry-trends/keeping-up-with-performance-demands-of-encrypted-web-traffic (accessed on 6 February 2023).

16. Google Transparency Report: HTTPS Encryption on the Web. Available online: https://transparencyreport.google.com/https/overview?hl=en (accessed on 6 February 2023).
17. Cisco Encrypted Traffic Analytics. Available online: https://www.cisco.com/c/en/us/solutions/collateral/enterprise-networks/enterprise-network-security/nb-09-encrytd-traf-anlytcs-wp-cte-en.pdf (accessed on 6 February 2023).
18. ENISA Threat Landscape—Malware. Available online: https://www.enisa.europa.eu/publications/malware/at_download/fullReport (accessed on 6 February 2023).
19. Taylor, R.W.; Fritsch, E.J.; Liederbach, J. *Digital Crime and Digital Terrorism*; Prentice Hall Press: Hoboken, NJ, USA, 2014.
20. Cyber Security Review. Available online: https://www.treasuryandrisk.com/2012/02/01/cyber-security-review/ (accessed on 6 February 2023).
21. Yadav, T.; Mallari, R.A. Technical aspects of cyber kill chain. *arXiv* **2016**, arXiv:1606.03184.
22. Applying Machine Learning to Network Anomalies. Available online: https://www.youtube.com/watch?v=qOfgNd-qijI (accessed on 6 February 2023).
23. Wang, Y.; Zhou, A.; Liao, S.; Zheng, R.; Hu, R.; Zhang, L. A comprehensive survey on DNS tunnel detection. *Comput. Netw.* **2021**, *197*, 108322. [CrossRef]
24. Do, V.T.; Engelstad, P.; Feng, B.; van Do, T. Detection of DNS Tunneling in Mobile Networks Using Machine Learning. In Proceedings of the Information Science and Applications, Macau, China, 20–23 March 2017; Kim, K., Joukov, N., Eds.; Springer: Singapore, 2017; pp. 221–230.
25. Buczak, A.L.; Hanke, P.A.; Cancro, G.J.; Toma, M.K.; Watkins, L.A.; Chavis, J.S. Detection of Tunnels in PCAP Data by Random Forests. In Proceedings of the CISRC'16 11th Annual Cyber and Information Security Research Conference, Oak Ridge, TN, USA, 5–7 April 2016. [CrossRef]
26. Lambion, D.; Josten, M.; Olumofin, F.; De Cock, M. Malicious DNS Tunneling Detection in Real-Traffic DNS Data. In Proceedings of the 2020 IEEE International Conference on Big Data (Big Data), Atlanta, GA, USA, 10–13 December 2020; pp. 5736–5738. [CrossRef]
27. Palau, F.; Catania, C.; Guerra, J.; Garcia, S.; Rigaki, M. DNS tunneling: A deep learning based lexicographical detection approach. *arXiv* **2020**, arXiv:2006.06122.
28. Zhang, J.; Yang, L.; Yu, S.; Ma, J. A DNS tunneling detection method based on deep learning models to prevent data exfiltration. In Proceedings of the Network and System Security: 13th International Conference, NSS 2019, Sapporo, Japan, 15–18 December 2019; Springer: Berlin/Heidelberg, Germany, 2019; pp. 520–535.
29. Ahmed, J.; Gharakheili, H.H.; Raza, Q.; Russell, C.; Sivaraman, V. Real-time detection of DNS exfiltration and tunneling from enterprise networks. In Proceedings of the 2019 IFIP/IEEE Symposium on Integrated Network and Service Management (IM), Arlington, VA, USA, 8–12 April 2019; pp. 649–653.
30. Sanjay; Rajendran, B.; Pushparaj Shetty, D. DNS amplification & DNS tunneling attacks simulation, detection and mitigation approaches. In Proceedings of the 2020 International Conference on Inventive Computation Technologies (ICICT), Coimbatore, India, 26–28 February 2020; pp. 230–236.
31. Vapnik, V. *The Nature of Statistical Learning Theory*; Springer Science & Business Media: Berlin/Heidelberg, Germany, 2013.
32. Swersky, L.; Marques, H.O.; Sander, J.; Campello, R.J.; Zimek, A. On the evaluation of outlier detection and one-class classification methods. In Proceedings of the 2016 IEEE International Conference on Data Science and Advanced Analytics (DSAA), Montreal, QC, Canada, 17–19 October 2016; pp. 1–10. [CrossRef]
33. Abiodun, O.I.; Jantan, A.; Omolara, A.E.; Dada, K.V.; Mohamed, N.A.; Arshad, H. State-of-the-art in artificial neural network applications: A survey. *Heliyon* **2018**, *4*, e00938. [CrossRef] [PubMed]
34. A Statistical Test Suite for Random and Pseudorandom Number Generators for Cryptographic Applications. Available online: https://nvlpubs.nist.gov/nistpubs/legacy/sp/nistspecialpublication800-22r1a.pdf (accessed on 6 February 2023).
35. Chawla, N.V.; Bowyer, K.W.; Hall, L.O.; Kegelmeyer, W.P. SMOTE: Synthetic Minority over-Sampling Technique. *J. Artif. Int. Res.* **2002**, *16*, 321–357. [CrossRef]
36. Shannon, C.E. A Mathematical Theory of Communication. *Bell Syst. Tech. J.* **1948**, *27*, 379–423. [CrossRef]
37. Berg, A.; Forsberg, D. Identifying DNS-tunneled traffic with predictive models. *arXiv* **2019**, arXiv:1906.11246.
38. Mahdavifar, S.; Hanafy Salem, A.; Victor, P.; Razavi, A.H.; Garzon, M.; Hellberg, N.; Lashkari, A.H. Lightweight Hybrid Detection of Data Exfiltration Using DNS Based on Machine Learning. In Proceedings of the ICCNS 2021: The 11th International Conference on Communication and Network Security, Weihai, China, 3–5 December 2021; pp. 80–86. [CrossRef]
39. Iodine DNS Tunnel. Available online: https://github.com/elastic/examples/blob/master/Security%20Analytics/dns_tunnel_detection/dns-tunnel-iodine.pcap (accessed on 6 February 2023).
40. Ali, S.; Rehman, S.U.; Imran, A.; Adeem, G.; Iqbal, Z.; Kim, K.I. Comparative Evaluation of AI-Based Techniques for Zero-Day Attacks Detection. *Electronics* **2022**, *11*, 3934. [CrossRef]

Journal of
Cybersecurity and Privacy

MDPI

Article

Power-Based Side-Channel Attacks on Program Control Flow with Machine Learning Models

Andey Robins [1,*], Stone Olguin [2], Jarek Brown [2], Clay Carper [2] and Mike Borowczak [1]

1   Department of Electrical and Computer Engineering, University of Central Florida, Orlando, FL 32816, USA; mike.borowczak@ucf.edu
2   Department of Electrical Engineering and Computer Science, University of Wyoming, Laramie, WY 82070, USA; aolguin1@uwyo.edu (S.O.); jbrow125@uwyo.edu (J.B.); ccarper2@uwyo.edu (C.C.)
*   Correspondence: ja548335@ucf.edu

Abstract: The control flow of a program represents valuable and sensitive information; in embedded systems, this information can take on even greater value as the resources, control flow, and execution of the system have more constraints and functional implications than modern desktop environments. Early works have demonstrated the possibility of recovering such control flow through power-based side-channel attacks in tightly constrained environments; however, they relied on meaningful differences in computational states or data dependency to distinguish between states in a state machine. This work applies more advanced machine learning techniques to state machines which perform identical operations in all branches of control flow. Complete control flow is recovered with 99% accuracy even in situations where 97% of work is outside of the control flow structures. This work demonstrates the efficacy of these approaches for recovering control flow information; continues developing available knowledge about power-based attacks on program control flow; and examines the applicability of multiple standard machine learning models to the problem of classification over power-based side-channel information.

Keywords: side-channel attack; machine learning; power analysis; cybersecurity; control flow; dynamic program analysis

Citation: Robins, A.; Olguin, S.; Brown, J.; Carper, C.; Borowczak, M. Power-Based Side-Channel Attacks on Program Control Flow with Machine Learning Models. *J. Cybersecur. Priv.* **2023**, *3*, 351–363. https://doi.org/10.3390/jcp3030018

Academic Editors: Phil Legg and Giorgio Giacinto

Received: 27 May 2023
Revised: 22 June 2023
Accepted: 28 June 2023
Published: 7 July 2023

1. Introduction

A finite-state machine (FSM) is a computation model commonly used within the embedded system space; program control flow in embedded devices is often handled by an FSM. Smaller state machines, those with fewer states and transitions, can exist in limited purpose devices, such as vending machines, or more complex devices such as telecommunications devices. Such devices are often the target of Side-Channel Analysis (SCA), which aims to recover information from an embedded device. Power-based side-channel data are most commonly measured directly from the device via an instrumented VCC line. While this method requires direct access to the victim device, it is the most common method for gathering data for SCA. Other common side-channels utilized in SCA include system byproducts such as electromagnetic radiation, sound, and heat.

With a constant increase in consumer usage of Internet of Things (IoT) devices, low-power embedded systems are constantly being put into operation. One popular example of such a system making use of an FSM are smart locks. Often, these devices allow an end-user to configure multiple access codes and enable logging when a code is used. Access may be controlled remotely, allowing for on-the-fly adjustments to user access permissions. With the growing popularity of smart locks and similar smart devices, if an attacker were able to reverse-engineer the control flow inherent to the device, they may be able to influence behavior within the FSM. One informational prerequisite to building out such an attack would likely include identifying and characterizing the FSM responsible for whether or not the lock is engaged. Further, being able to exfiltrate sensitive data, such as the secret key that determines the lock's activation state, could allow an attacker to bypass the smart lock, granting them unimpeded access to the end-user's home.

This work extends the previous work of Carper et al. [1], which performed Differential Power Analysis (DPA) on data collected through the use of the ChipWhisperer hardware platform [2]. Specifically, the ChipWhisperer Nano was used to gather power-trace data. An FSM that consisted of two states conducting identical operations, in conjunction with an oracle-based input guiding program control flow, was utilized for data collection. The resulting power-traces were used to train multiple machine learning classification algorithms. These trained algorithms were then used to differentiate between state transitions occurring during code execution on the microcontroller. Further, recovery was successful when applied to 256 distinct classes of state transitions, resulting in the identification of the underlying process control flow. This work deviates from the prior foundational work by exploring additional machine learning backed solutions to the problem of control flow recovery, as well as exploring homogeneous operations within an individual state's computations to experimentally determine what degree of divergence in state behavior is necessary to ensure program control flow recovery.

Contributions of this work seek to answer three research questions. First, is different behavior required in each state of an embedded state machine in order to completely recover the transitions? Second, to what degree does the proportion of time spent in control flow and in a particular state of the FSM impact the recoverability of the state transition ordering? Finally, how effective are "off-the-shelf," meaning algorithms with no manual configuration, machine learning models when applied to the task of recovering control flow information?

This work is organized as follows. Section 2 motivates the side-channel analysis space and establishes relevant background information. Section 3 outlines the data collection and classification process undertaken in this work. Section 4 outlines the classification accuracy and Section 5 examines the application of results to the research questions. Section 6 concludes this work with an acknowledgment of limitations binding this work and commentary on future research directions required to better understand the control flow recovery space using power-based side-channels.

2. Related Works

The history of power-based side-channel attacks has had a number of meaningful advances coming in the last few decades. Despite the coming exploration into the efficacy of such power-based attacks, recovery of higher-order, control-level information such as the execution path through a state machine was under-explored until very recently. Thus, this section presents a brief overview of relevant findings in power-based side-channels, along with its applications and crossover with the field of Automated Machine Learning (AutoML), and characterizes the relevant previous work to motivate the experiments conducted herein. AutoML, the practice of automatically searching machine learning pipelines for effective ML configurations, has begun to be applied to other side-channel problems such as cryptographic key recovery with high success, motivating attempts to apply AutoML findings to the problem of program control flow recovery.

2.1. SCA Backgrounds

Common side-channel attacks involve attacks on the power usage of a device. The most common of these are simple power analysis (SPA) and differential power analysis (DPA) [3]. These methods of side-channel analysis inspired research in device-level SCA; they have even been referred to as the "bedrock" for SCA research [4]. The direct analysis of power usage by gathering power traces allows for a user to be able to understand the implementations of cryptographic operations of a device, and it can allow for the extraction of a secret key. SPA and DPA are both considered passive attacks as they entail only observing various properties of the device; however, active attacks are another avenue explored in the literature. Fault injection attacks, a breadth of attacks which span voltage glitching to temperature extremes, are another frequently explored avenue for SCA [5,6]. Other powerful techniques exist, such as combining different passive and active attack strategies. For example, a novel analysis tool Differential Behavioral Analysis (DBA) is a combination of a Safe Error Attack (SEA) and DPA [7]. DBA can be defended against using traditional bit-masking strategies. This work makes use of passive attacks exclusively, and specifically employs simple power analysis as a means to recover control flow information.

One of the most common applications of side-channel attacks is in the subversion of cryptographic systems. These attacks on crypto-schema employ both active and passive attacks. The injection of faults has been shown to be able to effectively recover a secret AES key, and the power observation making use of DPA similarly is able to recover a secret AES key [8,9]. Many of the early works in SCA demonstrated various ways to recover secret cryptographic information, either keys or text, to some degree; however, with the advent of post-quantum cryptography, many of the crypto-systems currently employed will become insecure and obsolete [10]. For more discussion of the topic, we refer the curious reader to one of the surveys on the state-of-the-art in the field [11,12]. The realm of side-channels is evolving in cooperation with these searches for quantum-resistant algorithms, and early works have demonstrated strong recovery attacks for cryptographic secrets in post-quantum, lattice-based cryptographic systems [13].

The rising prevalence of SCA in cryptographically sensitive applications and its impact to the security of a device led to development of different countermeasures against SCA. Borowczak and Vemuri developed a method to create side-channel resistant finite-state machines (S*FSMs) [14]. This introduced an algorithm to transform FSMs to side-channel resistant FSMs. The method of Random Process Interrupts (RPIs) allows for some of the operations in cryptographic devices to be less vulnerable to timing attacks by implementing strategic delays in execution [15]. In addition to the RPI method, two other popular methods of implementing countermeasures against side-channel power include masking and hiding [16]. Masking involves generating a random "mask" value that will attempt to conceal any intermediate value during cryptographic operations. Masking removes correlations between the gathered traces and the cryptographic secret information. Hiding involves trying to make traces appear to be random. This randomness can appear by adding noise to the power or implementing random delays or desynchronization. As a result, the gathered traces are harder to extract secret information. Therefore, many countermeasures against SCA have been devised, but DPA methods would still find secure information even with countermeasures in place. In the same work that introduced RPIs, the countermeasure is still shown to be vulnerable to DPA [15]. Thus, even with countermeasures in place, improvements of applications of SCA can circumvent these protections and secret information can still be extracted.

Instead of collecting and analyzing arbitrary power traces to determine the leakage of information Test Vector Leakage Assessment (TVLA) can be used [17]. TVLA involves using statistical tests to determine if there is significant evidence to determine if the device had any leakage. Goodwill et al. utilized the Welch's t-test to determine if there is a significant difference between two groups. The hypothesis tested whether the gathered traces are truly random or if there is leakage present within traces. While this methodology can be beneficial and has been used recently to show side-channel vulnerabilities in some of the NIST lightweight cryptography round 2 candidate s-boxes [18,19], TVLA can have issues demonstrated by relatively high rates of false negatives or false positives, even when using different tests such as the Pearson χ^2 test [20].

Signal Processing also can be used for SCA both as an attack vector and for defensive countermeasures, as mentioned by Le et al. [21]. In addition, Le et al. also demonstrates how three different signal processing techniques could be applied to SCA, which would allow for more ways to implement it. The work also defends using signal processing to mitigate SCA. There is also a precedent for AutoML being utilized for signal processing; an example uses the AutoML procedure of acquiring correct hyperparameters for deep learning to classify Electroencephalography (EEG) signals [22]. The work also claims that EEG signal classification is complex enough that machine learning techniques such as deep learning are "appropriate to find the best solutions". The hyperparameter tuning and deep learning from AutoML were stated to have less overfitting, and thus, yielded more optimized models for classifying the EEG signals.

Time-series forecasting, although prominently implemented with traditional machine learning methods, has significantly less implementation within AutoML toolchains, being cited as "still in the development stage" [23]. It is demonstrated in their review article that there are gaps in traditional time-series forecasting with machine learning in terms of reapplying AutoML to time-series methods that used traditional machine learning [23]. The article showcases that there are research avenues, such as deep learning or neural architecture search (NAS), to implement AutoML for time-series analysis.

AutoML has been implemented in analyzing time-series data, as experimented previously in comparison to rigorous, hand-crafted machine learning models [24]. In this paper, its authors conclude that in short-term models for time-series predictions, AutoML does not outperform traditional methods of using Machine Learning by manually tuning hyperparameters and preprocessing data. However, suggestions for time-series analysis with AutoML are: validation on the selection strategy with statistical significance tests; adding permutation strategies; and considering the cost of using AutoML with the benefit of its implementation. Additional implementation of AutoML utilize the process of NAS to efficiently search for an effective neural network architecture for utilization on time-series data [25]. It mentions that AutoML significantly improved the performance of searching a data-augmented time-series neural network architecture. The significance of NAS's performance boost was such that it outperformed other "best" statistical models. In terms of future possible improvements, the authors mention that further performance enhancements on the data augmentation could come from using other deep learning models such as GRU-AE and ConvLSTM.

One of the implementations of machine learning for side-channel analysis is named Deep Learning-based Side-Channel Analysis (DL-SCA) [26]. DL-SCA is a new area of research, which is signified by a large increase of papers on this topic. An advantage of DL-SCA includes more powerful analysis by taking up to a factor of five times less data to break through targets with countermeasures as compared to template attacks. DL-SCA also requires little to no effort when it comes to preprocessing and preparing the attack of the side-channel measurements. Related to this deep learning AutoML approach of side-channel analysis is the Deep Learning Leakage Assessment (DL-LA), a method of verifying that a trace has significant leakage information [27]. DL-LA implements AutoML only for the analysis aspect of SCA. An open challenge to using DL-LA is that there are no clear advantages to DL-LA for the significance of side-channel traces [26]. This challenge demonstrates that if a significant advantage to leakage assessment is gained by utilizing DL-LA, then the DL-SCA techniques can also be used with DL-LA.

The increase in popularity of SCA in security has led to developments in both attack vectors and defensive countermeasures. Starting from DPA [3], to implementing AutoML methods of deep learning with TVLA [27], the security aspect of SCA from a defensive and offensive standpoint have increased in scope from simple power analysis to implementations of machine learning, demonstrating a considerable growth of the research area. The idea of utilizing AutoML for DPA is a growing research area that has openings for finding research in time-series data as well as with signal processing. AutoML techniques are therefore well suited to further application in time-series related tasks for state of the art DPA and SCA.

2.2. Foundational Experiments

This experiment is conceptualized as an extension to prior control flow recovery experiments [1]. Power-based side-channel attacks were used to extract information by using properties from a FSM. In this foundational work, the original experiment made use of a single classifier, the k-nearest neighbors (KNN) classifier with heterogeneous states for the FSM. KNN was able to achieve 81% or higher accuracy of transition classification. Accuracy would increase as the number of classes decreased. As a result, FSM components that handle sensitive information could be vulnerable to power-based side-channel attacks, even with only a single classifier being used to analyze the state machine.

The future work section in this foundational work [1] mentions how an avenue of research could be with how modifying the input to the states could be explored. In particular, the modifications to the states to also include homogeneous states as well as implementing tests using more than a single classifier were used as motivation for the extensions and further experimentation presented herein.

3. Methods

Analyzing the ability for program control flow to be recovered via power-based SCA required the creation and capture of a dataset encompassing numerous execution paths through a program while being able to associate the captured power traces with a training label for later machine-learning backed analysis of transition order. We explore both aspects of these experiments in two methodology sub-sections. The first details the adaptation of data collection from prior works [1] for the purposes of this experiment. The second details the training and evaluation of various machine learning models for the recovery of control flow information from the gathered trace data. Additionally, in the absence of a standard SCA benchmarking suite, and in the interests of reproducability, the entire code base is made available through a public GitLab repository [28]. Code made available in this manner is licensed under the GPLv3.

3.1. Data Generation

Data generation made use of the ChipWhisperer [2] family of devices. These are purpose-built microcontrollers for SCA data collection which contain all of the processing on-board for the collection of power traces. The ChipWhisperer Nano (CW Nano) is one such device backed by an STM32F0 microcontroller.

Each instance of the CW Nano device was programmed with a minimal C program which emulated a two-state state machine. See Figure 1 for a depiction of the FSM. The device was fed a transition sequence from a host device which communicated with the CW Nano before and after experimentation to send the oracle transition sequence and retrieve the power trace captured onboard the device during execution. The state machine transitioned through eight states in accordance with each bit of the oracle: a bit of 0 at position i of the oracle indicates that the i-th state was state 1 while a 1 indicates the state was state 2. Both states performed integer addition a specific number of times where this number was determined during compilation and will be referred to as the value w for the firmware. A firmware where $w = 1$ indicates that the firmware performed a single addition in each state while a firmware with $w = 16$ indicates that the states of that firmware performed the addition a total of 16 times.

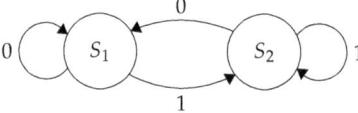

Figure 1. A diagram of the state machine executed by the target board. Transitions represent the next value in the oracle text. For instance, if the FSM was in state S_1 and the next digit was a "1", then the state machine would transition to state S_2 and execute the code associated with that state. If the FSM was in state S_1 and the next digit was a "0", then the state would transition to state S_1 and repeat the previously executed code.

Each CW Nano was paired with a Lenovo ThinkCentre running Ubuntu LTS 22.10. All collection used Python v3.10.6 and the ChipWhisperer library version 5.7.0 distributed by PyPi. The CW Nano device was programmed with firmware version 5.1.0. All version numbers presented were the latest releases at the time of data collection. The code for handling the state transitions is presented in Figure 2 and an example of the state code for firmware ($w = 2$) is presented in Figure 3.

State Transition Code

```c
for (uint8_t i = 0; i < 8; i++ ) {
    uint8_t state = transitions & 0x1;
    transitions >>= 1;
    if (state == 0 ) {
        worker(one_zero, zero_one, dest);
    } else {
        worker(one_zero, zero_one, dest);
    }
}
```

Figure 2. The C code for turning an oracle byte previously received by the CWNano into a series of state transitions on the device. The values one_zero, zero_one, and dest are discussed in Section 3.1.

State Code

```c
void worker(int* x, int* y, int* total) {
    *total = *x + *y;
    *total = *x + *y;
}
```

Figure 3. The C code executed in the body of the state-machine. Figure 2 invokes this function with specially crafted arguments as discussed in Section 3.1. The number of times *total = *x + *y; is repeated is identified as w, so the code snippet above has a w value of 2.

The inputs to the worker function of each state were specially crafted to ensure an equal hamming weight of all inputs to prevent the inference of the state transitions from the contents of the state by the machine learning models later trained. For further discussion of experiments which utilize differences in state behavior to enable related analysis, see [1]. The value of one_zero is 16 ones followed by 16 zeros, or 4,294,901,760 (base ten). The value of zero_one was the opposite, 16 zeros followed by 16 ones, or 65,535 (base ten). Thus, the total hamming weight of operands utilized across the body of the worker function is constant between states.

All potential oracle values, representing all 256 potential permutations of state transitions, were executed 100 times. Firmware was generated for all $w \in 1, 2, 4, 8, 16, 32, 64, 128$ and traces were captured across all oracles and 100 repeated executions and stored for later analysis. Labeling incorporated both the number of operations executed within each state of the firmware and the oracle used to generate the trace as well as the order in the 100 samples to uniquely identify each trace. The resulting data was 5.8 GB for each firmware, resulting in a total data set measuring approximately 40 GB in size.

3.2. Machine Learning Classification

For the task of recovering control flow information, we reduce the task to one of multi-class classification; this makes it a suitable task for applied machine learning classifiers. Each trace is labeled with the oracle byte used to dictate the state transitions, thus a proper classification would represent a complete recovery of the state transitions executed by the CW Nano device. As an example, consider a trace labeled with the oracle byte of $11001100_2 = 204_{10}$. The power-trace presented to the ML model would either be correctly classified as class 204, indicating a complete recovery of the control flow of

J. Cybersecur. Priv. **2023**, *3*

the program, or be incorrectly classified into another class, representing an inability to completely recovery the control flow of the application.

Classification was completed by a number of classifiers provided by the Scikit-learn [29] (SKL) library (version 0.24.2 as packaged by conda forge). The selected classifiers had minimal configuration beyond the defaults provided by SKL, so further hyperparameter optimization may find ways to improve the models created by the process described herein.

Each training process was repeated across five folds of cross validation to address concerns of over-fitting. Eighty percent of the available data was used for training the classifier while another 20% was used for testing the complete classifier. Unless otherwise specified, all results presented in the rest of this work refer to metrics obtained by evaluating the testing dataset. The process was repeated in its entirety for each distinct firmware.

Data were taken directly from the dataset previously generated and split into cross-validation folds using a stratified k-fold method provided by SKL. No preprocessing was performed on the data. Four classifiers were then fit to the training data: a random forest classifier, a decision tree classifier, a KNN classifier, and a logistic regression classifier. The only configuration provided was to the logistic regression classifier; both a solver and maximum number of iterations were provided since without them, the process of fitting data caused convergence failure errors. Convergence failure errors emerged due to the fact that the provided number of iterations was insufficient to converge to a reasonable solution and the solver was needed to match the types of data generated by the CW Nano. Execution of these classification tasks was aided through parallel computation by placing the entire workflow for each distinct firmware on separate threads (i.e., $w = 1$ on one thread, $w = 2$ on another, etc.).

4. Results

For each firmware, with the exception of firmware where a single execution is performed ($w = 1$), classification accuracy values approaching 100% are observed for the random forest classifiers. Accuracy values of 98%+ are seen for decision trees and logistic regression. The KNN classifier is the outlier with an observed lower bound on accuracy values that was slightly greater than 80%.

Firmware with only a single execution of the addition operation ($w = 1$) was the exception to these metrics of accuracy. The resulting skew in overall performance is illustrated in Figure 4 while the exact performance of all four classifiers on each of the folds of testing is illustrated in Figure 5. The highest observed accuracy for this firmware ($w = 1$) was associated with a single fold of validation and the KNN classifier; it was only able to achieve a maximum accuracy of 3.26%. While this is nearly an order of magnitude more accurate than randomly guessing the class, it is far from a desirable accuracy. Preprocessing, ensemble classification, and hyperparameter optimization would be relevant approaches to addressing this concern if the classification of this firmware were the primary goal; however, as the goal is characterization of the bounds of potential classification, this is left for future work. Therefore, we can conclude that when the amount of work performed in each branch of control flow (i.e., when the amount of work performed by each state) is low, "off-the-shelf" machine learning models will struggle to determine the underlying program execution flow.

In stark contrast to the classification accuracy of traces obtained from this firmware ($w = 1$), as the w value of the firmware increases, the performance capabilities of simple machine learning classifiers are well suited to the classification task set before them. For firmware with w values of 2, 4, and 8, a random forest classifier was able to correctly recover the program execution flow in all five folds of cross-validation with 100% accuracy. For algorithm specific and cross-fold specific performances on firmware with two executions of addition operations ($w = 2$), see Figure 6. While all other classifiers achieved high levels of accuracy on average (99%+) over the same firmware, only the random forest classifier achieved this level of performance.

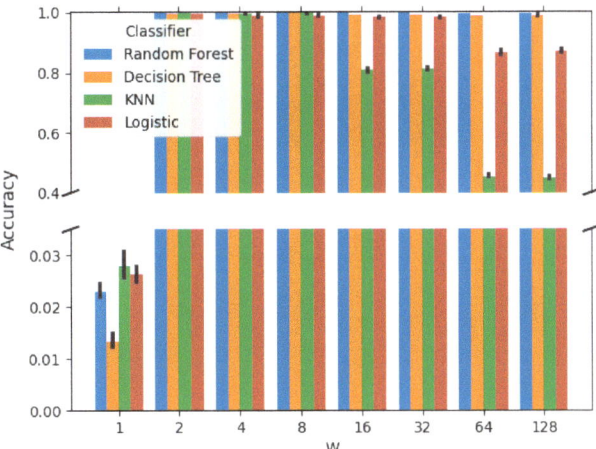

Figure 4. A figure which demonstrates the variance, or lack of variance, exhibited by each classification algorithm depending upon the number of operations performed by the firmware. The y-axis is split to emphasize the difference between $w = 1$ and the other $w \geq 2$.

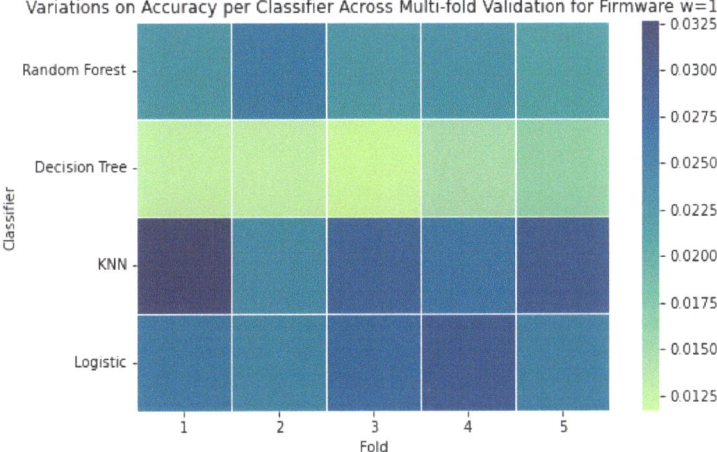

Figure 5. A heatmap demonstrating the accuracy of the testing phase for firmware with a single operation in each state ($w = 1$). Most notable is that, while results are better than random guessing, classification accuracy of 2% is extremely different than the 98%+ accuracy achieved for all other tested firmware.

Across all classifiers, a decrease in overall accuracy was observed moving from firmware with 8 executions ($w = 8$) to firmware with 16 ($w = 16$). In the case of random forest classifiers, this is a decrease from an average accuracy of 100% to 99.92%. Both the decision tree classifiers and logistic regression had their accuracy decrease as the number of operations performed by the firmware increased, but both remained over 98% classification accuracy on average. The KNN classifier saw vastly diminishing performance in the move to firmware with more operations, only achieving a maximum accuracy of 81.4% with an average accuracy of 80.8%. Similar decreases in performance were observed when moving to the next level of firmware ($w = 32$). A visual presentation of the average performance across these various firmware with more than two operations is available in Figure 7.

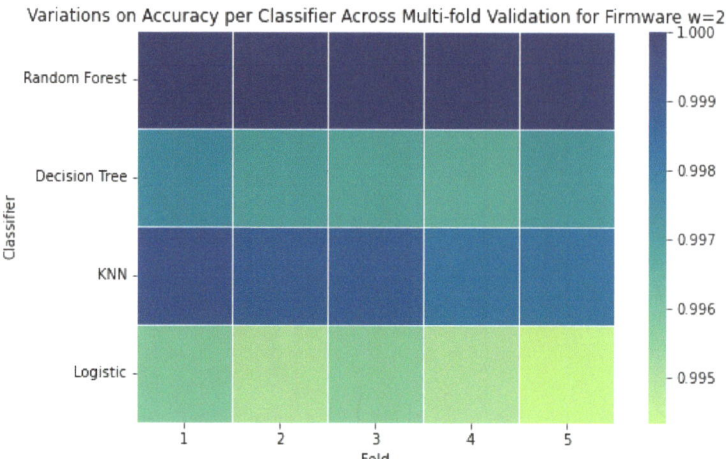

Figure 6. A heatmap demonstrating the accuracy of the testing phase for firmware with two operations executed in each state ($w = 2$). This firmware exhibits a similar difference between each classifier as seen in Figure 5 but shifted to the high end of classification accuracy. The random forest classifier maxes out at 100% accuracy for this firmware.

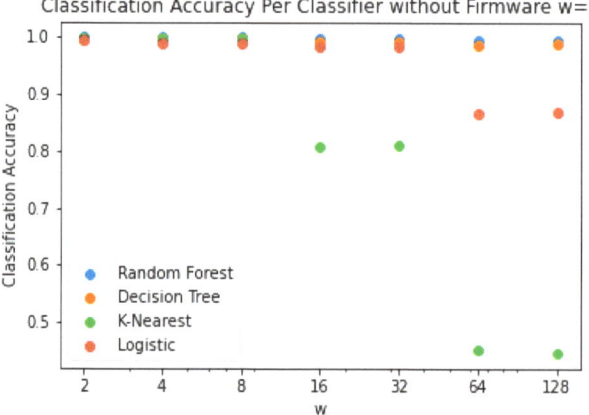

Figure 7. A series of dot plots which illustrate the performance of various classifiers for firmware with various amounts of computation. Accuracy for firmware of $w = 1$ is not included since it was less than 3% for all four tested classifiers. See Figure 5 for specific performance on firmware with $w = 1$ for each classification algorithm.

Further hyperparameter optimization might be effective in improving accuracy in firmware where more operations are performed in each state of the state machine, and automated approaches to the machine learning for this task could find effective preprocessing and postprocessing to improve the overall results. However, as a proof of concept and demonstration that the work performed in each branch of the state machine is not required to be different in order to recover the transitions, these results are highly significant.

5. Discussion

A number of conclusions can be drawn from the results achieved across these classification problems. Beyond the minimal proof of concept that control flow can be significantly recovered even when the work in different states of a limited purpose finite-state machine are identical, these findings suggest that obfuscation techniques may be necessary to obscure the control flow of the program when said control flow conveys security-relevant information. As an example, an attacker should not be able to purchase a smart lock, determine the device's control flow from the embedded finite-state machine, and then gain the ability to access a home using the same smart lock model. Since the results show that this information was exfiltrated from the underlying micro-controller, this is a potential vulnerability that may require more sophisticated protections than traditional, software-based ones.

One surprising result was the extremely low accuracy while applying machine learning classifiers to the firmware which has only one operation ($w = 1$). It was hypothesized before data analysis was completed that the average accuracy would decrease monotonically as the number of operations increased. The intuition used to develop this hypothesis was that as the proportional time spent in the control flow code sections increased, the more accurate the transition recovery would be. This followed from the observation that, when more relative time is spent in control flow, more of the data points captured within the power trace would be directly related to the process of determining state machine transitions. The subversion of this hypothesized outcome indicates that the number of operations has much less influence in the classification of transitions than it was initially assumed. It is clear that the amount of work performed in a state still has influence, as evidenced by the variation in classification accuracy in correlation with the number of operations within each state. However, this role may not be nearly as important as the actual work performed and the state transitions executed by a low-powered device.

The first research question sought to identify whether different behavior is required in each state of an embedded state machine in order to completely recover the transitions. This question is answered firmly in the negative. While prior works made use of the different behavior of a heterogeneous, two-state FSM to more easily perform the classification [1], this difference is not required. This work clearly demonstrates that, while differences in state behavior can allow for recoverable transition sequences, it is not strictly necessary since high transition recovery accuracy was achieved with homogeneous state behavior. Even when applying the same techniques and classifiers as were used in prior work, meaningful levels of accuracy were achieved with said states.

This finding suggests that power-based side-channel attacks will be an applicable tool to recover state transition information regardless of what kind of work is performed by the states within an FSM. For devices with minimal numbers of states which do a meaningful amount of work (i.e., they are not comparable to the $w = 1$ firmware tested in these experiments), these results suggest it is possible to recover the transition order of the underlying FSM. As of the time of writing, such behavior is also consistent with speculation in current literature. Further work will be necessary to determine if these findings are consistent when expanded to state machines with many states.

The second research question sought to address to what degree the proportion of time spent in control flow and in a particular state of an FSM would impact the recoverability of the state transition ordering. It was initially hypothesized that the ratio of time spent in the state machine versus in the control flow would be the primary predictor of classification accuracy. While this held true for firmware with more than one operation ($w \geq 2$) from 2 to 128, the special case was the firmware with a single operation ($w = 1$). It can therefore be concluded that there is a bounded range in which the control flow can be recovered without more advanced means than are presented here. Further research will be necessary to determine whether the lower bound is one which can be encountered in production grade FSM. However, the lower bound of recoverability suggests that minimized states may evade detection, recovery, and classification. This is demonstrated by the low accuracy associated with classifying for firmware with a single operation.

The final research question examined how effective "off-the-shelf" machine learning models are when applied to the task of recovering control flow information. "Off-the-shelf" machine learning models, specifically more light-weight ones than the deep learning approaches common in power-based side-channel attacks, show much promise in their ability to capture high-level control flow information. Even without hyperparameter optimization, high levels of accuracy were achieved. With this optimization, it may be possible to achieve similar accuracy on firmware with more operations. Situations in which "off-the-shelf" solutions are not sufficient to achieve high classification accuracy must be further explored to motivate the need for hyperparameter optimization.

The efficacy of random forest algorithms for classification tasks is well known. Yet even with this reputation, these algorithms' performance on the collected data is important as it may suggest their applicability and strong performance on more complex state machines. When paired with optimization algorithms such as Bayesian Optimization, their capabilities may continue to be relevant, potentially minimizing the need for more computationally challenging solutions which make use of deep learning such as DL-SCA.

6. Conclusions

In this work, the program control flow was able to be recovered using SPA. The classification models used were able to achieve a high level of accuracy, with the random forest model reaching 100% accuracy for three of the values of w tested; the other models also reached very high classification accuracy, with several averaging over 98% on firmware operations with more than one execution ($w \geq 2$). This level of performance was achieved without hyperparameter optimization begin applied, an approach which could lead to improvements in some situations.

Power-based side-channel analysis is a new potential tool for attackers looking to recover control flow information from an embedded or otherwise low-powered system. Due to the recent nature of the development of meaningful recovery attacks on program control flow information, it remains to be seen to what degree existing counter-measures will be applicable to the protection of this information. Contrary to the intuition of this research team, short sections of code were able to evade detection with meaningful impacts on the accuracy of recovery as exhibited by the results surrounding firmware with a single execution of operations in this work.

Looking to the future, most current work in power-based control flow recovery has been done with state machines which have only two states; however, in practice, nearly all state machines have many more states. Future work should explore the potential for the current two-state techniques to be extended to multiple homogeneous states as well as multiple heterogeneous states and variations between the two. Furthermore, the applicability of automated machine learning pipelines for the task of classifying state transitions is another avenue for future exploration. While current "off-the-shelf" machine learning classifiers are sufficient to classify the states under consideration, the ability of these findings to be transferred to more complex state machines must be examined to discern where their application breaks down and traditional AutoML pipelines must be employed. Overall, with the ability for FSM transitions to be recovered clearly established now, the task must turn to more firmly defining the capabilities and bounds on this avenue of attack. Variable transition counts, wildly different state computations, more complex state machines, and further perturbations on the environments data is collected within are all promising future directions of research at this time. This work should seek to qualify the limitations of SPA approaches for FSM transition recovery through power analysis. Finally, historic mitigation techniques applied to combat side-channel attacks must be re-evaluated to determine to what extent existing mitigations protect against this control flow recovery attack.

One primary limitation is that the comparative time spent in each state, a by-product of the number of operations in each state, is constant across a sample. While the question of whether a simple machine learning model would be sufficient for recovering the control flow of a program with identical work in each state has been answered in the affirmative in this paper, future work should certainly address this limitation by determining if a consistent time in each state is necessary for these results to be widely transferable. Perhaps more specialized machine learning may be able to improve the classification, but in comparison to the other models created throughout this process, it is clear that the data captured itself is the limitation directly responsible for reducing general classifier accuracy.

Additionally, while attempting to make use of "off-the-shelf" machine learning models was a key research question, it does assume that the benefits of deep learning approaches, or other AutoML approaches such as NAS, are not of enough importance to justify the computational trade-offs. The strong performance of the algorithms examined in this work may justify this restriction in this specific scenario, but further examination of their limitations will be necessary to determine if more modern, advanced, or complex machine learning pipelines allow for more meaningful state transition recovery in more complex applications.

Author Contributions: Conceptualization, A.R. and C.C.; Methodology, A.R.; Software, A.R.; Validation, S.O.; Investigation, A.R. and S.O.; Resources, M.B.; Data curation, A.R.; Writing—original draft, A.R., S.O., J.B., C.C. and M.B.; Writing—review & editing, A.R., S.O., J.B., C.C. and M.B.; Visualization, A.R., S.O. and J.B.; Project administration, M.B.; Funding acquisition, M.B. All authors have read and agreed to the published version of the manuscript.

Funding: This work was supported through various contracts and gifts including INL Laboratory Directed Research & Development (LDRD) Program under the DOE Battelle Energy Alliance Standard Research Contract #249922, IOG, and the University of Wyoming's Nell Templeton Endowment.

Data Availability Statement: The data presented in this study are openly available in FigShare at 10.6084/m9.figshare.23635623.

Acknowledgments: The research team would like to acknowledge and thank the Secure Systems Collaborative for their assistance in revisions and presentation of information.

Conflicts of Interest: Any opinions, findings, and conclusions or recommendations expressed in this material are those of the author(s) and do not necessarily reflect the views of any agency, sponsor, or corporate entity.

References

1. Carper, C.; Robins, A.; Borowczak, M. Transition Recovery Attack on Embedded State Machines Using Power Analysis. In Proceedings of the 2022 IEEE 40th International Conference on Computer Design (ICCD), Olympic Valley, CA, USA, 23–26 October 2022; pp. 572–576.
2. O'flynn, C.; Chen, Z. Chipwhisperer: An open-source platform for hardware embedded security research. In *Constructive Side-Channel Analysis and Secure Design, Proceedings of the 5th International Workshop, COSADE 2014, Paris, France, 13–15 April 2014;* Revised Selected Papers 5; Springer: Berlin/Heidelberg, Germany, 2014; pp. 243–260.
3. Kocher, P.; Jaffe, J.; Jun, B. Differential power analysis. In *Advances in Cryptology—CRYPTO '99, Proceedings of the Annual International Cryptology Conference, Santa Barbara, CA, USA, 15–19 August 1999;* Springer: Berlin/Heidelberg, Germany, 1999; pp. 388–397.
4. Randolph, M.; Diehl, W. Power side-channel attack analysis: A review of 20 years of study for the layman. *Cryptography* **2020**, *4*, 15. [CrossRef]
5. Gangolli, A.; Mahmoud, Q.H.; Azim, A. A systematic review of fault injection attacks on IOT systems. *Electronics* **2022**, *11*, 2023. [CrossRef]
6. Kim, C.H.; Quisquater, J.J. Faults, injection methods, and fault attacks. *IEEE Des. Test Comput.* **2007**, *24*, 544–545. [CrossRef]
7. Balasch, J.; Gierlichs, B.; Reparaz, O. Differential Behavioral Analysis. In Proceedings of the Cryptographic Hardware and Embedded Systems, Vienna, Austria, 10–13 September 2007.
8. Tunstall, M.; Mukhopadhyay, D.; Ali, S. Differential fault analysis of the advanced encryption standard using a single fault. In *Information Security Theory and Practice. Security and Privacy of Mobile Devices in Wireless Communication, Proceedings of the 5th IFIP WG 11.2 International Workshop, WISTP 2011, Heraklion, Crete, Greece, 1–3 June 2011;* Proceedings 5; Springer: Berlin/Heidelberg, Germany, 2011; pp. 224–233.
9. Lo, O.; Buchanan, W.J.; Carson, D. Power analysis attacks on the AES-128 S-box using differential power analysis (DPA) and correlation power analysis (CPA). *J. Cyber Secur. Technol.* **2017**, *1*, 88–107. [CrossRef]
10. Bernstein, D.J.; Lange, T. Post-quantum cryptography. *Nature* **2017**, *549*, 188–194. [CrossRef] [PubMed]
11. Roy, K.S.; Kalita, H.K. A survey on post-quantum cryptography for constrained devices. *Int. J. Appl. Eng. Res.* **2019**, *14*, 2608–2615.
12. Nejatollahi, H.; Dutt, N.; Ray, S.; Regazzoni, F.; Banerjee, I.; Cammarota, R. Post-quantum lattice-based cryptography implementations: A survey. *ACM Comput. Surv. (CSUR)* **2019**, *51*, 1–41. [CrossRef]
13. Mujdei, C.; Wouters, L.; Karmakar, A.; Beckers, A.; Mera, J.M.B.; Verbauwhede, I. Side-channel analysis of lattice-based post-quantum cryptography: Exploiting polynomial multiplication. *ACM Trans. Embed. Comput. Syst.* **2022**. [CrossRef]

14. Borowczak, M.; Vemuri, R. S*FSM: A paradigm shift for attack resistant FSM designs and encodings. In Proceedings of the 2012 ASE/IEEE International Conference on BioMedical Computing (BioMedCom), Washington, DC, USA, 14–16 December 2012; pp. 96–100.
15. Clavier, C.; Coron, J.S.; Dabbous, N. Differential power analysis in the presence of hardware countermeasures. In Proceedings of the International Workshop on Cryptographic Hardware and Embedded Systems, Worcester, MA, USA, 17–18 August 2000; Springer: Berlin/Heidelberg, Germany, 2000; pp. 252–263.
16. Mangard, S.; Oswald, E.; Popp, T. *Power Analysis Attacks*; Springer: Boston, MA, USA, 2007.
17. Goodwill, G.; Jun, B.; Jaffe, J.; Rohatgi, P. *A Testing Methodology for Side-Channel Resistance Validation*; Cryptography Research Inc.: San Francisco, CA, USA, 2011; p. 15.
18. Unger, W.; Babinkostova, L.; Borowczak, M.; Erbes, R. Side-channel Leakage Assessment Metrics: A Case Study of GIFT Block Ciphers. In Proceedings of the 2021 IEEE Computer Society Annual Symposium on VLSI (ISVLSI), Tampa, FL, USA, 7–9 July 2021; pp. 236–241.
19. Unger, W.; Babinkostova, L.; Borowczak, M.; Erbes, R.; Srinath, A. TVLA, Correlation Power Analysis and Side-Channel Leakage Assessment Metrics. In Proceedings of the Lightweight Cryptography Workshop 2022, Virtual, 9–11 May 2022; NIST: Gaithersburg, MD, USA, 2022.
20. Moradi, A.; Richter, B.; Schneider, T.; Standaert, F.X. Leakage Detection with the x2-Test. *IACR Trans. Cryptogr. Hardw. Embed. Syst.* **2018**, *2018*, 209–237. [CrossRef]
21. Le, T.H.; Clédière, J.; Servière, C.; Lacoume, J.L. How can signal processing benefit side channel attacks? In Proceedings of the 2007 IEEE Workshop on Signal Processing Applications for Public Security and Forensics, Washington, DC, USA, 11–13 April 2007; pp. 1–7.
22. Aquino-Brítez, D.; Ortiz, A.; Ortega, J.; León, J.; Formoso, M.; Gan, J.Q.; Escobar, J.J. Optimization of Deep Architectures for EEG Signal Classification: An AutoML Approach Using Evolutionary Algorithms. *Sensors* **2021**, *21*, 2096. [CrossRef] [PubMed]
23. Alsharef, A.; Aggarwal, K.; Sonia.; Kumar, M.; Mishra, A. Review of ML and AutoML Solutions to Forecast Time-Series Data. *Arch. Comput. Methods Eng.* **2022**, *29*, 5297–5311. [CrossRef] [PubMed]
24. Paldino, G.M.; De Stefani, J.; De Caro, F.; Bontempi, G. Does AutoML Outperform Naive Forecasting? *Eng. Proc.* **2021**, *5*, 36.
25. Javeri, I.Y.; Toutiaee, M.; Arpinar, I.B.; Miller, T.W.; Miller, J.A. Improving Neural Networks for Time Series Forecasting using Data Augmentation and AutoML. In Proceedings of the IEEE International Conference on Big Data Computing Service and Applications (BigDataService), Oxford, UK, 23–26 August 2021.
26. Picek, S.; Perin, G.; Mariot, L.; Wu, L.; Batina, L. SoK: Deep Learning-based Physical Side-channel Analysis. *ACM Comput. Surv.* **2023**, *55*, 1–35. [CrossRef]
27. Moos, T.; Wegener, F.; Moradi, A. DL-LA: Deep Learning Leakage Assessment: A modern roadmap for SCA evaluations. *IACR Trans. Cryptogr. Hardw. Embed. Syst.* **2021**, *2021*, 552–598. [CrossRef]
28. Side Channel State Machines. 2023. Available online: https://gitlab.com/UWyo-SSC/side-channel-state-machines (accessed on 19 June 2023).
29. Pedregosa, F.; Varoquaux, G.; Gramfort, A.; Michel, V.; Thirion, B.; Grisel, O.; Blondel, M.; Prettenhofer, P.; Weiss, R.; Dubourg, V.; et al. Scikit-learn: Machine Learning in Python. *J. Mach. Learn. Res.* **2011**, *12*, 2825–2830.

Journal of
Cybersecurity and Privacy

MDPI

Review

Cybersecurity for AI Systems: A Survey

Raghvinder S. Sangwan, Youakim Badr * and Satish M. Srinivasan

School of Graduate Professional Studies, The Pennsylvania State University, 30 E. Swedesford Road, Malvern, PA 19355, USA
* Correspondence: yzb61@psu.edu

Abstract: Recent advances in machine learning have created an opportunity to embed artificial intelligence in software-intensive systems. These artificial intelligence systems, however, come with a new set of vulnerabilities making them potential targets for cyberattacks. This research examines the landscape of these cyber attacks and organizes them into a taxonomy. It further explores potential defense mechanisms to counter such attacks and the use of these mechanisms early during the development life cycle to enhance the safety and security of artificial intelligence systems.

Keywords: machine learning; cybersecurity; AI attacks; defense mechanism

Citation: Sangwan, R.S.; Badr, Y.; Srinivasan, S.M. Cybersecurity for AI Systems: A Survey. *J. Cybersecur. Priv.* **2023**, *3*, 166–190. https://doi.org/10.3390/jcp3020010

Academic Editor: Giorgio Giacinto

Received: 24 January 2023
Revised: 8 March 2023
Accepted: 11 March 2023
Published: 4 May 2023

1. Introduction

Advances in Artificial Intelligence (AI) technology have contributed to the enhancement of cybersecurity capabilities of traditional systems with applications that include detection of intrusion, malware, code vulnerabilities and anomalies. However, these systems with embedded machine learning models have opened themselves to a new set of vulnerabilities, commonly known as AI attacks. Currently, these systems are prime targets for cyberattacks, thus compromising the security and safety of larger systems that encompass them. Modern day AI attacks are not only limited to just coding bugs and errors. They manifest due to the inherent limitations or vulnerabilities of systems [1]. By exploiting the vulnerabilities in the AI system, attackers aim at either manipulating its behavior or obtaining its internal details by tampering with its input, training data, or the machine learning (ML) model. McGraw et al. [2] have classified AI attacks broadly as manipulation and extraction attacks. Based on the inputs given to the system, the training dataset used for learning, and manipulation of the model hyperparameters, attacks on AI systems can manifest in different types, with different degrees of severity. For example, adversarial or evasion attack can be launched by manipulating the input to the AI system, which results in the system producing an unintended outcome. A poisoning or causative attack can be launched by tainting the training dataset, which would result in the AI system exhibiting unethical behavior.

Therefore, it is important that we start thinking about designing security into AI systems, rather than retrofitting it as an afterthought. This research addresses the following research questions:

RQ1: What are the cyberattacks that AI systems can be subjected to?

RQ2: Can the attacks on AI systems be organized into a taxonomy, to better understand how the vulnerabilities manifest themselves during the system development.

RQ3: What are possible defense mechanisms to prevent AI systems being subjected to cyberattacks?

RQ4: Is it possible to devise a generic defense mechanism against all kinds of AI attacks.

To address these research questions and determine the extent of risk to safety and security of AI systems, we first conducted a systematic literature review looking for AI attacks on systems reported in the literature. We then organized these attacks into a taxonomy to not only understand the types of vulnerabilities, but also the stage in the development of AI systems when these vulnerabilities manifest themselves. We then conducted further literature search looking for any defense mechanisms to counter these attacks and improve the safety and security of AI systems.

This study is organized as follows. In Section 2, we report the results of the systematic literature review and identify the attacks, from an AI system development perspective, and their vulnerabilities. In Section 3, we introduce a taxonomy of AI attacks along with defense mechanisms and countermeasures to mitigate their threats. Section 4 concludes the study and highlights major findings.

2. Literature Review

This survey was founded on searching, by keywords, to find related articles to cybersecurity of AI systems. The top most used keywords are as follow: cybersecurity, cyberattack, and vulnerabilities. We searched Scopus, an Elsevier abstracts and citation database, for articles having titles that matched the search query ("cyber security" OR "cybersecurity" OR "security" OR "cyberattack" OR "vulnerability" OR "vulnerabilities" OR "threat" OR "attack" OR "AI attack") AND ("AI" OR "ML" OR "Artificial Intelligence" OR "Machine Learning") AND ("system")).

The search resulted in a total of 1366 articles. Within these articles, we looked for those in computer science or computer engineering subject areas that were published in journals in the English language, leaving us with 415 manuscripts. We carefully reviewed the abstracts of the papers to determine their relevance. Only articles that discussed the vulnerabilities of AI systems to attacks and/or their defense mechanisms were considered.

During the learning or training stage, an AI system needs data for training a machine learning model. The training data are subject to manipulation attacks, requiring that their integrity be verified. Ma et al. [3] used a visual analytics framework for explaining and exploring ML model vulnerabilities to data poisoning attacks. Kim and Park [4] proposed a blockchain-based environment that collects and stores learning data whose confidentiality and integrity can be guaranteed. Mozaffari-Kermani et al. [5] focused on data poisoning attacks on, and the defenses for, machine learning algorithms in healthcare.

During the inference or testing stage, an AI system can be subjected to manipulation attacks by presenting falsified data to be classified as legitimate data. Adversarial or evasion attacks and/or potential defenses against such attacks are discussed in [6–14]. Chen et al. [15] looked at such attacks in the context of reinforcement learning. Li et al. [16] proposed a low latency decentralized framework for identifying adversarial attacks in deep learning-based industrial AI systems. Garcia-Ceja et al. [17] described how biometric profiles can be generated to impersonate a user by repeatedly querying a classifier and how the learned profiles can be used to attack other classifiers trained on the same dataset. Biggio et al. [18] examined vulnerabilities of biometric recognition systems and their defense mechanisms. Ren et al. [19] also looked at querying-based attacks against black-box machine learning models and potential defense mechanisms against such attacks. Wang et al. [20] looked at a variant, termed the Man-in-the-Middle attack, using generative models for querying. Threats from, and potential defense against, attacks on machine learning models in 5G networks is discussed in [21,22]. Apruzzese et al. [23] provided an approach to mitigating evasion attacks on AI-based network intrusion detection systems. Zhang et al. [24] explored adversarial attacks against commonly used ML-based cybersecurity systems. Liu et al. [25] discussed how to improve robustness of ML-based CAD systems against adversarial attacks. Building malware detection systems that are more resilient to adversarial attacks was the focus of [26,27], and Gardiner and Nagaraja [28] provided a comprehensive survey on vulnerabilities of ML models in malware detection systems. Dasgupta and Collins [29] surveyed game theoretical approaches that can be used to make ML algorithms robust against adversarial attacks.

During the inference or testing stage, extraction attacks are possible using the feature vector of a model for model inversion or reconstruction and gaining access to private data that was used as input or for training an AI system [30].

Hansman and Hunt [31] and Gao et al. [32] proposed a taxonomy of network and computer attacks to categorize different attack types. Their taxonomy includes four dimensions to categorize attacks on AI systems, including attack classes, attack targets, vulnerabilities and exploits used by the attacks and whether the attack has a payload or effect beyond itself. Their taxonomical structure is very comprehensive and can be used to analyze a system for its dependability, reliability and security.

Despite the benefits of machine learning technologies, the learning algorithms can be abused by cybercriminals to conduct illicit and undesirable activities. It was shown in [33,34] that attackers might gain a significant benefit by exploiting vulnerabilities in the learning algorithms, which can sometimes become a weakest link in the security chain. Several studies related to attacks on machine learning algorithms have been reported in the literature using different threat models. Barreno et al. [35,36], Huang et al. [36], Biggio et al. [37] and Munoz-Gonzalez et al. [38] discussed different attack scenarios against machine learning models with different attack models. The frameworks they proposed characterize the attacks according to the attacker's goal, their capabilities to manipulate the data and influence the learning system, familiarity with the algorithms, the data used by the defender and the attacker's strategy. For example, data poisoning attacks, also known as causative attacks, are a major emerging security threat to data-driven technologies. In these types of attacks, it can be assumed that the hacker has control over the training dataset that is being used by the learning algorithm. The hacker can actively influence the training dataset in order to subvert the entire learning process, thus decreasing the overall performance of the system, or to produce particular types of errors in the system output. For example, in a classification task, the hacker may poison the data to modify the decision boundaries learned by the learning algorithm, thus resulting in misclassification of instances, or a higher error rate for a specific type of class. This is a kind of threat that is related to the reliability of the large amount of data collected by the systems [38,39].

This survey is distinct from [31,39] in studying attacks on an AI system from the perspective of a software engineering team, that organizes its work around different stages of an AI system's development life cycle. For these different stages of an AI system, and their corresponding attacks, potential defense mechanisms are also provided. Organizing the literature using this perspective can be valuable to systematically study the design of AI systems for security purposes, to explore the trade offs that result from using different defense mechanisms, and to develop a catalog of patterns and tactics for designing AI systems for security purposes.

Table 1 lists various attacks carried out at different stages of the AI system development processes and the countermeasures that are taken against these attacks.

Table 1. Attacks on AI systems at different stages of its development.

Attacks	AI System Development	Vulnerabilities	Defense Mechanisms
Poisoning attacks [1,37]	During training of the model	Weakness in the federated learning algorithms, resulting in stealing of the data and algorithm from individual user devices.	See list of defense mechanisms for both the data and model poisoning attacks.
Data poisoning attacks [38–40]	During the training stage	Tampering of the features and class information in the training dataset	Adversarial training, Feature squeezing, Transferability blocking, MagNet, Defense-GAN, Local intrinsic dimensionality, Reject On Negative Impact (RONI), L-2 Defense, Slab Defense, Loss Defense and K-NN Defense.

Table 1. *Cont.*

Attacks	AI System Development	Vulnerabilities	Defense Mechanisms
Model poisoning attacks [41–44]	During the training stage	Trust ability of the trainer, based on a privately held validation dataset. Use of pre-trained models that are corrupted.	Securely hosting and disseminating pre-trained models in virtual repositories that guarantee integrity to preclude benevolent models from being manipulated. Identifying backdoors in malevolently trained models acquired from untrustworthy trainers by fine-tuning untrusted models.
Transfer learning attacks [42,44–46]	During the training stage	Similarity of the model structures.	Obtain pre-trained models from trusted source. Employ activation-based pruning with different training examples.
Model poisoning in federated learning [41,45,47,48]	During the training stage	Obstruct the convergence of the execution of the distributed Stochastic Gradient Descent (SGD) algorithm,	Robust aggregation methods, robust learning rate.
Model inversion attack [49–52]	During Inference and/or testing stage	Models are typically trained on rather small, or imbalanced, training sets.	L2 Regularizer [49], Dropout and Model Staking [50], MemGuard [51] and Differential privacy [52].
Model extraction attack [53,54]	During Inference and/or training stage	Models having similar characteristics (parameters, shape and size, similar features etc.)	Hiding or adding noises to the output probabilities while keeping the class label of the instances intact. Suppressing suspicious queries or input data.
Inference attack [55]	During Inferencing, Training, and Testing	Model Leaking information leading to inferences being made on private data.	Methods proposed in [55] have leveraged heuristic correlations between the records of the public data and attribute values to defending against inference attacks. Modifying the identified k entries that have large correlations with the attribute values to any given target users.

The following section systematically explores attacks on AI systems and their defenses in more detail.

3. AI Attacks and Defense Mechanisms

Research has been carried out to identify new threats and attacks on different levels of design and implementation of AI systems. Kaloudi and Li [56], stressed the dearth of proper understanding of the malicious intention of the attacks on AI-based systems. The authors introduced 11 use cases divided into five categories: (1) next generation malware, (2) void synthesis, (3) password-based attacks, (4) social bots, and (5) adversarial training. They developed a threat framework to categorize the attacks. Turchin [57] pointed out the lack of desired behaviors of AI systems that could be exploited to design attacks in different phases of system development. The research lists the following modes of failure of AI systems:

- The need for better resources for self-upgradation of AI systems can be exploited by adversaries
- Implementation of malicious goals make the AI systems unfriendly
- Flaws in the user-friendly features
- Use of different techniques to make different stages of AI free from the boundaries of actions expose the AI systems to adversaries

Similar research is carried out by Turchin and Denkenberger [58] where the classification of attacks was based on intelligence levels of AI systems. The authors introduced three levels of AI intelligence with respect to human intelligence: (1) "Narrow AI" which requires human assistance, (2) "Young AI" which has capability a bit better than human, and (3) "Mature AI" whose intelligence is super-human. While classifying the intelligence levels of AI systems, the authors investigated several vulnerabilities during the evolution of capabilities of AI systems. Yampolsky [59] projected a holistic view of tracks as to why an AI system could be malicious, classifying the tracks into two stages: (1) Pre-deployment and

(2) Post-deployment. This includes the intrinsic and extrinsic reasons for AI technologies to be malicious, such as design flaws, intentional activities, or environmental factors.

3.1. Types of Failures

Shiva Kemar et al. [60] discussed two modes of failures of machine learning (ML) systems. They claimed that AI systems can fail either due to the inherent design of the systems (unintentional failures) or by the hand of an adversary (intentional failures).

Unintentional Failures: The unintentional failure mode leads to the failure of an AI/ML system when the AI/ML system generates formally correct, but completely unsafe, behavior.

Intentional failures: Intentional failures are caused by the attackers attempting to destabilize the system either by (a) misclassifying the results, by introducing private training data, or b) by stealing the foundational algorithmic framework. Depending on the accessibility of information about the system components (i.e., knowledge), intentional failures can be further subdivided into different subcategories.

3.1.1. Categories of Unintentional Failures

Unintentional failures happen when AI/ML systems produce an unwanted or unforeseen outcome from a determined action. It happens mainly due to system failures. In this research we further categorize different types of unintentional failures.

- **Reward Hacking:** Reward hacking is a failure mode that an AI/ML system experiences when the underlying framework is a reinforcement learning algorithm. Reward hacking appears when an agent has more return as reward in an unexpected manner in a game environment [61]. This unexpected behavior unsettles the safety of the system. Yuan et al. [62] proposed a new multi-step reinforcement learning framework, where the reward function generates a discounted future reward and, thus, reduces the influence of immediate reward on the current state action pair. The proposed algorithm creates the defense mechanism to mitigate the effect of reward hacking in AI/ML systems.
- **Distributed Shift:** This type of mode appears when an AI/ML model that once performed well in an environment generates dismal performance when deployed to perform in a different environment. One such example is when the training and test data come from two different probability distributions [63]. The distribution shift is further subdivided into three types [64]:

1. Covariate Shift: The shifting problem arises due to the change in input features (covariates) over time, while the distribution of the conditional labeling function remains the same.
2. Label Shift: This mode of failure is complementary to covariate shift, such that the distribution of class conditional probability does not change but the label marginal probability distribution changes.
3. Concept Shift: Concept shift is a failure related to the label shift problem where the definitions of the label (i.e., the posteriori probability) experience spatial or temporal changes.

Subbaswamy and Saria proposed an operator-based hierarchy of solutions that are stable to the distributed shift [65]. There are three operators (i.e., conditioning, intervening and computing counterfactuals) that work on a graph specific to healthcare AI. These operators effectively remove the unstable component of the graph and retain the stable behavior as much as possible. There are also other algorithms to maintain robustness against the distributed shift. Rojas-Carulla et al. [66] proposed a data-driven approach, where the learning of models occurs using data from diverse environments, while Rothenhausler et al. [67] devised bounded magnitude-based robustness, where the shift is assumed to have a known magnitude.

- **Natural Adversarial Examples:** The natural adversarial examples are real-world examples that are not intentionally modified. Rather, they occur naturally, and result in considerable loss of performance of the machine learning algorithms [68]. The instances are semantically similar to the input, legible and facilitate interpretation (e.g., image data) of the outcome [69]. Deep neural networks are susceptible to natural adversarial examples.

3.1.2. Categories of Intentional Failures

The goal of the adversary is deduced from the type of failure of the model. Chakraborty et al. [70] identify four different classes of adversarial goals, based on the machine learning classifier output, which are the following: (1) confidence reduction, where the target model prediction confidence is reduced to a lower probability of classification, (2) misclassification, where the output class is altered from the original class, (3) output misclassification, which deals with input generation to fix the classifier output into a particular class, and (4) input/output misclassification, where the label of a particular input is forced to have a specific class.

Shiv Kumar et al. [60] identified the taxonomy of intentional failures/attacks, based on the knowledge of the adversary. It deals with the extent of knowledge needed to trigger an attack for the AI/ML systems to fail. The adversary is better equipped with more knowledge [70] to perform the attack.

There are three types of classified attacks based on the adversary's access to knowledge about the system.

1   **Whiteb ox Attack:** In this type of attack, the adversary has access to the parameters of the underlying architecture of the model, the algorithm used for training, weights, training data distribution, and biases [71,72]. The adversary uses this information to find the model's vulnerable feature space. Later, the model is manipulated by modifying an input using adversarial crafting methods. An example of the whitebox attack and adversarial crafting methods are discussed in later sections. The researchers in [73,74] showed that adversarial training of the data, filled with some adversarial instances, actually helps the model/system become robust against whitebox attacks.

2   **Blackbox Attack:** In blackbox attacks the attacker does not know anything about the ML system. The attacker has access to only two types of information. The first is the hard label, where the adversary obtained only the classifier's predicted label, and the second is confidence, where the adversary obtained the predicted label along with the confidence score. The attacker uses information about the inputs from the past to understand vulnerabilities of the model [70]. Some blackbox attacks are discussed in later sections. Blackbox attacks can further be divided into three categories:

- **Non-Adaptive Blackbox Attack:** In this category of blackbox attack, the adversary has the knowledge of distribution of training data for a model, T. The adversary chooses a procedure, P, for a selected local model, T', and trains the model on known data distribution using P for T' to approximate the already learned T in order to trigger misclassification using whitebox strategies [53,75].
- **Adaptive Blackbox Attack:** In adaptive blackbox attack the adversary has no knowledge of the training data distribution or the model architecture. Rather, the attacker approaches the target model, T, as an oracle. The attacker generates a selected dataset with a label accessed from adaptive querying of the oracle. A training process, P, is chosen with a model, T', to be trained on the labeled dataset generated by the adversary. The model T' introduces the adversarial instances using whitebox attacks to trigger misclassification by the target model T [70,76].
- **Strict Blackbox Attack:** In this blackbox attack category, the adversary does not have access to the training data distribution but could have the labeled dataset (x, y) collected from the target model, T. The adversary can perturb the input to identify the changes in the output. This attack would be successful if the adversary has a large set of dataset (x,y) [70,71].

Grayb ox attacks: In whitebox attacks the adversary is fully informed about the target model, i.e., the adversary has access to the model framework, data distribution, training procedure, and model parameters, while in blackbox attacks, the adversary has no knowledge about the model. The graybox attack is an extended version of either whitebox attack or blackbox attack. In extended whitebox attacks, the adversary is partially knowledgeable about the target model setup, e.g, the model architecture, T, and the training procedure, P, is known, while the data distribution and parameters are unknown. On the other hand, in the extended blackbox attack, the adversarial model is partially trained, has different model architecture and, hence, parameters [77].

3.2. Anatomy of Cyberattacks

To build any machine learning model, the data needs to be collected, processed, trained, and tested and can be used to classify new data. The system that takes care of the sequence of data collection, processing, training and testing can be thought of as a generic AI/ML pipeline, termed the attack surface [70]. An attack surface subjected to adversarial intrusion may face poisoning attack, evasion attack, and exploratory attack. These attacks exploit three pillars of the information security, i.e., Confidentiality, Integrity, and Availability, known as the CIA triad [78]. Integrity of a system is compromised by the poisoning and evasion attacks, confidentiality is subject to intrusion by extraction, while availabilty is vulnerable to poisoning attacks. The entire AI pipeline, along with the possible attacks at each step, are shown in Figure 1.

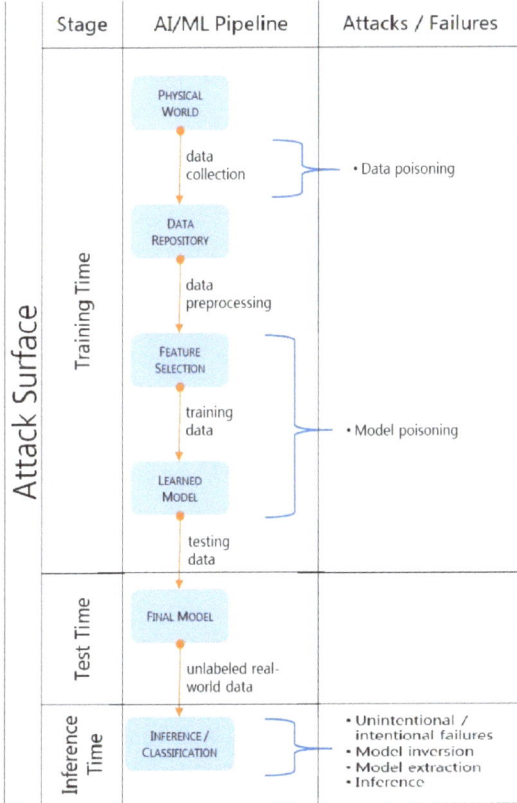

Figure 1. ML Pipeline with Cyberattacks Layout.

3.3. Poisoning Attack

Poisoning attack occurs when the adversary contaminates the training data. Often ML algorithms, such as intrusion detection systems, are retrained on the training dataset. In this type of attack, the adversary cannot access the training dataset, but poisons the data by injecting new data instances [35,37,40] during the model training time. In general, the objective of the adversary is to compromise the AI system to result in the misclassification of objects.

Poisoning attacks can be a result of poisoning the training dataset or the trained model [1]. Adversaries can attack either at the data source, a platform from which a defender extracts its data, or can compromise the database of the defender. They can substitute a genuine model with a tainted model. Poisoning attacks can also exploit the limitations of the underlying learning algorithms. This attack happens in federated learning scenarios where the privacy on individual users' dataset is maintained [47]. The adversary takes advantage of the weakness of federated learning and may take control of both the data and algorithm on an individual user's device to deteriorate the performance of the model on that device [48].

3.3.1. Dataset Poisoning Attacks

The major scenarios of data poisoning attacks are error-agnostic poisoning attacks and error-specific poisoning attacks. In the error-agnostic type of poisoning attack the hacker aims to cause a Denial of Service (DOS) kind of attack. The hacker causes the system to produce errors, but it does not matter what type of error it is. For example, in a multi-class classification task a hacker could poison the data leading to misclassification of the data points irrespective of the class type, thus maximizing the loss function of the learning algorithm. To launch this kind of attack, the hacker needs to manipulate both the features and the labels of the data points. On the other hand, in error-specific poisoning attacks, the hacker causes the system to produce specific misclassification errors, resulting in security violation of both integrity and availability. Here, the hacker aims at misclassifying a small sample of chosen data points in a multi-class classification task. The hacker aims to minimize the loss function of the learning algorithm to serve the purpose, i.e., to force the system into misclassifying specific instances without compromising the normal system operation, ensuring that the attack is undetected [38,39].

A model is built up from a training dataset. So, attacking the dataset results in poisoning the model. By poisoning the dataset, the adversary could manipulate to generate natural adversarial examples, or inject instances with incorrect labels into the training dataset. The model may learn the pattern on misclassified examples in the data that serves the goal of the adversary. The dataset poisoning attacks can be further subdivided into two categories [79].

- **Data Modification**: The adversary updates or deletes training data. Here, the attacker does not have access to the algorithm. They can only manipulate labels. For instance, the attacker can draw new labels at random from the training pool, or can optimize the labels to cause maximum disruption.

- **Data Injection:** Even if the adversary does not have access to the training data or learning algorithm, he or she can still inject incorrect data into the training set. This is similar to manipulation, but the difference is that the adversary introduces new malicious data into the training pool, not just labels.

Support Vector Machines (SVMs) are widely used classification models for malware identification, intrusion detection systems, and filtering of spam emails, to name a few applications. Biggio, Nelson and Laskov [40] illustrated poisoning attacks on the SVM classifier, with the assumption that the adversary has information about the learning algorithm, and the data distribution. The adversary generates surrogate data from the data distribution and tampers with the training data, by introducing the surrogate data, to drastically reduce the model training accuracy. The test data remains untouched. The authors formed an equation, expressing the adversarial strategy, as:

$$MAX_x \; A(x) = \sum_{i=1}^{k}(1 - y_i f_x(x_i)) = \sum_{i=1}^{k}(-g_i)$$

where $x_l \leq x \leq x_u$ and D = $(x_i, \; y_i)_{i=1}^{k}$ is the validation data.

The goal of the adversary is to maximize the loss function $A(x)$ with the surrogate data instance $(x, \; y)$ to be added into the training set D_{tr} in order to maximally reduce the training accuracy of classification. g_i is the status of the margin, influenced by the surrogate data instance $(x, \; y)$.

Rubinstien et al. [80] presented the attack on SVM learning by exploiting training data confidentiality. The objective is to access the features and the labels of the training data by examining the classification on the test set.

Figure 2 explains the poison attack on the SVM classifier. The left sub-figure indicates the decision boundary of the linear SVM classifier, with support vectors and classifier margin. The right sub-figure shows how the decision boundary is drastically changed by tampering with one training data instance without changing the label of the instance. It was observed that the classification accuracy would be reduced by 11% by a mere 3% manipulation of the training set [81]. Nelson et al. [39] showed that an attacker can breach the functionality on the spam filter by poisoning the Bayesian classification model. The filter becomes inoperable under the proposed Usenet dictionary attack, wherein 36% of the messages are misclassified with 1% knowledge regarding the messages in the training set.

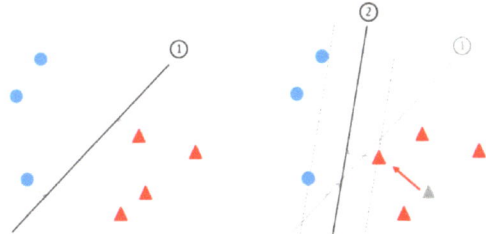

Figure 2. Poisoning attack changing the decision boundary.

Munoz-Gonzalez et al. [38] illustrated poisoning attacks on multi-class classification problems. The authors identified two attack scenarios for the multi-class problems: (1) error-generic poisoning attacks and (2) error-specific poisoning attacks. In the first scenario, the adversary attacks the bi-level optimization problem [40,82], where the surrogate data is segregated into training and validation sets. The model is learned on the generated surrogate training dataset with the tampered instances. The validation set measures the influence of the tampered instances on the original test set, by maximizing the binary class loss function. It is expressed in the following equation:

$$D_x^* = argmax_{D_x'} A\left(D_x', \sigma\right) = L(\widehat{D_{val}}, \; \widehat{\theta})$$

$$Such \; as \; \widehat{\theta} = min_{w^*} L(\widehat{D_{tr}} \; U \; D_x', \; \theta^*)$$

The surrogate data $\widehat{D}$ is segregated into training $\widehat{D_{tr}}$ and validation sets $\widehat{D_{val}}$. The model is trained on $\widehat{D_{tr}}$ along with D_x' (i.e., the tampered instances). $\widehat{D_{val}}$ is used to measure the influence of the tainted samples on the genuine data via the function $A\left(D_x', \sigma\right)$ that explains the loss function, L, with respect to the validation dataset $\widehat{D_{val}}$ and the parameters $\widehat{\theta}$ of the surrogate model. In the multi-class scenario, the multi-class loss function is used for error-generic poisoning attacks.

In error-specific poisoning attacks, the objective remains to change the outcome of specific instances in a multi-class scenario. The goal of desired misclassification is expressed with the equation:

$$\left(D'_x, \sigma\right) = -L(\overbrace{\widehat{D^*_{val}}, \ \widehat{\theta}})$$

$\widehat{D^*_{val}}$ is the same as the $\widehat{D_{val}}$ with different labels for desired misclassified instances that the adversary chose. The attacker aims to minimize the loss of the chosen misclassified samples.

In separate research, Kloft and Laskov [83] explained the adversarial attack on detection of outliers (anomalies), where the adversary is assumed to have knowledge about the algorithm and the training data. Their work introduced a finite sliding window, while updating the centre of mass iteratively for each new data instance. The objective is to accept the poisoned data instance as a valid data point, and the update on the center of mass is shifted in the direction of the tainted point, that appears to be a valid one. They show that relative displacement, d, of the center of mass under adversarial attack is lower bounded by the following inequality when the training window length is infinite:

$$d_i \leq ln(1 + \frac{i}{n})$$

where i and n are the number of tampered points and number of training points, respectively.

The intuition behind the use of anomaly detection is to sanitize the data by removing the anomalous data points, assuming the distribution of the anomalies is different from that of the normal data points. Koh, Steinhardt, and Liang [84] presented data poisoning attacks that outsmart data sanitization defenses for traditional anomaly detection, by nearest neighbors, training loss and singular value decomposition methods. The researchers divided the attacks into two groups:

- **High Sensitive**: An anomaly detector usually considers points as anomalous when the point is far off from its closest neighbors. The anomaly detector cannot identify a specific point as abnormal if it is surrounded by other points, even if that tiny cluster of points are far off from remaining points. So, if an adversary/attacker concentrates poison points in a few anomalous locations, then the anomalous location is considered benign by the detector.
- **Low Sensitive** : An anomaly detector drops all points away from the centroid by a particular distance. Whether the anomaly detector deems a provided point as abnormal does not vary much by addition or deletion of some points, until the centroid of data does not vary considerably.

Attackers can take advantage of this low sensitivity property of detectors and optimize the location of poisoned points such that it satisfies the constraints imposed by the defender.

Shafahi et al. [85] discussed how classification results can be manipulated just by injecting adversarial examples with correct labels. which is known as the clean-label attack. The clean-label attack is executed by changing the normal ("base") instance to reflect the features of another class, as shown in Figure 3. The Gmail image is marked with blue dots and lies on the feature space of the target dataset. This poisoned data is used for training and shifts the decision boundary, as shown in Figure 4.

Due to the shift, the target instance is classified as "base" instance. Here, the adversary tries to craft a poison instance such that it is indistinguishable from the base instance, i.e., the instance looks similar, and also minimizes the feature representation between the target and poison instances so that it triggers misclassification while training. This attack can be crafted using the optimization problem by means of the following equation:

$$p = argmin_x \, ||f(x) - f(t)||_2^2 + \beta * ||x - b||_2^2$$

where b is the base instance, and t and p are the target and poison instances, respectively. The parameter β identifies the degree to which p appears to be a normal instance to the human expert.

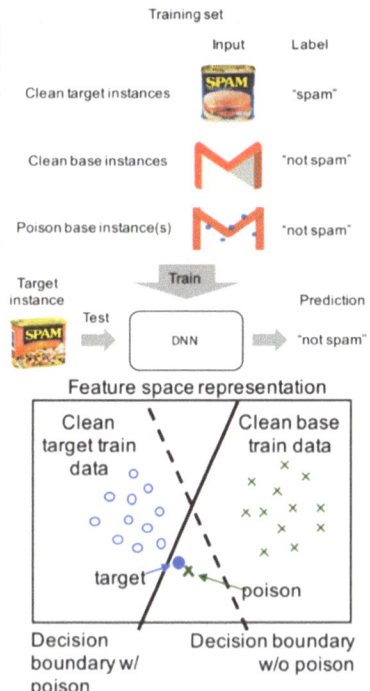

Figure 3. Clean-label attack procedure and example.

Figure 4. Badnet of MINST sample [42].

Suciu et al. [86] presented a similar type of attack on neural networks, but with the constraint that at least 12.5% of every mini-batch of training data should have tainted examples.

3.3.2. Data Poisoning Defense Mechanisms

There are studies that propose potential defense mechanisms to resolve the problems related to the data poisoning attacks discussed thus far. Devising a generic defense strategy against all attacks is not possible. The defense strategies are specific to the attack and a defense scheme specific to an attack makes the system susceptible to a different kind of attack. Some advanced defense strategies include:

1. **Adversarial Training :** The goal of adversarial training is to inject instances generated by the adversary into the training set to increase the strength of the model [87,88]. The defender follows the same strategy, by generating the crafted samples, using the

brute force method, and training the model by feeding the clean and the generated instances. Adversarial training is suitable if the instances are crafted on the original model and not on a locally-trained surrogate model [89,90].

2. **Feature Squee zing:** This defense strategy hardens the training models by diminishing the number of features and, hence, the complexity of data [91]. This, in turn, reduces the sensitivity of the data, which evades the tainted data marked by the adversary.

3. **Transferability blocking:** The true defense mechanism against blackbox attacks is to obstruct the transferability of the adversarial samples. The transferability enables the usage of adversarial samples in different models trained on different datasets. Null labeling [92] is a procedure that blocks transferability, by introducing null labels into the training dataset, and trains the model to discard the adversarial samples as null labeled data. This approach does not reduce the accuracy of the model with normal data instances.

4. **MagNet:** This scheme is used to arrest a range of blackbox attacks through the use of a detector and a reformer [93]. The detector identifies the differences between the normal and the tainted samples by measuring the distance between them with respect to a threshold. The reformer converts a tampered instance to a legitimate one by means of an autoencoder.

5. **Defense-GAN:** To stave off both blackbox and whitebox attacks, the capability of General Adversarial Network (GAN) [94] is leveraged [95]. GAN uses a generator to construct the input images by minimizing the reconstruction error. The reconstructed images are fed to the system as input, where the genuine instances are closer to the generator than the tainted instances. Hence, the performance of the attack degrades.

6. **Local Intrinsic Dimensionality:** Weerashinghe et al. [96] addressed resistance against data poisoning attack on SVM classifiers during training. They used Local Intrinsic Dimensionality (LID), a metric of computing dimension of local neighborhood subspace for each data instance. They also used K-LID approximation for each sample to find the likelihood ratio of K-LID values from the distribution of benign samples to that from tainted samples. Next, the function of the likelihood ratio is fitted to predict the likelihood ratio for the unseen data points' K-LID values. The technique showed stability against adversarial attacks on label flipping.

7. **Reject On Negative Impact (RONI):** The functioning of the RONI technique is very similar to that of the Leave-One-Out (LOO) validation procedure [97]. Although effective, this technique is computationally expensive and may suffer from overfitting if the training dataset used by the algorithm is small compared to the number of features. RONI defense is not well suited for applications that involve deep learning architectures, as those applications would demand a larger training dataset [39]. In [98], a defensive mechanism was proposed based on the k-Nearest Neighbors technique, which recommends relabeling possible malicious data points based on the labels of their neighboring samples in the training dataset. However, this strategy fails to detect attacks in which the subsets of poisoning points are close. An outlier detection scheme was proposed in [99] for classification tasks. In this strategy, the outlier detectors for each class are trained with a small fraction of trusted data points. This strategy is effective in attack scenarios where the hacker does not model specific attack constraints. For example, if the training dataset is poisoned only by flipping the labels, then this strategy can detect those poisoned data points which are far from the genuine ones. Here, it is important to keep in mind that outlier detectors used in this technique need to first be trained on small curated training points that are known to be genuine [99].

In many studies, the defense strategies are for the time of filtering of data during anomaly detection (i.e., before the model is trained). Koh, Steinhardt, and Liang [84] considered data sanitization defenses of five different types, from the perspective of anomaly detection, each with respective anomaly detection parameters β and parametrarized scores

S_β which identify the degree of anomaly. D_{clean} and D_{poison} are the datasets for clean and poisoned instances $D = D_{clean} \cup D_{poisin}$ and β is derived from D.

(1) **L-2 Defense:** This type of defense discards the instances that are distant from the center of the corresponding class they belong to, from the perspective of the L-2 distance measure. The outlier detection parameter and parametrarized score for the L-2 defense are expressed as:

$$\beta_y = Expectation_D(x|y)$$

$$S_\beta(x, y) = ||x - \beta_y||_2$$

(2) **Slab Defense:** Slab defense [81] draws the projections of the instances on the lines or planes joining the class centers and discards those that are too distant from the centers of the classes. Unlike the L-2 defense, this mechanism considers only the distances between the class centers as pertinent dimensions. The outlier detection parameter and parametrarized score for the slab defense are expressed as:

$$\beta_y = Expectation_D(x|y)$$

$$S_\beta(x, y) = |(\beta_1 - \beta_{-1})^T (x - \beta_y)|$$

where θ is the learning parameter that minimizes the training loss, x denotes the data point and y is the class.

(3) **Loss Defense:** Loss defense removes points that are not fitted well by the trained model on D. The feature dimensions are learned based on loss function l. The outlier detection parameter and parametrarized score for the loss defense are expressed as:

$$\beta_y = argmin_\theta Expectation_D l_\theta[(x|y)]$$

$$S_\beta(x, y) = l_\beta(x|y)$$

(4) **SVD Defense :** SVD defense is the mechanism that works on the basis of sub-space assumption [100]. In this defense mechanism the normal instances are assumed to lie in low-ranked sub-space while the tampered instances have components that are too large to fit into this sub-space. The outlier detection parameter and parametrarized score for the loss defense are expressed as:

$$\beta = |M|_{RSV}^k$$

$$S_\beta(x, y) = ||\left(I - \beta\beta^T\right)x||_2$$

The term $|M|_{RSV}^k$ is the matrix of $S_\beta(x, y) = |((I - \beta\beta^T)x||_2$ right singular vector of data matrix d.

(5) **K-NN Defense:** The K-NN defense discards data instances that are distant from the K nearest neighbors. The outlier detection parameter and parametrarized score for the k-NN defense are expressed as:

$$\beta = D$$

$$S_\beta(x, y) = dist_{k\text{-NN}} \in \beta$$

Koh, Steinhardt, and Liang [84] have tested these 5 types of data sanitization defenses on four types of datasets: The MNIST dataset [101], Dogfish [102], Enron spam detection [103] and the IMDB sentiment classification datasets [104]. The first two datasets are image datasets. The results showed that these defenses could still be evaded with concentrated attacks where the instances concentrated in a few locations appear to be normal. However, it was observed that L-2, slab and loss defenses still diminished the test error (which is exploited by the adversary to launch a data poisoning attack) considerably, compared to the SVD and k-NN defenses.

Peri et al. [105] proposed a defense mechanism resisting clean-label poison attacks, based on k-NN, and identified 99% of the poisoned instances, which were eventually discarded before model training. The authors claimed that this scheme, known as Deep K-NN, worked better than the schemes provided by [84], without reducing the model's performance.

3.3.3. Model Poisoning Attacks

Poisoning of models is more like a traditional cyberattack. If attackers breach the AI system, then either they can compromise the existing AI model with the poisoned one or they can execute "A man in the middle" attack [106] to have the wrong model downloaded, while transferring learning.

Model poisoning is generally done using Backdoored Neural Network (BadNet) attack [45]. BadNets are modified neural networks, in which the model is trained on clean and poisoned inputs. In this, the training mechanism is fully or partly outsourced to the adversary, who returns the model with secret backdoor inputs. Secret backdoor inputs are inputs added by the attacker which result in misclassification. The inputs are known only to the attacker. BadNet is categorized into two related classes:

1. **Outsource training attack**, when training is outsourced, and
2. **Transfer learning attack**, when a pre-trained model is outsourced and used.

In the following subsections, we also explore model poisoning attacks on the federated learning scenario, where the training of the model is distributed on multiple computing devices and the results of the training are aggregated from all the devices to form the final training model. Bhagoji et al. [41] classified the model poisoning attack strategies on federated learning scenarios as: (1) explicit boosting, and (2) alternating minimization.

Outsourced Training Attack

We want to train the parameters of a model, M. using the training data. We outsource the description of M to the trainer who sends the learned parameters back to us β_M. Our trustability of the trainer depends on a privately held validation dataset, with a targeted accuracy, or on the service agreement between us and the trainer.

The objective of the adversary is to return a corrupted model with backdoored trained parameters β'_M. This is different from β_M and either should not lower the validation accuracy or decrease the model accuracy of the inputs with a backdoor trigger. Thus, the training attack can be targeted or untargeted. In a targeted attack, the adversary switches the label of the outputs for specific inputs, while in an untargeted attack, the input of the backdoored property remains misclassified to degrade the overall model accuracy.

Figure 4 depicts an example of backdoor attacks where the second and third images are the original image's backdoored version, whereas Figure 5 depicts an example of BadNet attacks on traffic images.

Figure 5. Badnet Example [42].

Figure 6 illustrates a special type of potential BadNet (i.e., BadNet with backdoor detector) which makes use of a parallel link to identify the backdoor trigger. It also uses a combining layer to produce misclassifications if the backdoor appears. This perturbed model would not impact the results on a cleaned dataset, so the user would not be able to identify if the model has been compromised.

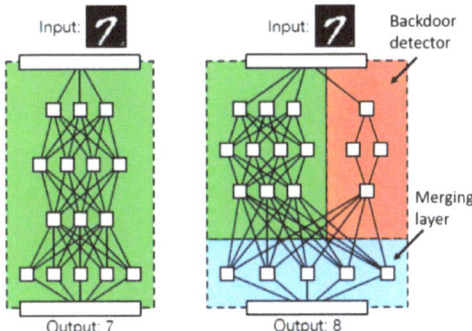

Figure 6. Badnet Model [42].

In terms of defense mechanisms, Backdoor attacks like BadNet happen when we use pre-trained models. So, the less pre-trained the model, the less the attack. However, today, almost all networks are built using pre-trained models.

To make the models robust against backdoor attacks, Gu et al. [42] proposed the following defense strategies:

- Securely hosting and disseminating pre-trained models in virtual repositories that guarantee integrity, to preclude benevolent models from being manipulated. The security is characterized by the fact that virtual archives should have digital signatures of the trainer on the pre-trained models with the public key cryptosystem [43].
- Identifying backdoors in malevolently trained models acquired from an untrustworthy trainer by retraining or fine-tuning the untrusted model with some added computational cost [44,46]. These researchers considered fully outsourced training attacks. Another research [107], proposed a defense mechanism with an assumption that the user has access to both clean and backdoored instances.

Transfer Learning Attack

The objective of transfer learning is to save computation time, by transferring the knowledge of an already-trained model to the target model [45]. The models are stored in online repositories from where a user can download them for an AI/ML application. If the downloaded model, M_{cor}, is a corrupted model, then, while transferring learning, the user generates his/her model and parameters based on M_{cor}. In transfer learning attacks, we assume that the newly adapted model, M_{cor}, and the uncorrupted model have the same input dimensions but differ in number of classes.

Figure 7 compares a good network (left), that rightly classifies its input, to BadNet (right), that gives misclassifications but has the same architecture as the good network.

Figure 8 describes the transfer learning attack setup with backdoor strengthening factor to enhance the impact of weights.

In terms of potential defense mechanisms, the obvious defense strategy is to obtain pre-trained models from trusted online sources, such as Caffe Model Zoo and Keras trained Model Library [108], where a secure cryptographic hashing algorithm (e.g., SHA-1) is used as a reference to verify the downloads. However, the researchers in [42] showed that downloaded BadNet from "secure" online model archives can still hold the backdoor property, even when the user re-trains the model to perform his/her tasks.

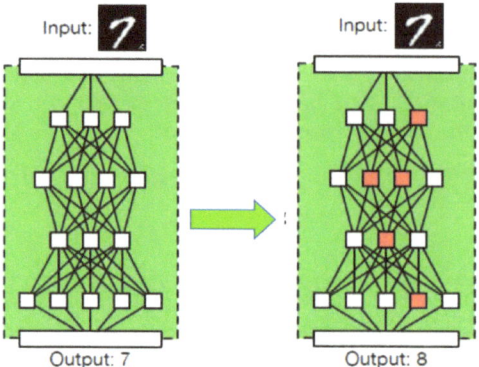

Figure 7. Transfer learning using the BadNet [42].

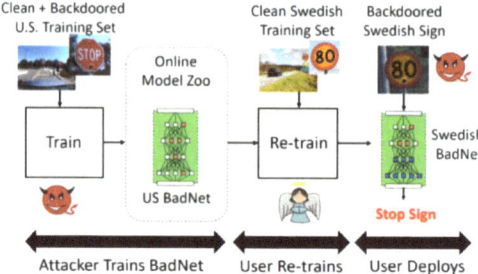

Figure 8. Transfer Learning set up attacks [42].

Wu et al. [109] devised methodologies to resolve transfer learning attacks related to misclassification. They proposed activation-based pruning [110] and developed the distilled differentiator, based on pruning. To augment strength against attacks, the ensemble construct from the differentiators is implemented. As the individual distilled differentiators are diverse, in activation-based pruning, different training examples promote divergence among the differentiators; hence, increasing the strength of ensemble models. Pruning changes the model structure and arrests the portability of attack from one system to the other [44,46]. Network pruning removes the connectives between the model and generates a sparse model from a dense network model. The sparsity helps in fine tuning the model and eventually discarding the virulence of the attacks. Comprehensive evaluations, based on classification accuracy, success rate, size of the models, and time for learning, regarding the defense strategies suggested by the authors, on image recognition showed the new models, with only five differentiators, to be invulnerable against more than 90% of adversarial inputs, with accuracy loss less than 10%.

Attack on Federated Learning

In the federated learning scenario, each and every individual device has its own model to train, securing the privacy of the data stored in that device [47]. Federated learning algorithms are susceptible to model poisoning if the owner of the device becomes malicious. Research [111,112] introduced a premise for federated learning, where a single adversary attacks the learning by changing the gradient updates to arbitrary values, instead of introducing the backdoor property into the model. The objective of the attacker is to obstruct the convergence of the execution of the distributed Stochastic Gradient Descent (SGD) algorithm. In a similar study, Bagdasaryan et al. [48] proposed a multi-agent framework, where multiple adversaries jointly conspired to replace the model during model covergence. Bhagoji et al. [41] worked on targeted misclassification by introducing a sequence of attacks induced by a single adversary: (1) explicit boosting, and (2) alternating minimization. The underlying algorithm is SGD.

- **Explicit Boosting:** The adversary updates the boosting steps to void the global aggregated effect of the individual models locally distributed over different devices. The attack is based on running of boosting steps of SGD until the attacker obtains the parameter weight vector, starting from the global weight, to minimize the training loss over the data and the class label. This enables the adversary to obtain the initial update, which is used to determine the final adversarial update. The final update is obtained by the product of the final adversarial update and the inverse of adversarial scaling (i.e., the boosting factor), so that the server cannot identify the adversarial effect.

- **Alternating Minimization:** The authors in [45] showed that, in an explicit boosting attack, the malicious updates on boosting steps could not evade the potential defense related to measuring accuracy. Alternating minimization was introduced to exploit the fact that it is updates related only to the targeted class that need to be boosted. This strategy improves adversarial attack that can bypass the defense mechanism with the goal of minimizing training loss and boosting parameter updates for the adversarial goals and achieved a high success rate.

In terms of potential defense mechanisms, two typical strategies are deployed, depending on the nature of the attacks on federated learning: (1) robust aggregation methods, and (2) robust learning rate.

- **Robust aggregation methods:** These methods incorporate security into federated learning by exploring different statistical metrics that could replace the average (mean) statistic, while aggregating the effects of the models, such as trimmed mean, geometric median, coordinate-median, etc [47,111,113–116]. Introducing the new statistic while aggregating has the primary objective of staving off attacks during model convergence. Bernstein et al. [117] proposed a sign aggregation technique on the SGD algorithm, distributed over individual machines or devices. The devices interact with the server by communicating the signs of the gradients. The server aggregates the signs and sends this to the individual machines, which use it to update their model weights. The weight update rule can be expressed by the following equation:

$$w_{t+1} = w_t + \gamma(sgn \sum\nolimits_{i \in A_t} sgn(\Delta_t^i))$$

where Δ_t^i is the weight update of the device i at time t. $\Delta_t^i = w_t^k - w_t.w_t$ is the weight the server sent to the set of devices A_t at time t and γ is the server learning rate.

This approach is robust against convergence attacks, but susceptible to backdoor attacks in federated learning scenarios.

In a recent study, [118] the authors modified the mean estimator of the aggregate by introducing weight-cutoff and addition of noise [119] during weight update to deter backdoor attacks. In this method, the server snips the weights when the L2 norm of a weight update surpasses a pre-specified threshold, and then aggregates the snipped weights, along with the noise, during aggregation of weights.

- **Robust Learning Rate:** Ozdayi, Katancioglu, and Gel [120] introduced the defense mechanism by making the model learning rate robust with a pre-specified boundary of malicious agents. With the help of the updated learning rate, the adversarial model weight approaches the direction of the genuine model weight. This work is an extension of the signed aggregation proposed in [117]. The authors proposed a parameter-learning threshold δ. The learning rate for the i-th dimension of the data can be represented as:

$$\gamma_{\delta,i} = \begin{cases} \gamma & \text{if } \left| \sum_{k \in S_t} \text{sgn}\left(\Delta_{t,i}^k\right) \right| \geq \delta \\ -\gamma & \text{otherwise} \end{cases}$$

The server weight update at time $t + 1$ is

$$w_{t+1} = w_t + \gamma_\delta \odot \frac{\sum_{k \in S_t} n_k \triangle_t^k}{\sum_{k \in S_t} n_k}$$

where γ_δ is the overall learning rate, including all dimensions, and $\odot$ is the feature-wise product operation. Δ^k is the update on the gradient descent update of the k-th player in the system, and k may be the adversary or the regular user.

3.4. Model Inversion Attack

The model inversion attack is a way to reconstruct the training data, given the model parameters. This type of attack is a concern for privacy, because there are a growing number of online model repositories. Several studies related to this attack hve been under both the blackbox and whitebox settings. Yang et al. [121] discussed the model inversion attack in the blackbox setting, where the attacker wants to reconstruct an input sample from the confidence score vector determined by the target model. In their study, they demonstrated that it is possible to reconstruct specific input samples from a given model. They trained a model (inversion) on an auxiliary dataset, which functioned as the inverse of the given target model. Their model then took the confidence scores of the target model as input and tried to reconstruct the original input data. In their study, they also demonstrated that their inversion model showed substantial improvement over previously proposed models. On the other hand, in a whitebox setting, Fredrikson et al. [122] proposed a model inversion attack that produces only a representative sample of a training data sample, instead of reconstructing a specific input sample, using the confidence score vector determined by the target model. Several related studies were proposed to infer sensitive attributes [122–125] or statistical information [126] about the training data by developing an inversion model. Hitaj et al. [71] explored inversion attacks in federated learning where the attacker had whitebox access to the model.

Several defense strategies against the model inversion attack have been explored that include L2 Regularizer [49], Dropout and Model Staking [50], MemGuard [51], and Differential privacy [52]. These defense mechanisms are also well-known for reducing overfitting in the training of deep neural network models.

3.5. Model Extraction Attack

A machine learning model extraction attack arises when an attacker obtains black-box access to the target model and is successful in learning another model that closely resembles. or is exactly the same as, the target model. Reith et al. [54] discussed model extraction against the support vector regression model. Juuti et al. [127] explored neural networks and showed an attack, in which an adversary generates queries for DNNs with simple architectures. Wang et al., in [128], proposed model extraction attacks for stealing hyperparameters against a simple architecture similar to a neural network with three layers. The most elegant attack, in comparison to the others, was shown in [129]. They showed that it is possible to extract a model with higher accuracy than the original model. Using distillation, which is a technique for model compression, the authors in [130,131], executed model extraction attacks against DNNs and CNNs for image classification.

To defend against model extraction attacks, the authors in [53,132,133] proposed either hiding or adding noises to the output probabilities, while keeping the class label of the instances intact. However, such approaches are not very effective in label-based extraction attacks. Several others have proposed monitoring the queries and differentiating suspicious queries from others by analyzing the input distribution or the output entropy [127,134].

3.6. Inference Attack

Machine learning models have a tendency to leak information about the individual data records on which they were trained. Shokri et al. [49] discussed the membership inference attack, where one can determine if the data record is part of the model's training dataset or not, given the data record and blackbox access to the model. According to them, this is a concern for privacy breach. If the advisory can learn if the record was used as part of the training, from the model, then such a model is considered to be leaking information. The concern is paramount, as such a privacy beach not only affects a single observation, but the entire population, due to high correlation between the covered and the uncovered dataset [135]. This happens particularly when the model is based on statistical facts about the population.

Studies in [136–138] focused on attribute inference attacks. Here an attacker gets access to a set of data about a target user, which is mostly public in nature, and aims to infer the private information of the target user. In this case, the attacker first collects information from users who are willing to disclose it in public, and then uses the information as a training dataset to learn a machine learning classifier which can take a user's public data as input and predict the user's private attribute values.

In terms of potential defense mechanisms, methods proposed in [55,139] leveraged heuristic correlations between the records of the public data and attribute values to defend against attribute inference attacks. They proposed modifying the identified k entries that have large correlations with the attribute values to any given target users. Here k is used to control the privacy–utility trade off. This addresses the membership inference attack.

4. Conclusions

Using an extensive survey of the literature, this research addresses two research questions regarding attacks on AI systems and their potential defense mechanisms.

RQ1: What are the cyberattacks that AI systems can be subjected to?

To answer this question, we discussed different categories of intentional and unintentional failures, along with the details of poisoning attacks on data and machine learning models. We also introduced backdoored neural network (discussing it from the perspective of research carried out on outsourced training attacks, transfer learning attack and federated learning attacks), model inversion, model extraction and inference attacks.

RQ2: Can the attacks on AI systems be organized into a taxonomy, to better understand how the vulnerabilities manifest themselves during system development?

Upon reviewing the literature related to attacks on AI systems, it was evident that, at different stages of the AI/ML pipeline development, vulnerabilities manifest; thus, providing an opportunity to launch attacks on the AI system. Table 1 and Figure 1 organize the AI attacks into a taxonomy, to better understand how vulnerabilities manifest and how attacks can be launched during the entire system development process.

RQ3: What are possible defense mechanisms to defend AI systems from cyberattacks?

While addressing the second research question, we reviewed multiple state of the art methods that are used as potential defense mechanisms for each type of attack.

RQ4: Is it possible to device a generic defense mechanism against all kinds of AI attacks?

Based on the literature review of cyberattacks on AI systems. it is clearly evident that there is no single. or generic, defense mechanism that can address diverse attacks on AI systems. Vulnerabilities that manifest in AI systems are more specific to the system design and its composition. Therefore, a defense mechanism has to be tailored, or designed, in such a way that it can suit the specific characteristics of the system.

This survey sheds light on the different types of cybersecurity attacks and their corresponding defense mechanisms in a detailed and comprehensive manner. Growing threats and attacks in emerging technologies, such as social media, cloud computing, AI/ML systems, data pipelines and other critical infrastructures, often manifest in different forms. It is worth noting that it is challenging to capture all patterns of threats and attacks. Therefore, this survey attempted to capture a common set of general threat and attack patterns that are specifically targeted towards AI/ML systems. Organizing this body of knowledge. from the perspective of an AI system's life cycle, can be useful for software engineering teams when designing and developing intelligent systems. In addition, this survey offers a profound benefit to the research community focused on analyzing the cybersecurity of AI systems. Researchers can implement and replicate these attacks on an AI system, systematically apply defenses against these attacks, understand the trade offs that arise from using defense mechanisms, and create a catalog of patterns or tactics for designing trustworthy AI systems.

Author Contributions: Conceptualization, Y.B., R.S.S. and S.M.S.; methodology, Y.B., R.S.S. and S.M.S.; writing and editing, Y.B. and R.S.S.; review, R.S.S. and S.M.S., funding acquisition, Y.B. All authors have read and agreed to the published version of the manuscript.

Funding: This research was funded by the Penn State InudstryXchange 2021.

Acknowledgments: In memoriam: "Partha, the bond between friends cannot be broken by death. You will be greatly missed." (Y.B.).

Conflicts of Interest: The authors declare no conflict of interest.

References

1. Comiter, M. Attacking artificial intelligence: AI's security vulnerability and what policymakers can do about it. *Harv. Kennedy Sch. Belfer Cent. Sci. Int. Aff.* **2019**, 1–90. Available online: https://www.belfercenter.org/sites/default/files/2019-08/AttackingAI/AttackingAI.pdf (accessed on 8 March 2023) .
2. Mcgraw, G.; Bonett, R.; Figueroa, H.; Shepardson, V. Security engineering for machine learning. *IEEE Comput.* **2019**, *52*, 54–57. [CrossRef]
3. Ma, Y.; Xie, T.; Li, J.; Maciejewski, R. Explaining vulnerabilities to adversarial machine learning through visual analytics. *IEEE Trans. Vis. Comput. Graph.* **2019**, *26*, 1075–1085. [CrossRef] [PubMed]
4. Kim, J.; Park, N. Blockchain-based data-preserving AI learning environment model for AI cybersecurity systems in IoT service environments. *Appl. Sci.* **2020**, *10*, 4718. [CrossRef]
5. Mozaffari-Kermani, M.; Sur-Kolay, S.; Raghunathan, A.; Jha, N.K. Systematic poisoning attacks on and defenses for machine learning in healthcare. *IEEE J. Biomed. Health Inform.* **2014**, *19*,1893–1905. [CrossRef] [PubMed]
6. Sadeghi, K.; Banerjee, A.; Gupta, S.K.S. A system-driven taxonomy of attacks and defenses in adversarial machine learning. *IEEE Trans. Emerg. Top. Comput. Intell.* **2020**, *4*, 450–467. [CrossRef]
7. Sagar, R.; Jhaveri, R.; Borrego, C. Applications in security and evasions in machine learning: A survey. *Electronics* **2020**, *9*, 97. [CrossRef]
8. Pitropakis, N.; Panaousis, E.; Giannetsos, T.; Anastasiadis, E.; Loukas, G. A taxonomy and survey of attacks against machine learning. *Comput. Sci. Rev.* **2019**, *34*, 100199. [CrossRef]
9. Cao, N.; Li, G.; Zhu, P.; Sun, Q.; Wang, Y.; Li, J.; Yan, M.; Zhao, Y. Handling the adversarial attacks. *J. Ambient. Intell. Humaniz. Comput.* **2019**, *10*, 2929–2943. [CrossRef]
10. Wang, X.; Li, J.; Kuang, X.; Tan, Y.; Li, J. The security of machine learning in an adversarial setting: A survey. *J. Parallel Distrib. Comput.* **2019**, *130*, 12–23. [CrossRef]
11. Rouani, B.D.; Samragh, M.; Javidi, T.; Koushanfar, F. Safe machine learning and defeating adversarial attacks. *IEEE Secur.* **2019**, *17*, 31–38. [CrossRef]
12. Qiu, S.; Liu, Q.; Zhou, S.; Wu, C. Review of artificial intelligence adversarial attack and defense technologies. *Appl. Sci.* **2019**, *9*, 909. [CrossRef]
13. Biggio, B.; Roli, F. Wild patterns: Ten years after the rise of adversarial machine learning. *Pattern Recognit.* **2018**, *84*, 317–331. [CrossRef]
14. Sethi, T.S.; Kantardzic, M.; Lyu, L.; Chen, J. A dynamic-adversarial mining approach to the security of machine learning. *Wiley Interdiscip. Rev. Data Min. Knowl. Discov.* **2018**, *8*, e1245. [CrossRef]
15. Chen, T.; Liu, J.; Xiang, Y.; Niu, W.; Tong, E.; Han, Z. Adversarial attack and defense in reinforcement learning-from AI security view. *Cybersecurity* **2019**, *2*, 1–22. [CrossRef]
16. Li, J.; Ota, K.; Dong, M.; Wu, J.; Li, J. DeSVig: Decentralized swift vigilance against adversarial attacks in industrial artificial intelligence systems. *IEEE Trans. Ind. Inform.* **2019**, *16*, 3267–3277. [CrossRef]
17. Garcia-Ceja, E.; Morin, B.; Aguilar-Rivera, A.; Riegler, M.A. A Genetic Attack Against Machine Learning Classifiers to Steal Biometric Actigraphy Profiles from Health Related Sensor Data. *J. Med. Syst.* **2020**, *44*, 1–11. [CrossRef]
18. Biggio, B.; Russu, P.; Didaci, L.; Roli, F. Adversarial biometric recognition: A review on biometric system security from the adversarial machine-learning perspective. *IEEE Signal Process. Mag.* **2015**, *32*, 31–41. [CrossRef]
19. Ren, Y.; Zhou, Q.; Wang, Z.; Wu, T.; Wu, G.; Choo, K.K.R. Query-efficient label-only attacks against black-box machine learning models. *Comput. Secur.* **2020**, *90*, 101698. [CrossRef]
20. Wang, D.; Li, C.; Wen, S.; Nepal, S.; Xiang, Y. Man-in-the-middle attacks against machine learning classifiers via malicious generative models. *IEEE Trans. Dependable Secur. Comput.* **2020**, *18*, 2074–2087. [CrossRef]

21. Qiu, J.; Du, L.; Chen, Y.; Tian, Z.; Du, X.; Guizani, M. Artificial intelligence security in 5G networks: Adversarial examples for estimating a travel time task. *IEEE Veh. Technol. Mag.* **2020**, *15*, 95–100. [CrossRef]
22. Benzaid, C.; Taleb, T. AI for beyond 5G networks: a cyber-security defense or offense enabler? *IEEE Networks* **2020**, *34*, 140–147. [CrossRef]
23. Apruzzese, G.; Andreolini, M.; Marchetti, M.; Colacino, V.G.; Russo, G. AppCon: Mitigating Evasion Attacks to ML Cyber Detectors. *Symmetry* **2020**, *12*, 653. [CrossRef]
24. Zhang, S.; Xie, X.; Xu, Y. A brute-force black-box method to attack machine learning-based systems in cybersecurity. *IEEE Access* **2020**, *8*, 128250–128263. [CrossRef]
25. Liu, K.; Yang, H.; Ma, Y.; Tan, B.; Yu, B.; Young, E.F.; Karri, R.; Garg, S. Adversarial perturbation attacks on ML-based cad: A case study on CNN-based lithographic hotspot detection. *ACM Trans. Des. Autom. Electron. Syst.* **2020**, *25*, 1–31. [CrossRef]
26. Katzir, Z.; Elovici, Y. Quantifying the resilience of machine learning classifiers used for cyber security. *Expert Syst. Appl.* **2018**, *92*, 419–429. [CrossRef]
27. Chen, S.; Xue, M.; Fan, L.; Hao, S.; Xu, L.; Zhu, H.; Li, B. Automated poisoning attacks and defenses in malware detection systems: An adversarial machine learning approach. *Comput. Secur.* **2018**, *73*, 326–344. [CrossRef]
28. Gardiner, J.; Nagaraja, S. On the security of machine learning in malware c&c detection: A survey. *ACM Comput. Surv.* **2016**, *49*, 1–39.
29. Dasgupta, P.; Collins, J. A survey of game theoretic approaches for adversarial machine learning in cybersecurity tasks. *AI Mag.* **2019**, *40*, 31–43. [CrossRef]
30. Al-Rubaie, M.; Chang, J.M. Privacy-preserving machine learning: Threats and solutions. *IEEE Secur. Priv.* **2019**, *17*, 49–58. [CrossRef]
31. Hansman, S.; Hunt, R. A taxonomy of network and computer attacks. *Comput. Secur.* **2005**, *24*, 31–43. [CrossRef]
32. Gao, J.B.; Zhang, B.W.; Chen, X.H.; Luo, Z. Ontology-based model of network and computer attacks for security assessment. *J. Shanghai Jiaotong Univ.* **2013**, *18*, 554–562. [CrossRef]
33. Gonzalez, L.M.; Lupu, E.; Emil, C. The secret of machine learning. *ITNow* **2018**, *60*, 38–39. [CrossRef]
34. Mcdaniel, P.; Papernot, N.; Celik, Z.B. Machine learning in adversarial settings. *IEEE Secur. Priv.* **2016**, *14*, 68–72. [CrossRef]
35. Barreno, M.; Nelson, B.; Joseph, A.D.; Tygar, J.D. The security of machine learning. *Mach. Learn.* **2010**, *81*, 121–148. [CrossRef]
36. Barreno, M.; Nelson, B.; Sears, R.; Joseph, A.D.; Tygar, J.D. Can machine learning be secure? In Proceedings of the 2006 ACM Symposium on Information, Computer and Communications Security, Taipei, Taiwan, 21–24 March 2006; pp. 16–25.
37. Biggio, B.; Fumera, G.; Roli, F. Security evaluation of pattern classifiers under attack. *IEEE Trans. Knowl. Data Eng.* **2013**, *26*, 984–996. [CrossRef]
38. Muñoz-González, L.; Biggio, B.; Demontis, A.; Paudice, A.; Wongrassamee, V.; Lupu, E.C.; Roli, F. Towards poisoning of deep learning algorithms with back-gradient optimization. In Proceedings of the 10th ACM Workshop on Artificial Intelligence and Security, Dallas, TX, USA, 3 November 2017; pp. 27–38.
39. Nelson, B.; Barreno, M.; Chi, F.J.; Joseph, A.D.; Rubinstein, B.I.; Saini, U.; Sutton, C.; Tygar, J.D.; Xia, K. Exploiting machine learning to subvert your spam filter. In Proceedings of First USENIX Workshop on Large Scale Exploits and Emergent Threats, **2008**, *8*, 1–9.
40. Biggio, B.; Nelson, B.; Laskov, P. Poisoning attacks against support vector machines. *arXiv* **2012**, arXiv:1206.6389.
41. Bhagoji, A.N.; Chakraborty, S.; Mittal, P.; Calo, S. Model poisoning attacks in federated learning. In Proceedings of the Workshop on Security in Machine Learning (SecML), collocated with the 32nd Conference on Neural Information Processing Systems, Montreal, QC, Canada, 7 December 2018.
42. Gu, T.; Liu, K.; Dolan-Gavitt, B.; Garg, S. Badnets: Evaluating backdooring attacks on deep neural networks. *IEEE Access* **2019**, *7*, 47230–47244. [CrossRef]
43. Samuel, J.; Mathewson, N.; Cappos, J.; Dingledine, R. Survivable key compromise in software update systems. In Proceedings of the 17th ACM conference on Computer and communications security, Chicago, IL, USA, 4–8 October 2010; pp. 61–72.
44. Liu, K.; Dolan-Gavitt, B.; Garg, S. Fine-pruning: Defending against backdooring attacks on deep neural networks. In Proceedings of the International Symposium on Research in Attacks, Intrusions, and Defenses, Heraklion, Crete, Greece, 10–12 September 2018; pp. 273–294.
45. Gu, T.; Dolan-Gavitt, B.; Garg, S. Badnets: Identifying vulnerabilities in the machine learning model supply chain. *arXiv* **2017**, arXiv:1708.06733.
46. Wang, B.; Yao, Y.; Shan, S.; Li, H.; Viswanath, B.; Zheng, H.; Zhao, B.Y. Neural cleanse: Identifying and mitigating backdoor attacks in neural networks. In Proceedings of the IEEE Symposium on Security and Privacy (SP), San Francisco, CA, USA, 19–23 May 2019; pp. 707–723.
47. Mcmahan, B.; Moore, E.; Ramage, D.; Hampson, S.; Arcas, B.A. Communication-efficient learning of deep networks from decentralized data. In Proceedings of the 20th International Conference of Artificial Intelligence and Statistics, Fort Lauderdale, FL, USA, 20–22 April 2017; pp. 1273–1282.
48. Bagdasaryan, E.; Veit, A.; Hua, Y.; Estrin, D.; Shmatikov, V. How to backdoor federated learning. In Proceedings of International Conference on Artificial Intelligence and Statistics, Online, 26–28 August 2020; pp. 2938–2948.
49. Shokri, R.; Stronati, M.; Song, C.; Shmatikov, V. Membership inference attacks against machine learning models. In Proceedings of the 2017 IEEE Symposium on Security and Privacy (SP), San Jose, CA, USA, 22–26 May 2017; pp. 3–18

50. Salem, A.; Zhang, Y.; Humbert, M.; Berrang, P.; Fritz, M.; Backes, M. ML-Leaks: Model and Data Independent Membership Inference Attacks and Defenses on Machine Learning Models. *arXiv* **2018**, arXiv:1806.01246.
51. Jia, J.; Salem, A.; Backes, M.; Zhang, Y.; Gong, N.Z. Memguard: Defending against black-box membership inference attacks via adversarial examples. In Proceedings of the 2019 ACM SIGSAC Conference on Computer and Communications Security, London, UK, 11–15 November 2019; pp. 259–274.
52. Dwork, C.; Mcsherry, F.; Nissim, K.; Smith, A. Calibrating noise to sensitivity in private data analysis. *Theory Cryptogr. Conf.* **2006**, *3876*, 265–284.
53. Tramèr, F.; Zhang, F.; Juels, A.; Reiter, M.K.; Ristenpart, T. Stealing machine learning models via prediction apis. *USENIX Secur. Symp.* **2016**, *16*, 601–618.
54. Reith, R.N.; Schneider, T.; Tkachenko, O. Efficiently stealing your machine learning models. In Proceedings of the 18th ACM Workshop on Privacy in the Electronic Society, London, UK, 11 November 2019; pp. 198–210.
55. Weinsberg, U.; Bhagat, S.; Ioannidis, S.; Taft, N. BlurMe: Inferring and obfuscating user gender based on ratings. In Proceedings of the sixth ACM conference on Recommender systems, Dublin, Ireland, 9–13 September 2012; pp. 195–202.
56. Kaloudi, N.; Li, J. The AI-based cyber threat landscape: A survey. *ACM Comput. Surv.* **2020**, *53*, 1–34. [CrossRef]
57. Turchin, A. A Map: AGI Failures Modes and Levels, 2023. Available online: https://www.lesswrong.com/posts/hMQ5 iFiHkChqgrHiH/a-map-agi-failures-modes-and-levels (accessed on 8 March 2023).
58. Turchin, A.; Denkenberger, D. Classification of global catastrophic risks connected with artificial intelligence. *AI Soc.* **2020**, *35*, 147–163. [CrossRef]
59. Yampolskiy, R.V. Taxonomy of pathways to dangerous artificial intelligence. In Proceedings of the Workshops at the Thirtieth AAAI Conference on Artificial Intelligence, Phoenix, AZ, USA, 12–13 February 2016; pp. 143–158.
60. Kumar, R.S.S.; Brien, D.O.; Albert, K.; Viljöen, S.; Snover, J. 2019. Failure Modes in Machine Learning. Available online: https://arxiv.org/ftp/arxiv/papers/1911/1911.11034.pdf (accessed on 8 March 2023).
61. Hadfield-Menell, D.; Milli, S.; Abbeel, P.; Russell, S.; Dragan, A. Inverse Reward Design. *Adv. Neural Inf. Process. Syst.* **2017**, *30*. Available online: https://proceedings.neurips.cc/paper/2017/hash/32fdab6559cdfa4f167f8c31b9199643-Abstract.html (accessed on 8 March 2023)
62. Yuan, Y.; Yu, Z.L.; Gu, Z.; Deng, X.; Li, Y. A novel multi-step reinforcement learning method for solving reward hacking. *Appl. Intell.* **2019**, *49*, 2874–2888. [CrossRef]
63. Leike, J.; Martic, M.; Krakovna, V.; Ortega, P.A.; Everitt, T.; Lefrancq, A.; Orseau, L.; Legg, S. AI safety Gridworlds. *arXiv* **2017**, arXiv:1711.09883.
64. Zhang, A.; Lipton, Z.C.; Li, M.; Smola, A. Dive into Deep Learning. *arXiv* **2021**, arXiv:2106.11342.
65. Subbaswamy, A.; Saria, S. From development to deployment: dataset shift, causality, and shift-stable models in health AI. *Biostatistics* **2020**, *21*, 345–352. [CrossRef]
66. Rojas-Carulla, M.; Schölkopf, B.; Turner, R.; Peters, J. Invariant models for causal transfer learning. *J. Mach. Learn. Res.* **2018**, *19*, 1309–1342.
67. Rothenhäusler, D.; Meinshausen, N.; Bühlmann, P.; Peters, J. Anchor regression: Heterogeneous data meet causality. *J. R. Stat. Soc. Ser. B* **2021**, *83*, 215–246. [CrossRef]
68. Gilmer, J.; Adams, R.P.; Goodfellow, I.; Andersen, D.; Dahl, G.E. Motivating the Rules of the Game for Adversarial Example Research. *arXiv* **2018**, arXiv:1807.06732.
69. Zhao, Z.; Dua, A.; Singh, S. Generating natural adversarial examples *arXiv* **2017**, arXiv:1710.11342.
70. Chakraborty, A.; Alam, M.; Dey, V.; Chattopadhyay, A.; Mukhopadhyay, D. Adversarial attacks and defences: A survey. *arXiv* **2018**, arXiv:1810.00069
71. Hitaj, B.; Ateniese, G.; Perez-Cruz, F. Deep models under the GAN: information leakage from collaborative deep learning. In Proceedings of the 2017 ACM SIGSAC Conference on Computer and Communications Security, Dallas, TX, USA, 30 October–3 November 2017; pp. 603–618.
72. Tramèr, F.; Kurakin, A.; Papernot, N.; Goodfellow, I.; Boneh, D.; Mcdaniel, P. Ensemble adversarial training: Attacks and defenses. *arXiv* **2017**, arXiv:1705.07204.
73. Szegedy, C.; Zaremba, W.; Sutskever, I.; Bruna, J.; Erhan, D.; Goodfellow, I.; Fergus, R. Intriguing properties of neural networks. *arXiv* **2013**, arXiv:1312.6199.
74. Madry, A.; Makelov, A.; Schmidt, L.; Tsipras, D.; Vladu, A. Towards deep learning models resistant to adversarial attacks. *arXiv* **2017**, arXiv:1706.06083.
75. Papernot, N.; Mcdaniel, P.; Goodfellow, I. Transferability in Machine Learning: from Phenomena to Black-Box Attacks using Adversarial Samples. *arXiv* **2016**, arXiv:1605.07277.
76. Pang, R.; Zhang, X.; Ji, S.; Luo, X.; Wang, T. AdvMind: Inferring Adversary Intent of Black-Box Attacks. In Proceedings of the 26th ACM SIGKDD International Conference on Knowledge Discovery & Data Mining, Virtual Event, 6–10 July 2020; pp. 1899–1907.
77. Vivek, B.; Mopuri, K.R.; Babu, R.V. Gray-box adversarial training. In Proceedings of the European Conference on Computer Vision, Munich, Germany, 8–14 September 2018; pp. 203–218.
78. Fenrich, K. Securing your control system. *Power Eng.* **2008**, *112*, 1–11.

79. Ilmoi. Poisoning attacks on Machine Learning: A 15-year old security problem that's making a comeback. *Secur. Mach. Learn.* **2019**. Available online: https://towardsdatascience.com/poisoning-attacks-on-machine-learning-1ff247c254db (accessed on 8 March 2023)

80. Rubinstein, B.I.; Bartlett, P.L.; Huang, L.; Taft, N. Learning in a large function space: Privacy-preserving mechanisms for SVM learning. *J. Priv. Confidentiality* **2012**, *4*, 65–100. [CrossRef]

81. Steinhardt, J.; Koh, P.W.; Liang, P. Certified defenses for data poisoning attacks. In Proceedings of the 31st International Conference on Neural Information Processing Systems, Long Beach, CA, USA, 4–9 December 2017; pp. 3520–3532.

82. Mei, S.; Zhu, X. Using machine teaching to identify optimal training-set attacks on machine learners. In Proceedings of the Twenty-Ninth AAAI Conference on Artificial Intelligence, Austin, TX, USA, 25–30 January 2015; pp. 2871–2877.

83. Kloft, M.; Laskov, P. Online anomaly detection under adversarial impact. In Proceedings of the 13th International Conference on Artificial Intelligence and Statistics, Sardinia, Italy, 13–15 May 2010; pp. 405–412.

84. Koh, P.W.; Steinhardt, J.; Liang, P. Stronger data poisoning attacks break data sanitization defenses. *Mach. Learn.* **2022**, *111*, 1–47. [CrossRef]

85. Shafahi, A.; Huang, W.R.; Najibi, M.; Suciu, O.; Studer, C.; Dumitras, T.; Goldstein, T. Poison frogs! targeted clean-label poisoning attacks on Neural Networks. In Proceedings of the 32nd International Conference on Neural Information Processing Systems, Montréal, Canada, 3–8 December 2018; pp. 6106–6116.

86. Suciu, O.; Marginean, R.; Kaya, Y.; Daume, H.; Iii.; Dumitras, T. When does machine learning {FAIL}? generalized transferability for evasion and poisoning attacks. In Proceedings of the 27th Security Symposium, USENIX, Baltimore, MD, USA, 15–17 August 2018; pp. 1299–1316.

87. Goodfellow, I.J.; Shlens, J.; Szegedy, C. Explaining and harnessing adversarial examples. *arXiv* **2014**, arXiv:1412.6572.

88. Lyu, C.; Huang, K.; Liang, H.N. A unified gradient regularization family for adversarial examples. In Proceedings of the 2015 IEEE international conference on data mining, Atlantic City, NJ, USA, 14–17 November 2015; pp. 301–309.

89. Papernot, N.; Mcdaniel, P. Extending defensive distillation. *arXiv* **2017**, arXiv:1705.05264.

90. Papernot, N.; Mcdaniel, P.; Goodfellow, I.; Jha, S.; Celik, Z.B.; Swami, A. Practical black-box attacks against machine learning. In Proceedings of the 2017 ACM on Asia conference on computer and communications security, Abu Dhabi, United Arab Emirates, 2–6 April 2017; pp. 506–519.

91. Xu, W.; Evans, D.; Qi, Y. Feature squeezing: Detecting adversarial examples in deep neural networks. *arXiv* **2017**, arXiv:1704.01155.

92. Hosseini, H.; Chen, Y.; Kannan, S.; Zhang, B.; Poovendran, R. Blocking transferability of adversarial examples in black-box learning systems. *arXiv* **2017**, arXiv:1703.04318.

93. Meng, D.; Chen, H. Magnet: A two-pronged defense against adversarial examples. In Proceedings of the 2017 ACM SIGSAC Conference on Computer and Communications Security, Dallas, TX, USA, 30 October–3 November 2017; pp. 135–147.

94. Goodfellow, I.; Pouget-Abadie, J.; Mirza, M.; Xu, B.; Warde-Farley, D.; Ozair, S.; Courville, A.; Bengio, Y. Generative adversarial networks. *Commun. ACM* **2020**, *63*, 139–144. [CrossRef]

95. Samangouei, P.; Kabkab, M.; Chellappa, R. Defense-gan: Protecting classifiers against adversarial attacks using generative models. *arXiv* **2018**, arXiv:1805.06605.

96. Weerasinghe, S.; Alpcan, T.; Erfani, S.M.; Leckie, C. Defending Distributed Classifiers Against Data Poisoning Attacks. *arXiv* **2020**, arXiv:2008.09284.

97. Efron, B. The jackknife, the bootstrap and other resampling plans. In *CBMS-NSF Regional Conference Series in Applied Mathematics*; Society for Industrial and Applied Mathematics: Philadelphia, PA, USA, 1982.

98. Paudice, A.; Muñoz-González, L.; Lupu, E.C. Label sanitization against label flipping poisoning attacks. In *Joint European Conference on Machine Learning and Knowledge Discovery in Databases*; Springer: Berlin/Heidelberg, Germany, 2018; pp. 5–15.

99. Paudice, A.; Muñoz-González, L.; Gyorgy, A.; Lupu, E.C. Detection of adversarial training examples in poisoning attacks through anomaly detection. *arXiv* **2018**, arXiv:1802.03041.

100. Rubinstein, B.I.; Nelson, B.; Huang, L.; Joseph, A.D.; Lau, S.; Rao, S.; Taft, N.; Tygar, J.D. Antidote: Understanding and defending against poisoning of anomaly detectors. In Proceedings of the 9th ACM SIGCOMM Conference on Internet Measurement, Chicago, IL, USA, 4–6 November 2009; pp. 1–14.

101. Lecun, Y.; Bottou, L.; Bengio, Y.; Haffner, P. Gradient-based learning applied to document recognition. *Proc. IEEE* **1998**, *86*, 2278–2324. [CrossRef]

102. Koh, P.W.; Liang, P. Understanding black-box predictions via influence functions. In Proceedings of the International Conference on Machine Learning, Sydney, NSW, Australia, 6–11 August 2017; pp. 1885–1894.

103. Liubchenko, N.; Podorozhniak, A.; Oliinyk, V. Research Application of the Spam Filtering and Spammer Detection Algorithms on Social Media. *CEUR Workshop Proc.* **2022**, *3171*, 116–126.

104. Wang, Q.; Yuying, G.; Ren, J.; B., Z. An automatic classification algorithm for software vulnerability based on weighted word vector and fusion neural network. *Comput. Secur.* **2023**, *126*, 103070. [CrossRef]

105. Peri, N.; Gupta, N.; Huang, W.R.; Fowl, L.; Zhu, C.; Feizi, S.; Goldstein, T.; Dickerson, J.P. Deep k-NN defense against clean-label data poisoning attacks. In Proceedings of the European Conference on Computer, Glasgow, UK, 23–28 August 2020; pp. 55–70.

106. Natarajan, J. AI and Big Data's Potential for Disruptive Innovation. Cyber secure man-in-the-middle attack intrusion detection using machine learning algorithms. In *AI and Big Data's Potential for Disruptive Innovation*; IGI Global: Hershey, PA, USA, 2020; pp. 291–316.

107. Tran, B.; Li, J.; Madry, A. Spectral Signatures in Backdoor Attacks. In Proceedings of the 32nd International Conference on Neural Information Processing Systems, Montréal, Canada, 3–8 December 2018; pp. 8011–8021

108. Nguyen, G.; Dlugolinsky, S. ; Bobak, M.; Tran, V.; Garcia, A.; Heredia, I.; Malik, P.; Hluchy, L. Machine Learning and Deep Learning frameworks and libraries for large-scale. *Artif. Intell. Rev.* **2019**, *52*, 77–124. [CrossRef]

109. Wu, B.; Wang, S.; Yuan, X.; Wang, C.; Rudolph, C.; Yang, X. Defending Against Misclassification Attacks in Transfer Learning. *ArXiv*, **2019**, arXiv:1908.11230

110. Polyak, A.; Wolf, L. Channel-level acceleration of deep face representations. *IEEE Access* **2015**, *3*, 2163–2175. [CrossRef]

111. Blanchard, P.; Mhamdi, E.M.; Guerraoui, R.; Stainer, J. Machine learning with adversaries: Byzantine tolerant gradient descent. *31st Conf. Neural Inf. Process. Syst.* **2017**, *30*, 118–128.

112. Chen, Y.; Su, L.; Xu, J. Distributed statistical machine learning in adversarial settings: Byzantine gradient descent. *Proc. Acm Meas. Anal. Comput. Syst.* **2017**, *1*, 1–25. [CrossRef]

113. Lundberg, S.M.; Lee, S.I. A unified approach to interpreting model predictions. In Proceedings of the 31st International Conference on Neural Information Processing Systems, Long Beach, CA, USA, 4–9 December 2017; pp. 4768–4777.

114. Guerraoui, R.; Rouault, S. The hidden vulnerability of distributed learning in byzantium. In Proceedings of the International Conference on Machine Learning; Stockholm, Sweden, 10–15 July 2018; pp. 3521–3530.

115. Pillutla, K.; Kakade, S.M.; Harchaoui, Z. Robust aggregation for federated learning. *IEEE Trans. Signal Process.* **2022**, *70*, 1142–1154. [CrossRef]

116. Yin, D.; Chen, Y.; Kannan, R.; Bartlett, P. Byzantine-robust distributed learning: Towards optimal statistical rates. In Proceedings of the International Conference on Machine Learning, Stockholm, Sweden, 10–15 July 2018; pp. 5650–5659.

117. Bernstein, J.; Wang, Y.X.; Azizzadenesheli, K.; Anandkumar, A. signSGD: Compressed optimisation for non-convex problems. In Proceedings of the International Conference on Machine Learning, Stockholm, Sweden, 10–15 July 2018; pp. 560–569.

118. Fung, C.; Yoon, C.J.; Beschastnikh, I. Mitigating sybils in federated learning poisoning. *arXiv* **2018**, arXiv:1808.04866.

119. Liu, Y.; Yi, Z.; Chen, T. Backdoor attacks and defenses in feature-partitioned collaborative learning. *arXiv* **2020**, arXiv:2007.03608.

120. Ozdayi, M.S.; Kantarcioglu, M.; Gel, Y.R. Defending against Backdoors in Federated Learning with Robust Learning Rate. 2020. Available online: https://ojs.aaai.org/index.php/AAAI/article/view/17118/16925 (accessed on 8 March 2023).

121. Yang, Z.; Zhang, J.; Chang, E.C.; Liang, Z. Neural network inversion in adversarial setting via background knowledge alignment. In Proceedings of the 2019 ACM SIGSAC Conference on Computer and Communications Security, London, UK, 11–15 November 2019; pp. 225–240.

122. Fredrikson, M.; Lantz, E.; Jha, S.; Lin, S.; Page, D.; Ristenpart, T. Model inversion attacks that exploit confidence information and basic countermeasures. In Proceedings of the 22nd ACM SIGSAC Conference on Computer and Communications Security, Denver, CO, USA, 12–16 October 2015; pp. 1322–1333.

123. Hidano, S.; Murakai, T.; Katsumata, S.; Kiyomoto, S.; Hanaoka, G. Model inversion attacks for prediction systems: Without knowledge of non-sensitive attributes. In Proceedings of the 2017 15th Annual Conference on Privacy, Security and Trust (PST), Calgary, AB, Canada, 28–30 August 2017; pp. 115–11509.

124. Wu, X.; Fredrikson, M.; Jha, S.; Naughton, J.F. A methodology for formalizing model-inversion attacks. In Proceedings of the 2016 IEEE 29th Computer Security Foundations Symposium (CSF), Lisbon, Portugal, 27 June–1 July 2016; pp. 355–370.

125. Zhang, Y.; Jia, R.; Pei, H.; Wang, W.; Li, B.; Song, D. The secret revealer: Generative model-inversion attacks against deep neural networks. In Proceedings of the IEEE/CVF Conference on Computer Vision and Pattern Recognition, Seattle, WA, USA, 13 June–19 June 2020; pp. 250–258.

126. Ateniese, G.; Mancini, L.V.; Spognardi, A.; Villani, A.; Vitali, D.; Felici, G. Hacking smart machines with smarter ones: How to extract meaningful data from machine learning classifiers. *Int. J. Secur. Networks* **2015**, *10*, 137–150. [CrossRef]

127. Juuti, M.; Szyller, S.; Marchal, S.; Asokan, N. PRADA: protecting against DNN model stealing attacks. In Proceedings of the 2019 IEEE European Symposium on Security and Privacy (EuroS&P), Stockholm, Sweden, 17–19 June 2019; pp. 512–527.

128. Wang, B.; Gong, N.Z. Stealing hyperparameters in machine learning. In Proceedings of the 2018 IEEE Symposium on Security and Privacy (SP), San Francisco, CA, USA, 21–23 May 2018; pp. 36–52.

129. Takemura, T.; Yanai, N.; Fujiwara, T. Model Extraction Attacks on Recurrent Neural Networks. *J. Inf. Process.* **2020**, *28*, 1010–1024. [CrossRef]

130. Hinton, G.; Vinyals, O.; Dean, J. Distilling the knowledge in a neural network. *arXiv* **2015**, arXiv:1503.02531.

131. Hsu, Y.C.; Hua, T.; Chang, S. ; Lou, Q.; Shen, Y.; Jin, H. Language model compression with weighted low-rank factorization, *arXiv* **2022**, arXiv:2207.00112. 10.48550/arXiv.2207.00112, 2022.

132. Chandrasekaran, V.; Chaudhuri, K.; Giacomelli, I.; Jha, S.; Yan, S. Exploring connections between active learning and model extraction. In Proceedings of the 29th Security Symposium (USENIX), Boston, MA, USA, 12–14 August 2020; pp. 1309–1326.

133. Lee, T.; Edwards, B.; Molloy, I.; Su, D. Defending against neural network model stealing attacks using deceptive perturbations. In Proceedings of the 2019 IEEE Security and Privacy Workshops (SPW), San Francisco, CA, USA, 20–22 May 2019; pp. 43–49.

134. Kesarwani, M.; Mukhoty, B.; Arya, V.; Mehta, S. Model extraction warning in MLaaS paradigm. In Proceedings of the 34th Annual Computer Security Applications Conference, San Juan, PR, USA, 3–7 December 2018; pp. 371–380.

135. Fredrikson, M.; Lantz, E.; Jha, S.; Lin, S.; Page, D.; Ristenpart, T. Privacy in Pharmacogenetics: An End-to-End Case Study of Personalized Warfarin Dosing. *Proc. Usenix Secur. Symp.* **2014**, *1*, 17–32.

136. Chaabane, A.; Acs, G.; Kaafar, M.A. You are what you like! information leakage through users' interests. In Proceedings of the 19th Annual Network & Distributed System Security Symposium (NDSS), San Diego, CA, USA, 5–8 February 2012.
137. Kosinski, M.; Stillwell, D.; Graepel, T. Private traits and attributes are predictable from digital records of human behavior. *Proc. Natl. Acad. Sci. USA* **2013**, *110*, 5802–5805. [CrossRef] [PubMed]
138. Gong, N.Z.; Talwalkar, A.; Mackey, L.; Huang, L.; Shin, E.C.R.; Stefanov, E.; Shi, E.; Song, D. Joint link prediction and attribute inference using a social-attribute network. *Acm Trans. Intell. Syst. Technol.* **2014**, *5*, 1–20. [CrossRef]
139. Reynolds, N.A. An Empirical Investigation of Privacy via Obfuscation in Social Networks, 2022. Available online: https://figshare.mq.edu.au/articles/thesis/An_empirical_investigation_of_privacy_via_obfuscation_in_social_networks/19434461/1 (accessed on 8 March 2023).

Journal of
*Cybersecurity
and Privacy*

MDPI

Article

Characterizing the Impact of Data-Damaged Models on Generalization Strength in Intrusion Detection

Laurens D'hooge *, Miel Verkerken, Tim Wauters, Filip De Turck and Bruno Volckaert

IDLab-Imec, Department of Information Technology, Ghent University, 9052 Gent, Belgium
* Correspondence: laurens.dhooge@ugent.be

Abstract: Generalization is a longstanding assumption in articles concerning network intrusion detection through machine learning. Novel techniques are frequently proposed and validated based on the improvement they attain when classifying one or more of the existing datasets. The necessary follow-up question of whether this increased performance in classification is meaningful outside of the dataset(s) is almost never investigated. This lacuna is in part due to the sparse dataset landscape in network intrusion detection and the complexity of creating new data. The introduction of two recent datasets, namely CIC-IDS2017 and CSE-CIC-IDS2018, opened up the possibility of testing generalization capability within similar academic datasets. This work investigates how well models from different algorithmic families, pretrained on CICIDS2017, are able to classify the samples in CSE-CIC-IDS2018 without retraining. Earlier work has shown how robust these models are to data reduction when classifying state-of-the-art datasets. This work experimentally demonstrates that the implicit assumption that strong generalized performance naturally follows from strong performance on a specific dataset is largely erroneous. The supervised machine learning algorithms suffered flat losses in classification performance ranging from 0 to 50% (depending on the attack class under test). For non-network-centric attack classes, this performance regression is most pronounced, but even the less affected models that classify the network-centric attack classes still show defects. Current implementations of intrusion detection systems (IDSs) with supervised machine learning (ML) as a core building block are thus very likely flawed if they have been validated on the academic datasets, without the consideration for their general performance on other academic or real-world datasets.

Keywords: intrusion detection; network security; supervised machine learning; generalization strength; CIC-IDS2017; CSE-CIC-IDS2018

Citation: D'hooge, L.; Verkerken, M.; Wauters, T.; De Turck, F.; Volckaert, B. Characterizing the Impact of Data-Damaged Models on Generalization Strength in Intrusion Detection. *J. Cybersecur. Priv.* **2023**, *3*, 118–144. https://doi.org/10.3390/jcp3020008

Academic Editors: Giorgio Giacinto and Phil Legg

Received: 21 December 2022
Revised: 28 February 2023
Accepted: 5 March 2023
Published: 3 April 2023

1. Introduction

The digital attack surface is expanding. Every day, more devices are connected to the Internet. Malicious actors also have access to this global network and leverage it for nefarious purposes. Identifying and tracking packets or flows on the network that are (part of) a cyberattack is of obvious utility. Researchers have been working on this problem since at least 1985 [1,2]. During that period, network connectivity was not ubiquitous so researchers started their analysis on the hosts under attack, not looking at network traffic. This type of intrusion detection is called host-based intrusion detection (HIDS). As more and more clients became part of networks, it became necessary to add a second branch to intrusion detection. Network-based intrusion detection (NIDS) tries to model the attacks from network traffic.

These models can exist at different levels of abstraction. Deep packet inspection works based on the data encapsulated in the network packets. Packet-level IDS broadens its view by including features extracted from protocol headers and other metadata [3]. Flow-level IDS does not look at individual packets, but treats them as aggregated in flows.

At every level, a further distinction can be made between rule-based systems and anomaly detection systems. Rule-based systems have the advantage of being able to identify specific intrusion patterns. These methods are built on signature databases. Malicious activity that has been reported on is transformed into a unique signature. Further occurrences of that pattern will be picked up by the system. The biggest downside to this tailored approach is that it is thwarted by alterations to the attack patterns. This has created an arms race between the malicious actors who employ obfuscation and evolutionary strategies to create mismatches with the existing rules and the defense researchers who combat them with novel techniques to generalize the rules [4]. Anomaly detection systems take a different approach. These try to model behavior and report on deviations from normality. This branch is currently the most popular, because it promises models that have a solid general representation and are thus less likely to be fooled by attackers.

1.1. Problem Statement

Almost all ML-IDS research is aimed at improving the state-of-the art classification scores on especially crafted, academic datasets. These contributions are easily recognized as improvements if they outperform previous methods [5–9]. However, model evaluation is only performed within the dataset. Models are never exposed to compatible samples from other intrusion detection datasets. This evaluation strategy cannot answer how well these systems would perform when deployed on real networks. This work is a larger-scale continuation of [10] which found generalization issues when exposing CIC-IDS2017 models to CSE-CIC-IDS2018 data (small experiment, few ML methods, did not include all attack classes).

1.2. Research Contribution

This work is the first comprehensive test of how well existing machine learning methods are able to learn meaningful representations of network attacks, tested on related academic datasets. Pure classification results obtained in a previous work [11] show that these methods are very capable of classifying the network attacks contained in the individual subsets of CIC-IDS2017. Even more impressive is that these results were stable even when aggressively reducing the amount of data that the learning algorithms had at their disposal. In this article, a fresh set of models is trained on CIC-IDS2017 with the same data reduction methods to verify the earlier results after which the main contribution of this article is presented. The models, pretrained on CIC-IDS2017, are tasked with classifying the new samples of CSE-CIC-IDS2018. In theory, this should go well, because the results within CICIDS2017 are excellent. In reality, it is shown that the models most often do not learn good higher-order representations of attack traffic (classes). In the cases where they do, there are complications that restrict the practical utility of the tested methods.

1.3. Article Outline

The experimental design and results for global binary models and attack-class-specific binary models are the main parts of this article. They are described in Sections 2, 4 and 5. The result sections have intermediate conclusions to make the material more accessible. Section 6 largely centers on a simplified view of the results in which only the generalized performance of the best three models per attack class is considered. To conclude, the key observations and contributions are summarized in Section 7.

1.4. Related Work

The related work examines the lack of research into model generalization for ML-NIDS from practical, experimental and theoretical perspectives, as shown in Section 1.4.1, Section 1.4.2 and Section 1.4.3, respectively. It also informs the reader of more fundamental critiques of applying machine learning to the intrusion detection problem. Finally, a few noteworthy attempts at solving the generalization issue from the dataset side are highlighted in Section 1.4.4.

1.4.1. Practical: Lack of Interoperable Datasets

A practical reason for the lack of generalization testing in ML-NIDS is the difficulty of obtaining permission to set up capturing experiments on live, corporate, or academic networks. The next-best option is to test between different academic datasets. That too was almost impossible until recently. Few datasets have been created to test intrusion detection systems and typically neither the experiment design nor the feature extraction process are public. This is starting to change, which in large part is thanks to the efforts made by the Canadian Institute for Cybersecurity, operating at the University of New Brunswick. Their data generation experiments have matured and produced two high-quality datasets in 2017 [12] and 2018 [13]. A 2019 [14,15] iteration that specifically focuses on distributed denial of service attacks (DDoS) has just been published.

1.4.2. Experimental: Defining the Scope of Generalization

Publications such as those by Govindarajan et al. [16] and Lu et al. [17] specifically mention improved generalization by employing ensembles of methods and or preprocessing steps (Kuang et al. [18]). Unfortunately, their definition of generalization is too narrow, because they treat it as synonymous with the test set error. Generalization outside of the (often single) dataset on which the proposed methods have been validated is only ever implied.

A recent survey of the proposed deep learning IDSs which specifically selected approaches that mention improved generalization similarly equates generalization with obtaining improved results on a single dataset [19]. The authors of the survey observed three candidate generalization measurements from the literature: model complexity, stability and robustness. Grouped under the umbrella term regularization, several methods are discussed. Some, such as weight decay, dropout, pooling, or weight sharing apply to neural network-based methods, while others such as data augmentation or adversarial training can be applied more broadly. The main concern of the authors is the trial-and-error that is common in deep learning, brought on by the lack of fundamental understanding of why these models outperform. A mention is given to data augmentation as one of the promising routes to increase generalization.

1.4.3. Theoretical and Fundamental Critiques of ML-NIDS

Applying machine learning altogether as a potential solution to intrusion detection has been questioned in the past, most succinctly by the proponents of rule-based systems. The best phrasing of the issue can be read in a landmark article by Sommer et al. [20] stating that: "It is crucial to acknowledge that the nature of the domain is such that one can *always* find schemes that yield marginally better ROC curves than anything else has for a specific given setting. Such results however do not contribute to the progress of the field without any semantic understanding of the gain." Foregoing the operational perspective in favor of slight increases in classification scores on purely academic datasets without insight into what drives the increase is of little utility. Throughout the text, the authors point at the disjoint between the academic community that envisions models that exhibit generality and the functional but highly specialized tooling that is used in real-world settings.

A well-founded but opinionated piece by Gates et al. [21] challenged the paradigm in network anomaly detection by critically examining the underlying assumptions that have been (and still are) relied on. The authors questioned the copying of the requirements and methods put forth by Denning et al. [1], intended for host-based intrusion detection, to network intrusion detection. Three categories covering nine assumptions are discussed. These include issues with the problem domain (network attacks are anomalous, rare and anomalous activity is malicious), the training data (attack-free data are available, simulated data are representative and network traffic is static) and with operational usability (choice of false alarm rate, the definitions of malicious are universal and administrators can interpret anomalies). Based on their challenges to the assumptions, the authors recommend moving away from equating anomalous traffic with malicious traffic, employing hybrid methods (classification and anomaly detection), community-based sourcing and the labeling of real samples and periodic redefinition of malicious behavior. Some of these points have since been addressed, but the data aspect remains an active issue, which is why recent critiques of the lack of modern, high-quality data are readily available (2015 [22], 2016 [23] 2019 [24]).

1.4.4. Reaching Generalization by Augmenting Datasets

A largely theoretical attempt at actually generalizing data for use in signature-based intrusion detection has been described by Li et al. [25]. They propose three tiers to artificially create a more complete input space. The first level (L1) is to generalize the feature ranges for which they propose strategies for both discrete and continuous extension in a realistic manner. This idea is still actively being pursued but with more advanced methods to model the input–output relation (mostly generative adversarial networks (GANs) [26,27]). Generalization testing by augmenting datasets to create new, compatible test sets has also been performed in other areas where machine learning is dominant with surprising results [28].

2. Materials and Methods

The methodology section focuses on two aspects: the data on which the models have been trained (Section 2.1) and the training/evaluation procedures themselves (Section 2.2). The evaluation procedure that was developed for this work is new, but it does reuse the data preprocessing and performance measuring components of the training framework [11]. This is intentional, because changing these components or introducing new parts would influence the results. The evaluation code for unseen data sets includes no retraining components. Pretrained models are kept unmodified to evaluate the new samples.

2.1. Included Data Sets

The dataset landscape in intrusion detection is sparsely populated. Many papers published today still work with the KDD collection, recorded in 1998 and published in 1999 or its refresh NSL-KDD (2009-revision). Most of the recent innovation is performed by the Canadian Institute for Cybersecurity. After publishing NSL-KDD, researchers at the institute noted that the lack of up-to-date datasets that can be dynamically (re)generated is a serious problem for the research field. The first iteration of a dynamically generated dataset was presented in 2012. ISCXIDS2012 includes baseline traffic that spans multiple protocols (HTTP, SMTP, SSH, etc.). Profiles for the baseline traffic were derived per protocol from real user activity (called B-profiles). Inside a testbed, these profiles can be used to create more benign traffic. In parallel to this, various attacks were performed (M-profiles). Some of these are complex and multi-stage (such as system infiltration), while others are generated by running existing tools (e.g., HTTP-DoS). This controlled separation enables the requirement to machine-label the data. The researchers make the raw PCAP data available as well as CSV files with the processed, labeled samples. This work relies on the two datasets which were built on the ISCXIDS2012 foundation, CIC-IDS2017 (Section 2.1.1) and CSE-CIC-IDS2018 (Section 2.1.2).

2.1.1. CIC-IDS2017

The initial experiment was expanded with more protocols (including HTTPS), a greater variety of attacks, more types of clients and larger networks. A new tool to process the PCAP files (CICFlowMeterV3) was also introduced and made open source (https://github.com/ahlashkari/CICFlowMeter, accessed on 7 December 2022). CIC-IDS2017 contains 5 days of traffic, split into seven subsets. The individual subsets contain attacks from different classes spanning DoS, DDoS, port scanning, botnet, infiltration, web attack and brute force traffic [29,30]. Processed CSV file sizes range from 64 to 270 MB. A merged version of all files was created that contains all 2.8 million samples (1.1 GB).

2.1.2. CSE-CIC-IDS2018

The next iteration was published only a year later. CSE-CIC-IDS2018 expands the infrastructure and moves it to Amazon Web Services instead of an on-site experimental setup. It also contains 10 days with samples from the same classes as those present in CIC-IDS2017. A mapping of this restructuring is shown before the attack-specific results in Table 1. Most of the attack scenarios keep using the same tools as those used to generate CIC-IDS2017. The total volume increased drastically with file sizes between 108 and 384 MB. The merged version contains no less than 9.3 million samples (3.5 GB).

Compatible follow-up versions to network intrusion detection datasets are very rare, but they are required to execute the proposed model evaluation strategy. CIC-IDS datasets were chosen for this analysis because they fit the following criteria: they are large-scale, labeled network intrusion detection dataset with compatible feature sets and extracted with the same tooling and with high consistency between the 2017 and 2018 versions (in both attack classes and tools).

Table 1. Mapping of the subsets of CIC-IDS2017 to their counterpart in CSE-CIC-IDS2018.

Attack Class	2017	Tools	2018	Tools
FTP/SSH brute force	0	Patator.py (FTP / SSH)	0	Patator.py (FTP / SSH)
DoS layer-7	1	Slowloris Slowhttptest Hulk Goldeneye	1	Slowloris Slowhttptest Hulk Goldeneye
Heartbleed	1	Heartleech	2	Heartleech
Web attacks	2	Custom Selenium XSS+bruteforce, SQLi vs. DVWA	5	same types, tools undocumented
Web attacks	2	Custom Selenium XSS+bruteforce, SQLi vs. DVWA	6	same types, tools undocumented
Infiltration	3	Metasploit, Dropbox download, cool disk MAC	7	Nmap, Dropbox download
Infiltration	3	Metasploit, Dropbox download, cool disk MAC	8	Nmap, Dropbox download
Botnet	4	ARES	9	Zeus, ARES
DDoS	5	Low Orbit Ion Cannon (LOIC) HTTP	3	LOIC HTTP
DDoS	5	LOIC HTTP	4	LOIC-UDP, High Orbit Ion Cannon (HOIC)
Port scan	6	Various Nmap commands	-	-

2.2. Training and Evaluation Procedure

A small core framework has previously been developed to evaluate IDS datasets. On top of a common core, there are several modifications, all located in the preprocessing steps to accommodate the specifics of the individual data sets. This experiment is supported by a new code that keeps the specific dataset preprocessing code for CIC-IDS2017 and CSE-CIC-IDS2018, followed by new code that channels the unseen samples to the appropriate pretrained models for classification. An overview of the flow of the experiment is given in Figure 1. Classification is performed by the models without any retraining. The collection of classification metrics by which the models' performance is evaluated are standards in data science (i.e., precision, recall, F1-score, balanced accuracy and ROC-AUC). For clarity, most mentions in this article are in terms of precision recall pairs or balanced accuracy. The remainder of this subsection briefly introduces the twelve supervised learners in Section 2.2.1 and the ways in which the difficulty of the classification was increased in Section 2.2.2.

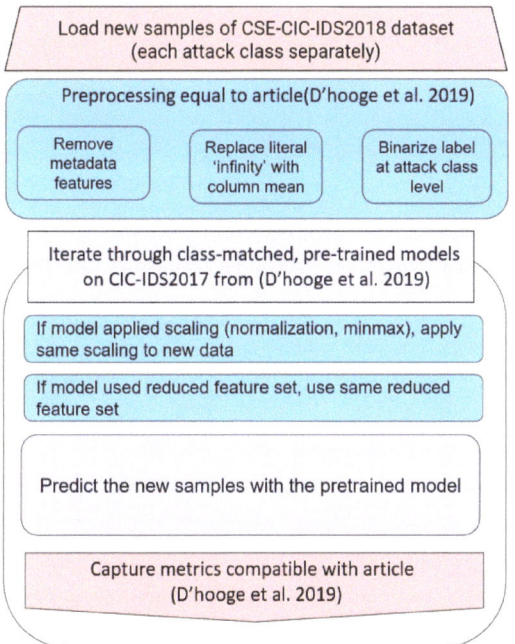

Figure 1. A visual overview of the experiment's architecture [11].

2.2.1. Included Algorithms

Pretrained models for a total of twelve supervised classifiers were included. The algorithms are separable into three families. All tree-based methods used gini-impurity to make splitting decisions. The abbreviations next to the methods are used throughout the rest of the text and in the figures. The sequence of decision tree-based classifiers includes important innovations made to them over time. The methods from other families were added for comparative purposes. Detailed information on the inner workings of every algorithm can be read in these references [31–33].

1 Tree-based methods:
- Decision tree (dtree);
- Decision trees with bagging (bag);
- Adaboost (ada);
- Gradient-boosted trees (gradboost);
- Regularized gradient boosting (xgboost);
- Random forest (rforest);
- Randomized decision trees (extratree).

2 Neighbor methods:
- K-nearest-neighbors (knn);
- Nearest-centroid (ncentroid).

3 Other methods:
- Linear kernel SVM (linsvc);
- RBF-kernel SVM (rbfsvc);
- Logistic regression (binlr).

2.2.2. Increasing the Learning Difficulty

The results obtained with the earlier implementation of this framework on NSL-KDD, ISCXIDS2012, CIC-IDS2017 and CSE-CIC-IDS2018, as documented in [11], showed great classification results. The consistency with which these results occurred in tandem with manual inspection of the intermediate cross-validation results allowed us to conclude that these results are stable and valid. That work already included measures to increase the learning difficulty in an effort to try to invalidate or reinforce the conclusions from a first examination of CICIDS2017 [34].

Data-reduced models are a central component in this work. That reduction was carried out along two axes. The most straightforward of the two is vertical data reduction. This entails reducing the number of samples to learn from through stratified sampling inside a train–test–validation splitter. The models were trained at different points of training volume ranging from (0.1% sample usage to 50% sample usage). The data were first split into a training and test set, with a further split happening on the training set into actual training and validation. Instead of using a fixed portion to test, the complement of the initial split was always taken (e.g., 5% training, 95% test, training further split into training and validation). The second axis is that of horizontal data reduction (i.e., feature reduction). Instead of applying this to strip out the inconsequential features, the opposite was carried out. A list was compiled of the features on which splits were chosen most often in the trees which classified the entire dataset. These top features of CIC-IDS2017 are shown in Table 2. Some features that would obviously contaminate the classification results were removed from the data prior to any training. For CIC-IDS2017/8, these include *Flow ID*, *Source IP*, *Source Port* and *Destination IP*. On a total of 79 remaining features, the 20 most discriminative features were removed before training. This procedure happened in blocks of 5, starting with the best 5 features first, then expanding to remove the 5 next best and so on. Previous findings showed the remarkable resilience of most methods to both horizontal and vertical data reduction [11].

Table 2. Most discriminative features of CIC-IDS2017.

Dataset		Most Discriminative
CIC-IDS2017	1–5	Timestamp, Init Win bytes forward, Destination Port, Flow IAT Min, Fwd Packets/s
	5–10	Fwd Packet Length Std, Avg Fwd Segment Size, Flow Duration, Fwd IAT Min, ECE Flag Count
	10–15	Fwd IAT Mean, Init Win bytes backward, Bwd Packets/s, Idle Max, Fwd IAT Std
	15–20	FIN Flag Count, Fwd Header Length, SYN Flag Count, Fwd Packet Length Max, Flow Packets

3. Note on Obtained Results and Graphics

Before presenting the results of this analysis, it needs to be stressed that this article is extensively supported by visualizations to summarize more than 150,000 data points in the result collection. The most interesting results are described in this article, but the total collection is much larger. All visualizations are interactive with the option of changing the parameters and re-render. The result files (grouped in folders D2017-M2017 and D2018-M2017) and associated plotting code are available publicly with documentation on how to run them at https://gitlab.ilabt.imec.be/lpdhooge/reduced-unseen-testing, last accessed on 10 March 2023. In the interest of replication ability, the repository also contains the experiment code required to obtain new results. It is highly recommended to read this article side-by-side with the visualizations.

The results are presented in two separate sections: first the global, binary models' standard intra-dataset performance (Section 4.1) and the same models' performance on unseen, related samples (Section 4.2). Second, because the global, binary models did not remain sufficiently effective, the results of attack-class-specific models are presented in the same way with standard intra-dataset performance first (Section 5.1) and inter-dataset generalized performance second (Section 5.2). Both sections end with brief intermediate conclusions Sections 4.2.4 and 5.2.9.

4. Results of Global Two-Class Models

The most hopeful hypothesis is one in which models trained on a large corpus of attack- and baseline traffic would learn an overarching representation between the two classes. This first subsection puts that hypothesis to the test by exposing the models trained on the merged CIC-IDS2017 dataset to itself and then to the merged data of CSE-CIC-IDS2018. The next two subsections delved into the detailed results, while Section 6 offers a summary and short discussion of the best results which is less verbose.

4.1. Internal Retest

Retesting the models that have been trained on the merged version of CIC-IDS2017 with their own data shows that these models are consistent with the results described in [11]. This is as expected and it is a necessary requirement to start evaluating the models with samples from CSE-CIC-IDS2018. During the evaluation, five classification metrics were taken into consideration: balanced accuracy, precision, recall, F1-score and standard accuracy.

Every tree-based classifier has classification metrics that converge above 99% with as little as 10% of the data used for training. The neighbor-based methods also stay consistent with previous findings, with knn converging on classification metrics above 98% with 10% of data used fir training. The nearest-centroid classifier fares much worse with a metric profile that is invariant to the amount of data used for training, reaching F1-scores of only 45% (hampered by low precision, and recall is relatively high at 70%). Similarly flat profiles have been observed for the linear support vector machine and the logistic regression. With these models, the F1-score does reach 82%. The RBF-kernel SVM does improve when given access to more training data, reaching an F1-score above 90%.

All models were found to be resistant to feature removal. All tree-based and neighbor methods never lost more than a flat 5% on any metric, even on the most aggressive feature reduction setting, with the removal of the 20 most discriminative features (on a total of 79 available features). The logistic regression and linear SVM did lose up to 10% in flat metrics (i.e., X-10% as opposed to X-(X*10%). The RBF-kernel SVM never lost more than 5%. Different methods of feature scaling typically had a limited effect on these results. Overall, a case could be made for the normalization of the data over min–max or no scaling, because normalization worked best and most stably for all methods, regardless of algorithmic class.

4.2. Exposure to Unseen Data

As stated in Section 2.1.2, CSE-CIC-IDS2018 is very similar to CIC-IDS2017. The 2018 version has the same attacks, executed with the same tools in a different network architecture. One difference is that the 2018 version has a finer division of the attacks, resulting in more dataset fragments (7 in 2017 and 10 in 2018, details in Table 1). This section looks only at the performance of the models trained on the merged version of CIC-IDS2017, tasked with classifying the merged version of CSE-CIC-IDS2018. Based on previous work (summarized in Section 4.1), the expectation is that these pretrained models will work well on the new samples.

4.2.1. Tree-Based Classifiers

Starting with single decision trees immediately shows that the assumption is challenged, because the results are very erratic. The best result is obtained at the 30% training data point, with an F1-score at 63%. Removing the best features incrementally introduces even more variability in the metrics while pushing them downward overall. Using feature removal with min–max-scaling or no scaling at all consistently drops recall below 20%.

A single decision tree was an unlikely candidate to be a good model. Therefore, the analysis included various tree-based ensemble learners. Results for the bagging classifier were not obtained because of insufficient memory on the experiment server (16 GB).

Adaboost had an F1-score at the 30% training data point of 61.0% (recall: 63.0%, precision: 78.3%), close to the performance of the single decision tree. Interestingly, removing the five most discriminative features, improves this point to an F1-score of 65.3% (recall: 71.7%, precision: 82.4%). This lonely peak is gone after removing the top-10 features or more. These observations only exist if the data had been normalized. Min–max or no scaling pushes recall below 20% almost without exception. Precision can be high (80+%) but paired with low recall and thus not useful.

Random forest performs worse, with F1 metric profiles very low (<20%) at almost every point of training volume, especially when applying min–max or no scaling. A singular peak that is similar to the ones for a single decision tree and adaboost happens once more at 30% training volume, but only when removing the top-15 features.

Randomized trees have a worse performance profile than all previous methods with F1-scores stably around 0%, regardless of the training volume or removed features. The "best" result is a meager 10% recall when no scaling is applied, which is invariant to feature removal or training volume. The discrepancy between the performance of this classifier within CIC-IDS2017 and on the related CSE-CIC-IDS2018 is staggering (Figure 2a,b). This method is especially bothersome because of the low time required to build a set of randomized trees. This clearly demonstrates that no learning happens. It is peculiar that a method trained on a thousandth of CIC-IDS2017 (2830 samples) is able to generalize from that to classify the other 99.9% (2,827,913 samples) with an F1-score of more than 98.5%, while completely tanking on the data of CSE-CIC-IDS2018.

Gradient-boosted trees show peaks in recall above 90% when applying normalization or min–max-scaling. One observable pattern from the results is a tendency for these peaks to happen with almost no training data (0.1%). The only downside is the low precision that goes along with the high recall, once again voiding the usefulness of this classifier. Feature removal had inconsistent results for this classifier.

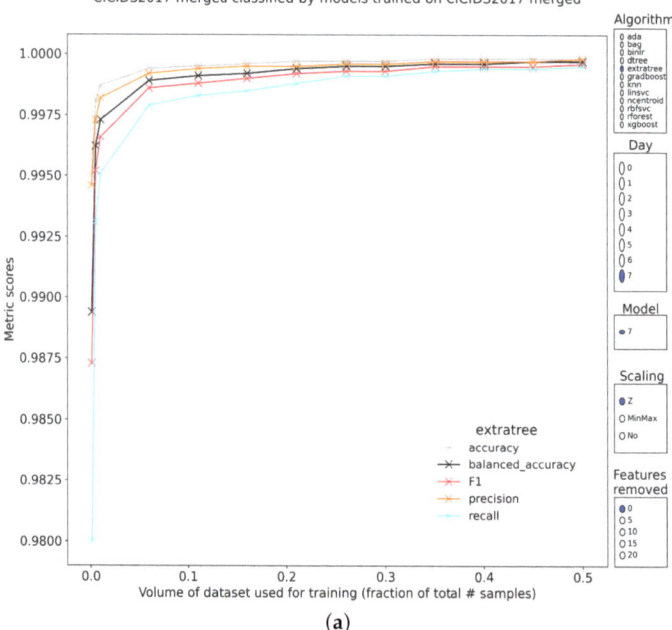

(a)

Figure 2. *Cont.*

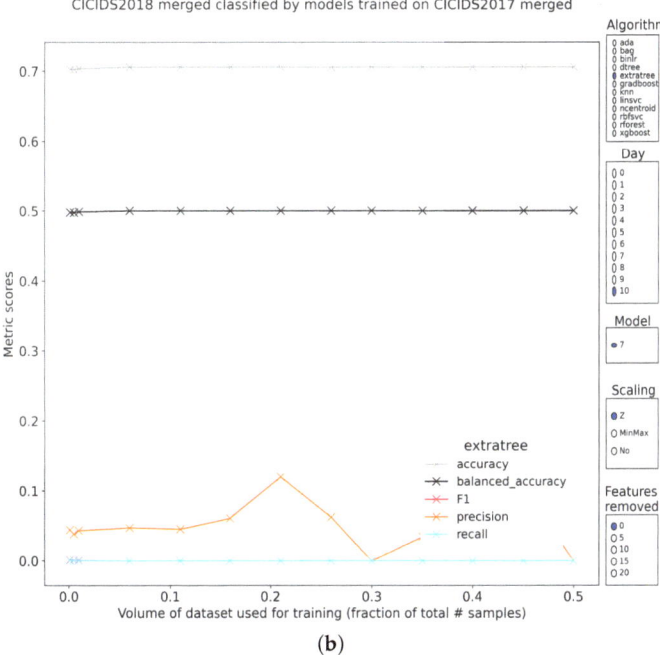

(b)

Figure 2. Contrast between intra-dataset generalization (**a**); and inter-dataset generalization (**b**) of randomized decision trees on the merged versions of CIC-IDS2017 and CSE-CIC-IDS2018.

Regularized, gradient-boosted trees (XGBoost framework) is the last and most theoretically potent version of a tree-based ensemble classifier in this analysis. Overall, it shows more grouped peaks (decent recall and precision) than the other tree-based classifiers. These results only occur when employing normalization or min–max scaling. The impact of feature reduction is interesting, because the best results are not found when zero feature reduction was applied, but rather when they are found at varying points of top feature removal. The overall conclusion for xgboost remains that it is excessively inconsistent to be usable.

4.2.2. Neighbor-Based Classifiers

The simple nearest neighbor algorithm is much more consistent than the tree-based methods. It is only usable when employing normalization, but under that constraint, it reaches F1-scores of approximately 65%. For this algorithm, a clear upward trend in the metrics is observed when increasing the training volume, with diminishing returns starting after 0.5%. Knn is computationally expensive to run, but it can be included in an ensemble, based on these results. Removing the best features in a step-wise manner has the expected result of lowering the classification metrics, but the effect is not drastic and the upward trend stays intact.

The nearest-centroid classifier had the interesting property of having high recall (only for normalized or min–max-scaled features) on CIC-IDS2017. This property stays intact when evaluating the samples of CSE-CIC-IDS2018 with the pretrained models. With normalization and no feature removal, recall stably sits at 70%, as does balanced accuracy (precision 49%). Min–max scaling has even higher recall 87%, but worse balanced accuracy (57.6%, precision 33.7%). Feature removal does not alter the performance when used with normalization, but the models trained on min–max-scaled features significantly improve after removing the first five features. This is most probably due to the removal of the problematic timestamp feature, which was the most discriminative feature in CIC-

IDS2017. Recall now maxes out at 92.8% with balanced accuracy at 57.8% and precision at 33.5%. Removing even more of the most discriminative features does not alter this result. CSE-CIC-IDS2018 has 3.3x the amount of samples that are in CIC-IDS2017 and more importantly, this classifier converges almost immediately (at 0.5% of the samples of CIC-IDS2017 used to train).

4.2.3. Other Classifiers

The metrics for a logistic regression show that the features must be normalized to be a decent classifier. It has an upward trend with respect to the training volume, but it is not steep. Generally speaking, this upward trend stays intact when removing features. As expected, the absolute values for the metrics are lowered when reducing features, albeit not by much. At 30% training volume and top-5 features being removed (among others contaminating timestamp being removed) on CIC-IDS2017, it manages to classify the samples of CSE-CIC-IDS2018 with a recall score of 90.3%, precision of 53.8% and balanced accuracy of 77%. The class separation is well above chance, but still not sufficiently high to be able to recommend the method as a reliable classifier.

A support vector machine with a linear kernel has results similar to those of the logistic regression, but there is almost no upward trend and its classification performance is damaged more by feature removal. Its best result is obtained with normalized features, the top-5 of which have been removed and at training volumes of between 0.1 and 1% (recall: 90.5%, precision: 51.5%, balanced accuracy: 77%).

Switching the kernel to the radial basis function has the interesting property of topping out higher, but only for min–max-scaled features. Recall and precision move in opposite directions to one another with regard to the amount of data used for training, regardless of feature removal. With 25% training volume on CIC-IDS2017, recall climbs from 92.2 (top-0 features removed) to 99.45% (top-10 features removed), while precision at the same points drops from 60.5% to 50.3%. A minority of result points have not been collected for this algorithm due to the excessive run time of the algorithm (>1 day per run, caused by the implementation that locks execution to a single core). This classifier could benefit from feature selection in the standard manner (with the removal of poor features instead of the removal of top features). It scores the highest overall, but the time required to train and subsequently evaluate samples holds this algorithm back.

4.2.4. Intermediate Conclusion

From these results, it should be clear that generalization is poor at best and dismal at worst. The set of tested algorithm families certainly do not provide a silver bullet algorithm that can be trained to distinguish between benign and malign traffic. Some do have very high recall, but the accompanying precision is lackluster. Tree-based methods have an issue of overfitting despite having great intra-dataset generalization, even under strict limiting conditions. Further research is needed to constrain the tree-based methods to make them more robust. The neighbor-based methods fall into two classes, knn most consistently had the highest F1-scores (between 65 and 70%). Furthermore, it did not require many data points to reach these scores, which is essential for knn, because this is computationally expensive. The method opposite in run time to it, that of nearest centroids, is better in terms of recall and worse in terms of precision. This makes it less usable overall. For the remaining methods, the logistic regression and RBF-kernel SVM have the best results because of their high recall (90–99%), paired with moderate precision (50–60%), but these results are not sufficient to be used in real defense systems. The next section presents the results of testing models specifically trained for each attack class.

5. Results of Attack-Specific Two-Class Models

The inability of overarching models to generalize well or at all leads to a new hypothesis in which models trained on specific attack classes may exhibit a better performance. This hypothesis was been tested by tasking the models trained on the individual days (each containing samples from a distinct attack class) with the data on which they have been trained, as well as the corresponding data from CSE-CIC-IDS2018. This section's subdivisions are rather verbose and therefore quite dense. The summary and discussion of only the best-overall results are in Section 6.

5.1. Internal Retest

This section describes the results of making the pretrained models reclassify the samples of the attack class on which they were trained. This is included to test whether the newly trained models do not suffer from a regression in their performance. The classification performance should mirror the results described in this earlier work [11]. The fresh models tested less points of vertical data reduction over a larger range (13 points between 0.1 and 50% of data used for training, versus 35 points between 0.1 and 33%). No other variables were altered in the training methodology.

After comparing the original classification results to the new set of results, no performance regressions were found in the class-specific models. A short reiteration of the results is in order to have a baseline for comparison. CIC-IDS2017 has three classes of attack traffic that were universally well recognized by the tested algorithms.

Models trained on the DDoS, HTTP-DoS and port-scanning traffic subsets are insensitive to reduction in training volume and removal of discriminative features. Put another way: increasing the learning difficulty by scaling back the amount of data for training on while also removing the best features from the data, did not hurt the models' classification scores much or at all. It logically follows that these models are expected to perform well on the samples of these classes from CSE-CIC-IDS2018.

Models trained to recognize FTP/SSH brute force attacks, web attack and botnet traffic are extremely well recognized by tree-based methods, but algorithms from other families have mixed results. Recall tends to stay high, but precision is lost. For all learners, these classes were more sensitive to data reduction, with horizontal data reduction having the biggest negative impact.

The final class, infiltration, is problematic because the subset in CIC-IDS2017 contains a mere 36 positive samples out of a total of 288,602. Results on the CSE-CIC-IDS2018 of these models will be reported, but are unlikely to be good.

5.2. Exposure to Unseen Data

The conclusions in Section 5.1 should be promising signs of the good generalization performance of pretrained models when tasked with classifying unseen samples from a closely related dataset. This assumption is only slightly undercut to date by the results from Section 4. Nevertheless, models with increased resolution (i.e., trained to classify only samples from specific attack classes) could perform better. As mentioned in Section 2.1, CIC-IDS2017 and CSE-CIC-IDS2018 are very similar, but the latter has more subsets and volume overall than the former. The mapping between the subsets of these datasets is shown in Table 1.

5.2.1. FTP/SSH Brute Force

Days 0 of both CSE-CIC-IDS2018 and CIC-IDS2017 contain brute force attacks targeted at an FTP or an SSH server. These samples serve as a proxy for brute force traffic in general, because many more service endpoints, both public and non-public exist on the internet that are susceptible to brute force attempts (e.g., API servers, VPN access points, databases, RDP servers, etc.).

The very weak performance for most tree-based models is observed with class separability (balanced accuracy) often at 50%, indicating that the models are no better than chance. The results are worse when employing normalization, because the values are squeezed into a range that is too narrow. Even the models trained on very low training volumes (high vertical data reduction) still overfit on the data. There are some exceptions (subfigures of Figure 3), most notably (and expectedly) when using very low training volumes (0.1%).

Recall is typically very low, but the malicious samples in that recalled percentage are classified with high precision. Models that were trained with the most discriminative features removed fail immediately.

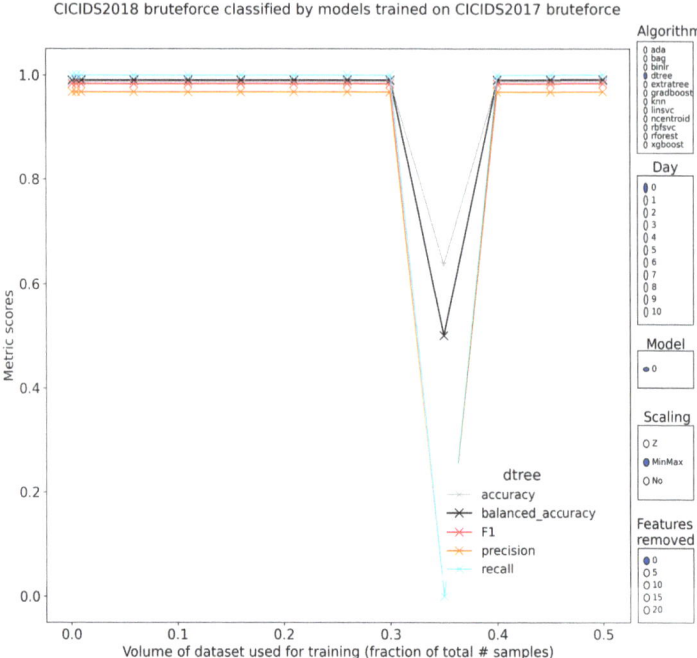

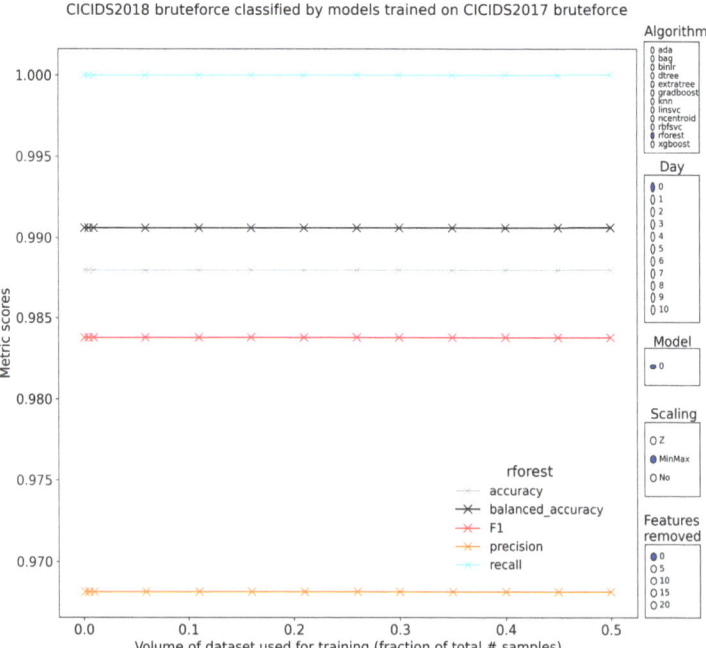

Figure 3. Performance metrics of two tree-algorithms trained on FTP-SSH brute force (CIC-IDS2017), evaluating FTP-SSH brute force from CSE-CIC-IDS2018.

A very similar conclusion is reached for the RBF-SVC. It manages to reach moderate recall (71%) with a high precision of 93.8%, but only with normalized features, and 0.1% training volume. Increases in training volume lead to very low recall with high precision. It is more resistant to feature removal than the tree-based methods. The logistic regression and linear SVM do not have noteworthy results.

Nearest neighbors is useless, because it has low precision and recall, regardless of the scaling and invariant to training volume. Nearest centroids has stable sections with precision–recall pairs at approximately 60% and 75%, respectively. These are maintained fairly well when reducing features, but only if the features were normalized or min–max-scaled. Without feature scaling, lots of performance is lost quickly after removing top-features. The classifier seems brittle overall. Curiously, the best recall results, up to perfect recall, happen when using only 0.1% of data for training.

5.2.2. Layer-7 Denial of Service

CSE-CIC-IDS2018 contains two days of denial of service attacks. The first of which has malicious packets generated by tools such as slowloris or HULK that abuse web servers by exhausting their resources. The second day contains traffic exclusively from exploiting the Heartbleed vulnerability on the affected implementation of OpenSSL (1.0.1-1.0.1f). CIC-IDS2017 bundles both types of attacks in a single day, using the same tooling. Because the attacks exist in one day in the 2017-version, the attack types got squashed into binary classification. It is a good use-case to test whether these attacks should be treated as the same category or not.

All tree-based methods overfit heavily, as they did on the brute force traffic. Good performance is only ever recorded for models that had very little data available to train on. Making matters worse is the inconsistency with which these results occur. In numerical terms, recall–precision pairs above 60% are very rare for any of the pretrained models. Once more, the worst results are obtained on models that had normalized features.

Nearest-neighbors has balanced accuracy scores consistently falling in the 70–80% range. Changes in scaling, training volume or feature reduction do not significantly alter this result. It is not good enough to be considered. Nearest-centroids separates the classes worse, indicated by the balanced accuracy of 50–60%. The only results that are better than chance were observed when using normalized features. Higher training volume or less feature reduction, do not affect the results.

The logistic regression models trained on min–max-scaled features follow the pattern that the section introduction put forward. Great generalization performance, with a stable, straightforward relationship between training volume and classification metrics (Figure 4). Those metrics are a stable 97.5% recall, paired with 70–75% precision yielding a total of 97.9% balanced accuracy (5 features removed). This amount of class separation is enough to recommend the classifier as a genuine method to classify unseen layer-7 DoS traffic. A linear support vector classifier or rbf-kernel SVM (with the same parameters) have nearly identical results. All models in the other category perform poorly if the features were standardized.

5.2.3. DoS Heartbleed

Although technically a form of information disclosure and not denial of service, Heartbleed traffic was included in the DoS category by the authors of both datasets.

Decision trees typically have very erratic metric graphs for this day of traffic. Models at peak performance in these graphs manage to achieve 80–95% balanced accuracy. Adaboost has the highest scores, both in absolute terms as well as averaged across the tested parameters. The changes in classification metrics can be as large as 50% flat and the relationship to training volume and feature removal is unclear. This unpredictability considerably lowers the real applicability of these models. The lowest variability models are randomized decision trees. These reach a flat profile after 1% training volume, with recall at 72.4% and precision at 99.5% (Figure 5). This result is also stable with regard to feature removal. It should be noted that with 0 features removed (which includes the problematic timestamp feature from CIC-IDS2017), this model performs no better than chance. Performance numbers are only good if this feature was removed ('timestamp' is first in the list of top-5 features).

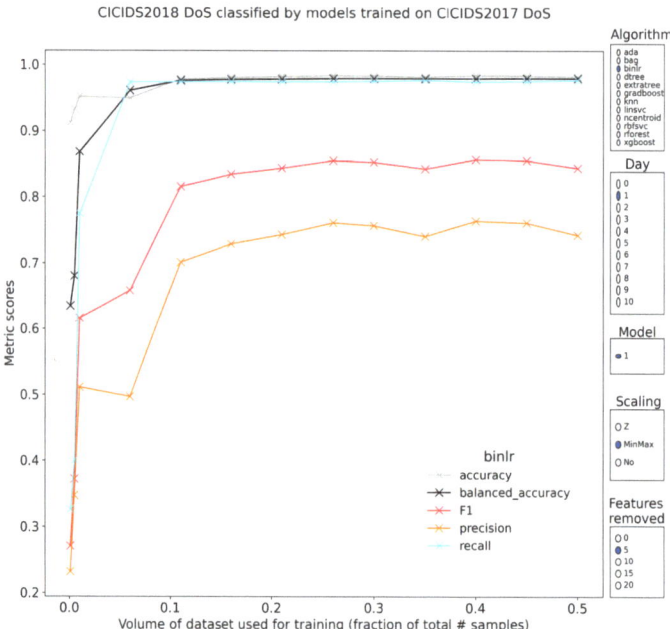

Figure 4. A rare occurrence of the expected relation between training volume and generalized model performance.

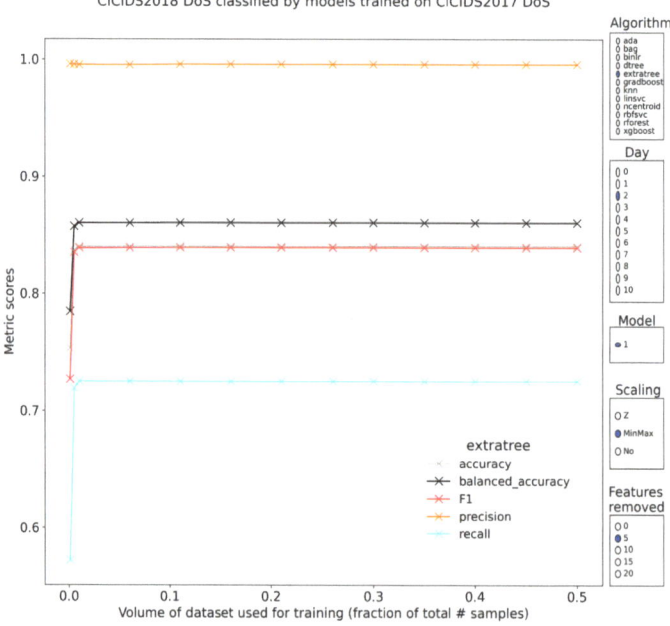

Figure 5. A subset of the randomized trees trained to recognize Heartbleed traffic perform stably well.

Nearest neighbors is an unusable classifier. It has very low recall/precision for all methods of feature scaling, across all points of feature reduction. It also shows a sudden decline in performance when using more than 1% of data as training samples. Nearest-centroids had recall–precision pairs of 60 and 95% within the relevant day of CIC-IDS2017, on the day containing Heartbleed samples, the model performance drops to precision recall pairs of 15 and 0% moving balanced accuracy close to blind guessing. This shows just how brittle the classifier is.

The logistic regression was very performant within CIC-IDS2017 with stable metric clusters above 95%, step-wise gain with increased training volume up to limit and step-wise loss in these metrics with increasingly aggressive removal of top features. It has this profile on the new samples of CSE-CIC-IDS2018. The model only starts to become performant with at least 5% data as training volume. The method is stable with perfect precision and 95% recall (Figure 6). This would be usable in a real-world system. Removing features has the expected effect of lowering the overall metrics, but stability is kept. A linear support vector machine has similar results, but requires normalized features. The RBF-kernel SVM required min–max-scaling and feature removal impacted precision much more negatively than it did for binlr.

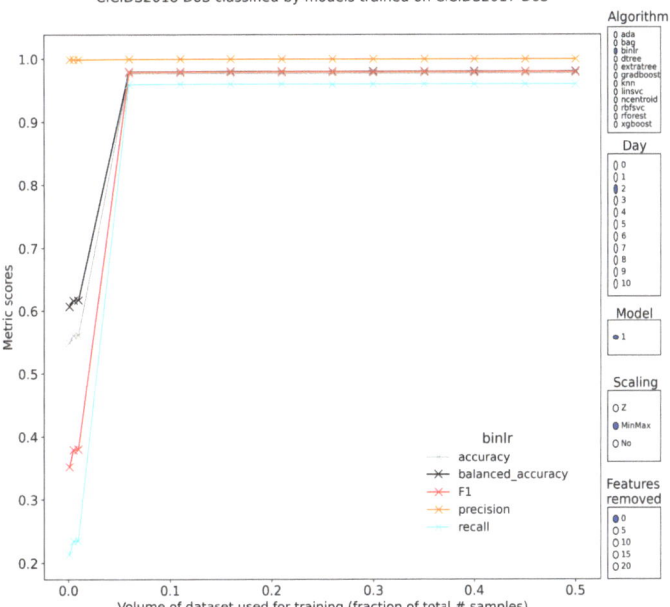

Figure 6. A subset of the logistic regression models trained to recognize Heartbleed traffic also have stable, high-performance scores.

Whether it is justified to clump layer-7 DoS and Heartbleed together in CIC-IDS2017 is unclear. The models might be more performant on the individual attacks if they were trained exclusively on them. The argument in favor of keeping the grouping is that there are iterations of the models that manage to classify both types. Testing the exact entanglement could not be deduced from these data, but it is possible by testing models pretrained on CSE-CIC-IDS2018.

5.2.4. DDoS Part 1

As with DoS traffic, CSE-CIC-IDS2018 also splits DDoS traffic over two days, whereas CIC-IDS2017 bundled them. The tooling used in both datasets is the same. The first day of DDoS samples in the 2018 version contains traffic generated by the Low-Orbit Ion Cannon (LOIC) tool, with both UDP and HTTP floods. These attacks do not rely on deviant protocol use, but simply overwhelm the web server(s) on the receiving end. The second day uses the High-Orbit Ion Cannon tool which also employs HTTP (GET and POST), as well as LOIC UDP.

All single decision tree models trained on non-scaled features have mirror-image metrics on the DDoS traffic from CIC-IDS2017 and the first day of CSE-CIC-2018 (Figure 7). Adaboost has some models with normalized features that are very performant with tight metric clusters at approximately 97%. Reducing features lowers this performance pulling precision and recall apart to 100% and 80%, respectively. While this could be interpreted as a good result, the unpredictable pattern of these metrics in relationship to the training volume significantly lowers the practical utility of this method. The bagging classifier built on decision trees shows signs of overfitting. It has good stability (normalized features) as long as no more than 10% of the DDoS data in CIC-IDS2017 has been used to train the model. In that low training volume region, the classifier has perfect recall, matched by 80+% precision. Randomized decision trees, random forests and gradient boosted trees, both standard and regularized, do not perform well enough to be considered real contenders.

Lots of tree-based methods show signs of overfitting beyond using more than 5% of data to train on. Methods to improve generalization for tree-based classifiers in intrusion detection are worth investigating.

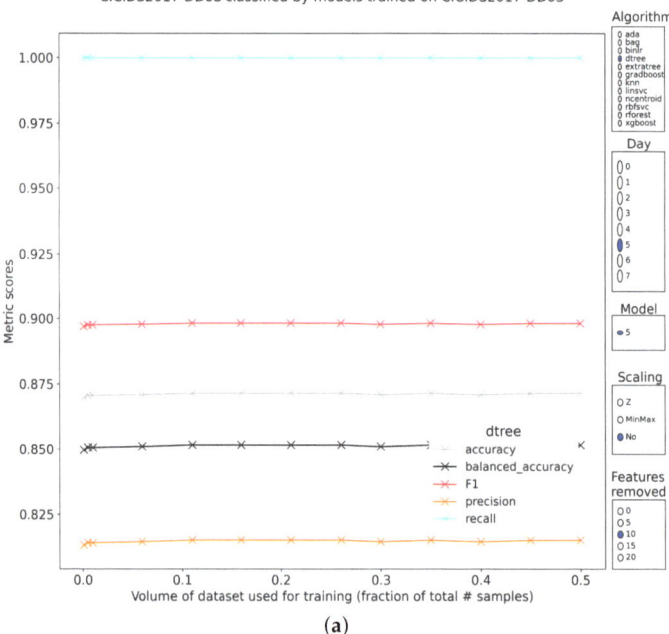

(a)

Figure 7. *Cont.*

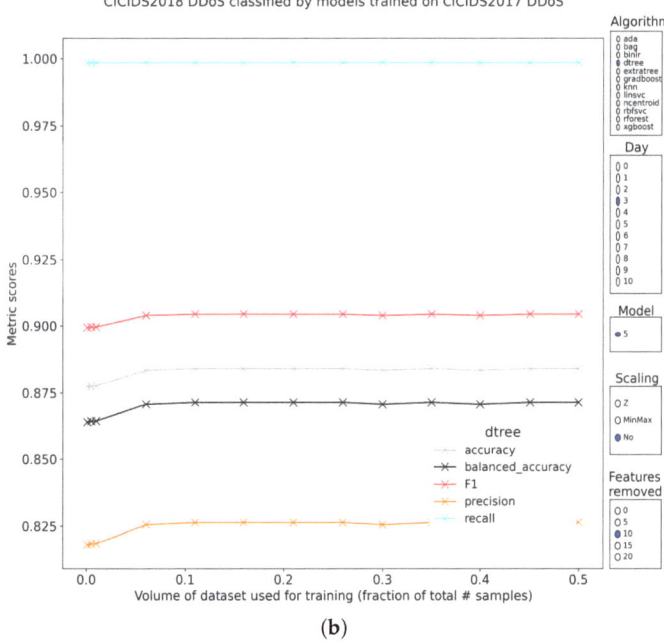

(b)

Figure 7. A rare occurrence of perfect consistency by pretrained IDS2017 DDoS models the respective IDS2018 DDoS samples. (**a**) Singular decision trees within CIC-IDS2017 DDoS; and (**b**) the same set of models summarized in figure (**a**) when evaluating CSE-CIC-ÍDS2018 DDoS part 1.

Nearest neighbors with normalized features has perfect recall and reaches 89.5% precision with 10% data used for training. At least a flat 10% loss in precision is observed compared to the classification performance on CIC-IDS2017. Min–max-scaled models also perform well, but not beyond 1% training volume. The nearest centroids loses a flat 10–15% on all metrics compared to the same model's performance on DDoS 2017, but the stability is retained. Recall is poor at only 50%.

The logistic regression models work with little training data reaching perfect recall and 80+% associated precision (only with min–max scaling). Intermittently, there are signs of overfitting at higher training volumes. The linear support vector classifiers obtain equal results, but with less stability. The rbf-kernel SVMs have similar results with both types of scaling. In terms of generalization strength, these methods definitely achieve more stable and thus better results than the other algorithms.

DDoS was one of the easiest classes within CIC-IDS2017. This does not translate into one-to-one to classification strength on CSE-CIC-IDS2018 DDoS. The remarkable resistance to data reduction in all methods of the DDoS class does not hold up. These methods need more robustness to be practical. Evaluated on the whole, classification strength on this easy class is better than it is on the harder classes.

5.2.5. DDoS Part 2

The second day of DDoS traffic in CSE-CIC-IDS2018 has very similar traffic. Only one new tool is introduced, and behind the scenes, it generates requests with the same protocol. It is odd to split the DDoS traffic over two days, because as the results will show, performance is alike.

Single decision trees have zones with adequate performance that are interwoven with zones with very poor performance metrics. It is not exclusively due to overfitting either, because regions with good performance do exist at higher training volumes. Adaboost models only work with normalized features, maximally reaching perfect precision and 80%

recall. As a standalone result, this would make adaboost a viable option, but once again, the unpredictability with regard to training volume hampers viability. The pretrained bagging classifiers perform like adaboost at low to very low training volumes and exclusively with normalized features, however, with even less stability. Conclusions for randomized trees, random forests and normal gradient-boosted trees can be summarized as lackluster across all parameters (again with an exception for very low training volumes). Regularized gradient-boosted trees perform stably with 80% recall and 100% precision insensitive to feature reduction.

Nearest neighbors has the same result as in the previous section, but with a worse precision (70+%). HOIC combined with LOIC UDP seems to be harder to classify, because the centroid suffers from very low (<25%) recall compared to the previous section (regardless of parameter selection).

Both methods of feature scaling obtain good results for the logistic regression models, with those trained on min–max-scaled features reaching clusters of perfect metrics. The best scores are obtained at the lowest training volumes, but the differential is tiny in most cases (0.5%). The linear kernel SVM has the same performance profile as binlr, with good results for the models trained on normalized features, but better results on models trained with min–max-scaled features. Once more, the highest performance is obtained with the lowest amounts of training data. The ideal classifier for this attack class is the RBF-kernel SVM with stable, perfect scores. This does require at least 1% data to train on, but shows no signs of overfitting (min–max-scaling).

It could be concluded that ML-based models are able to distinguish well between regular and multiple types of DDoS traffic. Unfortunately, due to the loud nature of DDoS attacks, they are easily detectable by other mechanisms. It might be useful at an aggregate level (service providers), but an individual business suffering from a DDoS attack will not need a machine learning model to confirm that.

5.2.6. Web Attacks

The web attacks are a harder attack type to classify within CIC-IDS2017. Most methods were not able to reach perfect classification scores. Although day 5 and 6 contain web attacks, the dataset documentation does not mention what the differences between the two days are. They both contain web brute force attempts, cross-site scripting (XSS) and structured query language injections (SQLis).

The poor generalization obtained by single decision trees is the root cause for the feeble results of the methods that build on top of it. Recall is so consistently below 40%, with spiking precision scores making it impossible to recommend any of these methods. These results did not improve with more training, different scaling or less feature reduction. The worst performers are randomized decision trees. There is no learning, because they do not try to set optimal splitting points. It is clear that for a harder-to-classify attack class, this method does not work. The web attack models built on decision trees typically had 90–100% recall after some training within CIC-IDS2017. The relative 50% drop-off is disconcerting.

Nearest neighbors starts off with some signs of learning, but levels off quickly at low to very low precision–recall pairs. The method had good scores within CIC-IDS2017 (85–95% recall and 75–85% precision), but that performance does not carry over into CSE-CIC-IDS2018. Nearest centroids had robust 85+% recall on the web attack traffic of CIC-IDS2017, at all combinations of training volume, scaling and feature reduction. The associated precision was never good, so it is expected that this will continue. Unfortunately, the nearest centroids loses much in terms of recall. Only the models with min–max-scaled features stay stable at 57%. Other methods of scaling have recall stable at 15%. All precision is lost.

The near-perfect recall and moderate precision of logistic regression models within CIC-IDS2017 is not retained on CSE-CIC-IDS2018. Recall drops below 40%, often crashing to 0%, and precision is at 0% more often than not. This conclusion also applies to a linear

SVM and rbf SVM. All of these methods struggled in terms of precision within CIC-IDS2017, but did reach near-perfect recall. None of this translates into generalization performance when classifying the web attacks in CSE-CIC-IDS2018, despite the fact that both datasets contain the same types of web attacks.

It is clear that, for this type of attack, which typically has a lower network footprint (unless it is a brute force login), is much harder to classify from network-related features. Within the dataset, however, the performance can be very good and a subsequent recommendation for use in real-world systems would be logical, but ultimately misguided.

5.2.7. Infiltration

Like web attacks, CSE-CIC-IDS2018 contains two days with infiltration traffic. The documentation does not mention what the differences are between the two days. The labeling in the data does not provide any additional information apart from 'infiltration'. A major caveat when analyzing these results is the lack of samples on which the models were trained. Day 3 of CIC-IDS2017 has infiltration traffic, but the distribution between benign and malicious is extremely skewed (288602-36). Generalization performance is thus not expected.

None of the tested algorithms perform at acceptable rates, and metrics are consistently below 20%. Sometimes, precision spikes high, but the associated recall is so close to zero that the high precision is meaningless. These results do not vary with changes in the training volume, feature scaling choice or feature reduction. The results for both days are close to identical. Some models, especially those built on decision trees, show climbing trends within CIC-IDS2017, but this is just the classifiers fitting any pattern and certainly not one that is significant or general.

It will be interesting to investigate whether models trained on the infiltration days of CSE-CIC-IDS2018 perform well when retested on each other's data as well as the 2017 infiltration samples.

5.2.8. Botnet Traffic

The botnet class in CIC-IDS2017 is one of the medium-difficulty classes, mainly because non-tree-based models had low precision and all models suffered from the removal of good features from the training set. The documentation for the 2017 data lists Ares [35] as the tested botnet. The 2018 version adds the Zeus [36] botnet.

Single decision trees have very irregular performance. At some points, the metrics almost reach perfect classification, but it is impossible to reliably tell which parameters are required. Feature reduction tanks performance across all trained models, most notably when using min–max-scaling or no scaling. There is one decent set of models (adaboost) and it requires normalized features and no feature reduction. The resulting models have an early peak at 0.5–1% training volume of perfect recall and 75% precision. Giving access to more training data still yields stable models, but the recall is only 50% with 95+% precision. As soon as features are removed, the classification scores plummet almost to 0. Changing how the features are preprocessed also had a major impact (summarized in Figure 8). The bagging classifier built on decision trees, gradient-boosted trees, random forests and extreme gradient-boosted trees also behave unexpectedly and are not sufficiently potent to be used as a classifier. Randomized decision trees generate no false positives, but no true positives either. All normal traffic is properly classified, but the models miss all malicious instances, leading to a false negative rate of 100% and a total balanced accuracy of 50%. This happens regardless of the training volume, scaling or feature removal (with very few exceptions).

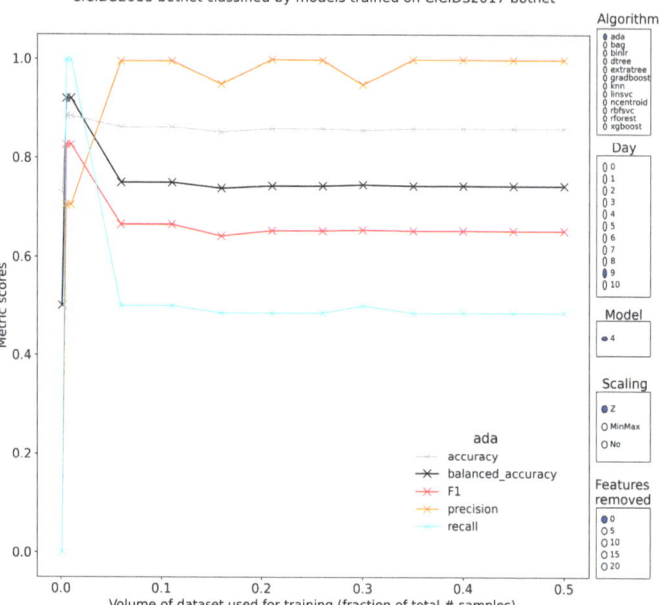

(**a**) Adaboost botnet normalized features, no feature reduction

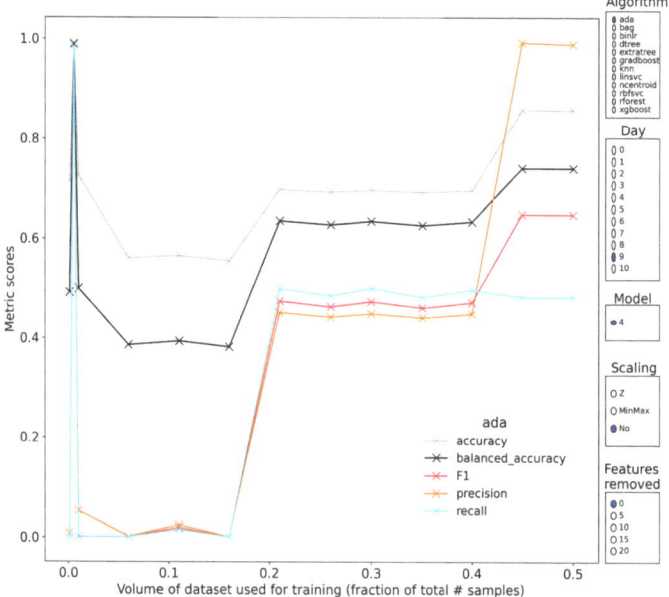

(**b**) Adaboost, pretrained for botnet, no scaling

Figure 8. *Cont.*

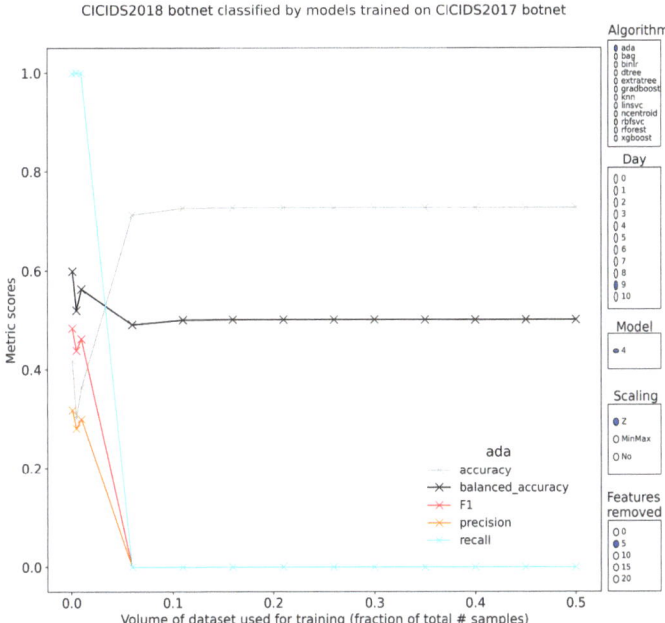

(**c**) Adaboost, pretrained for botnet, still normalized, top 5 features removed

Figure 8. The wild fluctuations between pretrained models when employing different scaling methods during preprocessing or when removing top-features when classifying a medium-difficulty class (botnet).

Nearest neighbors has an inverse relationship with training volume because precision–recall most often stays below 50% and it is not worth considering. The nearest centroids classifier has many good models that manage a balanced accuracy score of 75–80% and with very high stability. These models were trained with normalized features and have recall stable near 100%. Min–max-scaled features yield models with recall at a stable 50%. Not scaling features before training yields models with a stable recall of 0%. What is most interesting is that this happened at all considered points of training volume. Even within CIC-IDS2017, it was not advisable to use it as a classifier for malicious samples, due to its low precision. This remains unchanged on the botnet data of CSE-CIC-IDS2018.

The results of the logistic regression models and linear SVM are not good enough, but that was expected because these models performed poorly on the botnet data in CIC-IDS2017. The only interesting conclusion is the complete loss of recall on the botnet data in CSE-CIC-IDS2018, whereas these models trained to very high recall values on the 2017 data. Rbf-svc models have great performance (85% balanced accuracy, perfect recall with 55% precision) at very low training volumes (mostly with minmax-scaled features). This drops to approximately 70% balanced accuracy with increased training volume. These results are stable with regard to feature reduction. The loss in performance is mostly due to a sharp decline in recall.

5.2.9. Intermediate Conclusion

After the disappointing generalization strength of the global models, as discussed in Sections 4.2.4, a new hypothesis was formulated which states that models trained on specific attack classes might generalize better than their global two-class counterparts. This hypothesis is proven wrong by the results in the previous subsections (Sections 5.2.1–5.2.8). Model generalization rarely happens and when the pretrained models achieve stable, high classification metrics, it is most often on the easy classes of CIC-IDS2017.

There are three major issues that make the use of pretrained models so weak when it comes to generalization. First, how the features are scaled before training has a large impact on the model's performance, but there is no best choice that can be reasonably recommended. This was no issue for the models when they had to classify the test sets from CIC-IDS2017. Second, the relationship between training volume and classification scores is inverted more often than not, leading to a situation wherein models trained on 0.1–1% of the samples in CIC-IDS2017 perform best. The third and final nail in the coffin is the rapid loss in classification metrics when the most discriminative features are incrementally removed. Most models were very robust to this within CIC-IDS2017, especially to classify the easy classes, but this desirable property does not hold.

6. Discussion

The scope of this investigation has led to a substantial set of results. In the results (Sections 4 and 5), the classification results for all attack classes as well as the trends observed from the visualizations are described in detail. Even though both sections end with intermediate conclusions, they remain dense. This section was included to give a straightforward view of the results and their implications. Table 3 shows the best three models per attack class from both a baseline perspective (B rows) and a generalized performance perspective (G rows). What is best is determined by the ranking of the models based on an equally weighted combination of balanced accuracy, F1-score and use of training data (less is better). The numeric columns (except for reduction) are percentages with a maximum of 100.

Several points stand out in this table. First the baseline scores for all classes except infiltration (due to poor representation in CIC-IDS2017) are extremely high. Second and most importantly, pretrained models generalized well to the classes with clear network footprints such as bruteforce, L7-DoS, DDoS and botnet to some extent. These results are without any additional training and most often achieved by models that had little access to training data (% training at or below 1%, further broken down into one third training–two thirds validation). Third, although tree-based models typically have the highest baseline scores, the best generalizing models are not always tree-based. There are, however, more than enough tree-based models that do have great general performance (hence, they did not overfit) so it is possible. This is mainly interesting from a model interpretability perspective. Fourth and finally, the discrepancy between the baseline performance and the general performance for the web attacks would go unnoticed in most analyses, erroneously concluding that the models perform well on the class. This conclusion also applies to the global 2-class models.

One crucial remark about Table 3 is that it obfuscates whether the models had a stable, generalized performance. This is most often not the case (as shown in the detailed results in Section 5). Improvements that guarantee stable, general class-level models after training should be sought after. These improvements could come from changes in data preparation and model selection based on generalization potential (either during or after training) or algorithmic modifications that improve robustness.

Table 3. Classification metrics for the best 3 models per attack class, both for baseline (B) and generalized (G) classification, with the mention of the preprocessing parameters.

B/G	Class	Algorithm	Balanced Acc.	F1	Precision	Recall	Scaling	Reduction	% Train
B	0.Bruteforce	gradboost	99.84	99.06	98.40	99.73	No	0	0.5
		extratree	99.63	99.24	99.21	99.28	Z	0	0.5
		extratree	99.64	99.63	99.97	99.28	Z	0	1.0
G	0.Bruteforce	xgboost	100	100	100	100	No	0	0.5
		xgboost	99.97	99.95	99.90	100	No	0	1.0
		gradboost	99.06	98.38	96.81	100	MinMax	0	0.1

Table 3. *Cont.*

B/G	Class	Algorithm	Balanced Acc.	F1	Precision	Recall	Scaling	Reduction	% Train
B	1.L7-DoS	xgboost	99.85	99.79	99.71	99.88	No	0	0.5
		xgboost	99.85	99.77	99.66	99.89	Z	0	0.5
		xgboost	99.84	99.76	99.61	99.91	MinMax	0	0.5
G	1.L7-DoS	linsvc	97.80	82.59	71.57	97.63	MinMax	5	1.0
		linsvc	97.98	84.93	75.14	97.65	MinMax	5	6.0
		linsvc	97.75	81.63	70.10	97.70	MinMax	5	11.0
G	2.L7-DoS (HeartBleed)	rforest	99.75	99.81	99.65	99.78	Z	20	1.0
		linsvc	99.49	99.50	99.95	99.04	MinMax	0	0.5
		gradboost	99.65	99.72	99.60	99.85	MinMax	10	1
B	2.Web Attacks	xgboost	97.58	96.92	98.72	95.18	MinMax	0	1.0
		xgboost	98.83	98.75	99.86	97.66	MinMax	0	6.0
		extratree	98.89	98.27	98.75	97.80	MinMax	0	6.0
G	5.Web Attacks	gradboost	64.23	43.37	91.15	28.45	No	10	0.5
		dtree	77.74	38.69	29.69	55.52	No	0	11.0
		ada	64.36	41.35	73.76	28.73	No	0	1.0
G	6.Web Attacks	extratree	61.75	38.05	100	23.50	MinMax	5	0.5
		gradboost	61.66	36.92	88.59	23.32	No	10	0.5
		xgboost	61.66	36.82	87.42	23.32	MinMax	10	0.5
B	3.Infiltration	dtree	88.89	71.79	66.67	77.78	MinMax	10	11.0
		xgboost	93.06	91.18	96.88	86.11	Z	0	35.0
		extratree	88.89	86.15	96.55	77.78	MinMax	15	26.0
G	7.Infiltration	ncentroid	50.19	17.50	11.33	38.42	Z	20	6.0
		binlr	50.46	14.86	11.71	20.34	Z	0	6.0
		binlr	49.93	15.22	11.18	23.82	Z	20	6.0
G	8.Infiltration	ncentroid	57.75	42.42	35.74	52.16	Z	20	6.0
		binlr	55.23	43.21	31.58	68.38	MinMax	15	11.0
		linsvc	51.09	43.11	28.62	87.29	MinMax	10	11.0
B	4.Botnet	xgboost	98.42	98.19	99.58	96.85	MinMax	0	6.0
		xgboost	98.14	97.65	99.06	96.29	Z	0	6.0
		xgboost	97.53	97.32	99.68	95.07	No	0	6.0
G	9.Botnet	ada	98.90	98.40	98.39	98.41	No	0	0.5
		gradboost	92.11	82.67	70.51	99.91	Z	0	0.5
		ada	92.11	82.67	70.51	99.91	Z	0	0.5
B	5.DDoS	extratree	99.89	99.89	99.96	99.82	Z	5	0.1
		extratree	99.87	99.88	99.96	99.79	Z	10	0.1
		extratree	99.84	99.86	99.88	99.83	No	10	0.1
G	3.DDoS	dtree	96.30	96.75	96.09	97.42	Z	0	0.5
		ada	96.30	96.75	96.09	97.42	Z	0	1.0
		bag	95.96	96.49	95.58	97.42	Z	0	0.5
G	4.DDoS	binlr	99.86	99.87	99.99	99.75	MinMax	0	0.1
		binlr	99.86	99.87	99.99	99.75	MinMax	5	0.1
		binlr	99.86	99.87	99.99	99.75	MinMax	10	0.1
B	7.Global	xgboost	99.82	99.73	99.75	99.70	No	0	0.5
		xgboost	99.68	99.62	99.84	99.40	Z	0	0.5
		xgboost	99.86	99.80	99.85	99.75	Z	0	1.0
G	10.Global	knn	81.36	71.98	64.46	81.47	Z	0	0.1
		knn	79.23	69.06	60.65	80.18	Z	10	1.0
		knn	79.03	68.45	58.49	82.50	Z	10	0.5

7. Conclusions and Future Work

ML-based intrusion detection systems have to be able to accurately classify new samples to protect live networks. Getting access to these new samples can be tricky, but an intermediate evaluation is possible. This article tested whether a suite of supervised ML algorithms trained on CIC-IDS2017 (both global and class-specific models) effectively generalizes to the very similar, compatible CSE-CIC-IDS2018.

Unfortunately, our experiments demonstrated that the global, two-class models which had excellent performance on CIC-IDS2017 [11] do not generalize to the follow-up dataset CSE-CIC-IDS2018.

Even the most data-constrained trained models show clear signs of overfitting (best results at very low training volume) and an overall very weak performance. The best two-class models are the logistic regression and linear- and rbf-kernel SVMs. These reach between 90 and 100% recall with 50–60% precision. This leads to overall class separability in the 70% range. This is not sufficiently reliable to be used in real network defense systems.

Because the global models are too unreliable, specialized models for all shared attack classes between CIC-IDS2017 and CSE-CIC-IDS2018 have also been tested. Those results have pockets of good performance, mostly on the network-centric classes. Some models are able to classify the novel DoS, DDoS, botnet and brute force samples of CSE-CIC-IDS2018 with the retention of their strong performance metrics from classification within CIC-IDS2017 (F1-score > 95%). Section 6 provides a condensed version of the top results and their implications.

Three key issues still undermine a recommendation to use the tested algorithms in real network defense systems. First, how features are scaled has a major impact on the models' performance and the best choice varies too much to give a solid recommendation. This was no issue for the same models when only classifying the test sets of the data on which they were trained. Second, almost every model significantly struggles to maintain performance if a selection of top-features was removed prior to training. This too was much less of an issue for the models during standard intra-dataset testing. Third, the best-performing models were most often those trained on very little data (0.1–1% training volume). This clear sign of overfitting was most prominent for tree-based learners, but affected all other methods to some extent. Performance regressions by the numbers were erratic and could dip down to balanced accuracies of 50%.

Losing this invariance to scaling, training volume and feature reduction that made the models so attractive when classifying only within CIC-IDS2017 has a big implication. A large collection of models have to be trained and tested before the best models are cherry-picked. Such a large expenditure of time and computational resources for a relatively low yield is not defensible.

To summarize: this article experimentally demonstrates that ML-NIDS methods fail to generalize even just across tightly coupled datasets. Consequently, it is highly unlikely that they will perform well when deployed on real-world networks. We urge researchers in the ML-NIDS domain to execute this article's more rigorous model evaluation strategy to avoid publishing potentially misleading and overly optimistic results.

Future Work and Hypotheses

Our future research will investigate potential solutions to improve ML-based NIDS systems until they can consistently classify related and compatible datasets.

An obvious first attempt would be to investigate more powerful classification methods. Recent ML-NIDS literature borrows neural network architectures that dominate pattern recognition tasks in other fields [37–39]. Although the results are great, no literature exists that tests whether they are better at generalization.

Alternatively, more stringent model regularization techniques and/or feature selection can be tested as potential solutions. Because the feature selection method of [11] was counter-intuitive, there is room to test optimized models that only kept the most potent features.

Finally, instead of trying to build global two-class models or attack-class specific models, the models could be trained to recognize attacks within specific domains (e.g., simultaneously training with differentiation at the protocol and attack level or training models to recognize traffic from a specific botnet). The major downside to this approach is that it reduces the range of attacks that it covers, thereby moving closer to signature-based methods.

Author Contributions: Conceptualization, L.D.; methodology, L.D.; software, L.D.; validation, L.D.; formal analysis, L.D.; investigation, L.D.; resources, L.D. and IDLab-Imec; data curation, L.D.; writing—original draft preparation, L.D.; writing—review and editing, L.D., M.V., T.W. and B.V.; visualization, L.D.; supervision, T.W., B.V. and F.D.T.; project administration, L.D.; funding acquisition, T.W., B.V. and F.D.T. All authors have read and agreed to the published version of the manuscript.

Funding: This research received no external funding.

Institutional Review Board Statement: Not applicable.

Informed Consent Statement: Not applicable.

Data Availability Statement: The datasets, both raw and cleaned up, are publicly available at https://gitlab.ilabt.imec.be/lpdhooge/ids-dataset-collection. The full source code of the analysis and the complete set of visualizations is available at https://gitlab.ilabt.imec.be/lpdhooge/reduced-unseen-testing. (both URLs checked on 10 March 2023).

Conflicts of Interest: The authors declare no conflict of interest.

References

1. Denning, D.; Neumann, P.G. *Requirements and Model for IDES-a Real-Time Intrusion-Detection Expert System*; SRI InternationalL: Menlo Park, USA 1985; Volume 8.
2. Denning, D.E. An intrusion-detection model. *IEEE Trans. Softw. Eng.* **1987**, *13*, 222–232. [CrossRef]
3. Duessel, P.; Gehl, C.; Flegel, U.; Dietrich, S.; Meier, M. Detecting zero-day attacks using context-aware anomaly detection at the application-layer. *Int. J. Inf. Secur.* **2017**, *16*, 475–490. [CrossRef]
4. Kolias, C.; Kolias, V.; Kambourakis, G. TermID: A distributed swarm intelligence-based approach for wireless intrusion detection. *Int. J. Inf. Secur.* **2017**, *16*, 401–416. [CrossRef]
5. Shone, N.; Ngoc, T.N.; Phai, V.D.; Shi, Q. A deep learning approach to network intrusion detection. *IEEE Trans. Emerg. Top. Comput. Intell.* **2018**, *2*, 41–50. [CrossRef]
6. Sethi, K.; Sai Rupesh, E.; Kumar, R.; Bera, P.; Venu Madhav, Y. A context-aware robust intrusion detection system: A reinforcement learning-based approach. *Int. J. Inf. Secur.* **2020**, *19*, 657–678. [CrossRef]
7. Quadir, M.A.; Christy Jackson, J.; Prassanna, J.; Sathyarajasekaran, K.; Kumar, K.; Sabireen, H.; Ubarhande, S.; Vijaya Kumar, V. An efficient algorithm to detect DDoS amplification attacks. *J. Intell. Fuzzy Syst.* **2020**, *39*, 8565–8572. [CrossRef]
8. Kannari, P.R.; Shariff, N.C.; Biradar, R.L. Network intrusion detection using sparse autoencoder with swish-PReLU activation model. *J. Ambient. Intell. Humaniz. Comput.* **2021**, *12*, 1–13. [CrossRef]
9. Badji, J.C.J.; Diallo, C. A CNN-based Attack Classification versus an AE-based Unsupervised Anomaly Detection for Intrusion Detection Systems. In Proceedings of the 2022 International Conference on Electrical, Computer and Energy Technologies (ICECET), Prague, Czech Republic, 20–22 July 2022; pp. 1–7. [CrossRef]
10. D'hooge, L.; Wauters, T.; Volckaert, B.; De Turck, F. Inter-dataset generalization strength of supervised machine learning methods for intrusion detection. *J. Inf. Secur. Appl.* **2020**, *54*, 102564. [CrossRef]
11. D'hooge, L.; Wauters, T.; Volckaert, B.; De Turck, F. Classification hardness for supervised learners on 20 years of intrusion detection data. *IEEE Access* **2019**, *7*, 167455–167469. [CrossRef]
12. Sharafaldin, I.; CIC. CIC-IDS2017. 2017. Available online: https://www.unb.ca/cic/datasets/ids-2017.html (accessed on 15 November 2022).
13. Sharafaldin, I.; CIC. CIC-IDS2018. 2018. Available online: https://www.unb.ca/cic/datasets/ids-2018.html (accessed on 15 November 2022).
14. Sharafaldin, I.; CIC. CIC-DDoS2019. 2019. Available online: https://www.unb.ca/cic/datasets/ddos-2019.html (accessed on 15 November 2022).
15. Sharafaldin, I.; Lashkari, A.H.; Hakak, S.; Ghorbani, A.A. Developing realistic distributed denial of service (DDoS) attack dataset and taxonomy. In Proceedings of the 2019 International Carnahan Conference on Security Technology (ICCST), Chennai, India, 1–3 October 2019; pp. 1–8.
16. Govindarajan, M.; Chandrasekaran, R. Intrusion detection using an ensemble of classification methods. In Proceedings of the World Congress on Engineering and Computer Science (WCECS), San Francisco, USA, 24–26 October 2012 Volume 1, pp. 459–464.

17. Lu, L.; Teng, S.; Zhang, W.; Zhang, Z.; Fei, L.; Fang, X. Two-Layer Intrusion Detection Model Based on Ensemble Classifier. In Proceedings of the CCF Conference on Computer Supported Cooperative Work and Social Computing, Kunming, China, 16–18 August 2019; Springer: Singapore, 2019; pp. 104–115.
18. Kuang, F.; Xu, W.; Zhang, S.; Wang, Y.; Liu, K. A novel approach of KPCA and SVM for intrusion detection. *J. Comput. Inf. Syst.* **2012**, *8*, 3237–3244.
19. Wickramasinghe, C.S.; Marino, D.L.; Amarasinghe, K.; Manic, M. Generalization of deep learning for cyber-physical system security: A survey. In Proceedings of the IECON 2018-44th Annual Conference of the IEEE Industrial Electronics Society, Washington, DC, USA, 21–23 October 2018, pp. 745–751.
20. Sommer, R.; Paxson, V. Outside the closed world: On using machine learning for network intrusion detection. In Proceedings of the 2010 IEEE Symposium on Security and Privacy, Oakland, CA, USA, 16–19 May 2010, pp. 305–316.
21. Gates, C.; Taylor, C. Challenging the anomaly detection paradigm: A provocative discussion. In Proceedings of the 2006 Workshop on NEW Security Paradigms, Schloss Dagstuhl, Germany, 19–22 September 2006; pp. 21–29.
22. Małowidzki, M.; Berezinski, P.; Mazur, M. Network intrusion detection: Half a kingdom for a good dataset. In Proceedings of the NATO STO SAS-139 Workshop, Lisbon, Portugal, 1 December 2015.
23. Vasilomanolakis, E.; Cordero, C.G.; Milanov, N.; Mühlhäuser, M. Towards the creation of synthetic, yet realistic, intrusion detection datasets. In Proceedings of the NOMS 2016-2016 IEEE/IFIP Network Operations and Management Symposium, Istanbul, Turkey, 25–29 April 2016; pp. 1209–1214.
24. Ring, M.; Wunderlich, S.; Scheuring, D.; Landes, D.; Hotho, A. A survey of network-based intrusion detection data sets. *Comput. Secur.* **2019**, *86*, 147–167. [CrossRef]
25. Li, Z.; Das, A.; Zhou, J. Model generalization and its implications on intrusion detection. In Proceedings of the International Conference on Applied Cryptography and Network Security, New York, NY, USA, 7–10 June 2005; pp. 222–237.
26. Lin, Z.; Shi, Y.; Xue, Z. Idsgan: Generative adversarial networks for attack generation against intrusion detection. In Proceedings of the Pacific-Asia Conference on Knowledge Discovery and Data Mining, Chengdu, China, 16–19 May 2022, pp. 79–91.
27. Newlin, M.; Reith, M.; DeYoung, M. Synthetic Data Generation with Machine Learning for Network Intrusion Detection Systems. In Proceedings of the European Conference on Cyber Warfare and Security, Coimbra, Portugal on 4– 5 July 2019; pp. 785–XVII.
28. Recht, B.; Roelofs, R.; Schmidt, L.; Shankar, V. Do imagenet classifiers generalize to imagenet? In Proceedings of the International Conference on Machine Learning, PMLR, Long Beach, CA, USA, 9–15 June 2019; pp. 5389–5400.
29. Sharafaldin, I.; Lashkari, A.H.; Ghorbani, A.A. Toward generating a new intrusion detection dataset and intrusion traffic characterization. *ICISSp* **2018**, *1*, 108–116.
30. Sharafaldin, I.; Gharib, A.; Lashkari, A.H.; Ghorbani, A.A. Towards a reliable intrusion detection benchmark dataset. *Softw. Netw.* **2018**, *2018*, 177–200. [CrossRef]
31. Hastie, T.; Tibshirani, R.; Friedman, J.H.; Friedman, J.H. *The Elements of Statistical Learning: Data Mining, Inference, and Prediction*; Springer: Berlin/Heidelberg, Germany, 2009; Volume 2.
32. Chen, T.; Guestrin, C. Xgboost: A scalable tree boosting system. In Proceedings of the 22nd Acm Sigkdd International Conference on Knowledge Discovery and Data Mining, San Francisco, CA, USA, 13–17 August 2016; pp. 785–794.
33. Geurts, P.; Ernst, D.; Wehenkel, L. Extremely randomized trees. *Mach. Learn.* **2006**, *63*, 3–42. [CrossRef]
34. D'hooge, L.; Wauters, T.; Volckaert, B.; De Turck, F. In-depth comparative evaluation of supervised machine learning approaches for detection of cybersecurity threats. In Proceedings of the 4th International Conference on Internet of Things, Big Data and Security (IoTBDS), Crete, Greece, 2–4 May 2019; pp. 125–136.
35. Sweetsoftware. Ares. 2017. Available online: https://github.com/sweetsoftware/Ares (accessed on 18 November 2022).
36. Touyachrist. Evo-Zeus. 2017. Available online: https://github.com/touyachrist/evo-zeus (accessed on 18 November 2022).
37. Young, T.; Hazarika, D.; Poria, S.; Cambria, E. Recent trends in deep learning based natural language processing. *IEEE Comput. IntelligenCe Mag.* **2018**, *13*, 55–75. [CrossRef]
38. Zhao, Z.Q.; Zheng, P.; Xu, S.t.; Wu, X. Object detection with deep learning: A review. *IEEE Trans. Neural Networks Learn. Syst.* **2019**, *30*, 3212–3232. [CrossRef] [PubMed]
39. Mighan, S.N.; Kahani, M. A novel scalable intrusion detection system based on deep learning. *Int. J. Inf. Secur.* **2021**, *20*, 387–403. [CrossRef]

Journal of
*Cybersecurity
and Privacy*

MDPI

Article

ReMouse Dataset: On the Efficacy of Measuring the Similarity of Human-Generated Trajectories for the Detection of Session-Replay Bots

Shadi Sadeghpour * and Natalija Vlajic

Department of Electrical Engineering and Computer Science, York University, Toronto, ON M3J 1P3, Canada
* Correspondence: shadisa@cse.yorku.ca

Abstract: Session-replay bots are believed to be the latest and most sophisticated generation of web bots, and they are also very difficult to defend against. Combating session-replay bots is particularly challenging in online domains that are repeatedly visited by the same genuine human user(s) in the same or similar ways—such as news, banking or gaming sites. In such domains, it is difficult to determine whether two look-alike sessions are produced by the same human user or if these sessions are just bot-generated session replays. Unfortunately, to date, only a handful of research studies have looked at the problem of session-replay bots, with many related questions still waiting to be addressed. The main contributions of this paper are two-fold: (1) We introduce and provide to the public a novel real-world mouse dynamics dataset named ReMouse. The ReMouse dataset is collected in a guided environment, and, unlike other publicly available mouse dynamics datasets, it contains repeat sessions generated by the same human user(s). As such, the ReMouse dataset is the first of its kind and is of particular relevance for studies on the development of effective defenses against session-replay bots. (2) Our own analysis of ReMouse dataset using statistical and advanced ML-based methods (including deep and unsupervised neural learning) shows that two different human users cannot generate the same or similar-looking sessions when performing the same or a similar online task; furthermore, even the (repeat) sessions generated by the same human user are sufficiently distinguishable from one another.

Keywords: behavioral biometrics; mouse dynamics; feature learning; convolutional neural network; clustering algorithms

Citation: Sadeghpour, S.; Vlajic, N. ReMouse Dataset: On the Efficacy of Measuring the Similarity of Human-Generated Trajectories for the Detection of Session-Replay Bots. *J. Cybersecur. Priv.* **2023**, *3*, 95–117. https://doi.org/10.3390/jcp3010007

Academic Editors: Giorgio Giacinto and Phil Legg

Received: 12 January 2023
Revised: 22 February 2023
Accepted: 27 February 2023
Published: 2 March 2023

1. Introduction

Behavioral biometrics measure and analyze user interactions in the online domain so as to recognize or verify a person's unique identity, with the ultimate goal of providing an imperceptible layer of security to systems and applications [1]. The best-known forms of behavioral biometrics involve the monitoring and analysis of the following modalities: mouse cursor movement, keystroke or voice dynamics, the appearance and speed of signing, etc. The main advantages of mouse movement analysis relative to the other forms of behavioral biometrics include: (a) mouse movement can be monitored in a manner that is entirely unobtrusive for the end user; (b) monitoring of mouse movement does not require the use of additional hardware or software and thus does not incur additional cost; (c) from the perspective of user privacy, sharing mouse dynamics data is far less problematic than sharing keystrokes, signatures or voice data [2]; (d) mouse movement has already proven to be effective, not only in the identification or authentication of end users but also in the process of determining users' age and gender [3], as well as their emotions and work productivity [4].

A number of previous studies on mouse dynamics have looked at the importance of different mouse movement characteristics for the purpose of user identification/authentication, such as hesitation patterns, random and straight movements, etc. [5]. Some of these studies have also looked at the use of different machine learning methods in user identification/authentication systems; however, they often rely only on a limited number of handpicked features extracted from their respective mouse movement datasets. To avoid the pitfalls of manual feature extraction processes, in this study we propose to tackle the problem of mouse trajectory classification by using a deep neural network (convolutional neural network) that utilizes all of the raw mouse movement data. That is, instead of handpicking the most important features for a set of mouse movement trajectories, we let the convolution neural network identify these features in an unsupervised manner. Furthermore, we investigate the use of mouse movement analysis in another important application area—malicious web-bot detection. Malicious web bots are known to pose a significant threat to the entire Internet community. One particularly challenging form of malicious bot are the bots capable of impersonating human behavior in terms of mouse movement. The latest generation of such human-mimicking malicious bots are synthesized by means of 'session replays' [6–8]. That is, these bots programmatically replay a browsing session, including the mouse movement trajectory, that was previously executed (and recorded) by a genuine human visitor to a target/victim web site. The specific goal of this study is to offer a better insight into: (a) the statistical similarities and differences between browsing sessions (mouse movement trajectories) generated by different genuine users on the same target web page; (b) the statistical similarities and differences between browsing sessions (mouse movement trajectories) repeated by the same genuine user on the same target web page. We believe that a better understanding of these similarities and differences is of critical importance for the creation of more effective techniques of malicious bot detection—in particular the detection of session-replay bots—which in turn can ensure a safer Internet for everyone.

The specific contributions of the research work presented in this paper can be summarized as follows: (i) We developed an interactive web platform capable of collecting a number of different mouse movement actions and features, including trajectory, point-click, drag-and-drop, velocity, etc. The platform has been deployed on MTurk (https://www.mturk.com/, accessed on 25 February 2023) and has allowed us to collect mouse movement data from several hundred genuine human users (i.e., participants) while repeating the same/similar online task. We named this dataset ReMouse and are making it available to the research community on IEEE DataPort [9]. (ii) We conducted statistical and ML-based analyses of the ReMouse dataset. The results of this analysis have shown that all mouse dynamics sessions coming from the same genuine human user are relatively different from each other and that it is highly unlikely that different genuine human users produce 'same-looking' sessions when completing the same/similar online task.

To the best of our knowledge, the ReMouse dataset is the first publicly available mouse dynamics dataset with repeat sessions generated by the same human user(s). As such, this dataset can be a very valuable resource for any future research dealing with the problem of session-replay bots, which are currently known to be the most advanced form of web bots on the Internet. In this work, we make the first step towards the ReMouse dataset analysis using statistical and advanced ML-based methods, including deep and unsupervised neural learning. Given the fact that no prior research on the topic of repeat sessions and/or session-replay bots has been conducted (i.e., that is available in the literature), we needed to develop an entirely new research methodology. With this manuscript, we not only try to close the current research and literature gap, we also highlight the need for further development and hope to inspire other researchers to work alongside us on this important area of study.

The remainder of this paper is organized as follows: In Section 2, we provide an overview of previous relevant works on the use of mouse dynamics for the purpose of user authentication and bot detection, as well as an overview the existing publicly available mouse dynamics datasets, including our novel ReMouse dataset. In Section 3, we introduce the web platform that has been used to collect the ReMouse dataset. In Section 4, we present the results of our analysis of the ReMouse dataset using statistical analysis techniques, while in Sections 5 and 6, we summarize our approach and main findings obtained on the ReMouse dataset using advanced ML techniques. Finally, conclusions and directions for future work are presented in Section 7.

2. Related Work

Understanding users' behavior on one or a set of related web pages, including the usage of mouse cursors, has been essential in many application domains, including educational technology, web analytics, e-commerce, digital advertising, and especially bot detection and user authentication [10,11]. To date, a substantial number of published works has looked at the importance of mouse dynamics from a number of different research perspectives. In this section, we provide a survey of a subset of works which are more closely related to the topic of our own research. In particular, we provide an overview of published works that have studied mouse dynamics in the context of user authentication and bot detection. We also give an overview of several publicly available mouse dynamics datasets.

2.1. Mouse Dynamics for User Authentication

A number of research works have proven the general usefulness of mouse dynamics in the domain of user authentication. Some of these works have also turned to the use of machine learning as a promising approach to increasing the accuracy of mouse-movement-based authentication.

In [12], the authors have provided a comprehensive study on the use of several different deep learning architectures, i.e., 1D-CNN (convolutional neural network), 2D-CNN, LSTM (long short-term memory) and a hybrid CNN-LSTM in biometric-based authentication systems deploying mouse dynamics data. In particular, the authors have combined convolutional layers with LSTM layers to build a hybrid neural network capable of modeling temporal sequences on a larger but fixed time scale. Another deep learning approach has been proposed in [13] to address the problem of biometric-based user authentication in systems with an insider threat. Specifically, to preserve the mouse movement features of each individual user, a unique mapping method was developed to map all the basic actions, such as move, click, drag, scroll and stay, into images. The obtained (images) dataset was then used to train seven-layer CNN classification models.

An authentication system based on a weighted multi-classifier voting technique and deploying different mouse movement operations (such as movement direction and elapsed time) has been described in [14]. In [15], the authors have applied a semi-supervised learning method using a novel feature extraction technique for authentication via mouse dynamics. The authors of [16] have introduced a user authentication system comprising two components named 'enrollment', responsible for feature learning, and 'verification', which performs the actual authentication. The authors have employed an FCN (fully convolutional neural network) for feature learning and an OCSVM (one-class support vector machine) for authentication.

The use of the Random Forest algorithm for the purpose of user authentication has been studied in [17]. To predict/determine one's identity, this study suggests using approximately 1000 mouse actions (60 min of the user's active mouse movements on average) to train the model. The findings of this study imply that mouse dynamics should be considered as an additional security service in the systems, not a single verification indicator.

In [18], the researchers have improved the results of user authentication based on mouse dynamics by replacing the raw coordinates with directional velocities. Finally, the effectiveness of using ensemble learning and frequency-domain representations of mouse dynamics for continuous authentication tasks have been studied in [19].

2.2. Mouse Dynamics for Bot Detection

To date, the use of mouse movement analysis in another important application area—malicious web-bot detection—has been investigated by several researchers. Acien et al. [20] have presented a bot detector called BeCAPTCHA-Mouse, which is trained on data generated by the neuromotor modeling of mouse dynamics and is claimed to be capable of detecting highly realistic bot trajectories. To detect web bots, Iliou et al. [21] have proposed a framework that combines two web-bot detection modules: a web-logs detection module and a mouse movement detection module. Each module has its own classifier. The fundamental idea of the proposed approach is to capture the different temporal properties of web logs and mouse movements, plus the spatial properties of mouse movements, with the ultimate goal of creating a more robust detection framework that would be hard to evade.

Other researchers have proved the usefulness of mouse dynamics in detecting malicious bots by employing a deep neural network approach [22]; C4.5 algorithm [8]; a combined model of unsupervised and supervised ML techniques, including the K-Nearest-Neighbors algorithm and naïve Bayes classifier [23], a classification algorithm based on distance measures adapted from the Kolmogorov–Smirnov non-parametric test [24] and sequence learning [25]. Importantly, in [26], the authors have proposed a new web forensic framework for bot crime investigations. The framework is based on four different types of human behavioral patterns (timing, movement, pressure and error) to provide evidence of bad bot activity on web applications.

Although there exists a broad list of machine learning algorithms and data mining techniques that have been applied to the problem of bot detection, the question/problem of advanced session-replay web bots remains largely unanswered. According to our knowledge, the only two research studies that have tackled the problem of session replays and have attempted to build adequate ML-based countermeasures are [8,27]. However, the focus of [27] is on session replays in the context of user authentication (and not malicious web bots), while the results of [8] are based on a proprietary dataset involving blog bots (one very narrow subcategory of web bots). Moreover, a common drawback of both studies is that they omit to consider the possibility of web-sites (i.e., online services) in which genuine human users end up generating similar/repeat sessions, as in the case of news, banking or gaming web-sites.

2.3. Mouse Dynamics Datasets

In terms of the actual mouse movement datasets analyzed in their studies, different researchers have employed different approaches to acquiring human-generated mouse trajectories. They have either used existing publicly available datasets (e.g., [17,28–32]) or they have collected their own. In general, there are two different approaches to collecting a mouse movement dataset: (1) by creating a 'guided environment', where the users are asked to perform a specific (same) task with the mouse, or (2) by creating a 'non-guided environment', where users are not guided (i.e., instructed) on how to perform a particular task [33].

Some of the most commonly studied publicly available mouse movement datasets include: Balabit [28], Bogazici [29], the Attentive Cursor dataset [30], SapiMouse [31], Chao Shen [32] and DFL [17]. The following provides a brief description of each dataset.

2.3.1. Balabit Dataset

Published in 2016, the Balabit dataset falls in the category of 'non-guided environment' datasets and includes mouse pointer positioning and timing information for 10 users working over remote desktop clients connected to a remote server. During data collection, users were asked to perform their regular daily activities. Mouse events were stored in tuples containing the following data: timestamp, pressed button, mouse state and mouse pointer coordinates. The primary purpose of collecting the Balabit dataset was to learn how the involved users utilize their mouse so as to be able to protect them from unauthorized usage of their accounts. Both training and test data are presented as sessions in the dataset; however, the test sessions are much shorter than the training sessions.

2.3.2. Bogazici Mouse Dynamics Dataset

The Bogazici dataset [29], published in 2021, also falls into the category of 'non-guided environment' datasets and comprises mouse usage behavior patterns of 24 users gathered over a one-month period. The data collection participants were selected from different positions in a software company in order to acquire different patterns of user behavior while interacting with different programs and tools in the office environment. Each user's machine was loaded with a specially designed program that would launch at startup and would collect the user's mouse movements without being tied to a specific task and without preventing the user from performing their regular daily activities. The specific information contained in the dataset includes mouse action type, timestamp, spatial coordinates, button, state and application window name. The dataset was collected for the purpose of training several neural network and deep learning models, which were then deployed to identify/verify the involved users.

2.3.3. The Attentive Cursor Dataset

This is a large-scale 'guided environment' dataset of mouse cursor movements during a web search task, and the set was collected in 2020 for the purposes of inferring a user's attention and demographic information. Nearly 3000 participants were recruited from the FIGURE EIGHT (https://www.figure-eight.com, accessed on 25 February 2023) crowdsourcing platform. Using an injected custom JavaScript code, the authors captured the real-world behavior of individuals completing a transactional web search task. The captured information includes the following: mouse cursor position, timestamp, event name, XPath of the DOM element related to the event and the DOM element attributes (if any).

2.3.4. SapiMouse Dataset

The dataset was collected at Sapientia University in 2020 and also falls into the category of 'guided environment' datasets. It contains mouse dynamics data from 120 subjects (92 males and 28 females between 18 and 53 years of age). Using a JavaScript web application running on the user's computer, mouse movements were sampled by an event-driven sampling technique. The participants were asked to perform four different actions, and each was associated with geometrical shapes in a web page, including right and left clicks and drag and drop actions. In the dataset, two files were associated with each participant, with each file corresponding to one- and three-minute-long sessions, respectively. Individual lines in the two files capture information pertaining to one mouse event, such as mouse cursor position, button type, event type (move, drag, press or release) and respective timestamp. The authors have presented user authentication results obtained on this dataset in [31].

2.3.5. Chao Shen Dataset

This 'non-guided environment' dataset was collected in 2017 and consists of mouse dynamics information pertaining to 28 users, with each user completing at least 30 separate data sessions over a two-month period. Each session consisted of about thirty minutes of the respective user's mouse activity. In the dataset, each mouse operation was represented as a tuple of multi-attributes (action type, application type, screen area and window position) and their respective timestamps. The dataset was collected for the purpose of continuous user authentication.

2.3.6. DFL Dataset

This dataset was collected in 2018 from 21 participants in a non-guided environment. The participants were asked to install a background service on their computers (which collected their mouse activity data) and perform their daily activities. The dataset contains the following information about the users' mouse activities: timestamp, button (left, right, no-button), state (move, pressed, released, drag) and coordinates. The dataset was used to evaluate a user verification system, as described in [17].

Our novel mouse dynamics dataset (ReMouse), which we are introducing in this paper and making available to the public, has been collected by means of a web platform developed using the Django REST framework. To collect mouse data from genuine human participants, the platform was deployed on MTurk (for more details, see Section 3.2).

The main differences between our ReMouse dataset and the mouse dynamics datasets previously released by other researchers are as follows: (i) The ReMouse dataset contains the mouse dynamics information of 100 users of mixed nationality, residing in diverse geographical regions, and using different devices (hardware and software components). (ii) The dataset contains dozens of 'repeat sessions' per each user, where 'repeat sessions' are sessions during which the user is asked to complete the same logical task in a guided online environment (e.g., play an online game involving the same sequence of steps and intermediate objectives). Through analysis of such 'repeat sessions', it is possible to obtain a better insight into the actual impact of 'repetition' on the user's mouse behavior (e.g., mouse trajectory and speed). According to our knowledge, this is the first dataset of this kind offered to the public. (iii) Each session in the ReMouse dataset is depicted with more granular information relative to the sessions in other datasets. Namely, in addition to the timing and positioning information of the mouse cursor, our dataset also contains mouse movement speed/velocity, the applications' window size (the height and width), as well as the anonymized IP addresses of the participants as user IDs.

Table 1 compares the characteristics of the most commonly studied publicly available dataset with those of our novel ReMouse dataset.

Table 1. The characteristics of the most prevalent publicly available dataset, including our novel ReMouse dataset.

Name	Ref.	# User	Data Collection	Period of Observing Each User's Activity	Action	Session Fields	Task	Repeat Sessions
Balabit	[28]	10	N/A	N/A	Mouse movement, point click, drag and drop	Timestamp, coordinates, pressed button, state of the mouse	Non-guided	No
Bogazici	[29]	24	1 month	2550 h	Mouse movement, point click, drag and drop	Timestamp, coordinates, button, state of the mouse, application window name	Non-guided	No
The Attentive Cursor	[30]	3K	N/A	2 h	Mouse movement, point click	Timestamp, coordinates, event name, XPath of the DOM element that relates to the event, the DOM element attributes (if any)	Guided	No
SapiMouse	[31]	120	N/A	4 min of each user's activity	Mouse movement, point click, drag and drop	Timestamp, coordinates, button, state of the mouse	Guided	No
Chao Shen	[32]	28	2 months	30 sessions of 30 min	Mouse movement, point click, drag and drop	Timestamp, action type, application type, screen area, window position	Non-guided	No
DFL	[17]	21	7 months	Daily users' mouse activities for 7 months	Mouse movement, point click, drag and drop	Timestamp, coordinates, button, state of the mouse	Non-guided	No
ReMouse	[9]	100	2 Days	5 min of each user's activity	Mouse movement, point click, drag and drop	User ID, session ID, timestamp, coordinates, button, event type, state of the mouse, speed, screen size	Guided	Yes

3. ReMouse Dataset

3.1. Web Platform for Data Collection

Our interactive web platform, which was developed for the purpose of mouse dynamics data collection, is hosted on AWS (Windows Server IIS) and is accessible through the following URL: http://human-likebots.com (accessed on 25 February 2023). On the front/user-facing end, the platform simulates a simple 'Catch Me If You Can!' online game (refer to Figure 1). The game web-page contains a JavaScript code which captures the actual mouse dynamics data (i.e., mouse move, load, click, scroll, … events) as well as the associated metadata. Specifically, in the time interval during which the user stays on the web-site and plays the 'Catch Me If You Can!' game, the script preforms a discrete 'event polling' of various event listeners every 30 ms. In addition to recording the mouse-dynamics-related events, the script also captures the timestamps and x–y coordinates of the recorded events, mouse speed, session ID and screen size. The data collected by the script are first buffered and then sent to the back-end server every few seconds (we decided against shorter sampling and transmission intervals to avoid unnecessary data overhead). Using the Django Rest Framework [34], the server-side web application is able to receive and store the recorded event data in a log file (CSV format). The client- and server-side applications do not record any personal information about the users interacting with the human-likebots.com site.

Figure 1. The web-site 'Catch Me if You Can!'.

3.2. ReMouse Dataset Acquisition

In order to collect real human-user data, our interactive human-likebots.com page was deployed on the Amazon MTurk platform (MTurk is a crowdsourcing marketplace that allows researchers to hire anonymous virtual workers to complete human intelligence tasks for pay. Currently, MTurk offers access to over 500,000 virtual workers from 190 countries). We specifically requested 100 MTurk users to visit and interact with our 'Catch Me If You Can!' site by playing multiple rounds of the game—for a total duration of 5 min. In each round of the game, the users were asked to follow six steps and perform three different actions, including left-click, right-click and drag-and-drop actions. We considered each round played by a particular user as a separate mouse movement session. Figure 2 shows the total number of sessions generated by each participating user, while Figure 3 shows the minimum, maximum and average session counts over all 100 users.

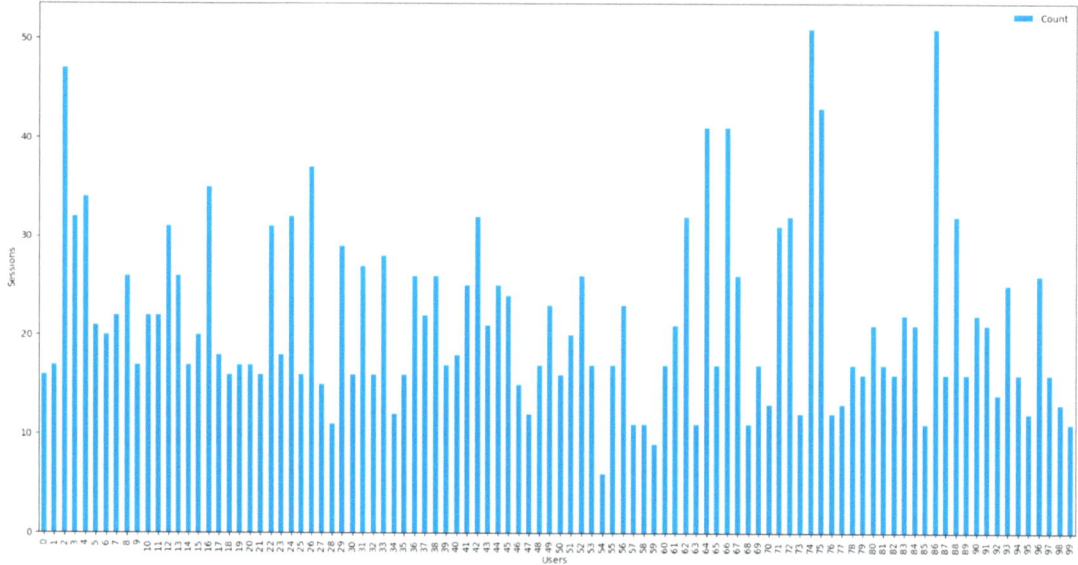

Figure 2. The number of sessions generated by each user.

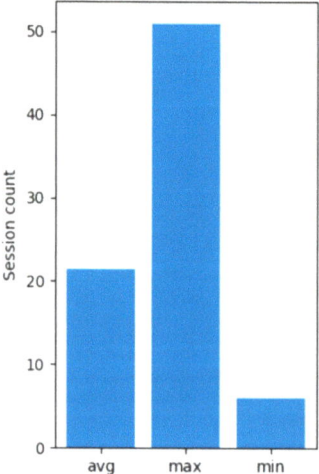

Figure 3. Session status.

4. ReMouse Dataset Analysis

4.1. Sessions Generated by The Same User

In the first stage of our ReMouse dataset study, we focused on analyzing the sessions generated by each individual user in isolation from other users. For the purpose of this analysis, a mouse cursor trajectory of a particular session was modeled by means of two time-dependent variables: (1) 2D coordinates/position of the mouse cursor; (2) speed of mouse cursor. As an illustration, Figure 4 displays the trajectories comprising only the mouse coordinates (i.e., positional information) of session number 3 for ReMouse users 90 to 98.

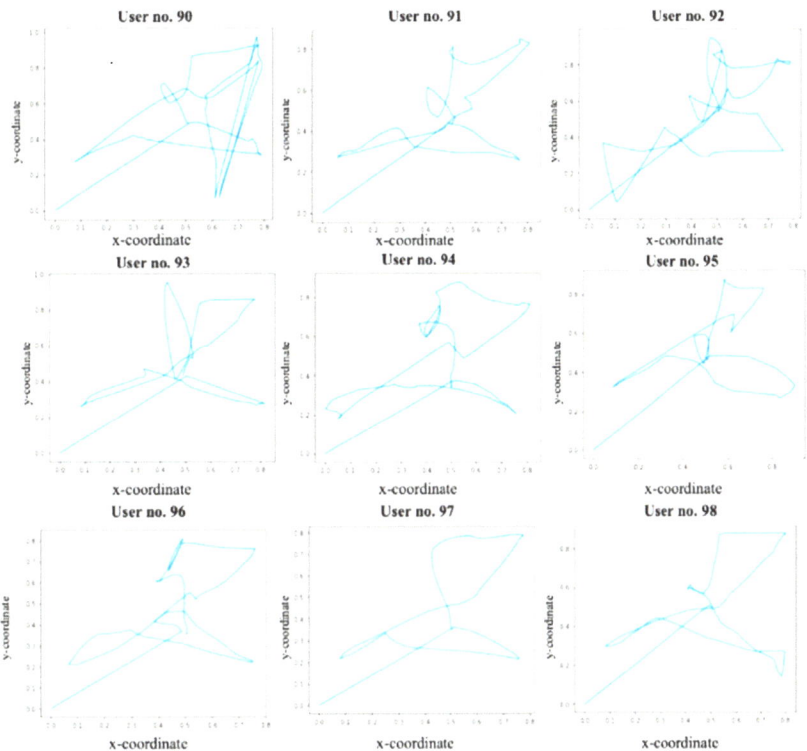

Figure 4. Visual representation of mouse cursor trajectory in the session with order number 3 for users 90 to 98.

Our analysis of single-user sessions led to some interesting observations:

Observation 1.1: It is evident from the collected data that by repeating the same online task over time (i.e., repeating multiple rounds of our 'Catch Me If You Can!' game), each user generally becomes faster and able to complete every subsequent round of the game in a progressively shorter amount of time. These findings are illustrated in Figure 5, which displays the 'time taken' and the 'average mouse movement speed' for user 82 (which is randomly chosen among the 100 participants) across each of the 16 rounds/sessions of the game that this particular user has performed. The same observation is also evident from Figure 6, which shows the dynamic time warping (DTW) distances [35] between the trajectories of subsequent pairs of sessions generated by user 82 (e.g., trajectories of first and second session, second and third session, etc.). As can be seen in Figure 6, the DTW distances between the trajectories of subsequent sessions become closer and shorter as the user keeps repeating the same task.

Note that we opted for the use of the DTW distance metric in our analysis as it has allowed us to measure the distance between two sessions (two time series) of different lengths and different time-wise alignments (DTW re-aligns two feature vector sequences by warping the time axis iteratively until an optimal match between the two sequences is found [35]). Figure 7 provides a closer look into the trajectories of two particular sessions (number 13 and 14) of user 82 and their respective DTW cumulative distance.

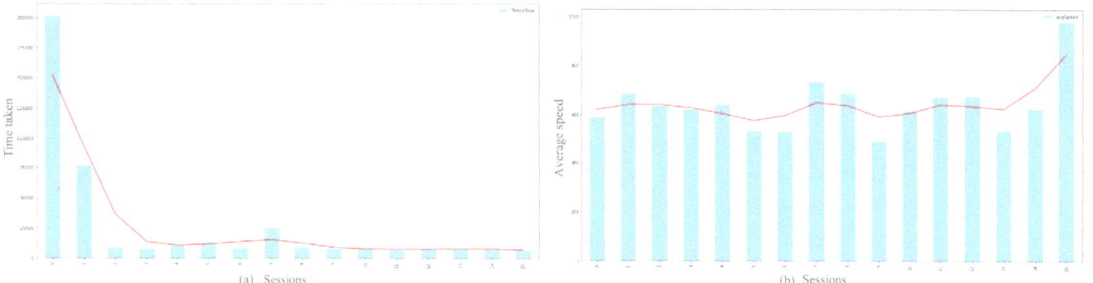

Figure 5. (**a**) Time taken to complete each of 16 conducted sessions for user number 82; (**b**) Average mouse movement speed for each of 16 conducted sessions.

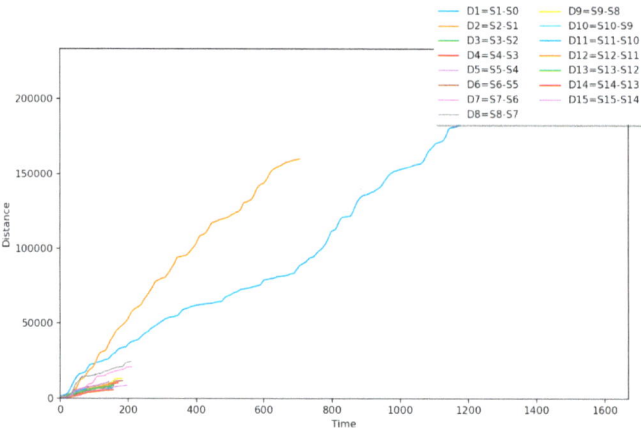

Figure 6. Cumulative difference/distance between subsequent pairs of sessions generated by user 82.

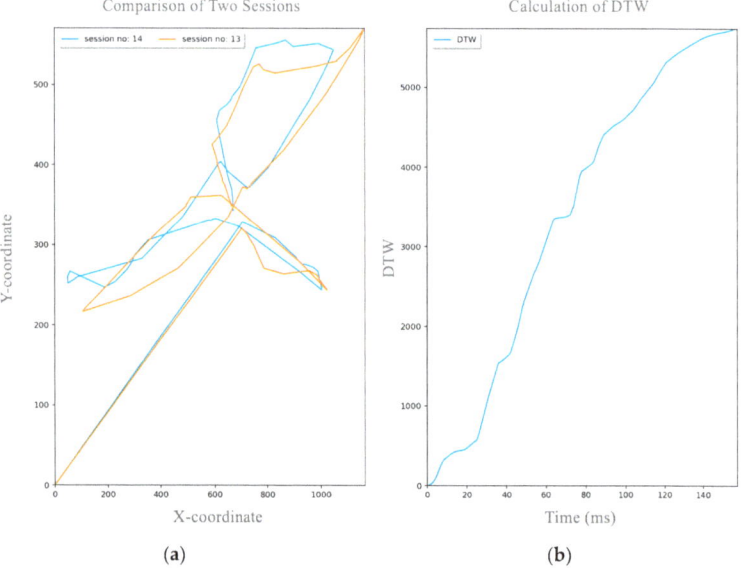

Figure 7. (**a**) Trajectories of sessions 13 and 14 of user 82; (**b**) Cumulative DTW distance between two sessions.

To confirm Observation 1.1, we also deployed simple 'trend line analysis' [36] on the ReMouse dataset. A trend line is a bounding line that captures a trend and rallying patterns in a given dataset. If the slope of the line is a positive value, it indicates the trend is increasing, and a negative value implies that the trend is decreasing. We employed this analysis to discover the trend in 'time taken to complete a session' and 'average mouse speed' in relation to the session order number for each participating user. The average value of the slope in 'time taken to complete a session' trend lines, when calculated across all the users, was 417.0, which is a good indication that with every subsequent session/repetition the users generally spent less time completing the task. On the other hand, the average value of the slope in the 'speed of mouse movement' trend lines, when calculated across all users, was 10.0, which is further proof that users generally became faster in completing a similar online task with every subsequent session/repetition.

Observation 1.2: Even though the repeat sessions generated by each particular user became progressively 'closer' (as illustrated in Figure 6), no user is able to produce two entirely identical consecutive mouse trajectories when repeating the same online task. This observation is illustrated in Table 2, which shows the ids of the two closest consecutive sessions generated by each respective user in the ReMouse dataset when measured using the minimum normalized cumulative DTW distance. Moreover, since the overall cumulative DTW distances will be greater when the sessions are longer—cumulating over time—we normalized the DTW distance values by the time taken to complete each pair of sessions (i.e., the trajectory time-wise length). That way, the time component does not affect the results, and the minimum DTW distances show the actual trajectories' closeness. A closer inspection of the values in Table 2 reveals that user 74 produced the most similar consecutive trajectories in the ReMouse dataset (corresponding to sessions number 39 and 40), with a normalized cumulative DTW distance of 64.23521268 (note that two identical sessions would produce a DTW distance of 0). The graph shown in Figure 8 plots the minimum normalized cumulative DTW distance values from Table 2, confirming Observation 1.2. Figure 9 provides a closer look at the trajectories of sessions 39 and 40 of user 74, as well as their respective normalized cumulative DTW.

Observation 1.3: Through the analysis of ReMouse dataset, we further observed that in the initial sessions the users acted generally more confused, i.e., their cursors exhibited more 'erratic' behavior until the users finally figured out what exactly they were expected to do. However, even in these initial sessions, the mouse speed was not considerably slower than in the later session, which is indicated through a relatively small positive slope value obtained from the 'trend line analysis'.

Table 2. The most similar trajectories generated by each participating user in the ReMouse dataset with their respective DTW values—the minimum DTW normalized cumulative distance between the closest sessions.

Users	Sessions	Min DTW Normalized Cumulative Distance	Users	Sessions	Min DTW Normalized Cumulative Distance
0	7,8	591.6516	50	2,3	303.9826
1	5,6	295.2985	51	4,5	291.6989
2	35,36	147.0755	52	7,8	272.5094
3	13,14	192.1207	53	13,14	196.9675
4	9,10	180.0245	54	2,3	1490.494
5	4,5	398.1191	55	13,14	421.657
6	8,9	272.4871	56	11,12	276.5871
7	19,20	293.7516	57	8,9	1387.489
8	17,18	192.9701	58	8,9	634.1661
9	11,12	345.1108	59	6,7	777.4243
10	5,6	308.2797	60	6,7	174.8066

Table 2. *Cont.*

Users	Sessions	Min DTW Normalized Cumulative Distance	Users	Sessions	Min DTW Normalized Cumulative Distance
11	3,4	572.3161	61	17,18	232.3106
12	2,3	107.556	62	27,28	126.1892
13	21,22	262.7717	63	3,4	1112.61
14	4,5	297.0564	64	33,34	142.0399
15	2,3	287.2074	65	9,10	301.4555
16	9,10	116.766	66	33,34	199.8493
17	10,11	247.4575	67	14,15	137.9862
18	12,13	275.4263	68	3,4	1728.454
19	9,10	371.7259	69	4,5	427.3393
20	7,8	175.7365	70	9,10	1201.285
21	11,12	280.7912	71	17,18	126.8211
22	23,24	127.987	72	16,17	211.9789
23	7,8	343.7548	73	5,6	487.4164
24	28,29	198.9364	**74**	**39,40**	**64.23521**
25	12,13	358.7146	75	24,25	85.11796
26	29,30	204.9529	76	8,9	402.6993
27	11,12	241.8954	77	3,4	623.3006
28	7,8	462.876	78	10,11	412.5679
29	26,27	110.2986	79	11,12	355.0567
30	5,6	210.5634	80	18,19	488.2605
31	11,12	203.5428	81	7,8	315.7737
32	5,6	213.7062	82	13,14	383.0098
33	14,15	258.7817	83	9,10	262.1923
34	8,9	503.8331	84	6,7	275.4376
35	2,3	241.2987	85	8,9	2391.673
36	23,24	210.416	86	48,49	174.3101
37	10,11	305.7957	87	11,12	422.6979
38	23,24	112.3997	88	24,25	113.6169
39	4,5	191.0098	89	7,8	354.2762
40	7,8	429.8543	90	17,18	134.8357
41	17,18	143.9127	91	6,7	299.5449
42	21,22	318.2114	92	5,6	792.4915
43	18,19	226.5839	93	7,8	292.0623
44	4,5	446.748	94	8,9	282.6595
45	6,7	181.1306	95	9,10	432.2253
46	6,7	240.4841	96	23,24	210.416
47	5,6	630.878	97	13,14	261.8753
48	12,13	294.704	98	2,3	753.1881
49	2,3	315.2712	99	8,9	386.572

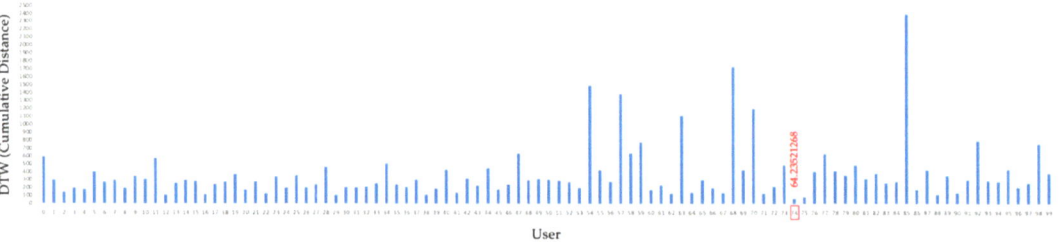

Figure 8. Minimum DTW normalized cumulative distances across sessions of each individual user.

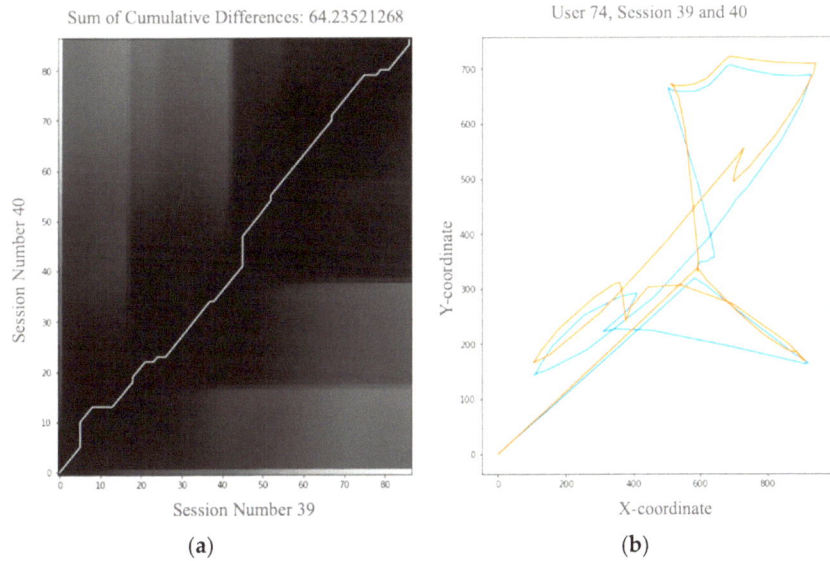

Sum of Cumulative Differences: 64.23521268

User 74, Session 39 and 40

(a)

(b)

Figure 9. (**a**) Sum of cumulative DTW distance value in sessions generated by the same user, user 74; (**b**) Sessions 39 (blue) and 40 (orange) of user 74.

4.2. Sessions Generated by Different User

In the second stage of our ReMouse dataset study, the focus was on the pairwise analysis of sessions generated by different users. The findings of this analysis are summarized below:

Observation 2.1: Different users produced different-looking sessions when completing the same/similar online task.

The validity of this observation was confirmed by comparing all users' sessions in our dataset (i.e., by calculating the cross-user pairwise minimum DTW distance). Table 3 shows the minimum normalized cumulative DTW distance value between two sessions of two distinct users out of all users' sessions. As shown, the most similar trajectories generated by two distinct users are sessions 6 and 29 of users 1 and 2, respectively. The actual DTW distance between these sessions is 21.94, which suggests that, although similar, these two sessions are not identical. This observation can be further generalized, implying that even though sessions generated by two distinct human users while completing the same/similar online task may exhibit a high degree of similarity, they are also likely to be sufficiently distinct from each other.

Table 3. Cross-user pairwise DTW normalized cumulative distance calculation result.

Min DTW	Users	Sessions
21.941833	1 and 2	6 and 29

Observation 2.2: There are no two sessions created by two distinct users that are closer to each other than (any) two sessions created by the same user when completing the same/similar online task.

To confirm this observation, in addition to calculating the distance between sessions generated by different users, we also computed the minimum normalized cumulative DTW distance between ANY two (not just consecutive) sessions generated by the same user in the ReMouse dataset. Table 4 summarizes these results, and it shows that out of the entire ReMouse dataset, user 1 has generated two most similar trajectories (corresponding to sessions number 16 and 28) with a respective distance of 20.376812.

Table 4. Pairwise DTW normalized cumulative distance calculation result—the same user.

Min DTW	Users	Sessions
20.376812	1 and 1	16 and 28

The observations of this section can be further generalized and put in the context of session-replay bots. Namely, the numerical results obtained through the analysis of ReMouse dataset imply that no two sessions (i.e., mouse trajectories) generated on a static web-site—regardless of whether they are generated by the same or two distinct users—can be identical. Based on this, we further hypothesize that only pre-programmed session-replay bots are theoretically able to produce identical browsing sessions (i.e., mouse trajectories). Or, put another way, any occurrence/observation of 'identical' or 'almost identical' browsing sessions (i.e., mouse trajectories) in a web-site should be taken with caution, potentially warranting further investigation for the presence of session-replay bots.

5. Feature Engineering—Preparing ReMouse Dataset for Machine-Learning-Based Analysis

In previous studies on mouse dynamics, researchers have commonly relied on heuristics-based (i.e., manually selected) mouse movement features, such as 2D cursor position, mouse speed, click frequency, etc. The results of our own ReMouse dataset analysis using manually selected features are presented in Section 4. However, some known challenges of manual features selection are: (1) manual feature selection requires in-depth expert knowledge of the specific dataset at hand and the ultimate application environment; (2) there is often a need to fine-tune the number and type of manually selected features for each dataset, which tends to be a time-consuming process; (3) the generalization value of the results obtained using manual feature selection is often questionable. One of the objectives of our work was to analyze the ReMouse dataset by means of advanced machine learning (ML) techniques. However, for the reasons outlined above, we were determined to avoid basing our ML analysis on manually selected features. Additionally, due to the different durations of individual user sessions in the ReMouse dataset, we were facing very heterogeneous 'mouse location' and 'mouse speed' feature vector representations (i.e., the feature vectors representing different sessions were of variable/non-fixed length). Training an ML algorithm using such non-uniform set of feature vectors would have required additional expert-knowledge decision making and the manual re-engineering of input data.

As an alternative to manual feature selection and feature vector re-engineering, and inspired by works [2,22], we pursued a novel approach to representing individual user sessions in the ReMouse dataset. Namely, in this part of our analysis, rather than manually extracting features to describe a user's unique mouse behavior characteristics, we mapped the mouse trajectories into pictures. In order to conduct automated feature extraction on image representations of user sessions from the ReMouse dataset, we deployed a pre-trained deep learning model—VGG16 [37]. In particular, we used the VGG16 library implemented in Keras [38]. VGG16 is a convolutional neural network model well known for its ability to perform very-high-accuracy feature extraction on image datasets [39]. The reason why we resorted to deploying a pre-trained VGG16 model is the fact that working with a 'from-scratch' convolutional neural network may require days of training and millions of images to achieve a high accuracy in real-world applications [40] (from the perspective of image processing, our ReMouse dataset is of relatively small size, containing the sessions of 'only' 100 users). For the purposes of our research, we acquired the generic pre-trained VGG16 model from [38] and retrained it on our own image representations of web sessions from the ReMouse dataset (the process of re-using the weights from a pre-trained model is called 'Transfer Learning' [41]). The original VGG16 model used in our work was trained on standard computer vision benchmark datasets, including ImageNet [42].

Using VGG16, we ended up with each image (i.e., user session) being represented as a vector with 1000 features [43]. To further reduce the number of features identified with VGG16, next, we used principal component analysis (PCA) [44]. PCA produced 100 eigenvectors over the VGG16 feature space. Nevertheless, as shown in Figure 10, not all of the 100 identified PCA eigenvectors are of the same significance, as 95% of data variance occurs over the first 57 eigenvectors. Thus, for the purpose of our ML-based analysis (as discussed in the next section) we opted to map our original ReMouse dataset into a set of feature vectors over the first 57 most significant PCA eigenvectors.

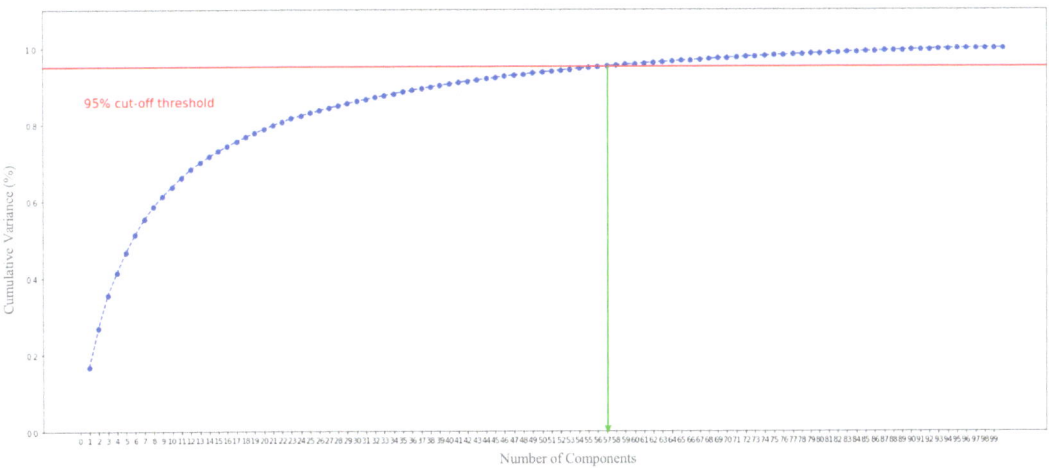

Figure 10. The number of components needed to explain the variance.

6. ML-Based Analysis of ReMouse Dataset: Focusing on Sessions Generated by Different Users

The objective of our ML-based analysis of the curated image-based ReMouse dataset (as explained in Section 5) was to investigate the (dis)similarities between comparable (same-order number) web sessions generated by different users. We specifically decided to look at the third session generated by each of the 100 participating ReMouse users (forming one data subset, which we will refer to as 'ReMouse Subset-3' in the reminder of this article), as well as the fifth session generated by each of the 100 participating ReMouse users (forming the second data subset, which we will refer to as 'ReMouse Subset-5'). We opted to look at the third and fifth sessions due to our observation that for most ReMouse users some of the originally exhibited 'erratic' mouse behavior largely disappears after the first two rounds/repetitions of the 'Catch Me If You Can!' game (see Section 3). In other words, the user behavior and mouse trajectory in these sessions are generally 'stable' and thus likely to produce more accurate results. To conduct the cross-user session (dis)similarity analysis, we specifically decided to deploy unsupervised ML learning, including the Self-Organizing Map (SOM) and several unsupervised clustering ML algorithms.

The SOM algorithm is typically used to build a topology-preserving mapping of high-dimensional input data to 2D or 3D space, where the similarity of individual input points can be assessed in more intuitive (visual and non-visual) ways. Unsupervised clustering is known for its ability to decompose a dataset into subgroups based on their similarity so that data points in the same cluster are more closely related to each other than data points in different clusters [45].

According to our knowledge, this is the first research study that has looked into the use of unsupervised clustering on the image representation of user sessions for the purpose of cross-user session (dis)similarity analysis. Additionally, the only other work that has pursued image-based web-session representation and analysis [22] was specifically concerned with the problem of malicious web-bot detection through session classification, and thus ultimately opted for the use of supervised deep learning—as opposed to the question of session similarity, which is the focus of our work and requires the use of unsupervised techniques.

6.1. Data Analysis Using SOM Map

The Self-Organizing Map (SOM) algorithm [46] is generally used to create a 2D topology-preserving and density-mapping representation of a multi-dimensional input (i.e., training) dataset. The topology preservation property implies that if two input points end up firing nearby nodes in the trained SOM map during the deployment phase then the two points are relatively close to each other (i.e., are similar) in the original input space. On the other hand, the density-mapping property means that the regions of high-input-dataset density are mapped to SOM regions with more neurons.

For the purposes of our research, we trained two 15-by-15-sized SOM maps (experimentally), one using the ReMouse Subset-3 and the other using ReMouse Subset-5. We used the SOM implementation from the Python SOMPY package [47], which has a structure similar to *somtoolbox* in MATLAB. In terms of functionalities, the package uses only batch training (which is faster than online training) and *sklearn* or random initialization.

The heatmaps generated on each of the two trained SOM maps are shown in Figures 11a and 11b, respectively. An SOM heatmap is produced by displaying how many of the training inputs are associated with each node in the trained SOM map [48]. It is very evident from the two heatmaps that there are no actual (i.e., distinguishable) clusters in either ReMouse Subset-3 or ReMouse Subset-5—as most neurons are 'fired' by no/one single-input point, and only a handful of neurons are fired by two or more (distinct) input points. It should also be noted that the neurons with an input-data membership of two or more are largely distributed at the edges of the respective SOM maps, which suggests that the actual 'closeness' of the input points that fire these neurons may not be significant. Border neurons in an SOM map do not 'stretch out' during the training process as much as they should, and as a result they tend to 'attract' many potentially very different/distant points located on the 'outside' of the SOM border. This phenomenon in known in the literature as the 'SOM border effect' [49].

(a)   (b)

Figure 11. Users' data points map: (**a**) session number 3; (**b**) session number 5.

From a practical point of view, that such a disperse distribution of data points form ReMouse Subset-3 and ReMouse Subset-5 (as shown in Figure 11a,b) is a clear indication that individual users—when performing the same general online task—are likely to end up producing very different/distinct mouse trajectories. When put in the context of session-replay bots, this further suggests that any session/trajectory that shows a significant similarity with an already-observed session/trajectory should be flagged as potentially 'malicious', since (according to our results) the likelihood that both of such sessions are genuinely human is rather small.

As part of our future work, we plan to deploy different variants of the SOM algorithm (e.g., growing SOM map [50] and evolving SOM algorithm [51]) in order to further address the issue of the 'border effect' observed in our dataset.

6.2. Data Analysis Using Unsupervised Clustering Techniques

In order to validate our initial findings obtained by means of SOM heatmaps, we further performed an unsupervised clustering of ReMouse Subset-3 and ReMouse Subset-5 using the SOM clustering [47] (the python package provides an additional feature which enables automated identification of the main clusters within the formed map using K-means clustering algorithm), K-means clustering [52], and agglomerative clustering [53] algorithms.

An important result coming out of this stage of our research is obtaining the Silhouette and Davies–Bouldin scores, which were obtained by performing clustering on the two data subsets with a gradually increasing number of assumed clusters [54,55]. The Silhouette score measures how similar an object is to its own cluster (cohesion) compared with other clusters (separation). A higher Silhouette value implies that points are well matched to their own cluster and poorly matched to neighboring clusters. The Davies–Bouldin score is the average similarity measure of each cluster with its most similar cluster. Clusters that are farther apart and less dispersed will result in a higher Davies–Bouldin score.

Figures 12 and 13 depict the Silhouette and Davies–Bouldin score obtained using K-means clustering algorithms. Similar results have been obtained with the other two clustering algorithms. In the cases of all three algorithms, the highest values of the two scores are recorded for k = 2, suggesting that the optimal number of clusters is two. Figures 14–16 provide 2D and 3D visualizations of the actual clustering results obtained on ReMouse Subset-3 and ReMouse Subset-5 using the three selected clustering algorithms and assuming k = 2. All three figures provide clear evidence that, even under the optimal number of clusters (k = 2), the input data is pretty spread out throughout the input space, and many points that formally belonging to the same cluster are at a significant distance from each other. This further supports our earlier hypothesis that session trajectories generated by different users while completing the same online task are sufficiently distinguishable from each other.

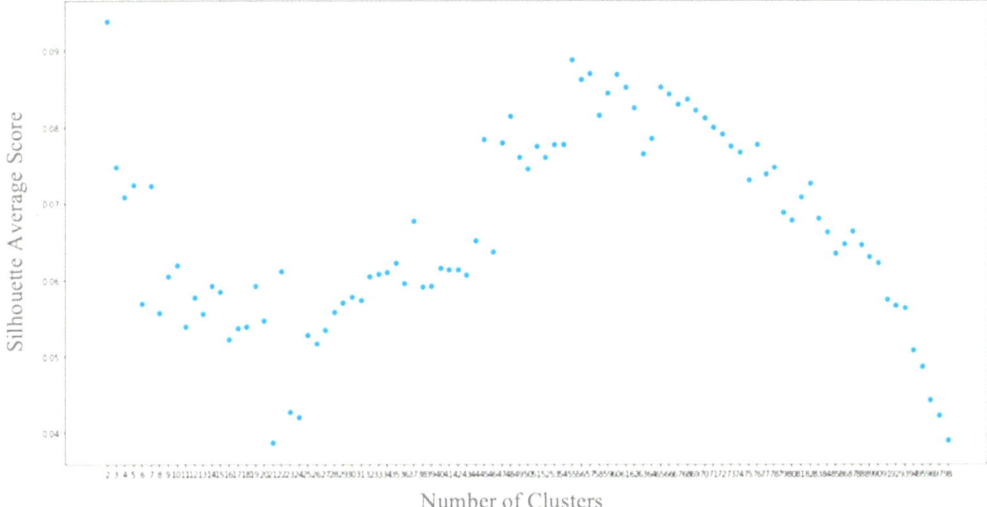

Figure 12. Silhouette average score.

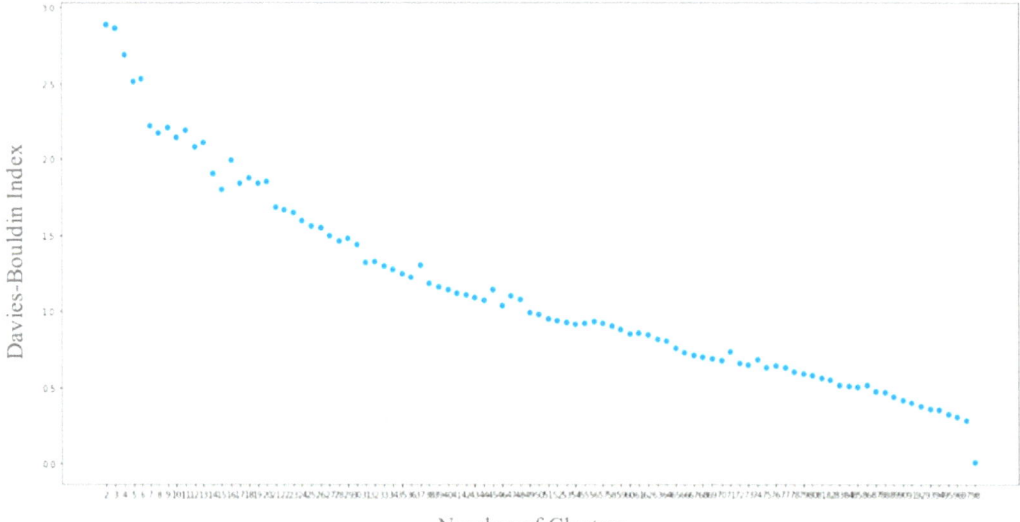

Figure 13. Davies–Bouldin index.

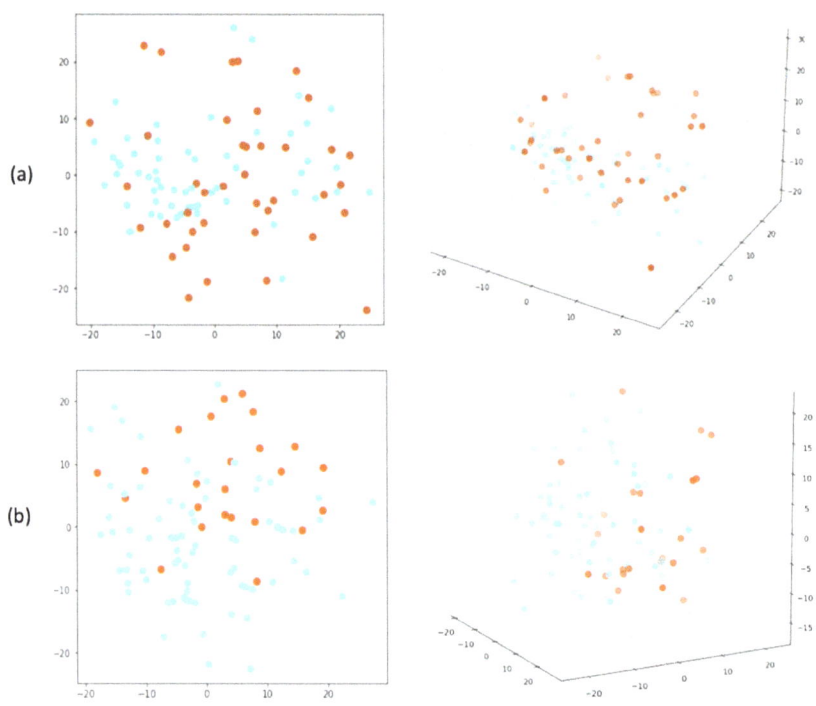

Figure 14. Unsupervised clustering visualization using SOM: (**a**) session number 3 and (**b**) session number 5 of all users.

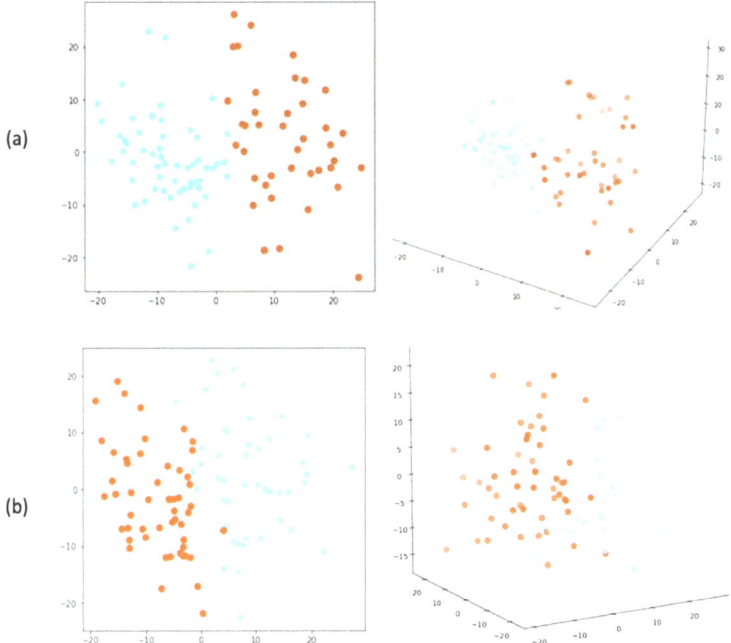

Figure 15. Unsupervised clustering visualization using K-means clustering algorithm, (**a**) session number 3 and (**b**) session number 5 of all users.

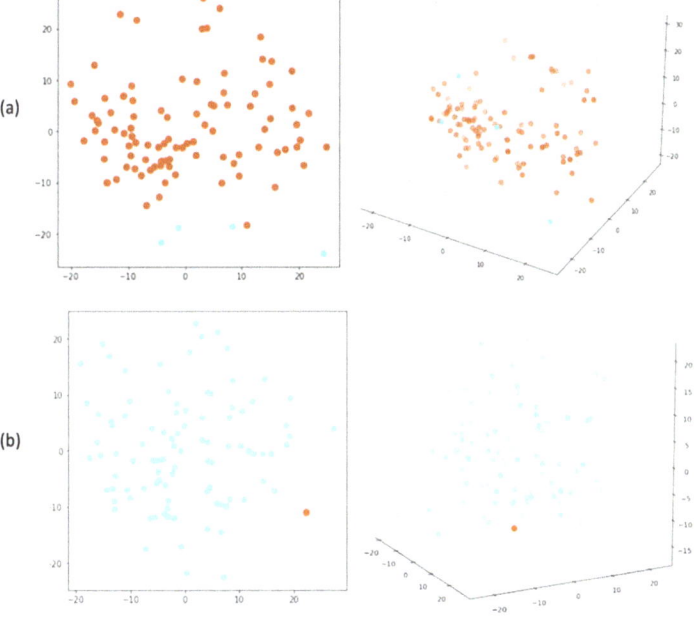

Figure 16. Unsupervised clustering visualization using agglomerative clustering algorithm, (**a**) session number 3 and (**b**) session number 5 of all users.

7. Conclusions and Future Work

In this work, we presented an in-depth analysis of our novel real-world mouse dynamics dataset, the ReMouse dataset. We began by reviewing the literature that investigated mouse dynamics in the context of user authentication and bot detection. We also provided a summary of several publicly available mouse dynamics datasets. We then analyzed the ReMouse dataset using statistical and advanced ML-based methods, including deep and unsupervised neural learning.

In the first stage of the preliminary analysis using statistical methods, we focused on analyzing the sessions generated by each individual user in isolation from other users. Second, the focus was on the pairwise analysis of sessions generated by different users. Based on the preliminary analysis of our novel ReMouse dataset, we concluded that although sessions generated by genuine human users are relatively similar to each other, there always exist some minimum distinguishable differences between them. We showed that sessions whose 'difference' from each other is below the determined threshold should potentially be flagged as 'replay' sessions generated by session-replay bots.

Considering the fact that the generalization value of the results obtained using manual feature selection is often questionable, we then investigated the (dis)similarities between comparable (same-order number) web sessions generated by different users by means of advanced machine learning techniques. The results further supported our earlier hypothesis that session trajectories generated by different users while completing the same online task are sufficiently distinguishable from each other.

According to our knowledge, the ReMouse dataset is the first publicly available mouse dynamics dataset containing repeat sessions generated by the same human user(s). As such, this dataset can be a very valuable resource for research studies that aim to improve our understanding of (human) user behavior during repetitive interactions with the same web-site, with the ultimate goal of developing effective techniques for the detection of, and defense against, sessions-replay bots.

We believe that the ReMouse dataset contains enough statistical data to facilitate unbiased and high-quality research in the above-mentioned research areas. However, we also would like to point out a few possible, though minor, limitations of our dataset and work. One potential limitation of our dataset/work can be related to the platform we used to collect the data, MTurk. Although MTurk workers are generally pretty diverse when it comes to their place of residence or profession, they tend to be less diverse in terms of their age, education, computer-use proficiency, etc. [56]. This can complicate how data can be interpreted, affecting the reliable and validity of our conclusions, as well as the generalizability of such results.

Nevertheless, more importantly, this study is the first of its kind, so it effectively demonstrates the importance of filling the literature gaps, highlighting the need for further development in the area of our study. This work aims to bring more attention to the problems/threats posed by session-replay web bots, which carry out the most advanced types of malicious web bot attacks. Therefore, we invite other researchers to work alongside us. We made some progress in providing the data and tools and hope to facilitate further studies by other researchers.

For future work, we plan to extend our image-based ML analysis of the ReMouse dataset by considering other aspects of mouse dynamics rather than just trajectory (e.g., by additionally embedding the information on time, mouse velocity and click events into the image representation of a user session). We are also currently working on incorporating the malicious sessions generated by actual session-replay bots into the ReMouse dataset. Finally, we plan to experiment with different variants of the SOM algorithm (e.g., growing an SOM map and evolving the SOM algorithm) in order to further address the issue of the 'border effect', which has been observed in our preliminary analysis.

Author Contributions: Conceptualization, S.S. and N.V.; methodology, S.S.; validation, S.S. and N.V.; writing—original draft preparation, S.S.; writing—review and editing, S.S. and N.V.; supervision, N.V.; project administration, N.V. All authors have read and agreed to the published version of the manuscript.

Funding: This research received no external funding.

Institutional Review Board Statement: The study was conducted in accordance with the Declaration of Helsinki, and approved by the Institutional Review Board (OFFICE OF RESEARCH ETHICS (ORE)) of York University (certificate #: e2022-374 issued on 4 August 2022).

Informed Consent Statement: Informed consent was obtained from all subjects involved in the study.

Data Availability Statement: Our novel ReMouse dataset presented in this study is openly available in the IEEE Dataport at https://dx.doi.org/10.21227/jkmt-za31, accessed on 25 February 2023.

Conflicts of Interest: The authors declare no conflict of interest.

References

1. Maureen. What Is Behavioral Biometric Authentication? 1Kosmos. 2022. Available online: https://www.1kosmos.com/biometric-authentication/what-is-behavioral-biometrics-authentication/ (accessed on 25 February 2023).
2. Thomas, P.A.; Mathew, K.P. A Broad Review on Non-Intrusive Active User Authentication in Biometrics. *J. Ambient. Intell. Human Comput.* **2023**, *14*, 339–360. [CrossRef] [PubMed]
3. Leiva, L.A.; Arapakis, I.; Iordanou, C. My Mouse, My Rules: Privacy Issues of Behavioral User Profiling via Mouse Tracking. In Proceedings of the 2021 Conference on Human Information Interaction and Retrieval, 51–61. CHIIR '21, Canberra, ACT, Australia, 14–19 March 2021; Association for Computing Machiner: New York, NY, USA, 2021. [CrossRef]
4. Kaklauskas, A. Web-based Biometric Computer Mouse Advisory System to Analyze a User's Emotions and Work Productivity. In *Biometric and Intelligent Decision Making Support*; Kaklauskas, A., Ed.; Intelligent Systems Reference Library; Springer International Publishing: Cham, Switzerland, 2014; Volume 81, pp. 137–173. [CrossRef]
5. Katerina, T.; Nicolaos, P. Mouse behavioral patterns and keystroke dynamics in End-User Development: What can they tell us about users' behavioral attributes? *Comput. Hum. Behav.* **2018**, *83*, 288–305. [CrossRef]
6. Rahman, R.U.; Tomar, D.S. Threats of price scraping on e-commerce websites: Attack model and its detection using neural network. *J. Comput. Virol. Hacking Tech.* **2020**, *17*, 75–89. [CrossRef]
7. Nick, R. How Attackers Use Request Bots to Bypass Your Bot Mitigation Solution. Security Boulevard (Blog). 2021. Available online: https://securityboulevard.com/2021/07/how-attackers-use-request-bots-to-bypass-your-bot-mitigation-solution/ (accessed on 14 June 2022).
8. Chu, Z.; Gianvecchio, S.; Wang, H. Bot or Human? A Behavior-Based Online Bot Detection System. In *From Database to Cyber Security: Essays Dedicated to Sushil Jajodia on the Occasion of His 70th Birthday*; Pierangela, S., Indrajit, R., Indrakshi, R., Eds.; Lecture Notes in Computer Science; Springer International Publishing: Cham, Switzerland, 2018; pp. 432–449. [CrossRef]
9. Sadeghpour, S.; Vlajic, N. *ReMouse-Mouse Dynamic Dataset*; IEEE: New York, NY, USA, 2022; Available online: https://ieee-dataport.org/documents/remouse-mouse-dynamic-dataset (accessed on 24 August 2022).
10. Jaiswal, A.K.; Tiwari, P.; Hossain, M.S. Predicting users' behavior using mouse movement information: An information foraging theory perspective. *Neural Comput. Appl.* **2020**, 1–14. [CrossRef]
11. Kirsh, I.; Joy, M. Exploring Pointer Assisted Reading (PAR): Using Mouse Movements to Analyze Web Users' Reading Behaviors and Patterns. In *HCI International 2020-Late Breaking Papers: Multimodality and Intelligence*; Constantine, S., Masaaki, K., Helmut, D., Lauren, R.-J., Eds.; Lecture Notes in Computer Science; Springer International Publishing: Cham, Switzerland, 2020; pp. 156–173. [CrossRef]
12. Chong, P.; Elovici, Y.; Binder, A. User Authentication Based on Mouse Dynamics Using Deep Neural Networks: A Comprehensive Study. *IEEE Trans. Inf. Forensics Secur.* **2019**, *15*, 1086–1101. [CrossRef]
13. Hu, T.; Niu, W.; Zhang, X.; Liu, X.; Lu, J.; Liu, Y. An Insider Threat Detection Approach Based on Mouse Dynamics and Deep Learning. *Secur. Commun. Netw.* **2019**, *2019*, 1–12. [CrossRef]
14. Kaixin, W.; Liu, H.; Wang, B.; Hu, S.; Song, J. A User Authentication and Identification Model Based on Mouse Dynamics. In Proceedings of the 6th International Conference on Information Engineering, online, 19–20 November 2022; 2017; pp. 1–6.
15. Yildirim, M.; Anarim, E. Novel Feature Extraction Methods for Authentication via Mouse Dynamics with Semi-Supervised Learning. In Proceedings of the 2019 Innovations in Intelligent Systems and Applications Conference (ASYU), Izmir, Turkey, 31 October–2 November 2019; 2020; pp. 1–6. [CrossRef]
16. Antal, M.; Fejer, N.; Buza, K. SapiMouse: Mouse Dynamics-based User Authentication Using Deep Feature Learning. In Proceedings of the 2021 IEEE 15th International Symposium on Applied Computational Intelligence and Informatics (SACI), Timisoara, Romania, 19–21 May 2021; pp. 61–66. [CrossRef]

17. Antal, M.; Denes-Fazakas, L. User Verification Based on Mouse Dynamics: A Comparison of Public Data Sets. In Proceedings of the 2019 IEEE 13th International Symposium on Applied Computational Intelligence and Informatics (SACI), Timisoara, Romania, 23–31 May 2019; pp. 143–148. [CrossRef]
18. Antal, M.; Fejér, N. Mouse dynamics based user recognition using deep learning. *Acta Univ. Sapientiae Inform.* **2020**, *12*, 39–50. [CrossRef]
19. Yildirim, M.; Anarim, E. Mitigating insider threat by profiling users based on mouse usage pattern: Ensemble learning and frequency domain analysis. *Int. J. Inf. Secur.* **2021**, *21*, 239–251. [CrossRef]
20. Acien, A.; Morales, A.; Fierrez, J.; Vera-Rodriguez, R. BeCAPTCHA-Mouse: Synthetic mouse trajectories and improved bot detection. *Pattern Recognit.* **2022**, *127*, 108643. [CrossRef]
21. Iliou, C.; Kostoulas, T.; Tsikrika, T.; Katos, V.; Vrochidis, S.; Kompatsiaris, I. Detection of Advanced Web Bots by Combining Web Logs with Mouse Behavioural Biometrics. *Digit. Threat. Res. Pract.* **2021**, *2*, 1–26. [CrossRef]
22. Wei, A.; Zhao, Y.; Cai, Z. A Deep Learning Approach to Web Bot Detection Using Mouse Behavioral Biometrics. In *Biometric Recognition*; Zhenan, S., Ran, H., Jianjiang, F., Shiguang, S., Zhenhua, G., Eds.; Lecture Notes in Computer Science; Springer International Publishing: Cham, Switzerland, 2019; pp. 388–395. [CrossRef]
23. Rahman, R.U.; Tomar, D.S. New biostatistics features for detecting web bot activity on web applications. *Comput. Secur.* **2020**, *97*, 102001. [CrossRef]
24. Chuda, D.; Peter, K.; Jozef, T. Mouse Clicks Can Recognize Web Page Visitors! In Proceedings of the 24th International Conference on World Wide Web, Florence, Italy, 18–22 May 2015; pp. 21–22.
25. Niu, H.; Chen, J.; Zhang, Z.; Cai, Z. Mouse Dynamics Based Bot Detection Using Sequence Learning. In *Biometric Recognition*; Jianjiang, F., Junping, Z., Manhua, L., Yuchun, F., Eds.; Lecture Notes in Computer Science; Springer International Publishing: Cham, Switzerland, 2021; pp. 49–56. [CrossRef]
26. Rahman, R.U.; Tomar, D.S. A new web forensic framework for bot crime investigation. *Forensic Sci. Int. Digit. Investig.* **2020**, *33*, 300943. [CrossRef]
27. Solano, J.; Lopez, C.; Esteban, R.; Alejandra, C.; Lizzy, T.; Martin, O. SCRAP: Synthetically Composed Replay Attacks vs. Adversarial Machine Learning Attacks against Mouse-Based Biometric Authentication. In Proceedings of the 13th ACM Workshop on Artificial Intelligence and Security, Virtual Event, USA, 13 November 2020; pp. 37–47.
28. Fülöp, Á.; Kovács, L.; Kurics, T.; Windhager-Pokol, E. Balabit Mouse Dynamics Challenge Data Set. 2016. Available online: https://github.com/balabit/Mouse-Dynamics-Challenge (accessed on 14 June 2022).
29. Kılıç, A.A.; Yıldırım, M.; Anarım, E. Bogazici mouse dynamics dataset. *Data Brief* **2021**, *36*, 107094. [CrossRef] [PubMed]
30. Leiva, L.A.; Arapakis, I. The Attentive Cursor Dataset. *Front. Hum. Neurosci.* **2020**, *14*, 565664. [CrossRef]
31. Antal, M. Sapimouse. Python. 2021. Available online: https://github.com/margitantal68/sapimouse (accessed on 14 June 2022).
32. Shen, C.; Cai, Z.; Guan, X. Continuous authentication for mouse dynamics: A pattern-growth approach. In Proceedings of the IEEE/IFIP International Conference on Dependable Systems and Networks (DSN 2012), Boston, MA, USA, 25–28 June 2012; pp. 1–12. [CrossRef]
33. Karim, M. Hasanuzzaman A Study on Mouse Movement Features to Identify User. *Sci. Res. J.* **2020**, *8*, 77–82. [CrossRef]
34. Django REST Framework. 2011. Available online: https://www.django-rest-framework.org/ (accessed on 14 June 2022).
35. INFORMS. A Measure of Distance between Time Series: Dynamic Time Warping. INFORMS. 2022. Available online: https://www.informs.org/Publications/OR-MS-Tomorrow/A-measure-of-distance-between-time-series-Dynamic-Time-Warping (accessed on 21 June 2022).
36. Morse, G. Programmatic Identification of Support/Resistance Trend Lines with Python. Medium. 2019. Available online: https://towardsdatascience.com/programmatic-identification-of-support-resistance-trend-lines-with-python-d797a4a90530 (accessed on 21 June 2022).
37. Simonyan, K.; Andrew, Z. Very Deep Convolutional Networks for Large-Scale Image Recognition. *arXiv* **2014**, arXiv:1409.1556. [CrossRef]
38. Keras-Applications/Vgg16.Py at Master Keras-Team/Keras-Applications. 2020. GitHub. Available online: https://github.com/keras-team/keras-applications (accessed on 21 June 2022).
39. Liu, F.; Wang, Y.; Wang, F.-C.; Zhang, Y.-Z.; Lin, J. Intelligent and Secure Content-Based Image Retrieval for Mobile Users. *IEEE Access* **2019**, *7*, 119209–119222. [CrossRef]
40. Hands-on Transfer Learning with Keras and the VGG16 Model. Available online: https://www.learndatasci.com/tutorials/hands-on-transfer-learning-keras/ (accessed on 21 June 2022).
41. Brownlee, J. Transfer Learning in Keras with Computer Vision Models. Machine Learning Mastery (Blog). 2019. Available online: https://machinelearningmastery.com/how-to-use-transfer-learning-when-developing-convolutional-neural-network-models/ (accessed on 21 June 2022).
42. Deng, J.; Dong, W.; Socher, R.; Li, L.-J.; Li, K.; Fei-Fei, L. ImageNet: A large-scale hierarchical image database. In Proceedings of the 2009 IEEE Conference on Computer Vision and Pattern Recognition, Miami, FL, USA, 20–25 June 2009; pp. 248–255. [CrossRef]
43. Keras, T. Keras Documentation: Keras Applications. 21 June 2022. Available online: https://keras.io/api/applications/#vgg16 (accessed on 25 February 2023).

44. Cunningham, P. Dimension Reduction. In *Machine Learning Techniques for Multimedia: Case Studies on Organization and Retrieval, Matthieu Cord and Pádraig Cunningham*; Cognitive Technologies; Springer: Berlin/Heidelberg, Germany, 2008; pp. 91–112. [CrossRef]
45. Salgado, C.M.; Vieira, S.M. Machine Learning for Patient Stratification and Classification Part 2: Unsupervised Learning with Clustering. In *Leveraging Data Science for Global Health*; Leo Anthony, C., Maimuna, S.M., Patricia, O., Juan Sebastian, O., Kenneth, E.P., Melek., S., Eds.; Springer International Publishing: Cham, Switzerland, 2020; pp. 151–168. [CrossRef]
46. Penn, B.S. Using self-organizing maps to visualize high-dimensional data. *Comput. Geosci.* **2005**, *31*, 531–544. [CrossRef]
47. Moosavi, V. Sevamoo/SOMPY. Jupyter Notebook. 2014. Available online: https://github.com/sevamoo/SOMPY (accessed on 21 June 2022).
48. Gupta, R. Deeper Dive into Self-Organizing Maps (SOMs). Water Programming: A Collaborative Research Blog (Blog). 2020. Available online: https://waterprogramming.wordpress.com/2020/07/20/deeper-dive-into-self-organizing-maps-soms/ (accessed on 21 June 2022).
49. Marzouki, K.; Takeshi, Y. Novel Algorithm for Eliminating Folding Effect in Standard SOM. In *ESANN*; Citeseer: Princeton, NJ, USA, 2005; pp. 563–570.
50. Dittenbach, M.; Dieter, M.; Andreas, R. The Growing Hierarchical Self-Organizing Map. In Proceedings of the IEEE-INNS-ENNS International Joint Conference on Neural Networks. IJCNN 2000. Neural Computing: New Challenges and Perspectives for the New Millennium, Como, Italy, 27 July 2000; IEEE: Piscataway, NJ, USA, 2000; pp. 15–19.
51. Deng, D.; Kasabov, N. On-line pattern analysis by evolving self-organizing maps. *Neurocomputing* **2003**, *51*, 87–103. [CrossRef]
52. Sklearn.Cluster.KMeans. Scikit-Learn. Available online: https://scikit-learn/stable/modules/generated/sklearn.cluster.KMeans.html (accessed on 22 June 2022).
53. Sklearn.Cluster.AgglomerativeClustering. Scikit-Learn. Available online: https://scikit-learn/stable/modules/generated/sklearn.cluster.AgglomerativeClustering.html (accessed on 21 June 2022).
54. Davies, D.L.; Bouldin, D.W. A Cluster Separation Measure. *IEEE Trans. Pattern Anal. Mach. Intell.* **1979**, *2*, 224–227. [CrossRef]
55. Georgios, D. Geodra/Articles. Jupyter Notebook. 2019. Available online: https://github.com/geodra/Articles/blob/85a4d13e060d45129af7b62174ea28619f4d9cf8/Davies-Bouldin%20Index%20vs%20Silhouette%20Analysis%20vs%20Elbow%20Method%20Selecting%20the%20optimal%20number%20of%20clusters%20for%20KMeans%20clustering.ipynb (accessed on 22 June 2022).
56. Aguinis, H.; Villamor, I.; Ramani, R.S. MTurk Research: Review and Recommendations. *J. Manag.* **2020**, *47*, 823–837. [CrossRef]

Journal of
Cybersecurity and Privacy

MDPI

Article

Detection of SQL Injection Attack Using Machine Learning Techniques: A Systematic Literature Review

Maha Alghawazi, Daniyal Alghazzawi and Suaad Alarifi *

Information Systems Department, Faculty of Computing and Information Technology, King Abdulaziz University, Jeddah 80200, Saudi Arabia
* Correspondence: salarifi@kau.edu.sa

Abstract: An SQL injection attack, usually occur when the attacker(s) modify, delete, read, and copy data from database servers and are among the most damaging of web application attacks. A successful SQL injection attack can affect all aspects of security, including confidentiality, integrity, and data availability. SQL (structured query language) is used to represent queries to database management systems. Detection and deterrence of SQL injection attacks, for which techniques from different areas can be applied to improve the detect ability of the attack, is not a new area of research but it is still relevant. Artificial intelligence and machine learning techniques have been tested and used to control SQL injection attacks, showing promising results. The main contribution of this paper is to cover relevant work related to different machine learning and deep learning models used to detect SQL injection attacks. With this systematic review, we aims to keep researchers up-to-date and contribute to the understanding of the intersection between SQL injection attacks and the artificial intelligence field.

Keywords: SQL injection; machine learning; deep learning; adversarial attacks

Citation: Alghawazi, M.; Alghazzawi, D.; Alarifi, S. Detection of SQL Injection Attack Using Machine Learning Techniques: A Systematic Literature Review. *J. Cybersecur. Priv.* **2022**, *2*, 764–777. https://doi.org/10.3390/jcp2040039

Academic Editor: Marina L. Gavrilova

Received: 31 July 2022
Accepted: 14 September 2022
Published: 20 September 2022

Publisher's Note: MDPI stays neutral with regard to jurisdictional claims in published maps and institutional affiliations.

1. Introduction

Most cyber-physical system (CPS) applications are safety-critical; misbehavior caused by random failures or cyber-attacks can considerably restrict their growth. Thus, it is important to protect CPS from being damaged in this way [1]. Current security solutions have been well-integrated into many networked systems including the use of middle boxes, such as antivirus protection, firewall, and intrusion detection systems (IDS). A firewall controls network traffic based on the source or destination address. It alters network traffic according to the firewall rules. Firewalls are also limited to their knowledge of the hosts receiving the content and the amount of state available. An IDS is a type of security tool that scans the system for suspicious activity, monitors the network traffic, and alerts the system or network administrator [2]. In this context, a number of frameworks and mechanisms have been suggested in recent papers.

In this paper, we have considered SQL injection attacks that target the HTTP/HTTPS protocol, which aim to pass through the web application firewall (WAF) and obtain an unauthorized access to proprietary data. SQL injection belongs to the injection family of web attacks, wherein an attacker inserts inputs into a system to execute malicious statements. The victim system is usually not ready to process this input, typically resulting in data leakage and/or granting of unauthorized access to the attacker; in this case, the attacker can access and/or modify the data, affecting all aspects of security, including confidentiality, integrity, and data availability [3].

In an SQL injection, the attacker inserts an SQL statement into an exchange between a client and database server [3]. SQL (structured query language) is used to represent queries to database management systems (DBMSs). The maliciously injected SQL statement is designed to extract or modify data from the database server. A successful injection can result in authentication and bypass and changes to the database by inserting, modifying, and/or deleting data, causing data loss and/or destruction of the entire database. Furthermore, such an attack could overrun and execute commands on the hosted operating system, typically leading to more serious consequences [4].

Thus, SQL injection attacks present aserious threats to organizations. A variety of research has been undertaken to address this threat, presenting various artificial intelligence (AI)techniques for detection of SQL injection attacks using machine learning and deep learning models [5]. AI techniques to facilitate the detection of threats are usually implemented via learning from historical data representing an attack and/or normal data. Historical data are useful for learning, in order to recognize patterns of attacks, understanding detected traffic, and even predicting future attacks before they occur [6].

SQL injection attackers and defenders must understand how SQL language works to know how it can be misused [3]. To extract data from a database or modify the data, queries must be written using SQL language and they must follow a standard syntax, such as:

"SELECT * FROM books WHERE author = 'MAHA'"

The above query will return all books authored by MAHA. Queries are submitted to the DBMS and are usually written through a web browser. For the query to be transmitted to the database server through the web browser, it has to be encoded through a long URL string, such as: http://www.xyz_website.com?QUERY=SELECT%20*%20FROM%20 books%20WHERE%20author=7453.

What if the attacker adds to the previous SQL query? For example:

"SELECT * FROM books WHERE author = 'MAHA' OR '1' = '1'"

As the statement 1 = 1 is always true, the query will return all books in the database, not just the books authored by MAHA.

The previous example might not represent a threat, especially if the stored list of books is not confidential. However, it could be applied to valuable using different syntax, and if successful, it might return sensitive data, such as passwords, bank accounts, trade secrets, and personal data, which might be considered a privacy breach, among other consequences.

In some research, injecting a code using 'OR' followed by a TRUE statement, such as 1 = 1 is called "tautology" [7]. Methods other than tautology can be used, such as when an attacker intentionally injects an incorrect query to force the database server to return a default error page, which might contain valuable information that could help an attacker to understand the database to form a more advance attack [7]. The SQL syntax "UNION" can also be used to extract information, in addition to many other methods based on the same idea, of misusing SQL syntax to extract or even update the data in the targeted database.

This is how SQL injection works; the question then becomes: how does one detect this type of attack using deep learning methods?

Deep learning is a machine learning and artificial intelligence method. It can be used to support the detection of SQL injection attacks by training a classifier to achieve the ability to recognize and therefore detect an attack. The classifier is trained using deep learning models and can be used to classify new data, such as traffic or data in log files. If the classifier is passive, it will alert the administrator; if it is active, it will prevent data from passing to the database server. The classifier can be trained to recognize and detect SQL injection attacks using three different learning methods [8].

First is, unsupervised learning, where features are extracted from unclassified data, i.e., data that are labelled as neither normal nor abnormal. Using information and the Bayesian probability theory, the classifier detects hidden structures in the unclassified dataset. An unclassified dataset means that it is not known whether these data are normal or abnormal (malicious). Different techniques can be used in unsupervised learning, such as clustering and density estimation [8].

The second is, supervised learning, whereby a labelled training dataset is used to train the classifier. As the input data are labelled, i.e., normal or abnormal, the output is known beforehand. Therefore, the process involves simple mapping between the input training data and the known output, followed by continuous modification of the algorithm and changing of the weights until an acceptable classification accuracy is achieved. Then, a test dataset is used to test the classifier; if the result is with an acceptable accuracy range, the classifier is ready to detect novel data, i.e., data not previously used in training or testing. The main drawback of supervised learning is generating and labelling the training and testing data, which might consume processing time, especially for complex attacks. Supervised learning is categorized into classification and regression algorithms. The most common supervised learning algorithms include Bayesian networks, decision trees, support vector machines (SVMs), K-nearest neighbors, and neural networks. Third is, semi-supervised learning, which use combination of supervised and unsupervised learning methods [8].

The main contribution of this paper is to provide a systematic review of the machine learning and deep learning solutions that, are used to improve the detectability of SQL injection attacks. With this systematic review, we aim to keep researchers up-to-date and contribute to the understanding of the intersection between an SQL injection attack and artificial intelligence.

The paper is organized as follows. Section 1 is an introduction to SQL injection attacks and deep learning algorithms. In Section 2, we discuss related studies and consider previous systematic reviews. In Section 3, we present the research method and planning of the systematic review. In Section 4, highlights the results and review all related studies. In Section 5, presents the discussion and answers to research questions. Finally, in Section 6, we present our conclusions.

2. Related Studies

In this section, four published systematic reviews were considered. Newer systematic reviews typically include both recent and older studies in the area under investigation. Therefore, all of the papers we considered were relatively recent. The first was published in 2017 [9] and it covered previous primary studies on SQL injection attacks, techniques, and tools. In [9], forty-six primary studies were analyzed related to SQL injection attacks, tools, and techniques, in addition to the impact of the attack. We adapted the same methodology as that used in [9] due to its comprehensiveness and because it achieves satisfying results, in addition, this research was similar to that in [9] in terms of objectives, ideas, and the area of research.

Qiu et al. [10] provided a comprehensive review of using artificial intelligence in attacking and defending against security attacks, concentrating on the training and testing stages. In their study, they sorted technologies and applications of adversarial attacks in terms of natural language processing, cyberspace security, computer vision, and the physical world. Furthermore, the authors considered defense strategies in their research and proposed methods to deal with specific types of adversarial attack. Martins et al. [11] explored more than 15 papers that applied adversarial machine learning techniques used in intrusion and malware detection models. In their study, the authors summarized the most common adversarial attacks and defense mechanisms for intrusion and malware detection.

Muslihi et al. [12] conducted a review of more than 14 studies published using deep learning methods to detect SQL injection attacks, including CNN, LSTM, DBN, MLP, and Bi-LSTM. They also provided a comparison of methods in terms of objectives, techniques, features, and datasets. Muhammad et al. [13] reviewed and analytically evaluated the methods and tools that are commonly used to detect and prevent SQL injection attacks, considering a total of 82 studies. Their review results showed that most researchers focused on proposing approaches to detect and mitigate SQL injection attacks (SQLIAs) rather than evaluating the effectiveness of existing SQLIA detection methods.

3. Research Method

This systematic literature review was conducted in four main phases: (A) planning the systematic review; (B) conducting the review; (C) reporting the results; and (D) discussing the results. In the planning phase, research questions and the research strategy were set. Section 4 outlines the systematic review. We discuss our results in Section 5. Figure 1 is a representation of the phases of this research.

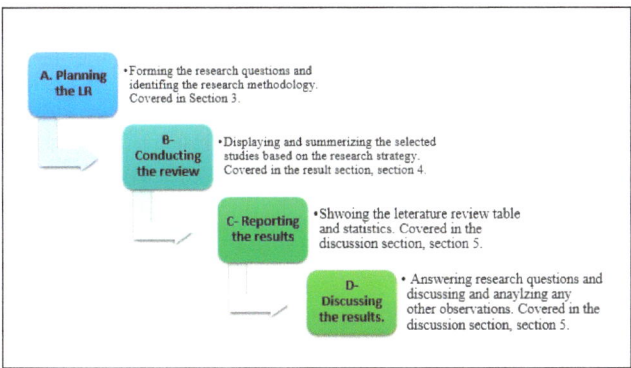

Figure 1. Research phases.

3.1. Planning the Systematic Review

Research Questions

Q1: What are the machine learning and deep learning methods used to detect SQL injection attacks?

Q2: How are SQL injection attack datasets generated using machine learning techniques?

Q3: How can machine learning be used to generate adversarial SQL injection attacks?

The first question was the main question decided upon before starting the review, whereas the second and third questions were added later after reviewing other systematic reviews covered in Section 4.

3.2. Research Strategy

The libraries used to retrieve the research papers were ACM, IEEE, Springer and Science Direct. The main search topics were SQL injection attacks and machine learning models. The search was configured to retrieve papers published between 2012 and 2021, and we retrieved conference papers, journal articles, and review articles. Some inclusion criteria were defined to select relevant papers among the publications retrieved at the time of the search. These criteria were used to decide which papers to review and which to discard and not include for further study.

3.2.1. Inclusion Criteria

- Papers related to SQL injection attacks;
- Papers that included our search keywords;
- Papers from the scientific databases ACM, IEEE, SpringerLink, and ScienceDirect.
- Papers on the topic of machine learning and the security domain.

3.2.2. Exclusion Criteria

- Papers not covering machine learning techniques and SQL injection attacks;
- Papers published before 2012; and
- Papers that are not available in full-text format.

4. Results

Conducting the Review

After filtering retrieved studies according to the inclusion criteria, 36 studied were retained. Selected studies were reviewed, as they could possibly provided answers to the research questions.

Q1: What are the machine learning and deep learning methods used to detect SQL injection attacks?

Many researchers have demonstrated the use of machine learning and deep learning algorithms to detect SQL injection attacks [14]. Hasan and Tarique [14] tested and compared 23 machine learning classifiers using MATLAB. They generated their own datasets, into which they injected abnormal SQL syntax. They checked and manually verified the SQL statements. A total of 616 SQL statements were used to train the test classifiers. The used the following machine learning algorithms: "coarse k-NN, bagged trees, linear SVM, fine k-NN, medium k-NN, RUS boosted trees, subspace discriminant, boosted trees, weighted k-NN, cubic k-NN, linear discriminant, medium tree, subspace k-NN, simple tree, quadratic discriminant, cubic SVM, fine Gaussian SVM, cosine k-NN, complex tree, logistic regression, coarse Gaussian SVM, medium Gaussian, and SVM". The five best models in terms of accuracy were determined to be ensemble boosted, bagged trees, linear discriminant, cubic SVM, and fine Gaussian SVM.

Gao et al. [15] proposed a model called ATTAR to detect SQL injection attacks by analyzing web access logs to extract SQL injection attack features. The features were chosen based on access behavior mining and a grammar pattern recognizer. The main target of this model was detection of unknown SQL injection statements that had not been previously used in the training data. Five machine learning algorithms were used for training: naive Bayesian, random forest, SVM, ID3, and k-means. The experimental results showed that the accuracy of the models based on random forest and ID3 achieved the best results in detecting SQL injection attacks. We could not find what ATTAR stands for in [15].

Gandhi et al. [16] proposed a hybrid CNN-BiLSTM-based model for SQL injection attack detection. The authors presented a detailed comparative analysis of different types of machine learning algorithms used for detection of SQL injection attacks. The CNN-BiLSTM approach provided accuracy of approximately 98%, compared withother described machine learning algorithms.

Zhang [17] presented a machine learning classifier to detect SQL injection vulnerabilities in PHP code. Multiple machine learning algorithms were trained and evaluated, including random forest, logistic regression, SVM, multilayer perceptron (MLP), long short-term memory (LSTM), and a convolutional neural network (CNN). Zhang found that CNN provided the best precision of 95.4%.

Gi Li et al. [18] proposed an adaptive deep forest model (ADF) with the integration of the AdaBoost algorithm. AdaBoost stands for adaptive boosting, which is a statistical classification algorithm, and the deep forest model is a layered model based on a deep neural network. The adaptive deep forest model proposed in [16] achieved high efficiency, comparable to that of traditional machine learning models, such as decision trees, and a better performance compared with regular deep neural network models, such as RNN and CNN.

Uwagbole et al. [19] created a dataset using symbolic finite automata to train a classifier to detect SQL injection attacks. The generated data were labelled, and training was conducted with a supervised learning model with an ML algorithm of two-class support vector machine (TC SVM) and two-class logistic regression (TC LR). The generated models were evaluated using a receiver operating characteristic (ROC) curve.

Ahmed et al. [20] proposed an SQL injection detection method using an ensemble learning algorithm and natural language processing (NLP) to generate a bag-of-words model used to train a random forest classifier. Prediction was also considered in this research to improve the detection ability of the classifier. In this study, decision tree, naïve Bayes, SVM, and k-NN classification models were also trained to classify the same testing dataset, and their performances were compared with that of the proposed method. The experimental results showed that the proposed method achieved better accuracy, higher TPR, and lower FNR than the other four classifiers. Evaluation metrics were used to measure the performance of the classifier. The measurements were based on a confusion matrix, accuracy, precision, true-positive rate, false-positive rate, true-negative rate, false-negative rate, receiver operating characteristic curve, and area under the curve.

Tripathy et al. [21] created a dataset by gathering and combining a large number of smaller datasets. The generated dataset was labelled, and the learning model was supervised learning. They trained seven machine learning models: decision tree, AdaBoost, random forest, optimized linear, TensorFlow linear, deep ANN, and a boosted trees classifier. Then, they compared the seven algorithms in terms of performance and accuracy. The results showed that the random forest classifier outperformed all other classifiers and achieved an accuracy of 99.8%.

Chinmay and Kulkarni [22] proposed a novel approach to detection of SQL injection attacks using a human agent knowledge transfer (HAT) and TD machine learning algorithm. In this model, a machine learning agent acted as a maze game to differentiated between normal SQL queries and malicious SQL queries. If the incoming SQL query was an SQL injection attack query, then it gained more rewards and was deemed an SQL injection attack query before achieving the final state. This machine learning approach achieved an accuracy of 95%.

Makiou et al. [23] proposed a detection system based on two approaches. The first detection method was based on pattern matching, which is the same as a signature-based detection system whereby the classifier has a database of SQL attack signatures and only inspects the HTTP URL in an attempt to find a match. The second detection method used was based on machine learning techniques. To build this model, the authors collected malicious data and trained the classifier with these data by extracting the features representing attacks. The following algorithms were employed: SVM, naïve Bayes, and K-nearest neighbor. The performance of the classifier was measured using the total cost ratio (TCR).

Kar et al. [24] trained a support vector machine (SVM) to detect malicious SQL queries by modelling the WHERE clause of a query as an interaction network of tokens and computing the centrality of the nodes. Node centralities were used to quantify the degree of importance or centrality of a node in the network. The experimental results obtained on a dataset collected from five web applications using some automated attack tools, confirmed that three of the centrality measures used in this study can effectively detect SQL injection attacks with minimal impact on performance.

Wang et al. [25] analyzed the existing SQL injection detection algorithms in an intelligent transportation system. The authors proposed a long short-term memory (LSTM)-based SQL injection attack detection method and a method of generating SQL injection samples to augment the dataset. This method can simulate SQL injection attacks and generate valid positive samples to solve the problem of overfitting caused by a lack of positive samples. The experimental results showed that the accuracy, precision, and F1 score of the proposed method were all above 92%.

Kamtuo and Soomlek. [26] proposed a framework for SQL injection prevention via server-side scripting using machine learning and compiler platforms. A dataset of 1100 samples of SQL commands were trained in four machine learning models: boosted decision tree, decision tree, support vector machine (SVM), and an artificial neural network. The results indicate that the decision tree algorithm achieved the highest prediction efficiency among the tested models.

Sivasangari et al. [27] used the AdaBoost algorithm to detect SQL injection attacks. In this study, the data were converted into stumps, which were classified as weak stumps providing less weight to the output or strong stumps providing the highest weight in the overall output. The experimental result showed that the proposed algorithm accurately and effectively detected injection attacks.

Daset al. [28] proposed a method for classifying dynamic SQL queries as either attacks or normal based on a web profile prepared during the training phase. Naïve Bayes, SVM, and parse tree approaches were used for the classification process. The overall detection rate using the two datasets was 91% and 90%, respectively.

Kasim [29] designed a method to detect malicious SQL queries. Decision tree algorithms were used for the classification processes to detect different levels of SQL injection. The proposed model maintained an accuracy more than 98% in detecting SQL injection attacks and an accuracy of 92% in classifying the level of attack as simple, unified, or lateral.

Tanget et al. [30] presented a simple method for SQL injection attack detection based on an artificial neural network. First, a large amount of SQL injection data were analyzed to extract the relevant features. Then, a variety of neural network models, such as MLP and LSTM, were trained. The experimental results showed that the detection rate of MLP was better than that of LSTM.

Erdődiet al. [31] automatized the process of exploiting SQL injection attacks through reinforcement learning agents. In this study, the problem was modelled as a Markov decision process. The experimental results show that reinforcement learning agents can be used in the future to perform security assessment and penetration testing.

Kar et al. [32] presented a detection method by modeling SQL queries as a graph of tokens and utilized the centrality measure of tokens to train single and multiple SVM classifiers. The system was tested using directed and undirected graphs with different SVM classifiers. The experimental results demonstrated that the proposed technique is able to effectively identify malicious SQL queries.

Solomon et al. [33] presented a model of a two-class support vector machine (TCSVM) to predict binary labelled outcomes concerning whether an SQL injection attack was positive or negative in a web request. This model intercepted web requests at the proxy level and applied ML predictive analytics to predict SQL injection attacks.

Mcwhirter et al. [34] presented a novel approach for classifying SQL queries. A gap-weighted string subsequence kernel algorithm was used to compute the similarity metric between the query strings. Then, the support vector machine was trained on the similarity metrics to determine whether the query strings was normal or malicious. The proposed approach was evaluated using a number of datasets and achieved 92.48% accuracy.

Mejia-Cabrera et al. [35] presented a new approach to the construction of a dataset with a NoSQL query database. Six classification algorithms were trained and evaluated to identify SQL injection attacks, which included: decision tree, SVM, random forest, k-NN, neural network, and multilayer perceptron. The experimental results showed that the last two algorithms obtained an accuracy of 97.6%.

Pathak et al. [36] trained a progressive neural network model with a naïve Bayesian classifier to successfully detect SQL injection attacks. Progressive neural networks were trained using parameters such as error-based, time-based, SQL query and, union-based SQL injection attacks. The proposed method achieved an accuracy of 97.897%.

Wang et al. [37] proposed a hybrid approach using tree-vector kernels in SVM to learn SQL statements. The authors used both the parse tree structure of SQL queries and the query value similarity characteristic to distinguish between malicious and benign queries. The results confirmed the benefit of incorporation to efficiently and accurately identify abnormal queries.

Fang et al. [38] proposed a tool based on LSTM neural networks and the word vectors of SQL tokens. According to the syntactic functions of the SQL queries, each query was converted into sequences of tokens to build an SQL word vector model. Then, the LSTM neural network was trained. The results of the experiment showed that the proposed tool achieved an accuracy of 98.60%.

Zhang et al. [39] proposed a deep learning-based approach to detect SQL injection attacks in network traffic. The proposed approach selected only the target features needed by the model to be trained using a deep belief network (DBN) model. The authors also employed test data to test the performance of different models, including LSTM, CNN, and MLP. According to the experimental results, DBN achieved an accuracy of 96%.

Priyaa et al. [40] proposed a framework that combined the EDADT (efficient data adaptive decision tree) algorithm and the SVM classification algorithm to detect SQL injection attacks. The employed dataset was created using the MovieLens dataset system for movie recommendations, which included user login and movie details. The experimental results showed that the proposed approach achieved an accuracy of 99.87%.

Joshi et al. [41] proposed a method for detecting SQL injection using the naïve Bayes machine learning algorithm. The authors applied a tokenization process to break the query into meaningful elements called tokens. Then, the list of tokens became an input for the further classification processes. The result of the naïve Bayes approach was analyzed using precision, recall, and accuracy.

Q2: How are SQL injection attack datasets generated using machine learning techniques?

Many researchers have been developed and generated their SQL injection datasets instead of using existing datasets [42]. Islam et al. [43] developed a training dataset for NoSQL injection to manually design important features using various supervised learning algorithms. In this study, the authors generated a dataset including approximately 75% benign and 25% injection queries, which was tested on a local server.

Appelt et al. [44] proposed automated testing techniques that generated SQL injection attacks, bypassing web application firewalls (WAFs). The authors developed SQL injection grammar based on existing SQL injection attacks, as well as an automated input generation technique to automatically generate attack payloads. Then, machine learning was used to efficiently generate additional payloads and new successful attacks with a high probability of bypassing the firewall.

Ross et al. [42] proposed a system consisting of three phases to generate data: traffic generation, capture, and preprocessing. In the traffic generation phase, the simulated normal and malicious traffic was generated from the scripts located on the traffic generation server. Then, the traffic was captured by the webapp server and at the Datiphy appliance. Finally, data preprocessing was achieved with bash shell scripts on the webapp server. The resulting data from preprocessing was imported into Weka, which is a machine learning framework that includes many ML tools. The data were processed into word vectors using the weak filter StringToVec. Then correlated feature selection was employed to reduce the number of features for efficient machine learning.

Liu et al. [45] proposed a tool called DeepSQLi to generate test cases for detection of SQL injection attacks using a deep learning model and sequence-of-words prediction. DeepSQLi used the neural language model, which can be trained to learn semantic features of SQL attacks to translate the test case (or user input) into a new test case. Therefore, DeepSQLi is able to generate SQL injection attacks that have not been captured by patterns in the training datasets. Siddiq et al. [46] proposed a learning-based SQL injection fix tool called SQLIFIX. This tool creates an abstraction of SQL injection code from a training dataset that consists of 14 projects and then clusters them using hierarchical clustering. The proposed approach generated correct solutions for 67.52% of cases for Java and 41.33% of correct solutions for PHP on an independent test set.

Naghmeh [47] proposed a model for the detection of SQLI attacks using artificial intelligence (AI) techniques. This model consisted of three main components: uniform resource locator (URL) generator to generate thousands of normal and malicious URLs; a URL classifier to classify all generated URLs as either normal or malicious; and a neural network (NN) model to detect whether a given URL was a malicious, or benign URL. The model was first trained and then evaluated by employing both benign and malicious URLs. URL classifiers were also used to convert all generated URLs into strings of logic (1 = malicious; 0 = benign).

Q3:How can machine learning be used to generate adversarial SQL injection attacks?

Adversarial machine learning (AML) is based on the threats posed by an attacker with the aim of being incorrectly classified by the victim machine learning algorithm. Generating an adversarial SQL injection dataset starts with a target malicious query that was correctly detected. And then, a set of mutation operators was iteratively applied in order to generate new queries [48].

Demetrio and Valenza [48] developed a tool named WAF-A-MoLE to generate adversarial examples against web application firewalls (WAFs) by applying a set of syntactic mutations. The authors produced a dataset of SQL injection queries through an automatic procedure. To evaluate the effectiveness of the proposed tool, it was applied to different ML-based WAFs and evaluated in terms of their robustness against WAF-A-MoLE.

Appelt et al. [49] proposed a black-box automated technique, named 4SQLi, for generating test inputs that could bypass security filters, resulting in executable SQL queries. This technique was based on a set of multiple mutation operators that manipulated inputs to produce new test inputs to trigger SQLi attacks, making it possible to create inputs that contained new attack patterns, thus increasing the possibility of generating a successful SQLi attacks.

5. Discussion

5.1. Machine Learning and Deep Learning Techniques for Detection of SQL Injection Attacks (Related to Q1)

In this section, the results reported in Section 4 are discussed. In related studies, various algorithms and techniques can be used for detecting SQL injection attacks. Table 1 summarizes the algorithms under review, in addition to the employed datasets and evaluation methods.

Table 1. Summary of the Machine learning algorithms, Datasets, and Evaluation Methods.

Ref.	Algorithm	Dataset	Dataset Size	Accuracy	FPR	FNR	TP	FN	FP	TN	Precision	Recall	F1 Score	AUC
[13]	Naïve Bayesian	Collected from access logs	58,000 log records	-	10.9% 16.7%	34.5% 18.2%	-	-	-	-	-	-	-	-
	SVM			-	4.1% 8.3%	41.4% 18.2%	-	-	-	-	-	-	-	-
	ID3			-	0.0% 0.0%	41.4% 18.2%	-	-	-	-	-	-	-	-
	RF			-	0.68% 0.0%	37.9% 9.1%	-	-	-	-	-	-	-	-
	K-means			-	0.68% 0.0%	37.9% 9.1%	-	-	-	-	-	-	-	-
[14]	CNN-BiLSTM	Collected from various websites	4200 queries (3072 SQL injections,1128 normal data	98%	-	-								-
[15]	Decision Tree	Collected from two sources	950 vulnerable PHP cases, 8800 non-vulnerable files	93.4%	-	-				-	76.6%	56.5%	0.650%	-
	Random Forest			93.6%	-	-				-	77.4%	57.7%	0.660%	-
	SVM			95.4%	-	-				-	98.6%	58.3%	0.732%	-
	Logistic Regression			95.1%	-	-				-	98.5%	56.0%	0.713%	-
	Multilayer Perceptron			95.3%	-	-				-	91.0%	63.7%	0.746%	-
	RNN			95.3%	-	-				-	92.2%	62.4%	0.742%	-
	LSTM			95.2%	-	-				-	91.9%	61.4%	0.734%	-
	CNN			95.3%	-	-				-	95.4%	59.9%	0.734%	-
[16]	ADF	Collected from vulnerability submission platforms	10,000 negative samples and 10,000 positive samples	Not clear	-	-				-	-		-	-
	AdaBoost													
[17]	Two-Class Logistic Regression		Dataset of 725,206 attribute values	96.4%	-	-				-	0.971	0.957	0.964	0.984
	Two-Class Support Vector Machine			98.6%	-	-				-	0.974	0.998	0.986	0.986
[18]	Random Forest + NLP	Open-source tools, such as Libinjection and Sqlmap	17,266 thousand SQL injection payloads and 19,303 thousand normal payloads	98.1515	0.96137	0.03862	4182	168	1	4792	0.9997%	-	-	0.99
[19]	RF	Collected from datasets available in public repositories	7576 malicious SQL queries and 100,496 legal inputs	99.8%	-	-				-	0.999	0.999	0.999	-
	TensorFlow Boosted Trees Classifier			99.6%	-	-				-	0.989	0.961	0.998	-
	AdaBoost Classifier			99.5%	-	-				-	0.997	0.996	0.997	-
	Decision Tree			99.5%	-	-				-	0.998	0.997	0.997	-
	SGD Classifier			98.6%	-	-				-	0.988	0.997	0.992	-
	Deep ANN			98.4%	-	-				-	0.934	0.820	0.873	-
	TensorFlow Linear Classifier			97.8%	-	-				-	0.908	0.759	0.988	-

Table 1. *Cont.*

Ref.	Algorithm	Dataset	Dataset Size	Evaluation Methods										
				Accuracy	FPR	FNR	TP	FN	FP	TN	Precision	Recall	F1 Score	AUC
[12]	Ensemble Boosted Trees	Open-source datasets	616 SQL statements	93.8%	-	-	-	-	-	-	-	-	-	-
	Bagged Trees			93.8%	-	-	-	-	-	-	-	-	-	-
	Linear Discriminant			93.7%	-	-	-	-	-	-	-	-	-	-
	Cubic SVM			93.7%	-	-	-	-	-	-	-	-	-	-
	Gaussian SVM			93.5%	-	-	-	-	-	-	-	-	-	-
[20]	TD Machine Learning Technique	Not mentioned	Not mentioned	95%.	-	-	-	-	-	-	-	-	-	-
[21]	SVM, Naïve Bayes, K-Nearest Neighbor	Open-source datasets	Not mentioned	Not clear	-	-	-	-	-	-	-	-	-	-
[22]	SVM classifier	Dataset generated using a honeypot-based technique.	4610 injected and 4884 genuine token sequences	92.84%	1.33%	86.66%	914	8	8	969	98.40%	86.66%	-	-
				99.16%	0.82%	99.13%	799	123	13	964	99.13%	99.31%	-	-
				99.37%	0.72%	99.46%	917	5	7	970	99.24%	99.46%	-	-
				99.05%	1.02%	99.13%	914	8	10	967	98.92%	99.13%	-	-
[23]	LSTM	Open-source datasets	Not mentioned	93.47%	-	-	-	-	-	-	93.56%	92.43%	92.99%	-
[24]	SVM, Boosted Decision Tree, Artificial Neural Network, Decision Tree	Open-source datasets	1100 vulnerable SQL commands	99.68%	-	-	-	-	-	1.000	-	-	-	-
[25]	AdaBoost algorithm	Not mentioned	Not mentioned	Not Clear	-	-	-	-	-	-	-	-	-	-
[26]	Naïve Bayesian	Not mentioned	Not mentioned	90%	-	-	-	-	-	-	-	-	-	-
	SVM			91%										
	Parse Tree			91%										
[27]	Decision tree	OWASP dataset	332 malicious codes and 52 the clean codes	98%	-	-	-	-	-	97%	98%	97%	-	98.2%
[28]	MLP	Open-source datasets	820 SQL injection samples and 8925 normal samples	99.67%	0.00%	-	-	-	-	100%	99.41%	-	-	-
	LSTM			97.68%	0.13%	-	-	-	-	99.86%	95.49%	-	-	-
[29]	Markov Decision Processes (MDPs)	Not mentioned	1000 SQL environments	-	-	-	-	-	-	-	-	-	-	-
[30]	SVM	Open-source datasets	4610 injected queries and 4884 genuine queries	99.37%	0.31%	-	-	-	-	-	99.35%	99.35%	99.46%	-
				99.73%	0.31%	-	-	-	-	-	99.67%	99.78%	99.73%	-
				99.63%	0.31%	-	-	-	-	-	99.67%	99.57%	99.62%	-
[31]	TCSVM	Dataset from MicrosoftSQL reserved keywords website	362,603 attack items and 362,603 non-attack items	98.60%	-	-	-	-	-	-	97.4%	99.7%	98.5%	98.6%
[32]	SVM	Amnesia testbed dataset	46 legitimate queries and 40 malicious SQL injection attacks	-	-	-	-	-	-	-	65.9%	98.3%	78.9%	-
											68%	100%	81%	
[33]	Support Vector Machine	Novel datasets	450 malicious and 59 benign queries	84.9%	-	-	-	-	-	-	84.8%	91.1%	87.6%	83.3%
	K-Nearest Neighbor			87.6%	-	-	-	-	-	-	84.8%	96.7%	90.4%	96.6%
	Neural Network			97.6%	-	-	-	-	-	-	98.7%	97.4%	98.0%	98.9%
	Multilayer Perceptron			97.6%	-	-	-	-	-	-	98.7%	97.4%	98.0%	98.9%
	Decision Tree			89.4%	-	-	-	-	-	-	96.3%	85.6%	90.6%	94.6%
	Random Forest			89.6%	-	-	-	-	-	-	87.5%	96.4%	91.7%	97.4%
[34]	Progressive Neural Network, Naïve Bayes	Open-source dataset	A 62.2 KB SQL query and a 4.86 KB SQL injection exploitation	97.897%	-	-	193	0	0	5	-	-	-	-
[35]	SVM	Open-source dataset	1000 benign and 1000 malicious HTTP requests	-	0.982	0.000	-	-	-	-	-	-	-	-
[36]	LSTM	Open-source dataset	43,167 injected query strings and 32,486 genuine query strings	98.60%	-	-	-	-	-	-	99.17%	99.20%,	99.17%	99%
[37]	LSTM, MLP, CNN, Deep Belief Network (DBN)	Datasets collected from HTTP requests	118,529 normal data points and 21,810 SQL injection data points	-	-	-	-	-	-	-	-	-	-	-
[38]	EDADT and SVM	Dataset created based on the MovieLens dataset	Not mentioned	99.87%	-	-	-	-	-	-	-	-	-	-
[39]	Naïve Bayes	Not mentioned	101 normal codes and 77 malicious codes	93.3%	-	-	-	-	-	-	1.0	0.89	-	-

Table 1 shows that most of the studies focused on using supervised machine learning to detect and classify SQL injection attacks; 89% of the studies used supervised learning, and 4% used unsupervised learning and mixed learning, whereas 3% used other types of learning, as shown in Figure 2.

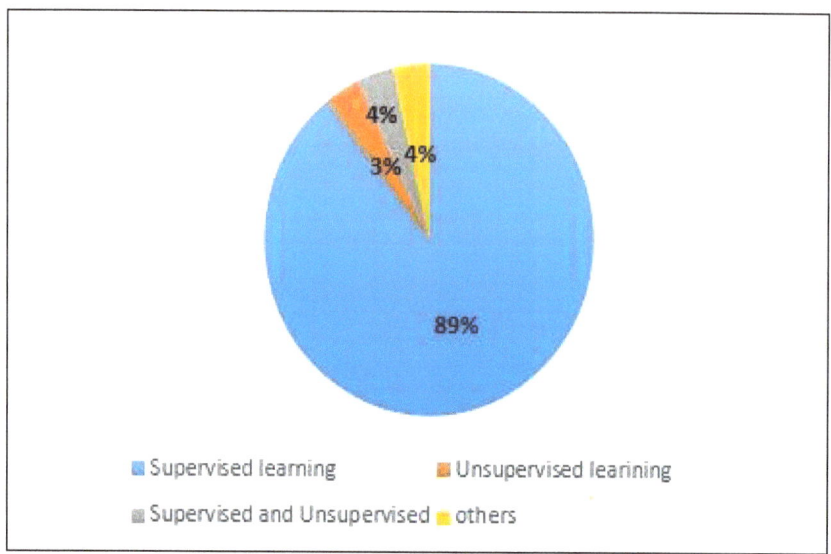

Figure 2. Percentage of the mchine learning and deep learning techniques used idetecting SQL injection attacks.

5.2. Generating SQL Injection Attack Datasets Using Machine Learning Techniques (Related to Q2)

A high-quality dataset for training is essential for machine learning and deep learning methods to achieve effective detection performance. It is difficult to identify suitable datasets with patterns to train classifiers in SQL injection attack research [30]. The results of the studies reviewed in Section 4 showed that, after automatically generating SQL injection attack payloads from different web applications, machine learning techniques can learn incrementally learn the payloads that are passed or blocked by the firewalls and can be used to efficiently generate additional payloads with high probability of bypassing the firewall. A total of 83% of the reviewed studies used datasets collected from public repositories and HTTP requests. The remaining 17% of the reviewed studies used datasets created by the authors using deep learning models that can be trained to learn the semantic features of SQL attacks to generate new test cases from user inputs.

5.3. Generating Adversarial SQL Injection Attacks Using ML Techniques (Related to Q3)

The result reported in Section 4 showed that adversarial SQL injection attacks can be generated using mutation operators, which are a set of operators that alter the syntax of the original payload without affecting its semantics. Such operators can be classified into three classes based on their purpose: behavior-changing, syntax-repairing, and obfuscating operators [49,50]. Table 2 provides a summary of the mutation operators.

Table 2. Summary of mutation operators (adopted from [50]).

MO Class	MO Name	Description	Example
Behavior-Changing Operators	MO or	Adds an OR clause to the input	Original input: "SELECT * FROM table WHERE id= " the input will change the logic of the statement and turns it as follows: "SELECT * FROM table WHERE id = 1 OR 1 = 1
	MO and	Adds an AND clause to the input	
	MO semi	Adds a semicolon followed by an additional clause	
Syntax-Repairing Operators	MO par	Appends a parenthesis to a valid input	Original inpt: "SELECT * FROM table WHERE character = CHR(" + input + ")" The changed SQL statement: SELECT * FROM table WHERE character = CHR(67) OR 1 = 1 ().
	MO cmt	Adds a comment command (– or #) to an input	
	MO qot	Adds a single or double quote to an input	
Obfuscating Operators	MO wsp	Changes the encoding of white spaces	Original input: 1 OR 1 = 1, mutated input: 1+– OR + 1 = 1. This changes the predefined statement: "SE- LECT * FROM table WHERE id = " + input to SELECT * FROM table WHERE id = 1 + OR + 1 = 1
	MO chr	Changes the encoding of a character literally enclosed in quotes	
	MO html	Changes the encoding of an input to HTML entity encoding	
	MO per	Changes the encoding of an input to percentage encoding	
	MO bool	Rewrites a Boolean expression while preserving its truth value	
	MO keyw	Obfuscates SQL keywords by randomizing the capitalization and inserting comments	

6. Conclusions

SQL injection attacks represent a major threat to web applications, and this may have major implications for privacy and security. Machine learning and deep learning applications have achieved considerable success in detecting this type of web attack. In this study, we conducted a systematic literature review of 36 articles related to research on SQL injection attacks and machine learning techniques. We identified the most commonly used machine learning techniques to detect all types of SQL injection attacks. The review results showed that few studies used machine learning tools and methods to generate new SQL injection attack datasets. Similarly, the results showed that only a few studies focused only on using mutation operators to generate adversarial SQL injection attack queries. In future work, we aim to cover the use of other machine learning and deep learning models to generate and detect SQL injection attacks., In addition to investigating the use of other AI techniques to generate adversarial SQL injection attacks, such as generative adversarial networks (GANs).

Author Contributions: Conceptualization, M.A. and D.A.; methodology, M.A.; software, M.A.; validation, M.A., D.A. and S.A.; formal analysis, O.R.; investigation, M.A.; resources, M.A.; data curation, M.A.; writing—original draft preparation, M.A.; writing—review and editing, S.A.; visualization, M.A.; supervision, D.A. All authors have read and agreed to the published version of the manuscript.

Funding: This research was funded by the Deanship of Scientific Research (DSR) at King Abdulaziz University, Jeddah, under Grant No. IFPDP-284-22. The authors, therefore, acknowledge with thanks to DSR technical and financial support.

Institutional Review Board Statement: Not applicable.

Informed Consent Statement: Not applicable.

Data Availability Statement: Not applicable.

Conflicts of Interest: The authors declare no conflict of interest.

References

1. Han, S.; Xie, M.; Chen, H.-H.; Ling, Y. Intrusion Detection in Cyber-Physical Systems: Techniques and Challenges. *IEEE Syst. J.* **2014**, *8*, 1049–1059. [CrossRef]
2. Mishra, P.; Varadharajan, V.; Tupakula, U.; Pilli, E.S. A Detailed Investigation and Analysis of using Machine Learning Techniques for Intrusion Detection. *IEEE Commun. Surv. Tutor.* **2018**, *21*, 686–728. [CrossRef]
3. Charles, M.J.; Pfleeger, P.; Pfleeger, S.L. *Security in Computing*, 5th ed.; Springer: Berlin/Heidelberg, Germany, 2004.

4.   Son, S.; McKinley, K.S.; Shmatikov, V. Diglossia: Detecting code injection attacks with precision and efficiency. *Proc. ACM Conf. Comput. Commun. Secur.* **2013**, *2*, 1181–1191. [CrossRef]
5.   Yan, R.; Xiao, X.; Hu, G.; Peng, S.; Jiang, Y. New deep learning method to detect code injection attacks on hybrid applications. *J. Syst. Softw.* **2018**, *137*, 67–77. [CrossRef]
6.   Vähäkainu, P.; Lehto, M. Artificial intelligence in the cyber security environment. In Proceedings of the 14th International Conference on Cyber Warfare and Security, ICCWS 2019, Stellenbosch, South Africa, 28 February–1 March 2019; pp. 431–440.
7.   Satapathy, S.C.; Govardhan, A.; Raju, K.S.; Mandal, J.K. SQL Injection Detection and Correction Using Machine Learning Techniques. *Adv. Intell. Syst. Comput.* **2015**, *337*, 435–442. [CrossRef]
8.   Marashdeh, Z.; Suwais, K.; Alia, M. A Survey on SQL Injection Attacks: Detection and Challenges. In Proceedings of the 2021 International Conference on Information Technology (ICIT), Amman, Jordan, 14–15 July 2021; pp. 957–962. [CrossRef]
9.   Faker, S.A.; Muslim, M.A.; Dachlan, H.S. A systematic literature review on sql injection attacks techniques and common exploited vulnerabilities. *Int. J. Comput. Eng. Inf. Technol.* **2017**, *9*, 284–291.
10.   Qiu, S.; Liu, Q.; Zhou, S.; Wu, C. Review of artificial intelligence adversarial attack and defense technologies. *Appl. Sci.* **2019**, *9*, 909. [CrossRef]
11.   Martins, N.; Cruz, J.M.; Cruz, T.; Abreu, P.H. Adversarial Machine Learning Applied to Intrusion and Malware Scenarios: A Systematic Review. *IEEE Access* **2020**, *8*, 35403–35419. [CrossRef]
12.   Muslihi, M.T.; Alghazzawi, D. Detecting SQL Injection on Web Application Using Deep Learning Techniques: A Systematic Literature Review. In Proceedings of the 2020 Third International Conference on Vocational Education and Electrical Engineering (ICVEE), Surabaya, Indonesia, 3–4 October 2020. [CrossRef]
13.   Aliero, M.S.; Qureshi, K.N.; Pasha, M.F.; Ghani, I.; Yauri, R.A. Systematic Review Analysis with SQLIA Detection and Prevention Approaches. *Wirel. Pers. Commun.* **2020**, *112*, 2297–2333. [CrossRef]
14.   Hasan, M.; Tarique, M. Detection of SQL Injection Attacks: A Machine Learning Approach. In Proceedings of the 2019 International Conference on Electrical and Computing Technologies and Applications (ICECTA), Ras Al Khaimah, United Arab Emirates, 19–21 November 2019.
15.   Gao, H.; Zhu, J.; Liu, L.; Xu, J.; Wu, Y.; Liu, A. Detecting SQL Injection Attacks Using Grammar Pattern Recognition and Access Behavior Mining. In Proceedings of the 2019 IEEE International Conference on Energy Internet (ICEI), Nanjing, China, 27–31 May 2019. [CrossRef]
16.   Gandhi, N. A CNN-BiLSTM based Approach for Detection of SQL Injection Attacks. In Proceedings of the 2021 International Conference on Computational Intelligence and Knowledge Economy (ICCIKE), Dubai, United Arab Emirates, 17–18 March 2021; pp. 378–383.
17.   Zhang, K.; Dataset, A.T. A Machine Learning based Approach to Identify SQL Injection Vulnerabilities. In Proceedings of the 2019 34th IEEE/ACM International Conference on Automated Software Engineering (ASE), San Diego, CA, USA, 11–15 November 2019; pp. 2019–2021. [CrossRef]
18.   Li, Q.I.; Li, W.; Wang, J. A SQL Injection Detection Method Based on Adaptive Deep Forest. *IEEE Access* **2019**, *7*, 145385–145394. [CrossRef]
19.   Uwagbole, S.O.; Buchanan, W.J.; Fan, L. An Applied Pattern-Driven Corpus to Predictive Analytics in Mitigating SQL Injection Attack. In Proceedings of the 2017 Seventh International Conference on Emerging Security Technologies (EST), Canterbury, UK, 6–8 September 2017; pp. 12–17.
20.   Ahmed, M. Cyber Attack Detection Method Based on NLP and Ensemble Learning Approach. In Proceedings of the 2020 23rd International Conference on Computer and Information Technology (ICCIT), Dhaka, Bangladesh, 19–21 December 2020; pp. 19–21.
21.   Tripathy, D.; Gohil, R.; Halabi, T. Detecting SQL Injection Attacks in Cloud SaaS using Machine Learning. In Proceedings of the 2020 IEEE 6th Intl Conference on Big Data Security on Cloud (BigDataSecurity), IEEE Intl Conference on High Performance and Smart Computing, (HPSC) and IEEE Intl Conference on Intelligent Data and Security (IDS), Baltimore, MD, USA, 25–27 May 2020; pp. 145–150. [CrossRef]
22.   Kulkarni, C.C.; Kulkarni, S.A. Human agent knowledge transfer applied to web security. In Proceedings of the 2013 Fourth International Conference on Computing, Communications and Networking Technologies (ICCCNT), Tiruchengode, India, 4–6 July 2013; pp. 14–17. [CrossRef]
23.   Makiou, A.; Begriche, Y.; Serhrouchni, A. Hybrid approach to detect SQLi attacks and evasion techniques. In Proceedings of the 10th IEEE International Conference on Collaborative Computing: Networking, Applications and Worksharing, Miami, FL, USA, 22–25 October 2014; pp. 452–456. [CrossRef]
24.   Kar, D.; Sahoo, A.K.; Agarwal, K.; Panigrahi, S.; Das, M. Learning to Detect SQLIA Using Node Centrality with Feature Selection. In Proceedings of the 2016 International Conference on Computing, Analytics and Security Trends (CAST), Pune, India, 19–21 December 2016; pp. 18–23.
25.   Li, Q.; Wang, F.; Wang, J.; Li, W. LSTM-Based SQL Injection Detection Method for Intelligent Transportation System. *IEEE Trans. Veh. Technol.* **2019**, *68*, 4182–4191. [CrossRef]
26.   Kamtuo, K.; Soomlek, C. Machine Learning for SQL Injection Prevention in Server-Side Scripting. In Proceedings of the 2016 International Computer Science and Engineering Conference (ICSEC), Chiang Mai, Thailand, 14–17 December 2016; pp. 1–6.
27.   Sivasangari, A. SQL Injection Attack Detection using Machine Learning Algorithm. In Proceedings of the 2021 5th International Conference on Trends in Electronics and Informatics (ICOEI), Tirunelveli, India, 3–5 June 2021; pp. 1166–1169.

28. Das, D.; Sharma, U.; Bhattacharyya, D.K. Defeating SQL injection attack in authentication security: An experimental study. *Int. J. Inf. Secur.* **2019**, *18*, 1–22. [CrossRef]
29. Kasim, Ö. An ensemble classification-based approach to detect the attack level of SQL injections. *J. Inf. Secur. Appl.* **2021**, *59*, 102852. [CrossRef]
30. Tang, P.; Qiu, W.; Huang, Z.; Lian, H.; Liu, G. Detection of SQL injection based on artificial neural network. *Knowl.-Based Syst.* **2020**, *190*, 105528. [CrossRef]
31. Erdődi, L.; Sommervoll, Å.Å.; Zennaro, F.M. SQL injection vulnerability exploitation using Q-learning reinforcement learning agents. *J. Inf. Secur. Appl. Simulating* **2021**, *61*, 102903. [CrossRef]
32. Kar, D.; Panigrahi, S.; Sundararajan, S. SQLiGoT: Detecting SQL injection attacks using the graph of tokens and SVM. *Comput. Secur.* **2016**, *60*, 206–225. [CrossRef]
33. Uwagbole, S.O.; Buchanan, W.J.; Fan, L. Applied Machine Learning Predictive Analytics to SQL Injection Attack Detection and Prevention. In Proceedings of the 2017 IFIP/IEEE Symposium on Integrated Network and Service Management (IM), Lisbon, Portugal, 8–12 May 2017; pp. 1087–1090. [CrossRef]
34. Mcwhirter, P.R.; Kifayat, K.; Shi, Q.; Askwith, B. SQL Injection Attack classification through the feature extraction of SQL query strings using a Gap-Weighted String Subsequence Kernel. *J. Inf. Secur. Appl.* **2018**, *40*, 199–216. [CrossRef]
35. Mejia-Cabrera, H.I.; Paico-Chileno, D.; Valdera-Contreras, J.H.; Tuesta-Monteza, V.A.; Forero, M.G. *Automatic Detection of Injection Attacks by Machine Learning in NoSQL Databases*; Springer: Berlin/Heidelberg, Germany, 2021; pp. 23–32.
36. Pathak, R.K.; Yadav, V. *Handling SQL Injection Attack Using Progressive Neural Network*; Springer: Singapore, 2020; Volume 1170.
37. Wang, Y.; Li, Z. SQL injection detection via program tracing and machine learning. In *Lecture Notes in Computer Science*; 7646 LNCS; Springer: Berlin/Heidelberg, Germany, 2012; pp. 264–274. [CrossRef]
38. Fang, Y.; Peng, J.; Liu, L.; Huang, C. WOVSQLI: Detection of SQL injection behaviors using word vector and LSTM. In Proceedings of the ICCSP 2018: Proceedings of the 2nd International Conference on Cryptography, Security and Privacy, Guiyang, China, 16–19 March 2018; pp. 170–174. [CrossRef]
39. Zhang, H.; Zhao, J.; Zhao, B.; Yan, X.; Yuan, H.; Li, F. SQL injection detection based on deep belief network. In Proceedings of the CSAE 2019: Proceedings of the 3rd International Conference on Computer Science and Application Engineering, Sanya, China, 22–24 October 2019. [CrossRef]
40. Priyaa, B.D.; Student, P.G.; Devi, M.I. Hybrid SQL Injection Detection System. In Proceedings of the 2016 3rd International Conference on Advanced Computing and Communication Systems (ICACCS), Coimbatore, India, 22–23 January 2016.
41. Joshi, A. SQL Injection Detection using Machine Learning. In Proceedings of the 2014 International Conference on Control, Instrumentation, Communication and Computational Technologies (ICCICCT), Kanyakumari, India, 10–11 July 2014; Volume 2, pp. 1111–1115.
42. Ross, K.; Moh, M.; Yao, J.; Moh, T.S. Multi-source data analysis and evaluation of machine learning techniques for SQL injection detection. In Proceedings of the ACMSE 2018 Conference, Richmond, KY, USA, 29–31 March 2018; pp. 1–8. [CrossRef]
43. Islam, M.R.U.; Islam, M.S.; Ahmed, Z.; Iqbal, A.; Shahriyar, R. Automatic detection of NoSQL injection using supervised learning. In Proceedings of the 2019 IEEE 43rd Annual Computer Software and Applications Conference (COMPSAC), Milwaukee, WI, USA, 15–19 July 2019; Volume 1, pp. 760–769. [CrossRef]
44. Appelt, D.; Nguyen, C.D.; Briand, L. Behind an application firewall, are we safe from SQL injection attacks? In Proceedings of 2015 IEEE 8th International Conference on Software Testing, Verification and Validation (ICST), Graz, Austria, 13–17 April 2015. [CrossRef]
45. Liu, M.; Li, K.; Chen, T. DeepSQLi: Deep semantic learning for testing SQL injection. In Proceedings of the ISSTA 2020: Proceedings of the 29th ACM SIGSOFT International Symposium on Software Testing and Analysis, Virtual Event, 18–22 July 2020; pp. 286–297. [CrossRef]
46. Siddiq, M.L.; Jahin, R.R.; Rafid, M.; Islam, U. SQLIFIX: Learning-Based Approach to Fix SQL Injection Vulnerabilities in Source Code. In Proceedings of the 2021 IEEE International Conference on Software Analysis, Evolution and Reengineering (SANER), Honolulu, HI, USA, 9–12 March 2021; pp. 354–364. [CrossRef]
47. Sheykhkanloo, N.M. Employing Neural Networks for the detection of SQL injection attack. In Proceedings of the SIN '14: Proceedings of the 7th International Conference on Security of Information and Networks, Glasgow, UK, 9–11 September 2014; pp. 318–323. [CrossRef]
48. Demetrio, L.; Valenza, A.; Costa, G.; Lagorio, G. WAF-A-MoLE: Evading web application firewalls through adversarial machine learning. In Proceedings of the SAC '20: Proceedings of the 35th Annual ACM Symposium on Applied Computing, Brno, Czech Republic, 30 March–3 April 2020; pp. 1745–1752. [CrossRef]
49. Appelt, D.; Nguyen, C.D.; Briand, L.C.; Alshahwan, N. Automated testing for SQL injection vulnerabilities: An input mutation approach. In Proceedings of the 2014 International Symposium on Software Testing and Analysis, San Jose, CA, USA, 21–25 July 2014; pp. 259–269.
50. Appelt, D. Automated Security Testing of Web-Based Systems against SQL Injection Attacks. Ph.D. Thesis, University of Luxembourg, Luxembourg, 2016.

Journal of
Cybersecurity and Privacy

MDPI

Review

Contactless Fingerprint Recognition Using Deep Learning—A Systematic Review

A M Mahmud Chowdhury and Masudul Haider Imtiaz *

Department of Electrical and Computer Engineering, Clarkson University, Potsdam, NY 13699, USA
* Correspondence: mimtiaz@clarkson.edu

Abstract: Contactless fingerprint identification systems have been introduced to address the deficiencies of contact-based fingerprint systems. A number of studies have been reported regarding contactless fingerprint processing, including classical image processing, the machine-learning pipeline, and a number of deep-learning-based algorithms. The deep-learning-based methods were reported to have higher accuracies than their counterparts. This study was thus motivated to present a systematic review of these successes and the reported limitations. Three methods were researched for this review: (i) the finger photo capture method and corresponding image sensors, (ii) the classical preprocessing method to prepare a finger image for a recognition task, and (iii) the deep-learning approach for contactless fingerprint recognition. Eight scientific articles were identified that matched all inclusion and exclusion criteria. Based on inferences from this review, we have discussed how deep learning methods could benefit the field of biometrics and the potential gaps that deep-learning approaches need to address for real-world biometric applications.

Keywords: biometrics; contactless fingerprint; deep learning; fingerprint analysis; fingerprint recognition

Citation: Chowdhury, A.M.M.; Imtiaz, M.H. Contactless Fingerprint Recognition Using Deep Learning—A Systematic Review. *J. Cybersecur. Priv.* **2022**, *2*, 714–730. https://doi.org/10.3390/jcp2030036

Academic Editor: Danda B. Rawat

Received: 17 July 2022
Accepted: 23 August 2022
Published: 8 September 2022

Publisher's Note: MDPI stays neutral with regard to jurisdictional claims in published maps and institutional affiliations.

1. Introduction

Contactless fingerprint identification technology has the potential to be one of the most reliable techniques for biometric identification [1,2]. The first contactless fingerprint recognition system was introduced in 2004 [3] as an alternative to traditional contact-based fingerprinting [4]. Since then, interest has grown, as shown by a continually growing number of publications by different research groups. This publication corroborates that the demand for contactless fingerprint recognition systems is increasing rapidly [5]. The National Institute of Standards and Technology (NIST) has also reported that contactless fingerprint recognition system is an important component of next-generation fingerprint technologies [6]. Generally, a contactless fingerprint system involves a high-resolution camera [7,8]. The captured images provide the details of fingerprints (ridge, valleys) and wrinkles, etc. [9]. One of the challenges of the traditional contact-based fingerprint recognition system is fingerprint capturing [10]. During the acquisition of a contact-based fingerprint, issues such as a latent fingerprint left by a previous user on the sensor surface lead to low fingerprint quality [10–12]. Also, deformation and distortion of fingerprints occur because of the pressure on the sensor surface [12]. Distortions can be caused by non-uniformity of the finger pressure on the device, finger ridge changes due to heavy labor or injuries, different illumination on finger skin, or motion artifacts during image capturing [13]. When fingerprints contact the scanner, the ridge flow may become discontinuous. A lot of background noise might also be introduced during capture [14]. Often, only a partial fingerprint is obtained because the rest might be either lost or smudged during capture [8], as shown in Figure 1. This process is subject to partial information, poor quality, distortions, and variations, including background and illumination [15]. The variations in sensors and the acquisition environment may introduce a wide range of intra-

and inter-class variability in the captured fingerprint in terms of resolution, orientation, sensor noise, and skin conditions. A finger photo acquired by a contactless sensor does not suffer from deformation or latent, hidden fingerprints [7,10]. However, new challenges are also present here. For example, captured images can be of poor quality, with different size, low resolution, background segmentation, or uncontrolled illumination, and face difficulty in extracting features like minutiae, finger enhancement, etc. [16]. According to the NIST, a standard fingerprint image, generally the frontal region of the finger, requires 500 dpi imaging sensors for a good-quality application [17]. These can be captured by smartphones or a handheld electronic device [7,18–20].

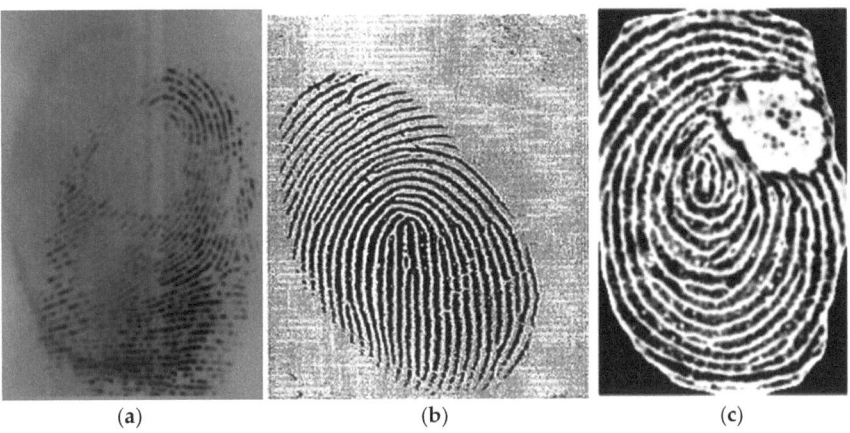

(a)　　　　　　　　　　(b)　　　　　　　　　　(c)

Figure 1. Different challenges for contact-based fingerprint images: (**a**) blurry images, (**b**) distorted image capture, (**c**) deformed images [21–23].

The contactless finger image obtains ridge–valley contrast that is different from a print made from the contact of a finger on a live-scan capture device [24]. To address this, different technologies for acquiring finger photos, such as 2D and 3D fingerprints, have been introduced [13,16,25,26]. Image processing can solve some issues, while the rest of them remain in contactless 2D and 3D fingerprint areas [27]. In recent years, deep-learning technology has demonstrated success in image recognition, classification, and feature representation [28–37]. These deep-learning models have also been employed in contactless fingerprint-based biometric technologies [38]. It is necessary to conduct a comprehensive survey on the latest research findings on 2D and 3D contactless fingerprint recognition systems based on deep-learning technology to understand those models and point out the future development direction. It is useful to note that there is a particular system of capturing contactless finger photo images that might impact the performance of the deep-learning models. Also, it will be useful to know how the limitations of classical machine-learning open the door for deep learning in the contactless fingerprint area. This study explored deep neural network (DNN) methods for contactless fingerprint recognition. For this, we needed to analyze the machine learning (ML)-based algorithms to compare with DNN methods. Photo capture and image processing are the first steps for contactless fingerprint recognition. We have explored the steps of feature extraction and recognition based on ML and DNN methods. Various test outputs with their performance were analyzed to validate the feasibility of the suggested DNN methods. This paper has investigated fingerprint capturing methods, fingerprint preprocessing, and feature extraction in both classical image processing and machine learning, as well as replacement of classical methods by deep learning. A total of 32 papers (without duplication) were found related to these topics. Following the application of inclusion and exclusion criteria, eight papers were selected for a full-text review.

The paper is organized as follows: first, the systematic review procedure is represented in Section 2 along with the description of three research questions (RQ). Section 3 presents a detailed investigation of the image-capturing method using image sensors. Section 4 explores relevant classical methods. Section 5 analyzes the deep neural network methods in contactless fingerprint recognition systems. Section 6 provides a discussion and Section 7 ends with conclusions for future work.

2. Review Methodology

The key focus of this review is an up-to-date summary of recent novel approaches. The systematic search procedure was set primarily following the Preferred Reporting Items for Systematic Reviews and Meta-Analyses (PRISMA) [23]. This methodology used the following processes: (a) identifying research question (RQ), (b) source of study (c) search strategy: setting inclusion/exclusion criteria, (d) results.

2.1. Research Questions

(1) RQ1. How do different sensor systems capture finger images to ensure the acceptable quality of fingerprints? Research findings will help to investigate whether the capturing systems have any impact on the model architecture or the recognition performance.
(2) RQ2. How does the classical machine-learning method preprocess the contactless finger images and prepare for recognition algorithms? Research findings explore the classical methods used for feature extraction, image segmentation, minutiae point extraction, image deblur, background noise removal, particular portion segmentation, and suitable feature extraction from finger images.
(3) RQ3. How do deep neural networks replace the classical recognition models? The answer will explore the architecture of related deep neural networks and their performance improvement over traditional methods.

2.2. Source of Studies

The search for relevant literature was performed across six repositories: Google Scholar, Science Direct, Wiley Online Library, ACM Digital library, MDPI, and IEEE. Search dates ranged from inception to 30 April 2022.

2.3. Search Strategy

The following 'free- text search terms' were used: 'finger photo recognition', 'finger-print identification', 'touchless fingerprint recognition'. The search results were strictly restricted to the English language. References from selected primary full-text articles were further analyzed for relevant publications. The selection was further narrowed by applying the eligibility criteria described in Table 1. Articles fulfilling the inclusion criteria were considered in this review, and those fulfilling the exclusion criteria were filtered out.

Table 1. Inclusion and Exclusion Criteria for this systematic review.

Inclusion Criteria	Exclusion Criteria
Article published in peer-reviewed venues	Papers not written in English
Article published since 2010	Traditional contact-based fingerprint method
Articles must address a certain combination of words i.e., deep learning + contactless fingerprint recognition	
Automate + fingerprint identification, 3D + contactless identification, smartphone/mobile + capture, contactless + finger photo	

A total of 49 publications were identified through the database search and three from the bibliography of those publications; however, 33 failed to satisfy the eligibility criteria and were excluded. Thus, 16 publications ultimately fulfilled the eligibility criteria for this review. Figure 2 illustrates the methodology and results of the review process.

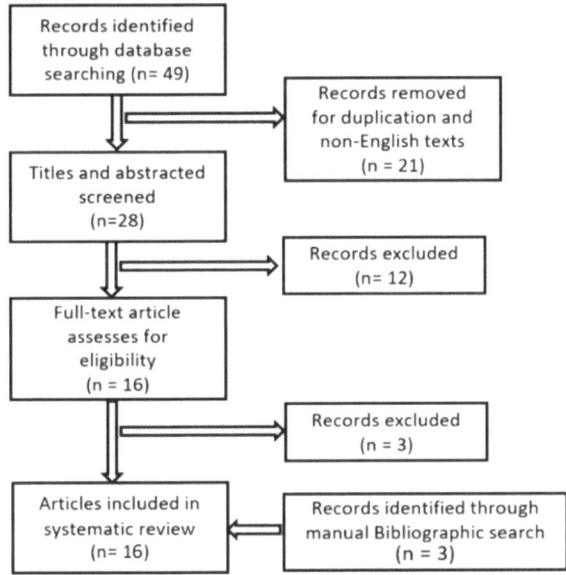

Figure 2. Flow diagram depicting the systematic review strategy.

2.4. Review Outcome

There are two types of contactless fingerprint capturing techniques: 2D and 3D. Smartphones and digital cameras can take 2D and 3D photos [17,39]; 3D contactless fingerprints can also be acquired with photometric stereo-based cameras [39], 3D fingerprint reconstruction, structured light-scanning-based 3D fingerprint reconstruction, etc. [40–47]. The general biometric workflow of a contactless fingerprint recognition system is described in Figure 3.

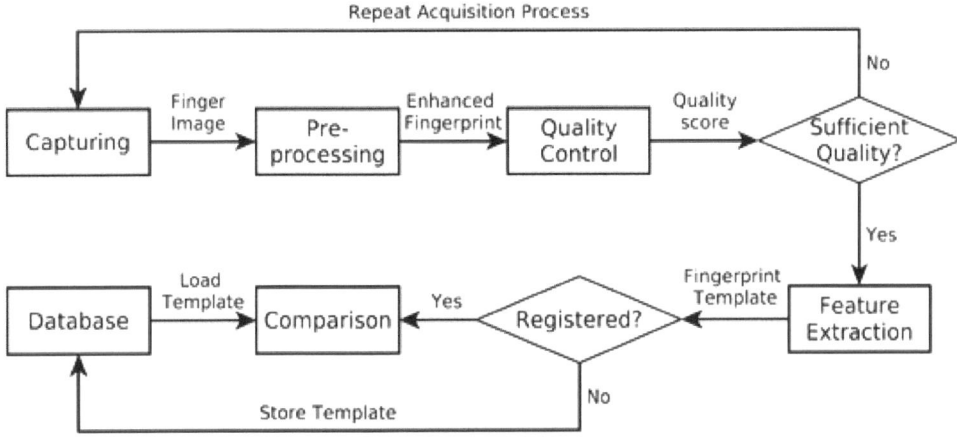

Figure 3. Overview of the sub-systems of a generic contactless fingerprint recognition system [10].

3. Contactless Fingerprint Capturing Methods

3.1. 2D Contactless Fingerprint Capturing Methods

During a contactless fingerprint capture, one or multiple fingers are presented to an optical device like a camera or lens. These devices can be (a) prototype hardware designs developed by researchers or (b) general-purpose devices customized to meet the unique needs for contactless fingerprint recognition [48].

Smartphone-based image acquisition is one of the widely available techniques to capture 2D contactless finger photos [4]. The NIST [17] published a document to assess contactless fingerprint capturing methods; the document provides proper instructions for contactless fingerprint capturing devices. It describes the smartphone's uniform light lighting, backdrop segmentation, and motion reduction during capture. Multi-finger capturing techniques can also be used with smartphones [49]. The advantage of multi-finger capture is the efficiency since feature extraction of all five fingers can occur from one single image [50]. To evaluate the performance of Nokia N95 and HTC Desire mobile phone for this, 1320 fingerprints were captured. A flashlight-enabled phone was used for appropriate illumination and to cover the entire finger area. However, the image quality was reported to be poor, as a flashlight performs well only in a dark setting [22]. To improve image quality and to reduce camera noise, dark environments might play a very important role. Auto-focus and maintenance of a standard distance from hand to phone may also be useful strategies. Figure 4 shows the identical distance and illumination from hand to phone.

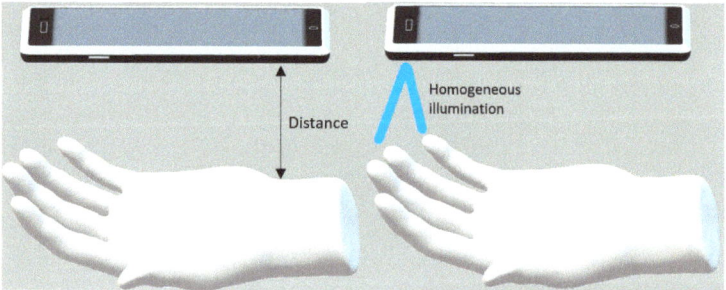

Figure 4. Homogeneous distance illumination with auto focus capturing by smartphone.

Figure 5 illustrates the impressions of a fingerprint taken with a contact-based fingerprint device (Figure 5a) and the corresponding finger image acquired using a non-contact device (Galaxy S8). (Figure 5b). The contact-based fingerprint can directly be used for finding feature such as: ridge, valley, delta cores, minutiae etc., whereas the corresponding contactless fingerprint image would need additional processing.

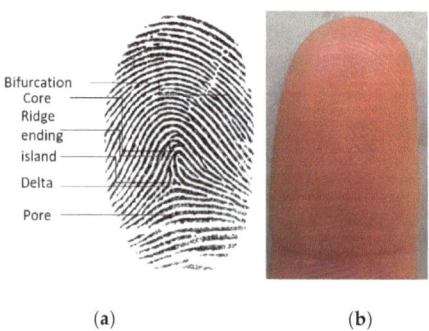

(**a**)   (**b**)

Figure 5. (**a**) Contact-based fingerprint, (**b**) contactless fingerprint (Samsung Galaxy S8) [15].

A digital camera is another tool to capture contactless 2D finger photos. The main feature of this system is white-color- and LED-color-based image sensors [10]. A three-camera-based system with blue LED is much more comfortable than a white LED for the user to acquire fingerprints. The charge-coupled camera device emits a green LED, and there is a stepper motor with a mirror that can capture five fingers at a time, making it convenient [11].

3.2. 3D Contactless Fingerprint Capturing Methods

Researchers have used lab-developed prototypes of the 3D fingerprint capture approach, which requires (i) photometric stereo techniques, (ii) structured light scanning, and (iii) stereo vision [51]. The photometric stereo-based 3D fingerprint method captures multiple 2D images under heterogeneous illumination using a high-speed camera. Time-of-flight (ToF) is the main principle of this technique, where surface reflectance is measured from fingerprint to light source [52]. This system is low-cost because it uses only one high-speed camera and multiple LEDs. Figure 6 shows the capturing method with camera and finger position.

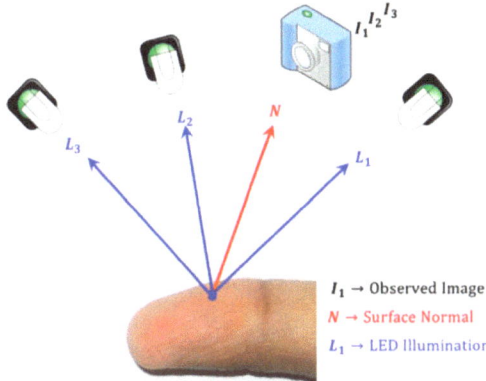

Figure 6. Acquisition of 3D fingerprint using photometric stereo techniques [39].

The structured light-scanning method consists of several high-speed cameras and a digital light-processing projector [53,54]. During the capture process, multiple 2D fingerprint images are captured under pattern illuminations, and 3D depth information is calculated through triangulation according to the point correspondences between images [55]. This method can recover ridge-valley details and achieve relatively accurate 3D depth information. However, the hardware system is expensive and bulky [39].

The stereo-vision-based 3D contactless fingerprint method is usually comprised of two or more cameras [51,56,57]. During the capture process, 2D fingerprint images are captured from different views. The 3D fingerprints are reconstructed by calculating 3D depth information between corresponding points according to the triangulation principle. The advantage is that the systems are simple, low-cost, and relatively compact. However, current methods are usually time-consuming because of the extensive computation of the correspondences between pixel points [58]. Table 2 shows the 2D and 3D capturing devices and their approximate cost, with light environment, etc.

Table 2. Overview of contactless 2D and 3D capturing devices and their properties.

Capturing Device	Authors	Cost	Light Environment	Finger Type
Mobile Phone (2D)	Lee et al. [19]	Low cost	No extra illumination	Single Finger
Digital Camera (2D)	Hiew et al. [59]	Low cost	Table lamp illumination	Single Finger
Digital Camera (2D)	Genovese et al. [60]	Medium cost	Green Light illumination	Finger slap
Webcam (2D)	Piuri et al. [61]	Low cost	Different illumination (white light, no light)	Single Finger
Webcam	Kumar and Zhou [9]	Low cost	No illumination	Finger slap
Smartphone (2D)	Derawi et al. [18]	Low cost	No illumination	Finger slap
Smartphone (2D)	Canrey et al. [49]	Low cost	Screen guidance. If flash required (Y/N)	Finger slap
Smartphone (2D)	Deb et al. [61]	Medium cost	3 smartphones in different illumination	Thumb and index finger
Smartphone (3D)	Xie et al. [51]	Medium cost	2 cameras with depth information	Finger slap

4. Classical Method to Extract Features from Contactless Fingerprints

The basic steps for contactless fingerprint recognition pipeline are shown in Figure 7 as a flowchart:

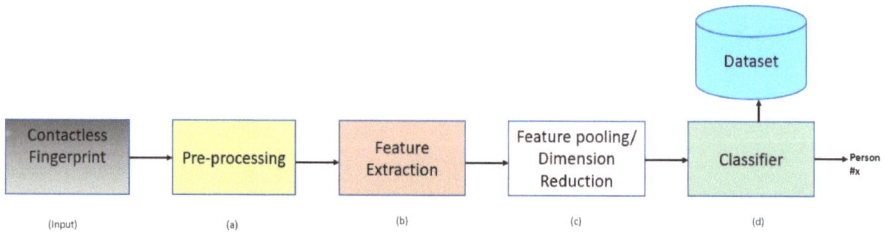

Figure 7. The fundamental steps for contactless fingerprint recognition from input to (**a**) preprocess the images; (**b**) Feature extraction (**c**) Dimension reduction; and (**d**) classified the person.

Most of the contact-based fingerprint images captured from the devices are grayscale and ready for feature extraction [62]. In contrast, most contactless finger-imaging solutions provide color RGB images that require preprocessing before feature extraction [63]. The primary challenges of preprocessing contactless finger images and recommended methods to overcome these challenges are shown in Table 3.

Table 3. Overview of challenges during the preprocessing of contactless finger images and proposed approaches.

Challenge	Authors	Year	Approach
Finger Segmentation	Wang et al. [62]	2017	Hand color estimation in YCbCr
Rotated pitched principal orientation estimation	Zaghetto et al. [9]	2015	Artificial neural network
Low contrast	Wang et al. [62]	2016	CLAHE and extensions
Distance to the sensor, ridge line frequency	Zaghetto et al [9]	2017	Frequency map, sensor-finger distance approximation
Core/principal singular point detection	Labati et al. [64]	2010	Poincare-based ridge orientation analysis
Deformation correction	Lin et al. [11]	2018	Robust thin-plate splines, deformation correction model

When processed with the classical methods, both contactless 2D and 3D images have issues with low focus of ridge/valley and blurred ROI (background) [57]. Misplaced or rotated fingers and the lack of skin deformation also cause processing issues [65]. An image processing pipeline must be developed based on the selected equipment and the environmental conditions needed during the image acquisition process. Image processing begins with the following common preprocessing steps:

Finger Segmentation and Detection: The initial step is to detect the finger based on color and shape. Sharpness, shape, color contrast, and image depth information are four different categories for improving contactless 2D and 3D finger detection and image segmentation [13]. Sharpness-based strategies utilize the difference between the focused, blurred background and the sharp finger area. This effect works best with images obtained with a very small finger-to-sensor distance and a wide-open aperture. One experiment showed that the variance-modified Laplacian of Gaussian (VMLOG) algorithm is best suited for contactless 2D fingerprint-capturing devices [10,66,67]. All finger shapes, from thumb to little finger, are highly similar for all finger position codes. A machine-learning-based algorithm has been applied to a binarized image in the LUV color model [10]. To make the skin color contrast and segment the skin and background color, the analysis of the YCbCr color space represents a very vital approach [64,68]. A different method of image segmentation and image depth information approach combined an RGB image via a smartphone [69]. These were able to extract the finger slap (the four fingers except the thumb) from busy backgrounds for further processing.

Minutiae-Based Feature Extraction: One of the main conditions for pre-processed contactless fingerprints is that images must be converted from RGB to greyscale [70]. Thus, ROI such as minutiae, ridge valley extraction, and finger orientation estimation must also be handled with a machine-learning approach. After detecting the finger, the ROI must be extracted, which involves the normalization of width, height, and resolution. This 3D contactless fingerprint preprocessing stage implies an extracted finger image as input. It should be noted that finger detection and ROI extraction are done in output. The color-based segmentation of ROI extraction constrained setups depends on contactless 3D finger geometry [10]. Several operations used the ridge–line orientation and shape to detect the core point [71]. Using a support vector machine (SVM) [72], it is easy to classify minutiae-based fingerprints and to detect the minutiae points as the detection points to refer to as a category [73]. SVM can determine the image quality with five feature vector lengths such as gray mean, gray variance, contrast, coherence, and the main energy ratio. These features take much training time to implement.

Fingerprint Image Enhancement: To improve image contrast and sharpness, image enhancement techniques such as spatial domain techniques and frequency domain techniques can be used to improve the quality [74,75]. Finger image enhancement should result in a fingerprint image with uniform illumination. Three different methods to achieve this appeared in the literature: a normalization using mean and variance filters [30], histogram enhancements like contrast-limited adaptive histogram equalization (CLAHE) [76], and local binary patterns (LBP) for enhancing the ridge–valley contrast of the 2D contactless fingerprint system [77]. Reducing the blurred image from the original image is another challenge in contactless 3D fingerprint enhancement [14]. A combination of image-processing algorithms and machine learning for extracting sweat pores of fingerprint patterns level-3 has been proposed by Genovese et al. [78].

5. Analyzing the Deep Neural Networks Methods Proposed for the Contactless Fingerprint Recognition Systems

Simple convolutional and pooling layers were utilized to create deep-learning models in many articles, but a multi-task fully convolutional network was used in three of them. The architecture for the multi-task deep convolutional network is shown in Figure 8.

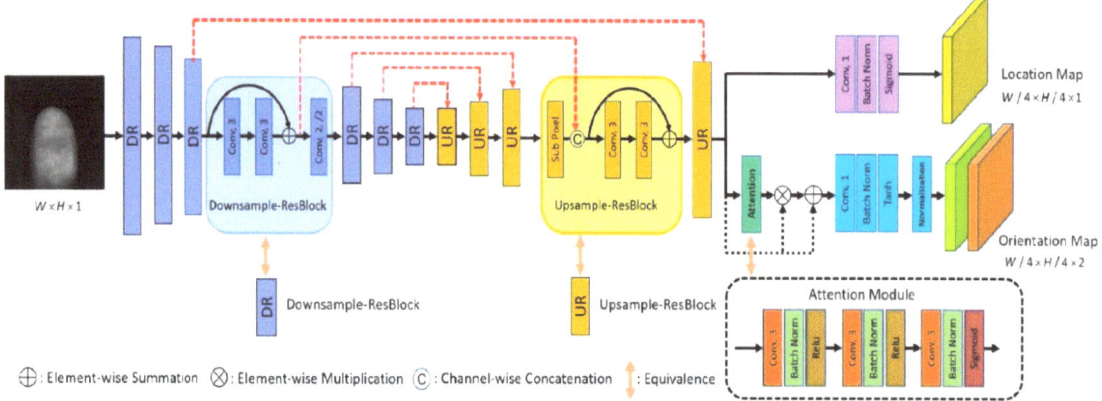

Figure 8. An architecture of multi-task deep convolutional networks [79].

Matching the contactless fingerprint with a traditional contact-based fingerprint using deep learning is a new domain in biometrics research. In order to recognize contactless fingerprints, this paper [67] described a convolutional neural network (CNN) framework. The convolutional and pooling layers are the two main layers of the algorithm. The convolutional layers were used to execute low-level features such as edges, corners, etc. Pooling layers enabled correct operations such as reducing the dimension of feature maps. Ten images were provided to the CNN model as an input batch for training. A training accuracy of 100 percent was attained after four iterations. At 95 percent of testing accuracy, 140 out of 275 images were used for testing purpose.

A fully convolutional network was applied for minutiae detection and extraction in [79]. The minute point and its corresponding direction were processed and analyzed using contactless grayscale fingerprint images from two different public datasets [12,80]. Images were assessed online after being trained offline. A full-sized contactless fingerprint from two different datasets (9000, 6000) was applied as an input and its corresponding minute ground truth was indicated as an output in the offline portion. In conjunction with a novel loss function, this method concurrently learns the minutiae detection and orientation. One of the main claims of this study is that a multi-task technique outperforms any single minutiae detection task. An hourglass-shaped encoder–decoder network [81] structure was applied for a multi-task deep neural network called ContactlessMinuNet architecture [79]. To process the input fingerprint images, a shared encoder subnetwork was used. For up-sampling, the subnetwork was decoded to expand the image. Lastly, the network split into two branches for minutiae detection and direction computation.

Minutiae point detection branch: In this network [79], the input feature represents the detection of minutiae points, and the output represents the probability of each pixel's minutiae points. The network is very simple, with a 1×1 convolutional layer, a batch normalization layer that standardizes the input layer, and a sigmoid layer. A non-linear activation function sigmoid layer is used to generate minutiae location.

Minutiae direction regression branch: This network [79] is designed to predict the minutiae direction. Pixel-by-pixel images were extracted with a phase angle $oi \in (0,2\pi)$. The subnetwork works as input features, and the output layer predicts minutiae direction. A convolutional layer (1×1), batch normalization, and non-linear activation function *tanh* layer were used to predict the minutiae path.

Using 3×3 CNN layers, the final convolution has been used with (stride = 1) and padding to keep the height and width constant. For testing, the proposed method was compared with the benchmark dataset of the PolyU dataset [12]. The accuracy of minutiae detection and its location increased to 94.10% compared to 89.61%. The proposed method of this study is shown in Figure 9.

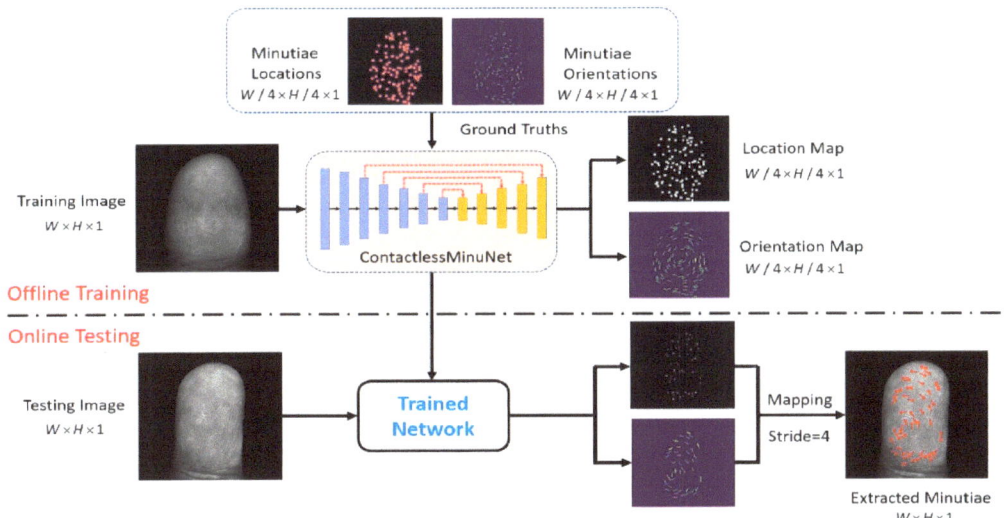

Figure 9. Overview of the minutiae extraction algorithm for contactless fingerprints based on multi-task fully deep convolutional neural network [2].

A study reported in [82] suggested how to extract a minutiae point from an input image without preprocessing. To train the model and obtain the output without any preprocessing, a number of deep neural networks have been deployed. Initially, JudgeNet was trained to locate the minutiae regions and picked a general overview of detecting minutiae points. The original image resolution was 640×640 and 500 ppi with 200 labeled images. A max pooling was used to reduce the image dimensions, and it showed image dimensions of 45×65. Using multiscale input and four CNN layers, the network performed very well to get the accurate output. Later, another deep CNN layer named LocalNet specifically indicated the directions of minutiae with a more concise image dimension of 45×45 and decided the specific location. Lastly, a comprehensive estimation and decision were made to add or eliminate the minutiae location. The overview of the network architecture is shown in Figure 10.

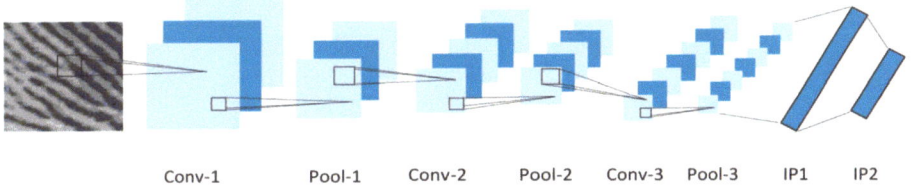

| Conv-1 | Pool-1 | Conv-2 | Pool-2 | Conv-3 | Pool-3 | IP1 | IP2 |

Figure 10. JudgeNet and LocalNet share a similar convolutional architecture [82].

A method was proposed [83] to get the proper position of the contactless fingerprint of multi-view 3D fingerprint features using CNN. A fully convolutional network (FCN) was applied with this model for automatic fingerprint segmentation and three Siamese networks for fingerprint multi-view. Various convolutional neural network models such as VGG net [31], AlexNet [84], and GoogleNet [85] are introduced in this work. These architectures are very well-trained pixel-to-pixel deep networks. For foreground and background segmentation, semantic segmentation architecture was applied. This model clusters the same image together with a different class. To predict each pixel from the top-view of the fingerprint, they used the softmax loss function. The Siamese convolutional network worked very well to match image pairs (matched and unmatched) in the same network. Three Siamese networks indicated the positions: top view, side 1 view, side 2 view. The network is structured with six convolutional layers with one fully connected layer. One to five layers are followed by max-pooling, where the input patch size was 256×192.

The kernel size was 3×3 with stride value 2. The output numbers from the feature map were 64, 96, 128, 256, and 512, generated from the 48-feature map in the first convolutional layer. The final result was presented in the receiving operating characteristic (ROC) curve and the equal error rate (EER) curve to evaluate performance. Using computing matching scores from CNN-based features and minutiae-based features, another Siamese convolutional neural network was applied to extract the global feature from a finger photo. They mentioned that fingerprint images have many global features that ease extraction of the features using CNN. Using an input image size of 310×240, the first convolutional layer was introduced with a kernel size of 3×3 with batch normalization. By evaluating the ROC curve and EER curve, they showed the estimation of EER; minutiae matching rate was 11.39% and 4.09%, respectively. Figure 11 shows how a fully convolutional network segments the fingerprint background and directs the capturing methods of multi-view with deep representation:

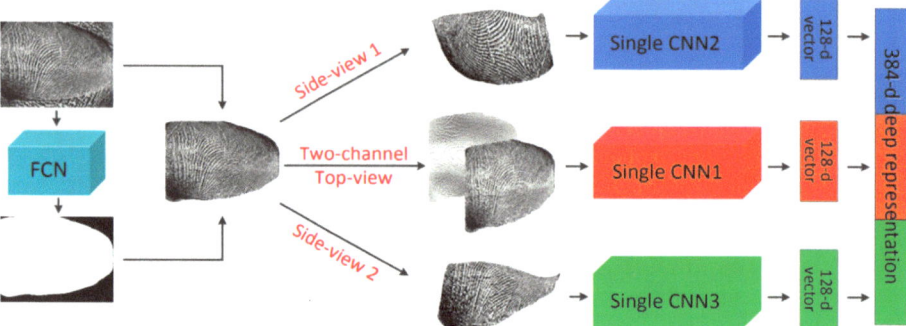

Figure 11. Automatic learning of 3D fingerprint features via deep representation [86].

A CNN-based framework has been applied [78] to make an accurate comparison between contactless fingerprints and contact-based fingerprints. Minutiae points, ridge maps, and specific regions are the targeted metrics to establish the comparison [83]. A multi-Siamese network was used to train and learn the minutiae features. As the image dataset was collected from different sensors, a CNN-based cross-comparison framework was used to compare contactless and contact-based fingerprints. Figure 12 shows the deep-feature representation generation process:

A data augmentation process was used in 5780 contactless and contact-based images from 320 fingers [78]; 3840 images were used in the training set while the rest were used for testing purposes. The image size remained 192×192 in every image. A public dataset was used to determine the performance and to compare and validate the dataset. The dataset contains 1500 fingers data with 3000 contactless fingerprint samples. For the performance metrics and evaluation, the ROC method (receiver operating characteristics) and EER (equal error rate) were used. To obtain the fingerprint recognition, CMC (cumulative match characteristics) and rank-one accuracy methods were applied. The comparative experimental evaluations are shown in Table 4. Also, in Table 5 shows the total summary of the described articles of deep learning in Section 5.

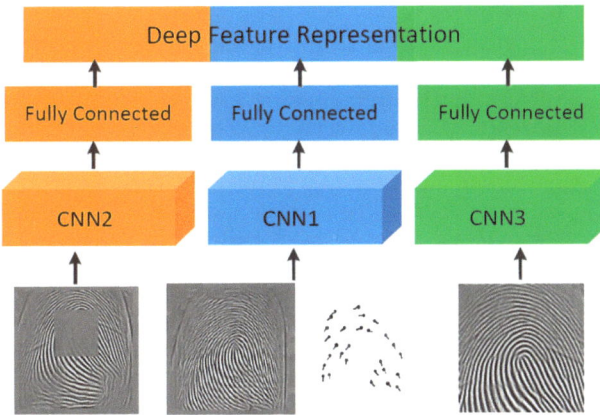

Figure 12. Deep-feature representation generation process using three multi-Siamese networks [83].

Table 4. Experimental evaluation of two datasets.

Experiments	Equal Error Rate (ERR)	Rank-One Accuracy
Deformation correction model [87] on dataset A	16.17%	41.82%
Minutiae matcher in NIST [88] on dataset A	43.83%	10.99%
Proposed method on dataset A	7.93%	64.59%
Deformation correction model [87] on dataset B	21.60%	38.90%
Minutiae matcher in NIST [88] on dataset B	38.01%	24.92%
Proposed method on dataset B	7.11%	58.87%

Table 5. The following table describes the summary of the analysis.

Study	Database	Training Data	Purpose of Deep Learning	Input to Deep Neural Network	Output from Deep Neural Network	Performance Metrics
[67]	Private	275 images with 55 different people	Fingerprint Recognition	RGB to Gray scale images	Feature matching	Classification (Metric Accuracy)
[78]	Public	5760 images from 320 fingers	Minutiae Extraction	Gray scale images	Extracted minutiae images	AUC, EER
[79]	Private + Public	9000/6000/1320 images	Multiview fingerprint recognition	Gray scale images	Feature (Ridge, valley) representation	EER
[80]	Public	100 images	Minutiae Extraction	Gray scale images	Extracted Minutiae images	Classification (Metric Accuracy)
[82]	Private + Public	500 images	CNN based framework for Contactless fingerprint	HSV images	Similarity distance between two images	ROC curve
[83]	Public	9920 images	To correct fingerprint viewpoint	Gray scale images	Correct images	ROC and CMC curve

6. Discussion

This review is intended to provide a systematic survey of the deep-learning approaches employed for contactless fingerprint processing. The review surveyed eight full-text scientific research articles showing how deep learning can replace machine learning in contactless fingerprint contexts. This review was focused on three major research questions: the contactless finger photo capturing method, the classical approach of fingerprint recognition, and the use of deep learning. The first research question shows the direction of the different capturing methods and various camera sensors. This analysis might help researchers to understand divergent capturing methods and their limitations. Also, they might be motivated to employ smartphone-based finger photo capturing. In the second research question, we explained how classical machine-learning techniques have been introduced into contactless fingerprint recognition methods. This review covered feature extraction, image segmentation, and blur reduction; however, systems like data acquisition, data cleaning, data labeling, etc. were beyond the scope of this review.

The main contribution of this paper is the review of the use of deep learning, specifically, its impact and usability in the field of contactless fingerprints. We have discussed how a contactless recognition system can benefit from using deep learning. In addition, we have also pointed out potential vulnerabilities in classical methods and shown the applicability of deep learning to real-world applications. Research Question 3 shows that the following factors can impact the research of contactless fingerprint recognition systems:

Feature learning: Deep-learning methods have an advantage over previous state-of-the-art methods because they can learn features from data. Contactless fingerprint recognition systems require both local and global features [89] and are compatible with hierarchical and structural feature learning enabled by deep learning [90]. In addition to processing and labeling with the handcrafting data, some tools like labelme and image-label will be difficult in most cases. Therefore, deep learning can assist in preprocessing or extraction of the features of fingerprint images. The learned features can be generalized to previously unseen datasets and other related tasks (for example, features learned for contactless fingerprint recognition can also be used for fingerprint attribute estimation, e.g., ridge, minutiae pattern). In addition, pre-training improves feature-learning by large amounts of unlabeled data when using smaller training datasets.

Concentration on Identification: Authentication and recognition have been the primary focus of deep-learning research in the contactless fingerprint context. Authentication is a comparably easy problem and estimates well for a large number of subjects. However, the more challenging part is the identification problem. The biometric system needs to distinguish between potentially millions of identities for large-scale identification. This system requires complex deep-learning architectures to capture definite interclass differences and handle large intra-class variability. Consequently, much training data would be required to capture these variations.

Large-scale datasets: Though deep-learning approaches have already exceeded human performance on some in-the-wild, large-scale datasets, these datasets do not meet the requirements of real-world, high-security applications. In addition, there is a lack of large-scale datasets for contactless fingerprint modalities in biometrics to benefit from deep learning. Even if large datasets are available, each individual needs to have sufficient representative samples to consider for various influencing factors.

Dataset quality: Existing fingerprint recognition datasets are mostly gathered from the public dataset. It is important to use large-scale datasets that capture real-world variations for biometrics to benefit from deep learning, especially in the contactless fingerprint area.

Computing resources: Along with the increased use of mobile devices, secure authentication commercial devices have become necessary modern technologies. However, if complex deep-learning architectures are required for authentication, such devices might not have the necessary computing resources for storing the dataset. A cloud-based system could be a solution for restoring the data collected from those devices.

Training deep-learning models with proper computing resources: The success of deep learning has been largely demonstrated by industries with access to large amounts of data and computational resources. For most other researchers, computing resources are limited, and it is imperative to speed up the training of deep-learning approaches. We need to strive for data-efficient learning algorithms.

7. Conclusions

This review focused on three major research questions: the contactless finger photo capturing method, the classical approach to fingerprint recognition, and the use of deep learning. Specifically, we have detailed deep-learning methods, as these methods have shown development in contactless fingerprint recognition, though little has been explored. The accuracy of contactless fingerprints is increasing day by day and they have facilitated a new range of fingerprinting applications. They have increased the security system threats with respect to terrorism and cyber-crime development. Commercial facilities, border crossing areas, airports, and government access points are also employing contactless fingerprint biometrics. Further, credit card account fraud, hijacking of websites, and most importantly, the critical corruption of governmental agencies such as the Department of Defense and the Department of Homeland Security require the development of systems for which contactless fingerprint biometrics can be a solution. These deep-learning methods have demonstrated good generalization capability for different datasets. We have summarized their architecture and implementation at various sub-stages, including pre-processing, features extraction, classification, or matching. This study also covered the possible drawbacks of deep-learning models.

In summary, deep-learning-based contactless 3D fingerprint identification systems have shown enhanced usability, and soon they will be a widely used biometric performance modality. Therefore, our future research will be focused on creating new or existing deep-learning techniques to address certain upcoming contactless fingerprint challenges, such as speeding up feature extraction, reducing the amount of time required to process images, and improving identification accuracy. Additionally, other biometric characteristics such as patterns in palmprints will be taken into consideration as applications of deep-learning techniques.

Author Contributions: A.M.M.C. prepared the article and M.H.I. Supervised him. All authors have read and agreed to the published version of the manuscript.

Funding: This research received no external funding.

Institutional Review Board Statement: Not applicable.

Informed Consent Statement: Not applicable.

Data Availability Statement: Not applicable.

Conflicts of Interest: The authors declare that no conflict of interest.

References

1. Maltoni, D.; Maio, D.; Jain, A.K.; Prabhakar, S. Synthetic fingerprint generation. In *Handbook of Fingerprint Recognition*; Springer: London, UK, 2009; pp. 271–302.
2. Choi, H.; Choi, K.; Kim, J. Mosaicing touchless and mirror-reflected fingerprint images. *IEEE Trans. Inf. Forensics Secur.* **2010**, *5*, 52–61. [CrossRef]
3. Song, Y.; Lee, C.; Kim, J. A new scheme for touchless fingerprint recognition system. In Proceedings of 2004 International Symposium on Intelligent Signal Processing and Communication Systems, ISPACS, Seoul, Korea, 18–19 November 2004.
4. Kumar, A. Introduction to trends in fingerprint identification. In *Contactless 3D Fingerprint Identification*; Springer: Berlin/Heidelberg, Germany, 2018; pp. 1–15.
5. Oduah, U.I.; Kevin, I.F.; Oluwole, D.O.; Izunobi, J.U. Towards a high-precision contactless fingerprint scanner for biometric authentication. *Array* **2021**, *11*, 100083. [CrossRef] [PubMed]
6. Stanton, B.C.; Stanton, B.C.; Theofanos, M.F.; Furman, S.M.; Grother, P.J. *Usability Testing of a Contactless Fingerprint Device: Part 2*; US Department of Commerce, National Institute of Standards and Technology: Gaithersburg, MD, USA, 2016.

7. Raghavendra, R.; Busch, C.; Yang, B. Scaling-robust fingerprint verification with smartphone camera in real-life scenarios. In Proceedings of the 2013 IEEE Sixth International Conference on Biometrics: Theory, Applications and Systems (BTAS), Arlington, VA, USA, 29 September–2 October 2013.
8. Mil'shtein, S.; Paradise, M.; Bustos, P.; Baier, M.; Foret, S.; Kunnil, V.O.; Northrup, J. Contactless challenges. *Biom. Technol. Today* **2011**, *2011*, 10–11. [CrossRef]
9. Kumar, A.; Zhou, Y. Contactless fingerprint identification using level zero features. In Proceedings of the IEEE CVPR 2011 Workshops, Colorado Springs, CO, USA, 20–25 June 2011.
10. Priesnitz, J.; Rathgeb, C.; Buchmann, N.; Busch, C.; Margraf, M. An overview of touchless 2D fingerprint recognition. *EURASIP J. Image Video Process.* **2021**, *2021*, 1–28. [CrossRef]
11. Noh, D.; Choi, H.; Kim, J. Touchless sensor capturing five fingerprint images by one rotating camera. *Opt. Eng.* **2011**, *50*, 113202. [CrossRef]
12. Lin, C.; Kumar, A. Matching contactless and contact-based conventional fingerprint images for biometrics identification. *IEEE Trans. Image Process.* **2018**, *27*, 2008–2021. [CrossRef]
13. Wang, Y.; Hassebrook, L.G.; Lau, D.L. Data acquisition and processing of 3-D fingerprints. *IEEE Trans. Inf. Forensics Secur.* **2010**, *5*, 750–760. [CrossRef]
14. Tang, Y.; Jiang, L.; Hou, Y.; Wang, R. Contactless fingerprint image enhancement algorithm based on Hessian matrix and STFT. In Proceedings of the 2017 2nd International Conference on Multimedia and Image Processing (ICMIP), Wuhan, China, 17–19 March 2017.
15. Dharavath, K.; Talukdar, F.A.; Laskar, R.H. Study on biometric authentication systems, challenges and future trends: A review. In Proceedings of the 2013 IEEE International Conference on Computational Intelligence and Computing Research, Enathi, India, 26–28 December 2013.
16. Parziale, G.; Chen, Y. Advanced technologies for touchless fingerprint recognition. In *Handbook of Remote Biometrics*; Springer: London, UK, 2009; pp. 83–109.
17. Libert, J.; Grantham, J.; Bandini, B.; Wood, S.; Garris, M.; Ko, K.; Byers, F.; Watson, C. Guidance for evaluating contactless fingerprint acquisition devices. *NIST Spec. Publ.* **2018**, *500*, 305.
18. Derawi, M.O.; Yang, B.; Busch, C. Fingerprint recognition with embedded cameras on mobile phones. In *Proceedings of the International Conference on Security and Privacy in Mobile Information and Communication Systems*; Springer: Berlin/Heidelberg, Germany, 2011.
19. Lee, C.; Lee, S.; Kim, J.; Kim, S.J. Preprocessing of a fingerprint image captured with a mobile camera. In *International Conference on Biometrics*; Springer: Berlin/Heidelberg, Germany, 2006.
20. Su, Q.; Tian, J.; Chen, X.; Yang, X. A fingerprint authentication system based on mobile phone. In *International Conference on Audio-and Video-Based Biometric Person Authentication*; Springer: Berlin/Heidelberg, Germany, 2005.
21. Agarwal, A.; Singh, R.; Vatsa, M. Fingerprint sensor classification via mélange of handcrafted features. In Proceedings of the 2016 23rd International Conference on Pattern Recognition (ICPR), Cancun, Mexico, 4–8 December 2016.
22. Zhao, Q.; Jain, A.; Abramovich, G. 3D to 2D fingerprints: Unrolling and distortion correction. In Proceedings of the 2011 International Joint Conference on Biometrics (IJCB), Washington, DC, USA, 11–13 October 2011.
23. Drahansky, M.; Dolezel, M.; Urbanek, J.; Brezinova, E.; Kim, T.H. Influence of skin diseases on fingerprint recognition. *J. Biomed. Biotechnol.* **2012**, *2012*, 626148. [CrossRef]
24. Pillai, A.; Mil'shtein, S. Can contactless fingerprints be compared to existing database? In Proceedings of the 2012 IEEE Conference on Technologies for Homeland Security (HST), Waltham, MA, USA, 13–15 November 2012.
25. ISO/IEC 2382-37; Biometrics, I.I.J.S. 2017 Information Technology-Vocabulary-Part 37: Biometrics. International Organization for Standardization: Geneva, Switzerland, 2017.
26. Yin, X.; Zhu, Y.; Hu, J. A Survey on 2D and 3D Contactless Fingerprint Biometrics: A Taxonomy, Review, and Future Directions. *IEEE Open J. Comput. Soc.* **2021**, *2*, 370–381. [CrossRef]
27. Shafaei, S.; Inanc, T.; Hassebrook, L.G. A new approach to unwrap a 3-D fingerprint to a 2-D rolled equivalent fingerprint. In Proceedings of the 2009 IEEE 3rd International Conference on Biometrics: Theory, Applications, and Systems, Washington, DC, USA, 28–30 September 2009.
28. Affonso, C.; Rossi, A.L.D.; Vieira, F.H.A.; de Leon Ferreira, A.C.P. Deep learning for biological image classification. *Expert Syst. Appl.* **2017**, *85*, 114–122. [CrossRef]
29. Cai, L.; Gao, J.; Zhao, D. A review of the application of deep learning in medical image classification and segmentation. *Ann. Transl. Med.* **2020**, *8*, 713. [CrossRef] [PubMed]
30. Wu, M.; Chen, L. Image recognition based on deep learning. In Proceedings of the 2015 IEEE Chinese Automation Congress (CAC), Wuhan, China, 27–29 November 2015.
31. Pak, M.; Kim, S. A review of deep learning in image recognition. In Proceedings of the 2017 4th International Conference on Computer Applications and Information Processing Technology (CAIPT), Kuta Bali, Indonesia, 8–10 August 2017.
32. Wu, R.; Yan, S.; Shan, Y.; Dang, Q.; Sun, G. Deep image: Scaling up image recognition. *arXiv* **2015**, arXiv:1501.02876.
33. Li, Y. Research and application of deep learning in image recognition. In Proceedings of the 2022 IEEE 2nd International Conference on Power, Electronics and Computer Applications (ICPECA), Shenyang, China, 21–23 January 2022.

34. Jia, X. Image recognition method based on deep learning. In Proceedings of the 2017 29th Chinese Control and Decision Conference (CCDC), Chongqing, China, 28–30 May 2017.
35. Cheng, F.; Zhang, H.; Fan, W.; Harris, B. Image recognition technology based on deep learning. *Wirel. Per. Commun.* **2018**, *102*, 1917–1933. [CrossRef]
36. Coates, A.; Ng, A.Y. Learning feature representations with k-means. In *Neural Networks: Tricks of the Trade*; Springer: Berlin/Heidelberg, Germany, 2012; pp. 561–580.
37. Zhong, G.; Wang, L.N.; Ling, X.; Dong, J. An overview on data representation learning: From traditional feature learning to recent deep learning. *J. Financ. Data Sci.* **2016**, *2*, 265–278. [CrossRef]
38. Minaee, S.; Abdolrashidi, A.; Su, H.; Bennamoun, M.; Zhang, D. Biometrics recognition using deep learning: A survey. *arXiv* **2019**, arXiv:1912.00271.
39. Kumar, A. *Contactless 3D Fingerprint Identification*; Springer: Cham, Switzerland, 2018.
40. Jia, W.; Yi, W.J.; Saniie, J.; Oruklu, E. 3D image reconstruction and human body tracking using stereo vision and Kinect technology. In Proceedings of the 2012 IEEE International Conference on Electro/Information Technology, Indianapolis, IN, USA, 6–8 May 2012.
41. Yin, X.; Zhu, Y.; Hu, J. 3D fingerprint recognition based on ridge-valley-guided 3D reconstruction and 3D topology polymer feature extraction. *IEEE Trans. Pattern Anal. Mach. Intell.* **2019**, *43*, 1085–1091. [CrossRef]
42. Song, P.; Yu, H.; Winkler, S. Vision-based 3D finger interactions for mixed reality games with physics simulation. In Proceedings of the 7th ACM SIGGRAPH International Conference on Virtual-Reality Continuum and Its Applications in Industry, Singapore, 8–9 December 2008.
43. Liu, F.; Zhang, D. 3D fingerprint reconstruction system using feature correspondences and prior estimated finger model. *Pattern Recognit.* **2014**, *47*, 178–193. [CrossRef]
44. Liu, F.; Zhang, D.; Shen, L. Study on novel curvature features for 3D fingerprint recognition. *Neurocomputing* **2015**, *168*, 599–608. [CrossRef]
45. Nayar, S.K.; Gupta, M. Diffuse structured light. In Proceedings of the 2012 IEEE International Conference on Computational Photography (ICCP), Seattle, WA, USA, 28–29 April 2012.
46. Zhang, L.; Curless, B.; Seitz, S.M. Rapid shape acquisition using color structured light and multi-pass dynamic programming. In Proceedings of the First International Symposium on 3D Data Processing Visualization and Transmission, Padova, Italy, 19–21 June 2002.
47. Kumar, A.; Kwong, C. Towards contactless, low-cost and accurate 3D fingerprint identification. In Proceedings of the IEEE Conference on Computer Vision and Pattern Recognition, Portland, OR, USA, 23–28 June 2013.
48. Parziale, G. Touchless fingerprinting technology. In *Advances in Biometrics*; Springer: London, UK, 2008; pp. 25–48.
49. Carney, L.A.; Kane, J.; Mather, J.F.; Othman, A.; Simpson, A.G.; Tavanai, A.; Tyson, R.A.; Xue, Y. A multi-finger touchless fingerprinting system: Mobile fingerphoto and legacy database interoperability. In Proceedings of the 2017 4th International Conference on Biomedical and Bioinformatics Engineering, Seoul, Korea, 12–14 November 2017.
50. Rilvan, M.A.; Chao, J.; Hossain, M.S. Capacitive swipe gesture based smartphone user authentication and identification. In Proceedings of the 2020 IEEE Conference on Cognitive and Computational Aspects of Situation Management (CogSIMA), Victoria, BC, Canada, 24–29 August 2020.
51. Xie, W.; Song, Z.; Chung, R.C. Real-time three-dimensional fingerprint acquisition via a new photometric stereo means. *Opt. Eng.* **2013**, *52*, 103103. [CrossRef]
52. Zhang, D.; Lu, G. 3D biometrics technologies and systems. In *3D Biometrics*; Springer: New York, NY, USA, 2013; pp. 19–33.
53. Jecić, S.; Drvar, N. The assessment of structured light and laser scanning methods in 3D shape measurements. In Proceedings of the 4th International Congress of Croatian Society of Mechanics, Bizovac, Croatia, 18–20 September 2003.
54. Bell, T.; Li, B.; Zhang, S. Structured light techniques and applications. In *Wiley Encyclopedia of Electrical and Electronics Engineering*; John Wiley & Sons, Inc.: Hoboken, NJ, USA, 1999; pp. 1–24.
55. Salih, Y.; Malik, A.S. Depth and geometry from a single 2D image using triangulation. In Proceedings of the 2012 IEEE International Conference on Multimedia and Expo Workshops, Melbourne, Australia, 9–13 July 2012.
56. Labati, R.D.; Genovese, A.; Piuri, V.; Scotti, F. Toward unconstrained fingerprint recognition: A fully touchless 3-D system based on two views on the move. *IEEE Trans. Syst. Man Cybern. Syst.* **2015**, *46*, 202–219. [CrossRef]
57. Liu, F.; Zhang, D.; Song, C.; Lu, G. Touchless multiview fingerprint acquisition and mosaicking. *IEEE Trans. Instrum. Meas.* **2013**, *62*, 2492–2502. [CrossRef]
58. Sero, D.; Garachon, I.; Hermens, E.; Liere, R.V.; Batenburg, K.J. The study of three-dimensional fingerprint recognition in cultural heritage: Trends and challenges. *J. Comput. Cult. Herit.* **2021**, *14*, 1–20. [CrossRef]
59. Genovese, A.; Munoz, E.; Piuri, V.; Scotti, F.; Sforza, G. Towards touchless pore fingerprint biometrics: A neural approach. In Proceedings of the 2016 IEEE Congress on Evolutionary Computation (CEC), Vancouver, BC, Canada, 24–29 July 2016.
60. Piuri, V.; Scotti, F. Fingerprint biometrics via low-cost sensors and webcams. In Proceedings of the 2008 IEEE Second International Conference on Biometrics: Theory, Applications and Systems, Washington, DC, USA, 29 September–1 October 2008.
61. Deb, D.; Chugh, T.; Engelsma, J.; Cao, K.; Nain, N.; Kendall, J.; Jain, A.K. Matching fingerphotos to slap fingerprint images. *arXiv* **2018**, arXiv:1804.08122.

62. Priesnitz, J.; Huesmann, R.; Rathgeb, C.; Buchmann, N.; Busch, C. Mobile contactless fingerprint recognition: Implementation, performance and usability aspects. *Sensors* **2022**, *22*, 792. [CrossRef] [PubMed]

63. Wang, K.; Jiang, J.; Cao, Y.; Xing, X.; Zhang, R. Preprocessing algorithm research of touchless fingerprint feature extraction and matching. In *Chinese Conference on Pattern Recognition*; Springer: Singapore, 2016.

64. Liu, K.; Gong, D.; Meng, F.; Chen, H.; Wang, G.G. Gesture segmentation based on a two-phase estimation of distribution algorithm. *Inf. Sci.* **2017**, *394*, 88–105. [CrossRef]

65. Bhattacharyya, D.; Ranjan, R.; Alisherov, F.; Choi, M. Biometric authentication: A review. *Int. J. u- e-Serv. Sci. Technol.* **2009**, *2*, 13–28.

66. Khalil, M.S.; Wan, F.K. A review of fingerprint pre-processing using a mobile phone. In Proceedings of the 2012 International Conference on Wavelet Analysis and Pattern Recognition, Xi'an, China, 15–17 July 2012.

67. Khalil, M.S.; Kurniawan, F.; Saleem, K. Authentication of fingerprint biometrics acquired using a cellphone camera: A review. *Int. J. Wavelets Multiresolut. Inf. Process.* **2013**, *11*, 1350033. [CrossRef]

68. Kaur, A.; Kranthi, B. Comparison between YCbCr color space and CIELab color space for skin color segmentation. *Int. J. Appl. Inf. Syst.* **2012**, *3*, 30–33.

69. Tassis, L.M.; de Souza, J.E.T.; Krohling, R.A. A deep learning approach combining instance and semantic segmentation to identify diseases and pests of coffee leaves from in-field images. *Comput. Electron. Agric.* **2021**, *186*, 106191. [CrossRef]

70. Priesnitz, J.; Rathgeb, C.; Buchmann, N.; Busch, C. Touchless fingerprint sample quality: Prerequisites for the applicability of NFIQ2. 0. In Proceedings of the 2020 International Conference of the Biometrics Special Interest Group (BIOSIG), Darmstadt, Germany, 16–18 September 2020.

71. Chinnappan, C.; Porkodi, R. Fingerprint Recognition Technology Using Deep Learning: A Review. *SSRN Electron. J.* **2021**, *9*, 4647–4663.

72. Wu, Q.; Zhou, D.-X. Analysis of support vector machine classification. *J. Comput. Anal. Appl.* **2006**, *8*.

73. Zhang, Y. Support vector machine classification algorithm and its application. In *International Conference on Information Computing and Applications*; Springer: Berlin/Heidelberg, Germany, 2012.

74. Gowri, D.S.; Amudha, T. A review on mammogram image enhancement techniques for breast cancer detection. In Proceedings of the 2014 International Conference on Intelligent Computing Applications, Coimbatore, India, 6–7 March 2014.

75. Fenshia Singh, J.; Magudeeswaran, V. A machine learning approach for brain image enhancement and segmentation. *Int. J. Imaging Syst. Technol.* **2017**, *27*, 311–316. [CrossRef]

76. Gragnaniello, D.; Poggi, G.; Sansone, C.; Verdoliva, L. Local contrast phase descriptor for fingerprint liveness detection. *Pattern Recognit.* **2015**, *48*, 1050–1058. [CrossRef]

77. Hu, Z.; Li, D.; Isshiki, T.; Kunieda, H. Hybrid Minutiae Descriptor for Narrow Fingerprint Verification. *IEICE Trans. Inf. Syst.* **2017**, *100*, 546–555. [CrossRef]

78. Svoboda, J. *Deep Learning for 3D Hand Biometric Systems*; Università della Svizzera Italiana: Lugano, Switzerland, 2020.

79. Zhang, Z.; Liu, S.; Liu, M. A multi-task fully deep convolutional neural network for contactless fingerprint minutiae extraction. *Pattern Recognit.* **2021**, *120*, 108189. [CrossRef]

80. Zhou, W.; Hu, J.; Petersen, I.; Wang, S.; Bennamoun, M. A benchmark 3D fingerprint database. In Proceedings of the 2014 11th International Conference on Fuzzy Systems and Knowledge Discovery (FSKD), Xiamen, China, 19–21 August 2014.

81. Melekhov, I.; Ylioinas, J.; Kannala, J.; Rahtu, E. Image-based localization using hourglass networks. In Proceedings of the IEEE International Conference on Computer Vision Workshops, Venice, Italy, 22–29 October 2017.

82. Jiang, L.; Zhao, T.; Bai, C.; Yong, A.; Wu, M. A direct fingerprint minutiae extraction approach based on convolutional neural networks. In Proceedings of the 2016 International Joint Conference on Neural Networks (IJCNN), Vancouver, BC, Canada, 24–29 July 2016.

83. Lin, C.; Kumar, A. A CNN-based framework for comparison of contactless to contact-based fingerprints. *IEEE Trans. Inf. Forensics Secur.* **2018**, *14*, 662–676. [CrossRef]

84. Yu, W.; Yang, K.; Bai, Y.; Xiao, T.; Yao, H.; Rui, Y. Visualizing and comparing AlexNet and VGG using deconvolutional layers. In Proceedings of the 33rd International Conference on Machine Learning, New York City, NY, USA, 19–24 June 2016.

85. Ballester, P.; Araujo, R.M. On the performance of GoogLeNet and AlexNet applied to sketches. In Proceedings of the Thirtieth AAAI Conference on Artificial Intelligence, Pelotas, Brazil, 21 February 2016.

86. Lin, C.; Kumar, A. Contactless and partial 3D fingerprint recognition using multi-view deep representation. *Pattern Recognit.* **2018**, *83*, 314–327. [CrossRef]

87. Lin, C.; Kumar, A. Improving cross sensor interoperability for fingerprint identification. In Proceedings of the 2016 23rd International Conference on Pattern Recognition (ICPR), Cancun, Mexico, 4–8 December 2016.

88. Watson, C.I.; Garris, M.D.; Tabassi, E.; Wilson, C.L.; McCabe, R.M.; Janet, S.; Ko, K. *User's Guide to NIST Biometric Image Software (NBIS)*; NIST: Gaithersburg, MD, USA, 2007.

89. Tan, H.; Kumar, A. Minutiae attention network with reciprocal distance loss for contactless to contact-based fingerprint identification. *IEEE Trans. Inf. Forensics Secur.* **2021**, *16*, 3299–3311. [CrossRef]

90. Sundararajan, K.; Woodard, D.L. Deep learning for biometrics: A survey. *ACM Comput. Surv. CSUR* **2018**, *51*, 1–34. [CrossRef]

Journal of
Cybersecurity and Privacy

MDPI

Article

Improved Detection and Response via Optimized Alerts: Usability Study

Griffith Russell McRee

Center for Cybersecurity Research and Analysis, Capitol Technology University, 11301 Springfield Road, Laurel, MD 20708, USA; russ@holisticinfosec.io

Abstract: Security analysts working in the modern threat landscape face excessive events and alerts, a high volume of false-positive alerts, significant time constraints, innovative adversaries, and a staggering volume of unstructured data. Organizations thus risk data breach, loss of valuable human resources, reputational damage, and impact to revenue when excessive security alert volume and a lack of fidelity degrade detection services. This study examined tactics to reduce security data fatigue, increase detection accuracy, and enhance security analysts' experience using security alert output generated via data science and machine learning models. The research determined if security analysts utilizing this security alert data perceive a statistically significant difference in usability between security alert output that is visualized versus that which is text-based. Security analysts benefit two-fold: the efficiency of results derived at scale via ML models, with the additional benefit of quality alert results derived from these same models. This quantitative, quasi-experimental, explanatory study conveys survey research performed to understand security analysts' perceptions via the Technology Acceptance Model. The population studied was security analysts working in a defender capacity, analyzing security monitoring data and alerts. The more specific sample was security analysts and managers in Security Operation Center (SOC), Digital Forensic and Incident Response (DFIR), Detection and Response Team (DART), and Threat Intelligence (TI) roles. Data analysis indicated a significant difference in security analysts' perception of usability in favor of visualized alert output over text alert output. The study's results showed how organizations can more effectively combat external threats by emphasizing visual rather than textual alerts.

Keywords: user acceptance; user experience; security alert; detection; data science; visualization; visual alert output; text alert output

Citation: McRee, G.R. Improved Detection and Response via Optimized Alerts: Usability Study. *J. Cybersecur. Priv.* **2022**, 2, 379–401. https://doi.org/10.3390/jcp2020020

Academic Editor: Sokratis Katsikas

Received: 5 April 2022
Accepted: 25 May 2022
Published: 31 May 2022

Publisher's Note: MDPI stays neutral with regard to jurisdictional claims in published maps and institutional affiliations.

1. Introduction

The compounding challenges for security analysts working in the modern threat landscape include excessive events and alerts, a high volume of false-positive alerts, the treatment of time as a critical resource, threat actor innovation, and a high volume of unstructured data [1]. One solution is the use of data science and machine learning to relieve pressure for security analysts, where models and automation can be deployed to ingest and prioritize security event and threat data. Further, machine learning can enable pattern and trend analysis to better identify adversarial behavior [1]. Most importantly, the way the results of these data science (DS) and machine learning (ML) methods are presented to security analysts can have a direct impact on performance and efficacy. Interactive security data visualization via the likes of graph and timeline visualization are methods known to be of benefit to security analysts [2]. This study specifically considered security analysts' perceptions of usability and ease of use of security alert output from DS and ML methods. This study's findings provide useful data points for organizations seeking to improve the working experience for security analysts with the hope of increasing organizational safety and security.

1.1. Background

Many organizations must deal with a high volume of security alert and event data derived from security devices and detective capabilities [3]. A Dimensional Research study found that these organizations face a large burden due to alert overload, where 99% of security professionals surveyed acknowledge that high volumes of security alerts are problematic. The Dimensional Research study also determined that primary challenges include many minor problems or noise (68%), wasted time chasing false positives (66%), team members who feel overwhelmed (50%), excessive time spent triaging alerts (47%), and an increased overall security risk (42%) [4]. Bartos found that one of the core issues an analyst faces is the large number of alerts generated by numerous cybersecurity tools. When considering additional data received via various sharing and collaborative platforms, the issue is further amplified. As such, for security analysts, data prioritization and summarization are essential to reduce the excessive amount of information presented. Prioritization is consistently identified as a core tenet of security incident handling in numerous studies [5]. A lack of prioritization can result in security data fatigue, analyst burnout, and ineffective or insufficient incident response [6]. Organizations face increased risk and liability if their capacity to respond to high-fidelity detections is reduced by excessive alert noise [7]. As indicated by FireEye data, in organizations that receive 17,000 alerts weekly, more than 51% of the alerts are false positives, and only 4% of the alerts are thoroughly investigated [8]. More narrowly, Seals found that 80% of organizations who receive 500 or more severe/critical alerts per day investigate fewer than 1% of them [9]. The issue is exacerbated by data volumes. Oltsik reported that, as part of security operations, 38% of organizations collect, process, and analyze more than 10 terabytes monthly. As of 2017, 28% of organizations collect, process, and analyze substantially more data than in the two years prior, while another 49% of organizations collect, process, and analyze somewhat more data today than the two years prior [10]. A recent survey of 50 SOC professionals, Managed Security Services Providers (MSSP), and Managed Detection and Response (MDR) providers evaluated the state of incident response within SOCs and found numerous causes for concern. Nearly half of respondents reported a false-positive rate of 50% or higher, which was so high because security information and event management (SIEM) and incident response tools are improperly tuned and alert on known-good activity, resulting in investigations with a high rate of false positives [11]. Respondents reported that when their SOC had too many alerts for analysts to process, 38% either turn off high-volume alerting features or hire more analysts. Additionally, respondents felt that their main job responsibility was less to analyze and remediate security threats and more to reduce alert investigation time or the volume of alerts [11]. All of this results in significant security analyst turnover. A large majority (80%) of respondents indicated that their SOC had experienced at least 10% analyst turnover. The largest pool of respondents (45%) indicated a 10–25% turnover, and more than a third (35%) lost a quarter or more of their SOC analysts in less than 12 months [11]. Slatman's research focused on data-driven security operations and security analytics to investigate and address the investigation challenges security analysts face [3]. The challenges are categorized into four main categories: an increasingly complex IT environment, limited business alignment, ever-evolving adversaries and corresponding attacks, and inadequate resources with respect to people and technology. The concept of data-driven security operations is the seminal starting point for this research. A focus on data-driven security operations addresses and enables discussions related to challenges that security analysts face, as well as opportunities for improvements such as applied machine learning and visualization.

The specific business problem is: organizations risk data breach, loss of valuable human resources, reputation, and revenue due to excessive security alert volume and a lack of fidelity in security event data. A Cloud Security Alliance survey illuminated the problem further. With an average of two billion transactions a month at the average enterprise, IT security professionals say that 40.4% of alerts received lack actionable intelligence to investigate, and another 31.9% report ignored alerts due to false positives [12]. Chickowski stated that as much as 25% of a security analyst's time is spent processing false-positive alerts, commonly erroneous security alerts or false indicators of confidence, before focusing on true-positive findings. Every hour an analyst spends on the job, 15 min are wasted on false positives, leading the typical organization to waste between 286 and 424 h per week on false positives [13]. In addressing this problem, improving the efficiency of security analysts can be helpful. In a survey that examines specific areas where high- and low-performing SOCs diverge, with a focus on the challenges both groups struggle with, Ponemon found key data points in the differences and similarities between the two classes of SOCs. Even highly effective SOCs suffer from job-related stress affecting security analysts, where 55% of respondents from high-performing SOCs rated their stress level as a 9 or 10 on a 10-point scale. Twenty-two percent of survey respondents rated their SOC as ineffective, citing a lack of visibility into the attack surface and a lack of timely remediation as the core factors [14]. To examine opportunities for increased efficiencies, this study used a survey questionnaire based on the Technology Acceptance Model (TAM) to test for statistical differences between security analysts' responses regarding perception and usability of text-based alert output (TAO) versus visualized alert output (VAO).

1.2. Research Purpose

The purpose of this quantitative, quasi-experimental, explanatory study was to determine if security analysts utilizing this security alert data perceive a statistically significant difference in usability between security alert output that is visualized versus that which is text-based. Prior studies have found that study participants using a visual analytics (VA) interface performed better than those on the text-oriented interface and that the visual analytic interface yielded performance that was quicker and more accurate than the text interface [15]. This study built on these findings to assess security analysts' preferences specific to both usability and ease of use of security alert output from various models and security data analytics.

1.3. Research Question

The research question that guided the proposed study was:

- Is there a difference in the level of acceptance of security alert output between those with a preference for visual alert outputs (VAO) and those with a preference for text alert outputs (TAO), with VAO and TAO generated via data science/machine learning methods, as predicted by the TAM?

Sub-questions were:

- Does the adoption of VAO have a significant impact on the four individual TAM components: perceived usefulness (PU), perceived ease of use (PEU), attitude toward using (AU), and intention to use (IU)?
- Does the adoption of TAO have a significant impact on the four individual TAM components: perceived usefulness (PU), perceived ease of use (PEU), attitude toward using (AU), and intention to use (IU)?

1.4. Theoretical Framework

Figure 1 illustrates the theoretical framework by which the research question will be explored.

The TAM asserts that the behavioral intention to use a system is determined by PU and PEU [16]. PU is the extent to which a person believes that using the system will enhance his or her job performance, while perceived ease of use (PEU) is the extent to which a person believes that using the system will be effortless [17]. TAM additionally asserts that the effects of external variables (system characteristics) on intention to use are mediated by PU and PEU. Finally, PU is also influenced by PEU because the easier a system is to use, the more useful it can be [18].

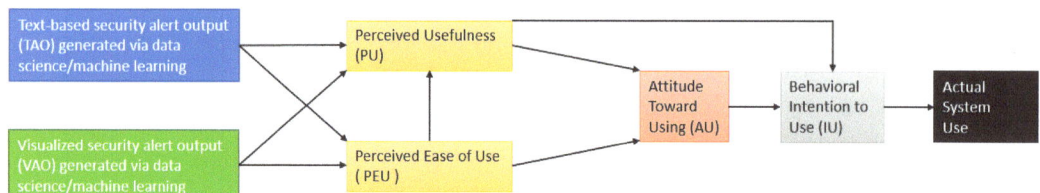

Figure 1. Theoretical Framework: Technology Acceptance Model. Adapted from "Perceived Usefulness, Perceived Ease of Use, and User Acceptance of Information Technology" [17].

Section 1 provided an overview of the study with the context and background for the research problem and statement, as well as purpose and significance. Section 2 includes details of the methodological approach used by the researcher for this study. Section 3 offers background on the research results and provides a description of the sample as well as hypothesis testing, inclusive of a summary and data analysis. Section 4 concludes the study with a discussion of the research results, coupled with its conclusions, limitations, implications for practice, and recommendations for future research.

2. Material and Methods

2.1. Design and Methodology

The researcher utilized a quantitative, quasi-experimental, explanatory methodology for the envisioned study, using survey research to better understand related phenomena. Quantitative methods are used to measure behavior, knowledge, opinions, or attitudes in business research, as is pertinent when the Technology Acceptance Model is the utilized instrument. An online survey was used to test for statistically significant differences in the level of acceptance of alert output between those choosing VAO in all scenarios and those having some or complete preference for TAO, with VAO and TAO being generated via data science/machine learning methods as predicted by the TAM. In pursuit of further insights relevant to potential differences in security analysts' perceptions of visual and text analytics, the research question that guides this study was:

- RQ1: Is there a difference in the level of acceptance of security alert output between those with a preference for VAO and those with a preference for TAO, with VAO and TAO generated via data science/machine learning methods, as predicted by the TAM?
    - Sub-questions were:
        - SQ1: Does the adoption of VAO have a significant impact on the four individual TAM components: PU, PEU, AU, and IU?
        - SQ2: Does the adoption of TAO have a significant impact on the four individual TAM components: PU, PEU, AU, and IU?

The online survey utilized for this study incorporated visual images as part of the questioning process, to create clarity and compel answering in full. To further minimize non-response, and to prepare data for testing, the following were included:

- As part of this quantitative, quasi-experimental, explanatory study, the online survey for data collection utilized a 7-point Likert scale.
- The online survey questionnaire and survey experiment, given that this research was specifically focused on visualization versus text, incorporated visual elements, which lead to a higher response quality and generate interesting interaction effects [19].

The target population for this study was global information security analysts working in a blue team (defender) capacity, analyzing security monitoring data and alerts. This is an appropriate population given the significant challenges the industry faces due to the sheer scale of security data, and the resulting difficulties security analysts face seeking precise and efficient answers to alert-related questions. Participants were solicited from this population via social media, including LinkedIn and Twitter, mailing lists, industry partners, and contact lists. The researcher ensured prequalification with a job and role-specific question. Survey participants who did not meet population requirements were disqualified.

Data analysis for this study utilized a mixed ANOVA because it enables efficiency while keeping variability low [20]. In other words, given the within-subjects component of this study where all participants undertook the same three scenarios, a mixed ANOVA allowed for partitioning out variability as a function of individual differences. Additionally, a mixed ANOVA provided the benefit of efficiency while keeping variability low, thereby keeping the validity of the results higher yet allowing for smaller subject groups [20].

2.2. Data Collection

SurveyMonkey was utilized to create survey hyperlinks for social media and e-mail dissemination to prospective participants and solicit their responses. The criteria for inclusion in the sample were as follows: (a) information security analysts, (b) working in a security monitoring role as part of a security operations center or fusion center, and (c) responding to security alert data. Participants were prequalified to meet these criteria and those who did not were excluded. Any survey results received from participants determined not to meet the criteria for inclusion were eliminated. Participants were required to provide their informed consent before responding to the survey. An opt-out option was available for participants while taking the survey.

The defined variables, related constructs, applied scale, and data types for each variable are listed in Table 1.

Table 1. Variable and data types.

RQ	Construct	Variable	Scale	Data
RQ1	Level of acceptance	DV	Likert	Interval
RQ1	Scenario (within-subjects)	IV	Likert	Interval
RQ1	Alert output (between-subjects)	IV	Likert	Interval
SQ1	Impact of adoption	DV	Likert	Interval
SQ1	Scenario (within-subjects)	IV	Likert	Interval
SQ1	Alert output (between-subjects)	IV	Likert	Interval
SQ2	Impact of adoption	DV	Likert	Interval
SQ2	Scenario (within-subjects)	IV	Likert	Interval
SQ2	Alert output (between-subjects)	IV	Likert	Interval

2.3. Instrumentation

The TAM implies that positive perception of usefulness and ease of use (perceived usability) influence intention to use, which in turn influences the actual likelihood of use [21]. Original construction of the TAM for measurement of PU and PEU resulted in a 12-item instrument that was shown to be reliable [22]. It consisted of the two factors PU and PEU and was correlated with intentions to use and self-report usage [17]. This quantitative, quasi-experimental, explanatory study utilized a 7-point Likert scale to assess the level of acceptance and the perceived ease of use and perceived usefulness of alerts in three scenarios (the within-subjects independent variable). The preferred alert output (VAO or TAO) forms the basis of the between-subjects independent variable. Likert-type scale response anchors set the range between agreement and disagreement; as an example, 1 indicated strong disagreement and 7 indicated strong agreement with a statement.

2.4. Hypotheses

The following research questions served to determine if a relationship exists between the dependent variable, which is the level of acceptance of alert output, and the two independent variables, which are Session (1, 2, or 3) and Maximum Visual. Maximum

Visual had two levels: one where VAO was chosen for all scenarios and one where TAO was chosen for some or all scenarios.

- Is there a difference in the level of acceptance of alert outputs between those preferring VAO in all scenarios and those preferring TAO in some or all scenarios, as predicted by the TAM?
  - ○ Sub-questions:
    - Does the adoption of VAO have a significant impact on the four individual TAM components: PU, PEU, AU, and IU?
    - Does the adoption of TAO have a significant impact on the four individual TAM components: PU, PEU, AU, and IU?

The following research hypotheses explored the research questions for a relationship between the independent variable of Maximum Visual (a preference for VAO in all scenarios versus a preference for TAO in some or all scenarios), and the dependent variable, which is the level of acceptance of alert outputs. The dependent variable is specific to security analysts' perception of machine learning (ML)- and data science (DS)-generated alert output.

The null and alternative hypotheses are stated as:

H1: *There is no significant difference in the level of acceptance of alert outputs between those preferring VAO in all scenarios and those preferring TAO in some or all scenarios, as predicted by the TAM.*

H2: *There is a significant difference in the level of acceptance of alert outputs between those preferring VAO in all scenarios and those preferring TAO in some or all scenarios, as predicted by the TAM.*

Omnibus tests are applicable to these hypotheses, where H1: R-squared is equal to 0 and H2: R-squared is greater than 0. Table 2 highlights the relationship between the research questions and the hypotheses.

Table 2. Research question and hypotheses testing.

RQ	Type of Analysis	Variable	Scale	Data
RQ1	Variance	IV-DV	Likert	H1, H2
SQ1	Variance	IV-DV	Likert	H1, H2
SQ2	Variance	IV-DV	Likert	H1, H2

Note. RQ = research question; SQ = sub-question; DV = dependent variable; IV = independent variable; H1 = null hypothesis; H2 = alternative hypothesis.

2.5. Data Analysis

The data collected for analysis from the results of a SurveyMonkey online questionnaire were processed with IBM SPSS software and R, a programming language for statistical computing, machine learning, and graphics. The analysis focused on data exploration of dependent and independent variables. The main dependent variable was the level of acceptance of the security alert output and was based on the four individual TAM components: PU, PEU, AU, and IU. Each component was derived from responses to groups of Likert-style statements (scored 1 through to 7, with 7 representing the most favorable response). PU and PEU had a total of six statements, and AU and IU had three statements. The level of acceptance of the alert output was calculated by adding all 18 scores together, with a maximum score of 126 and a minimum score of 18. The sub-scores for PU, PEU, AU, and IU represent secondary dependent variables. The within-subjects independent variable was scenario. It had three levels, Scenario 1, Scenario 2, and Scenario 3, with all participants being subject to all scenarios. The between-subjects independent variable was Maximum Visual. This had two levels: a preference for VAO in all three scenarios, and a preference for TAO in at least one of the scenarios.

Both parametric and non-parametric tests were performed. Mixed ANOVA tested whether the level of acceptance of alert outputs is influenced by the within-subjects variable Scenario and the between-subjects variable Maximum Visual. Mixed ANOVA was also repeated for the four sub-scales of PU, PEU, AS, and IU, with Bonferroni corrections for multiple comparisons. Additionally, a Mann–Whitney U test was performed, comparing the level of acceptance of alert outputs of the two levels of Maximum Visual, and a Friedman test compared the level of acceptance across the three scenarios.

2.6. Validity and Reliability

The study's dependent variables are derived from the TAM. As such, the validity and reliability of TAM are paramount. Davis developed and validated scales for two variables, perceived usefulness (PU) and perceived ease of use (PEU), as basic determinants of user acceptance. Davis used definitions for PU and PEU to develop scale markers pretested for content validity, as well as tested for reliability and construct validity [17].

Davis found that the PU scale attained a Cronbach's alpha reliability of 0.97 for both systems tested, while PEU achieved a reliability of 0.86 for one system tested and 0.93 for the other. Upon pooling observations for the two systems, Cronbach's alpha was found to be 0.97 for usefulness and 0.91 for ease of use [17].

Davis tested for convergent and discriminant validity using multi-trait–multimethod (MTMM) analysis, where the MTMM matrix contained the intercorrelations of items (methods) applied to the two different test systems (traits). Davis indicated that convergent validity determines if items making up a scale behave as if measuring a common underlying construct. Convergent validity is demonstrated when items that measure the same trait correlate highly with one another [17]. Davis' study found that 90 mono-trait–heteromethod correlations for PU were all significant at the 0.05 level, while for PEU, 86 out of 90, or 95.56%, of the mono-trait–hetero-method correlations were significant. These data support the convergent validity of TAM's two scales: PU and PEU [17].

3. Results

3.1. Background

The specific business problem that oriented this study is: organizations risk data breach, loss of valuable human resources, reputation, and revenue due to excessive security alert volume and a lack of fidelity in security event data. To determine means of support for security analysts experiencing these security event-specific challenges, the study asked if there is a difference in the level of acceptance of security alert outputs between those preferring VAO in all scenarios, and those preferring TAO in some or all scenarios, as predicted by the TAM. The dependent variable was participants' level of acceptance of security alert output: the within-subjects independent variable is Scenario, and the between-subjects independent variable is Maximum Visual (preference for VAO in all scenarios versus preference for TAO in some or all scenarios). SurveyMonkey was utilized to deliver an online survey to participants, from which the collected data were analyzed. The survey queried a population of cybersecurity analysts and managers in SOC, DFIR, DART, and TI roles, targeted for participation via social media. Twitter and LinkedIn were utilized. The LinkedIn campaign included the use of Linked Helper to create a list of potential participants whose profiles matched the desired role descriptions from connections in the researcher's network of 1411 connections as of this writing. The final filtered list resulted in 234 potential participants to whom an invitation to participate was sent. A 7-point Likert scale survey queried participants regarding their perspectives on perceived ease of use and perceived usefulness of ML and DS-generated alert output across three scenarios with TAO and VAO results [23]. Of 119 respondents, 24 disqualified themselves and 95 identified themselves as qualified, 81 of whom completed all 3 scenarios.

3.2. Description of the Sample

Data collected from cybersecurity analysts and managers in SOC, DFIR, DART, and TI roles resulted in 95 qualified respondents. A total of 95 qualified respondents is in keeping with estimates of an appropriate sample size. Where 2018 Bureau of Labor Statistics data indicate that there were 112,300 information security analysts, and this specific target population is a subpopulation of the larger 112,300 security analysts, if 5% of the larger 112,300 population is applied, a target population of 5615 is appropriate [24]. With a 95% confidence level, and 10% confidence interval (margin of error), then the ideal sample size is 94 [25]. Of the 95 respondents to this survey, 81 completed all 3 scenarios presented in the survey. The 14 incomplete survey results were discarded, resulting in an 85.20% completion rate. The 14 incomplete surveys were discarded due to missing data and to enable analysis of two complete and distinct groups, namely respondents who chose VAO across all three scenarios, and those who selected a mix of VAO and TAO or all TAO results across all three scenarios. The 81 respondents, as broken down into their 2 distinct groups, are defined under the Maximum Visual variable (Vis_max), where the participants who said yes to VAO in all three scenarios were labeled *Yes* (N = 59), and the participants who selected a mix of VAO and TAO or all TAO results across all three scenarios were labeled *No* (N = 22).

3.3. Hypothesis Testing

Given that the data collected for this study did not meet the standard for normality, both parametric and non-parametric tests were performed. Parametric statistical procedures depend on assumptions about the shape of the distribution (assume a normal distribution) in the population and the form or parameters (means and standard deviations) of the assumed distribution [26]. On the other hand, nonparametric statistical procedures depend on few or no assumptions about the shape (normality) or parameters of the population distribution from which the sample was taken [26]. Nonparametric tests include the Mann–Whitney U test and the Friedman test. Parametric tests can be conducted via a mixed analysis of variance (ANOVA) with a Bonferroni correction. The mixed ANOVA tests included an approach for treatment of the dependent variable: security analysts' level of acceptance of the alert output. First, mixed ANOVA was performed across the TAM-based questionnaire categories, namely perceived usefulness (PU), perceived ease of use (PEU), attitude towards using (AU), and intent to use (IU), where the scores for all sub-scales were summed. Second, mixed ANOVA was performed on each sub-scale. For the individual sub-scales, statistical significance was set at $\alpha/4$, or 0.0125.

3.4. Validating Assumptions

When assessing normality, the distributions were not normally distributed. Standardized residuals for each of the three scenarios do not appear normally distributed, as seen in the histograms in Figure 2.

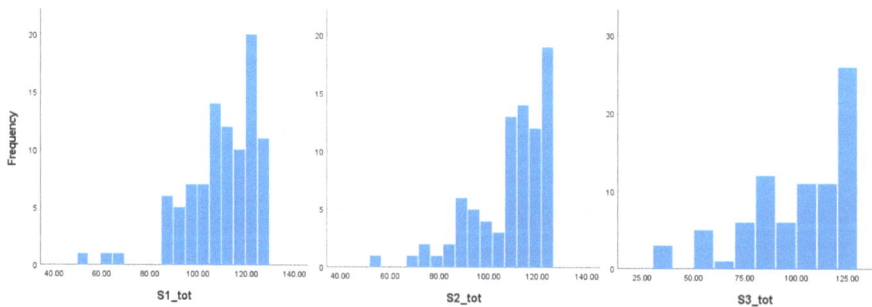

Figure 2. Standardized residual normality for Scenarios 1–3.

Given that the residuals are skewed, Friedman's test was also conducted, as a non-parametric equivalent of a within-subjects one-way ANOVA. It only considers the impact of the within-subjects variable Scenario.

Finally, reliability was assumed where Cronbach's alpha measures the internal consistency of questions related to the same issues across each of the three scenarios. If Cronbach's alpha ranged from 0 to 1 and scores were expected to be between 0.7 and 0.9, the result for this study represents good consistency [27]. Using a scale comprised of 18 TAM questions for each scenario, and 81 valid cases, with 14 excluded (n = 95), the reliability statistic for each scenario as indicated by Cronbach's alpha was 0.958 for Scenario 1, 0.971 for Scenario 2, and 0.986 for Scenario 3.

3.5. Descriptive Statistics

Survey respondents were categorized as follows:

- For each of the three scenarios, a scenario variable:
  - ○ 0 = no response
  - ○ 1 = text response
  - ○ 2 = visual response
- A scenario product variable (product of all scenario variables):
  - ○ All visual responses: $2 * 2 * 2 = 8$
  - ○ 2 visual responses, 1 text response: $2 * 2 * 1 = 4$
  - ○ 1 visual response, 2 text responses: $2 * 1 * 1 = 2$
  - ○ All text responses: $1 * 1 * 1 = 1$

The results using these variables are seen in Table 3.

Table 3. Response products.

Valid	Frequency	Percent	Valid %	Cumulative %
0	14	14.7	14.7	14.7
1	2	2.1	2.1	16.8
2	4	4.2	4.2	21.1
4	16	16.8	16.8	37.9
8	59	62.1	62.1	100
Total	95	100	100	

The dependent variable is represented by survey scenario question response totals as summed from Likert-scale responses ranging from 1 (strongly disagree) to 7 (strongly agree). These are represented for each scenario presented to participants as *S1_tot* for Scenario 1, *S2_tot* for Scenario 2, and *S3_tot* for Scenario 3. For the mixed ANOVA, these represent the within-subjects factors seen in Table 4.

Table 4. Factors and descriptive statistics.

Within-Subjects Factors			
Scenarios		Dependent Variable	
1		S1_tot	
2		S2_tot	
3		S2_tot	
Between-Subjects Factors			
		Value Label	N
Maximum Visual	0.00	No	22
	1.00	Yes	59

Table 4. *Cont.*

Descriptive Statistics

	Maximum Visual	Mean	Std. Deviation	N
	No	107.7273	11.65856	22
S1_tot	Yes	110.2034	15.15754	59
	Total	109.5309	14.26454	81
	No	104.7727	14.91223	22
S2_tot	Yes	109.9661	15.87556	59
	Total	108.5556	15.70032	81
	No	88.6364	29.03618	22
S3_tot	Yes	104.6102	21.62136	59
	Total	100.2716	24.7255	81

The Maximum Visual variable (*Vis_max*) defined the participants who said yes to VAO in all three scenarios, labeled *Yes* (N = 59), and the participants who selected a mix of VAO and TAO or all TAO results across all three scenarios, labeled *No* (N = 22). Maximum Visual is the study's between-subjects independent variable. It was one of the main factors in the mixed ANOVA, as can be seen in Table 5.

Table 5. Maximum Visual IVs (between-subjects factors).

		Frequency	Percent	Valid Percent	Cumulative Percent
	No	22	23.2	27.2	27.2
Valid	Yes	59	62.1	72.8	100.0
	Total	81	85.3	100.0	
Missing	999.00	14	14.7		
Total		95	100.0		

3.6. Mann–Whitney U Test

A Mann–Whitney U test of independent samples had participants' level of acceptance of alert output as its dependent variable, which is the ranked, summed scores across all scenarios (*S_tot*). The independent variable is Maximum Visual (*Vis_max*). The test determines whether the group who prefer VAO across all scenarios have a significantly different acceptance score than those who prefer TAO in some or all scenarios. Score totals are noted in Figure 3, while Table 6 provides a statistical summary.

The Mann–Whitney U test indicates that there is a significant difference ($U = 863.5$, $p = 0.023$) in the level of acceptance of alert output between the respondents who selected visual output across all scenarios ($n = 59$) as compared to the respondents who provided mixed responses ($n = 22$). As such, the null hypothesis, that there is no statistically significant difference in the level of acceptance of alert output between those who preferred VAO in all scenarios and those preferring TAO in some or all scenarios, is rejected.

The effect size is calculated by dividing the Standardized Test Statistic, Z, by the square root of the number of pairs: $\frac{Z}{\sqrt{n}} = \frac{2.279}{\sqrt{81}} = 0.253$. The effect size, according to Cohen's classification of effect, is moderate, given 0.1 (small effect), 0.3 (moderate effect), and 0.5 and above (large effect).

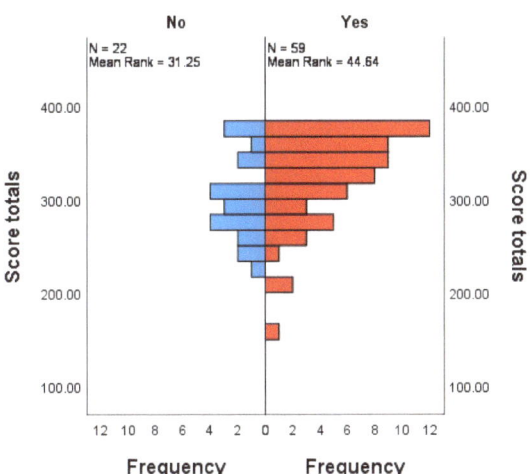

Figure 3. Independent samples Mann–Whitney U test results.

Table 6. Independent samples Mann–Whitney U test summary.

Total N	81
Mann–Whitney U	863.500
Test Statistic	863.500
Standard Error	94.140
Standardized Test Statistic	2.279
Asymptotic Sig. (2-sided test)	0.023

3.7. Friedman Test

A related samples Friedman test was conducted to assess the measurements of the same dependent variable under different conditions for each participant, namely the three scenarios for this study defined by the variables *S1_tot*, *S2_tot*, and *S3_tot*. Rank frequencies are shown in Figure 4 and the statistical summary is represented in Table 7.

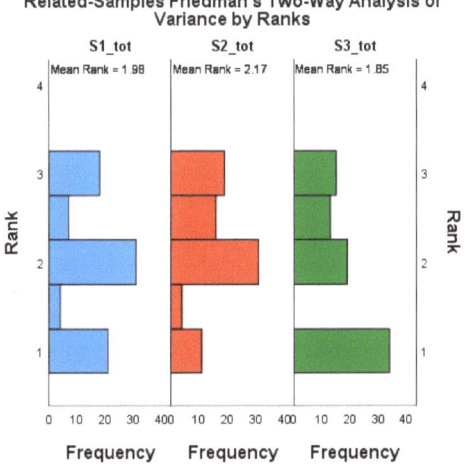

Figure 4. Related samples Friedman's two-way ANOVA by ranks.

Table 7. Related samples Friedman's two-way ANOVA by ranks, summary.

Total N	81
Test Statistic	5.496
Degree of Freedom	2
Asymptotic Sig. (2-sided test)	0.064

The Friedman test carried out to compare the score ranks for the three scenarios found there to be no significant difference between scenarios: $x^2(2) = 5.496$, $p < 0.064$. The result indicates that scenario mean ranks did not differ significantly from scenario to scenario when not also factoring for responses based on output preference (Maximum Visual).

Effect size was not applicable as no measurable significance was found.

3.8. Mixed ANOVA—All Measures (PU, PEU, AU, IU Combined)

A two-way mixed ANOVA was conducted, with a Bonferroni correction for the within-subjects variable. The dependent variable was the level of acceptance of alert output, with all items of all TAM sub-scales summed.

While considered more conservative, most authorities suggest the Greenhouse–Geisser correction when the epsilon (ε) estimate is below 0.75. As noted in Table 8, $\varepsilon = 0.727$, and thus the Greenhouse–Geisser correction was utilized.

Table 8. Mauchly's test of sphericity.

Within-Subjects Effect	Mauchly's W	Approx. Chi-Square	df	Sig.	Greenhouse–Geisser
Scenarios	0.625	36.652	2	0.000	0.727

As indicated in Table 8, sphericity cannot be assumed as $p < 0.001$. As such, the Greenhouse–Geisser correction was applied.

The within-subjects variable, equating to score totals for each of the three study scenarios, is represented by Scenarios (*S1_tot*, *S2_tot*, and *S3_tot)*. The between-subjects variable was Maximum Visual (Vis_max), labeled as *Yes* ($n = 59$) and *No* ($n = 22$). Again, the Maximum Visual variable (*Vis_max*) differentiates between the participants who said yes to VAO in all three scenarios, labeled *Yes* (N = 59), and the participants who selected a mix of VAO and TAO, or all TAO results, across all three scenarios, labeled *No* ($n = 22$). Maximum Visual is the statistical analogy for the study's between-subjects independent variable, specifically (a) ML/DS-generated TAO, and (b) ML/DS-generated VAO.

Participants were presented with three scenarios exhibiting security alert output for the results of applied models, where the output was both VAO and TAO. A mixed ANOVA using $\alpha = 0.05$ with a Greenhouse–Geisser correction showed that scores varied significantly across Scenarios in tests of within-subject effects, and there was also a significant interaction with Maximum Visual:

Scenarios: (F (1.455, 114.915) = 19.925, $p < 0.001$, ηp2 = 0.201)
Scenarios∗Vis_max: (F (1.455, 114.915) = 5.634, $p = 0.010$, ηp2 = 0.067)

The impact of Maximum Visual (vis_max) on the level of acceptance of output was mediated by Scenarios. The difference of the level of acceptance was more significant for Scenario 3, as an example. Post hoc tests using the Bonferroni correction revealed that favorable scores declined insignificantly from Scenario 1 to Scenario 2 by an average of 1.596 points ($p = 0.702$) but declined significantly from Scenario 1 to Scenario 3 by 12.342 points ($p < 0.001$). Scenario 2 to Scenario 3 saw an additional significant decrease of 10.746 points ($p < 0.001$). The differences in scores were not particularly meaningful between or within Scenarios 1 and 2 (*S1_tot* and *S2_tot*) and Maximum Visual (*Vis_max*) = Yes or No. However, a significant difference was noted in Scenario 3 (*S3_tot*) compared to Scenarios 1 and 2, as well as Maximum Visual = Yes versus Maximum Visual = No. Most noteworthy is a 15% decrease in mean score for Maximum Visual = No in Scenario 3 as compared to Scenario 2, indicating a noteworthy decrease in PU, PEU, AU, and IU for participants selecting TAO.

Via estimated marginal means between-subjects, where Maximum Visual = Yes or Maximum Visual = No, inclusive of all TAM components with $\alpha = 0.05$ and Bonferroni correction, pairwise comparisons yielded a 7.881 point mean difference in favor of VAO, significant at $p = 0.046$. As such, there was a significant main effect of Maximum Visual scores ($F (1, 79) = 4.111$, $p = 0.046$, $\eta p2 = 0.049$) on the level of acceptance of alert output, as indicated by the sum of participants' scores for all TAM components (PU, PEU, AU, and IU). These results are represented visually in Figure 5.

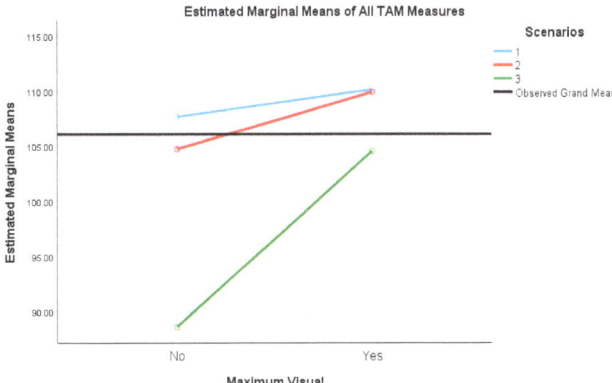

Figure 5. Estimated marginal means of all measures.

3.9. Mixed ANOVA—Perceived Usefulness (PU)

Two-way mixed ANOVA with Bonferroni correction, computed using $\alpha = 0.0125$, was performed for PU in isolation. $\alpha = 0.0125$ was appropriate to avoid family-wise errors by adjusting to be more conservative, where four tests at $\alpha = 0.05$ implies the use of $\alpha = 0.0125$. The measures related to PU represented one of four TAM-specific comparisons, and thus a conservative but accurate method to compensate for multiple tests was required.

Mixed ANOVA was again applied, where the within-subjects variables equating to score totals for each of the three study scenarios were represented by Perceived_Usefulness (*PUS1_tot*, *PUS2_tot*, and *PUS3_tot*), and between-subjects factors were again represented by Maximum Visual (Vis_max), labeled as Yes ($n = 59$) and No ($n = 22$).

Participants were presented with three scenarios exhibiting security alert output for the results of applied models, where the output was both VAO and TAO. A mixed ANOVA computed using $\alpha = 0.0125$ with a Greenhouse–Geisser correction showed that scores varied significantly across scenarios specific to Perceived_Usefulness (*PUS1_tot*, *PUS2_tot*, and *PUS3_tot*) in tests of within-subject effects, and less significantly when differentiated for Maximum Visual:

Scenarios: ($F (1.637, 129.311) = 16.999$, $p < 0.001$, $\eta p2 = 0.177$)
Scenarios∗Vis_max: ($F (1.637, 129.311) = 4.017$, $p = 0.028$, $\eta p2 = 0.048$)

Post hoc tests using the Bonferroni correction revealed that favorable scores for PU declined insignificantly from Scenario 1 to Scenario 2 by an average of 0.076 points ($p = 1.000$), but then declined significantly from Scenario 1 to Scenario 3 by 3.999 points ($p = < 0.001$) and from Scenario 2 to Scenario 3 by an additional 3.924 points ($p < 0.001$). The differences in scores were not particularly meaningful between or within Scenarios 1 and 2 (*PUS1_tot* and *PUS2_tot*) and Maximum Visual (*Vis_max*) = Yes or No. A significant difference was, however, noted in Scenario 3 (*PUS3_tot*) compared to Scenarios 1 and 2, as well as Maximum Visual = Yes versus Maximum Visual = No. Again, a 15% decrease in mean score for Maximum Visual = No was noted in Scenario 3 as compared to Scenario 2, indicating a significant decrease in PU for participants selecting TAO. Interestingly, there was a 1% increase in PU for participants selecting TAO for Scenario 2 as compared to Scenario 1.

Via estimated marginal means between-subjects, where Maximum Visual = Yes or Maximum Visual = No, inclusive only of PU data with $\alpha = 0.0125$ and Bonferroni correction, pairwise comparisons yielded a 3.642 point mean difference in favor of VAO, significant at $p = 0.007$. As such, there was a significant main effect of Maximum Visual scores ($F (1, 79) = 7.643$, $p = 0.007$, ηp2 = 0.088) on the level of acceptance of alert output, as indicated by sum of participants' scores for PU. These results are best represented visually, as noted in Figure 6.

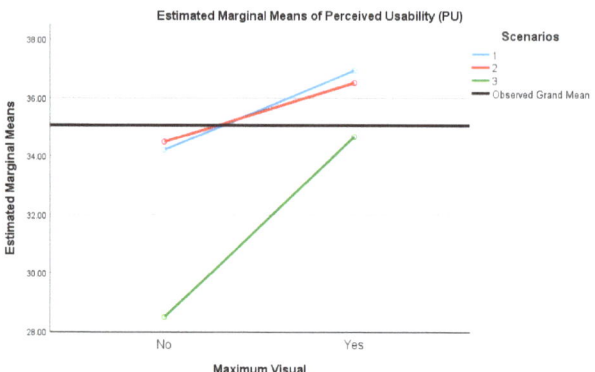

Figure 6. Estimated marginal means—PU.

3.10. Mixed ANOVA—Perceived Ease of Use (PEU)

Two-way mixed ANOVA with Bonferroni correction, computed using $\alpha = 0.0125$, was performed for PEU in isolation. $\alpha = 0.0125$ was applicable as one quarter of $\alpha = 0.05$ given that the TAM components related to PEU represent one of four tests of related measures.

Mixed ANOVA was again applied, where the within-subjects variables equating to score totals for each of the three study scenarios are represented by *Perceived_EaseOfUse* (*PEUS1_tot*, *PEUS2_tot*, and *PEUS3_tot*), and between-subjects factors were again represented by Maximum Visual (Vis_max), labeled as Yes ($n = 59$) and No ($n = 22$).

Participants were presented with three scenarios exhibiting security alert output for the results of applied models, where the output was both VAO and TAO. A mixed ANOVA computed using $\alpha = 0.0125$ with a Greenhouse–Geisser correction showed that scores varied significantly across scenarios specific to perceived ease of use (*PEUS1_tot*, *PEUS2_tot*, and *PEUS3_tot*) in tests of within-subject effects, and insignificantly when differentiated for Maximum Visual:

Scenarios: ($F (1.658, 130.988) = 8.752$, $p = 0.001$, ηp2 = 0.100)
Scenarios∗Vis_max: ($F (1.658, 130.988) = 3.548$, $p = 0.040$, ηp2 = 0.043)

Post hoc tests using the Bonferroni correction revealed that favorable scores for PEU decreased insignificantly from Scenario 1 to Scenario 2 by an average of 1.020 points ($p = 0.294$) but declined significantly from Scenario 1 to Scenario 3 by an average of 3.357 points ($p = 0.002$). An insignificant decrease was noted from Scenario 2 to Scenario 3 by an additional 2.337 points ($p = 0.033$). The differences in scores were meaningful between Scenarios 1 and 2 (*PEUS1_tot* and *PEUS2_tot*) and Maximum Visual (*Vis_max*) = No and again between Scenarios 2 and 3 (*PEUS2_tot* and *PEUS3_tot*) and Maximum Visual (*Vis_max*) = No. A significant difference was, however, noted in Scenario 3 (*PEUS3_tot*) compared to Scenarios 1 and 2, as well as Maximum Visual = Yes versus Maximum Visual = No. Again, a 10% decrease in mean score for Maximum Visual = No was noted in Scenario 3 as compared to Scenario 2, indicating a significant decrease in PEU for participants selecting TAO. Interestingly, there was a 1% increase in PEU for participants selecting VAO for Scenario 2 as compared to Scenario 1. Additionally, for the first time in this analysis, within Scenario 1, TAO outscored VAO within a specific TAM component (PEU).

Via estimated marginal means between-subjects, where Maximum Visual = Yes or Maximum Visual = No, inclusive only of PEU data with $\alpha = 0.0125$ and Bonferroni correction, pairwise comparisons yielded only a 1.229 point mean difference in favor of VAO, insignificant at $p = 0.362$. As such, there was not a significant main effect of Maximum Visual scores ($F(1, 79) = 0.842$, $p = 0.362$, $\eta p2 = 0.011$) on the level of acceptance of alert output, as indicated by the sum of participants' scores for PEU. These results are best represented visually, as noted in Figure 7.

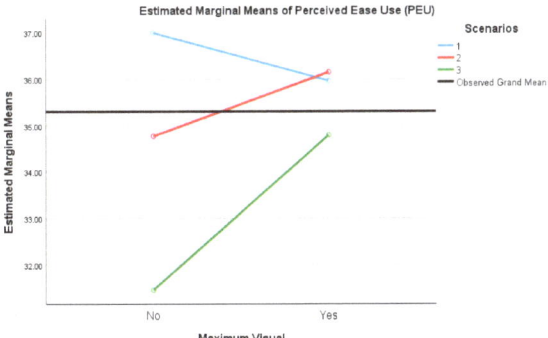

Figure 7. Estimated marginal means—perceived ease use (PEU).

3.11. Mixed ANOVA—Attitude toward Using (AU)

Two-way mixed ANOVA with Bonferroni correction, computed using $\alpha = 0.0125$, was performed for AU in isolation. $\alpha = 0.0125$ was applicable as one quarter of $\alpha = 0.05$ given that the TAM measures related to AU represented one of four tests of related measures.

Mixed ANOVA was again applied, where the within-subjects variables equating to score totals for each of the three study scenarios were represented by *Attitude2Use* (*AUS1_tot*, *AUS2_tot*, and *AUS3_tot*), and between-subjects factors were again represented by Maximum Visual (*Vis_max*), labeled as Yes ($n = 59$) and No ($n = 22$).

Participants were presented with three scenarios exhibiting security alert output for the results of applied models, where the output was both VAO and TAO. A mixed ANOVA computed using $\alpha = 0.0125$ with a Greenhouse–Geisser correction showed that scores varied significantly across scenarios specific to attitude toward using (*AUS1_tot*, *AUS2_tot*, and *AUS3_tot*) in tests of within-subject effects, and significantly again when differentiated for Maximum Visual:

Scenarios: ($F(1.669, 131.861) = 20.605$, $p < 0.001$, $\eta p2 = 0.207$)
Scenarios∗Vis_max: ($F(1.669, 130.988) = 8.159$, $p = 0.001$, $\eta p2 = 0.094$)

Post hoc tests using the Bonferroni correction revealed that favorable scores for AU decreased insignificantly from Scenario 1 to Scenario 2 by an average of 0.196 points ($p = 1.000$) but declined significantly from Scenario 1 to Scenario 3 by an average of 2.293 points ($p < 0.001$). A significant decrease was noted from Scenario 2 to Scenario 3 by an additional 2.097 points ($p < 0.001$). The differences in scores were not meaningful between Scenarios 1 and 2 (*AUS1_tot* and *AUS2_tot*) and Maximum Visual (*Vis_max*) = No, but were quite impactful between Scenarios 2 and 3 (*AUS2_tot* and *AUS3_tot*) and Maximum Visual (*Vis_max*) = No. As is consistent throughout this analysis, there was a significant difference noted in Scenario 3 (*AUS3_tot*) compared to Scenarios 1 and 2, as well as Maximum Visual = Yes versus Maximum Visual = No. A stark 19% decrease in mean score for Maximum Visual = No was noted in Scenario 3 as compared to Scenario 2, indicating a significant decrease in AU for participants selecting TAO. No change in AU was noted for participants selecting VAO for Scenario 2 as compared to Scenario 1. Also noteworthy was the lowest mean scores of all results recorded, specifically for TAO in Scenario 3, indicating a particularly poor attitude towards using TAO.

Via estimated marginal means between-subjects, where Maximum Visual = Yes or Maximum Visual = No, inclusive only of AU data with $\alpha = 0.0125$ and Bonferroni correction, pairwise comparisons yielded a small 1.587 point mean difference in favor of VAO, insignificant at $p = 0.036$. As such, there was not a significant main effect of Maximum Visual scores ($F (1, 79) = 4.566$, $p = 0.036$, $\eta p2 = 0.055$) on the level of acceptance of alert output, as indicated by the sum of participants' scores for AU. These results are best represented visually, as noted in Figure 8.

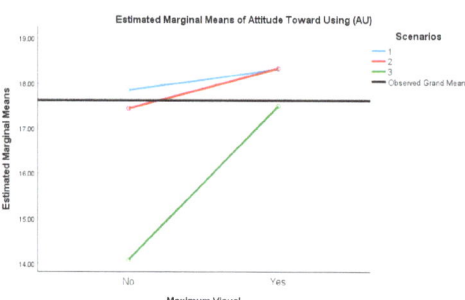

Figure 8. Estimated marginal means—attitude toward using (AU).

3.12. Mixed ANOVA—Intention to Use (IU)

Two-way mixed ANOVA (mixed ANOVA) with Bonferroni correction, computed using $\alpha = 0.0125$, was performed for IU in isolation. $\alpha = 0.0125$ was applicable as one quarter of $\alpha = 0.05$ given that the TAM measures related to IU represent one of four tests of related measures.

Mixed ANOVA was again applied, where the within-subjects variables equating to score totals for each of the three study scenarios were represented by *Intention2Use* (*IUS1_tot*, *IUS2_tot*, and *IUS3_tot*), and between-subjects factors were again represented by Maximum Visual (*Vis_max*), labeled as Yes ($n = 59$) and No ($n = 22$).

Participants were presented with three scenarios exhibiting security alert output for the results of applied models, where the output was both VAO and TAO. A mixed ANOVA computed using $\alpha = 0.0125$ with a Greenhouse–Geisser correction showed that scores varied significantly across scenarios specific to Intention to Use (*IUS1_tot*, *IUS2_tot*, and *IUS3_tot*) in tests of within-subject effects, and significantly again when differentiated for Maximum Visual:

Scenarios: ($F (1.447, 114.327) = 24.493$, $p < 0.001$, $\eta p2 = 0.237$)
Scenarios∗Vis_max: ($F (1.447, 114.327) = 5.728$, $p = 0.009$, $\eta p2 = 0.068$)

Post hoc tests using the Bonferroni correction revealed that favorable scores for IU decreased insignificantly from Scenario 1 to Scenario 2 by an average of 0.304 points ($p = 0.758$) but declined significantly from Scenario 1 to Scenario 3 by an average of 2.692 points ($p < 0.001$). A significant decrease was noted from Scenario 2 to Scenario 3 by an additional 2.388 points ($p < 0.001$). The differences in scores were not meaningful between Scenarios 1 and 2 (*IUS1_tot* and *IUS2_tot*) and Maximum Visual (*Vis_max*) = No, but were quite impactful between Scenarios 2 and 3 (*IUS2_tot* and *IUS3_tot*) and Maximum Visual (*Vis_max*) = No. As is consistent throughout this analysis, there was a significant difference noted in Scenario 3 (*IUS3_tot*) compared to Scenarios 1 and 2, as well as Maximum Visual = Yes versus Maximum Visual = No. Again, a substantial 19% decrease in mean score for Maximum Visual = No was noted in Scenario 3 as compared to Scenario 2, indicating a significant decrease in IU for participants selecting TAO. As is the case for AU, no change in IU was noted for participants selecting VAO for Scenario 2 as compared to Scenario 1. Also noteworthy was the largest percentage of decrease in mean scores of all results recorded, specifically for Scenario 3, indicating that intention to use was low for any aspect of Scenario 3, TAO, or VAO.

Via estimated marginal means between-subjects, where Maximum Visual = Yes or Maximum Visual = No, inclusive only of IU data with $\alpha = 0.0125$ and Bonferroni correction, pairwise comparisons yielded a small 1.423 point mean difference in favor of VAO, insignificant at $p = 0.040$. As such, there was not a significant main effect of Maximum Visual scores (F (1, 79) = 4.378, $p = 0.040$, $\eta p2 = 0.053$) on the level of acceptance of alert output, as indicated by the sum of participants' scores for IU. These results are represented visually in Figure 9.

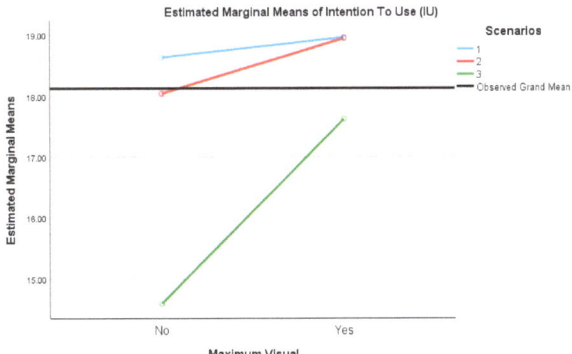

Figure 9. Estimated marginal means—intention to use (IU).

3.13. Summary of Hypothesis Testing

The null hypothesis states that there is no statistically significant difference in the level of acceptance of alert output between those choosing VAO and those having some or complete preference for TAO, with VAO and TAO being generated via data science/machine learning methods as predicted by the TAM. The null hypothesis was rejected via nonparametric and parametric methods. Table 9 represents non-parametric outcomes per an independent samples Mann–Whitney U test.

Table 9. Means' analysis—intention to use (IU).

Maximum Visual		Mean	Std. Deviation	N
	No	18.6364	2.05971	22
IUS1_tot	Yes	18.9661	2.66501	59
	Total	18.8765	2.50690	81
	No	18.0455	2.60909	22
IUS2_tot	Yes	18.9492	2.80039	59
	Total	18.7037	2.76335	81
	No	14.5909	5.11449	22
IUS3_tot	Yes	17.6271	4.16843	59
	Total	16.8025	4.61633	81

The Mann–Whitney U test indicates that there was a significant difference ($U = 863.5$, $p = 0.023$) between the respondents who selected visual output across all scenarios ($n = 59$) as compared to the respondents who provided mixed responses ($n = 22$).

Table 10 represents the outcomes for parametric tests of within-subjects effects.

Table 10. Tests of within-subjects effects.

Source		df	F	Sig.	Partial Eta Squared	Observed Power
Scenarios $*$ Vis_max	Greenhouse–Geisser	1.455	5.634	0.010	0.067	0.763

$\alpha = 0.05$. $*$ = The impact of vis_max on the level of acceptance of output as mediated by Scenarios.

The mixed ANOVA using $\alpha = 0.05$ with a Greenhouse–Geisser correction was significant when differentiated for Maximum Visual: $F (1.455, 114.915) = 5.634$, $p = 0.010$.

Table 11 represents the outcomes for parametric tests of between-subjects effects.

Table 11. Tests of between-subjects effects.

Source		df	F	Sig.	Partial Eta Squared	Observed Power
Vis_max	Bonferroni	1	4.111	0.046	0.049	0.517

$\alpha = 0.05$.

The mixed ANOVA using $\alpha = 0.05$ with Bonferroni adjustment was significant: $(F (1, 79) = 4.111$, $p = 0.046$.

In summary, the null hypothesis was rejected, as follows:

- **Non-parametric:** $U = 863.5$, $p = 0.023$
- **Parametric:**
  - **Within-subjects:** $(F (1.455, 114.915) = 5.634$, $p = 0.010$, $\eta p2 = 0.067)$
  - **Between-subjects:** $(F (1, 79) = 4.111$, $p = 0.046$, $\eta p2 = 0.049)$

As such, for RQ1: is there a difference in the level of acceptance of security alert output between those with a preference for VAO and those with a preference for TAO, with VAO and TAO generated via data science/machine learning methods, as predicted by the TAM? the answer is yes.

Additional sub-questions were examined in this analysis. Specifically, the sub-questions are stated as:

- SQ1: Does the adoption of VAO have a significant impact on the four individual TAM components: PU, PEU, AU, and IU?
- SQ2: Does the adoption of TAO have a significant impact on the four individual TAM components: PU, PEU, AU, and IU?

Outcomes indicate mixed results in answering the sub-questions. Table 12 states the results of within-subjects effects per individual TAM components.

Table 12. Tests of within-subjects effects per individual TAM components.

TAM Factor	Adjustment	df	F	Sig.	Partial Eta Squared	Observed Power
PU	Greenhouse–Geisser	1.637	4.017	0.028	0.048	0.434
PEU	Greenhouse–Geisser	1.658	3.548	0.040	0.043	0.380
AU	Greenhouse–Geisser	1.669	8.159	0.001	0.094	0.819
IU	Greenhouse–Geisser	1.447	5.728	0.009	0.068	0.705

$\alpha = 0.0125$.

The within-subjects findings indicated that PU and PEU were not significantly influenced by the adoption of VAO or TAO, while AU and IU were significantly influenced by the adoption of VAO. Table 13 states the results of between-subjects effects per individual TAM components.

Table 13. Tests of between-subjects effects per individual TAM components.

TAM Factor	Adjustment	df	F	Sig.	Partial Eta Squared	Observed Power
PU	Bonferroni	1	7.643	0.007	0.088	0.584
PEU	Bonferroni	1	0.842	0.362	0.011	0.055
AU	Bonferroni	1	4.566	0.036	0.055	0.343
IU	Bonferroni	1	4.378	0.040	0.053	0.328

$\alpha = 0.0125$.

The between-subjects findings indicate that PU was the only TAM component to be significantly influenced by the adoption of VAO.

As a result, the answer to SQ1 is yes, in part:

- The TAM components PU and PEU were not significantly influenced by the adoption of VAO within-subjects, while AU and IU were significantly influenced by the adoption of VAO within-subjects.
- The TAM component PU was significantly influenced by the adoption of VAO between-subjects.

The answer to SQ2 is universally no. No individual TAM component was significantly influenced by TAO adoption, and TAO adoption trailed VAO in near totality.

3.14. Summary

The results indicate that there was a difference in acceptance as predicted by TAM. The dependent variable, security analysts' level of acceptance of security alert output, and the two independent variables, Scenario and ML/DS-generated alert output (TAO and VAO), were assessed with non-parametric and parametric methods. Both the Mann–Whitney U test and the mixed ANOVA determined that there was a difference between the acceptance of VAO and TAO in favor of VAO. The mixed ANOVA also demonstrated that two of the TAM factors, AU and IU, were influenced by the adoption of VAO and TAO.

4. Discussion

4.1. Discussion of the Results

This study sought to determine if there is a difference between the adoption of VAO and TAO generated via data science/machine learning methods as predicted by the TAM. The related hypothesis tested for significant differences in the level of acceptance of alert outputs between those preferring VAO in all scenarios and those preferring TAO in some or all scenarios, as predicted by the TAM. The null hypothesis was rejected. A non-parametric test, the Mann–Whitney test, indicated a significant difference in the level of acceptance of output between those preferring visual alerts in all scenarios, and other preferences ($U = 863.5$, $p = 0.023$). This result was repeated in the between-subjects element of a mixed ANOVA, $F (1, 79) = 4.111$, $p = 0.046$, $\eta p2 = 0.049$. The within-subjects element of the mixed ANOVA, relating to different responses to each scenario, was also statistically significant, $F (1.455, 114.915) = 5.634$, $p = 0.010$, $\eta p2 = 0.067$. These results indicate a statistically significant difference in perception that favors VAO.

4.2. Original Contribution to the Body of Knowledge

This study begins to close a gap in the body of knowledge and represents opportunities for additional research. Prior studies have focused exclusively on specific tenets discussed herein, but not in aggregate or totality. Studies focused on visual analytics versus text-oriented interfaces, while robust, did not factor for scale or usability, nor efficiencies gained from ML/DS. Other research focused on security operations at scale to address data overload and complexity but did not address solutions for an improved analyst experience and usability with visualization. More studies addressed detailed ML/DS opportunities leading to increased efficiency and detection, but again with no focus on alert output and usability. This research intentionally joined these tenets to improve security analysts' experience with optimized alert output derived from ML/DS to address challenges of scale, detection fidelity, and usability. This contribution to the body of knowledge enables industry and academia to further refine security detection methods and products to reduce risk and better protect organizations. Specific contributions follow, and are discussed further in Section 4.4:

- Enables industry, service, and application providers to develop, deploy, and utilize tools and capabilities that include visualizations for alert output.
- Indicates that the interface for security analysts working daily with such tools and capabilities offers a favorable user experience that is rich in visual features.
- Clarifies that issues specific to this study's problem statement can be rectified with visual alert output derived from machine learning and data science intended to reduce the burden on security analysts.

4.3. Limitations

This study's results did not conform to expectations for normality, exhibiting a noteworthy skew towards strongly agree, or a 7 on the Likert scale. Bias may have been introduced in two distinct ways. First, TAM-based user experience (UX) studies are best delivered using a left-to-right layout, where 1 = Extremely disagree and 7 = Extremely agree [18]. Additionally, Lewis suggested that all questionnaire items have a positive tone such that greater levels of agreement indicate a better user experience [18]. This could explain why the normality histograms as seen in Figures 2–4 show such a strong skew to the right (strongly agree). Second, the researcher may have introduced additional bias by describing the VAO with a caveat stating that users who selected visual output would have the ability to mouse over the graphical interface and interact with specific data points. No such additional benefit or opportunity was discussed for users who preferred TAO.

Scenario 3 included a dynamic, animated visualization, where alert counts moved through days of the month over a five-month period. The researcher asserts that this visual was not met with positive perception and likely viewed as of low quality and difficult to interpret as compared to the static visuals seen in Scenarios 1 and 2. Additionally, the researcher did not randomize the scenarios as delivered to participants. As such, all participants received the scenarios in the same order. Thus, order effects could explain the decline in positive perception of Scenario 3 for participants. Order effects refer to the phenomenon where different orders for the presentation of questions, or response alternatives, may systematically influence respondents' answers [28]. Scores may decrease over time from fatigue, or increase due to learning, and order effects can interfere with estimates of the effect of the treatment itself during analysis, a disadvantage of repeated measures designs [29].

4.4. Implications for Practice

The most significant implications for practice as determined from this study's results are simple. Develop, deploy, and utilize tooling and capabilities that include visualizations for alert output. Better still, ensure that the interface imposed on the security analysts working daily with such tooling and capabilities offers a favorable user experience that is rich in visual features, including additional right-click context (additional exploratory analytics available via a mouse right-click menu). Ben-Asher and Gonzalez determined that a high volume of intrusion alerts to be processed, coupled with excessive false-positive alerts, challenges human cognitive capabilities in accurately detecting an attack [30]. This study's findings indicate an opportunity to rectify these issues with the benefits of visual alert output derived from machine learning and data science intended to reduce the burden on security analysts.

4.5. Recommendations for Future Study

A future study that builds on this study's findings might incorporate a third option for participants: text alert output, visual alert output, or both. Security analysts would likely seek an initial visual alert inclusive of the options to dive deeper into the raw data. A future study could expose the degree to which analysts may seek such multifaceted options.

Results specific to Scenario 3 revealed a noteworthy decline in perception and satisfaction for the visual alert output included with the scenario. Given that this visual alert output was a dynamic animation unlike its static counterparts in Scenarios 1 and 2, a future study could further explore the perceptions of, and interactions with, dynamic visualizations versus static visualizations. Even more stark was the dip in perception and satisfaction for the text alert output included with Scenario 3. Future research could further explore the layout of data tables, including satisfaction with a variety of included fields and column headings.

Performance-based experimentation represents a potential focus area for future research, with attention to key performance indicators and metrics and analysis of the speed to conclusions as a comparison of TAO versus VAO. While this study's delimitations prevented true experimentation, the premise of presenting participants with actionable scenarios while measuring their response time, accuracy, and efficacy would provide more accurate assessment of VAO versus TAO's impact on performance.

5. Conclusions

Organizations dealing with a high volume of security alert and event data, that are also facing a high burden due to alert overload, should consider implementing features and capabilities that incorporate visual alert output. These organizations risk data breach, loss of valuable human resources, reputation, and revenue due to excessive security alert volumes and a lack of fidelity in security event data. Visualization can benefit security analysts faced with these burdens on behalf of their organizations. This quantitative, quasi-experimental, explanatory study determined that security analysts perceive improved usability of security alert output that is visualized rather than text-based. The related hypothesis tested for significant differences in the level of acceptance of output between those affirming a maximum visual preference (three out of three scenarios) and those showing a preference for text in at least one scenario. The results determined that those showing maximum visual preference had a significantly higher acceptance of alert output ($U = 863.5$, $p = 0.023$). This finding was also supported by the main between-subjects effect of a mixed ANOVA, $F(1, 79) = 4.111$, $p = 0.046$, $\eta p2 = 0.049$. The ANOVA's within-subjects main effect (scenario) was also statistically significant, $F(1.455, 114.915) = 5.634$, $p = 0.010$, $\eta p2 = 0.067$. All supporting data are available with Supplementary Martials, including a literature review. These findings represent an opportunity to enhance and enable higher-order analysis, including detection development, tuning, and validation, as well as threat hunting and improved investigations: cut the noise, hone the signal.

Supplementary Materials: The following supporting information can be downloaded at: https://github.com/holisticinfosec/Optimized-Alerts-Usability-Study (accessed on 24 May 2022).

Funding: This research received no external funding.

Institutional Review Board Statement: The study was conducted in accordance with the Declaration of Helsinki, and approved by the Institutional Review Board of Capitol Technology University (approved 28 September 2020).

Informed Consent Statement: Informed consent was obtained from all subjects involved in the study.

Conflicts of Interest: The author declares no conflict of interest.

References

1. Khan, M. Security Analysts Are Overworked, Understaffed and Overwhelmed—Here's How AI Can Help. Available online: https://securityintelligence.com/security-analysts-are-overworked-understaffed-and-overwhelmed-heres-how-ai-can-help (accessed on 21 September 2020).
2. Cambridge Intelligence. Visualizing Cyber Security Threats. Available online: https://cambridge-intelligence.com (accessed on 1 May 2021).
3. Slatman, H. *Unboxing Security Analytics: Towards Effective Data Driven Security Operations*; Computer Science, University of Twente: Enschede, The Netherlands, 2016.
4. Dimensional Research. 2020 State of SecOps and Automation. Available online: https://www.sumologic.com/brief/state-of-secops (accessed on 5 May 2021).
5. Bartos, V.; Zadnik, M.; Habib, S.M.; Vasilomanolakis, E. Network entity characterization and attack prediction. *Future Gener. Comput. Syst.* **2019**, *97*, 674–686. [CrossRef]
6. Sundaramurthy, S.C.; Bardas, A.G.; Case, J.; Ou, X.; Wesch, M.; McHugh, J.; Rajagopalan, S.R. A Human Capital Model for Mitigating Security Analyst Burnout. In Proceedings of the Symposium on Usable Privacy and Security, Ottawa, CA, USA, 22–24 July 2015.
7. Paul, C.L.; Dykstra, J. Understanding operator fatigue, frustration, and cognitive workload in tactical cybersecurity operations. *J. Inf. Warf.* **2017**, *16*, 1–11.
8. FireEye. The Numbers Game: How Many Alerts Is Too Many to Handle? Available online: https://www.fireeye.com/offers/rpt-idc-numbers-game-special-report.html (accessed on 11 June 2020).
9. Seals, T. Less Than 1% of Severe/Critical Security Alerts Are Ever Investigated. Available online: https://www.infosecurity-magazine.com/news/less-than-1-of-severe-critical (accessed on 12 July 2021).
10. Oltsik, J. The Problem with Collecting, Processing, and Analyzing More Security Data. Available online: https://www.esg-global.com/blog/the-problem-with-collecting-processing-and-analyzing-more-security-data (accessed on 10 April 2021).
11. CriticalStart. The Impact of Security Alert Overload. Available online: https://www.criticalstart.com (accessed on 10 April 2021).
12. Kohgadai, A. Alert Fatigue: 31.9% of IT Security Professionals Ignore Alerts. Available online: https://www.skyhighnetworks.com/cloud-security-blog/alert-fatigue-31-9-of-it-security-professionals-ignore-alerts (accessed on 10 April 2021).
13. Chickowski, E. Every Hour SOCs Run, 15 Minutes Are Wasted on False Positives. Available online: https://securityboulevard.com/2019/09/every-hour-socs-run-15-minutes-are-wasted-on-false-positives (accessed on 2 September 2019).
14. Ponemon. 2020 Devo SOC Performance Report: A Tale of Two SOCs. Available online: https://www.devo.com (accessed on 8 February 2021).
15. Giacobe, N.A. *Measuring the Effectiveness of Visual Analytics and Data Fusion Techniques on Situation Awareness in Cyber-Security*; Penn State University: State College, PA, USA, 2013.
16. Venkatesh, V.; Davis, D. A theoretical extension of the technology acceptance model: Four longitudinal field studies. *Inf. Syst. Res.* **2000**, *46*, 186–204. [CrossRef]
17. Davis, F.D. Perceived Usefulness, Perceived Ease of Use, and User Acceptance of Information Technology. *MIS Q.* **1989**, *13*, 319–340. [CrossRef]
18. Lewis, J.R. Comparison of Four TAM Item Formats: Effect of Response Option Labels and Order. *J. Usability Stud.* **2019**, *14*, 224–236.
19. Deutskens, E.; De Ruyter, K.; Wetzels, M.; Oosterveld, P. Response rate and response quality of Internet-based surveys: An experimental study. *Mark. Lett.* **2004**, *15*, 21–36. [CrossRef]
20. Lumen. Repeated-Measures ANOVA. *Boundless Statistics*. Available online: https://courses.lumenlearning.com/boundless-statistics/chapter/repeated-measures-anova (accessed on 19 August 2021).
21. Lewis, J.R.; Utesch, B.S.; Maher, D.E. Measuring Perceived Usability: The SUS, UMUX-LITE, and AltUsability. *Int. J. Hum. Comput. Interact.* **2015**, *31*, 496–505. [CrossRef]
22. Szajna, B. Software evaluation and choice: Predictive validation of the technology acceptance instrument. *MIS Q.* **1994**, *18*, 319. [CrossRef]
23. Shahrabi, M.A.; Ahaninjan, A.; Nourbakhsh, H.; Ashlubolagh, M.A.; Abdolmaleki, J.; Mohamadi, M. Assessing psychometric reliability and validity of Technology Acceptance Model (TAM) among faculty members at Shahid Beheshti University. *Manag. Sci. Lett.* **2013**, *3*, 2295–2300. [CrossRef]
24. U.S. Bureau of Labor Statistics. Information Security Analysts: Occupational Outlook Handbook: U.S. Bureau of Labor Statistics. Available online: https://www.bls.gov/ooh/computer-and-information-technology/information-security-analysts.htm (accessed on 14 June 2019).
25. Barlett, J.E.; Kotrlik, J.W.; Higgins, C.C. Organizational research: Determining appropriate sample size in survey research. *Inf. Technol. Learn. Perform. J.* **2001**, *19*, 43–50.
26. Hoskin, T. Parametric and Nonparametric: Demystifying the Terms. Available online: https://www.mayo.edu/research/documents/parametric-and-nonparametric-demystifying-the-terms/doc-20408960 (accessed on 19 August 2021).
27. Lane, D.M. Online Statistics Education: A Multimedia Course of Study. Available online: https://onlinestatbook.com (accessed on 19 August 2021).

28. Strack, F. Order Effects in Survey Research: Activation and Information Functions of Preceding Questions. In *Context Effects in Social and Psychological Research*; Schwarz, N., Sudman, S., Eds.; Springer: New York, NY, USA, 1992; pp. 23–34.

29. Minitab Blog Editor. Repeated Measures Designs: Benefits, Challenges, and an ANOVA Example. Available online: https://blog.minitab.com/en/adventures-in-statistics-2/repeated-measures-designs-benefits-challenges-and-an-anova-example (accessed on 19 August 2021).

30. Ben-Asher, N.; Gonzalez, C. Effects of cyber security knowledge on attack detection. *Comput. Hum. Behav.* **2015**, *48*, 51–61. [CrossRef]

Journal of
*Cybersecurity
and Privacy*

Article

Unsupervised Machine Learning Techniques for Detecting PLC Process Control Anomalies

Emmanuel Aboah Boateng and J. W. Bruce *

Department of Electrical and Computer Engineering, Tennessee Technological University,
Cookeville, TN 38505, USA; eaboahboa42@tntech.edu
* Correspondence: jwbruce@tntech.edu

Abstract: The security of programmable logic controllers (PLCs) that control industrial systems is becoming increasingly critical due to the ubiquity of the Internet of Things technologies and increasingly nefarious cyber-attack activity. Conventional techniques for safeguarding PLCs are difficult due to their unique architectures. This work proposes a one-class support vector machine, one-class neural network interconnected in a feed-forward manner, and isolation forest approaches for verifying PLC process integrity by monitoring PLC memory addresses. A comprehensive experiment is conducted using an open-source PLC subjected to multiple attack scenarios. A new histogram-based approach is introduced to visualize anomaly detection algorithm performance and prediction confidence. Comparative performance analyses of the proposed algorithms using decision scores and prediction confidence are presented. Results show that isolation forest outperforms one-class neural network, one-class support vector machine, and previous work, in terms of accuracy, precision, recall, and F1-score on seven attack scenarios considered. Statistical hypotheses tests involving analysis of variance and Tukey's range test were used to validate the presented results.

Keywords: cyber-physical systems; anomaly detection; programmable logic controllers (PLCs); one-class support vector machine (OCSVM); one-class neural network (OCNN); isolation forest (IF); unsupervised machine learning; cybersecurity

Citation: Aboah Boateng, E.; Bruce, J. W. Unsupervised Machine Learning Techniques for Detecting PLC Process Control Anomalies. *J. Cybersecur. Priv.* **2022**, *2*, 220–244. https://doi.org/10.3390/jcp2020012

Academic Editors: Phil Legg and Giorgio Giacinto

Received: 14 February 2022
Accepted: 17 March 2022
Published: 24 March 2022

Publisher's Note: MDPI stays neutral with regard to jurisdictional claims in published maps and institutional affiliations.

1. Introduction

The pervasiveness of Internet of Things technology and networked sensors in many industrial control systems (ICSs) have exposed critical infrastructure to malicious activities and cyber threats, leading to an increase in successful cyberattacks on critical infrastructure [1–4]. Programmable logic controllers (PLCs) are embedded devices that serve as major components in ICSs and are crucial to ICSs' network operation. PLCs control industrial systems by collecting input data from field devices such as sensors and sending commands to actuating devices for process execution [5,6]. ICSs monitor and control critical infrastructure such as nuclear facilities, electricity supply, and water management. PLCs are vulnerable to attacks, similar to other embedded devices. Because PLCs are widely used to control the physical processes of critical infrastructure, attacks against PLCs can cause irreparable damage to enterprises and even loss of human life [7].

In the past, PLCs operated as isolated and proprietary systems with no external connectivity [8,9]. As a result, PLC attacks were limited to insider intrusion, physical damage, and tampering [10]. PLCs are increasingly connected to the internet and corporate networks via transmission control protocol/internet protocol (TCP/IP) and wireless IP [11]. It is difficult to apply traditional techniques for detecting anomalous PLC behavior due to their unique architecture and proprietary operating systems. Therefore, it is crucial to protect PLCs against any forms of cyber-attack and anomalies such as hardware malfunction, accidental actions by insiders, and malicious intruders [12]. Figure 1 shows a typical ICS with interconnected network configuration. The human–machine interface (HMI) provides a visual view and process control commands. The PLCs contain the control logic that supervises the control process. The control process data logs are stored in the historian.

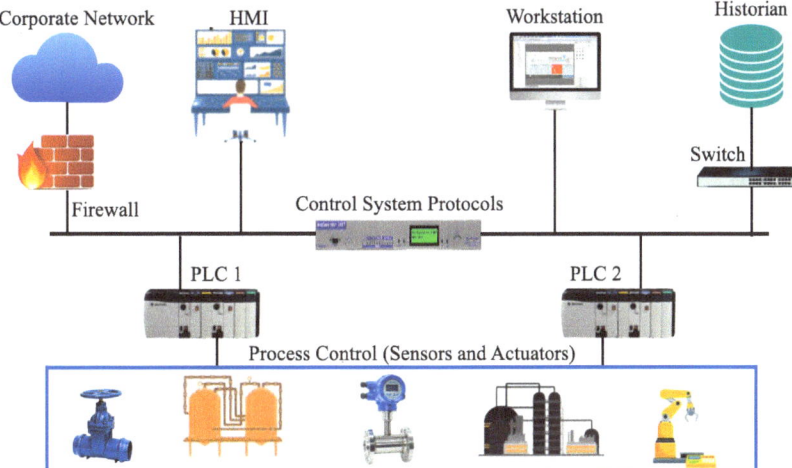

Figure 1. A typical ICS with interconnected network configuration.

Although both supervised and unsupervised ML techniques have been applied in PLC anomaly detection [13,14], it is usually difficult to rely on a supervised learning approach as real-world ICSs contain numerous sensor data that are tedious to label. Moreover, unsupervised ML techniques for anomaly detection in PLCs and ICSs have not been widely examined. This work explores one-class support vector machines (OCSVM), one-class neural network (OCNN) interconnected in a feed-forward manner, and isolation forest (IF) algorithms to verify PLC process integrity. In order to evaluate this concept, a traffic light control experiment similar to [13,15] was developed. Recent work has suggested that one-class support vector machines (OCSVM) are accurate for identifying anomalous PLC behavior and for identifying anomalies in other areas [16–18]. Research work in [19] shows that the future of deep neural networks for intelligent decision making in ICS looks promising. This is because anomaly-detection algorithms based on deep neural networks serve as a data-driven universal function approximation tool.

This work further extends unsupervised PLC anomaly detection techniques by using IF and OCNN. After training, the proposed models are intended to run on a dedicated or separate computer to monitor operations at the PLC memory addresses through real-time HMI historian logs. Results indicate that isolation forest techniques may reduce anomaly detection models' dependence on the specific data set locality. This work shows that IF outperforms OCNN and OCSVM in detecting PLCs anomalies.

1.1. Contributions

The novel contributions of this work can be summarized as follows:

1. Employ OCNN-based technique for detecting abnormal PLC behavior—the first known application of OCNN in the ICS domain;
2. Conduct comparative performance analysis between OCSVM, OCNN, and IF based on their decision scores instead of using traditional binary predictions and employing analysis of variance (ANOVA) and Tukey's range test for confirming validity of results;
3. Introduce a new histogram-based approach for visualizing anomaly-detection algorithm performance and prediction confidence.

1.2. Outline of the Paper

This paper is organized as follows. Section 2 presents a detailed overview of the related works, followed by Section 3, which discusses the details of the experimental setup and the approach to collecting data for training and evaluating the ML algorithms. Section 4 discusses the proposed unsupervised anomaly detection frameworks, and after that, Section 5 presents the results and analysis. Finally, Section 6 concludes the paper and provides recommendations for future work.

2. Related Work

Inoue et al. employed unsupervised ML algorithms for anomaly detection in water treatment systems [20]. They compared two unsupervised methods: a deep neural network consisting of feed-forward layers with multiple inputs and outputs and a one-class support vector machine (OCSVM). The authors claimed that the deep neural network model generated fewer false positives than the OCSVM, although the OCSVM could detect more anomalies. The authors report recall values less than 0.7 for both deep neural network and OCSVM.

Tomlin et al. [21] proposed a clustering approach for network intrusion-detection system implementation in ICS. Their experimental results highlighted the issues associated with using cluster analysis as a unique tool for anomaly-based intrusion detection. Although the work of Tomlin et al. seems promising, it focused on mainly simulated experimental data, which sometimes fail to represent an actual ICS setup.

Xiao et al. [22] proposed a noninvasive power-based anomaly-detection scheme for detecting attacks on PLCs using long short-term memory. Their work detected malicious software execution in a PLC by analyzing the PLC power consumption. Xiao et al. achieved accuracy as high as 99%. However, PLC power consumption is affected by power supply instability and electronics malfunction, and can produce false-positive values.

In [23], the authors used a fully connected neural network and an autoencoder to detect anomalies in network traffic. Their results demonstrated a higher detection rate and lowered false positive rate when compared with eight other modern anomaly detection techniques. Potluri et al. [24] also employed Artificial Neural Networks (ANN) for identifying false data injection attacks in ICS. The classification report obtained in [24] shows a promising detection accuracy with ANN.

In [25], Elnor et al. proposed a semisupervised dual isolation forest-based anomaly detection approach using the normal process operation data of the secure water treatment (SWaT) testbed and water distribution testbed. They compared their approach to other anomaly detection techniques for ICS in terms of precision, recall, and F1-score. They achieved a 7% improvement in the F1-score and detected 19 out of 36 SWaT attacks.

Ahmed et al. [26] proposed an unsupervised learning approach using isolation forest to detect covert data integrity assault on a smart grid communication network. Although they achieved an average accuracy of 93%, their approach focused on simulated experimental data and may not represent ICS accurately. From the aforementioned, it can be realized that isolation forest is a tremendous unsupervised learning approach with high performance in anomaly detection. However, there are not enough applications of isolation forest techniques for anomaly detection in PLCs and ICSs.

Liu et al. [27] proposed an anomaly detector based on subspace technique and quantization method for amplitude-frequency characteristic deviation of ICSs. Their approach is practical and may be readily deployed in real ICS. However, the work does not address ICS confidentiality attack. Reported results show an inability to detect anomalies in ICSs with aggressive disturbances and instabilities. The work in [27] highlights the general challenges associated with deploying anomaly detection models in resource-constrained embedded devices for ICS protection.

PLC protection has some challenges associated with applying anomaly detection techniques [27–30]. Most legacy PLCs in ICSs have insufficient low-level documentation making it challenging to perform forensic investigations in cases of cyber-attacks or anomalous events [31]. Security mechanisms and forensic tools dedicated for PLCs to perform comprehensive security investigations are lacking [32]. Lastly, PLC availability in an ICS environment is often paramount. Therefore, shutting down a PLC-based ICS for forensic investigations is often not feasible [28]. Therefore, robust detection techniques are required for real-time anomaly detection in PLCs and ICSs.

An unsupervised ML technique called OCSVM was employed to detect anomalies in PLCs successfully in [13]. Their experiment simulated a traffic light control system using a PLC. They captured relevant PLC memory addresses into a log file for real-time data recording from the traffic light operation. The captured data was normalized and used for training the OCSVM model. Training and test accuracies were 98% and 82%, respectively. However, OCSVM recall values on some test cases were as low as 75%, and the average accuracy over their three-test cases was 78%. The low-performance metrics of detection technique in [13] call for the need to investigate robust detection techniques for anomaly detection in PLCs.

While OCSVM has been used as an effective unsupervised technique for anomaly detection, OCSVM performance is unsatisfactory on complex, high-dimensional datasets [33,34]. A one-class neural network (OCNN) with a one-class objective function was used for anomaly detection in complex datasets [33]. Despite its great potential on complex datasets, OCNN has not been applied to ICS or PLC for anomaly detection purposes. This work examines OCSVM, OCNN, and IF ML techniques for detecting PLC anomalous behavior by tracking the operations at the PLC input and output memory addresses.

3. Experiment Setup

This section provides the details of the experimental setup used in this work to implement the traffic light system. The ICS used in this work is patterned after the one described in [13,15].

3.1. Description of Control Setup

Siemens's open-source traffic light control program [15] was used to implement a traffic light system to control vehicles and pedestrian traffic at a pedestrian crossing with red, yellow, and green signals. In addition to the traffic light signals, each pedestrian light was equipped with a pushbutton for pedestrians to request green light signals. The following safety requirements were taken into account in the control logic program in order to prevent any hazard to pedestrians or drivers:

1. The control system default operation should turn ON the green and red light signals for the vehicle traffic and pedestrian traffic, respectively, to define a safe starting point;
2. Whenever the program receives a green request from the pedestrian through the pushbutton, the vehicle traffic light signals must change from green to red via yellow.

Apart from the safety requirements, Figure 2 summarizes the control setup operation. In [13,15], a system was constructed using Siemens S&-1212C PLC loaded with the TLIGHT control program. This work implements the TLIGHT control logic using OpenPLC [35] and ScadaBR [36]. Figure 3 provides a block diagram of the experimental setup for recording training and test data. The experimental setup's main components are described below.

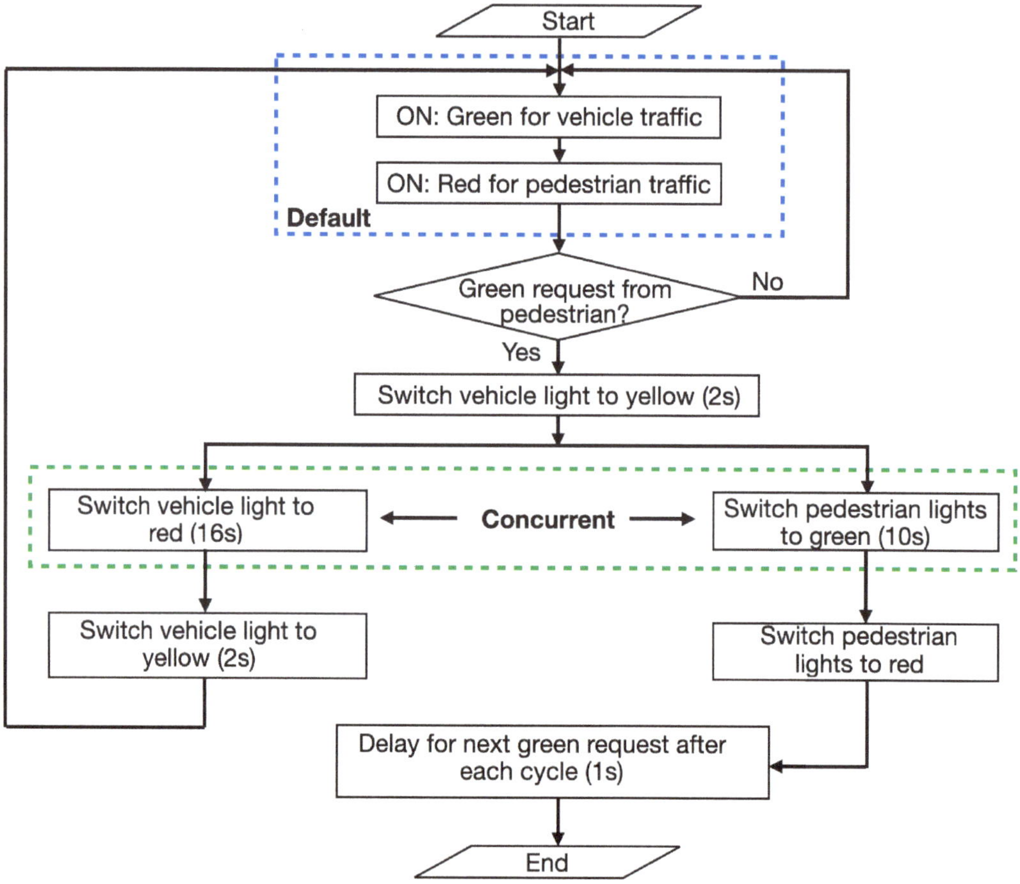

Start
ON: Green for vehicle traffic
ON: Red for pedestrian traffic
Default
Green request from pedestrian?
No
Yes
Switch vehicle light to yellow (2s)
Switch vehicle light to red (16s)
Concurrent
Switch pedestrian lights to green (10s)
Switch vehicle light to yellow (2s)
Switch pedestrian lights to red
Delay for next green request after each cycle (1s)
End

Figure 2. Flow chart of TLIGHT system operations.

TLIGHT SYSTEM
openPLC
scadaBR
Modbus TCP/IP
Soft PLC
HMI

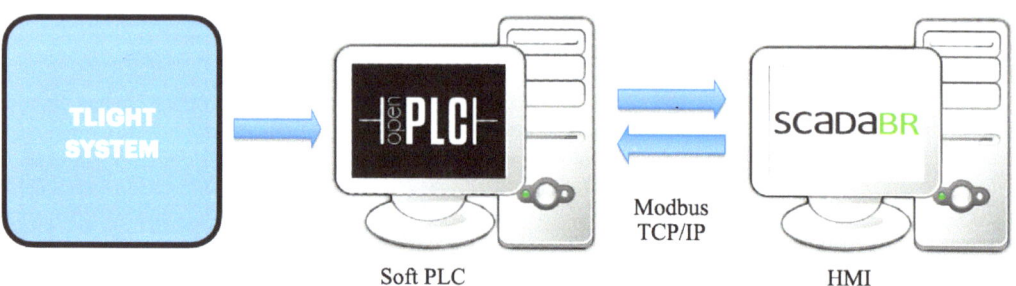

Figure 3. Diagram of the cyber-physical system network interconnection and information flow.

3.2. OpenPLC

OpenPLC is an open-source simulation environment for home and industrial automation systems development [35]. OpenPLC runtime is versatile, and it creates a virtual PLC architecture on supported hardware to mimic PLC behavior. OpenPLC supports several firm PLC devices [37–39] and personal computers (PC) running Linux and Windows operating systems to create flexible soft PLCs installations [35]. The TLIGHT system [15] was implemented in two parts in OpenPLC. The first part was the control program development similar to the description of Figure 2 in ladder logic form in OpenPLC editor. OpenPLC editor was used to simulate and test the TLIGHT system logic to ensure that the program was error-free and accurately represented the TLIGHT system description in [13,15]. The simulated program followed the IEC 61131-3 standard for PLC programs [40]. The ladder logic implementation is publicly available on [41]. Finally, the ladder logic was converted to a structured text format that can be run and interpreted by the OpenPLC runtime.

The soft PLC in Figure 3 was implemented with a PC running Linux version of OpenPLC. The experimental setup in this paper will work on all OpenPLC supported hardware devices [35,37–39]. The second part of the implementation was the program's deployment in structured text format onto the OpenPLC runtime for real-time program execution. PLC consists of a central processing unit (CPU), memory areas (also referred to as address space in OpenPLC), and input/output devices. Internally, the program works by continuously scanning the program for every 100 ms. Each scan cycle consists of three crucial steps: check inputs, execute program logic, and update outputs. The cyclical PLC runtime process continues so long as the runtime is set to running mode as described in Algorithm 1.

Algorithm 1: PLC runtime execution.

Input: Pushbuttons for green request from the pedestrians
Output: Light signals states for vehicles and pedestrians
Initialize Default TLIGHT system state
for *each 50 ms* **do**
   | sample inputs from PLC addresses
   | execute ladder logic
   | update PLC registers
   | process network transactions
end

3.3. Human Machine Interface (HMI)

ScadaBR [36], an open-source supervisory control and data acquisition (SCADA) system, was utilized as the HMI to monitor and control the PLC runtime. ScadaBR depicts the control system's state in real-time. It allows direct observation and execution of control commands to PLC. The PLC input and output memory addresses were mapped to corresponding Modbus input and output addresses in the HMI. At the end of every HMI cycle time (100 ms), ScadaBR records available data at the input and output Modbus addresses to a log file. Finally, TLIGHT system operations are exported from the HMI as CSV file for preprocessing and training of the detection models. The HMI application also operates independently of the PLC, as described in Algorithm 2.

Algorithm 2: HMI application execution.

Input: PLC inputs' states
Output: PLC outputs' states
for *each 100 ms* **do**
   | read PLC inputs' states
   | read PLC registers' states
   | **if** *an update from user* **then**
      | write change to settable PLC registers
   | **end**
   | process network transactions
end

---

4. Proposed Method

The proposed anomaly detection systems described here use the normal process data from TLIGHT system's input and output signals. Details about the data collection, anomalies, and theoretical background of the algorithms used in the proposed methods are described in this section. Figure 4 is a framework of the anomaly detection approach that shows how the proposed methods could be implemented in other real-world ICS scenarios. The process starts with offline training of OCSVM, OCNN, and IF using the dataset from HMI historian directly recorded from the PLC memory addresses. Training data consists of relevant features which are normalized to retain the minimum and maximum features values. The processed data are used to develop the detection models. The trained models are serialized onto a separate computer for real-time PLC anomaly detection. During testing or online detection, real-time measurement data is obtained from the HMI historian, and information about the training data normalization procedure is used to process the online data - indicated by the red dotted arrows in Figure 4. The final decision is made by each trained detection model for specified time frames.

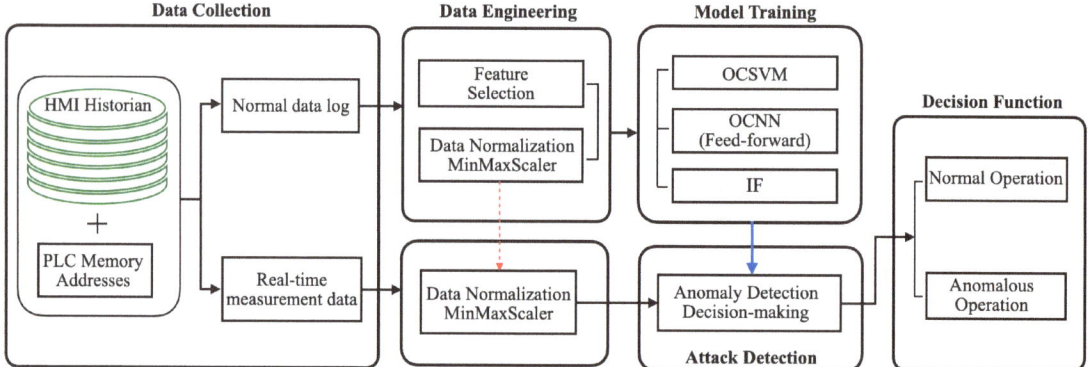

Figure 4. General framework of the anomaly detection approach.

4.1. Data Collection and Preprocessing

ML relies heavily on data by using statistical models and algorithms to build models capable of predicting outcomes for a given input [42]. As a result, data quality is critical to ML model robustness. Data is collected from the HMI historian. The HMI monitors and records the memory addresses with timestamps via the Modbus communication protocol. The data is recorded for about 4 days to ensure enough training and test data to evaluate the proposed techniques in this work. In order to ensure a fair comparison between this work and [13], the approach described here follows a similar approach in [13] as closely as possible. Figure 5 summarizes the approach to the data collection and preprocessing.

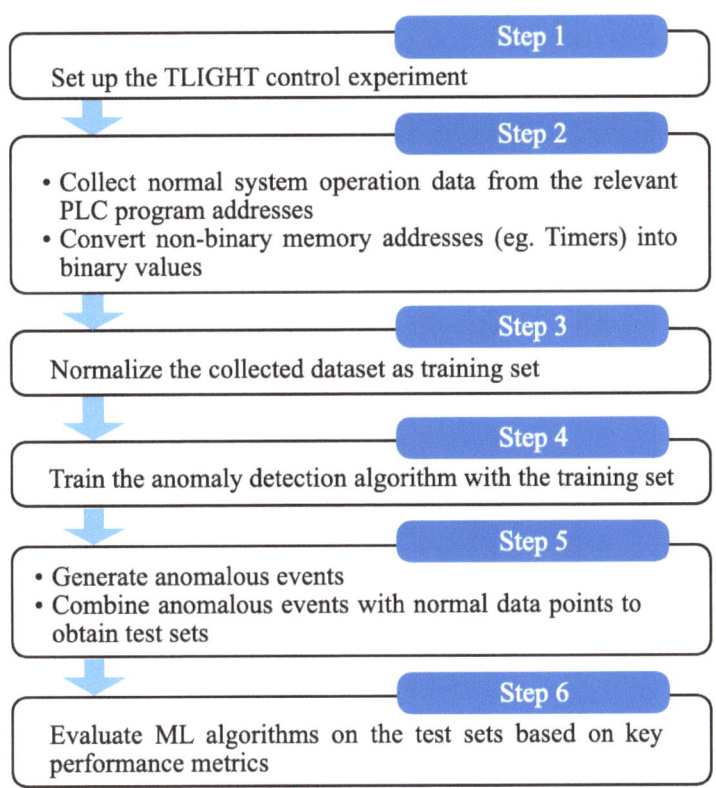

Figure 5. Description of the various steps involved in data collection, preprocessing, training and evaluation of the anomaly detection algorithms.

4.1.1. Anomalous Scenarios

In order to evaluate and compare the performance of the different anomaly-detection techniques proposed in this work, five different test sets are generated. Each set contains normal and anomalous TLIGHT system events. Anomalous system events for the five test sets are derived from seven scenarios. All seven attack scenarios could generally represent real-world scenarios resulting from malfunctioning sensors and actuators, such as broken connectors, damaged cable insulation, physical obstruction, or natural disasters. It is crucial to quickly identify the anomalies in all scenarios because they could indicate hardware failure mode or the need for system maintenance. Furthermore, each scenario can also represent a specific malicious attack on an ICS. The seven attack scenarios are outlined below.

- Anomalous scenario 1: All the vehicles and pedestrians' green lights are turned ON at the same time. The purpose of this anomalous event is to violate the TLIGHT system safety rules. This attack generally represents a real-world scenario in which an attacker has compromised the PLC operations through elevation of privileges attack with the aim of causing traffic collision between vehicles and pedestrians.
- Anomalous scenario 2: All the traffic lights are shut down. This attack aims to simulate an unnecessary traffic scenario for the vehicles and deny pedestrians' green light requests. This attack represents a real-world scenario in which an attacker has introduced logic bomb attack inside the PLC ladder logic with the aim of terminating TLIGHT system operations.

- Anomalous scenario 3: All pedestrians and vehicles' traffic light signals are turned ON. This attack scenario aims to violate the TLIGHT system safety requirements. This attack generally represents a real-world scenario in which an attacker has compromised the wired connection between the PLC and physical components with the aim of causing a denial-of-service attack. This attack could lead to traffic jams and delays.
- Anomalous scenario 4: Refuse all green light requests from the pedestrians. This attack scenario violates the TLIGHT system logic and operation cycle. This attack generally represents a real-world scenario in which an attacker tampered with the HMI communication protocol due to unencrypted communication with the aim of causing a denial-of-service attack.
- Anomalous scenario 5: All vehicles and pedestrians' red light signals are turned ON at the same time. The motive of this attack is to cause unnecessary traffic for both vehicles and pedestrians and violate the TLIGHT system's default setting. This attack generally represents a real-world scenario in which an attacker has introduced a hardware trojan inside the physical components causing the red light signals to respond differently from the PLC logic.
- Anomalous scenario 6: The vehicle's yellow signals timing bits are manipulated. This kind of anomaly is stealthy and subtle because all the traffic lights seem to be operating normally with manipulated timing bits. This attack generally represents a real-world scenario where an attacker has executed a man-in-the-middle attack by spoofing the vehicle and pedestrian timing bits signals.
- Anomalous scenario 7: Delay timing bits for subsequent pedestrian green requests, and pedestrians' green light phase duration are manipulated. This attack scenario is similar to attack scenario six in its subtlety and difficulty of detection from a human perspective. This attack generally represents a real-world scenario in which an attacker has executed a man-in-the-middle attack by spoofing the delay timing bits for pedestrian green request signals.

4.1.2. Test Cases

The details of the five test cases considered in this study are:

- Test set 1 contains 5000 normal and anomalous events samples, of which 10% are anomalous instances. The 10% of anomalous instances consists of 10% anomalous scenarios 1, 2, 3, 4, and 5;
- Test set 2 contains 7000 test samples, of which 10% are anomalous events. These anomalous events consist solely of anomalous scenario 3;
- Test set 3 contains 13,130 normal and anomalous samples. About 20% of the data contains anomalous instances sampled from anomalous scenarios 1 and 3. Anomalous scenarios 1 and 3 consist of 50% each of the total anomalous events in test set 3;
- Test set 4 contains 15,000 test samples of which anomalous instances in the test sample are 30%. These anomalous instances are sampled from anomalous scenarios 6 and 7. Moreover, anomalous scenarios 6 and 7 consist of 20% and 10% anomalies, respectively. This particular test set comprises only timing bits anomalies;
- Test set 5 is the most diverse and complicated test set. Test set 5 contains 18,270 normal and anomalous test samples. A total of 50% of the test data is anomalous instances sampled from anomalous scenarios 1, 2, 3, 5, 6, and 7. This test set is the only set with a mixture of timing bits anomalies and traffic light signals anomalies. It is also the test set with the highest number of anomalies. Anomalous scenario 1 comprises 5% of the test data, scenario 2 is 10%, scenario 3 is 10%, scenario 5 is 5%, scenario 6 is 5%, and anomalous scenario 7 is 15% of the test data.

The total training dataset samples and test sets 1-3 are consistent with the number of samples used in [13]. Test set 4 and 5 consist mainly of timing bits anomalies. Table 1 summarizes the number of records and proportion of anomalies in the training and test sets.

Table 1. Number of records and proportion of anomalies in training and test data sets.

Dataset	No. of Records	% Anomalies
Training set	41,580	n/a
Test Set 1	5000	10
Test Set 2	7000	10
Test Set 3	13,130	20
Test Set 4	15,000	30
Test Set 5	18,270	50

4.2. OCSVM-Based Detection Approach

Scholkopf et al. [43] proposed OCSVM, a maximum-based classifier established on support vector machines. The OCSVM is an unsupervised anomaly-detection algorithm that learns a decision function for separating the normal class from the anomalies [44]. Given a training dataset $\{X_i | i = 1, 2, 3 \cdots, n\}$ where $X_i \in R^d$, the OCSVM separates the data points from the origin in the feature space by a hyperplane and maximizes the distance from the hyperplane to the origin. OCSVM finds a decision function f_F that separates the data points into positive and negative scores. The positive scores represent the region in the feature space where $X_i \in F$, and F is the set that carries a high concentration of the data points, also known as the minimum-volume set. The negative scores represent all other data points or anomalies. High dimensional Hilbert space H, can be used to transform each data point X_i via a feature map $\Phi : R_d \leftarrow H$ generated by a positive-definite kernel, $k(X, X')$. The optimization problem for separating the data from the origin in the OCSVM is therefore given by

$$\min_{w,b} \frac{1}{2}\|w\|^2 - \frac{C}{N} \sum_{n=1}^{N} \xi - b$$
$$s.t : \langle w, \Phi(X_i) \rangle \geq b - \xi_i, \forall i,$$
$$\xi_i \geq 0, \forall i \tag{1}$$

where b is the variable that controls the algorithm's bias. The optimization problem is formulated such that $w \cdot \phi(X) - b$ is positive for as many N training examples as possible. The C value is a hyperparameter that serves as the differential weight of the normal data points compared to the anomalous data points. The value, $\nu = 1/C$ is regarded as the prior probability that a data point in the training set is an anomaly, thereby regulating the trade-off between false positives and false negatives in the model. The slack variable ξ allows some data points in a nonseparable dataset to be within the margin. As a result, for the given data X, the decision function $f_F(X_{n:})$ is

$$f_F(X_{n:}) = w^T \Phi(X_{n:}) - b \tag{2}$$

The function definition in (2) is responsible for separating the data points from the origin by determining whether a point is in the positive or negative set. The width of the margin is controlled by $b \in [0, 1]$ and w is the normal vector of the hyperplane. The input data is projected into a nonlinear high-dimensional space by $\Phi(X_{n:})$, and the slack variable ξ models the separation errors in the same way as the feature space of (1). Therefore, the overall OCSVM objective function is

$$\min_{w,b} \frac{1}{2}\|w\|^2 + \frac{1}{\nu N} \sum_{n=1}^{N} \max(0, b - \langle w, \Phi(X_{n:}) \rangle) - b \tag{3}$$

While the literature reports different variations of OCSVM, this work presents an OCSVM model that is developed by using the same model parameters in [13] to serve as a baseline upon which our proposed methods could be compared. OCSVM model learning process is controlled by using hyperparameters. Table 2 shows the hyperparameters for the OCSVM. According to [13], the modeling parameters in Table 2 were selected as optimal hyper-parameters for the OCSVM algorithm after investigating various hyperparameter ranges.

Table 2. Model hyperparameters for OCSVM.

Parameter	Description	Choice
kernel	Type of kernel used in the algorithm	polynomial
degree	Degree of polynomial kernel function	3
coef0	Controls how much the model is influenced by high-degree polynomials versus low-degree polynomials	4
nu(ν)	An upper bound on the fraction of training errors and a lower bound of the fraction of support vectors	0.1
gamma	Defines the level of a single training example's influence	0.1

4.3. OCNN-Based Detection Approach

Neural networks for one-class classification have been proposed in [45–47]. However, this work presents OCNN algorithm formulated on the foundation of OCSVM optimization problem [43], and a proposed alternating minimization algorithm in [33] to form a feed-forward neural network architecture capable of detecting PLC anomalies. OCNN combines the ability of feed-forward neural network to extract features from the data along with a one-class objective to become a universal anomaly detector. Given a feed-forward neural network with a hidden layer, activation function g, and an output node, the alternate minimization algorithm proposed by [33] is used to obtain the objective function. Derivation of the OCNN follows the overall OCSVM objective function in (3). The resulting objective function is used to solve the scalar output obtained from the hidden layer to the output layer w, and the weight matrix from the input to the hidden node V as

$$\arg\min_{w,V} \frac{1}{2}\|w\|^2 + \frac{\|V\|^2}{2} + \frac{1}{\nu N}\sum_{n=1}^{N} \ell(y_n, \hat{y}(w, V))$$

where

$$\ell(y, \hat{y}) = \max(0, y - \hat{y}), \ y_n = b, \text{ and } \hat{y}(w, V) = \langle w, g(VX_n)\rangle$$

Using the same alternate minimization approach as [33], the optimization problem for the bias, b is

$$\arg\min_{b} \left(\frac{1}{\nu N}\sum_{n=1}^{N} \max(0, b - \hat{y})\right) - b$$

Finally, the OCNN objective function generalization is

$$\min_{w,b,V} \frac{1}{2}\|w\|^2 + \frac{1}{2}\|V\|^2 \frac{1}{\nu N}\sum_{n=1}^{N} \max(0, b - \langle w, g(VX_{n:})\rangle) - b \tag{4}$$

where ν parameter controls the trade-off between maximizing the distance of the hyperplane from the origin and the number of data points allowed to cross the hyperplane. This approach allows the model to utilize rich features obtained from unsupervised transfer learning, particularly for anomaly detection in a complex dataset where the decision boundary between the normal data points is highly nonlinear. The solution to optimizing (4) is summarized in Algorithm 3.

Algorithm 3: OCNN Algorithm.

Input: Training dataset $\{X_i | i = 1, 2, 3..., n\}$
Output: Set of decision scores
Initialize b at $t \leftarrow 0$
while *(there is no convergence)* **do**
  Find (w^{t+1}, V^{t+1})
  Solve for b
  $t \leftarrow t + 1$
end
Compute decision scores (S_n) for each (X_i)
if $(S_n \geq 0)$ **then**
  X_i is normal instance;
else
  X_i is anomalous instance
end
return $\{S_n\}$

Given a training dataset $\{X_i | i = 1, 2, 3..., n\}$, the width b of the hyperplane margin is first initialized. The model uses backpropagation to learn the neural network parameters (w, V). The model then iteratively updates b to achieve convergence. Then, the scoring function S_n labels the data points as normal and anomalous instances based on the convergence criterion ϵ with:

$$y = \begin{cases} 1 & \text{if } S_n(x) > \epsilon \\ -1 & \text{if } S_n(x) \leq \epsilon \end{cases} \tag{5}$$

where y represents binary classes of the decision function scores, $S_n(x)$.

The OCNN architecture consisted of 32 hidden layers with rectified linear activation (ReLU) function. Various hyperparameters are used to configure the OCNN model. Table 3 shows the optimal hyperparameters chosen for the OCNN after hyperparameter tuning.

Table 3. Model hyperparameters for OCNN.

Activation Function	v	Learning Rate	No. of Hidden Layers
ReLU	0.04	0.0001	32

4.4. Isolation Forest-Based Detection Approach

Isolation forest (IF) is an unsupervised learning technique that builds binary trees ensemble for a given dataset for anomaly detection [48–50] IF assumes that anomalies make up the minority of a given dataset. As a result, anomalies have attribute values that are different from the normal instances. IF uses several isolation trees and trains each tree on a subset of the training dataset. IF uses the following parameters for constructing the binary trees:

1. Total number of isolation trees (n_t);
2. Sample size of training data subset used to train each isolation tree (n_{max});
3. Maximum number of features representing a subset of the data features used to train each tree (f_{max}).

Algorithm 4 summarizes the IF algorithm training process. During training, IF recursively partitions the training data with an axis-parallel cut at randomly chosen partition points in randomly selected attributes. Next, IF isolates the partitioned instances into nodes with fewer and fewer instances until the points are isolated into singleton nodes containing one instance [48]. IF randomly selects attributes splits q and a split subset p within a specified range, resulting in a left (X_l) and right (X_r) subsets of the data each time until all training samples are isolated into singleton nodes. Algorithm 5 summarizes the recursive binary splitting concept for separating anomalies by IF.

Algorithm 4: Train $IF(X, n_t, n_{max}, f_{max})$.

Input: X—input data, n_t—number of trees, n_{max}—sub-sampling size, f_{max}—attributes of data subset
Output: a set of n_t *iTrees*
Initialize *Forest*
for $(i = 1 \text{ to } n_t)$ **do**
  $X' \leftarrow sample(X, f_{max}, n_{max})$
  $Forest \leftarrow Forest \cup iTree(X')$
end
return *Forest*

Algorithm 5 shows that after each split, isolation tree (*iTree*) produces a node which is either an internal node (*inNode*) or external node (*exNode*) depending on whether there is a further possibility of splitting the former into subsequent split regions. Consequently, the two internal node subsets (X_l and X_r) are split further until they reach an external node. External nodes are considered as leaves of branches when the maximum tree depth is reached or the last nodes in branches when the data subset size of the region is one.

Algorithm 5: Train $iTree(X')$.

Input: X—input data, n_t—number of trees, n_{max}—sub-sampling size, f_{max}—attributes of data subset
Output: an *iTrees*
if X' *is a singleton node* **then**
  return $exNode\{Size \leftarrow |X|\}$;
else
  let Q be a list of attributes in X
  randomly select an attribute $q \in Q$ randomly select a split point p from max
    and min values of attributes q in X'
  $X_l \leftarrow filter(X', q < p)$
  $X_r \leftarrow filter(X, q \geq p)$
  return $inNode\{Left \leftarrow iTree(X_l),$
  $Right \leftarrow iTree(X_r), SplitAttribute \leftarrow q, SplitValue \leftarrow p\}$
end

Anomalous events are considerably different from the normal data points, and so the smaller paths in the isolation tree construction correspond to the lower dimensionality of the subspaces in which the anomalies have been isolated. IF works under the implicit assumption that it is more likely to isolate subspaces of lower dimensionality created by random splits [48]. The decision score $S_n(x)$ for a given data sample x based on a detection threshold ϵ is given by

$$S_n(x) = 2^{-\frac{\bar{h}(x)}{H}}$$

where H is the average expected path length of trees with anomalies considered as -1 while normal instances are labeled as 1 as follows

$$H = 2\ln f_{max} - 1 + 1.2 - 2\frac{f_{max} - 1}{f}$$

The average path length on all trees $\bar{h}(x)$ can be derived as

$$\bar{h}(x) = \frac{1}{n_t} \sum_{n=1}^{n_t} h_i(x)$$

where $h_i(x)$ is the *nth* tree path length established by the number of edges in the tree. The IF algorithm is developed into a model using optimized hyperparameters. Table 4 shows the IF model's optimal hyperparameters after tuning a range of hyper-parameters.

Table 4. Model hyperparameters for IF.

Parameter	Description	Value
$n_{estimators}$	Number of base estimators in the forest ensemble	156
n_{max}	Number of training samples to draw to train each estimator	180
f_{max}	Number of features to draw to train each estimator	10
contamination	Proportion of outliers in the data set	0.05

5. Results and Discussions

The evaluation is based on performance metrics, results from predictions on the test data, and comparison with previous work trained on a similar dataset. The dataset is an HMI historian log of operations at PLC memory addresses publicly available at [41]. Data of PLC memory addresses operations are obtained through the Modbus communication protocol between the PLC and HMI. Google's Tensorflow [51], an open-source deep neural network library, is used for training the OCNN model and subsequently serialized onto a separate computer for online TLIGHT system anomaly detection. Evaluation results and performance metrics calculations are performed by using the Scikit-learn library [52].

5.1. Performance Metrics

The performance metrics of the detection models in identifying anomalies in the TLIGHT dataset are derived from the confusion matrix. Totally, four evaluation outcomes are generated by the confusion matrix: true positive (TN), true negative (TN), false positive (FP), and false negative (FN). These outcomes are used for calculating the accuracy, precision, recall, and F1-score of anomaly detection models.

Accuracy measures the proportion of correct predictions on the test data given by

$$\text{Accuracy} = \frac{TP + TN}{\text{Real positives} + \text{Real negatives}}$$

Precision is a measure of the proportion of predicted positives that are true positives. Precision is defined as

$$\text{Precision} = \frac{TP}{TP + FP}$$

Recall measures the proportion of actual positives that are correctly classified. It represents the ability of the model to detect all positive samples. Recall is

$$\text{Recall} = \frac{TP}{TP + FN}$$

The F1-score is the harmonic mean of precision and recall. F1-score has its best value of 1, indicating perfect precision and recall, and its worst value of 0. It is defined as

$$\text{F1-score} = \frac{2 \times \text{precision} \times \text{recall}}{\text{precision} + \text{recall}}$$

5.2. Performance Evaluation

This work presents a new way of visualizing anomaly detection algorithm results using a histogram. Although histograms have been used in previous work to present detection algorithms results [53–56], the approach presented in this work is new and provides a better understanding of detection algorithms performance by revealing the exact proportions of true positives, true negatives, false positives, and false negatives of detection algorithms.

Visualization of results is done by first separating the decision scores (real numbers) into positive and negative scores represented by P_1 and N_1 respectively. Next, decision scores are separated into true positives, true negatives, false positives, and false negatives with associated notations x_{tp}, x_{tn}, x_{fp}, and x_{fn}, respectively, based on the ground truth of the test sets. Different algorithms provide different decision scores based on their objective functions, so the resulting x_{tp} and x_{fp} scores are normalized to a range between 0 and 1 using the maximum and minimum values in P_1. In contrast, x_{tn} and x_{fn} scores are normalized to range between 0 and 1 using the maximum and minimum values in N_1. Furthermore, to ensure an objective comparison of the different algorithms, the x_{tp} and x_{fn} quantities are normalized as a function of the total ground truth positives. Similarly, x_{tn} and x_{fp} are normalized as a function of the ground truth negatives. Let the normalized scores of x_{tp}, x_{tn}, x_{fp}, and x_{fn} be X_{tp}, X_{tn}, X_{fp}, and X_{fn} respectively. Finally, the normalized scores are used to plot a histogram of the distribution and proportion of decision scores.

Visualization of anomaly detection results requires methods different from previous work [33], where only positive P_1 and negative N_1 scores are presented. The approach in Figure 6 reveals the fractions of P_1, which corresponds to X_{tp} and X_{fp}, and the fractions of N_1 which are X_{tn} and X_{fn}. Moreover, the work in [33] only shows the proportions of P_1 and N_1 as a function of test data size on the histogram's y-axis, which makes it challenging to visualize the N_1 scores, primarily because test sets in anomaly detection mainly have smaller negative class proportions [45]. On the contrary, the proposed approach normalizes the histogram frequency (y-axis) to a range of 0 to 100% to present a better relative decision scores visualization. The visualization described here normalizes the x and y axes for easier comparison of different detection algorithms' performance. Finally, the proposed visualization approach may be applied to supervised ML algorithms for binary classification.

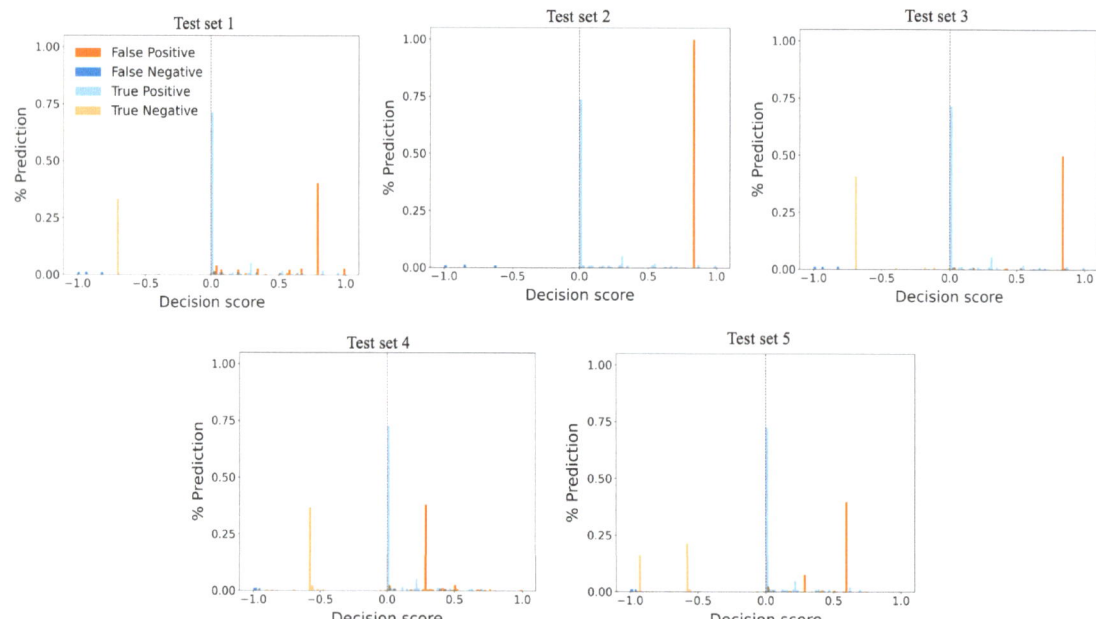

Figure 6. OCSVM results of the normalized TP, TN, FP, and FN values on test sets 1–5.

5.2.1. Performance of OCSVM

OCSVM's recall values on test sets 1, 2, 3, 4, and 5 are 90%, 87%, 86%, 81%, and 70%, respectively. Figure 6 illustrates the benefits of the proposed visualization as it reveals OCSVM's overall behavior on all test sets. A similar distribution of TP scores is observed on all test sets, showing how OCSVM learned the TLIGHT system's normal behavior during training process. OCSVM found detecting normal traffic transitions involving vehicles' green light signals challenging, leading to high TP scores that lie along the decision boundaries in all test cases. Again, FN scores of test sets 1 and 3 involve the same data records being misclassified as anomalies. Moreover, FN scores of test sets 4 and 5 represent identical normal data records misclassified as anomalies. The aforementioned show the importance of the proposed visualization in this work as Figure 6 reveals OCSVM's true performance on each data record, which would not be possible with the traditional histogram approach [33].

Although OCSVM's recall values decrease steadily from test sets 1 to 5, the normalized true positive scores are low in all test cases. In all test cases, OCSVM misclassifies over 30% anomalous instances as normal instances leading to high levels of FP in all test cases. In addition, Figure 6 shows that in all test cases in which OCSVM makes an accurate positive class (normal) prediction, the score (levels of confidence) of predictions are low and lie along the decision boundary. Although OCSVM detects several positive classes, it has a greater chance of misclassifying normal data points as anomalies because of the low confidence of the positive class prediction. Moreover, about 75% of correct positive class predictions occur close to the decisions boundary with low prediction confidence. The low prediction confidence makes OCSVM unstable for TLIGHT system anomaly detection. Figure 6 shows a histogram of normalized FP, FN, TP, and TN decision scores made by OCSVM on test sets 1–5.

OCSVM learns the TLIGHT system's normal behavior during training with a 100% precision and 98% F1-score. The results substantiate the procedure this work adopts in conducting the experiment and recording data as it is similar to the training results in [13]. Overall, OCSVM performs best on test set 1. OCSVM performance on test sets 2 and 3 are similar with an F1-score of 84%. OCSVM has its least performance on test sets 4 and 5, with F1-scores of 71% and 68% respectively. OCSVM model is unable to detect over 20% of anomalies in test sets 4 and 5 because of the large proportion of anomalies consisting of timing bits anomalies. Therefore, OCSVM appears to be ineffective at detecting TLIGHT system errors consisting of system timing bits manipulation. Table 5 summarizes the performance of the OCSVM described here and the OCSVM in [13]. Table 5 shows that the OCSVM reported here and in [13] have similar training performance due to the datasets and underlying TLIGHT experiment being designed identically. Test sets 1–3 in this work are created to be the same size as the test sets in [13]; however, the exact nature and distributions of errors in [13] are unknown and may be the reason for the slight differences seen in the Table 5.

Table 5. Performance of OCSVM described here and the reported results * of the OCSVM in [13].

Dataset	Accuracy		Precision		Recall		F1-Score	
	OCSVM	[13]	OCSVM	[13]	OCSVM	[13]	OCSVM	[13]
Training set	0.96	0.96 *	1.00	1.00 *	0.96	0.96 *	0.98	0.98 *
Test set 1	0.90	0.78 *	0.89	1.00 *	0.90	0.78 *	0.89	0.88 *
Test set 2	0.87	0.75 *	0.81	1.00 *	0.87	0.75 *	0.84	0.86 *
Test set 3	0.86	0.82 *	0.85	1.00 *	0.86	0.82 *	0.84	0.90 *
Test set 4	0.81	-	0.81	-	0.81	-	0.71	-
Test set 5	0.70	-	0.78	-	0.70	-	0.68	-

5.2.2. Performance of OCNN

OCNN's performance on all metrics is similar to OCSVM. OCNN's recall value on test set 1 is high at 91%, whereas the recall values on test sets 2 and 3 are similar at 88%. A closer observation of Figure 7 reveals that in all test sets, TP prediction scores by OCNN are close to the decision boundary signifying low confidence of the positive class prediction. Over all test cases, about 75% of the correctly predicted positive class have scores closer to the decision boundary, which shows that OCNN has potential instabilities similar to OCSVM.

In addition, OCNN misclassifies more than 25% of anomalies as normal instances, which is undesirable, especially in ICS anomaly detection. However, the TN and FP scores in all test sets are high, showing OCNN's robustness in detecting outliers. OCNN misclassifies several anomalies as normal instances, especially in test sets 2–5, leading to high false positive rates. Figure 7 shows a histogram of normalized FP, FN, TP, and TN decision scores made by OCNN on test sets 1–5.

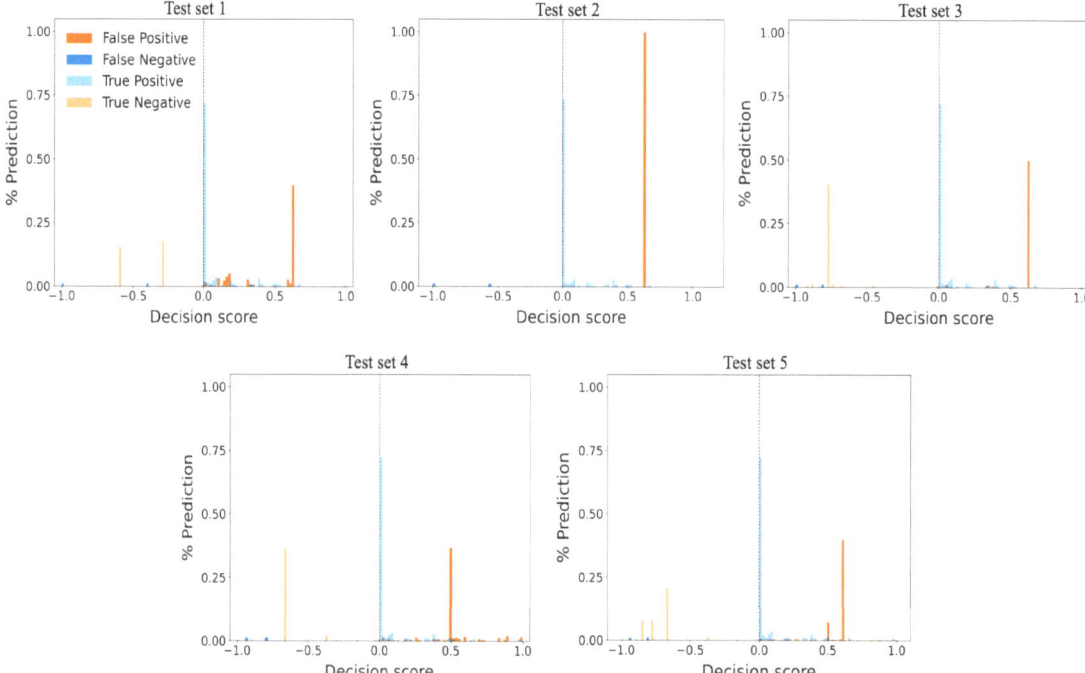

Figure 7. OCNN results of the normalized TP, TN, FP, and FN values on test sets 1–5.

OCNN has good performance on all metrics on test sets 1, 2, and 3, similar to OCSVM. OCNN learns the TLIGHT system's normal behavior well by having a training recall of 97%. However, OCNN's performance on test sets 4 and 5 is low with F1-scores of 79% and 68% respectively. Table 6 shows OCNN's ability to detect changes in the light signals behavior of the TLIGHT system and an inability to detect timing bits errors. OCSVM and OCNN have similar performance because the OCNN objective function is developed as an improvement upon the OCSVM optimization problem in Equation (3). Table 6 summarizes OCNN's performance on the five test sets.

Table 6. Summary of evaluation results for OCNN.

Dataset	Accuracy	Precision	Recall	F1-Score
Training set	0.97	1.00	0.97	0.99
Test set 1	0.91	0.90	0.91	0.90
Test set 2	0.88	0.81	0.88	0.84
Test set 3	0.88	0.87	0.88	0.86
Test set 4	0.81	0.82	0.81	0.79
Test set 5	0.70	0.79	0.70	0.68

5.2.3. Performance of Isolation Forest

Unlike OCSVM and OCNN, IF uses tree ensembles to isolate anomalies from the dataset instead of learning the system's normal behavior. IF achieves high recall rates on test sets 1 and 2 at 91% and 97%, respectively. IF misclassifies about 40% of anomalies as normal instances in test set 3, which resulted in a reduced recall rate of 88%. In test set 2, IF classifies normal and anomalous data points almost perfectly with high confidence, thereby achieving a precision of 98%. Unlike OCSVM and OCNN, IF's decision scores on TN and TP are consistently high, which means that whenever IF correctly predicts a normal instance, it is certain about the detection decision. In addition, Figure 8 shows that for more than 25% of the time, whenever IF correctly detects anomalous instances, the associated decision scores are high, signifying high detection confidence. Figure 8 shows that IF's decision scores are far away from the decision boundary, which makes IF a stable model for detecting anomalies in the TLIGHT system. IF decision scores are confident, therefore, it is an attractive approach for ICS anomaly detection. Figure 8 shows a histogram of normalized FP, FN, TP, and TN decision scores made by IF on test sets 1–5.

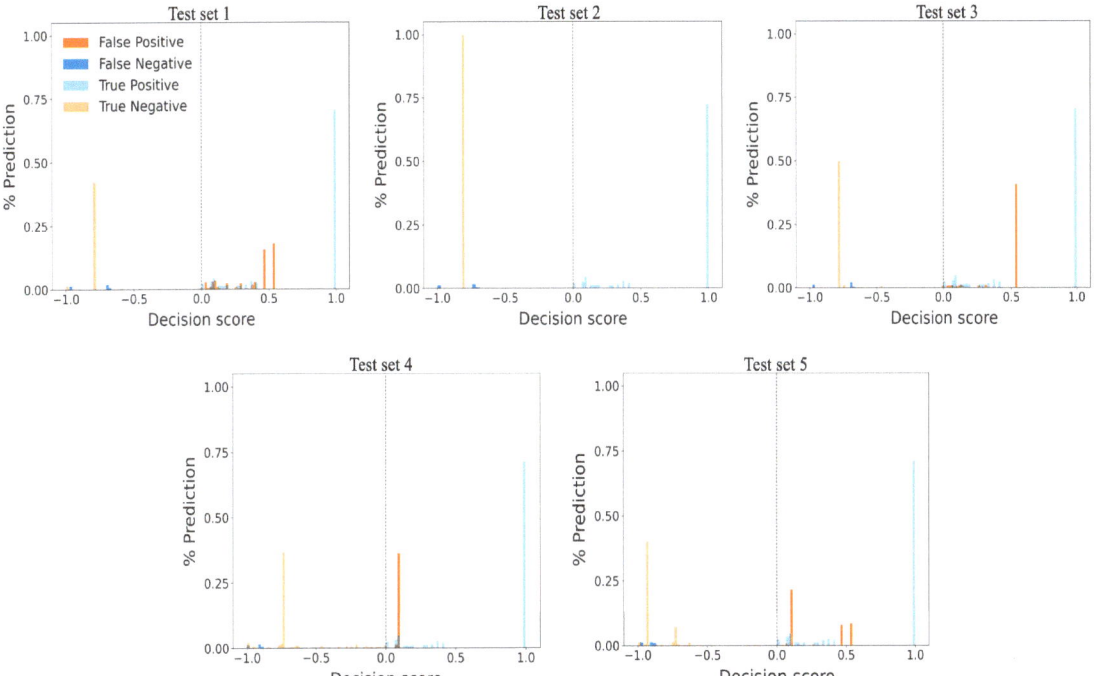

Figure 8. IF results of the normalized TP, TN, FP, and FN values on test sets 1–5.

Similar to OCSVM and OCNN, IF has an outstanding training performance. IF has an excellent performance on test sets 1 and 2 on all evaluation metrics. IF performance on test sets 3 and 4 are similar at an average recall value of 87%, whereas it has its lowest performance on test set 5. Test sets 4 and 5 consist of timing bits anomalies, and IF achieves recall rates of 86% and 82%, respectively. Results indicate that IF can detect timing bits errors better than OCSVM and OCNN. Table 7 shows a summary of evaluation results for IF.

Table 7. Summary of evaluation results for IF.

Dataset	Accuracy	Precision	Recall	F1-Score
Training set	0.95	1.00	0.95	0.98
Test set 1	0.91	0.90	0.91	0.91
Test set 2	0.97	0.98	0.97	0.97
Test set 3	0.88	0.87	0.88	0.87
Test set 4	0.86	0.86	0.86	0.85
Test set 5	0.78	0.82	0.78	0.77

5.3. Statistical Hypothesis Test

Statistical evidence about the best-performing detection model proposed in this work is conducted using Analysis of Variance Test and Tukey's range test. F1-score is selected as the evaluation metric in the hypothesis test because F1-score is a great measure of the trade-off between precision and recall, especially for imbalanced datasets.

5.3.1. Analysis of Variance Test (ANOVA)

ANOVA is a statistical model used to determine if a significant difference between the means of two or more data sets exists [57,58]. One-way ANOVA is chosen because of the interest in examining one independent variable's influence, which is F1-score. First, OSCVM, OCNN, and IF performances are evaluated on 20 different test samples of the exact sizes as test sets 1, 2, 3, 4, and 5. Next, each detection algorithm's F1-score is computed on 20 different samples of each test set. The assumptions about the data set are

- data points in each test sample are independent and identically distributed; and
- data points are normally distributed.

In addition, the hypotheses for the statistical test are

- null hypothesis (H_0): The mean F1-score of all detection algorithms are equal; and
- alternate hypothesis (H_a): One or more of the mean F1-score are unequal.

Based on the one-way ANOVA test, the F value is 14.972, and a p-value < 0.001 is achieved. One-way ANOVA shows significant evidence to reject the null hypothesis. Rejecting the null hypothesis indicates a considerable difference between at least two detection algorithms at a confidence level above 95%. Although one-way ANOVA reveals a difference in the three algorithms' performance, statistically, it is not clear which specific algorithm performs best or worst. Therefore, a post hoc analysis is required to identify the best-performing algorithm.

5.3.2. Tukey's Range Test

Tukey's range test is a statistical test used as post hoc analysis after one-way ANOVA [59]. Tukey's range test compares all possible mean F1-score pairs for all detection algorithms and precisely identifies differences between the pairs greater than the expected standard error. Tukey's range test is based on the same assumptions as ANOVA. Table 8 depicts Tukey's range test results at $\alpha = 0.05$.

Table 8. Multiple comparison of mean F1-score for OCSVM, OCNN, and IF using Tukey's range test at $\alpha = 0.05$.

Group 1	Group 2	Mean Diff.	p-Adjusted	Reject
OCNN	IF	5.320	0.001	True
OCNN	OCSVM	−0.587	0.862	False
IF	OCSVM	−5.907	0.001	True

The mean F1-score for IF significantly differs from OCNN; hence IF outperforms OCNN. However, the mean F1-score difference between OCNN and OCSVM is insignificant; therefore, OCNN and OCSVM perform at par. Lastly, Tukey's range test indicates sufficient statistical evidence to reject the null hypothesis between the group IF-OCSVM and conclude that IF outperforms OCSVM. Results in Table 8 indicate that IF is the superior detection model for the TLIGHT dataset, whereas OCNN and OCSVM have similar overall performance.

5.4. Summary of Results

The overall performance of the detection algorithms is summarized in this section. Figure 9 shows box plots of OCSVM, OCNN, and IF results distributions with the outlier test case labeled where applicable. IF has the highest median accuracy of 88%. Furthermore, accuracy and recall box plots in Figure 9 show that all methods have outlier performance more than 1.5 times the interquartile value on test set 5. However, the precision box plot of Figure 9 indicates that IF's precision value of 98% on test set 2 is an outlier. The precision box plot shows no outliers for OCSVM and OCNN. Lastly, the F1-score box plot in Figure 9 shows that the only F1-score outlier is OCNN's result on test set 5 and the F1-scores distribution of IF is right-skewed. Therefore, the overall results indicate that all the detection models find it challenging to detect anomalies in test set 5. Nevertheless, all the detection models have similar performance distributions on test sets 1–4.

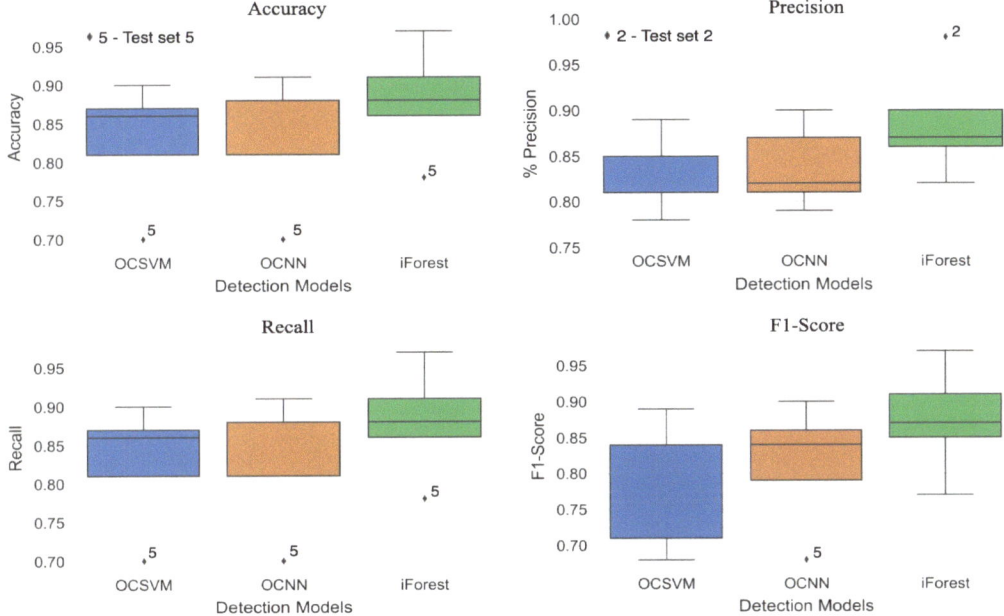

Figure 9. Box plot of OCSVM, OCNN, and IF performance distribution.

It is insightful to compare the detection models' average performance with the reported results in [13] on all evaluation across test sets 1–3: IF performs about 5% better than OCSVM, OCNN, and [13] in accuracy, precision, and recall. However, in terms of F1-score, IF averages about 7% over OCSVM, OCNN, and [13]. In all evaluation metrics, OCNN and OCSVM perform similarly. Figure 10 shows the comparison between the detection models in this work and the reported results in [13]. Test sets 1–3 in this work are created to be the same sizes as the test sets in [13]; however, the exact nature of anomalies and their relative distributions in the three test sets is not provided in [13]. It is surmised that the difference in validation performance between the OCSVM in this work and the reported results of the OCSVM in [13] is due to these anomalies variations. Moreover, the reported result in [13] has a precision of 100% in all test cases, but a low recall performance—below 83% in all three test sets—which could potentially indicate overfitting of their model. Overall, IF achieved the best performance on all three test sets.

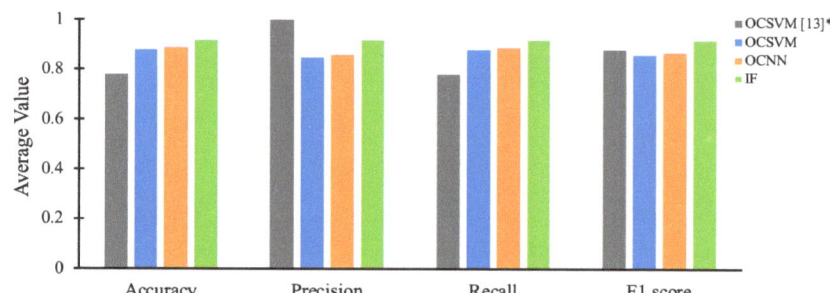

Figure 10. Average test sets 1–3 performance of the OCSVM reported results * in [13], and the OCSVM, OCNN, and IF approaches described in this paper.

Test sets 4 and 5 consist of timing bits anomalies unique to this work, and such errors were not considered in [13]. Figure 11 shows the average performance comparison between OCSVM, OCNN, and IF on test sets 4 and 5. IF's average performance is higher than that of OCNN and OCSVM on all the evaluation metrics, whereas OCNN and OCSVM perform similarly.

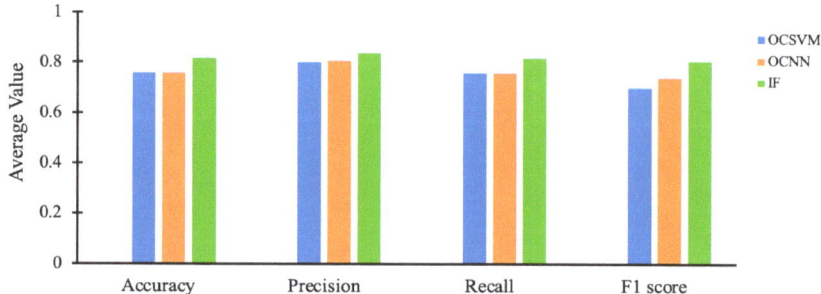

Figure 11. Average test sets 4–5 performance of OCSVM, OCNN, and IF.

5.5. Practical Considerations

This work focused on TLIGHT system experiments consisting of digital signals from sensors and actuators with the purpose of monitoring operations at the PLC memory addresses. The digital nature of the experiment ensures fair comparison with previous work developed with a similar experiment. However, the work presented here need not be constrained to digital signals. The algorithms presented in this work can be extended to PLC process control involving both analog and digital signals. The proposed algorithm's objective functions are adaptable to nonlinear scenarios; hence robust performance is expected in industrial practices involving analog control systems. The multilayer network of OCNN allows the computation of any nonlinear function [45]. OCSVM and IF have been employed to successfully detect PLC anomalies involving analog signals in [20,25,60].

The presented techniques are general methods that can be implemented in real-world ICS infrastructure with minimum effort. The outstanding performance of the proposed techniques can be realized on legacy and embedded PLCs. An approach may be to compile the trained models to C code using open-source compilers such as [61–63], which, as an example, support x86 and ARM64 processor architectures. The generated C code should be readily portable to dedicated ARM and general-purpose processors [64] for real-time inference. A similar approach to the experiment conducted in this work may also be employed. The trained models may be serialized onto a separate PC with a data pipeline to the HMI historian and PLC memory addresses to receive data and perform real-time anomaly detection.

5.6. Limitations

While this work makes significant contributions to the scientific body of ICS anomaly detection, there are some limitations to the proposed approaches. The proposed histogram-based visualization approach is limited to anomaly-detection algorithms with signed output results. A detection algorithm's output must be positive and negative real numbers representing normal and anomalous points or vice-versa in order for the proposed visualization approach to be effective. The histogram-based visualization plots reveal that OCSVM and OCNN make less-confident predictions. OCSVM and OCNN have similar decision scores distributions across all five test sets because they are both formulated from a similar optimization problem. Observing OCSVM and OCNN performance limitations may not have been possible without the proposed visualization approach. Furthermore, comparing anomaly-detection algorithms performances based on decision scores instead of traditional binary predictions requires decision scores normalization. Since different anomaly detectors might produce decision scores on different scales, decision scores normalization is required for fair comparison.

In addition, there are some limitations associated with the proposed techniques. OCSVM is sensitive to the choice of kernels, and ν parameters [45], hence OCSVM is not robust in ICS applications without a deeper understanding of the ICS. OCSVM limitation can partially be solved by using variable subsampling [65] during model training in the context of ICS with unpredictable behavior. The feed-forward nature of the neural network in OCNN makes the algorithm sensitive to noise [45]. Therefore, clean ICS data should be used for OCNN training to avoid model overfitting. Finally, IF algorithm's recursive data partitioning could lead to lower performance in high-dimensional ICS data due to the masking effect of locally noisy and irrelevant features. As a result, feature-selection techniques [66,67] should be employed in high-dimensional ICS data before IF model training.

Although IF has a stellar performance on key evaluation metrics on test sets 1–3, it achieved lower recall values on test sets 4–5, which contain timing bits error. Some anomalous data points are detected by either OCSVM or OCNN, but IF fails to detect them. This shows that the proposed algorithms have strengths and weaknesses on different subsets of the data, and hence, a single detection algorithm may not be able to generalize to an arbitrary ICS setup. However, aggregating the predictions from individual anomaly detection models could potentially result in a robust model capable of detecting anomalies in an arbitrary ICS setup.

6. Conclusions

This work presents unsupervised ML algorithms for anomaly detection, including cyber-attacks on PLCs and ICS. A previously studied TLIGHT ICS system was used. The control system's normal behavior is recorded through the PLC memory addresses. One-class support vector machine, one-class neural network, and isolation forest algorithms were developed using system process data. This work proposes a new histogram-based visualization technique for demonstrating true positives, true negatives, false positives, and false negatives proportions in anomaly detection models' performance. The proposed visualization technique can also be extended to supervised ML algorithms involving binary classification. Results indicate that OCSVM and OCNN have similar performance on all evaluation metrics, which are inferior to IF performance. A hypothesis test is conducted using one-way ANOVA and Tukey's range test to provide statistical evidence about the algorithm with the best performance. The hypothesis test indicates that IF has the best anomaly-detection rate on the TLIGHT system; however, there is insufficient statistical evidence to support any difference in performance between OCSVM and OCNN. Finally, IF achieved superior performance over results reported in prior work. The proposed techniques are generalized methods, which can be implemented in real-world ICS with minimal effort.

Recommendation

Based on the limitations outlined in this work, it is evident that some anomaly-detection algorithms will perform well on a particular subset of the dataset, whereas other algorithms will do better on other subsets of the dataset. Therefore, future work should focus on the following to address the challenge mentioned above and extend scientific knowledge:

- improving the anomaly-detection rate on the TLIGHT system through ensemble techniques;
- developing dual anomaly-detection algorithms that will focus on specific subsets of the dataset; and
- extending the proposed techniques in this work to other publicly available anomaly detection datasets.

Author Contributions: Conceptualization, E.A.B. and J.W.B.; software, E.A.B.; validation, E.A.B. and J.W.B.; investigation, E.A.B.; resources, J.W.B.; writing—original draft preparation, E.A.B.; writing—review and editing, E.A.B. and J.W.B. All authors have read and agreed to the published version of the manuscript.

Funding: This research was funded, in part, by the State of Tennessee and the Tennessee Technological University Center for Manufacturing Research.

Institutional Review Board Statement: Not applicable.

Acknowledgments: The views expressed in this paper are those of the authors, and do not reflect the official policy or position of the state of Tennessee and Tennessee Technological University.

Conflicts of Interest: The authors declare no conflict of interest.

References

1. Kello, L. *The Virtual Weapon and International Order*; Yale University Press: New Haven, CT, USA, 2019.
2. Yaacoub, J.P.A.; Salman, O.; Noura, H.N.; Kaaniche, N.; Chehab, A.; Malli, M. Cyber-physical systems security: Limitations, issues and future trends. *Microprocess. Microsyst.* **2020**, *77*, 103201. [CrossRef] [PubMed]
3. Thakur, K.; Ali, M.L.; Jiang, N.; Qiu, M. Impact of cyber-attacks on critical infrastructure. In Proceedings of the 2016 IEEE 2nd International Conference on Big Data Security on Cloud (BigDataSecurity), IEEE International Conference on High Performance and Smart Computing (HPSC), and IEEE International Conference on Intelligent Data and Security (IDS), New York, NY, USA, 9–10 April 2016; pp. 183–186.
4. Plėta, T.; Tvaronavičienė, M.; Casa, S.D.; Agafonov, K. Cyber-attacks to critical energy infrastructure and management issues: Overview of selected cases. *Insights Into Reg. Dev.* **2020**, *2*, 703–715. [CrossRef]
5. Wardak, H.; Zhioua, S.; Almulhem, A. PLC access control: A security analysis. In Proceedings of the 2016 World Congress on Industrial Control Systems Security (WCICSS), London, UK, 12–14 December 2016; pp. 1–6.
6. Abbasi, A.; Holz, T.; Zambon, E.; Etalle, S. ECFI: Asynchronous control flow integrity for programmable logic controllers. In Proceedings of the 33rd Annual Computer Security Applications Conference, Orlando, FL, USA, 4–8 December 2017; pp. 437–448.
7. Abbasi, A. Ghost in the PLC: stealth on-the-fly manipulation of programmable logic controllers' I/O. In Proceedings of the Black Hat EU, London, UK, 1–4 November 2016; pp. 1–4.
8. Yau, K.; Chow, K.P. PLC forensics based on control program logic change detection. *J. Digit. Forensics, Secur. Law* **2015**, *10*, 5. [CrossRef]
9. Langmann, R.; Stiller, M. The PLC as a smart service in industry 4.0 production systems. *Appl. Sci.* **2019**, *9*, 3815. [CrossRef]
10. Tsiknas, K.; Taketzis, D.; Demertzis, K.; Skianis, C. Cyber Threats to Industrial IoT: A Survey on Attacks and Countermeasures. *IoT* **2021**, *2*, 163–188. [CrossRef]
11. Spyridopoulos, T.; Tryfonas, T.; May, J. Incident Analysis & Digital Forensics in SCADA and Industrial Control Systems. In Proceedings of the 8th IET International System Safety Conference Incorporating the Cyber Security Conference, Cardiff, UK, 16–17 October 2013.
12. Boeckl, K.; Boeckl, K.; Fagan, M.; Fisher, W.; Lefkovitz, N.; Megas, K.N.; Nadeau, E.; O'Rourke, D.G.; Piccarreta, B.; Scarfone, K. *Considerations for Managing Internet of Things (IoT) Cybersecurity and Privacy Risks*; US Department of Commerce, National Institute of Standards and Technology: Gaithersburg, MD, USA, 2019.

13. Yau, K.; Chow, K.P.; Yiu, S.M.; Chan, C.F. Detecting anomalous behavior of PLC using semi-supervised machine learning. In Proceedings of the 2017 IEEE Conference on Communications and Network Security (CNS), Las Vegas, NV, USA, 9–11 October 2017; pp. 580–585.

14. Aboah, B.E.; Bruce, J.W. Anomaly Detection for Industrial Control Systems Based on Neural Networks with One-Class Objective Function. *Proc. Stud. Res. Creat. Inq. Day* **2021**, *5*, 86.

15. Siemens, S. *S7-300 Programmable Controller Quick Start, Primer, Preface*; Technical Report; C79000-G7076-C500-01; Siemens: Nuremberg, Germany, 1996.

16. Chen, Y.; Wu, W. Application of one-class support vector machine to quickly identify multivariate anomalies from geochemical exploration data. *Geochem. Explor. Environ. Anal.* **2017**, *17*, 231–238. [CrossRef]

17. Welborn, T. *One-Class Support Vector Machines Approach for Trust-Aware Recommendation Systems*; Shareok: Norman, OK, USA, 2021.

18. Hiranai, K.; Kuramoto, A.; Seo, A. Detection of Anomalies in Working Posture during Obstacle Avoidance Tasks using One-Class Support Vector Machine. *J. Jpn. Ind. Manag. Assoc.* **2021**, *72*, 125–133.

19. Ahmad, I.; Shahabuddin, S.; Malik, H.; Harjula, E.; Leppänen, T.; Loven, L.; Anttonen, A.; Sodhro, A.H.; Alam, M.M.; Juntti, M.; et al. Machine learning meets communication networks: Current trends and future challenges. *IEEE Access* **2020**, *8*, 223418–223460. [CrossRef]

20. Inoue, J.; Yamagata, Y.; Chen, Y.; Poskitt, C.M.; Sun, J. Anomaly detection for a water treatment system using unsupervised machine learning. In Proceedings of the 2017 IEEE International Conference on Data Mining Workshops (ICDMW), New Orleans, LA, USA, 18–21 November 2017; pp. 1058–1065.

21. Tomlin, L.; Farnam, M.R.; Pan, S. A clustering approach to industrial network intrusion detection. In Proceedings of the 2016 Information Security Research and Education (INSuRE) Conference (INSuRECon-16), Charleston, SC, USA, 30 September 2016.

22. Xiao, Y.j.; Xu, W.y.; Jia, Z.h.; Ma, Z.r.; Qi, D.l. NIPAD: A non-invasive power-based anomaly detection scheme for programmable logic controllers. *Front. Inf. Technol. Electron. Eng.* **2017**, *18*, 519–534. [CrossRef]

23. Muna, A.H.; Moustafa, N.; Sitnikova, E. Identification of malicious activities in industrial internet of things based on deep learning models. *J. Inf. Secur. Appl.* **2018**, *41*, 1–11.

24. Potluri, S.; Diedrich, C.; Sangala, G.K.R. Identifying false data injection attacks in industrial control systems using artificial neural networks. In Proceedings of the 2017 22nd IEEE International Conference on Emerging Technologies and Factory Automation (ETFA), Limassol, Cyprus, 12–15 September 2017; pp. 1–8.

25. Elnour, M.; Meskin, N.; Khan, K.; Jain, R. A dual-isolation-forests-based attack detection framework for industrial control systems. *IEEE Access* **2020**, *8*, 36639–36651. [CrossRef]

26. Ahmed, S.; Lee, Y.; Hyun, S.H.; Koo, I. Unsupervised machine learning-based detection of covert data integrity assault in smart grid networks utilizing isolation forest. *IEEE Trans. Inf. Forensics Secur.* **2019**, *14*, 2765–2777. [CrossRef]

27. Liu, B.; Chen, J.; Hu, Y. Mode division-based anomaly detection against integrity and availability attacks in industrial cyber-physical systems. *Comput. Ind.* **2022**, *137*, 103609. [CrossRef]

28. Ahmed, C.M.; MR, G.R.; Mathur, A.P. Challenges in machine learning based approaches for real-time anomaly detection in industrial control systems. In Proceedings of the 6th ACM on Cyber-Physical System Security Workshop, Taipei, Taiwan, 6 October 2020; pp. 23–29.

29. Priyanga, S.; Gauthama Raman, M.; Jagtap, S.S.; Aswin, N.; Kirthivasan, K.; Shankar Sriram, V. An improved rough set theory based feature selection approach for intrusion detection in SCADA systems. *J. Intell. Fuzzy Syst.* **2019**, *36*, 3993–4003. [CrossRef]

30. Raman, M.G.; Somu, N.; Mathur, A.P. Anomaly detection in critical infrastructure using probabilistic neural network. In *International Conference on Applications and Techniques in Information Security*; Springer: Berlin/Heidelberg, Germany, 2019; pp. 129–141.

31. Benkraouda, H.; Chakkantakath, M.A.; Keliris, A.; Maniatakos, M. Snifu: Secure network interception for firmware updates in legacy plcs. In Proceedings of the 2020 IEEE 38th VLSI Test Symposium (VTS), San Diego, CA, USA, 5–8 April 2020; pp. 1–6.

32. Wu, T.; Nurse, J.R. Exploring the use of PLC debugging tools for digital forensic investigations on SCADA systems. *J. Digit. Forensics, Secur. Law* **2015**, *10*, 7. [CrossRef]

33. Chalapathy, R.; Menon, A.K.; Chawla, S. Anomaly detection using one-class neural networks. *arXiv* **2018**, arXiv:1802.06360.

34. Bengio, Y.; LeCun, Y.; Scaling learning algorithms towards AI. *Large-Scale Kernel Mach.* **2007**, *34*, 1–41.

35. Alves, T.R.; Buratto, M.; De Souza, F.M.; Rodrigues, T.V. OpenPLC: An open source alternative to automation. In Proceedings of the IEEE Global Humanitarian Technology Conference (GHTC 2014), San Jose, CA, USA, 10–13 October 2014; pp. 585–589.

36. Mazurkiewicz, P. An open source SCADA application in a small automation system. *Meas. Autom. Monit.* **2016**, *62*, 199–201.

37. Unipi Neuron Kernel Description. Available online: https://www.unipi.technology/products/unipi-neuron-3 (accessed on 3 March 2022).

38. ZumIQ Edge Computer Kernel Description. Available online: https://www.freewave.com/products/zumiq-edge-computer/ (accessed on 3 March 2022).

39. Automation without Limits Kernel Description. Available online: https://www.unipi.technology/ (accessed on 3 March 2022).

40. Tiegelkamp, M.; John, K.H. *IEC 61131-3: Programming Industrial Automation Systems*; Springer: Berlin/Heidelberg, Germany, 2010.

41. TLIGHT SYSTEM Source Code to TLIGHT Experiment. Available online: https://github.com/emmanuelaboah/TLIGHT-SYSTEM (accessed on 17 January 2022).

42. Gollapudi, S. *Practical Machine Learning*; Packt Publishing Ltd.: Mumbai, India, 2016.
43. Schölkopf, B.; Platt, J.C.; Shawe-Taylor, J.; Smola, A.J.; Williamson, R.C. Estimating the support of a high-dimensional distribution. *Neural Comput.* **2001**, *13*, 1443–1471. [CrossRef] [PubMed]
44. Zhu, F.; Yang, J.; Gao, C.; Xu, S.; Ye, N.; Yin, T. A weighted one-class support vector machine. *Neurocomputing* **2016**, *189*, 1–10. [CrossRef]
45. Aggarwal, C.C. An introduction to outlier analysis. In *Outlier Analysis*; Springer: Berlin/Heidelberg, Germany, 2017; pp. 1–34.
46. Oza, P.; Patel, V.M. One-class convolutional neural network. *IEEE Signal Process. Lett.* **2018**, *26*, 277–281. [CrossRef]
47. Boehm, O.; Hardoon, D.R.; Manevitz, L.M. Classifying cognitive states of brain activity via one-class neural networks with feature selection by genetic algorithms. *Int. J. Mach. Learn. Cybern.* **2011**, *2*, 125–134. [CrossRef]
48. Liu, F.T.; Ting, K.M.; Zhou, Z.H. Isolation forest. In Proceedings of the 2008 Eighth IEEE International Conference on Data Mining, Washington, DC, USA, 15–19 December 2008; pp. 413–422.
49. Hariri, S.; Kind, M.C.; Brunner, R.J. Extended isolation forest. *IEEE Trans. Knowl. Data Eng.* **2019**, *33*, 1479–1489. [CrossRef]
50. Staerman, G.; Mozharovskyi, P.; Clémençon, S.; d'Alché Buc, F. Functional isolation forest. In Proceedings of the Asian Conference on Machine Learning, PMLR, Nagoya, Japan, 17–19 November 2019; pp. 332–347.
51. Abadi, M.; Agarwal, A.; Barham, P.; Brevdo, E.; Chen, Z.; Citro, C.; Corrado, G.S.; Davis, A.; Dean, J.; Devin, M.; et al. TensorFlow: Large-Scale Machine Learning on Heterogeneous Systems, 2015. Available online: tensorflow.org (accessed on 17 February 2021).
52. Pedregosa, F.; Varoquaux, G.; Gramfort, A.; Michel, V.; Thirion, B.; Grisel, O.; Blondel, M.; Prettenhofer, P.; Weiss, R.; Dubourg, V.; et al. Scikit-learn: Machine Learning in Python. *J. Mach. Learn. Res.* **2011**, *12*, 2825–2830.
53. Goldstein, M.; Dengel, A. Histogram-based outlier score (hbos): A fast unsupervised anomaly detection algorithm. In *KI-2012: Poster and Demo Track*; Citeseer: Princeton, NJ, USA, 2012; pp. 59–63.
54. Kind, A.; Stoecklin, M.P.; Dimitropoulos, X. Histogram-based traffic anomaly detection. *IEEE Trans. Netw. Serv. Manag.* **2009**, *6*, 110–121. [CrossRef]
55. Bansod, S.D.; Nandedkar, A.V. Crowd anomaly detection and localization using histogram of magnitude and momentum. *Vis. Comput.* **2020**, *36*, 609–620. [CrossRef]
56. Xie, M.; Hu, J.; Tian, B. Histogram-based online anomaly detection in hierarchical wireless sensor networks. In Proceedings of the 2012 IEEE 11th International Conference on Trust, Security and Privacy in Computing and Communications, Liverpool, UK, 25–27 June 2012; pp. 751–759.
57. Goldberg, D.E.; Scheiner, S.M. ANOVA and ANCOVA: Field competition experiments. *Des. Anal. Ecol. Exp.* **2001**, *2*, 69–93.
58. Rutherford, A. *ANOVA and ANCOVA: A GLM Approach*; John Wiley & Sons: Hoboken, NJ, USA, 2011.
59. Abdi, H.; Williams, L.J. Newman-Keuls test and Tukey test. In *Encyclopedia of Research Design*; Sage: Thousand Oaks, CA, USA, 2010; pp. 1–11.
60. Alqurashi, S.; Shirazi, H.; Ray, I. On the Performance of Isolation Forest and Multi Layer Perceptron for Anomaly Detection in Industrial Control Systems Networks. In Proceedings of the 2021 8th International Conference on Internet of Things: Systems, Management and Security (IOTSMS), Gandia, Spain, 6–9 December 2021; pp. 1–6.
61. Unlu, H. Efficient neural network deployment for microcontroller. *arXiv* **2020**, arXiv:2007.01348.
62. XLA: Optimizing Compiler for Machine Learning. Available online: https://www.tensorflow.org/xla (accessed on 3 March 2022).
63. NNCG: Neural Network Code Generator. Available online: https://github.com/iml130/nncg (accessed on 3 March 2022).
64. Urbann, O.; Camphausen, S.; Moos, A.; Schwarz, I.; Kerner, S.; Otten, M. AC Code Generator for Fast Inference and Simple Deployment of Convolutional Neural Networks on Resource Constrained Systems. In Proceedings of the 2020 IEEE International IOT, Electronics and Mechatronics Conference (IEMTRONICS), Vancouver, BC, Canada, 9–12 September 2020; pp. 1–7.
65. Aggarwal, C.C.; *Data Mining: The Textbook*; Springer: Berlin/Heidelberg, Germany, 2015; Volume 1.
66. Chandrashekar, G.; Sahin, F. A survey on feature selection methods. *Comput. Electr. Eng.* **2014**, *40*, 16–28. [CrossRef]
67. Kumar, V.; Minz, S. Feature selection: A literature review. *SmartCR* **2014**, *4*, 211–229. [CrossRef]

Journal of
Cybersecurity and Privacy

MDPI

Article

Association Rule Mining Meets Regression Analysis: An Automated Approach to Unveil Systematic Biases in Decision-Making Processes

Laura Genga [1,*], **Luca Allodi** [2] and **Nicola Zannone** [2]

1   Department of Industrial Engineering and Innovation Sciences, Eindhoven University of Technology,
    5612 AZ Eindhoven, The Netherlands
2   Department of Mathematics and Computer Science, Eindhoven University of Technology,
    5612 AZ Eindhoven, The Netherlands; l.allodi@tue.nl (L.A.); n.zannone@tue.nl (N.Z.)
*   Correspondence: l.genga@tue.nl

Citation: Genga, L.; Allodi, L.;
Zannone, N. Association Rule
Mining Meets Regression Analysis:
An Automated Approach to Unveil
Systematic Biases in Decision-Making
Processes. *J. Cybersecur. Priv.* **2022**, *2*,
191–219. https://doi.org/10.3390/
jcp2010011

Academic Editors: Phil Legg and
Giorgio Giacinto

Received: 28 December 2021
Accepted: 17 March 2022
Published: 21 March 2022

Publisher's Note: MDPI stays neutral
with regard to jurisdictional claims in
published maps and institutional affiliations.

Abstract: Decisional processes are at the basis of most businesses in several application domains. However, they are often not fully transparent and can be affected by human or algorithmic biases that may lead to systematically incorrect or unfair outcomes. In this work, we propose an approach for unveiling biases in decisional processes, which leverages association rule mining for systematic hypothesis generation and regression analysis for model selection and recommendation extraction. In particular, we use rule mining to elicit candidate hypotheses of bias from the observational data of the process. From these hypotheses, we build regression models to determine the impact of variables on the process outcome. We show how the coefficient of the (selected) model can be used to extract recommendation, upon which the decision maker can operate. We evaluated our approach using both synthetic and real-life datasets in the context of discrimination discovery. The results show that our approach provides more reliable evidence compared to the one obtained using rule mining alone, and how the obtained recommendations can be used to guide analysts in the investigation of biases affecting the decisional process at hand.

Keywords: decisional processes; bias discovery; association rule mining; regression analysis

1. Introduction

Decisional processes undertaken by humans are at the core of most organizations, from policy setting to IT and IT-security operations. These processes rely on cognitive resources (information, conceptual models, etc.) to help decision-makers in making appropriate decisions leading to meaningful courses of action. A prime example in the security domain is the operation of a security operation center, where technology (e.g., an SIEM—Security Information and Event Management system) supplies information to human operators who have to decide whether a specific event must be investigated [1]. The high complexity and repetitiveness of the information in input to these processes is known to lead to systematic biases in the analyst's decision-making process [2]. How to manage these shortcomings is still an open organizational issue [3], however, the identification of the sources of these biases is a first crucial step in that direction [1]. These issues are not unique to security decisions, and extend to other application domains, such as decisions for hiring or on loans requests, which have been shown to suffer from systematic, oftentimes implicit or unknown biases [4,5].

The common underlying thread is that any process relying on human judgment must be monitored to uncover unknown and implicit biases and that can only happen by systematically reviewing decisions through objective analyses that 'let the data speak'.

Uncovering biases from observational data is a broad and still open problem that requires a thorough exploratory analysis and understanding of the data, as well as rigorous estimations of effect sizes. The literature generally considers association rule mining for the former [6], while regression models are often used to evaluate effect sizes and rigorously evaluate evidence in the data [7]. However, when taken individually, these techniques are affected by intrinsic drawbacks. The outcome of association rule mining typically consists of several thousands of rules that cannot be easily operationalized. While a number of approaches have been proposed to prune the rule set, for instance by removing redundant rules [8] or assessing rule statistical significance [9], there is little or no support for analysts in delving deeper into the obtained outcome. Furthermore, different approaches typically lead to different outcomes, and there are no clear guidelines on how to determine the method and related parameters that best suit the data at hand, which require a deep understanding of the underlying statistical principles by the user. On the other hand, regression models are of little use without clearly defined hypotheses and a clear understanding of the data generation process.

In this work, we propose a novel methodology for uncovering systematic biases in data generating processes that combines the benefits of both worlds by leveraging principles from both association rule mining and regression analysis. We use association rule mining to extract the candidate hypotheses of biases from an exploration of data. These hypotheses are used to build regression models which provide us with statistical evidence for the presence/absence of biases in the decisional process, and effectively act as a cream-skimming mechanism to filter out hypotheses that are equivalent or that do not add significant information to uncover the data generation mechanism. This evidence can then be used by an analyst to take action and tackle the decision bias at the source.

We demonstrate our methodology in the context of discrimination detection to uncover the systematic use of sensitive data. In particular, we study the ability of the methodology to determine whether decisional processes are affected by biases that lead to unfair treatment because of personal characteristics or membership to certain (protected) societal groups. Nonetheless, our methodology is general and can be applied to the analysis of other decisional processes, e.g., for the security analysis of network traffic to uncover patterns of compromise. To evaluate the proposed methodology, we perform a set of experiments with both synthetic and real-world datasets to, respectively, validate our approach and showcase the methodology against real decision process outcomes.

This work extends our previous work [10], which only provides a high-level overview of the approach along with a proof-of-concept on a synthetic dataset. In particular, we refined the approach and extended the experimental evaluation to real-world datasets. The main contributions of this work can be summarized as follows:

- We identify general desiderata for a bias detection technique targeted at addressing sub-groups analysis;
- We propose a data-agnostic, evidence-based approach to identify well-grounded hypotheses of bias in any decisional process which aids policy makers identify potentially biased and systematic decisions affecting a group or sub-group(s) of entities of interest (e.g., sensitive subjects);
- We perform a set of experiments on synthetic data and showcase the application of our method in the domain of discrimination detection by employing two real-world datasets used in previous research on discrimination detection;
- We show that the descriptive statistics (mean, 95% confidence intervals) of the effects of interest returned by our approach can be used to further guide the policy maker in pertaining follow-up regulatory actions.

This paper is organized as follows. The next section provides background on association rule mining and regression analysis. Section 3 introduces our methodology and Section 4 presents its experimental evaluation. Section 5 provides a discussion of our method and results. Finally, Section 6 discusses related work and Section 7 provides conclusive remarks.

2. Background

We model a decision-making process as a set of records comprising a number of attributes (hereafter called *variables* or *features*) describing a given subject (e.g., a person applying for a loan) and the *outcome* of the process, i.e., the decision made for the subject. Intuitively, each record represents one observation of the process along with the data upon which it operated (i.e., the variables) and its outcome.

Table 1 provides a fictional example of a decision-making process of a financial institute aiming to determine whether a given applicant should be classified as a high-risk individual, i.e., they are likely unable to refund a loan. Each record corresponds to a single loan request where SubjID provides the ID of the applicant and Employed, Income, Gender, Ethnic Group are variables characterizing the applicant. HighRisk is the binary variable describing the outcome of the process (1 encoding a 'high-risk' evaluation for that subject).

Table 1. Example decisional process of a financial institute.

	Outcome	Variables			
SubjID	High Risk	Employed	Income	Gender	Ethnic Group
1	1	N	2000	M	Black
2	0	Y	10,000	F	White
⋮	⋮	⋮	⋮	⋮	⋮
100	1	N	5000	M	Asian

Decisional processes are often affected by human or algorithmic bias. In the example above, the data could reveal to an observer whether being currently employed is a relevant criterion for the bank's decision-making process. Similarly, it could reveal how the odds of being assigned to a risk category change for every additional dollar of income. Whereas these are relations that one could reasonably expect to find in any decision process of this type, other complex dynamics can have a 'hidden' impact on the decision. For example, Ethnic Group may have an impact, albeit perhaps more so below certain Income levels. A recent example of such potentially systematic biases can be found in the Netherlands; in January 2021, the national Dutch government resigned following a scandal involving unfair accusations against Dutch residents related to child benefit support. These accusations turned out to disproportionately target residents with dual nationalities and of specific ethnic origins requesting financial support for childcare from the Dutch government (https://www.theguardian.com/world/2021/jan/15/dutch-government-resigns-over-child-benefits-scandal, Last accessed 16 March 2022). Similarly, Gender or belief-related biases can interact with other variables, such as Ethnic Group or social status, to affect a decision.

To detect biases in decisional processes, one has to quantify to what extent the use of variables (e.g., Gender, Ethnic Group) has influenced the process outcome. A main challenge lies in the fact that the decisional process is often unknown. We only observe the output of a black-box process. Therefore, detecting biases in decisional processes requires reconstructing the decisional process from observational data and determining which variables were most likely used for decision making. Operationally, the problem can be formulated as deriving possible *correlations* between variables and the process outcome (i.e., to indicate the fact that individuals with certain attributes have higher chances of obtaining a certain outcome than individuals without those attributes).

We argue that any approach designed to tackle this challenge should meet a number of desiderata, as reported in Table 2.

The last three desiderata concern the capability of the approach to enable the understanding of how features and their values impact the outcome of the decisional process.

Two classes of techniques are widely used for the exploration of observational data: *(i)* approaches that use statistical tools, in particular *regression analysis*, to determine which variables are more likely able to explain the process outcome and *(ii)* approaches based on knowledge discovery, such as *association rule mining*, to measure possible differences in the proportions of positive/negative decisions on different groups of observations. We then introduce the basic concepts underlying these two lines of research and discuss their shortcomings with respect to the desiderata in Table 2.

Table 2. Desiderata for bias detection and investigation.

Desideratum	Description and Motivations
Data agnostic	The hypothesis generation should be agnostic of the *data-generation* process, i.e., the (often unknown) composition of decisional processes leading to a potentially biased outcome. Ideally, an approach to uncover these latent biases should be able to determine a set of hypotheses without requiring a priori knowledge of the composition of the underlying *data-generation* processes; indeed, in most contexts, little or no knowledge on how the decisions are taken is available, or the decisional environment is so complex that it is impossible to know, a priori, whether the decisions in outcome will be affected by biases (latent or explicitly manifest) in the process.
No parameter tuning	The solution should not require the tuning of parameters to avoid guess-work during the setup phase, and improve the stability and interpretability of the evaluation it generates, and operate.
Feature level and Feature value level	Biases can be analyzed at different levels of granularity. Capturing biases at a feature level would allow determining which (set of) variable(s) has an impact on the outcome, i.e., whether there is a significant correlation between the type of characteristics of an individual and the outcome variable. In certain domains such as in discrimination discovery, an analyst might require a more fine-grained analysis able to identify whether individuals with certain characteristics have been treated differently. To this end, it is desirable that the outcome of the analysis highlights possible correlations between feature *values* and the outcome variable.
Change impact	The solution should enable the analysis of the impact of changing the value of one (or more) feature(s) on the value of the outcome, allowing the user to assess both the direction (i.e., positive or negative) and the magnitude of this impact.

2.1. Association Rule Mining

The goal of association rule mining is to find correlations between variables [6]. When applied to decisional processes, association rule mining aims to derive rules describing the process from observational data.

A *decisional process* D can be represented as a set of *observations*, each describing a process instance for a given subject. Given a set of *variables* $\mathcal{V} = \{Var_1, \ldots, Var_n\}$, each representing a characteristic of the subject, an observation t is a tuple $(Var_1 = v_1, \ldots, Var_n = v_n)$, where $v_i \in dom(Var_i)$ is the value of variable Var_i in t. Every pair $Var_i = v_i$ is called *item*, and a set of items *itemset*.

An *association rule* r is an implication of the form $r : X \rightarrow Y$, where X and Y are two itemsets, respectively, called *antecedent* and *consequent* of the rule. Intuitively, an association rule indicates that if X occurs in a record, then Y will also likely occur in that record. In this work, we consider *class association rules* [11], i.e., association rules whose consequent consists of a single class item. For the sake of simplicity, hereafter we use the term 'rule' to refer to a class association rule.

To assess the *relevance* of the mined rules, in this work, we consider two well-known and largely adopted metrics [12]: *support*, which represents the percentage of records in the dataset covered by a rule, and *confidence*, which represents the percentage of records covered by the rule among those covered by its antecedent. Formally, the support and confidence of an association rule $r : X \rightarrow Y$ with respect to a dataset D are defined as

$$supp(r) = \frac{|\{t \in D \mid X \cup Y \subseteq t\}|}{|D|} \tag{1}$$

$$conf(r) = \frac{supp(r)}{supp(X)} \qquad (2)$$

It is worth noting that our approach is not constrained to the use of these metrics and other metrics could be employed to assess the relevance of the mined rules.

2.2. Regression Analysis

Regression analysis is a tool to evaluate the statistical association between at least one 'explanatory variable' and an 'outcome variable'. A regression model linking the explanatory variables to the outcome variable is generally formulated on the basis of hypotheses that the analyst makes about the underlying relation. A typical regression model assumes the following general form:

$$g(E(Y)) = c + \beta_1 Var_1 + \beta_2 Var_2 + \cdots + \beta_n Var_n + \epsilon \qquad (3)$$

where $g(\cdot)$ is the link function, Y is the outcome variable with mean $E(Y)$, c is the intercept, and $\beta_1, \ldots, \beta_n$ are the regression coefficients of the n explanatory variables $Var_1, \ldots, Var_n$, and ϵ is the error term. If the analyst believes that there are interactions between explanatory variables (i.e., they have a joint effect on the dependent variable), she can capture these interactions by considering the product of the explanatory variables, denoted by $Var_i \cdot Var_j$, as an additional explanatory variable. Equation (3) is called a *regression equation*; the estimation of the coefficients is the key aspect, and which link function one adopts depends on the nature of the data (e.g., a *logit* or a *probit* function for a binary outcome).

A model formulation (also called *parametrization*) is generally directly derived from the formulated hypotheses; however, in *exploratory* settings (where those hypotheses do not yet exist [7]) the model definition can generally be automated by employing techniques based on the analysis of variance (ANOVA). Again, the choice of the test to compare models depends on the type of model considered; logit models, for example, may be compared using likelihood ratio tests. to select the *explanatory variables* that have the highest *power* in 'explaining' the data. Given two models of the same power, the model with the fewer explanatory variables is preferred (principle of 'minimality'). Regardless of the adopted approach to parameterize a model, it is important to verify that the chosen explanatory variables are not highly correlated, to avoid model multicollinearity that may bias the coefficient estimation. This check can be performed by calculating a correlation matrix across the variables, or a variance inflation factor (VIF) for a given model.

2.3. Limitations of Association Rule Mining and Regression Analysis

Uncovering biases from observational data requires a thorough exploratory analysis of the data, as well as rigorous estimations of effect sizes. Whereas the literature generally considers association rule mining for the former, regression models are often used to evaluate effect sizes and rigorously evaluate evidence in the data. However, both methods have intrinsic shortcomings in our application. We then discuss these shortcomings, which are summarized in Table 3.

Table 3. Comparison of association rule mining and regression analysis with respect to the identified desiderata for bias detection in Table 2, where ● means "support" and ○ "no support".

	Data-Agnostic	No Param. Tuning	Feature Level	Feature Value Level	Change Impact
Assoc. Rule Mining	●	○	○	●	○
Regression Analysis	○	●	●	●	●

Association Rule Mining. First, rule mining requires an analyst to carefully tune the threshold parameters for the used relevance metrics without providing a rigorous way to 'prioritize' rules for a certain outcome. While selecting low threshold values can lead to a large number of rules, most of which are not interesting and/or not reliable, excessively high values can easily lead to missing relevant correlations. Rule mining also lacks support for the statistical validation of the associations detected among the variables. The use of metrics such as support and confidence does not guarantee preventing the generation of *false discoveries*, such as rules showing dependencies likely due by chance, or rules where the antecedent contains items that are actually independent of the consequent [13]. Moreover, association rule mining only allows analysts to explore relations among single feature values and class values (feature value level analysis), while feature level analysis is not supported.

Regression analysis. Compared to association rule mining, regression analysis provides a more robust approach to statistical validation. The output provided by regression techniques supports both feature level and feature value level analysis. Moreover, they do not require the tuning of parameters. However, regression (parametric) approaches require some type of hypothesis formulation to build a model to regress on. This is desirable in general as it attaches semantic meaning to the statistical evidence found in the data. However, for data exploration tasks such as the one at hand, regression approaches are very limited in nature. *Forward* or *backward* model selection procedures [7] can be applied to identify the 'best' model explaining the data, but the number of models to be compared explodes exponentially as the number of allowed variable interactions increases. More importantly, there is no 'guarantee' that the resulting selected 'best' model has any useful interpretation that can be used to take action and tackle the decision bias at the source.

3. A New Approach for Bias Detection Combining Rule Mining and Regression Analysis

To detect and investigate systematic biases in decisional processes, we propose to combine principles of rule mining with regression analysis. We note that a data sanitization process should start before the application of our methodology; for example, to identify highly correlated variables in a dataset that may create multicollinearity problems biasing estimated model coefficients. When two or more highly correlated variables are present, only one should be selected for inclusion in the analysis.

Our methodology is summarized in Figure 1. First, association rule mining is employed to generate the set of relevant rules (1). For our purpose, we treat each mined rule as a candidate hypothesis for bias. In step (2), we generate regression models by considering the variables included in each selected rule and regress over them to generate the model estimates of the considered outcome variable. In step (3), a model comparison is performed to eliminate 'redundant' models that do not add relatively more information to the prediction than a simpler model does. This leaves us with only 'winning' models that, among all evaluated candidates, provide the more convincing evidence for some effect, if any. Finally, in step (4), we extract the coefficients of these selected models to identify (sub)populations of interest for which there is statistical evidence of bias in the decision making. Then, we provide a detailed breakdown of each step of the methodology.

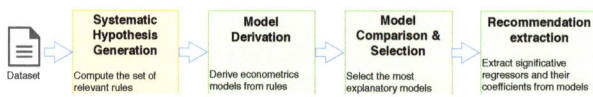

Figure 1. Depiction of the phases of the proposed methodology.

3.1. Systematic Hypothesis Generation

Given a decisional process D, we apply class association rule mining to derive the set of relevant rules R_{rel}. To measure the relevance of rules, we use *support* and *confidence*, as defined in Equations (1) and (2). Specifically, we say that a rule is relevant if its *support* and *confidence* levels are above some given thresholds ρ_{supp} and ρ_{conf}, respectively. Formally, $R_{rel} = \{r_i \mid supp(r_i) \geq \rho_{supp} \wedge conf(r_i) \geq \rho_{conf}\}$. Each rule in R_{rel} is considered a candidate hypothesis of biases in the decisional process.

Example 1. *Below, we show some example (relevant) rules that can be extracted by the application of association rule mining to the decisional process of Table 1:*

$$r_1: \quad \texttt{Income} = 5000, \texttt{EthnicGroup} = White \rightarrow \texttt{HighRisk} = 0$$
$$r_2: \quad \texttt{Gender} = M \rightarrow \texttt{HighRisk} = 1$$
$$r_3: \quad \texttt{Gender} = M, \texttt{Employed} = N \rightarrow \texttt{HighRisk} = 1$$
$$r_4: \quad \texttt{Income} = 2000, \texttt{EthnicGroup} = White \rightarrow \texttt{HighRisk} = 0$$

An analyst should investigate all the rules in R_{rel} to check whether they correspond to actual biases. However, as discussed earlier, association rule mining provides very little support for this. For instance, R_{rel} might contain rules that are not 'independent' from each other. In particular, many rules can be "subrules" of others, i.e., they extend other rules with additional itemsets as in the case of r_2 and r_3 above. Formally, a rule $r_i : X_i \rightarrow Y$ is a *subrule* of a rule $r_j : X_j \rightarrow Y$ if $X_i \subset X_j$. Thus, the analyst might not know whether the (possible) bias concerns the population characterized by a given rule (e.g., employed males) or whether it affects a larger population as characterized by a subrule (e.g., all males).

To find more reliable evidence of biases, in this work, we employ regression analysis to determine the statistical validity of the evidence found.

3.2. Model Derivation

To determine whether the candidate hypotheses extracted using rule mining corresponds to biases in the decisional process, we derive regression models from the set of relevant rules R_{rel}. Specifically, for each rule $r : Var_1 = v_1, \ldots, Var_N = v_N \rightarrow \texttt{Class} = Y$ in R_{rel}, we consider the set of explanatory variables occurring in the antecedent of the rule $V_i = \{Var_1, \ldots, Var_N\} \subseteq V$ and build a corresponding regression model M_i of the form of:

$$M_i : \texttt{Class} = c + \sum_{i=1}^{N} \beta_i \, Var_i + \sum_{1 \leq i < j \leq N} \beta_{ij} \, Var_i \cdot Var_j$$
$$+ \sum_{1 \leq i < j < k \leq N} \beta_{ijk} \, Var_i \cdot Var_j \cdot Var_k + \ldots + \beta_{1\ldots N} \, Var_1 \cdot \ldots \cdot Var_N \quad (4)$$

Example 2. *From the set of rules in Example 1, we can extract three models:*

$$M_1: \quad \texttt{HighRisk} = c_1 + \beta_{1,1} \, \texttt{Income} + \beta_{1,2} \, \texttt{EthnicGroup} + \beta_{1,3} \, \texttt{Income} \cdot \texttt{EthnicGroup}$$
$$M_2: \quad \texttt{HighRisk} = c_2 + \beta_{2,1} \, \texttt{Gender}$$
$$M_3: \quad \texttt{HighRisk} = c_3 + \beta_{3,1} \, \texttt{Gender} + \beta_{3,2} \, \texttt{Employed} + \beta_{3,3} \, \texttt{Gender} \cdot \texttt{Employed}$$

Note that some rules collapse in a single model as they contain exactly the same set of variables. In our example, this is the case for rules r_1 and r_4, which are both represented by model M_1.

To efficiently compare the 'credibility' of the obtained models (next step), we organize the derived models in a hierarchical structure. To this end, we introduce a partial order relation over regression models which resembles the subrule relation. Given two regression models M_i and M_j defined over the sets of explanatory variables V_i and V_j, respectively, we say that M_j is *nested* in M_i, denoted as $M_j \sqsubset M_i$, if and only if $V_i \subset V_j$. Whereas in the econometrics literature the term *nested* usually refers to the more general model (i.e., M_j is *nested* in M_i if $V_j \subset V_i$), here we adopt the opposite definition to remain consistent with the definition of *subrule* provided in Section 3.1. Moreover, we say that M_j is *directly nested* in M_i, denoted as $M_j \sqsubset M_i$, if and only if $M_j \subset M_i$ and there does not exist a model M_k such that $M_k \subset M_i$ and $M_j \subset M_k$. Based on the direct nesting relation, we construct a forest of models whereby the model at the root of each tree is the simplest model (i.e., with the smallest number of variables on the right hand side), and each child is a direct nested model of its parent(s).

Example 3. *The three models in Example 2 along with other hypothetical regression models can be represented in a hierarchy, as shown Figure 2. The hierarchy has two root nodes, i.e., M_5 and M_2, each with two children (M_1 and M_4 for M_5, M_3 and M_4 for M_2) among which one is in common (i.e., M_4). M_4 is further extended by M_6, which is also a child of M_3.*

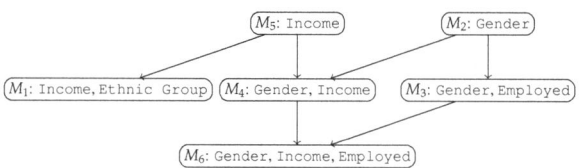

Figure 2. Example of a hierarchy of models.

3.3. Model Comparison and Selection

Once the hierarchical structure is in place, we apply a model selection procedure by comparing each parent with all its child models. Our pruning strategy consists of checking whether the addition of variables to a child model adds information that leads to a better description of the data, or whether the simpler model is preferable (in that it describes the data indistinguishably well with respect to the more complex model). This is operationalized through the ANOVA test. Alternatives to ANOVA for model comparison exist, such as AIC, BIC, or maximum likelihood; in this work, we adopt ANOVA for model comparison, but any other method could be used. The ANOVA test is a widely used statistical test that allows one to compare the fits of two regression models, one nested in the other, by comparing the (sum of squares of the) residuals (i.e., the errors) of the respective model predictions [14].

If the output of the ANOVA test indicates that the more complex model provides a significantly better explanation of the variance in the prediction, the child model is marked as preferable compared to the more general, simpler parent model. Otherwise, the parent model is marked as preferable. Formally, given a set $\mathcal{M}$ of regression models to test, we aim to derive the set $\mathcal{M}_{sel} = \{M_i \in \mathcal{M} \mid \nexists M_j \in \mathcal{M} \text{ s.t. } M_j \sqsubset M_i \wedge ANOVA(M_i, M_j) \leq \rho\}$, where ρ represents a threshold to determine whether $ANOVA(M_i, M_j)$ shows a statistically significant difference in the sum of the squared residuals between the two models.

Operationally speaking, the set $\mathcal{M}_{sel}$ was derived using the procedure shown in Algorithm 1.

Algorithm 1: Model Selection.

Input: Model hierarchy $(\mathcal{M}, \sqsubset)$ and significance threshold ρ
Output: $\mathcal{M}_{sel}$
1   $\mathcal{M}_{sel} \leftarrow \varnothing$;
2   $\mathcal{M}_p \leftarrow \{M_i \in \mathcal{M} \mid \nexists M_j \text{ s.t. } M_j \subset M_i\}$;
3   **while** $\mathcal{M}_p \neq \varnothing$ **do**
4     $M_i \leftarrow \mathcal{M}_p.pop()$;
5     $\mathcal{M}_{wc} \leftarrow \{M_j \mid M_j \sqsubset M_i \wedge ANOVA(M_i, M_j) \leq \rho\}$;
6   **if** $\mathcal{M}_{wc} = \varnothing$ **then**
7       $\mathcal{M}_{sel} \leftarrow \mathcal{M}_{sel} \cup \{M_i\}$;
8   **else**
9       $\mathcal{M}_p \leftarrow \mathcal{M}_p \cup \mathcal{M}_{wc}$;
10   **return** $\mathcal{M}_{sel}$

This procedure takes as input *(i)* a model hierarchy $(\mathcal{M}, \sqsubset)$, where $\mathcal{M}$ is the set of regression models and $\sqsubset$ is the directly nested relation on $\mathcal{M}$, and *(ii)* a threshold ρ determining whether the result of the ANOVA test is significant, and iteratively checks whether nested models provide more significant explanation of biases. At the beginning, the output set $\mathcal{M}_{sel}$ is initialized to the empty set, while the set of regression models to be analyzed is stored in a stack, $\mathcal{M}_p$, which is initialized to the root models (i.e., the models that are not nested in any other model) (lines 1–2).

The models in $\mathcal{M}_p$ are iteratively extracted from $\mathcal{M}_p$ and compared against their direct nested models using the ANOVA test (lines 4–5). Every child that is preferable compared to its parent(s) based on the ANOVA test is added to the set of *winner children* $\mathcal{M}_{wc}$ (line 5). If the set $\mathcal{M}_{wc}$ for a given parent M_i is empty, i.e., there are no better performing children models than M_i according to the ANOVA test, then M_i is added to the output set $\mathcal{M}_{sel}$ (lines 6–7). Otherwise, the models in $\mathcal{M}_{wc}$ are added to $\mathcal{M}_p$ in order to be analyzed in the next iterations of the algorithm, i.e., they are compared against their children (line 9). The procedure terminates when $\mathcal{M}_p$ is empty.

Example 4. *Consider the model hierarchy in Figure 2. By applying our model selection algorithm, at the beginning, we retrieve the two parent nodes, i.e., M_5 and M_2. Supposing that the ANOVA test indicates that M_1, M_3 are the only children scoring better than M_5, M_2, respectively, M_1 and M_3 are added to the stack $\mathcal{M}_p$. Since M_1 does not have any other child, it is added to $\mathcal{M}_{sel}$. Instead, M_3 has to be compared against M_6. If the ANOVA test determines that M_6 is better than M_3, M_6 is added to $\mathcal{M}_p$ and, since it has no children, in the next iteration, it is added to $\mathcal{M}_{sel}$. At this point the procedure terminates, since there are no more models to compare, returning $\mathcal{M}_{sel} = \{M_1, M_6\}$.*

It is worth noting that the proposed pruning procedure can theoretically lead to miss some interesting models. As the comparison only accounts for directly nested models, it is possible that models that score better than their ancestors but not than their direct parents are discarded. For example, since M_4 does not score better than M_5, it is not selected for the next iterations and, therefore, M_6 would have not been considered for the ANOVA test. However, it is reasonable to expect such loss to be limited. If a child model includes a variable providing a strong explanation of the observed effects, one can reasonably expect such variable(s) to have been picked up by other rules (step 1) and therefore to occur in other regression models. This leads to the otherwise discarded model being tested against different parents. This is the case, in our example, for M_6. While the procedure would have discarded M_6 if it had only M_4 as a parent, this model is still considered in the comparison against M_3 and, hence, it gets a chance to be selected.

3.4. Recommendation Extraction

The selected regression models $\mathcal{M}_{sel}$ obtained from step 3 provide the best 'explanation' of the decisional process. Each model comprises a set of coefficients $C_i = \{\beta_{i,1}, \beta_{i,2}, \dots, \beta_{i,k}\}$ together with an output of a statistical test determining whether each element of C_i is significantly different from zero (i.e., whether the associated variable in V_i is likely to have a significant effect on the outcome variable). The minimum level of statistical significance generally considered is 5% ($p \leq 0.05$).

By inspecting each model $M_i \in \mathcal{M}_{sel}$, in this phase, we extract regressors and associated coefficients $\langle \beta_{i,j}, Var_{i,j} = v_{i,j} \rangle$ with $p_{i,j} \leq 0.05$ for which there is enough evidence to consider possible effects on the outcome variable. Each extracted pair $\langle \beta_{i,j}, Var_{i,j} = v_{i,j} \rangle$ conveys information on the *direction* and *size* of the identified bias towards the group $Var_{i,j} = v_{i,j}$, represented, respectively, by the sign and magnitude of the coefficient $\beta_{i,j}$. The interpretation of this coefficient, in the case of discrete (as opposed to continuous) variables, is to be interpreted as the change in the outcome variable for observations that belong to the relevant category relative to observations in the baseline category (cf. Appendix A for a more detailed discussion).

We stress that 'hand-picking' variables with significant *p*-values is *not* a meaningful approach for model selection and interpretation. Differently, the goal of the proposed approach is to identify variables (possibly appearing across several selected models) for which there exists some evidence of correlation with the process outcome, and that may require additional, more rigorous investigation by an analyst or policy maker. To evaluate the strength of the emerging evidence, an analyst can, for example, compare how the associated coefficients for a variable vary across models (see analysis reported in Section 4.2 for an example), or evaluate cross-correlation effects with other variables in subsequent analyses. The output of the proposed approach serves, therefore, as an indication to guide further investigations of the data and the respective generative processes, and should *not* be considered as a means to automatically generate robust explanations for the data.

4. Experiments

This section discusses an application of our methodology to the problem of discrimination detection in decisional processes the Python implementation used for these experiments can be found at https://gitlab.tue.nl/lgenga/association-rule-mining-meets-regression-analysis (Last access 16 March 2022). We performed experiments with both synthetic datasets, to demonstrate the ability of our approach to detect situations in which discrimination occurred, and with real-life datasets, to evaluate the applicability of our approach to real-life scenarios. In the experiments, we assume that the policy maker knows the groups of protected subjects for which possible biases should be tested. Therefore, we only consider rules regarding these groups as initial input. This assumption is reasonable in the context of discrimination detection, where the protected groups are known a priori. Nonetheless, our approach is general and does not require a priori domain knowledge.

4.1. Approach Validation

4.1.1. Dataset and Settings

For the validation of our approach, we generated synthetic datasets to contain a known 'amount' of evidence of discrimination. To this end, we defined a simple decisional process regarding the hiring of candidates on the basis of their personal characteristics. Table 4 shows the variables characterizing the hiring process along with their domain. We consider the variable Age as a 'discriminatory variable', whereas the others are considered 'context variables'. We generate the synthetic data in two steps. First, we created the discriminated groups as groups of subjects sharing the same value of Age as well as a (randomly chosen) subset of context values; the values of the other context variables were randomly assigned from the respective domains. Discriminated subjects have a probability of 80% of being assigned to class "N". Second, we generated all 'non-discriminated' subjects simply by randomly selecting a value for each context variable and for the Age variable. Non-discriminated subjects have a 50% probability of being assigned to either the "N" or "Y" class.

Table 4. Variables used for the generation of the synthetic dataset along with their domain.

Variables	Variable Domain
Education	Doctorate, Master, Bachelor, HighSchool
Speak Language	Y, N
Previous Role	Employee, Manager, Self-Employed, Unemployed
Country	USA, Europe, SA, China, India
Age	25–50, 50+
Class	Y, N

In total, we generated 12 datasets by varying the number of discriminated groups (i.e., 1, 2 and 3) and the complexity of the dataset to test our methodology in different situations. The complexity of a dataset is defined over two dimensions: (1) presence/absence of *noise*, intended as subjects that do not belong to any of the generated context groups but in which one or more context variables assume a value used in one of the discriminated groups; and (2) the presence/absence of *overlapping*, meaning that subjects in two or more discriminated groups share at least a context variable and its value. Combining these two dimensions, we obtain four types of datasets: (i) without noise and overlapping, which represents the simplest situation; (ii) without noise but with overlapping; (iii) with noise but without overlapping; (iv) with noise and overlapping, which represents the most difficult situation to deal with, since spurious correlations can easily arise (note that the presence of overlapping only has an impact when more than one discriminated group exists). For every dataset, we generated a total of 10,000 subjects; among them, every discriminated group covered 25% of the dataset. We chose 25% to strike a balance between absolute minority ($<$50%) and small groups. For every dataset, we tested several configurations of support, which varied between 1% and 10% with a step of 1%, and confidence, which varied between 50% and 95% with a step of 5%. Note that when generating the regression models, we did not consider potential interactions among the variables in the experiments; namely, we used only factors of the first order when computing the regression models. While this choice can lead to lose some interesting correlation, it provides us with a good approximation of the relations characterizing the decisional process, and prevents the generation of noisy recommendations. Directionality is given by the sign of the corresponding coefficients.

4.1.2. Evaluation Metrics

To validate the approach, we compare the recommendations returned by our methodology and those returned by rule mining alone against the 'ground truth' used to generate the synthetic datasets. More precisely, we compute the fraction of correct models returned by our methodology as the ratio of the number of models involving significant regressors that indicate (at least some) true discriminatory factors among the variables over the total number of models returned by the approach. To compare this outcome with the one obtained using rule mining, we compute the ratio of the number of rules indicating (at least some) true discriminatory factors over the total number of mined rules.

To this end, we first derive for each model the set of significant regressors along with their coefficients. Then, we compare each regressor with the set of variables describing the discriminated groups. This comparison can return five different outcomes: *(a) Exact*, indicating that the set of significant regressors of the model involve all and only the variables characterizing one of the discriminated groups; *(b) Too general*, indicating that the set of explanatory variables in the regressors is a strict subset of the set of variables characterizing one of the discriminated groups; *(c) Too specific*, indicating that the set of explanatory variables in a regressor is a strict superset of the set of variables characterizing one of the discriminated groups; *(d) Partial*, indicating that the set of explanatory variables in the regressor overlaps with the set of variables characterizing one of the discriminated groups (but it is not a superset); *(e) Off target*, indicating that there are no significant regressors involving any variable characterizing a discriminated group. The output of rule mining is classified in the same way, by comparing the set of variables reported in a rule against the set of variables describing the discriminated groups. For a fair comparison, we only considered the variables involved in the antecedent of the rules; indeed, we are interested in determining whether a group shows signs of discrimination, rather than specifying whether it is a positive or negative discrimination.

We only consider *exact* and *too general* recommendations to be useful recommendations, since they include the true discriminated group, and therefore provide the analyst with a first, non-misleading indication of possible discriminatory relations. In contrast, the other categories of output are undesirable since, even if some do return part of the actual discriminatory group, the whole discriminated group cannot be identified as it is not included in the recommendation. Therefore, we compute the fraction of useful recommendations as the number of *Exact* and *Too general* models (rules) over all returned models (rules).

In addition to comparing the returned models against the ground truth, we also compare rule mining and regression analysis in terms of the number of output rules and regressors, respectively. The goal is to assess the capability of our approach to reduce the outcome complexity, thus making the analysis more accessible for a human analyst.

4.1.3. Results

Models vs. rules. Table 5 reports descriptive statistics of the results over all experiment runs.

Table 5. Min, max, mean, median, first and third quantile of the number of rules (first group of rows) and models (second group of rows) obtained in each experiment.

	Metric	Min	1st Q	Mean	Median	3rd Q	Max	sd
Rule mining	N_rules	0	0	12.87	4	13.25	139	23.74
	Exact	0	0	1.01	1	2	3	1.15
	Too general	0	0	1.77	0	3	7	2.38
	Too specific	0	0	3.52	0	2	64	9.99
	Partial	0	0	6.58	0	5	121	14.24
	Off target	0	0	0.00	0	0	0	0.00
Our approach	N_models_tot	0	0	4.98	4	8	16	4.72
	N_models_sel	0	0	1.05	1	2	6	1.11
	Exact	0	0	0.35	0	1	5	0.65
	Too general	0	0	0.53	0	1	6	1.03
	Too specific	0	0	0.18	0	0	2	0.39
	Partial	0	0	0.00	0	0	0	0.00
	Off target	0	0	0.00	0	0	0	0.00

The first set of rows reports the statistics for association rule mining, whereas the second set reports the statistics for our approach. We first observe that the number of rules is significantly larger than both the number of total models (i.e., the models derived from the set of rules) and that of selected models (i.e., the models returned in output by our approach). Furthermore, the number of the selected models is, on average, four times smaller than the overall number of models. The average experimental run produces approximately 12.87 rules, with a maximum of 139. The relatively high standard deviation (with respect to the mean) indicates that the number of rules in output can vary by large amounts across experimental setups. In contrast, the number of total (selected) models per experimental setup is, on average, more than two (twelve) times smaller, similarly to what can be observed for the maximum. The low standard deviation indicates a relatively stable output across experiments, especially for the selected models. Overall, this indicates that the model selection procedure appears to be removing a large number of rules but says little about the *correctness* of this process.

A first indication of the correctness of this process can be derived by evaluating of the number of *exact, too general, too specific, partial,* and *off target* rules/models in output of our method. Considering the obtained rules, we observed that association rule mining never returns *off target* recommendations. Moreover, it is able to identify, on average, at least one correct recommendation, either in terms of *exact* or *too general* recommendations. However, comparing these numbers with the overall average number of rules returned, these recommendations are likely to be hidden in a multitude of misleading recommendations. In fact, the results show that rule mining tends to return a much higher number of undesirable recommendations; on average, we obtain 3.52 *too specific* and 6.58 *partial* recommendations.

On the other hand, we observe that our approach returns a higher number of max *exact* recommendations. This is because a regressor (matching the ground truth) can be significant in multiple models. In general, we observe a similar distribution in the first and second quartile, even though the mean and median values show in general a lower overall capability of our approach to identify relevant groups under most circumstances (the median of *Exact* is 0). However, this minimal loss in detection is compensated by a large reduction in false positives to investigate. Moving to higher quartiles, we observe that our approach never returns *partial* or *off target* results, and generates much less *too specific* and *too general* recommendations. Overall, the results suggest that our approach is able to generate a more accurate output. However, this clearly depends on the number of discriminated groups, and results may vary significantly depending on the noise and overlap introduced in the synthetic datasets.

Figure 3 shows the density of 'useful' recommendations provided by rules mining and our approach, respectively, across our experimental conditions.

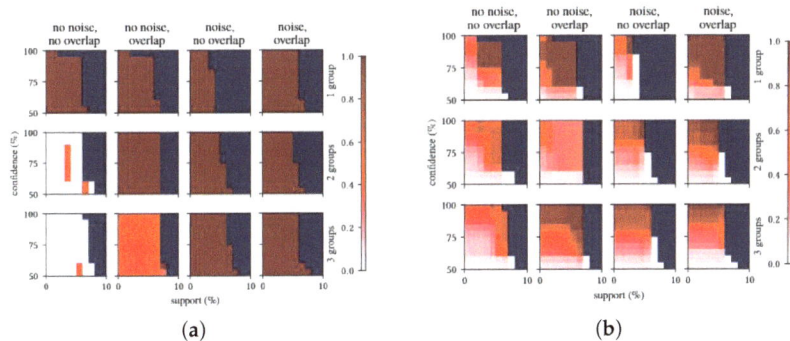

Figure 3. Density results for the synthetic dataset. (**a**) density results for models in the synthetic dataset; and (**b**) density results for rules in the synthetic datasets.

Results are arranged in a matrix, where each box represents a set of experiments with varying confidence and support levels (on the y and x axis, respectively, values are reported as percentages); the four columns correspond to the four combinations of noise and overlap, whereas the three rows correspond to the number of discriminated groups in the dataset. Recall that overlap does not impact the results when a single discriminated group is considered. The difference in the recommendations obtained for this dataset are mostly due to randomness in the data generation process. We reported them anyway for the sake of completeness. Within each box, each square corresponds to a combination of support and confidence thresholds. Squares are colored on the basis of the density of useful recommendations for the given combination of support and confidence. A darker color indicates a higher density (and vice versa). Blue cells represent support–confidence combinations from which no significant rules/regressors were obtained (resulting in a denominator of zero), and white cells represent support–confidence combinations for which no *exact* or *too general* recommendations were obtained.

We observe that, across almost all experimental setups, our approach produces a much higher density of relevant recommendations compared to rule mining alone. This confirms the observations made from Table 5; namely, rule mining tends to return a high number of recommendations, in which useful recommendations are hidden among the others. Our approach, instead, provides almost only useful recommendations in almost all performed experiments, with the exception of the experiments involving two and three discriminated groups with no noise and no overlap (first column of the second and third sets of experiments). While this might seem counter intuitive, delving into the corresponding dataset, we find that the over-imposed constraints for data generation turned out to produce unrealistic relations that significantly reduce the discriminating effects of the chosen variables. For more than one discriminated group, and in the absence of noise and overlap, the variable values used for the discriminated groups only occur for subjects fitting the related context. For example, in the experiments with two discriminated groups, we have discriminating context groups, "SpeakLanguage =Y" and "PreviousRole =*Employee*". Because of the generation constraints, there are no subjects assuming both these values. This creates the rather unrealistic situation whereby the value of one variable precludes another variable to assume some values. Our approach (correctly) detects a strong correlation among context variables SpeakLanguage and PreviousRole. This leads to the generation of *too specific* recommendations for most of the support–confidence thresholds, with some exceptions mostly due to the randomness of data. We observe a similar though not as strong effect on the experiments with overlap and no noise. The constraint on the noise led to obtain some correlations between some context group values which in turn led to generate some misleading recommendations. Nevertheless, the overall density values remain high. We point out that the presence of such correlations is a by-product of the data generation constraints and is unlikely to represent a realistic situation under real-life conditions. Therefore, we do not expect this behavior to affect the reliability of the recommendations provided by the approach in real-life contexts.

It is worth noting that, while we observe performance to significantly vary for rule mining depending on the support/confidence thresholds, our approach proved to be more stable, keeping a constant level of density in almost all cases. This is in line with previous observations that rule mining is sensitive to parameterization, and that choosing the correct parameter configuration largely depends on unknown structures in the data. By contrast, our approach performs well across the board. This effectively removes the need for fine-tuning the support and confidence thresholds for rule selection, with regression model selection doing the larger part of the heavy lifting required to cherry-pick relevant rules and discarding imprecise ones.

Regressors vs. rules. The previous paragraph discussed the results obtained at the regression models level. Here we focus on the obtained regressors. Table 6 shows descriptive statistics about rules and regressors obtained for the tested datasets.

Table 6. Descriptive statistics for rules and regressors in the experiment runs with synthetic data.

Metric	Min	1st Q	Mean	Median	3rd Q	Max	sd
N_rules	0	0	12.87	4	13.25	139	23.74
N_regr	0	0	2.11	2	4	6	1.93

The table shows some interesting trends. First, we observe much more variation in the number of rules than in the number of regressors (sd = 23.74 and 1.93, respectively), and that extreme values far away from the median are more likely to appear in the former than in the latter distribution. This confirms that the outcome of our approach is much more stable than the rule mining outcome. Furthermore, it is straightforward to see that, on average, the number of regressors is significantly lower than the number of rules. This is particularly evident from the mean value, equal to 12.87 for the rules, while the mean number of regressors is 2.11, with a six-fold reduction. An even stronger reduction can be observed considering the maximum values (139 for the rules, 6 for the regressors).

Figure 4 reports the relation between regressors and rules across the experiments for each dataset. Each grid corresponds to a single experimental setting (i.e., to one combination of support and confidence threshold); the x axis shows the number of extracted rules, while the y axis shows the number of extracted regressors. Different symbols and colors are used to represent the complexity of the dataset. A common trend for all datasets is that the number of rules exceeds the number of regressors for at least one order of magnitude at low support/confidence thresholds. Even when increasing the support/confidence thresholds, for most of the tested configurations, the number of rules was at least twice the number of regressors.

To visualize the order of magnitude in the difference between regressors and rules, Figure 5 reports (on a log scale) the ratio between regressors and rules for each experimental setting (without considering configurations where no rules were found). We observe that the datasets involving noise are also the ones in which we observe a stronger difference between the number of rules/regressors. In both datasets, we obtained at most the same numbers of regressors and rules, while in most of the configurations, the number of regressors is significantly lower (up to a three-fold reduction compared to the number of rules). For the datasets without noise, instead, while we still obtain overall less regressors than rules, this reduction is quite strong only for low support/confidence thresholds, and becomes less and less evident while increasing the thresholds. For the first dataset, the number of regressors exceeds, even though just slightly, the number of rules in few configurations. This is consistent with the characteristics of the used datasets; indeed, the datasets with no noise are also the ones more favorable to rule mining which, with high support/confidence thresholds, is able to return a limited number of rules. Nevertheless, overall these results show that the use of regression analysis reduces up to three times the number of generated bias candidates.

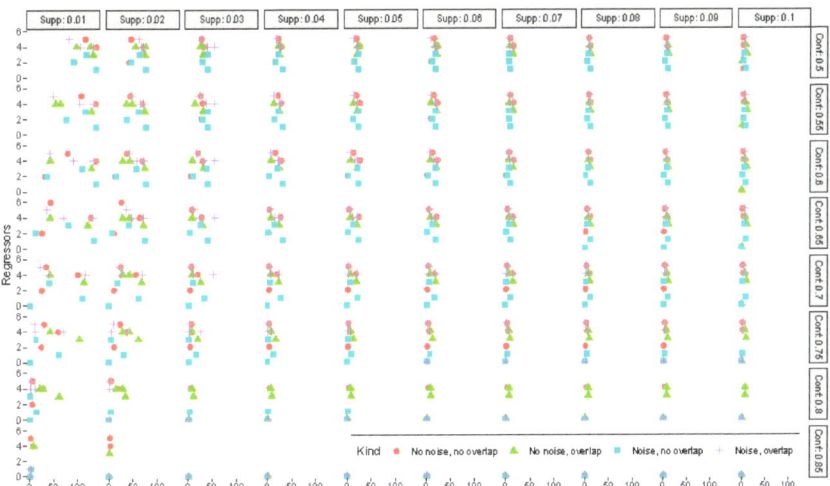

Figure 4. Rules and regressors for each experimental setting on all datasets. Results for confidence levels above 0.85 are removed as no rule is detected irrespective of the level of support.

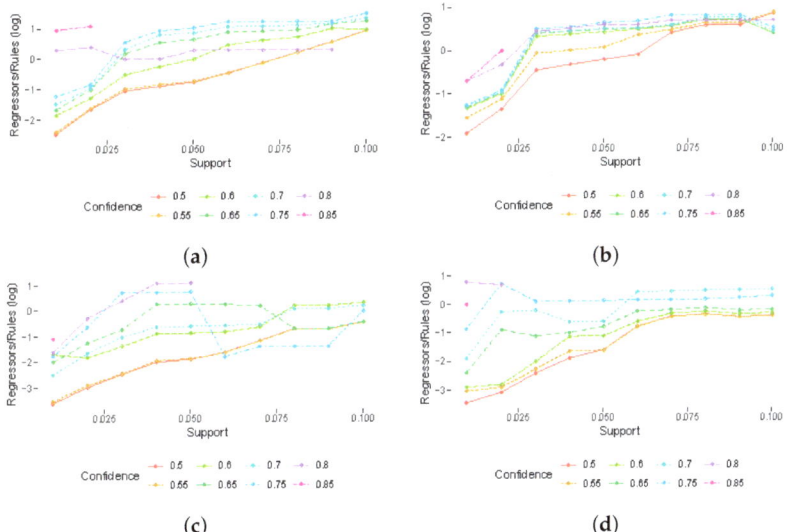

Figure 5. Fraction of obtained models per rules for all datasets: (**a**) no noise, no overlap; (**b**) no noise, overlap; (**c**) noise, no overlap; (**d**) noise, overlap.

Summarizing, the results show that our approach is able to significantly reduce the number of recommendations provided by rule mining without losing knowledge on the potential bias in the data. The approach also returned consistent results across varying support and confidence thresholds, thus showing to be robust with respect to parametrization. Interestingly, the cases where the approach showed more difficulties are the ones where the data generation procedure created very strong and undesired correlations among variables between which no correlation was intended. We discuss the limitations of the proposed method, such as spurious correlations, in Section 5.

4.2. Approach Application to Two Real-Life Use Cases

In this section, we discuss the results obtained by applying our approach to two real-life datasets which were used in previous work on discrimination detection: the German credit dataset [15], used, e.g., in [4,16,17], and the Crime and Communities dataset [18], used, e.g., in [16,19]. In the following, we present results related to configurations in which support varies between 3% and 10% with a step of 1% and confidence varies between 50% and 95% with a step of 5%. Exploring very low support values turned out to be not feasible with the current implementation of our approach, in terms of hardware and time constraints. Therefore, we did not test our approach for values of support equal to 1% and 2%. We argue that this choice does not significantly impact the validity of the performed results, since it is not unreasonable to discard very infrequent associations when addressing real-life cases. In addition, the validation of our approach on synthetic datasets has shown that it is robust with respect to the parameterization of support.

4.2.1. Use Case on Credit Risk

Dataset and Settings. The German dataset consists of 1000 records representing the assessment of credit risk (good or bad) of bank account holders [15]. The dataset encompasses 21 variables, grouped according to the following categories: personal properties (checking account status, duration, savings status, property magnitude, type of housing), properties related to past/current credits and requested credit (credit history, credit request purpose, credit request amount, installment commitment, existing credits, other parties, other payment plan), properties related to the employment status (job type, employment since, number of dependents, own telephone), and personal attributes (personal status and gender, age, resident since, foreign worker). We discretized the numeric attributes as suggested in [4]. Following [17], we considered the decisional process to be affected by discrimination if the final decision was influenced by the fact that the holder belongs to one or more of the following subgroups: non-single female, older than 52 years and foreign worker.

Results. Table 7 reports the descriptive statistics for the 80 experiment runs for varying levels of support ($[0.03, 0.10]$ with steps of 0.01) and confidence ($[0.5, 0.95]$ with steps of 0.5). We observe that the number of rules in the output is higher but resembles the same distribution as the number of derived regression models. Absolute values are, as one would expect, much higher for real datasets than for the experiment with synthetic data. The median experimental setting produces 5971.5 rules and 231.5 models. The stable ratio of models to rules between the two settings (synthetic and real) suggests that the pre-conditions for the two experiments are comparable. If we focus on the significant, unique regressors, we observe a stronger reduction; indeed, thanks to model selection, we obtain a median and a maximum of 26.5 and 32 regressors to consider (as opposed to, respectively, 5971.5 and 77,219 rules).

Table 7. Descriptive statistics of the experiment runs for the credit dataset.

Metric	Min	1st Q	Mean	Med.	3rd Q	Max	sd
#rul	54.0	2894.0	14,668.1	5971.5	19,166.5	77,219.0	20,004.6
#mod	12.0	117.25	373.1	231.5	491.25	1560.0	386.3
#regr	12.0	23.8	25.3	26.5	28.2	32	4.7

Figure 6 reports the relation between regressors and rules across experiments. We can observe that while the results obtained using rule mining vary significantly for different support and confidence settings, regressors turn out to be quite stable, with variations of the order of a few dozens across all experiments. Furthermore, the number of rules exceeds the numbers of regressors of a factor ranges from 10 to 1000, depending on the support level.

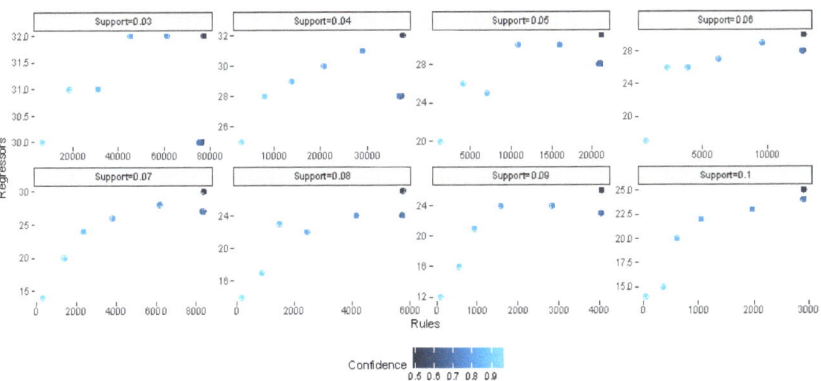

Figure 6. Rules and regressors for each experimental setting.

Figure 7 reports the (log) ratio between models and rules for each experimental setting. At every level of support and confidence, the number of regressors is, on average, notably smaller than the number of rules. The stability of the results given by our approach is consistent with what we observed in Section 4.1. Nevertheless, the reduction is especially strong at a low level of confidence and support. These results point out that the number of regressors remains manageable for being analyzed by a human policy maker, whereas the number of rules explodes. This suggests that our approach can be very effective in practice to obtain usable and statistically significant indications of biases in the data without the need to fine-tune the support/confidence levels in input to rule mining. The overhead in terms of output from low support and confidence levels is limited, whereas one is not incurred in the risk of removing potentially relevant rules.

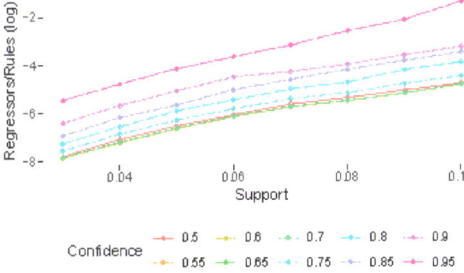

Figure 7. Fraction of obtained models per rule.

The results discussed to date show the capability of the approach to significantly reduce the space of candidate hypotheses, with respect to classic association rule mining. Exploring these hypotheses to detect the presence of actual biased relations is, at this point, up to the human policy makers. A detailed analysis of the detected regressors would not be possible here, for the sake of space. Nevertheless, in the following, we briefly discuss how regressor coefficients, together with their confidence intervals, can be used to further aid the policy maker in her analysis.

To this end, let us consider the configuration with support equal to 0.09 and confidence equal to 0.9. Figure 8 shows the confidence intervals of the corresponding regressors related to the three variables under investigation in our experiments, i.e., Age, Personal status and Foreign worker. The y axis shows the coefficient values; the blue cross represents the estimated value of the coefficient of one regressor and the blue line corresponds to its 95% confidence interval. The light-blue without crosses lines group regressors belonging to the same models. The number of lines per model depends on the domain of the corresponding variable. Both Age and Personal status have four different values; therefore, here we have three lines for every model corresponding to the values not used for the baseline in the regression. `Foreign worker`, instead, is a binary value; hence, each single line belongs to a different model.

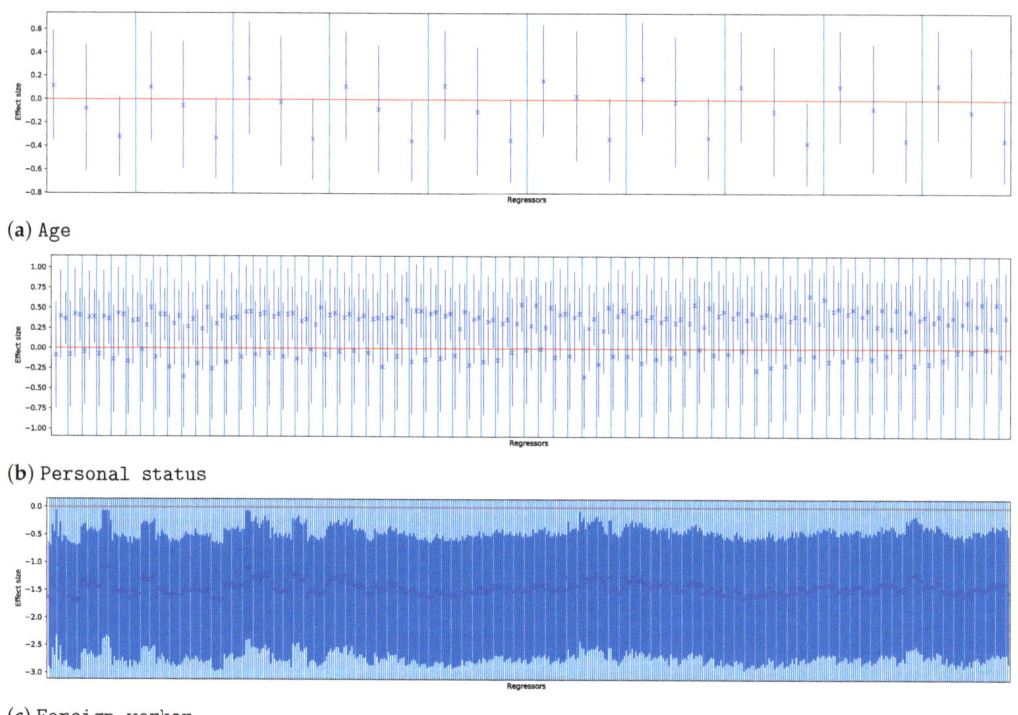

(a) `Age`

(b) `Personal status`

(c) `Foreign worker`

Figure 8. Coefficients confidence intervals for the three features under investigation in the experiment (support 0.09 and confidence 0.9). Variable `Age` can take four values: $[0, 30]$, $(30, 41]$, $(41, 52]$ and $(52, 100]$. The baseline value used in the regression model is $(30, 41]$. Variable `Personal status` can take four values: *male_single*, *female_div_or_dep_or_mar*, *male_div_or_sep* and *male_mar_or_wid*. The baseline value used in the regression model is *female_div_or_dep_or_mar*. Variable `Foreign worker` can take two values: Y, N. The baseline value used in the regression model is N.

First, we observe that the three variables occur in the result set with different frequencies: we found 10 models containing `Age`, 79 containing `Personal status` and 528 containing `Foreign worker`. By observing the trend of confidence intervals for each variable, one can already spot which candidate hypotheses look more interesting and which ones, instead, could likely be discarded. For instance, all confidence intervals for `Age` span across both negative and positive values, indicating no clear effect of `Age` on the outcome variable. This indicates that `Age` is not a discriminatory factor on its own. It is worth noting that the variable `Age` occurs in several rules. Therefore, by applying rule mining alone, one might deem this variable to be influential for the decision, although it has actually no statistically significant impact on the output.

The situation is different for the other two variables. For the sake of clarity, Figure 9 zooms in on some models for both the variables.

For `Personal status`, we focus on the first three models since we observe a stable trend from the overall figure, which suggests that similar insights can be derived from any group of models. For `Foreign worker`, instead, while we still observe a similar trend across the models, there seems to be more variability for the first few models; therefore, we decided to focus on the first ten. Figure 9a shows the third line of every model, corresponding to the value `male_single` which is always above 0. This suggests that this value of `Personal status` has a significant and positive impact on the decision, even though not a very strong one. This suggests that male, single candidates are significantly more likely to receive a positive risk class than the baseline group, i.e., non-single females. Similarly, for `Foreign worker`, we can see that the confidence interval is always below 0; namely, this regressor shows a significant and negative impact of being a foreign worker on the decision, with respect to the baseline group of non-foreign workers. Such an impact is relatively strong: in many cases, the likelihood of a positive decision was reduced up to 80%. These observations suggest that both these variables should be further investigated.

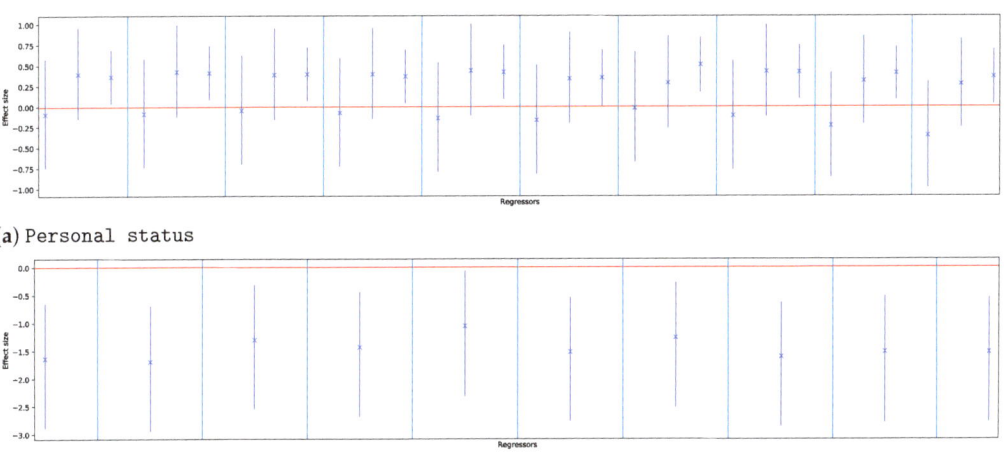

(a) `Personal status`

(b) `Foreign worker`

Figure 9. Zoom on the first models containing `Personal status` (**a**) and `Foreign worker` (**b**) in the experiment with support 0.09 and confidence 0.9.

Figure 8 also shows that the regressors exhibit the same trend for every model in the result set. This suggests that the behavior of these variables may somehow be considered as a global behavior or, at least, as a behavior valid for all identified groups of features. Further investigation may still be conducted to explain visible differences in terms of the coefficient values, for example, in the first set of models involving `Foreign worker`. We argue that such a representation would also provide the analyst with a valid means to detect groups in which regressors behave differently. In contrast, none of these considerations could have been drawn using rule mining alone. Using rule mining, the analyst can only derive the itemsets that are frequently related to a given value of the outcome variable, but no support was provided to analyze their statistical impact.

4.2.2. Use Case on Crime in Communities

Dataset and Settings. The Crime and Communities dataset contains 1994 records of communities described by socio-economic and demographic factors, including their crime rates [18]. In particular, the dataset involves 128 numerical variables, related to, e.g., average income, average household size, percentages of different ethnic groups, percentages of people at different degree of education and percentage of people using public transport. We preprocessed the dataset by performing common data cleaning tasks; namely, we removed variables involving missing values, as well as variables involving a single value, since they would have only led to noise in the analysis. The cleaned dataset involved 91 attributes. We applied supervised discretization to convert numerical variables into categorical; more precisely, we used the default settings of the supervised discretization technique implemented in Weka (https://www.cs.waikato.ac.nz/ml/weka/, Last access 16 March 2022), which strives to determine the most discriminative intervals with respect to the class.

As in [19], we selected variable `ViolentCrimePerPop` as the class attribute, where values lower than 20 represent the *positive* decision and values equal to or greater than 20 represent the *negative* decision. Among the four values of the variable `racePctBlack`, the sensitive item is: `racePctBlack = [0.375, 1]`. Accordingly, the decisional process is considered to be affected by discrimination if the fact that black people are the majority in the community has influenced the final decision.

Results. Table 8 reports the descriptive statistics for the 80 experiment runs for varying levels of support ($[0.03, 0.10]$ with steps of 0.01) and confidence ($[0.5, 0.95]$ with steps of 0.5). The number of models, while being consistently lower than the number of rules, is significantly higher those we obtained in the German dataset, approximately in the same order of magnitude as the number of rules. The number of regressors, on the other hand, shows a reduction in more than ten times with respect to the number of rules (models), along with a smaller standard deviation (and, therefore, a more stable output). The median obtained for rules and models in this experiment setting produces 1693 and 1565, respectively, while the median value for the regressors is 167. Moreover, we observe a maximum of 210 regressors to consider (as opposed to, respectively, 6355 rules and 3593 models).

Table 8. Descriptive statistics of the experiment runs for the Crime and Communities dataset.

Metric	Min	1st Q	Mean	Median	3rd Q	Max	sd
#rul	1.0	722.0	2245.0	1693.0	3153.0	6355.0	1879.7
#regr	9.0	108.0	157.4	167.0	205.0	210	52.1
#mod	1.0	658.0	1721.3	1565.0	2696.0	3570.0	1170.3

Figure 10 reports the relation between regressors and rules across experiments. We observe a trend similar to the one we observed for the German dataset, i.e., a strong variability in the rule mining results for different support and confidence settings, despite relatively stable regressor outputs. Furthermore, in this case, the number of rules exceeds the number of regressors of a factor ranging from 10 to 1000, depending on the support level. A notable exception, however, can be seen in the experiments with support higher than 0.8 and maximum confidence. This is due to the fact that, in these cases, only a few rules were mined, with the result that the output of rule mining is in this case comparable with that obtained using our approach. In one case, for the configuration with the highest threshold, only one rule was mined, from which nine significant regressors were extracted.

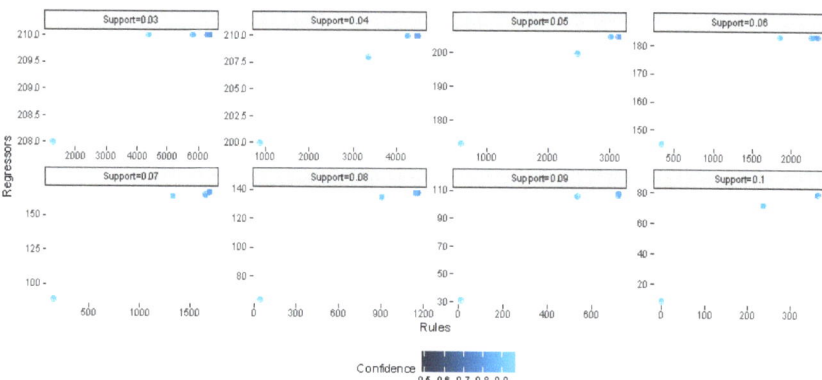

Figure 10. Rules and regressors for each experimental setting in the Crime and Communities dataset.

Figure 11 reports the (log) ratio between regressors and rules for each experiment setting. These results are consistent with what we observed for both the synthetic and German datasets: especially for low levels of these settings, there is a strong reduction in the candidates in the result set. Across all support levels, high confidence levels generate a higher number of regressors (with respect to generated rules) than at low confidence levels.

At a high confidence level, the number of regressors exceeds that of rules by a factor of 2–3 for support levels higher or equal to 0.8, and reduces well below zero at lower confidence levels. This is in line with the observation made for Figure 10 where we pointed out that in some settings, a few rules were obtained, which generated a comparable or higher number of regressors.

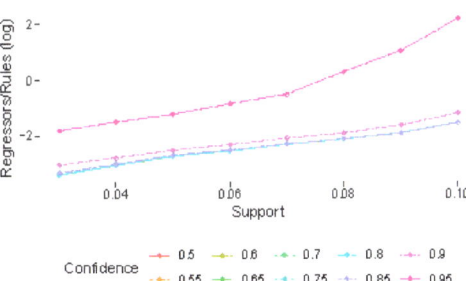

Figure 11. Fraction of obtained regressors per rule.

Figure 12 shows the confidence intervals for the regressors obtained for a support equal to 0.09 and confidence equal to 0.9. Among the 535 models containing the variable `racePctBlack`, the figure only reports the first 50 models for the sake of readability. These models show common trends among all models, but they also show some notable outliers. First, regressors in the first 42 models show a significant positive impact on the decision variable. Delving into greater detail, we observe that the third line of each model which corresponds to the highest percentage of black people in the community is the one with the largest impact on the class. Therefore, overall these models seem to suggest that if the percentage of black people increases, the possibility of being classified as a dangerous area also increases. However, the magnitude of the impact does seem to change in some models, moving from a strong impact (more than three-fold) to a marginal and even negative impact. For example, a model in Figure 12 shows that the first two values are close to zero; and the third line actually goes below 0, thus pointing out that this value is not significant at all for this model. It is worth noting that in the remaining set of models we analyzed (not reported here for the sake of space), the `racePctBlack` regressor always has a strong impact with the same dynamics we described above. Starting from these observations, the policy maker can actually recover the corresponding model to investigate the reasons underlying the observed differences.

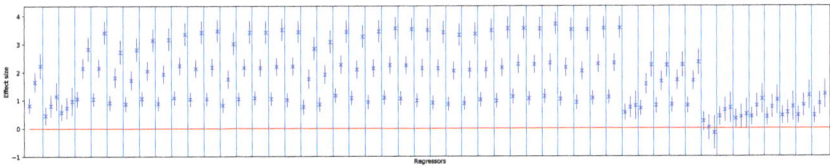

Figure 12. Coefficient confidence intervals for the `racePctBlack` regressors (first 50 models) in the experiment with support 0.09 and confidence 0.9. Variable `racePctBlack` can assume four values, namely $[0, 0.035]$, $[0.035, 0.165)$, $[0.165, 0.375]$), $[0.375, 1]$. The baseline value used in the regression model is $[0, 0.035]$.

5. Discussion

In this section, we elaborate upon some key observations obtained from our experiments and discuss the limitations of our approach.

Effective candidates generation. The results show how the combination of rules mining and regression analysis allow one to overcome the disadvantages of each method applied individually. First, we stress that, without the rule mining contribution to the methodology, the model testing using regression analysis would have failed to identify interesting relations. To double-check this, during the first stages of this work, we attempted to generate 'optimal' models through backward and forward model generation (ref. Section 2.2), leading to uninterpretable results, and oftentimes failing to target 'sensible' variables of interest. The systematic hypothesis generation process effectively implemented using rule mining allows focusing on models describing the phenomenon of interest (e.g., potential discrimination in a group or population). At the same time, the rigorous statistical evaluation employed for model selection allows our method to discard a large amount of 'false positives' returned by rule mining whose output, indeed, turned out to be very noisy (cf. Figure 3). Overall, we observe some improvements when increasing the support and confidence thresholds. However, being constrained to the use of high values of support and confidence is in general not desirable, since it can lead to some interesting dependencies being missed, especially when investigating possible discrimination cases. These limitations appear to be overcome or significantly reduced with the use of regression models for model derivation and selection. This approach scored relatively well in all experiment settings. Even though there are few configurations in which the approach could not detect any interesting bias, this was due to perfect correlations among unrelated variables, obtained by the data generation procedure and not so likely to occur in real scenarios.

Robustness with respect to parameter tuning. Another notable positive aspect of the approach is that performances are much less dependent on parameterization. In this respect, the forest structure used for model comparison requires pairwise comparisons between models, which rapidly increases as more models are generated by the rules. Nevertheless, our approach proved to be able to detect biased relations even with low values of confidence and support; this suggests that it is suitable also to explore bias-affecting minorities. Different data structures and heuristics for model comparison (e.g., eliminating models with irrelevant variables from different branches) could be employed to decrease the computational overhead. Nonetheless, the advantage of limiting the impact of blind fine-tuning from the procedural setup provides the desirable advantage of assuring that precise (as defined above) results can be expected as long as support is small. This gives the analyst some leeway on the concern about setting the thresholds for support and confidence.

Understandability of the extracted recommendation. Our experiments show that the number of regressors remains manageable for being analyzed by a human policy maker, whereas the number of rules explodes. This suggests that our approach can be very effective in practice to obtain usable and statistically significant indications of bias. We also show how plotting the obtained regression models represents a useful aid to the policy maker to grasp additional information on which variables/models can be shown to the class to have interesting correlations. In particular, we discussed how confidence intervals can be exploited to obtain an informative overview on relations existing within models of a single configuration, providing the base for further exploration.

Assumptions and limitations. The proposed approach can only detect the statistical evidence of bias in cases where the data generation process is sufficiently biased to generate that evidence. This is unavoidable in any empirical approach. In cases where little data exist for the investigation, the statistical detection of small bias effects may fail, as evidence may be attributed to chance alone. In those cases, other approaches such as qualitative methods may be more appropriate. Similarly, while our approach proved to be less sensible to parameter tuning than rule mining, the impact of tuning can still be relevant when addressing datasets with severely underrepresented groups. In the absence of a ground-truth on discrimination levels and groups, our approach to generate a synthetic dataset aims to striking a balance between extreme cases, and considering general guidelines for discriminative actions (e.g., the four-fifths rule [20]) as guiding principles. Whereas a more thorough sensitive analysis for tuning parameters may provide additional estimates of method performance in more extreme cases, those estimates are likely to be misleading because of unknown confounding factors affecting the data. To showcase the applicability of our method, we therefore decided to not make any strong assumptions about the nature of our synthetic dataset.

Another important observation concerns the presence of so-called "proxy" rules and "redundant" rules. The first ones are rules which, while not directly classifiable as biased decisions, actually lead to biased and unfair decisions [4,21]. Redundant rules, instead, are rules that cover the same (or a similar) set of samples of one or more other rules in the dataset. The presence of these rules is typically due to the presence of some correlations within the features and can lead to misleading and/or unreliable outcomes. In our experiments, we assume that all the features relevant for the decisions are present in the dataset, and there is no strong spurious correlation among the features set. We plan to investigate these aspects in future work. Nevertheless, we would like to point out that some mitigation strategies can be applied. For example, proxy rules could be detected by interviewing, when possible, domain experts to understand the relevance and possible hidden use of the features of the dataset. On the other hand, to prevent the generation of redundant rules, one can apply, for example, feature selection approaches, or pruning the redundant rules using approaches such as [22].

6. Related Work

This section provides an overview of the research related to *model transparency*, in particular *features selection, association rule mining*, and discusses approaches based on *combining* association rule mining and regression analysis. A summary of these approaches with respect to the desiderata in Section 2 is given in Table 9.

Table 9. Comparison of the related work with respect to the desiderata for bias detection presented in Section 2, where ● means "support", ◑ "partially support", ○ "no support". The asterisk ('*') indicates that the requirement is only supported by some approaches.

	Data Agnostic	No Param. Tuning	Feature Level	Feature Value Level	Change Impact
Association Rule Mining	●	○	○	●	○
Features selection					
Filter Methods	●	○	●	○ *	○
Wrapping Methods	◑	○	●	○	○
Embedded Methods	◑	○	◑	○	○
Combined approaches	◑	○	●	◑	●
Our work	●	◑	●	●	●

The increasing adoption of classifiers to support human decision-making processes has led to an increasing importance of the transparency of the models generated by machine learning techniques. A recent survey on this topic [23] identifies two categories of problems related to model interpretability, i.e., *a black-box explanation problem*, where decisions returned by a black-box classifier are analyzed to construct an explanation, and a *transparent box design problem*, where the goal is to develop interpretable, white-box classifiers. Our work is related to approaches in the first category, which can be further refined in three subgroups: *model explanation* aims to provide human-interpretable models capable of mimicking the behavior of the original classifiers [24–26]; *outcome explanation* aims to build local models explaining predictions made on single instances [27,28]; *model inspection* aims to provide a human understandable representation of some specific properties of the model and/or its predictions [29,30].

Our work is mainly related to model explanation, particularly so-called *agnostic* approaches (i.e., approaches that are not tailored to a specific classifier), which usually provide explanations in terms of features ranking. This problem overlaps with the *feature selection* problem, whose goal is to identify and remove those features that either do not have an impact on the classification or are "redundant", i.e., they are correlated to other features [31–34]. These methods can be grouped into three main categories. *Filter* methods evaluate the discriminative power of features exploiting exclusively intrinsic proprieties (e.g., the statistical properties) of the data [35,36]. The outcome of a filter method can consist of either the set of features showing a correlation with the class above a user-defined threshold (so-called "univariate" methods), or groups of features showing the best trade-off in terms of correlations with the class and minimum correlations among each other (named "multi-variate" methods) [31,37,38]. Another class of feature selection methods consists of *wrapping* methods. Given a classifier, they look for the subset of features that provide the best results in terms of a classification quality metric, e.g., accuracy [39,40]. The search is performed either by adding or removing one feature at each iteration, then evaluating the obtained improvements. Wrapper methods usually perform significantly better than filter approaches; however, they are computationally intensive and thus, unsuitable for real-world applications characterized by a large feature space. Finally, *embedded* methods are feature selection approaches embedded in the classification process itself; namely, these approaches exploit an intrinsic model building metric to assess the importance of features during the construction of decision trees [41].

All three classes of feature selection techniques do not completely meet the desiderata identified in Section 2. Change impact analysis is only addressed by some embedding and filtering approaches, e.g., [42], while wrapping approaches mainly rely on classification accuracy. Only multi-variate filter approaches are data-agnostic. Wrapping and embedding methods only partially meet this desideratum: to obtain the best results, one should know the classifier used for the decisions being analyzed. All feature selection methods require parameter tuning. Analysis at the feature level is fully supported only by wrapping methods. Indeed, many filter and embedded methods only return the correlation values for a single feature; only few methods in these groups allow one to assess correlations between the class and groups of features. It is worth noting that none of the methods support the analysis at the feature value level.

A recent model transparency approach alternative to feature selection is presented in [43]. This approach aims to provide explanations related to some *subspace* of interest, i.e., groups of samples of the population presenting some characteristics of interest, usually represented in terms of itemsets. A set of classification rules is then derived for samples in those groups by means of a multi-objective optimization function taking into account factors such as rules overlapping, fidelity to the original classifiers behaviors, precision, etc. This work, however, has the same advantages and disadvantages of association rule mining (see Section 2.3).

Association rule mining has been largely applied to analyze decisional processes, especially for discrimination discovery [4,22]. Several metrics tailored to measure the impact of sensitive itemsets on the class have been proposed. In a seminal work on discrimination discovery [4], Ruggeri and colleagues introduced the notion of *extended lift*. This metric measures how the rule confidence varies with/without the discriminatory itemset, thus providing an evaluation of the relevance of this itemset. This approach, however, does not support any statistical validation of the discovered associations. To address this issue, several approaches have been proposed. Some focus on mining non-redundant rules by comparing each rule with its generalizations and discarding those rules, not showing any improvement in terms of support [44] or confidence [8]. Other approaches, instead, fall within the field of *statistical association rule mining*, i.e., they focus on mining statistically significant positive associations, ensuring that these associations are unlikely to be due to chance. Some approaches apply statistical tests to rule assessment metrics, e.g., the confidence intervals [45]. Statistical tests have also been used to validate feature-class correlations, filtering rules involving features with an insufficient/not significant level of correlations [9], or assessing possible correlations between itemsets and the class by means of hypothesis testing (e.g., [46–48]).

While these approaches do improve the statistical robustness of the discovered set of rules, they come with some drawbacks. Approaches exploiting relevance metrics only indirectly assess the statistical significance of the impact of the feature values on the class values.

Moreover, the use of different metrics can lead to different results, and some commonly-used metrics also come with some drawbacks. For example, it is well known that rules whose consequent has a high support tend to have a high value of confidence, without this implying a real dependency among the antecedent and the consequent [46]. Furthermore, confidence allows measuring only one direction of the impact of feature values, i.e., positive correlations. In addition, all these approaches are mainly intended as filtering mechanisms. Overall, the support provided to the statistical validation of discovered association rules is still limited and not as mature as in other techniques, such as regression analysis. Indeed, the scope of the performed evaluation is only limited to the values of the explanatory variables that occur in the rule under analysis. Little or no support is provided to explore how the impact changes with respect to the different values of the variables.

The combination of associations rules and regression analysis is mostly unexplored; to date, only a few approaches have investigated potential advantages and applications. For instance, Changpetch and Lin [49] investigated the use of association rule mining to detect the set of the most interesting interactions to take into account when building a regression model. However, rule mining is only used to identify interactions among features. Moreover, only a single model is returned, which does not allow differentiating among different possible contexts in which discrimination could have occurred. It is also worth noting that a very aggressive rule filtering mechanism is adopted, so that only correlations with a strong support are considered, which is not always desirable when dealing with biases that involve small portions of the overall population. Other approaches exploit rule mining in the iterative building of the (best) regression model. For example, Jaroszewicz [50] defines so-called *polynomial association rules* to determine non-linear correlations among a set of (continuous) features and the class, and use an iterative regression model-building procedure that picks the best polynomial rule at each step to determine the factor to include in the regression model. Furthermore, in this case, the output consists of a single, 'optimal' model; moreover, polynomial rules are targeted to numerical domains. Other approaches combine their predictive capabilities in a single hybrid system to enhance classification performance. For example, Kamei et al. [51] showed an application to determine faulty modules, where samples described by a (set of) rules are classified accordingly, while samples for which no rules are available are classified according to a regression model. In this respect, the two classification models are built independently from each other. Combined approaches behave similarly to regression analysis, supporting statistical validation and analysis at both feature and feature values level. However, they require parameter tuning for the application of rule mining. They also bring some improvements in terms of data-agnostic requirement, since the use of rule mining enhances classic model selection techniques. However, as their goal is to detect the "best" model, it does not support the generation of multiple hypotheses, so that they cannot identify multiple contexts involving biases.

7. Conclusions

In this work, we proposed a methodology that leverages both association rule mining and regression analysis to uncover systematic biases in decisional processes. Specifically, our methodology uses association rule mining to systematically generate hypotheses of bias sources from an exploration of data. These hypotheses are then used to build regression models that provide statistically significant evidence about the impact of variables on the process outcome. The experiments show that our methodology overcomes the limitations of standard association rule mining and regression analysis. However, while being able to detect the population that is discriminated against, it tends to provide only an indication of the targeted set of observations, as opposed to giving a precise picture of targeted sub-groups. This is to be expected from any statistical analysis, as noisy data and sample sizes affect clearly have an impact on the prediction. Nonetheless, the ability of filtering out a large number of overly specific rules and focusing only on a few that are highly likely to cover the population of interest (or otherwise point towards it), enables policy makers and analysts to focus on groups of observations where future investigations and data collection are likely to uncover the specific effect. Furthermore, we showed how confidence intervals can be effectively exploited to grasp an overview of the most important detected relations, thus providing valuable guidance for the human analyst. In future work, we plan to address some of the limitations discussed in Section 5. In particular, we plan to investigate the combination of different rules' redundancy reduction techniques with our approach in order to improve its robustness with respect to undesired correlations among features. In addition, we plan to apply our method in other contexts, for example to uncover indicative patterns of compromise in network traffic based on a security event generated by network security sensors as recorded by a security operation center.

Author Contributions: Conceptualization, L.G. and L.A. and N.Z.; methodology, L.G. and L.A. and N.Z.; software, L.G. and L.A. and N.Z.; validation, L.G. and L.A. and N.Z.; formal analysis, L.G. and L.A. and N.Z.; investigation, L.G. and L.A. and N.Z.; resources, L.G. and L.A. and N.Z.; data curation, L.G. and L.A. and N.Z.; writing—original draft preparation, L.G. and L.A. and N.Z.; writing—review and editing, L.G. and L.A. and N.Z.; visualization, L.G. and L.A. and N.Z.; supervision, L.G. and L.A. and N.Z.; project administration, L.G. and L.A. and N.Z.; funding acquisition, none. All authors have read and agreed to the published version of the manuscript.

Funding: This research received no external funding.

Institutional Review Board Statement: Not applicable.

Informed Consent Statement: Not applicable.

Data Availability Statement: Publicly available datasets were analyzed in this study. These data can be found here: [15,18].

Conflicts of Interest: The authors declare no conflict of interest.

Appendix A. Regression Output Interpretation

The output of a regression is the estimation of which values of $c, \beta_1, \ldots, \beta_n$ provide the best prediction of Y. For example, consider the following regression on `HighRisk`:

$$\texttt{HighRisk} = c + \beta_1 \, \texttt{Employed} + \beta_2 \, \texttt{Gender} + \beta_3 \, \texttt{Employed} \cdot \texttt{Gender}$$

This model will generate an output of the type reported in Table A1 (also fictitious for the purpose of this explanation).

Table A1. Example of regression output

Regressor	Coeff.	*p*-Value
c	3	<0.05
Employed $= N$	1.4	<0.01
Gender $= F$	−1.2	0.10
Employed $= N \wedge$ Gender $= F$	1.1	<0.01

This output indicates that unemployed (and male) subjects have a 22% ($\exp(0.2) = 1.22$) (as the outcome variable of this example is binary, a logistic regression should be used. For a *logit* regression, the outcome is the log odd ratio of the observation ($\log(p(HighRisk)/(1 - p(HighRisk))$); therefore, regression coefficients should be exponentiated to reveal the change in the odds ratio caused by a unit variation, or change in category in that variable.) higher probability of being assigned to the category `HighRisk` than to the category `LowRisk`. Being female (*and* employed) decreases chances by 70% ($\exp(-1.2) = 0.3$). The coefficient for `Employed` $= N \wedge$ `Gender` $= F$ tells us that, however, being female *and* unemployed increases the baseline risk three times ($\exp(1.1) = 3.0$). The statistical significance of each coefficient serves as an indication to the analyst that an estimation of at least that magnitude is unlikely to be generated if no real effect exists: the smaller the probability of observing an estimation at least that large (i.e., the infamous p-value [52]), the highest the confidence one can have that, given the data, the effect exists in reality and is unlikely to be explainable by chance alone. Generally, the threshold for significance is set at $p \leq 0.05$, but this may vary considerably depending on the domain of application. In the example above, the p-values suggest that all coefficients are statistically significant, with the exception of the variable Gender for which no strong evidence of significance emerges ($p = 0.1$). If one would set the significance level at 0.05, one would not reject the null hypothesis that the variable Gender has no effect on the outcome variable.

References

1. Sundaramurthy, S.C.; McHugh, J.; Ou, X.; Wesch, M.; Bardas, A.G.; Rajagopalan, S.R. Turning contradictions into innovations or: How we learned to stop whining and improve security operations. In *Symposium on Usable Privacy and Security*; USENIX Association: Berkeley, CA, USA, 2016; pp. 237–251.
2. Sundaramurthy, S.C.; Bardas, A.G.; Case, J.; Ou, X.; Wesch, M.; McHugh, J.; Rajagopalan, S.R. A human capital model for mitigating security analyst burnout. In *Symposium On Usable Privacy and Security*; USENIX Association: Berkeley, CA, USA, 2015; pp. 347–359.
3. Chen, T.R.; Shore, D.B.; Zaccaro, S.J.; Dalal, R.S.; Tetrick, L.E.; Gorab, A.K. An organizational psychology perspective to examining computer security incident response teams. *IEEE Secur. Priv.* **2014**, *12*, 61–67. [CrossRef]
4. Ruggieri, S.; Pedreschi, D.; Turini, F. Data mining for discrimination discovery. *ACM Trans. Knowl. Discov. Data* **2010**, *4*, 9:1–9:40. [CrossRef]
5. Tversky, A.; Kahneman, D. Judgment under Uncertainty: Heuristics and Biases. *Science* **1974**, *185*, 1124–1131. [CrossRef]
6. Agrawal, R.; Imieliński, T.; Swami, A. Mining Association Rules Between Sets of Items in Large Databases. *SIGMOD Rec.* **1993**, *22*, 207–216. [CrossRef]
7. Field, A. *Discovering Statistics Using IBM SPSS Statistics*; Sage: Thousand Oaksm, MA, USA, 2013.
8. Bayardo, R.J.; Agrawal, R.; Gunopulos, D. Constraint-based rule mining in large, dense databases. *Data Min. Knowl. Discov.* **2000**, *4*, 217–240. [CrossRef]
9. Shaharanee, I.N.M.; Hadzic, F.; Dillon, T.S. Interestingness measures for association rules based on statistical validity. *Knowl.-Based Syst.* **2011**, *24*, 386–392. [CrossRef]
10. Genga, L.; Allodi, L.; Zannone, N. Unveiling systematic biases in decisional processes: An application to discrimination discovery. In Proceedings of the Asia Conference on Computer and Communications Security, Auckland, New Zeland, 7–12 July 2019; ACM: New York, NY, USA, 2019; pp. 67–72.
11. Liu, B.; Hsu, W.; Ma, Y. Integrating classification and association rule mining. In Proceedings of the International Conference on Knowledge Discovery and Data Mining; AAAI Press: Palo Alto, CA, USA, 1998; pp. 80–86.
12. Tan, P.N.; Kumar, V.; Srivastava, J. Selecting the right objective measure for association analysis. *Inf. Syst.* **2004**, *29*, 293–313. [CrossRef]
13. Webb, G.I. Discovering significant rules. In Proceedings of the SIGKDD International Conference on Knowledge Discovery and Data Mining; ACM: New York, NY, USA, 2006; pp. 434–443.
14. Agresti, A. *Categorical Data Analysis*; John Wiley & Sons: Hoboken, NJ, USA, 2003; Volume 482,
15. UCI. Statlog (German Credit Data) Data Set. Available online: http://archive.ics.uci.edu/ml/datasets/statlog+(german+credit+data) (accessed on 20 December 2021).
16. Nasiriani, N.; Squicciarini, A.C.; Saldanha, Z.; Goel, S.; Zannone, N. Hierarchical Clustering for Discrimination Discovery: A Top-Down Approach. In Proceedings of the International Conference on Artificial Intelligence and Knowledge Engineering, Sardinia, Italy, 3–5 June 2019; IEEE: Piscataway, NJ, USA, 2019; pp. 187–194.
17. Pedreschi, D.; Ruggieri, S.; Turini, F. Integrating induction and deduction for finding evidence of discrimination. In Proceedings of the International Conference on Artificial Intelligence and Law, Barcelona, Spain, 8–12 June 2009; ACM: New York, NY, USA, 2009; pp. 157–166.
18. UCI. Communities and Crime Data Set. Available online: https://archive.ics.uci.edu/ml/datasets/Communities+and+Crime (accessed on 20 December 2021).
19. Qureshi, B.; Kamiran, F.; Karim, A.; Ruggieri, S. Causal discrimination discovery through propensity score analysis. *arXiv* **2016**, arXiv:1608.03735.
20. Bobko, P.; Roth, P.L. The four-fifths rule for assessing adverse impact: An arithmetic, intuitive, and logical analysis of the rule and implications for future research and practice. In *Research in Personnel and Human Resources Management*; Emerald Group Publishing Limited: Bingley, UK, 2004.
21. Hajian, S.; Domingo-Ferrer, J. A Methodology for Direct and Indirect Discrimination Prevention in Data Mining. *IEEE Trans. Knowl. Data Eng.* **2013**, *25*, 1445–1459. [CrossRef]
22. Genga, L.; Zannone, N.; Squicciarini, A. Discovering reliable evidence of data misuse by exploiting rule redundancy. *Comput. Secur.* **2019**, *87*, 101577. [CrossRef]

23. Guidotti, R.; Monreale, A.; Ruggieri, S.; Turini, F.; Giannotti, F.; Pedreschi, D. A survey of methods for explaining black box models. *ACM Comput. Surv.* **2018**, *51*, 93. [CrossRef]
24. Augasta, M.G.; Kathirvalavakumar, T. Reverse engineering the neural networks for rule extraction in classification problems. *Neural Process. Lett.* **2012**, *35*, 131–150. [CrossRef]
25. Craven, M.; Shavlik, J.W. Extracting tree-structured representations of trained networks. In *Advances in Neural Information Processing Systems*; MIT Press: Cambridge, MA, USA, 1996; pp. 24–30.
26. Schetinin, V.; Fieldsend, J.E.; Partridge, D.; Coats, T.J.; Krzanowski, W.J.; Everson, R.M.; Bailey, T.C.; Hernandez, A. Confident interpretation of Bayesian decision tree ensembles for clinical applications. *IEEE Trans. Inf. Technol. Biomed.* **2007**, *11*, 312–319. [CrossRef] [PubMed]
27. Ribeiro, M.T.; Singh, S.; Guestrin, C. Why should i trust you: Explaining the predictions of any classifier. In Proceedings of the SIGKDD International Conference on Knowledge Discovery and Data Mining, San Francisco,CA, USA, 13–17 August 2016; ACM: New York, NY, USA, 2016; pp. 1135–1144.
28. Xu, K.; Ba, J.; Kiros, R.; Cho, K.; Courville, A.; Salakhudinov, R.; Zemel, R.; Bengio, Y. Show, attend and tell: Neural image caption generation with visual attention. In Proceedings of the International Conference on Machine Learning, Lille, France, 6–11 July 2015; pp. 2048–2057.
29. Datta, A.; Sen, S.; Zick, Y. Algorithmic transparency via quantitative input influence: Theory and experiments with learning systems. In Proceedings of the Symposium on Security and Privacy, San Jose, CA, USA, 22–26 May 2016; IEEE: Piscataway, NJ, USA, 2016; pp. 598–617.
30. Seifert, C.; Aamir, A.; Balagopalan, A.; Jain, D.; Sharma, A.; Grottel, S.; Gumhold, S. Visualizations of deep neural networks in computer vision: A survey. In *Transparent Data Mining for Big and Small Data*; Springer: Berlin/Heidelberg, Germany, 2017; pp. 123–144.
31. Hall, M.A. Correlation-Based Feature Selection for Machine Learning. Ph.D. Thesis, The University of Waikato, Hamilton, NewZealand, 1999 .
32. Molina, L.C.; Belanche, L.; Nebot, À. Feature selection algorithms: A survey and experimental evaluation. In Proceedings of the International Conference on Data Mining, Maebashi City, Japan, 9–12 December 2002; IEEE: Piscataway, NJ, USA, 2002; pp. 306–313.
33. Chandrashekar, G.; Sahin, F. A survey on feature selection methods. *Comput. Electr. Eng.* **2014**, *40*, 16–28. [CrossRef]
34. Hastie, T.; Tibshirani, R.; Friedman, J.; Franklin, J. The elements of statistical learning: data mining, inference and prediction. *Math. Intell.* **2005**, *27*, 83–85.
35. Lazar, C.; Taminau, J.; Meganck, S.; Steenhoff, D.; Coletta, A.; Molter, C.; de Schaetzen, V.; Duque, R.; Bersini, H.; Nowe, A. A survey on filter techniques for feature selection in gene expression microarray analysis. *IEEE/ACM Trans. Comput. Biol. Bioinform.* **2012**, *9*, 1106–1119. [CrossRef]
36. Duch, W.; Wieczorek, T.; Biesiada, J.; Blachnik, M. Comparison of feature ranking methods based on information entropy. In Proceedings of the International Joint Conference on Neural Networks, Budapest, Hungary, 25–29 July 2004; IEEE: Piscataway, NJ, USA, 2004; Volume 2, pp. 1415–1419.
37. Karegowda, A.G.; Manjunath, A.; Jayaram, M. Comparative study of attribute selection using gain ratio and correlation based feature selection. *Int. J. Inf. Technol. Knowl. Manag.* **2010**, *2*, 271–277.
38. Zien, A.; Krämer, N.; Sonnenburg, S.; Rätsch, G. The feature importance ranking measure. In Proceedings of the Joint European Conference on Machine Learning and Knowledge Discovery in Databases, Bled, Slovenia, 7–11 September 2009; Springer: Berlin/Heidelberg, Germany, 2009; pp. 694–709.
39. Kohavi, R.; John, G.H. Wrappers for feature subset selection. *Artif. Intell.* **1997**, *97*, 273–324. [CrossRef]
40. Henelius, A.; Puolamäki, K.; Boström, H.; Asker, L.; Papapetrou, P. A peek into the black box: Exploring classifiers by randomization. *Data Min. Knowl. Discov.* **2014**, *28*, 1503–1529. [CrossRef]
41. Ratanamahatana, C.; Gunopulos, D. Feature selection for the naive Bayesian classifier using decision trees. *Appl. Artif. Intell.* **2003**, *17*, 475–487. [CrossRef]
42. Cai, Y.; Chow, M.Y.; Lu, W.; Li, L. Statistical feature selection from massive data in distribution fault diagnosis. *IEEE Trans. Power Syst.* **2010**, *25*, 642–648. [CrossRef]
43. Lakkaraju, H.; Kamar, E.; Caruana, R.; Leskovec, J. Faithful and customizable explanations of black box models. In Proceedings of the AAAI/ACM Conference on AI, Ethics, and Society, Honolulu, HI, USA, 27–28 January 2019; pp. 131–138.
44. Bastide, Y.; Pasquier, N.; Taouil, R.; Stumme, G.; Lakhal, L. Mining minimal non-redundant association rules using frequent closed itemsets. In Proceedings of the International Conference on Computational Logic, London, UK, 24–28 July 2000; Springer: Berlin/Heidelberg, Germany, 2000; pp. 972–986.
45. Pedreschi, D.; Ruggieri, S.; Turini, F. Measuring discrimination in socially-sensitive decision records. In Proceedings of the International Conference on Data Mining, Miami, FL, USA, 6–9 December 2009; SIAM: Philadelphia, PA, USA, 2009; pp. 581–592.
46. Brin, S.; Motwani, R.; Silverstein, C. Beyond market baskets: Generalizing association rules to correlations. In Proceedings of the SIGMOD International Conference on Management of Data, Tucson, AZ, USA, 13–15 May 1997; ACM: New York, NY, USA, 1997; pp. 265–276.
47. Hämäläinen, W.; Nykänen, M. Efficient discovery of statistically significant association rules. In Proceedings of the International Conference on Data Mining; IEEE: Piscataway, NJ, USA, 2008; pp. 203–212.

48. Liu, B.; Hsu, W.; Ma, Y. Pruning and summarizing the discovered associations. In Proceedings of the SIGKDD International Conference on Knowledge Discovery and Data Mining; ACM: New York, NY, USA, 1999; pp. 125–134.
49. Changpetch, P.; Lin, D.K. Model selection for logistic regression via association rules analysis. *J. Stat. Comput. Simul.* **2013**, *83*, 1415–1428. [CrossRef]
50. Jaroszewicz, S. Polynomial association rules with applications to logistic regression. In Proceedings of the SIGKDD International Conference on Knowledge Discovery and Data Mining, Philadelphia, PA, USA, 20–23 August 2006; ACM: New York, NY, USA, 2006; pp. 586–591.
51. Kamei, Y.; Monden, A.; Morisaki, S.; Matsumoto, K.i. A hybrid faulty module prediction using association rule mining and logistic regression analysis. In Proceedings of the ACM-IEEE International Symposium on Empirical Software Engineering and Measurement; ACM: New York, NY, USA, 2008; pp. 279–281.
52. Goodman, S. A dirty dozen: twelve *p*-value misconceptions. In *Seminars in Hematology*; Elsevier: Amsterdam, The Netherlands, 2008; Volume 45; pp. 135–140.

Journal of
Cybersecurity and Privacy

MDPI

Article

Functionality-Preserving Adversarial Machine Learning for Robust Classification in Cybersecurity and Intrusion Detection Domains: A Survey

Andrew McCarthy *, Essam Ghadafi, Panagiotis Andriotis and Phil Legg *

Computer Science Research Centre, University of the West of England, Bristol BS16 1QY, UK; essam.ghadafi@uwe.ac.uk (E.G.); panagiotis.andriotis@uwe.ac.uk (P.A.)
* Correspondence: andrew6.mccarthy@uwe.ac.uk (A.M.); phil.legg@uwe.ac.uk (P.L.)

Abstract: Machine learning has become widely adopted as a strategy for dealing with a variety of cybersecurity issues, ranging from insider threat detection to intrusion and malware detection. However, by their very nature, machine learning systems can introduce vulnerabilities to a security defence whereby a learnt model is unaware of so-called adversarial examples that may intentionally result in mis-classification and therefore bypass a system. Adversarial machine learning has been a research topic for over a decade and is now an accepted but open problem. Much of the early research on adversarial examples has addressed issues related to computer vision, yet as machine learning continues to be adopted in other domains, then likewise it is important to assess the potential vulnerabilities that may occur. A key part of transferring to new domains relates to functionality-preservation, such that any crafted attack can still execute the original intended functionality when inspected by a human and/or a machine. In this literature survey, our main objective is to address the domain of adversarial machine learning attacks and examine the robustness of machine learning models in the cybersecurity and intrusion detection domains. We identify the key trends in current work observed in the literature, and explore how these relate to the research challenges that remain open for future works. Inclusion criteria were: articles related to functionality-preservation in adversarial machine learning for cybersecurity or intrusion detection with insight into robust classification. Generally, we excluded works that are not yet peer-reviewed; however, we included some significant papers that make a clear contribution to the domain. There is a risk of subjective bias in the selection of non-peer reviewed articles; however, this was mitigated by co-author review. We selected the following databases with a sizeable computer science element to search and retrieve literature: IEEE Xplore, ACM Digital Library, ScienceDirect, Scopus, SpringerLink, and Google Scholar. The literature search was conducted up to January 2022. We have striven to ensure a comprehensive coverage of the domain to the best of our knowledge. We have performed systematic searches of the literature, noting our search terms and results, and following up on all materials that appear relevant and fit within the topic domains of this review. This research was funded by the Partnership PhD scheme at the University of the West of England in collaboration with Techmodal Ltd.

Keywords: cybersecurity; adversarial machine learning; machine learning; intrusion detection; functionality-preservation

Citation: McCarthy, A.; Ghadafi, A.; Andriotis, P.; Legg, P. Functionality-Preserving Adversarial Machine Learning for Robust Classification in Cybersecurity and Intrusion Detection Domains: A Survey. *J. Cybersecur. Priv.* **2022**, *2*, 154–190. https://doi.org/10.3390/jcp2010010

Academic Editor: Danda B. Rawat

Received: 31 January 2022
Accepted: 15 March 2022
Published: 17 March 2022

Publisher's Note: MDPI stays neutral with regard to jurisdictional claims in published maps and institutional affiliations.

1. Introduction

Machine learning (ML) has become widely adopted as a strategy for dealing with a variety of cybersecurity issues. Cybersecurity domains particularly suited to ML include: intrusion detection and prevention [1], network traffic analysis [2], malware analysis [3,4], user behaviour analytics [5], insider threat detection [6], social engineering detection [7], spam detection [8], detection of malicious social media usage [9], health misinformation [10], climate misinformation [11], and more generally "Fake News" [12]. These are essentially classification problems. Papernot et al. [13] stated that most ML models can be described mathematically as functions $h_0(x)$ with an input x and parameterized by a vector $\theta \in \Theta$, although some models such as K nearest neighbor are non-paremetric. The output of the the function $h_0(x)$ is the model's prediction of some property of interest for the given input x. The input x is usually represented as a vector of values called features. The space of functions $h = x \mapsto h_0(x)|\theta \in \Theta$ defines the set of candidate hypotheses. In supervised learning, the parameters are adjusted to align model predictions $h_0(x)$ with the expected output y. This is achieved by minimizing a loss function that captures the dissimilarity of $h_0(x)$ and the corresponding y. Model performance must be validated against a separate training dataset to confirm if the model also generalizes well for unseen data. Classification ML systems find a function (f) that matches a vector ($\vec{x}$) to its corresponding class (y).

Dhar et al. [14] noted that few studies analyzed the complexity of models and associated trade-offs between accuracy and complexity. The complexity of an algorithm is often expressed in *Big-O notation*. They reviewed models, stating the number of features and activations have an effect on memory usage and computational complexity. Moreover, they argued that accuracy alone cannot justify the choice of model type, particularly in regard to DNN; however, we consider the risks involved for inaccurate predictions will vary across domains. In security domains, greater accuracy may be considered critical, possibly assuaging concerns regarding computational complexity of models.

Critically, ML systems are increasingly trusted within cyber physical systems [15], such as power stations, factories, and oil and gas industries. In such complex physical environments, the potential damage that could be caused by a vulnerable system might even be life threatening [16]. Despite our reliance and trust in ML systems, the inherent nature of machine learning—learning to identify patterns—is in itself a potential attack vector for adversaries wishing to circumvent ML-based system detection processes. Adversarial examples are problematic for many ML algorithms and models including random forests (RF) and naive Bayes (NB) classifiers; however, we focus on artificial neural networks and particularly deep neural networks. Artificial neural networks (ANN) are inspired by the network of neurons in the human brain. ANNs are useful because they can generalize from a finite set of examples, essentially mapping a large input space (infinite for continuous inputs) to a range of discrete outputs. Unfortunately, in common with other ML algorithms, neural networks are vulnerable to attacks using carefully crafted perturbations to inputs, including evasion and poisoning attacks. In recent work, carefully crafted inputs described as "adversarial examples" are considered possible in ANN because of these inherent properties that exist within neural networks [17], such as:

1. The semantic information of the model is held across the model and not localised to specific neurons;
2. Neural networks learn input–output mappings that are discontinuous (and discontiguous).

These properties mean that even extremely small perturbations of an input could cause a neural network to provide a misclassified output. Given that neural networks have these properties, we reasonably expect our biological neural networks to suffer misclassifications, and/or to have evolved mitigations. Human brains are more complex than current artificial neural networks, yet they suffer a type of misclassification (illusory perception), in the form of face pareidolia [18,19]. This strengthens the case that the properties of neural networks are a source of adversarial examples (AE). In cybersecurity-related domains it has been seen how adversaries exploit adversarial examples, using carefully-crafted noise to evade detection through misclassification [20,21].

In this way, an adversarial arms race exists between adversaries and defenders. The recent SolarWinds supply chain attack [22,23] identified in December 2020 indicates the reliance that organisations have on intrusion detection software, and the presence of advanced persistent threats (APTs) with the expertise and resources to attack organisations' network defenses. Adversarial machine learning is a critical area of research. If not addressed, there is increasing potential for novel attack strategies that seek to exploit the inherent weaknesses that exist within machine learning models. For this reason, this survey addresses the issues related to the robustness of machine learning models against adversarial attacks across the cybersecurity domain, where problems of functionality-preservation are recognized. While we use a case study of a network-based intrusion detection system (NIDS), these issues might be applicable in other areas where ML systems are used. We focus on papers detailing adversarial attacks and defenses. Attacks are further classified by attack type, attack objective, domain, model, knowledge required, and constraints. Defenses are further categorised by defense type, domain, and model. In the domain of network traffic analysis, adversaries need to evade detection methods. A suitable network firewall will reject adversarial traffic and malformed packets while accepting legitimate traffic. Therefore, successful adversarial examples must be crafted to comply with domain constraints such as those related to the transmission control protocol/internet protocol (TCP-IP) stack. Moreover, adversaries wish to preserve the functionality of their attacks. A successful attack must not lose functionality at the expense of evading a classifier. The essence of a simple adversarial attack is that a malicious payload evades detection by masquerading as benign. We refer to this characteristic as *functionality-preserving*. Compared to domains such as computer vision whereby the image modification is only to fool human vision sensors, adversarial attacks in other domains are significantly more challenging to fool both a human and/or system-based sensor.

The major contributions of this paper are:

- We conduct a survey of the literature to identify the trends and characteristics of published works on adversarial learning in relation to cybersecurity, addressing both attack vectors and defensive strategies;

- We address the issue of functionality-preservation in adversarial learning in contrast to domains such as computer vision, whereby a malformed input must suitably fool a system process as well as a human user such that the original functionality is maintained despite some modification;

- We summarise this relatively-new research domain to address the future research challenges associated with adversarial machine learning across the cybersecurity domain.

The remainder of this paper is structured as follows: Section 2 provides an overview of other important surveys; Section 3 discusses background material; Section 4 details the literature survey; Section 5 details our results; Section 6 provides our discussion, and the conclusion summarises our findings and identifies research challenges.

2. Related Works

Corona et al. [24] provided a useful overview of intrusion detection systems. They predicted greater use of machine learning for intrusion detection and called for further investigation into adversarial machine learning. We now consider a number of related academic surveys that have been presented in the last five years with a focus on adversarial examples, security, and intrusion detection.

2.1. Secure and Trustworthy Systems

Machine learning systems are used in increasingly diverse areas including those of cyber-security. Trust in these systems is essential. Hankin and Barrère [25] note that there are many aspects to trustworthiness: reliability, trust, dependability, privacy, resilience, and safety. Adversaries ranging from solo hackers to state-sponsored APTs have an interest in attacking these systems. Successful attacks against machine learning models mean that systems are vulnerable and therefore potentially dangerously deployed in cyber-security domains. Cho et al. [26] proposed a framework considering the security, trust, reliability and agility metrics of computer systems; however, they did not specifically consider adversarial machine learning, or robustness to adversarial examples.

2.2. Adversarial ML in General

Papernot et al. [13] noted that the security and privacy of ML is an active but nascent area of research. In this early work, they systematized their findings on security and privacy in machine learning. They noted that a science for understanding many of the vulnerabilities of ML and countermeasures is slowly emerging. They analysed ML systems using the classical confidentiality, integrity and availability (CIA) model. They analysed: training in adversarial settings; inferring adversarial settings; and robust, fair, accountable, and private ML models. Through their analysis, they identified a total of eight key takeaways that point towards two related notions of sensitivity. The sensitivity of learning models to their training data is essential to privacy-preserving ML, and similarly the sensitivity to inference data is essential to secure ML. Central to both notions of sensitivity is the generalization error (i.e., the gap between performance on training and test data). They focused on attacks and defenses for machine learning systems and hoped that understanding the sensitivity of modern ML algorithms to the data they analysed will foster a science of security and privacy in machine learning. They argued that the generalization error of models is key to secure and privacy-preserving ML.

Zhang and Li [27] discussed opportunities and challenges arising from adversarial examples. They introduced adversarial examples and surveyed state-of-the-art adversarial example generation methods and defenses, before raising future research opportunities and challenges. They noted three challenges for the construction of adversarial examples:

1. The difficulty of building a generalizable method;
2. The difficulty in controlling the size of perturbation (too small will not result in adversarial examples, and too large can easily be perceived);
3. Difficulty in maintaining adversarial stability in real-world applications (some adversarial examples do not hold for transformations such as blurring).

They identified two challenges for defense against adversarial examples. First, blackbox attacks do not require knowledge of the model architecture and therefore cannot be easily resisted by modifying the model architecture or parameters. Second, defenses are often specific to an attack method and are less suitable as a general defense. Defenses against one attack method do not easily defend against adversarial examples based on other methods for generating adversarial examples. They subsequently identified three opportunities:

1. Construction of adversarial examples with high transferability (high confidence);
2. Construction of adversarial examples without perturbing the target image; they suggested that perturbation size will affect the success rate and transferability of adversarial examples;
3. Considering and modeling physical transformations (translation, rotation, brightness, and contrast).

Their focus was on the visual domain and they did not specifically discuss IDS or functionality-preserving adversarial attacks.

Apruzzese et al. [28] examined adversarial examples and considered realistic attacks, highlighting that most literature considers adversaries with complete knowledge about the classifier and are free to interact with the target systems. They further emphasized that few works consider "relizable" perturbations that take account of domain and/or real-world constraints. There is perhaps a perception that the threat from adversarial attacks is low based on the assumption that much prior knowledge of the system is required. This approach has some merit; however, this could be an over-confident position to take. Their idea was that realistically the adversary has less knowledge of the system. This conflicts with Shannon's maxim [29] and Kerckhoff's second cryptographic principle [30], which states that the fewer secrets the system contains, the higher its safety. The pessimistic "complete knowledge" position is often used in cryptographic studies; in cryptographic applications it is considered safe because it is a bleak expectation. This expectation is also realistic since we must expect well-resourced adversaries to eventually discover or acquire all details of the system. Many adversarial example papers assume complete knowledge; this is however unlikely to always be the case, perhaps leading some to believe models are more secure against adversarial examples. However, the transferability property of adversarial examples means that complete knowledge is not required for successful attacks, and black-box attacks are possible with no prior knowledge of machine learning models. An adversary may only learn through interacting with the model. We must therefore account for the level of knowledge required by an adversary, including white-box, black-box, and gray-box knowledge paradigms.

2.3. Intrusion Detection

Wu et al. [31] considered several types of deep learning systems for network attack detection, including supervised and unsupervised models, and they compared the efficiency and effectiveness of different attack detection methods using two intrusion detection datasets: the "KDD Cup 99" dataset and an improved version known as NSL-KDD [32,33]. These two datasets have been used widely in the past by academic researchers; however, they do not fairly represent modern network traffic analysis problems due to concept-drift. Networks have increasing numbers of connected devices, increasing communications per second, and new applications using the network. The use of computer networks and the Internet has changed substantially in twenty years. The continued introduction of IPv6, network address translation, Wi-Fi, mobile 5G networks, and cloud providers has changed network infrastructure [34]. Furthermore, the Internet is now increasingly used for financial services. Akamai [35] reported that financial services now see millions or tens of millions of attacks each day. These attacks were less common twenty years ago. Furthermore, social media now constitutes much internet traffic and most social media platforms were founded after the KDD Cup 99 and NSL-KDD datasets were introduced. For example, Facebook, YouTube, and Twitter were founded in 2004, 2005, and 2006, respectively. This limits the validity of some research using outdated datasets. Therefore, we suggest research should use modern datasets that represent modern network traffic.

Kok et al. [36] analysed intrusion detection systems (IDS) that use a machine learning approach. They specifically considered the datasets used, the ML algorithms, and the evaluation metrics. They warned that some researchers are still using datasets first introduced decades ago (e.g., KDD Cup 99, NSL-KDD). They warned that this trend could result in no or insufficient progress on IDS. This would ultimately lead to the untenable position of obsolete IDS while intrusion attacks continue to evolve along with user behaviour and the introduction of new technologies. Their paper did not consider adversarial examples or robustness of ML models. Alatwi and Morisset [37] tabulated a list of network intrusion datasets in the literature that we extend in Table 1.

Table 1. Datasets used in the literature.

Work	Dataset	Network	Year	Attack Categories
[32]	KDD Cup 99	Traditional	1999	DoS, Probe, User 2 Root and Remote to User
[38]	NSL-KDD	Traditional	2009	DoS, Probe, User 2 Root and Remote to User
[39]	DARPA	Traditional	2009	DDoS, Malware, Spambots, Scans, Phishing
[40]	CTU-13	Traditional	2011	Botnet
[41]	Kyoto	Traditional	2015	Botnet
[42]	UNSW-NB15	Traditional	2016	Backdoors, Fuzzers, DoS, Generic, Shell code, Reconnaissance, Worms, Exploits, Analysis
[43]	WSN-D5	Wireless	2016	Greyhole, Blackhole, Scheduling, Flooding.
[44]	SDN Traffic	SDN	2016	DDoS
[45]	CICIDS2017	Traditional	2017	DoS, DDoS, SSH-Patator, Web, PortScan, FTP-Patator, Bot.
[46]	Mirai	IoT	2017	Botnet
[45]	CICIDS2018	Traditional	2018	Bruteforce Web, DoS, DDoS, Botnet, Infiltration.
[45]	CICDDoS2019	Traditional	2019	DDoS
[47]	Bot-IOT	IoT	2018	DDoS, DoS, OS Service Scan, Keylogging, Data exfiltration
[48]	Kitsune	IoT	2018	Recon, Man in the Middle, DoS, Botnet Malware
[49]	IEEE BigData Cup	Traditional	2019	N/A
[50]	HIKARI-2021	IoT	2021	Brute force attack, Brute force attack (XMLRPC), Vulnerability, probing, Synthetic Traffic

Martins et al. [51] considered adversarial machine learning for intrusion detection and malware scenarios, noting that IDS are typically signature-based, and that machine learning approaches are being widely employed for intrusion detection. They described five "tribes" of ML algorithms before detailing some fundamentals of adversarial machine learning, including commonly used distance metrics: L_∞, L_0, and L_2. They subsequently described common white-box methods to generate adversarial examples, including: Broyden–Fletcher–Goldfarb–Shanno algorithm (L-BFGS), the fast gradient sign method (FGSM), Jacobian-based saliency map attack (JSMA), Deepfool, and Carlini and Wagner attacks (C&W). They also considered black-box methods using generative adversarial networks (GANS). Traditional GANS sometimes suffer problems of mode collapse. Wasserstein generative adversarial networks (WGANS) solve some of these problems. They introduced Zeroth-order optimization attack (ZOO) as a black-box method. ZOO *estimates* the gradient and optimises an attack by iteratively adding perturbations to features. They noted that most attacks have been initially tested in the image domain, but can be applied to other types of data, which poses a security threat. Furthermore, they considered there is a trade-off when choosing an adversarial attack. For example, JSMA is more computationally intensive than FGSM but modifies fewer features. They considered JSMA to be the most realistic attack because it perturbs fewer features. When considering defenses, they tabulated advantages and disadvantages of common defenses. For example, feature squeezing is effective in image scenarios, but unsuitable for other applications because compression methods would result in data loss for tabular data. They noted that GANS are a very powerful technique that can result in effective adversarial attacks where the samples follow a similar distribution to the original data but cause misclassification.

2.4. Cyber-Physical Systems

Cyber-physical systems (CPSs) rely on computational systems to create actuation of physical devices. The range of devices is increasing from factory operations to power stations, autonomous vehicles, and healthcare operations. Shafique et al. [52] considered such smart cyber-physical systems. They discussed reliability and security vulnerabilities of machine learning systems, including hardware trojans, side channel attacks, and adversarial machine learning. This is important, because system aging and harsh operating environments mean CPSs are vulnerable to numerous security and reliability concerns. Advanced persistent threats could compromise the training or deployment of CPSs through stealthy supply-chain attacks. A single vulnerability is sufficient for an adversary to cause a misclassification that could lead to drastic effects in a CPS (e.g., an incorrect steering decision of an autonomous vehicle could cause a collision). We consider that vulnerabilities in ML could lead to a range of unwanted effects in CPSs, including those that could lead to life-threatening consequences [16]. The Stuxnet worm is an example of malware with dire consequences.

2.5. Contributions of This Survey

Our main objectives are:

- Collect and collate current knowledge regarding robustness and functionality-preserving attacks in cybersecurity domains;
- Formulate key takeaways based on our presentation of the information, aiming to assist understanding of the field.

This survey aims to complement existing work while addressing clear differences, by also studying the robustness of adversarial examples, specifically functionality-preserving use cases. Most previous work aimed to improve the accuracy of models or examine the effect of adversarial examples. Instead, we consider the robustness of models to adversarial examples.

Machine learning systems are already widely adopted in cybersecurity. Indeed, with increasing network traffic, automated network monitoring using ML is becoming essential. Modern computer networks carry private personal and corporate data including financial transactions. These data are an attractive lure to cyber-criminals. Adversaries may wish to steal or disturb data. Malware, spyware, and ransomware threats are endemic on many computer networks. IDS help keep networks safe; however, an adversarial arms race exists, and it is likely that adversaries, including advanced persistent threats, are developing new ways to evade network defenses. Some research has evaded intrusion detection classifiers using adversarial examples.

We identify that while adversarial examples in the visual domain are well understood, less work has focused on how adversarial examples can be applied to network traffic analysis and other non-visual domains, similarly to machine learning models used for image and object recognition. For example, convolutional neural networks (CNNs) are well researched, whereas other model types used for intrusion detection, e.g., recurrent neural networks (RNNs), receive less attention. The generation of adversarial examples to fool IDS is more complicated than visual domains because the features include discrete and non-continuous values [53]. Compounding the defense against adversarial examples is the overconfident assumption that successful adversarial examples require "complete knowledge" of the model and parameters. On the contrary, black-box attacks are possible with no or limited knowledge of the model. Most defenses so far proposed consider the visual domain and most are ineffective against strong and black-box attacks. This survey addresses the problem of adversarial machine learning across cyber-security domains. Further research is required to head off future mature attack methods that could facilitate more complex and destructive attacks.

3. Background

Here we provide further background on some key concepts that are related to adversarial learning, to support the reader of this survey. We cover the topics of model training, robustness, common adversarial example algorithms, adversary capabilities, goals, and attack methods.

3.1. Model Training

It is important to consider the dataset on which models are trained, because the trustworthiness and quality of a model is impacted by the distribution, quality, quantity, and complexity of dataset training samples [54]. Biased models are more susceptible to adversarial examples. Therefore, models must be trained on unbiased training data; however, Johnson et al. considered that the *absolute* number of training samples may be more important than the ratio of class imbalance [55]. For example, a small percentage of a large number of samples is sufficient to train a model regardless of high class imbalance (e.g., 1% malicious samples in 1 million network flows yields 10,000 samples). Unfortunately, cybersecurity datasets are often prone to bias, in part because of limited samples of some malicious traffic (e.g., *zero-day* attacks) and large amounts of benign traffic. Sheatsley et al. [56] state biased distributions enable successful adversarial examples with the modification of very few features.

3.1.1. Resampling

Three common data-level techniques tackle biased datasets by resampling:

- Oversampling: Random samples of minority classes are duplicated until the bias of majority classes is compensated;
- Undersampling: Random samples from the majority class are discarded until the bias of majority classes is compensated;
- Hybrid Sampling: Combines modest oversampling of minority classes and modest undersampling of majority classes aiming to give better model performance than applying either technique alone.

Algorithm-level techniques tackling dataset bias commonly employ cost-sensitive learning where a class penalty or weight is considered or decision thresholds are shifted to reduce bias [55].

3.1.2. Loss Functions

When training a model the goal is to minimize the loss function through use of an optimizer that adjusts the weights at each training step. Common optimizers include stochastic gradient descent (SGD), adaptive moments (Adam), and root mean squared propagation (RMSProp). Commonly, a regularizer is employed during training to ensure the model generalizes well to new data. A dropout layer is often employed as a regularizer.

The loss function must be chosen carefully: for binary classification binary_crossentropy (Equation (1)) is usual; for multiclass classification problems categorical_crossentropy (Equation (2)) or mean_squared_error (Equation (3)) are suitable.

$$f_{\text{binary\_crossentropy}}(y) = -y_i^{label} \log y_i i^{prediction} - \left(1 - y_i^{label}\right) \log \left(1 - y_i^{prediction}\right) \quad (1)$$

$$f_{\text{categorical\_crossentropy}}(y) = -\sum_{i=1}^{categories} y_i^{label} \log y_i^{prediction} \quad (2)$$

$$f_{\text{mean\_squared\_error}}(y) = \frac{1}{categories} \sum_{i=1}^{categories} \left(y_i^{label} - y_i^{prediction}\right)^2 \quad (3)$$

3.1.3. Cross Validation

Cross validation [57] is a widely used data resampling method to assess the generalizability of a model and to prevent over-fitting. Cross validation often involves stratified random sampling, meaning the sampling method retains the class proportions in the learning set. In leave-one-out cross validation, each sample is used in turn as the validation set. The test error approximates the true prediction error; however, it has high variance. Moreover, its computational cost can be high for large datasets. k-fold cross validation aims to optimise the bias/variance trade-off. In k-fold cross validation, the dataset is randomly split into k equal size partitions. A single partition is retained for test data, and the remaining $k-1$ partitions are used for training. The cross validation steps are reiterated until each partition is used once for validation, as shown in Figure 1. The results are averaged across all iterations to produce an estimation of the performance of the model (Equation (4)). Refaelzadeh et al. highlighted risks of elevated Type I errors (false positives). With larger values of k, variance is reduced. Moreover, bias also reduces because the model is trained on more of the dataset. We posit that resampling techniques could be used to improve robustness against adversarial examples.

$$CV_{(k)} = \frac{1}{k} \sum_{i=1}^{k} MSE_i \quad (4)$$

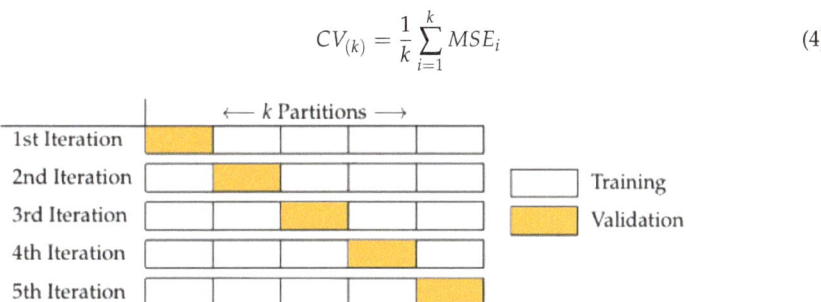

Figure 1. k-fold cross validation.

3.1.4. Bootstrapping

Bootstrapping is resampling with replacement, and is often used to statistically quantify the performance of a model, to determine if a model is statistically significantly better than other models.

3.2. Robustness

Robustness can be defined as the performance of well-trained models facing adversarial examples [58]. Essentially, robustness considers how sensitive a model's output is to a change in the input. The robustness of a model is related to the generalization error of the model. There is a recognised trade-off between accuracy and robustness in machine learning. That is, highly accurate models are less robust to adversarial examples. Machine learning models in adversarial domains must be both highly accurate and robust. Therefore, improving the robustness of machine learning models enables safer deployment of ML systems across a wider range of domains.

To critically evaluate and make fair comparisons, robustness metrics are necessary. Common metrics include precision (Equation (5)), recall (Equation (6)), and F1-score (Equation (7)).

$$Precision = \frac{TruePositives}{TruePositives + FalsePositives} \tag{5}$$

$$Recall = \frac{TruePositives}{TruePositives + FalseNegatives} \tag{6}$$

$$F1Score = 2 \times \frac{Precision \times Recall}{Precision + Recall} \tag{7}$$

Other possible useful metrics to evaluate robustness include: the Lipschitzian property, which monitors the changes in the output with respect to small changes to inputs; and CLEVER (cross-Lipschitz extreme value for network robustness), which is an extreme value theory (EVT)-based robustness score for large-scale deep neural networks (DNNs). The proposed CLEVER score is attack-agnostic and computationally feasible for large neural networks improving on the Lipschitzian property metric [59]. Table 2 details some advantages and disadvantages of some robustness metrics.

Table 2. Robustness metrics.

Work	Metric	Advantages	Disadvantages
N/A [59]	F1-Score CLEVER	Commonly used by researchers. Attack-agnostic and computationally feasible.	Biased by the majority class CLEVER is less suited to black-box attacks and where gradient masking occurs [60]; However, extensions to CLEVER help mitigate these scenarios [61].
[62]	Empirical robustness	Suitable for very deep neural networks and large datasets.	N/A

3.3. Common Adversarial Example Algorithms

There are numerous algorithms to produce adversarial examples. Szegedy et al. [17] used a box-constrained limited memory L-BFGS. Other methods include FGSM [63] and iterative derivatives, including the basic iterative method (BIM) and projected gradient descent (PGD). JSMA optimises for the minimal number of altered features (L_0). The Deepfool algorithm [62] optimises for the root-mean-square (Euclidean distance, L_2). Carlini and Wagner [64] proposed powerful C&W attacks optimizing for the L_0, L_2, and L_∞ distance metrics. There are many algorithms to choose from. Furthermore, Papernot et al. [65] developed a software library for the easy generation of adversarial examples. There are now a number of similar libraries that can be used to generate adversarial examples, as shown in Table 3.

Table 3. Libraries for Generating Adversarial Examples.

Work	Library Name	Year	Advantages	Disadvantages
[65]	CleverHans	2016	Recently updated to v4.0.0, well used by the community. MIT License	Can be complicated to configure.
[66]	Foolbox	2017	Fast generation of adversarial examples. MIT License	Large number of open issues.
[67]	Adversarial robustness toolbox	2018	Well maintained and supported. Supports most known machine learning frameworks. Extensive attacks and model robustness tools are supported.	Does not support all models.
[68]	Advertorch	2019	GNU lesser public license.	Few active contributors.

Moreover, algorithms such as FGSM that modify all features are unlikely to preserve functionality. Algorithms such as JSMA that modify a small subset of features are not guaranteed to preserve functionality; however, with fewer modified features, the likelihood improves. Checking for and keeping only examples that preserve functionality is possible, although it is a time-consuming and inelegant solution. A potentially better solution could ensure only functionality-preserving adversarial examples are generated.

When considering the robustness of machine learning models, we first must consider the threat model. We must consider how much the adversary knows about the classifier, ranging from *no knowledge* to *perfect knowledge*. Adversaries may have a number of different goals:

1. Accuracy degradation (where the adversary wants to sabotage the effectiveness of the overall classifier accuracy);
2. Target misclassification (where the adversary wants to misclassify a particular instance as another given class);
3. Untargeted classification (where the adversary wants to misclassify a particular instance to any random class).

We now consider the attack surface. In IDS, the attack surface can be considered as an end-to-end pipeline, with varying vulnerabilities and potential for compromise at each stage of the pipeline.

In one basic pipeline, as shown in Figure 2, the raw network traffic on network interfaces is collected as packet capture files (PCAPs), which are then processed into network flows. There are different applications that could be used to process PCAPs into network flows. CICFlowMeter [69] is a network traffic flow generator and analyser that has been used in cyber-security datasets [70,71] and produces bidirectional flows with over 80 statistical network traffic features. The generated flows are unlabelled and so must be labelled manually with the traffic type, typically benign/malicious, although multiclasses could be labelled given sufficient information including attack type, IP source and destination dyad, duration, and start time. Finally, the labelled flows are used to train the model. Repetitive training cycles could enable detection of new attacks; however, the cyclic nature of the training means that an adversary could attack any iteration of training. Furthermore, an adversary could choose to attack any point in the pipeline. The training data used to train the model generally consist of feature-vectors and expected outputs, although some researchers are considering unsupervised learning models. The collection and validation of these data offer an attack surface. Separately, the inference phase also offers an attack surface. It is interesting to note that the size of the feature set a machine learning model uses can be exploited as an attack surface. A fundamental issue is that each feature processed by a model may be modified by an adversary. Moreover, Sarker et al. [72] noted that the computational complexity of a model can be reduced by reducing the feature dimensions. Large feature sets include more features and hence provide more opportunities to an adversary for manipulation. Almomani et al. [73] indicated that accuracy can be maintained with fewer features, and McCarthy et al. [74] indicated that more features tend to reduce the necessary size of perturbations. Therefore, larger feature sets are more readily perturbed than smaller feature sets, which have fewer modifiable features and hence require larger perturbations.

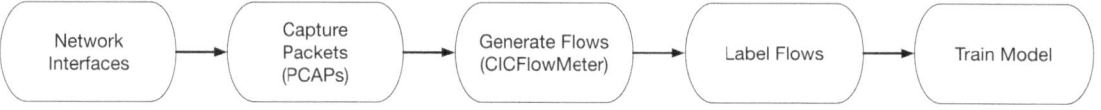

Figure 2. End-to-end pipeline for network intrusion detection system.

3.4. Threat Model—Adversary Capabilities

Adversaries are constrained by their skills, knowledge, tools, and access to the system under attack. An insider threat might have access to the classification model and other associated knowledge, whereas an external threat might only be able to examine data packets. While the attack surface may be the same for both adversaries, the insider threat is potentially a much stronger adversary because they have greater knowledge and access. Adversary capabilities mean that attacks can be split into three scenarios: white-box, black-box, and gray-box.

In white-box attacks, an adversary has access to all machine learning model parameters. In black-box attacks, the adversary has no access to the machine learning model's parameters. Adversaries in black-box scenarios may therefore use a different model, or no model at all, to generate adversarial examples. The strategy depends on successfully transferring adversarial examples to the target model. Gray-box attacks consider scenarios where an adversary has some, but incomplete, knowledge of the system. White-box and black-box are most commonly considered.

3.5. Threat Model—Adversary Goals

Adversaries aim to subvert a model through attacking its confidentiality, integrity, or availability. Confidentiality attacks attempt to expose the model or the data encapsulated within. Integrity attacks occur when an adversary attempts to control the output of the model, for example, to misclassify some adversarial traffic and therefore allow it to pass a detection process. Availability attacks could misclassify all traffic types, or deteriorate a model's confidence, consistency, performance, and access. In this way, an integrity attack resembles a subset of availability attack, since an incorrect response is similar in nature to a correct response being unavailable; however, the complete unavailability of a response would likely be more easily noticed than decreases in confidence, consistency, or performance. The goals of an adversary may be different but are often achieved with similar methods.

3.6. Threat Model—Common Attack Methods

Figure 3 shows some common categories of adversarial machine learning attack methods, that we explore in this section.

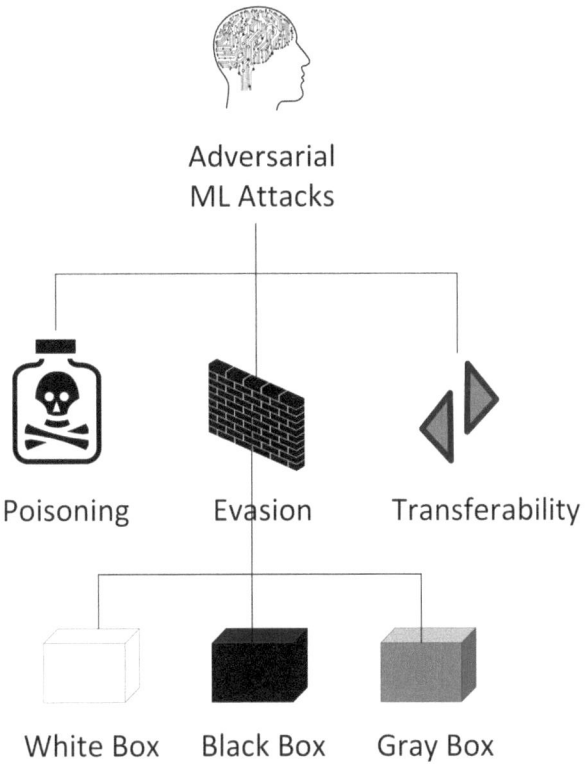

Figure 3. Common adversarial machine learning attacks.

3.6.1. Poisoning

An adversary with access to the training data or procedure manipulates it, implanting an attack during the training phase, when the model is trained on adversarial training data. This is achieved with carefully crafted noise or sometimes random noise. Unused or dormant neurons in a trained deep neural network (DNN) signify that a model can learn more; essentially, an increased number of neurons allows for a greater set of distinct decision boundaries forming distinct classifications of data. The under-utilised degrees of freedom in the learned model could potentially be used for unexpected classification of inputs. That is, the model could learn to provide selected outputs based on adversarial inputs. These neurons have very small weights and biases. However, the existence of such neurons allows successful poisoning attacks through training the model to behave differently for poisoned data. This suggests that distillation [75] could be effective at preventing poisoning attacks, because smaller models have lower knowledge capacity and likely fewer unused neurons. Distillation reduces the number of neurons that contribute to a model by transferring knowledge from a large model to a smaller model. Despite initial analysis indicating reduction in the success of adversarial attacks, Carlini [64] experimented with three powerful adversarial attacks and a high confidence adversarial example in a transferability attack, and found that distillation does not eliminate adversarial examples and provides little security benefit over undistilled networks in relation to powerful attacks. Unfortunately, they did not specifically consider poisoning attacks. Additional experiments could determine whether distillation is an effective defense against poisoning attacks.

3.6.2. Evasion

In evasion attacks, the adversary is often assumed to have no access to the training data. Instead, adversaries exploit their knowledge of the model and its parameters, aiming to minimise the cost function of adversarial noise, which, when combined with the input, causes changes to the model output. Untargeted attacks lead to a random incorrect output, targeted attacks lead to a specific incorrect output, and an attack may disrupt the model by changing the confidence of the output class. In the visual domain, the added noise is often imperceptible to humans. In non-visual domains such as intrusion detection, this problem may be much more challenging, since even small modifications may corrupt network packets and may cause firewalls to drop these malformed packets. This highlights the need for functionality preservation in adversarial learning as a clear distinction from vision-based attacks that exploit the human visual system.

3.6.3. Transferability

The transferability property of adversarial examples means that adversarial examples generated against one model will likely also work against other models trained for the same purpose. The second model need not have the same architecture or underlying model as the first and need not be trained on the same data. The transferability property of adversarial examples can form the basis for some black-box attacks where a surrogate model is used to generate adversarial examples that are subsequently presented to the target model.

4. Methodology

In this section, we describe our approach to surveying the literature so as to conduct an effective and meaningful survey of the literature.

Eligibility Criteria We determined our search terms leading to the most relevant articles. We chose the search terms detailed in Table 4.

Table 4. Topics and associated search terms used in this survey.

Topic	Search Query
Cyber security/intrusion detection	("cyber security" OR "intrusion detection" OR "IDS")
Adversarial machine learning attacks and defences	("adversarial machine learning" OR "machine learning" OR "adversarial example") and ("attack" OR "defence")
Robustness/Functionality Preservation	((("robustness" OR "generalization error" OR "accuracy" OR "f1score" OR "f-score" OR "TPR" OR "FPR") OR ((("functionality" OR "payload") AND "preservation")))

We expect these to result in good coverage of the relevant literature. We searched each database using the identified search terms. The literature search was conducted up to September 2021. Generally, we have chosen to exclude works that have not yet been peer-reviewed, such as those appearing on arXiv, unless deemed by the authors as a significant paper that makes a clear contribution to the subject domain. We collated the searches and any subsequent duplicates were removed. Each paper was screened by reading the title and abstract to determine the relevance. Inclusion criteria were: the article is related to functionality preservation in adversarial machine learning for cybersecurity or intrusion detection with insight into robust classification.

From this large list, we specifically focused on adversarial machine learning attacks and defenses, narrowing the literature down to relevant papers. Our selection process was roughly based on the preferred reporting items for systematic meta-analysis (PRISMA) framework [76]. Figure 4 details our selection process.

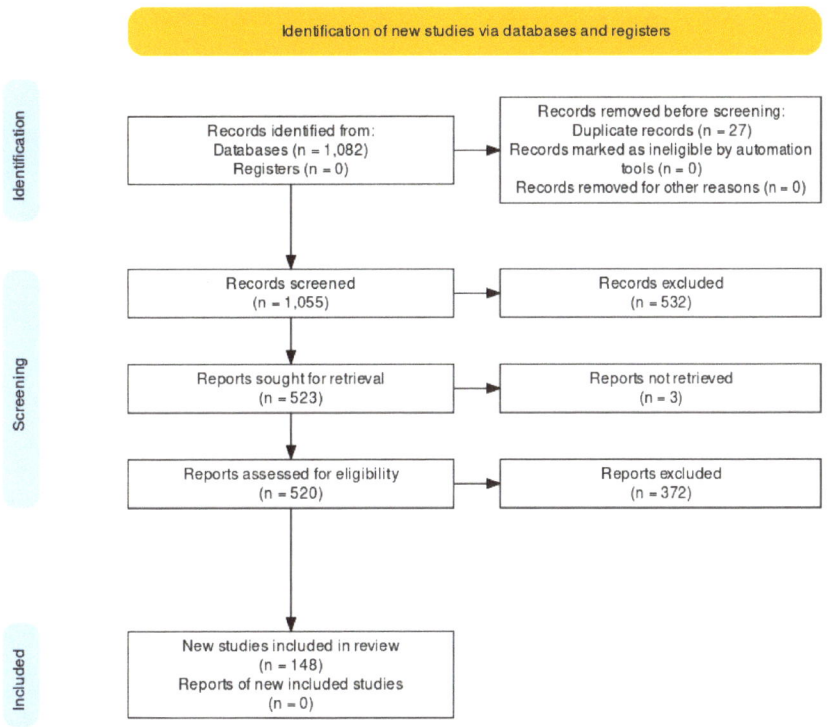

Figure 4. Preferred reporting items for systematic meta-analysis.

Information Sources We selected the following databases with a sizeable computer science element to search and retrieve literature: **IEEE Xplore**, **ACM Digital Library**, **ScienceDirect**, **Scopus**, **SpringerLink**, and **Google Scholar**.

5. Results

In this section, we describe the results of our search and selection process. We further describe our classification scheme, and tabulate and discuss our findings, including adversarial attacks in traditional and cybersecurity domains of malware, IDS, and CPS. We included 146 relevant papers in this survey.

5.1. Classification Scheme

We classify attacks by attack type, attack objective (targeted/untargeted), domain, model, knowledge required, and whether any constraints are placed on the adversarial examples. Defenses are classified by type, domain, and model. We summarise the attacks in Table 5.

Table 5. Chronologically ordered summary of adversarial example attacks.

Work	Year	Attack	Type			Obj		Domain			Model			Knowledge			Constraint		
			AE	Sequence of AEs	Transferability	Targeted	Untargeted	Visual	Cybersecurity	Text	MLP	CNN	RNN	White-Box	Black-box	Gray-Box	Box	Sparse	Func-Preserving
[17]	2014	L-BFGS	✓			✓		✓				✓		✓			✓		
[77]	2013	GradientDescent	✓			✓		✓				✓		✓		✓			
[78]	2016	Adversarial Sequences		✓			✓		✓				✓	✓					✓
[79]	2016	JSMA	✓			✓	✓	✓				✓		✓				✓	
[62]	2016	Deepfool	✓				✓	✓				✓		✓					
[80]	2017	AddSent,AddOneSent	✓	✓			✓			✓			✓			✓			
[81]	2018	GAN	✓				✓	✓				✓			✓				
[82]	2017	EnchantingAttack		✓		✓		✓		✓				✓					
[82]	2017	StrategicAttack	✓			✓		✓		✓				✓					
[64]	2017	C&W, L_0, L_2, L_∞	✓				✓	✓				✓		✓					
[83]	2017	FGSM,JSMA	✓				✓		✓		✓			✓					
[84]	2018	Generative RNN	✓				✓		✓				✓		✓				✓
[85]	2018	NPBO	✓				✓		✓		✓			✓					✓
[86]	2018	GADGET	✓				✓		✓				✓		✓				✓
[87]	2018	JSMA,FGSM,DeepFool,CW	✓			✓			✓		✓			✓					
[88]	2018	FGSM	✓				✓		✓		✓			✓					
[89]	2018	IDS-GAN	✓				✓		✓		✓				✓				
[90]	2018	ZOO,GAN	✓				✓		✓		✓				✓				
[91]	2019	One Pixel Attack	✓			✓		✓				✓		✓				✓	
[92]	2019	ManifoldApproximation	✓				✓		✓		✓				✓				✓
[93]	2019	FGSM,BIM,PGD	✓				✓		✓		✓			✓		✓			
[94]	2019	GAN Attack	✓				✓		✓		✓				✓				✓
[95]	2020	PWPSA	✓	✓	✓		✓		✓				✓	✓					✓
[95]	2020	GA	✓	✓	✓		✓		✓				✓	✓					✓
[96]	2020	One Pixel Attack	✓				✓		✓			✓		✓				✓	
[97]	2020	Opt Attack,GAN Attack	✓				✓		✓		✓				✓				✓
[98]	2021	GAMMA	✓				✓		✓						✓				✓
[99]	2021	UAP	✓				✓		✓		✓			✓		✓			✓
[100]	2020	Variational Auto Encoder	✓				✓		✓		✓			✓					✓
[101]	2021	Best-Effort Search	✓				✓		✓		✓	✓		✓	✓	✓	✓		✓

5.2. Adversarial Example Attacks

The attacks we focus on exploit adversarial examples that cause differences in the output of neural networks. Adversarial examples were discovered by Szegedy et al. [17]. Adversarial examples are possible in ANN as a consequence of the properties of neural networks; however, they are possible for other ML models. This complicates mitigation efforts, and adversarial examples can be found for networks explicitly trained on adversarial examples [102]. Furthermore, adversarial examples can be algorithmically generated, e.g., using gradient descent. Moreover, adversarial examples are often transferable, that is, an adversarial example presented to a second machine learning model trained on a subset of the original dataset may also cause the second network to misclassify the adversarial example.

5.2.1. Adversarial Examples—Similarity Metrics

In the visual domain, distance metrics are well used to judge how similar two inputs are, and therefore how easy the differences might be perceived. The following metrics are commonly used to describe the difference between normal and adversarial inputs:

- Number of altered pixels, (L_0);
- Euclidean distance (L_2, root-mean-square);
- Maximum change to any of the co-ordinates, (L_∞).

Human perception may not be the best criterion to judge a successful adversarial input. A successful attack in a vision ML task may be to fool a human. Success in an ML-based system is to fool some other detection routine, while conforming to the expected inputs of the system. For example, a malicious packet must remain malicious after any perturbation has been applied. If a perturbed packet is very close to the original packet, this would only be considered successful if it also retained its malicious properties, and hence its intended function.

5.2.2. Adversarial Examples-Types of Attack

White-Box Attacks: Most white-box attacks are commonly achieved through gradient descent to increase the loss function of the target model. The algorithmic generation of adversarial examples is possible. Moreover, Papernot et al. [65] developed a software library for the easy generation of adversarial examples and other libraries are now available. An early gradient descent approach was proposed by Szegedy et al. [17] using a box-constrained limited memory L-BFGS. Given an original image, this method finds a different image that is classified differently, whilst remaining similar to the original image. Gradient descent is used by many different algorithms; however, algorithms have been designed to be optimized for different distance metrics. There are numerous gradient descent algorithms that produce adversarial examples; they can differ in their optimization and computational complexity. We note the relative computational complexity of common adversarial example algorithms in Table 6 (adapted from [27]). High success rates correlate with high computational complexity. We expect this correlation to be more pronounced for functionality-preserving attacks. FGSM [63] was improved by Kurakin et al. [103], who refined the fast gradient sign by taking multiple smaller steps. This iterative granular approach improves on FGSM by limiting the difference between the original and adversarial inputs. This often results in adversarial inputs with a predictably smaller L_∞ metric. However, FGSM modifies all parameters. This is problematic for features that must remain unchanged or for discrete features such as application programming interface (API) calls. JSMA differs from FGSM in that it optimises to minimize the total number of modified features (L_0 metric). In this greedy algorithm, individual features are chosen with the aim of step-wise increasing the target classification in each iteration. The gradient is used to generate a saliency map, modelling each feature's impact towards the resulting classification. Large values significantly increase the likelihood of classification as the target class. Thus, the most important feature is modified at each stage. This process continues until the input is successfully classified as the target class, or a threshold number of pixels is reached. This algorithm results in adversarial inputs with fewer modified features. The Deepfool algorithm [62] similarly uses gradient descent but optimises for the root-mean-square, also known as Euclidean distance (L_2). This technique simplifies the task of shifting an input over a decision boundary by assuming a linear hyper-plane separates each class. The optimal solution is derived through analysis and subsequently an adversarial example is constructed; however, neural network decision boundaries are not truly linear. Therefore, subsequent repetitions may be required until a true adversarial image is found.

Table 6. Computational complexity of common adversarial example algorithms.

Method	Computational Complexity	Success Rate
L-BFGS	High	High
FGSM	Low	Low
JSMA	High	High
DeepFool	Low	Low
One-pixel	Low	Low
CW Attack	High	High

The optimizations for different distance metrics are types of constraint: maximum change to any feature (L_∞); minimal root-mean-square (L_2); minimal number of altered features (L_0). Constrained adversarial examples are important for functionality-preserving attacks. Additional constraints for specific domains are likely required, and this remains an open avenue for further research.

Most gradient descent algorithms were originally presented in the visual domain and used on images and pixel values. The pixel values of images are often presented as continuous values (0–255). The use of adversarial examples with discrete data values is less well explored and remains an interesting avenue for further research.

Black-Box Attacks: Researchers have also considered black-box attacks that do rely on gradient descent. Some black-box techniques commonly rely on the transferability of adversarial examples. Table 5 shows that few researchers employed the transferability of adversarial examples. Other common black-box techniques include GANS and genetic algorithms (GAs). Sharif et al. [104] proposed a method of attacking DNNs with a general framework to train an attack generator or generative adversarial network (GAN). GANs can be trained to produce new, robust, and inconspicuous adversarial examples. Attacks like Biggio et al. [77] are more suitable for the security domain, where assessing the security of algorithms and systems under worst-case attacks is needed [105,106].

An important consideration in attacks against intrusion detection systems is that attackers cannot perform simple oracle queries against an intrusion detection system and must minimize the number of queries to decrease the likelihood of detection. Apruzzese et al. [28] further note that the output of the target model is not directly observable by the attacker; however, exceptions occur where detected malicious traffic is automatically stopped or dropped, or where the attacker gains access to/or knowledge of the system.

Gray-box attacks consider scenarios where an adversary has only partial knowledge of the system. Biggio et al. [77] highlighted the threat from skilled adversaries with limited knowledge; more recently, gray-box attacks have received some attention: Kuppa et al. [92] considered malicious users of the system with knowledge of the features and architecture of the system, recognizing that attackers may differ in their level of knowledge of the system. Labaca-Castro et al. [99] used universal adversarial perturbations, showing that unprotected systems remain vulnerable even under limited knowledge scenarios. Li et al. [101] considered limited knowledge attacks against cyber physical systems and successfully deployed universal adversarial perturbations where attackers have incomplete knowledge of measurements across all sensors.

Building on Simple Adversarial Examples: Table 5 shows that much research considers simple adversarial examples, although less research considers sequences of adversarial examples or transferability. We chose to classify attacks as either a simple adversarial example, a sequence of adversarial examples, or a transferable adversarial example. A simple adversarial example is sufficient to alter the output of a simple classifier. Lin et al. [82] suggested that using adversarial examples strategically could affect the specific critical outputs of a machine learning system. Sequences of adversarial examples consist of two or more adversarial examples. Sequences of adversarial examples are more challenging than simple adversarial examples. Lin et al. [82] further suggested an *enchanting* attack to lure a machine learning system to a target state through crafting a series of adversarial examples. Table 5 shows that most research considers simple adversarial examples. Researchers are starting to consider sequences of adversarial examples and consider the transferability of adversarial examples. We chose to classify attacks in this way to clarify the complexity level of attack types. Furthermore, the table shows that sequences of adversarial examples and the transferability of adversarial examples is under-represented, providing opportunities for further research.

5.2.3. Adversarial Examples—Attack Objectives

There is a distinction between the objectives of attacks: targeted or untargeted. An attack objective might be to cause a classifier to misclassify an input as *any* other class (untargeted) or to misclassify an input as a *specific* class (targeted). In the cyber-security domain, IDS often focus on binary classification: malicious or benign. For binary classification the effect of targeted and untargeted attacks is the same. More complex multi-class IDS can help network analysts triage or prioritise different types of intrusions. Network analysts would certainly treat a distributed denial of service (DDoS) attack differently than a BotNet or infiltration attempt. Adversaries could gain significant advantage through *targeted* attacks, for example, by camouflaging an infiltration attack as a comparatively less serious network intrusion.

Recent research goes beyond adversarial examples causing misclassification of a single input. Moosavi-Dezfooli et al. [107] further showed the existence of untargeted *universal* adversarial perturbation (UAP) vectors for images, and ventured that this is problematic for classifiers deployed in real-world and hostile environments. In the cyber-security domain, Labaca et al. [99] demonstrated UAPs in the feature space of malware detection. They showed that UAPs have similar effectiveness to adversarial examples generated for specific inputs. Sheatsley et al. [56] looked at UAP in the constrained domain of intrusion detection. Adversaries need only calculate one UAP that could be applied to multiple inputs. Pre-calculation of a UAP could enable faster network attacks (DDoS) that would otherwise require too much calculation time. Table 5 shows that most research considers untargeted attacks. Targeted attacks are less represented in the literature. Furthermore, UAPs are a more recent avenue for research.

5.2.4. Adversarial Examples in Traditional Domains

Table 5 shows that attacks in the visual domain were the subject of much early research, and the visual domain continues to attract researchers; however, researchers are beginning to consider attacks against other DNN systems such as machine learning models for natural language processing, with some considering semantic preserving attacks.

In visual domains, features are generally continuous. For example, pixel values range from 0 to 255. A consensus exists in the visual domain that adversarial examples are undetectable to humans. Moreover, the application domain is clearly interrelated with the choice of machine learning model. Models such as CNNs are appropriate for visual-based tasks, whereas RNNs are appropriate for sequence-based tasks. We discuss model types in Section 5.2.6.

Some models, such as recurrent neural networks, cannot be attacked using traditional attack algorithms; however, some research aims to discover new methods to attack these systems. Papernot et al. [78] noted that because RNNs handle time sequences by introducing cycles to their computational graphs, the presence of these computation cycles means that applying traditional adversarial example algorithms is challenging because cycles prevent direct computation of the gradients. They adapted adversarial example algorithms for RNNs and evaluated the performance of their adversarial samples. If the model is differential, FGSM can be applied even to RNN models. They used a case study of a binary classifier (positive or negative) for movie reviews. They defined an algorithm that iteratively modifies words in the input sentence to produce an adversarial sequence that is misclassified by a well-trained model. They noted that their attacks are white-box attacks, requiring access to, or knowledge of, the model parameters. Szegedy [17] discovered the transferability of adversarial examples, noting that the same perturbation can cause a different network that was trained on a different subset of the dataset to misclassify the same input. This property of adversarial examples has serious implications because it means gaining access to a model is unnecessary to attack it. An adversary can employ the transferability of adversarial examples, where adversarial examples generated against a model under the adversary's control can be successfully used to attack the target model. The transferability of adversarial examples implies that an adversary does not need full access to a model to attack it (black-box).

5.2.5. Adversarial Examples in Cyber-Security Domains

Adversarial examples (AE) have been shown to exist in many domains. Indeed, no domain identified (so far) is immune to adversarial examples [56]. Researchers are beginning to consider cyber-security domains (Figure 5) where features are often a mixture of categorical, continuous, and discrete. Some research focuses on adversarial example attacks against IDS, although few studies specifically consider functionality-preserving attacks.

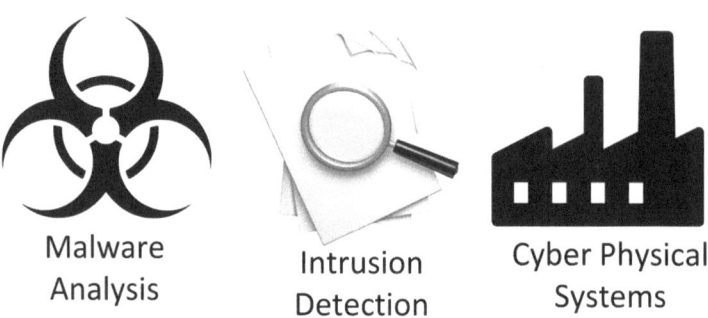

Figure 5. Common machine learning tasks in cyber security.

In the visual domain, we briefly discussed the consensus that adversarial examples are undetectable to humans. However, it is unclear how this idea should be translated to other domains. Carlini [64] held that, strictly speaking, adversarial examples must be similar to the original input. However, Sheatsley et al. [56] noted that research in non-visual domains provides domain-specific definitions: perturbed malware must preserve its malware functionality [56], perturbations in audio must be *nearly* inaudible [56], and perturbed text must preserve its meaning. Sheatsley et al. further offered a definition for adversarial examples in intrusion detection: perturbed network flows must maintain their attack behaviour. We consider that human perception may not be the best criterion for defining adversarial examples in cyber-security domains. Indeed, human perception in some domains might be immaterial. For example, only very skilled engineers could *perceive* network packets in any meaningful way even with the use of network analysis tools. Furthermore, users likely cannot perceive a difference between the execution of benign or malicious software. After malware is executed, the effects are clear; however, during malware execution users often suspect nothing wrong. We therefore consider that while fooling human perception remains a valid ambition, it is critical that adversarial perturbations in cyber-security domains preserve functionality and behaviour.

In the cyber-security domain, traditional gradient descent algorithms may be insufficient. Algorithms that preserve functionality are required. Moreover, some models used in the cyber-security domain are distinct from those used for purely visual problems. For example, RNNs are useful for time sequences of network traffic analysis. We now consider recent functionality-preserving attacks in the cybersecurity domains of malware, intrusion detection, and CPS. We further examine Functionality-preserving attacks in Table 7.

Table 7. Functionality-preservation in cybersecurity and intrusion detection.

Work	Year	Domain	Generation Method	Realistic Constraints	Findings
[53]	2019	Malware	Gradient-based	Minimal content additions/modification	Experiments showed that we are able to use that information to find optimal sequences of transformations without rendering the malware sample corrupt.
[94]	2019	IDS	GAN	Preserve functionality	The proposed adversarial attack successfully evades the IDS while ensuring preservation of functional behavior and network traffic features.
[108]	2019	IDS	Gradient-based	Respects mathematical dependencies and domain constraints.	Evasion attacks achieved by inserting a dozen network connections.
[109]	2019	IDS	Random modification ≤ 4 features: flow duration, sent bytes, received bytes, exchanged packets.	Retains internal logic	Feature removal is insufficient defense against functionality-preserving attacks, which may are possible by modifying very few features.
[110]	2019	IDS	Legitimate transformations: split, delay, inject	Packets must maintain malicious intent, transformations hold to underlying protocols.	Detection rate of packet-level features dropped by up to 70% and flow-level features dropped by up to 68%.
[56]	2020	IDS—Flows	Jacobian method (JSMA)	Obeys TCP/IP constraints	Biased distributions with low dimensionality enable constrained adversarial examples. Constrained to five random features, -50% adversarial examples succeed.
[95]	2020	IDS—packet	Valid packet	Minimal modification/insertion of packets	Experimental results show powerful and effective functionality-preserving attacks. More accurate models are more susceptible to adversarial examples.
[98]	2021	Malware	Injected unexecuted benign content	Minimal injected content	Section-injection attack can decrease the detection rate. Their analysis highlights that commercial products can be evaded via transfer attacks.
[101]	2021	CPS	Best-effort search	Real-world linear inequality	Best-effort search algorithms effectively generate adversarial examples meeting linear constraints. Their evaluation shows constrained adversarial examples significantly decrease detection accuracy.
[111]	2021	IDS	Minimal perturbation of each feature	FGSM	Functionality is not reported, but is less likely to preserve functionality because all features are perturbed.
[112]	2021	CPS/ICS	JSMA	Minimal number of perturbed features	Functionality is not reported, but is more likely to preserve functionality because relatively few features are perturbed.
[113]	2021	IDS	PSO-based mutation	Original traffic retained and packet order is unchanged	Measured attack effect, malicious behavior and attack efficiency
[114]	2021	IDS	GAN	preserving functional features of attack traffic	F1 score drop to zero from around 99% DIGFuPAS adversarial examples.
[115]	2021	IDS	PSO/GA/GAN	Only modifies features where network functionality is retained	In the network traffic data, it is unrealistic to assume an adversary can alter all traffic features—constraints on features that do not break functionality
[116]	2020	IDS	GAN/PSO	Original traffic and packet order is retained.	Detection performance and robustness should both be considered in feature extraction systems.

Malware: Hu and Tan [84] proposed a novel algorithm to generate adversarial sequences to attack an RNN-based malware detection system. They claimed that algorithms adapted for RNNs are limited because they are not truly sequential. They considered a system to detect malicious API sequences. Generating adversarial examples effective against such systems is non-trivial because API sequences are discrete values. There is a discrete set of API calls; changing any single letter in an API call will create an invalid API call and cause that API call to fail. This will result in a program crash. Therefore, any perturbation of an API call must result in a set of valid API calls. They proposed an algorithm based around a generative RNN and a substitute RNN. The generative RNN takes an API sequence as input and generates an adversarial API sequence. The substitute RNN is trained on benign sequences and the outputs of the generative RNN. The generative model aims to minimize the predicted malicious probability. Subsequently, adversarial sequences are presented to six different models. Following adversarial perturbation, the majority of the malware was not detected by any victim RNNs. The authors noted that even when the adversarial generation algorithm and the victim RNN were implemented with different models and trained on different training sets, the majority of the adversarial examples successfully attacked the victim RNN through the *transferability* property of adversarial examples. In MLP, they reported a TPR of 94.89% that fell to 0.00% under adversarial perturbations.

Demetrio et al. [98] preserved the functionality of malware while evading static windows malware detectors. Their attacks exploit the structure of the portable executable (PE) file format. Their framework has three categories of functionality-preserving manipulations: structural, behavioural, and padding. Some of their attacks work by injecting unexecuted (benign) content in new sections in the PE file, or at the end of the malware file. The attacks are a constrained minimization problem optimizing the trade-off between the probability of evading detection and the size of injected content. Their experiments successfully evaded two Windows malware detectors with few queries and a small payload size. Furthermore, they discovered that their attacks transferred to other Windows malware products. We note that the creation of new sections provides a larger attack surface that may be populated with adversarial content. They reported that their section-injection attack was able to drastically decrease the detection rate (e.g., from an original detection rate of 93.5% to 30.5%, also significantly outperforming their random attack at 85.5%).

Labaca-Castro et al. [53] presented a gradient-based method to generate valid executable files that preserve their intended malicious functionality. They noted that malware evasion is a current area of adversarial learning research. Evading the classifier is often the foremost objective; however, the perturbations must also be carefully crafted to preserve the functionality of malware. They noted that removing objects from a PE file often leads to corrupt files. Therefore, they only implement additive or modifying perturbations. Their gradient-based attack relies on *complete knowledge* of the system with the advantage that the likelihood of evasion can be calculated and maximised. Furthermore, they stated that their system only generates valid executable malware files.

Intrusion Detection: Usama et al. [94] used a generative adversarial network (GAN) to generate functionality-preserving adversarial examples. They noted that adversarial examples aiming to evade IDS should not invalidate network traffic features. A typical GAN composed of two neural networks, a generator G and discriminator D, was used to construct adversarial examples that masquerade as benign but functionally probe the network. Their attack was able to evade an IDS while preserving the intended behaviour. They suggested that adversarial training using GAN-generated adversarial examples improved the robustness of their model. They reported F1-scores of 89.03 (original), 40.86 (After attack), 78.49 (after adversarial training), and an improved 83.56 after GAN-based adversarial training.

Wang et al. [117] noted that relatively few researchers are addressing adversarial examples against IDS. They proposed an ensemble defense for network intrusion detection that integrates GANS and adversarial retraining. Their training framework improved robustness while maintaining accuracy of unperturbed samples. Unfortunately, they evaluated their defences against traditional attack algorithms: FGSM, basic iterative method (BIM), Deepfool, and JSMA. However, they did not specifically consider functionality-preserving adversarial examples. They further recognised the importance of using recent datasets for intrusion detection. They reported F1-scores for three classifiers and a range of adversarial example algorithms. For example, the F1-score for an ensemble classifier tested on clean data was 0.998 compared to 0.746 for JSMA. Among all classifiers, the ensemble classifier achieved superior F1-scores under all conditions.

Huang et al. [95] noted that it is more challenging to generate DDoS adversarial examples because of their discrete properties. They noted that work in the visual domain cannot be directly applied to adversarial examples for intrusion detection of DDoS. The input to their algorithm is a series of packets. This makes it difficult to optimize the distance between the original and adversarial sample while guaranteeing the validity of each packet. They proposed two black-box methods to generate DDoS adversarial examples against LSTM-based intrusion detection systems: genetic algorithm (GA) and probability weighted packet saliency attack (PWPSA). Each method modifies the original input, either inserting or modifying packets. The GA method evolves a population of DDoS samples and selects adversarial examples from the population. The PWPSA method finds the most important packet in the sequence and replaces it with a different "best packet" for this position. Both methods produce adversarial examples that can successfully evade their DDoS intrusion detection model. They reported success rates for their different attacks against different detectors. For example, success results for detector D: GA-Replace 91.37%, GA-Insert 74.5%, PWPSA-Replace 88.9%, and PWPSA-Insert 67.17%.

Cyber-Physical Systems: Cai et al. [100] warned that adversarial examples have consequences for system safety because they can cause systems to provide incorrect outputs. They presented a detection method for adversarial examples in CPS. They used a case study of an advanced emergency braking system, where a DNN estimates the distance to an obstacle. Their adversarial example detection method uses a variational auto-encoder to predict a target variable (distance) and compare it with a new input. Any anomalies are considered adversarial. Furthermore, adversarial example detectors for CPS must function efficiently in a real-time monitoring environment and maintain low false alarm rates. They reported that since the p-values for the adversarial examples are almost 0, the number of false alarms is very small and the detection delay is smaller than 10 frames or 0.5 s.

CPS include critical national infrastructure, such as power grids, water treatment plants, and transportation. Li et al. [101] asserted that adversarial examples could exploit vulnerabilities in CPS with terrible consequences; however, such adversarial examples must satisfy real-world constraints (commonly linear inequality constraints). For example, meter readings downstream may never be larger than meter readings upstream. Adversarial examples breaking constraints are noticeably anomalous. Risks to CPS arising from adversarial examples are not yet fully understood. Furthermore, algorithms and models from other domains may not readily apply because of distributed sensors and inherent real-world constraints. However, generated adversarial examples that meet such linear constraints were successfully applied to power grids and water treatment system case studies. The evaluation results show that even with constraints imposed by the physical systems, their approach still effectively generates adversarial examples, significantly decreasing the detection accuracy. For example, they reported the accuracy under adversarial conditions to be as low as 0%.

5.2.6. Adversarial Examples and Model Type

We classify models based on their architecture in four broad types: multi-layer perceptron (MLP), CNN, RNN, and RF. Ali et al. [118] observed that different deep learning architectures are more robust than others. They noted that CNN and RNN detectors are more robust than MLP and hybrid detectors, based on low attack success rates and high query counts. Architecture plays a role in the accuracy of these models because CNNs can learn contextual features due to their structure, and RNNs are temporally deeper, and thus demonstrate greater robustness.

Unsurprisingly, research on CNNs coincides with research in the visual domain, as shown in Table 5. The majority of adversarial example research on RNNs has until recently focused on the text or natural language domain; however, RNNs are also useful in the cybersecurity domain and researchers have recently considered adversarial example attacks against RNN-based IDS.

Other promising research shows that radial basis function neural networks (RBFNN) are more robust to adversarial examples [119]. RBFNNs fit a non-linear curve during training, as opposed to fitting linear decision boundaries. Commonly, RBFNNs transform the input such that when it is fed into the network it gives a linear separation. The non-linear nature of RBFNNs could be one potential direction for adversarial example research. Powerful attacks that are able to subvert RBFNNs would improve our understanding of decision boundaries. Goodfellow et al. [63] argued that the primary cause of neural networks' vulnerability to adversarial perturbation is their linear nature. However, RBFNNs are less commonly deployed and are therefore not further discussed.

5.2.7. Adversarial Examples and Knowledge Requirement

The majority of the research focus is on white-box attacks, as shown in Table 5, perhaps because such attacks are known to be efficient and effective. Less research focuses on black-box attacks and few studies recognise gray-box attacks that need only partial model knowledge. Gray-box attacks will likely have advantages over black-box attacks. Adversaries will undoubtedly use any and all information available to them.

We classify the attacks on the knowledge required by the adversary. White-box attacks are likely the most effective and efficient method of attack, because the adversary has *complete knowledge* of the model architecture, and information on how the model was trained. However, access to this knowledge is harder to attain, although it might also be gained through insider threats [120] or model extraction attacks [121]. Extracted models might be a feasible proxy on which to develop and test adversarial examples.

Notwithstanding the efficiency of white-box attacks, effective black-box attacks are possible. Black-box (or oracle) attacks require no knowledge of the model. Adversaries only need the ability to query the model and receive its output. Adversaries generate inputs and receive the output of the model. Typical black-box attacks include GA [95], and GANs [89,97].

Gray-box attacks require only limited model knowledge, perhaps including knowledge of the features used by the model. This is a realistic prospect, as adversaries will likely have or gain at least partial knowledge of the model.

5.2.8. Adversarial Example Constraints

Table 5 shows little research considering constraints of any sort. Much research on IDS ignores constraints; however, network traffic is highly constrained by protocols, and some network firewalls may drop malformed packets. Furthermore, it is insufficient that well-formed adversarial examples progress past firewalls. They must also retain their intended functionality.

Stringent constraints exist in the cyber-security domain. Extreme care must be taken to create valid adversarial examples. For example, in IDS, adversaries must conform the protocol specification of the TCP/IP stack.

We classify adversarial example constraints into three groups: (1) box constraints, simple constraints where values must remain within certain values; (2) sparse constraints, where a maximum number of features can be modified, the most extreme version being where only one feature can be modified; and (3) functionality-preserving constraints, where adversarial examples must retain their original functionality. For example, malware must function as malware when perturbed to evade a malware detector, and DDoS attacks must function as DDoS attacks when perturbed to evade detection. Functionality-preserving adversarial examples are an interesting avenue for further research.

5.3. Defenses Against Adversarial Examples

Figure 6 shows some common defence types that we explore in this section. We further detail proposed defenses against adversarial examples in Table 8.

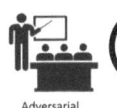

| Pre-processing | Detection | Adversarial Training | Testing | Architecture | Distillation | Game Theory | Ensemble Methods |

Figure 6. Common defence types against adversarial machine learning.

Table 8. Chronologically ordered summary of defenses against adversarial examples.

Work	Year	Defense	Type								Domain			Model			
			Pre-Process	Detection	Adv-Training	Testing	Architectural	Distillation	Ensemble	Game Theory	Visual	Cybersecurity	Text	MLP	CNN	RNN	RF
[63]	2014	Adversarial Training			✓						✓				✓		
[75]	2016	Distillation as defense						✓			✓				✓		
[122]	2016	Feedback Alignment					✓				✓				✓		
[123]	2016	Assessing Threat	✓								✓				✓		
[124]	2017	Statistical Test		✓							✓	✓		✓	✓		
[125]	2017	Detector SubNetwork		✓							✓				✓		
[126]	2017	Artifacts		✓							✓				✓		
[127]	2017	MagNet		✓							✓				✓		
[128]	2017	Feature Squeezing		✓							✓				✓		
[129]	2017	GAT			✓						✓				✓		
[102]	2018	EAT			✓						✓				✓		
[130]	2018	Defense-GAN			✓						✓				✓		
[103]	2018	Assessing Threat	✓								✓				✓		
[131]	2018	Stochastic Activation Pruning					✓				✓			✓	✓		
[132]	2018	DeepTest				✓					✓				✓		
[133]	2018	DeepRoad				✓					✓				✓		
[134]	2018	Defensive Dropout					✓				✓				✓		
[134]	2018	Def-IDS			✓							✓	✓				
[105]	2018	Multi-Classifier System							✓		✓				✓		
[135]	2019	Weight Map Layers					✓				✓				✓		
[136]	2019	Sequence Squeezing		✓								✓					✓
[109]	2019	Feature Removal	✓									✓	✓				
[137]	2020	Adversarial Training			✓							✓					✓
[138]	2020	Adversarial Training			✓							✓					✓
[139]	2019	Game Theory								✓		✓	✓				
[140]	2020	Hardening			✓					✓		✓					✓
[141]	2021	Variational Auto-encoder		✓							✓				✓		
[142]	2021	MANDA		✓								✓	✓				

It is hard to defend against adversarial examples. People expect ML models to give good outputs for all possible inputs. Because the range of possible inputs is so large, it is difficult to guarantee correct model behaviour for every input. Some researchers explored the possibility of exercising all neurons during training [132]. Furthermore, consideration must be given to how adversaries might react when faced with a defense. Researchers in secure machine learning must evaluate whether defenses remain secure against adversaries with knowledge of model defenses.

We classify the suggested defenses against adversarial examples into the following groups: pre-processing, adversarial training, architectural, detection, distillation, testing, ensembles, and game theory.

5.3.1. Pre-Processing as a Defense against Adversarial Examples

Some promising research considers transformations, such as translation, additive noise, blurring, cropping, and resizing. These often occur with cameras and scanners in the visual domain. Translations have shown initial success in the visual domain. Initial successes have prompted some researchers to discount security concerns. For example, Graese [123] overreached by declaring adversarial examples an "academic curiosity", not a security threat. This position misunderstands the threat from adversarial examples, which remain a concern for cyber-security researchers.

Eykolt et al. [143] noted the creation of perturbations in physical space that survive more challenging physical conditions (distance, pose, and lighting). Transformations are appropriate for images; however, such translations may make little sense in cyber-security domains. For example, what would it mean to rotate or blur a network packet? Nevertheless, inspiration could be taken from pre-processing methods in the visual domain. Adapting pre-processing methods to cyber-security and other non-visual domains is an interesting avenue for research.

5.3.2. Adversarial Training as a Defense against Adversarial Examples

Szegedy et al. [17] found that robustness to adversarial examples can be improved by training a model on a mixture of adversarial examples and unperturbed samples. Specific vulnerabilities in the training data can be identified through exploring UAPs. Identified vulnerabilities could potentially be addressed with adversarial training. We recognise that adversarial training is a simple method aiming to improve robustness; however, it is potentially a cosmetic solution: the problem of adversarial examples cannot be solved only through ever greater amounts of adversarial examples in the training data. Tramér et al. [102] found that adversarial training is imperfect and can be bypassed. Moreover, black-box attacks have been shown to evade models subject to adversarial training. Adversarial training has some merit because it is a simple method to improve robustness. It is unfortunately not a panacea and should be bolstered by other defenses. Research avenues could combine adversarial training with other techniques. We warn that models used in cyber-security or other critical domains should not rely solely on adversarial training.

5.3.3. Architectural Defenses against Adversarial Examples

Some research, rather than modifying a model's training data, investigated defenses through hardening the architecture of the model. This could involve changing model parameters or adding new layers. In Table 8, we classify such defenses as architectural.

Many white-box attacks rely on the quality of the gradient. Some research considers how the model's weights can be used to disrupt adversarial examples. Amer and Maul [135] modified convolutional neural networks (CNN), adding a weight map layer. Their proposed layer easily integrates into existing CNNs. A weight mapping layer may be inserted between other CNN layers, thus increasing the network's robustness to both noise and gradient-based adversarial attacks.

Other research aims to block algorithms from using weight transport and back-propagation to generate adversarial examples. Lillicrap et al. [122] proposed a mechanism called "feedback alignment", which introduces a separate feedback path via random fixed synaptic weights. Feedback alignment blocks the generation of adversarial examples that rely on the gradient because it uses the separate feedback path rather than weight transport.

Techniques to improve accuracy could similarly help harden models. For example, dropout can improve accuracy when used during training. It is particularly useful where there is limited training data and over-fitting is more likely to occur. Wang et al. [134] proposed hardening DNN using defensive dropout at test time. Unfortunately, there is inherently a trade-off between defensive dropout and test accuracy; however, a relatively small decrease in test accuracy can significantly reduce the success rate of attacks. Such hardening techniques force successful attacks to use larger perturbations, which in turn may be more readily recognized as adversarial.

Defenses that block gradient-based attacks complicate the generation of adversarial examples; however, like adversarial training, these defenses could be bypassed. In particular, black-box attacks and transferability-based attacks are not blocked by such defenses. A more promising defense, "defensive dropout", can block both black-box and transferability-based attacks.

5.3.4. Detecting Adversarial Examples

Much research has considered the best way to detect adversarial examples. If adversarial examples can be detected they could be more easily deflected, and perhaps even the original input could be salvaged and correctly classified. Grosse et al. [124] proposed a statistical test to detect adversarial examples before they are input into machine learning models. They observed that adversarial examples are unrepresentative of the distribution, and lie in unexpected regions of a model's output surface. Their proposed outlier detection system relies on the statistical separation of adversarial examples. They subsequently evaluated their model against adaptive strategies and strong black-box strategies.

Metzen et al. [125] proposed a binary classifier "detector subnetwork" aiming to distinguish between genuine data and adversarial examples. The detection of adversarial examples does not unequivocally lead to correct classification; however, the effect of adversarial examples could perhaps be mitigated through fallback solutions, for example, by requesting human intervention. After successfully detecting adversarial examples in their experiments, they later bypassed their defenses by generating adversarial examples that fool both detector and classifier. They further proposed a training procedure called "dynamic adversary training" as a countermeasure to their attack against the detector.

Feiman et al. [126] also detected adversarial examples by considering which artifacts of adversarial examples could help detection. They considered two complementary features used to detect adversarial examples: density estimates and Bayesian uncertainty estimates. They evaluated these features on CNNs trained on MNIST and CIFAR-10 datasets. They effectively detected adversarial examples with an ROC-AUC of 92.6%. They further suggested that their method could be used in RNNs. This suggestion is bolstered by Gal and Ghahramani's [144] assertion that Bayesian approximation using dropout can be applied to RNN networks.

Meng et al. [127] proposed a framework, "MagNET", to detect adversarial examples. This framework precedes the classifier it defends. The framework has two components: (1) A detector finds and discards any out-of-distribution examples (those significantly far from the manifold boundary); (2) A reformer that aims to find close approximations to inputs before forwarding the approximations to the classifier. Their system generalizes well because it learns to detect adversarial examples without knowledge of how they were generated. They proposed a defense against gray-box attacks where the adversary has knowledge of the deployed defenses. The proposed defense trains a number of auto-encoders (or *reformers*). At test-time a single auto-encoder is selected at random.

Xu et al. [128] proposed "feature squeezing" as a strategy to detect adversarial examples by squeezing out unnecessary features in the input. Through comparing predictions of the original and feature squeezed inputs, adversarial examples are identified if the difference between the two predictions meets a threshold. Two feature-squeezing methods are used: (1) Reducing the colour bit-depth of the image; (2) Spatial smoothing. An adversary may adapt and circumvent this defense; however, the defense may frustrate the adversary because it changes the problem the adversary must overcome.

Rosenberg et al. [136] considered the feature squeezing defense designed for CNNs and proposed "sequence squeezing", which is adapted for RNNs. Adversarial examples are similarly detected by running the classifier twice: once on the original sequence, and once for the sequence-squeezed input. An input is identified as adversarial if the difference in the confidence scores meets a threshold value.

Zhang et al. [141] proposed an image classifier based on a variational auto-encoder. They trained two models each on half the dataset: a target model and a surrogate model. On the surrogate model they generated three types of strong transfer-based adversarial examples: L_0, L_2, and L_∞. Analysis of their model using the CIFAR-10, MNIST, and Fashion-MNIST datasets found that their model achieves state-of-the-art accuracy with significantly better robustness. Their work is in the visual domain; however, perhaps their ideas can be applied to other domains such as intrusion detection.

We have discussed some architectural defenses against adversarial examples. In particular, we have considered methods for detecting adversarial examples. Carlini and Wagner [145] showed that adversarial examples are harder to detect and that adversarial examples do not exhibit intrinsic properties. Moreover, many detection methods can be broken by choosing good attacker-loss functions. Grosse et al. [124] noted that adversarial defenses exist within an arms race and that guarantees against future attacks are difficult because adversaries may adapt to the defenses by adopting new strategies. Meng et al. [127] advocated that defenses against adversarial examples should be independent of any particular attack. We have seen that human-in-the-loop solutions could be useful where few cases need human intervention; however, repeated requests might quickly overwhelm human operators given large numbers of adversarial examples, for example, as might be seen in network traffic analysis.

5.3.5. Defensive Testing

Adversarial examples cause unexpected behaviour. Recent research considers testing deep learning systems. Pei et al. [146] aimed to discover unusual or unexpected behaviour of a neural network through systematic testing. They produced test data by solving a joint optimization problem. Their tests aim to trigger different behaviours and activate a high proportion of neurons in a neural network. Their method finds corner-cases where incorrect behaviour is exhibited, for example, malware masquerading as benign. They claimed to expose more inputs and types of unexpected behaviour than adversarial examples. They further used the generated inputs to perform adversarial training. As a defense we question the practicability of triggering all neurons in larger neural networks; however, as an attack, their method could produce different types of adversarial inputs.

Other researchers are considering similar techniques to generate test data. Tian et al. [132] evaluated a tool for automatically detecting erroneous behaviour, generating test inputs designed to maximise the number of activated neurons using realistic driving conditions, including blurring, rain, and fog. Zhang et al. [133] proposed a system to automatically synthesize large amounts of diverse driving scenes, including weather conditions, using GANs. We consider GANs useful for generating adversarial inputs. GANs should implicitly learn domain constraints.

5.3.6. Multi-Classifier Systems

Biggio et al. [105] highlighted that robustness against adversarial examples can be improved through the careful use of ensemble classifiers, for example, by using rejection-based mechanisms. Indeed, Biggio et al. had implemented a multi-classifier system (MCS) [147], which was hardened using randomisation. Randomising the decision boundary makes a classifier harder to evade. Since the attacker has less information on the exact position of a decision boundary, they must make too conservative or too risky choices when generating adversarial examples.

5.3.7. Game Theory

Zhou et al. [139] consider game theoretic modeling of adversarial machine learning problems. Many different models have been proposed. Some aim to optimise the feature set using a set of high-quality features, thus making adversarial attacks more difficult. Game theoretic models are proposed to address more complex situations with many adversaries of different types. Equilibrium strategies are acceptable to both players and neither has an incentive to change. Therefore, assuming rational adversaries, game theory-based approaches allowing a Nash equilibrium could potentially end the evolutionary arms race.

5.3.8. Adversarial Example Defenses in Cybersecurity Domains

We discussed domains in Sections 5.2.4 and 5.2.5. Most research on defenses against adversarial examples has focused on the visual domain. Comparatively little research has so far considered defenses in cybersecurity domains such as intrusion detection and malware analysis. Applying current defenses in the visual domain to other domains might efficiently kickstart research into defenses for other domains. Effective defenses against adversarial examples could help enable the use of ML models in cybersecurity and other adversarial environments.

Different model types are more suited to domains. We consider that different model types may require different defenses. Again, we classify models into four types: MLP, CNN, RNN, and RF.

6. Discussion and Conclusions

ML systems are deployed in complex environments, including cybersecurity and critical national infrastructure. Such systems attract the interest of powerful advanced persistent threats that may target them. Crucially, we must address robustness against functionality-preserving adversarial examples before novel attack strategies exploit inherent weaknesses in critical ML models.

Machine learning and adversarial learning are becoming increasingly recognised by the research community, given the rapid uptake of ML models in a whole host of application domains. To put this in context, 2975 papers were published on arXiv in the last 12 months (October 2020–September 2021) related to machine learning and adversarial learning. Over recent years, the number of papers being published on this topic has grown substantially. According to Carlini, who maintains a blog post "A Complete List of All (arXiv) Adversarial Example Papers" [148], the cumulative number of adversarial example papers neared 4000 in the year 2021. It is therefore evident that there is a lot of interest and many researchers active in this area. Not all papers in this list are useful or relevant; we pass no judgement of their quality but merely aim to clarify the research landscape and draw important research to the fore. The majority of prior research has been applied to the visual domain. Seminal contributions have been made by Szegedy et al. [17], Goodfellow et al. [63], Carlini et al. [64], and Papernot [79]. It is clear that the visual domain continues to be well researched.

We conducted an extensive survey of the academic literature in relation to functionality-preservation in adversarial machine learning. We derived a classification based on both attack and defense. We consider edpossible robustness metrics. Moreover, we considered model training and data-level techniques that could help improve robustness through tackling biased datasets.

Analysis of functionality-preservation methods finds gradient-based methods may be less suitable for functionality-preservation and other constraints. Methods modifying large numbers of features are less likely to preserve functionality. We found that GANS and genetic algorithms are suitable for functionality-preserving attacks. We subsequently discussed defense strategies against functionality-preserving adversarial examples. We found that functionality-preserving adversarial machine learning is an open research topic. Finally, we will identify some key future directions and research challenges in functionality-preserving machine learning.

Future Directions and Research Challenges

We now discuss future research challenges. Few researchers address the problem of transferability, which remains a key area of concern because hard-to-attack models are nevertheless susceptible to *transferable* adversarial examples generated against easy-to-attack models. Breaking the transferability of adversarial examples is a key challenge for the research community. Currently, defensive dropout [134] at test time is a promising defense. Adversarial example detection is a useful area of research.

We consider the area of functionality-preserving adversarial examples under-explored. Research into improving robustness against such adversarial examples is an area requiring urgent research. We suggest that adapting defenses used in the visual domain and CNN models to other model types such as RNNs could offer potential solutions. Caution should be exercised when adapting defenses in the visual domain to other domains. For example, denoising defenses may not apply directly to discrete or noncontinuous data.

Constraints on adversarial examples are not limited to preserving the functionality of malware or IDS attacks. CPSs model the real world, where linear and other physical constraints must be respected. Adversarial examples that do not respect domain constraints risk marking themselves as obvious anomalies.

Concept-drift is a real concern for cybersecurity [1], as new attacks and techniques are discovered daily. As the model and the current state of the art diverge, the model suffers from hidden technical debt. Therefore, the model must be retrained to reflect the current state-of-the-art attacks and new network traffic patterns [149]. Researchers might develop and use more up-to-date datasets. Further avenues for research include semi-supervised/unsupervised ML and active learning methods that continuously update the underlying model and do not rely on labelled datasets.

We identify that data-level techniques such as resampling, balancing datasets, and cross validation could have effects on robustness against adversarial examples. Further research is required to explore how the bias-variance trade-off can effect robustness.

We prioritise the areas of future research, setting the agenda for research in this area. Critical areas of research include breaking the transferability of adversarial examples that would hopefully be applicable across domains. Non-visual domains including cybersecurity and cyber physical systems have been under-explored and this oversight should be rectified urgently. Further research on transformations in non-visual domains could provide useful knowledge. Detection of adversarial examples and pushing the fields of cybersecurity, intrusion detection, and cyber-physical systems will yield benefits beyond cybersecurity and may be applicable in other non-visual domains. Moreover, research is required in areas beyond instance classifiers. Areas of RNNs and reinforcement learning have been under-explored. More research is required to understand the use of domain constraints and functionality-preserving adversarial examples. Further research is needed towards effective countermeasures.

Additionally, we consider that more research attention could be given to dataset resampling strategies as a defence against adversarial examples. There is a need for better robustness metrics. Some researchers simply state accuracy, and others might state the better F1-score; however, the F1-score is biased by unbalanced datasets that are widespread in intrusion detection, partly due to large numbers of benign samples. Using F1-score could lead to a false sense of security. Researchers should adopt stronger metrics such as CLEVER [59] or empirical robustness [62].

Adversarial machine learning is a critical area of research. If not addressed, there is increasing potential for novel attack strategies that seek to exploit the inherent weaknesses that exist within machine learning models; however, few works consider *"realisable"* perturbations that take account of domain and/or real-world constraints. Successful adversarial examples must be crafted to comply with domain and real-world constraints. This may be challenging since even small modifications may corrupt network packets that are likely to be dropped by firewalls. This necessitates functionality preservation in adversarial learning.

We propose that human perception may not be the best criterion for analyzing adversarial examples. In cybersecurity domains we propose that adversarial examples must preserve functionality. Traditionally, adversarial examples are thought of as having imperceptible noise. That is, that humans cannot perceive the difference between the original and perturbed inputs. Indeed, human perception in some domains might be immaterial.

For example, strategic attacks triggered at crucial moments might cause damage to CPS before any human could reasonably act.

In cyber-security domains traditional gradient descent algorithms may be insufficient, although JSMA may be reasonable because it perturbs few features. Stringent constraints exist in the cyber-security domain and extreme care must be taken to create valid adversarial examples. We offer some guidelines for generating functionality-preserving adversarial examples. Functionality-preserving adversarial examples should: only perform legitimate transformations; respect mathematical dependencies, real-world, and domain constraints; minimize the number of perturbed features and restrict modification to non-critical features; and where possible retain the original payload and/or packet order.

Defences against adversarial examples must consider that adversaries are likely to adapt by adopting new strategies. Many researchers propose adversarial training to improve robustness. Adversarial training is a simple method aiming to improve robustness; however, it is potentially a cosmetic solution: the problem of adversarial examples cannot be solved only through ever greater numbers of adversarial examples in the training data. Adversarial training, if used, must be bolstered by other defenses. Interesting defence strategies include randomisation: randomising decision boundaries makes evasion more difficult because attackers have less information on the exact position of a decision boundary. They must therefore make too conservative or too risky choices when generating adversarial examples.

Game theoretic models could be used to address more complex situations with many adversaries of different types as found in intrusion detection. Equilibrium strategies acceptable to both defender and adversary mean neither has an incentive to change. Therefore, assuming rational opponents, game theory-based approaches allowing a Nash equilibrium could potentially end the evolutionary arms race, although it is difficult to conceive a world where no advantage is possible.

Current promising defenses such as dropout exchange a relatively small decrease in accuracy for a significant reduction of successful attacks, even successfully blocking black-box and transferability-based attacks. Hardening techniques force successful attacks to use larger perturbations, which in turn may be more readily recognized as adversarial.

In a broader cybersecurity context, risks arising from adversarial examples are not yet fully understood. Furthermore, algorithms and models from other domains may not readily apply because of distributed sensors and inherent real-world constraints. It is uncertain whether current defences are sufficient. Furthermore, adversarial example detectors must function efficiently in a real-time monitoring environment while maintaining low false alarm rates.

Many academic researchers use old datasets that do not fairly represent modern network traffic analysis problems due to concept-drift. Problems of labelling data and retraining systems provide an impetus to explore unsupervised and active learning. Unfortunately, adversarial attacks are possible on active learning systems [150]. Lin et al. [82] described an enchanting attack to lure a machine learning system to a target state through crafting a series of adversarial examples. It is conceivable that similar attacks could lure anomaly detection systems towards normalizing and accepting malicious traffic.

Key Future Research Challenges

Adversarial ML is a critical area of research. Researchers must address the robustness of ML models against adversarial examples allowing safer deployment of ML models across cybersecurity domains. Better robustness metrics should be used and developed. We find the traditional benchmark of human perception may be less relevant in functionality preservation. Moreover, traditional gradient descent algorithms may be insufficient to generate functionality-preserving attacks, and adversaries may use other methods such as GANS. Therefore, defences against gradient descent algorithms may likewise be insufficient. Defences must consider reactive adversaries who adapt to defences. Randomisation of decision boundaries can make evasion more difficult. Moreover, research into multi-classifier systems could help thwart evasion attacks, making it harder to evade classification. Dropout is currently a promising defense against adversarial examples, although multiple defenses may be required and a combination of defenses will likely offer better defense capability. Game-theory approaches could potentially end the adversarial arms race by achieving a Nash equilibrium. Concept-drift requires further research. Many researchers are using outdated datasets. Simply using newer datasets could postpone problems of concept-drift and is a good first step. Unsupervised/semi-supervised and active learning could potentially offer longer-term solutions to concept-drift, aiming for models to learn and detect novel attack methods. Transferability of adversarial examples remains an open issue, and more research here has the potential to disrupt many attack strategies. More research is required in the area of functionality-preserving adversarial attacks, recognising the limits and trade-offs between functionality-preserving adversarial examples and their ability to evade classification; moreover, research into adversarial attacks in other constrained domains could improve robustness against complex attacks.

We offer these insights and hope that this survey offers other researchers a base for exploring the areas of robustness and functionality-preserving adversarial examples.

Author Contributions: Conceptualization, A.M., P.A., E.G. and P.L.; methodology, A.M.; formal analysis, A.M.; investigation, A.M.; writing—original draft preparation, A.M.; writing—review and editing, A.M., P.A., E.G. and P.L.; visualization, A.M.; supervision, P.A., E.G. and P.L.; funding acquisition, P.L. All authors have read and agreed to the published version of the manuscript.

Funding: This research was funded by the Partnership PhD scheme at the University of the West of England in collaboration with Techmodal Ltd.

Institutional Review Board Statement: Not applicable.

Informed Consent Statement: Not applicable.

Data Availability Statement: Not applicable.

Conflicts of Interest: The authors declare no conflict of interest.

References

1. Andresini, G.; Pendlebury, F.; Pierazzi, F.; Loglisci, C.; Appice, A.; Cavallaro, L. INSOMNIA: Towards Concept-Drift Robustness in Network Intrusion Detection. In Proceedings of the 14th ACM Workshop on Artificial Intelligence and Security (AISec), ACM, Virtual Event, Korea, 15 November 2021.
2. Raghuraman, C.; Suresh, S.; Shivshankar, S.; Chapaneri, R. Static and dynamic malware analysis using machine learning. In *First International Conference on Sustainable Technologies for Computational Intelligence*; Springer: Berlin/Heidelberg, Germany, 2020; pp. 793–806.
3. Berger, H.; Hajaj, C.; Dvir, A. Evasion Is Not Enough: A Case Study of Android Malware. In *International Symposium on Cyber Security Cryptography and Machine Learning*; Springer: Berlin/Heidelberg, Germany, 2020; pp. 167–174.
4. Hou, R.; Xiang, X.; Zhang, Q.; Liu, J.; Huang, T. Universal Adversarial Perturbations of Malware. In *International Symposium on Cyberspace Safety and Security*; Springer: Berlin/Heidelberg, Germany, 2020; pp. 9–19.
5. Parshutin, S.; Kirshners, A.; Kornijenko, Y.; Zabiniako, V.; Gasparovica-Asite, M.; Rozkalns, A. Classification with LSTM Networks in User Behaviour Analytics with Unbalanced Environment. *Autom. Control. Comput. Sci.* **2021**, *55*, 85–91. [CrossRef]
6. Le, D.C.; Zincir-Heywood, N. Exploring anomalous behaviour detection and classification for insider threat identification. *Int. J. Netw. Manag.* **2021**, *31*, e2109. [CrossRef]
7. Biswal, S. Real-Time Intelligent Vishing Prediction and Awareness Model (RIVPAM). In Proceedings of the 2021 International Conference on Cyber Situational Awareness, Data Analytics and Assessment (CyberSA), Dublin, Ireland, 14–18 June 2021; pp. 1–2.
8. Kumar, N.; Sonowal, S.; Nishant. Email Spam Detection Using Machine Learning Algorithms. In Proceedings of the 2020 Second International Conference on Inventive Research in Computing Applications (ICIRCA), Coimbatore, India, 15–17 July 2020; pp. 108–113.
9. Kiela, D.; Firooz, H.; Mohan, A.; Goswami, V.; Singh, A.; Ringshia, P.; Testuggine, D. The hateful memes challenge: Detecting hate speech in multimodal memes. *arXiv* **2020**, arXiv:2005.04790.
10. Bin Naeem, S.; Kamel Boulos, M.N. COVID-19 misinformation online and health literacy: A brief overview. *Int. J. Environ. Res. Public Health* **2021**, *18*, 8091. [CrossRef]
11. Coan, T.; Boussalis, C.; Cook, J.; Nanko, M. Computer-assisted detection and classification of misinformation about climate change. *SocArXiv* **2021**, 1–12 .

12. Khanam, Z.; Alwasel, B.; Sirafi, H.; Rashid, M. Fake News Detection Using Machine Learning Approaches. In Proceedings of the IOP Conference Series: Materials Science and Engineering, Jeju Island, Korea, 12–14 March 2021; IOP Publishing: Jaipur, India, 2021; Volume 1099, p. 012040.
13. Papernot, N.; McDaniel, P.; Sinha, A.; Wellman, M.P. Sok: Security and privacy in machine learning. In Proceedings of the2018 IEEE European Symposium on Security and Privacy (EuroS&P), London, UK, 24–26 April 2018; pp. 399–414.
14. Dhar, S.; Guo, J.; Liu, J.; Tripathi, S.; Kurup, U.; Shah, M. On-device machine learning: An algorithms and learning theory perspective. *arXiv* **2019**, arXiv:1911.00623.
15. Gu, X.; Easwaran, A. Towards Safe Machine Learning for CPS: Infer Uncertainty from Training Data. In Proceedings of the 10th ACM/IEEE International Conference on Cyber-Physical Systems, Association for Computing Machinery, New York, NY, USA, 16–18 April 2019; pp. 249–258. [CrossRef]
16. Ghafouri, A.; Vorobeychik, Y.; Koutsoukos, X. Adversarial regression for detecting attacks in cyber-physical systems. In Proceedings of the International Joint Conference on Artificial Intelligence, Stockholm, Sweden, 13–19 July 2018.
17. Szegedy, C.; Zaremba, W.; Sutskever, I.; Bruna, J.; Erhan, D.; Goodfellow, I.; Fergus, R. Intriguing properties of neural networks. In Proceedings of the International Conference on Learning Representations, ICLR 2014, Banff, AB, Canada, 14–16 April 2014.
18. Wardle, S.G.; Taubert, J.; Teichmann, L.; Baker, C.I. Rapid and dynamic processing of face pareidolia in the human brain. *Nat. Commun.* **2020**, *11*, 1–14. [CrossRef]
19. Summerfield, C.; Egner, T.; Mangels, J.; Hirsch, J. Mistaking a house for a face: neural correlates of misperception in healthy humans. *Cereb. Cortex* **2006**, *16*, 500–508. [CrossRef]
20. Huang, Y.; Verma, U.; Fralick, C.; Infantec-Lopez, G.; Kumar, B.; Woodward, C. Malware Evasion Attack and Defense. In Proceedings of the 2019 49th Annual IEEE/IFIP International Conference on Dependable Systems and Networks Workshops (DSN-W), Portland, OR, USA, 24–27 June 2019; pp. 34–38. [CrossRef]
21. Ayub, M.A.; Johnson, W.A.; Talbert, D.A.; Siraj, A. Model Evasion Attack on Intrusion Detection Systems using Adversarial Machine Learning. In Proceedings of the 2020 54th Annual Conference on Information Sciences and Systems (CISS), Princeton, NJ, USA, 18–20 March 2020, pp. 1–6. [CrossRef]
22. Satter, R. *Experts Who Wrestled with SolarWinds Hackers say Cleanup Could Take Months-or Longer*; Reuters: New York, NY, USA, 2020.
23. Sirota, S. Air Force response to SolarWinds hack: Preserve commercial partnerships, improve transparency into security efforts. *Inside Cybersecur.* **2021**.
24. Corona, I.; Giacinto, G.; Roli, F. Adversarial attacks against intrusion detection systems: Taxonomy, solutions and open issues. *Inf. Sci.* **2013**, *239*, 201–225. [CrossRef]
25. Hankin, C.; Barrère, M. Trustworthy Inter-connected Cyber-Physical Systems. In *International Conference on Critical Information Infrastructures Security*; Springer: Berlin/Heidelberg, Germany, 2020; pp. 3–13.
26. Cho, J.H.; Xu, S.; Hurley, P.M.; Mackay, M.; Benjamin, T.; Beaumont, M. Stram: Measuring the trustworthiness of computer-based systems. *ACM Comput. Surv. (CSUR)* **2019**, *51*, 1–47. [CrossRef]
27. Zhang, J.; Li, C. Adversarial examples: Opportunities and challenges. *IEEE Trans. Neural Netw. Learn. Syst.* **2019**, *31*, 2578–2593. [CrossRef] [PubMed]
28. Apruzzese, G.; Andreolini, M.; Ferretti, L.; Marchetti, M.; Colajanni, M. Modeling Realistic Adversarial Attacks against Network Intrusion Detection Systems. *Digit. Threat. Res. Pract.* **2021**. [CrossRef]
29. Shannon, C.E. Communication theory of secrecy systems. *Bell Syst. Tech. J.* **1949**, *28*, 656–715. [CrossRef]
30. Taran, O.; Rezaeifar, S.; Voloshynovskiy, S. Bridging machine learning and cryptography in defence against adversarial attacks. In Proceedings of the European Conference on Computer Vision (ECCV) Workshops, Munich, Germany, 8–14 September 2018.
31. Wu, Y.; Wei, D.; Feng, J. Network attacks detection methods based on deep learning techniques: A survey. *Secur. Commun. Netw.* **2020**, *2020*, 8872923. [CrossRef]
32. Tavallaee, M.; Bagheri, E.; Lu, W.; Ghorbani, A.A. A detailed analysis of the KDD CUP 99 data set. In Proceedings of the 2009 IEEE Symposium on Computational Intelligence for Security and Defense Applications, Ottawa, ON, Canada, 8–10 July 2009; pp. 1–6.
33. McHugh, J. Testing intrusion detection systems: A critique of the 1998 and 1999 darpa intrusion detection system evaluations as performed by lincoln laboratory. *ACM Trans. Inf. Syst. Secur. (TISSEC)* **2000**, *3*, 262–294. [CrossRef]
34. Cerf, V.G. 2021 Internet Perspectives. *IEEE Netw.* **2021**, *35*, 3. [CrossRef]
35. McKeay, M. Akamai State of the Internet/Security: A Year in Review. Available online: http://akamai.com/soti (accessed on 15 September 2021).
36. Kok, S.; Abdullah, A.; Jhanjhi, N.; Supramaniam, M. A review of intrusion detection system using machine learning approach. *Int. J. Eng. Res. Technol.* **2019**, *12*, 8–15.
37. Alatwi, H.A.; Morisset, C. Adversarial Machine Learning In Network Intrusion Detection Domain: A Systematic Review. *arXiv* **2021**, arXiv:2112.03315.
38. Revathi, S.; Malathi, A. A detailed analysis on NSL-KDD dataset using various machine learning techniques for intrusion detection. *Int. J. Eng. Res. Technol. (IJERT)* **2013**, *2*, 1848–1853.
39. Gharaibeh, M.; Papadopoulos, C. DARPA 2009 intrusion detection dataset. *Colo. State Univ. Tech. Rep.* **2014**.
40. Garcia, S.; Grill, M.; Stiborek, J.; Zunino, A. An empirical comparison of botnet detection methods. *Comput. Secur.* **2014**, *45*, 100–123. [CrossRef]

41. Song, J.; Takakura, H.; Okabe, Y.; Eto, M.; Inoue, D.; Nakao, K. Statistical analysis of honeypot data and building of Kyoto 2006+ dataset for NIDS evaluation. In Proceedings of the first Workshop on Building Analysis Datasets and Gathering Experience Returns for Security, Salzburg, Austria, 10–13 April 2011; pp. 29–36.
42. Moustafa, N.; Slay, J. UNSW-NB15: A comprehensive data set for network intrusion detection systems (UNSW-NB15 network data set). In Proceedings of the 2015 military communications and information systems conference (MilCIS), Canberra, Australia, 10 November 2015; pp. 1–6.
43. Almomani, I.; Al-Kasasbeh, B.; Al-Akhras, M. WSN-DS: A dataset for intrusion detection systems in wireless sensor networks. *J. Sens.* **2016**, *2016*, 4731953. [CrossRef]
44. Niyaz, Q.; Sun, W.; Javaid, A.Y. A deep learning based DDoS detection system in software-defined networking (SDN). *arXiv* **2016**, arXiv:1611.07400.
45. Sharafaldin, I.; Lashkari, A.H.; Ghorbani, A.A. Toward generating a new intrusion detection dataset and intrusion traffic characterization. *ICISSp* **2018**, *1*, 108–116.
46. Antonakakis, M.; April, T.; Bailey, M.; Bernhard, M.; Bursztein, E.; Cochran, J.; Durumeric, Z.; Halderman, J.A.; Invernizzi, L.; Kallitsis, M.; et al. Understanding the mirai botnet. In Proceedings of the 26th USENIX Security Symposium (USENIX Security 17), Vancouver, BC, Canada, 16–18 August 2017; pp. 1093–1110.
47. Koroniotis, N.; Moustafa, N.; Sitnikova, E.; Turnbull, B. Towards the development of realistic botnet dataset in the Internet of things for network forensic analytics: Bot-iot dataset. *Future Gener. Comput. Syst.* **2019**, *100*, 779–796. [CrossRef]
48. Mirsky, Y.; Doitshman, T.; Elovici, Y.; Shabtai, A. Kitsune: An ensemble of autoencoders for online network intrusion detection. *arXiv* **2018**, arXiv:1802.09089.
49. Janusz, A.; Kałuza, D.; Chądzyńska-Krasowska, A.; Konarski, B.; Holland, J.; Ślęzak, D. IEEE BigData 2019 cup: Suspicious network event recognition. In Proceedings of the 2019 IEEE International Conference on Big Data (Big Data), Los Angeles, CA, 9–12 December 2019; pp. 5881–5887.
50. Ferriyan, A.; Thamrin, A.H.; Takeda, K.; Murai, J. Generating Network Intrusion Detection Dataset Based on Real and Encrypted Synthetic Attack Traffic. *Appl. Sci.* **2021**, *11*, 7868. [CrossRef]
51. Martins, N.; Cruz, J.M.; Cruz, T.; Abreu, P.H. Adversarial machine learning applied to intrusion and malware scenarios: A systematic review. *IEEE Access* **2020**, *8*, 35403–35419. [CrossRef]
52. Shafique, M.; Naseer, M.; Theocharides, T.; Kyrkou, C.; Mutlu, O.; Orosa, L.; Choi, J. Robust machine learning systems: Challenges, current trends, perspectives, and the road ahead. *IEEE Des. Test* **2020**, *37*, 30–57. [CrossRef]
53. Labaca-Castro, R.; Biggio, B.; Dreo Rodosek, G. Poster: Attacking malware classifiers by crafting gradient-attacks that preserve functionality. In Proceedings of the 2019 ACM SIGSAC Conference on Computer and Communications Security, London, UK, 11–15 November 2019; pp. 2565–2567.
54. Gonzalez-Cuautle, D.; Hernandez-Suarez, A.; Sanchez-Perez, G.; Toscano-Medina, L.K.; Portillo-Portillo, J.; Olivares-Mercado, J.; Perez-Meana, H.M.; Sandoval-Orozco, A.L. Synthetic minority oversampling technique for optimizing classification tasks in botnet and intrusion-detection-system datasets. *Appl. Sci.* **2020**, *10*, 794. [CrossRef]
55. Johnson, J.M.; Khoshgoftaar, T.M. Survey on deep learning with class imbalance. *J. Big Data* **2019**, *6*, 1–54. [CrossRef]
56. Sheatsley, R.; Papernot, N.; Weisman, M.; Verma, G.; McDaniel, P. Adversarial Examples in Constrained Domains. *arXiv* **2020**, arXiv:2011.01183.
57. Refaeilzadeh, P.; Tang, L.; Liu, H. Cross-validation. *Encycl. Database Syst.* **2009**, *5*, 532–538.
58. Bai, T.; Luo, J.; Zhao, J.; Wen, B. Recent Advances in Adversarial Training for Adversarial Robustness. *arXiv* **2021**, arXiv:2102.01356.
59. Weng, T.W.; Zhang, H.; Chen, P.Y.; Yi, J.; Su, D.; Gao, Y.; Hsieh, C.J.; Daniel, L. Evaluating the robustness of neural networks: An extreme value theory approach. *arXiv* **2018**, arXiv:1801.10578.
60. Goodfellow, I. Gradient masking causes clever to overestimate adversarial perturbation size. *arXiv* **2018**, arXiv:1804.07870.
61. Weng, T.W.; Zhang, H.; Chen, P.Y.; Lozano, A.; Hsieh, C.J.; Daniel, L. On extensions of clever: A neural network robustness evaluation algorithm. In Proceedings of the 2018 IEEE Global Conference on Signal and Information Processing (GlobalSIP), Anaheim, CA, USA, 26–28 November 2018; pp. 1159–1163.
62. Moosavi-Dezfooli, S.M.; Fawzi, A.; Frossard, P. DeepFool: A Simple and Accurate Method to Fool Deep Neural Networks. In Proceedings of the IEEE Conference on Computer Vision and Pattern Recognition (CVPR), Las Vegas, NV, USA, 27–30 June 2016.
63. Goodfellow, I.J.; Shlens, J.; Szegedy, C. Explaining and Harnessing Adversarial Examples. *arXiv* **2014**, arXiv:1412.6572.
64. Carlini, N.; Wagner, D. Towards evaluating the robustness of neural networks. In Proceedings of the 2017 IEEE Symposium on Security and Privacy (sp), San Jose, CA, USA, 22–26 May 2017; pp. 39–57.
65. Papernot, N.; Faghri, F.; Carlini, N.; Goodfellow, I.; Feinman, R.; Kurakin, A.; Xie, C.; Sharma, Y.; Brown, T.; Roy, A.; et al. Technical report on the cleverhans v2. 1.0 adversarial examples library. *arXiv* **2016**, arXiv:1610.00768.
66. Rauber, J.; Brendel, W.; Bethge, M. Foolbox: A python toolbox to benchmark the robustness of machine learning models. *arXiv* **2017**, arXiv:1707.04131.
67. Nicolae, M.I.; Sinn, M.; Tran, M.N.; Buesser, B.; Rawat, A.; Wistuba, M.; Zantedeschi, V.; Baracaldo, N.; Chen, B.; Ludwig, H.; et al. Adversarial Robustness Toolbox v1. 0.0. *arXiv* **2018**, arXiv:1807.01069.
68. Ding, G.W.; Wang, L.; Jin, X. AdverTorch v0. 1: An adversarial robustness toolbox based on pytorch. *arXiv* **2019**, arXiv:1902.07623.

69. Lashkari, A.H.; Zang, Y.; Owhuo, G.; Mamun, M.; Gil, G. CICFlowMeter. Available online: https://www.unb.ca/cic/research/applications.html (accessed on 19 February 2021).
70. Habibi Lashkari, A.; Draper Gil, G.; Mamun, M.S.I.; Ghorbani, A.A. Characterization of Tor Traffic using Time based Features. In Proceedings of the 3rd International Conference on Information Systems Security and Privacy-ICISSP, Porto, Portugal, 19–21 February 2017; pp. 253–262. [CrossRef]
71. Draper-Gil, G.; Lashkari, A.H.; Mamun, M.S.I.; Ghorbani, A. Characterization of Encrypted and VPN Traffic using Time-related Features. In Proceedings of the 2nd International Conference on Information Systems Security and Privacy-ICISSP, Rome, Italy, 19–21 February 2016; pp. 407–414. [CrossRef]
72. Sarker, I.H.; Abushark, Y.B.; Alsolami, F.; Khan, A.I. Intrudtree: A machine learning based cyber security intrusion detection model. *Symmetry* **2020**, *12*, 754. [CrossRef]
73. Almomani, O. A feature selection model for network intrusion detection system based on PSO, GWO, FFA and GA algorithms. *Symmetry* **2020**, *12*, 1046. [CrossRef]
74. McCarthy, A.; Andriotis, P.; Ghadafi, E.; Legg, P. Feature Vulnerability and Robustness Assessment against Adversarial Machine Learning Attacks. In Proceedings of the 2021 International Conference on Cyber Situational Awareness, Data Analytics and Assessment (CyberSA), Dublin, Ireland, 14–18 June 2021; pp. 1–8. [CrossRef]
75. Papernot, N.; McDaniel, P.; Wu, X.; Jha, S.; Swami, A. Distillation as a defense to adversarial perturbations against deep neural networks. In Proceedings of the 2016 IEEE Symposium on Security and Privacy (SP), San Jose, CA, USA, 22–26 May 2016; pp. 582–597.
76. Page, M.J.; McKenzie, J.E.; Bossuyt, P.M.; Boutron, I.; Hoffmann, T.C.; Mulrow, C.D.; Shamseer, L.; Tetzlaff, J.M.; Akl, E.A.; Brennan, S.E.; et al. The PRISMA 2020 statement: An updated guideline for reporting systematic reviews. *BMJ* **2021**, *372*, 1–9. [CrossRef]
77. Biggio, B.; Corona, I.; Maiorca, D.; Nelson, B.; Šrndić, N.; Laskov, P.; Giacinto, G.; Roli, F. Evasion attacks against machine learning at test time. In *Joint European Conference on Machine Learning and Knowledge Discovery in Databases*; Springer: Berlin/Heidelberg, Germany, 2013; pp. 387–402.
78. Papernot, N.; McDaniel, P.; Swami, A.; Harang, R. Crafting adversarial input sequences for recurrent neural networks. In Proceedings of the MILCOM 2016-2016 IEEE Military Communications Conference, Baltimore, MD, USA, 1–3 November 2016; pp. 49–54.
79. Papernot, N.; McDaniel, P.; Jha, S.; Fredrikson, M.; Celik, Z.B.; Swami, A. The Limitations of Deep Learning in Adversarial Settings. In Proceedings of the 2016 IEEE European Symposium on Security and Privacy (EuroS P), Saarbrucken, Germany, 21–24 March 2016; pp. 372–387.
80. Jia, R.; Liang, P. Adversarial Examples for Evaluating Reading Comprehension Systems. In Proceedings of the 2017 Conference on Empirical Methods in Natural Language Processing, Copenhagen, Denmark, 9–11 September 2017; pp. 2021–2031.
81. Zhao, Z.; Dua, D.; Singh, S. Generating Natural Adversarial Examples. In Proceedings of the International Conference on Learning Representations, Vancouver, BC, Canada, 30 April–3 May 2018.
82. Lin, Y.C.; Hong, Z.W.; Liao, Y.H.; Shih, M.L.; Liu, M.Y.; Sun, M. Tactics of adversarial attack on deep reinforcement learning agents. *arXiv* **2017**, arXiv:1703.06748.
83. Rigaki, M. *Adversarial Deep Learning against Intrusion Detection Classifiers*; Luleå University of Technology: Luleå, Sweden, 2017.
84. Hu, W.; Tan, Y. Black-box attacks against RNN based malware detection algorithms. In Proceedings of the Workshops at the Thirty-Second AAAI Conference on Artificial Intelligence, Orleans, LA, USA, 2–7 February 2018.
85. Homoliak, I.; Teknős, M.; Ochoa, M.; Breitenbacher, D.; Hosseini, S.; Hanacek, P. Improving Network Intrusion Detection Classifiers by Non-payload-Based Exploit-Independent Obfuscations: An Adversarial Approach. *EAI Endorsed Trans. Secur. Saf.* **2018**, *5*, e4. [CrossRef]
86. Rosenberg, I.; Shabtai, A.; Rokach, L.; Elovici, Y. Generic black-box end-to-end attack against state of the art API call based malware classifiers. In *International Symposium on Research in Attacks, Intrusions, and Defenses*; Springer: Berlin/Heidelberg, Germany, 2018; pp. 490–510.
87. Wang, Z. Deep learning-based intrusion detection with adversaries. *IEEE Access* **2018**, *6*, 38367–38384. [CrossRef]
88. Warzyński, A.; Kołaczek, G. Intrusion detection systems vulnerability on adversarial examples. In Proceedings of the 2018 Innovations in Intelligent Systems and Applications (INISTA), Thessaloniki, Greece, 3–5 July 2018, pp. 1–4.
89. Lin, Z.; Shi, Y.; Xue, Z. Idsgan: Generative adversarial networks for attack generation against intrusion detection. *arXiv* **2018**, arXiv:1809.02077.
90. Yang, K.; Liu, J.; Zhang, C.; Fang, Y. Adversarial examples against the deep learning based network intrusion detection systems. In Proceedings of the MILCOM 2018-2018 IEEE Military Communications Conference (MILCOM), Los Angeles, CA, USA, 29–31 October 2018; pp. 559–564.
91. Su, J.; Vargas, D.V.; Sakurai, K. One pixel attack for fooling deep neural networks. *IEEE Trans. Evol. Comput.* **2019**, *23*, 828–841. [CrossRef]
92. Kuppa, A.; Grzonkowski, S.; Asghar, M.R.; Le-Khac, N.A. Black box attacks on deep anomaly detectors. In Proceedings of the 14th International Conference on Availability, Reliability and Security, Canterbury, UK, 26–29 August 2019; pp. 1–10.

93. Ibitoye, O.; Shafiq, O.; Matrawy, A. Analyzing adversarial attacks against deep learning for intrusion detection in IoT networks. In Proceedings of the 2019 IEEE Global Communications Conference (GLOBECOM), Waikoloa, HI, USA, 9–13 December 2019; pp. 1–6.

94. Usama, M.; Asim, M.; Latif, S.; Qadir, J. Generative adversarial networks for launching and thwarting adversarial attacks on network intrusion detection systems. In Proceedings of the 2019 15th International Wireless Communications & Mobile Computing Conference (IWCMC), Tangier, Morocco, 24–28 June 2019; pp. 78–83.

95. Huang, W.; Peng, X.; Shi, Z.; Ma, Y. Adversarial Attack against LSTM-based DDoS Intrusion Detection System. In Proceedings of the 2020 IEEE 32nd International Conference on Tools with Artificial Intelligence (ICTAI), Baltimore, MD, USA, 9–11 November 2020; pp. 686–693.

96. Ogawa, Y.; Kimura, T.; Cheng, J. Vulnerability Assessment for Machine Learning Based Network Anomaly Detection System. In Proceedings of the 2020 IEEE International Conference on Consumer Electronics-Taiwan (ICCE-Taiwan), Taoyuan, Taiwan, 28–30 September 2020; pp. 1–2.

97. Chen, J.; Gao, X.; Deng, R.; He, Y.; Fang, C.; Cheng, P. Generating Adversarial Examples against Machine Learning based Intrusion Detector in Industrial Control Systems. *IEEE Trans. Dependable Secur. Comput.* 2020, *PrePrints*. [CrossRef]

98. Demetrio, L.; Biggio, B.; Lagorio, G.; Roli, F.; Armando, A. Functionality-preserving black-box optimization of adversarial windows malware. *IEEE Trans. Inf. Forensics Secur.* **2021**, *16*, 3469–3478. [CrossRef]

99. Labaca-Castro, R.; Muñoz-González, L.; Pendlebury, F.; Rodosek, G.D.; Pierazzi, F.; Cavallaro, L. Universal Adversarial Perturbations for Malware. *arXiv* **2021**, arXiv:2102.06747.

100. Cai, F.; Li, J.; Koutsoukos, X. Detecting adversarial examples in learning-enabled cyber-physical systems using variational autoencoder for regression. In Proceedings of the 2020 IEEE Security and Privacy Workshops (SPW), San Francisco, CA, USA, 21 May 2020; pp. 208–214.

101. Li, J.; Yang, Y.; Sun, J.S.; Tomsovic, K.; Qi, H. Conaml: Constrained adversarial machine learning for cyber-physical systems. In Proceedings of the 2021 ACM Asia Conference on Computer and Communications Security, Hong Kong, China, 7–11 June 2021; pp. 52–66.

102. Tramèr, F.; Kurakin, A.; Papernot, N.; Goodfellow, I.; Boneh, D.; McDaniel, P. Ensemble adversarial training: Attacks and defenses. In Proceedings of the 6th International Conference on Learning Representations, ICLR 2018, Vancouver, BC, Canada, 30 April–3 May 2018.

103. Kurakin, A.; Goodfellow, I.; Bengio, S.; Dong, Y.; Liao, F.; Liang, M.; Pang, T.; Zhu, J.; Hu, X.; Xie, C.; et al. Adversarial attacks and defences competition. In *The NIPS'17 Competition: Building Intelligent Systems*; Springer: Berlin/Heidelberg, Germany, 2018; pp. 195–231.

104. Sharif, M.; Bhagavatula, S.; Bauer, L.; Reiter, M.K. A General Framework for Adversarial Examples with Objectives. *ACM Trans. Priv. Secur.* **2019**, *22*. [CrossRef]

105. Biggio, B.; Roli, F. Wild patterns: Ten years after the rise of adversarial machine learning. *Pattern Recognit.* **2018**, *84*, 317–331. [CrossRef]

106. Gilmer, J.; Adams, R.P.; Goodfellow, I.; Andersen, D.; Dahl, G.E. Motivating the rules of the game for adversarial example research. *arXiv* **2018**, arXiv:1807.06732.

107. Moosavi-Dezfooli, S.M.; Fawzi, A.; Fawzi, O.; Frossard, P. Universal adversarial perturbations. In Proceedings of the IEEE Conference on Computer Vision and Pattern Recognition, Honolulu, HI, USA, 21–26 July 2017; pp. 1765–1773.

108. Chernikova, A.; Oprea, A. Fence: Feasible evasion attacks on neural networks in constrained environments. *arXiv* **2019**, arXiv:1909.10480.

109. Apruzzese, G.; Colajanni, M.; Marchetti, M. Evaluating the effectiveness of adversarial attacks against botnet detectors. In Proceedings of the 2019 IEEE 18th International Symposium on Network Computing and Applications (NCA), Cambridge, MA, USA, 26–28 September 2019; pp. 1–8.

110. Hashemi, M.J.; Cusack, G.; Keller, E. Towards evaluation of nidss in adversarial setting. In Proceedings of the 3rd ACM CoNEXT Workshop on Big DAta, Machine Learning and Artificial Intelligence for Data Communication Networks, Orlando, FL, USA, 9 December 2019, pp. 14–21.

111. Papadopoulos, P.; Essen, O.T.v.; Pitropakis, N.; Chrysoulas, C.; Mylonas, A.; Buchanan, W.J. Launching Adversarial Attacks against Network Intrusion Detection Systems for IoT. *J. Cybersecur. Priv.* **2021**, *1*, 14. [CrossRef]

112. Anthi, E.; Williams, L.; Rhode, M.; Burnap, P.; Wedgbury, A. Adversarial attacks on machine learning cybersecurity defences in industrial control systems. *J. Inf. Secur. Appl.* **2021**, *58*, 102717. [CrossRef]

113. Han, D.; Wang, Z.; Zhong, Y.; Chen, W.; Yang, J.; Lu, S.; Shi, X.; Yin, X. Evaluating and Improving Adversarial Robustness of Machine Learning-Based Network Intrusion Detectors. *IEEE J. Sel. Areas Commun.* **2021**, *39*, 2632–2647. [CrossRef]

114. Duy, P.T.; Khoa, N.H.; Nguyen, A.G.T.; Pham, V.H. DIGFuPAS: Deceive IDS with GAN and Function-Preserving on Adversarial Samples in SDN-enabled networks. *Comput. Secur.* **2021**, *109*, 102367. [CrossRef]

115. Alhajjar, E.; Maxwell, P.; Bastian, N. Adversarial machine learning in network intrusion detection systems. *Expert Syst. Appl.* **2021**, *186*, 115782. [CrossRef]

116. Han, D.; Wang, Z.; Zhong, Y.; Chen, W.; Yang, J.; Lu, S.; Shi, X.; Yin, X. Practical Traffic-Space Adversarial Attacks on Learning-Based Nidss. *arXiv* **2005**, arXiv:2005.07519.

117. Wang, J.; Pan, J.; AlQerm, I.; Liu, Y. Def-IDS: An Ensemble Defense Mechanism Against Adversarial Attacks for Deep Learning-based Network Intrusion Detection. In Proceedings of the 2021 International Conference on Computer Communications and Networks (ICCCN), Athens, Greece, 19–22 July 2021; pp. 1–9.
118. Ali, H.; Khan, M.S.; AlGhadhban, A.; Alazmi, M.; Alzamil, A.; Al-utaibi, K.; Qadir, J. Analyzing the Robustness of Fake-news Detectors under Black-box Adversarial Attacks. *IEEE Access* **2021**, 9, 81678–81692. [CrossRef]
119. Chenou, J.; Hsieh, G.; Fields, T. Radial Basis Function Network: Its Robustness and Ability to Mitigate Adversarial Examples. In Proceedings of the 2019 International Conference on Computational Science and Computational Intelligence (CSCI), Las Vegas, NV, USA, 5–7 December 2019; pp. 102–106.
120. Wei, W.; Liu, L.; Loper, M.; Truex, S.; Yu, L.; Gursoy, M.E.; Wu, Y. Adversarial examples in deep learning: Characterization and divergence. *arXiv* **2018**, arXiv:1807.00051.
121. Tramèr, F.; Zhang, F.; Juels, A.; Reiter, M.K.; Ristenpart, T. Stealing machine learning models via prediction apis. In Proceedings of the 5th USENIX Security Symposium (USENIX Security 16), Austin, TX, USA, 10–12 August 2016; pp. 601–618.
122. Lillicrap, T.P.; Cownden, D.; Tweed, D.B.; Akerman, C.J. Random synaptic feedback weights support error backpropagation for deep learning. *Nat. Commun.* **2016**, 7, 1–10. [CrossRef]
123. Graese, A.; Rozsa, A.; Boult, T.E. Assessing Threat of Adversarial Examples on Deep Neural Networks. In Proceedings of the 2016 15th IEEE International Conference on Machine Learning and Applications (ICMLA), Anaheim, CA, USA, 18–20 December 2016; pp. 69–74. [CrossRef]
124. Grosse, K.; Manoharan, P.; Papernot, N.; Backes, M.; McDaniel, P. On the (statistical) detection of adversarial examples. *arXiv* **2017**, arXiv:1702.06280.
125. Metzen, J.H.; Genewein, T.; Fischer, V.; Bischoff, B. On detecting adversarial perturbations. *arXiv* **2017**, arXiv:1702.04267.
126. Feinman, R.; Curtin, R.R.; Shintre, S.; Gardner, A.B. Detecting adversarial samples from artifacts. *arXiv* **2017**, arXiv:1703.00410.
127. Meng, D.; Chen, H. Magnet: A two-pronged defense against adversarial examples. In Proceedings of the 2017 ACM SIGSAC Conference on Computer and Communications Security, Dallas, TX, USA, 30 October–3 November 2017; pp. 135–147.
128. Xu, W.; Evans, D.; Qi, Y. Feature squeezing: Detecting adversarial examples in deep neural networks. *arXiv* **2017**, arXiv:1704.01155.
129. Lee, H.; Han, S.; Lee, J. Generative adversarial trainer: Defense to adversarial perturbations with gan. *arXiv* **2017**, arXiv:1705.03387.
130. Samangouei, P.; Kabkab, M.; Chellappa, R. Defense-gan: Protecting classifiers against adversarial attacks using generative models. *arXiv* **2018**, arXiv:1805.06605.
131. Dhillon, G.S.; Azizzadenesheli, K.; Lipton, Z.C.; Bernstein, J.; Kossaifi, J.; Khanna, A.; Anandkumar, A. Stochastic activation pruning for robust adversarial defense. *arXiv* **2018**, arXiv:1803.01442.
132. Tian, Y.; Pei, K.; Jana, S.; Ray, B. Deeptest: Automated testing of deep-neural-network-driven autonomous cars. In Proceedings of the 40th International Conference on Software Engineering, Gothenburg, Sweden, 27 May–3 June 2018; pp. 303–314.
133. Zhang, M.; Zhang, Y.; Zhang, L.; Liu, C.; Khurshid, S. DeepRoad: GAN-based metamorphic testing and input validation framework for autonomous driving systems. In Proceedings of the 2018 33rd IEEE/ACM International Conference on Automated Software Engineering (ASE), Montpellier, France, 3–7 September 2018; pp. 132–142.
134. Wang, S.; Wang, X.; Zhao, P.; Wen, W.; Kaeli, D.; Chin, P.; Lin, X. Defensive dropout for hardening deep neural networks under adversarial attacks. In Proceedings of the International Conference on Computer-Aided Design, San Diego, CA, USA, 5–8 November 2018; pp. 1–8.
135. Amer, M.; Maul, T. Weight Map Layer for Noise and Adversarial Attack Robustness. *arXiv* **2019**, arXiv:1905.00568.
136. Rosenberg, I.; Shabtai, A.; Elovici, Y.; Rokach, L. Defense methods against adversarial examples for recurrent neural networks. *arXiv* **2019**, arXiv:1901.09963.
137. Apruzzese, G.; Andreolini, M.; Marchetti, M.; Venturi, A.; Colajanni, M. Deep reinforcement adversarial learning against botnet evasion attacks. *IEEE Trans. Netw. Serv. Manag.* **2020**, 17, 1975–1987. [CrossRef]
138. Apruzzese, G.; Colajanni, M.; Ferretti, L.; Marchetti, M. Addressing adversarial attacks against security systems based on machine learning. In Proceedings of the 2019 11th International Conference on Cyber Conflict (CyCon), Tallinn, Estonia. 28–31 May 2019; Volume 900, pp. 1–18.
139. Zhou, Y.; Kantarcioglu, M.; Xi, B. A survey of game theoretic approach for adversarial machine learning. *Wiley Interdiscip. Rev. Data Min. Knowl. Discov.* **2019**, 9, e1259. [CrossRef]
140. Apruzzese, G.; Andreolini, M.; Colajanni, M.; Marchetti, M. Hardening random forest cyber detectors against adversarial attacks. *IEEE Trans. Emerg. Top. Comput. Intell.* **2020**, 4, 427–439. [CrossRef]
141. Zhang, C.; Tang, Z.; Zuo, Y.; Li, K.; Li, K. A robust generative classifier against transfer attacks based on variational auto-encoders. *Inf. Sci.* **2021**, 550, 57–70. [CrossRef]
142. Wang, N.; Chen, Y.; Hu, Y.; Lou, W.; Hou, Y.T. MANDA: On Adversarial Example Detection for Network Intrusion Detection System. In Proceedings of the IEEE INFOCOM 2021-IEEE Conference on Computer Communications, Vancouver, BC, Canada, 10–13 May 2021; pp. 1–10.
143. Song, D.; Eykholt, K.; Evtimov, I.; Fernandes, E.; Li, B.; Rahmati, A.; Tramer, F.; Prakash, A.; Kohno, T. Physical adversarial examples for object detectors. In Proceedings of the 12th USENIX Workshop on Offensive Technologies (WOOT 18), Baltimore, MA, USA, 13–14 August 2018.

144. Gal, Y.; Ghahramani, Z. Dropout as a bayesian approximation: Representing model uncertainty in deep learning. In *International Conference on Machine Learning*; PMLR: New York, NY, USA, 2016; pp. 1050–1059.
145. Carlini, N.; Wagner, D. Adversarial examples are not easily detected: Bypassing ten detection methods. In Proceedings of the 10th ACM Workshop on Artificial Intelligence and Security, Dallas, TX, USA, 3 November 2017; pp. 3–14.
146. Pei, K.; Cao, Y.; Yang, J.; Jana, S. Deepxplore: Automated whitebox testing of deep learning systems. In Proceedings of the 26th Symposium on Operating Systems Principles, Shanghai, China, 28–31 October 2017; pp. 1–18.
147. Biggio, B.; Fumera, G.; Roli, F. Adversarial pattern classification using multiple classifiers and randomisation. In *Joint IAPR International Workshops on Statistical Techniques in Pattern Recognition (SPR) and Structural and Syntactic Pattern Recognition (SSPR)*; Springer: Berlin/Heidelberg, Germany, 2008; pp. 500–509.
148. Carlini, N. A Complete List of All (Arxiv) Adversarial Example Papers. Available online: https://nicholas.carlini.com/writing/2019/all-adversarial-example-papers.html (accessed on 30 January 2022).
149. Sculley, D.; Holt, G.; Golovin, D.; Davydov, E.; Phillips, T.; Ebner, D.; Chaudhary, V.; Young, M.; Crespo, J.F.; Dennison, D. Hidden technical debt in machine learning systems. In Proceedings of the Advances in Neural Information Processing Systems, Montreal, QC, Canada, 7–12 December 2015; pp. 2503–2511.
150. Shu, D.; Leslie, N.O.; Kamhoua, C.A.; Tucker, C.S. Generative adversarial attacks against intrusion detection systems using active learning. In Proceedings of the 2nd ACM Workshop on Wireless Security and Machine Learning, Linz, Austria, 13 July 2020; pp. 1–6.

Journal of
*Cybersecurity
and Privacy*

MDPI

Article

Comparison of Deepfake Detection Techniques through Deep Learning

Maryam Taeb [1] and Hongmei Chi [2,*]

[1] Electrical and Computer Engineering, FAMU-FSU College of Engineering, Tallahassee, FL 32310, USA; mr21cg@my.fsu.edu
[2] Department of Computer Sciences, Florida A&M University, BBTA RM 309, 1333 Wahnish Way, Tallahassee, FL 32307, USA
* Correspondence: hongmei.chi@famu.edu; Tel.: +1-850-599-3050

Abstract: Deepfakes are realistic-looking fake media generated by deep-learning algorithms that iterate through large datasets until they have learned how to solve the given problem (i.e., swap faces or objects in video and digital content). The massive generation of such content and modification technologies is rapidly affecting the quality of public discourse and the safeguarding of human rights. Deepfakes are being widely used as a malicious source of misinformation in court that seek to sway a court's decision. Because digital evidence is critical to the outcome of many legal cases, detecting deepfake media is extremely important and in high demand in digital forensics. As such, it is important to identify and build a classifier that can accurately distinguish between authentic and disguised media, especially in facial-recognition systems as it can be used in identity protection too. In this work, we compare the most common, state-of-the-art face-detection classifiers such as Custom CNN, VGG19, and DenseNet-121 using an augmented real and fake face-detection dataset. Data augmentation is used to boost performance and reduce computational resources. Our preliminary results indicate that VGG19 has the best performance and highest accuracy of 95% when compared with other analyzed models.

Keywords: deepfake detection; digital forensics; media forensics; deep learning; VGG19; face-image manipulation

Citation: Taeb, M.; Chi, H. Comparison of Deepfake Detection Techniques through Deep Learning. *J. Cybersecur. Priv.* **2022**, 2, 89–106. https://doi.org/10.3390/jcp2010007

Academic Editors: Phil Legg and Giorgio Giacinto

Received: 10 January 2022
Accepted: 21 February 2022
Published: 4 March 2022

Publisher's Note: MDPI stays neutral with regard to jurisdictional claims in published maps and institutional affiliations.

1. Introduction

In the last few years, cybercrime, which accounts for a 67% increase in the incidents of security breaches, has been one of the most challenging problems that national security systems have had to deal with worldwide [1]. Deepfakes (i.e., realistic-looking fake media that has been generated by deep-learning algorithms) are being widely used to swap faces or objects in video and digital content. This artificial intelligence-synthesized content can have a significant impact on the determination of legitimacy due to its wide variety of applications and formats that deepfakes present online (i.e., audio, image and video).

Considering the quickness, ease of use, and impacts of social media, persuasive deepfakes can rapidly influence millions of people, destroy the lives of its victims and have a negative impact on society in general [1]. The generation of deepfake media can have a wide range of intentions and motivations, from revenge porn to political fake news. Rana Ayyub, an investigative journalist in India, became a target of this practice when a deepfake sex video showing her face on another woman's body was circulated on the Internet in April 2018 [2]. Deepfakes have also been published to falsify satellite images with non-existent landscape features for malicious purposes [3].

There are numerous captivating applications of deepfakery in video compositing and transfiguration in portraits, especially in identity protection as it can replace faces in photographs with ones from a collection of stock images. Cyber-attackers, using various strategies other than deepfakery, are always aiming to penetrate identification or authentication systems to gain illegitimate access. Therefore, identifying deepfake media using forensic methods remains an immense challenge since cyber-attackers always leverage newly published detection methods to immediately incorporate them in the next generation of deepfake generation methods. With the massive usage of the Internet and social media, and billions of images available on the Internet, there has been an immense loss of trust from social media users. Deepfakes are a significant threat to our society and to digital evidence in courts. Therefore, it is highly important to obtain state-of-the-art techniques to identify deepfake media under criminal investigation.

As demonstrated in Table 1 (inspired by the figure presented in [1]), tampering of evidence, scams and frauds (i.e., fake news), digital kidnapping associated with ransomware blackmailing, revenge porn and political sabotage are among the vast majority of types of deepfake activities with the highest level of intention to mislead [1].

Table 1. Deepfake Information trust Table.

Type of Media	Examples	Intention to Mislead	Level of Truth
Hoax	Tampering evidence Scam and Fraud Harming Credibility	High	Low
Entertainment	Altering movies Editing Special effects Art Demonstration	Low	Low
Propaganda	Misdirection Political Warfare Corruption	High	High
Trusted	Authentic Content	Low	High

The first deepfake content published on the Internet was a celebrity pornographic video that was created by a Reddit user (named deepfake) in 2017. The Generative Adversarial Network (GAN) was first introduced in 2014 and used for image-enhancement purposes only [4]. However, since the first published deepfake media, it has been unavoidable for deepfake and GAN technology to be used for malicious uses. Therefore, in 2017, GANs were used to generate new facial images for malicious uses for the first time [5]. Following that, there has been a constant development of other deepfake-based applications such as FakeApp and FaceSwap. In 2019, Deepnude was developed and provided undressed videos of the input data [6]. The widespread strategies used to manipulate multimedia files can be broadly categorized into the following major categories: copy–move, splicing, deepfake, and resampling [7]. Copy–move, splicing and resampling involve repositioning the contents of a photo, overlapping different regions of multiple photos into a new one, and manipulating the scale and position of components of a photo. The final goal is to manipulate the user by conveying the deception of having a larger number of components in the photograph than those that were initially present. Deepfake media, however, leveraging powerful machine-learning (ML) techniques, have significantly improved the manipulation of the contents. Deepfake can be considered to be a type of splicing, where a person's face, sound, or actions in media is swiped by a fake target [8]. A wide set of cybercrime activities are usually associated with this type of manipulation technique, and while spreading them is easy, correcting the records and avoiding deepfakes are harder [9]. Consequently, it is becoming harder for machine-learning techniques to identify convolutional traces of deepfake generation algorithms, as there needs to be frequency-specific anomaly analysis. The most basic algorithms that were being used to train models for the task of deepfake detection such as Support Vector Machine (SVM), Convolution Neural Network (CNN), and Recurrent Neural Network (RNN) are now being coupled with multi-attentional [10] or ensemble [11] methods to increase the performance and address weakness of other methods. As proposed by [12], by implementing an ensemble of standard and attention-based data-augmented detection networks, the generalization issue of the previous approaches can be avoided. As such, it is of high importance to identify the most suitable algorithms for the backbone layers in multi-attentional and ensembled architectures. As generation of deepfake media only started in 2017, academic writing on the problem is meager [13]. Most of the developed and published methods/techniques are focused on deepfake videos. The main difference between deepfake video- and image-detection methods is that video-detection methods can leverage spatial features [14], spatio-temporal anomalies [15] and supervised domain [16] to draw a conclusion on the whole video by aggregating the inferred output both in time and across multiple faces. However, deepfake image-detection techniques have access to one face image only and mostly leverage pixel- [17] and noise-level analysis [18] to identify the traces of the manipulation method.

Therefore, identifying the most reliable methods for face-image forgery detection that relies on convolutional neural networks (CNN) as the backbone for a binary classification task could provide valuable insight for the future direction in the development of deepfake-detection techniques. The overall approach taken in this work is illustrated in Figure 1.

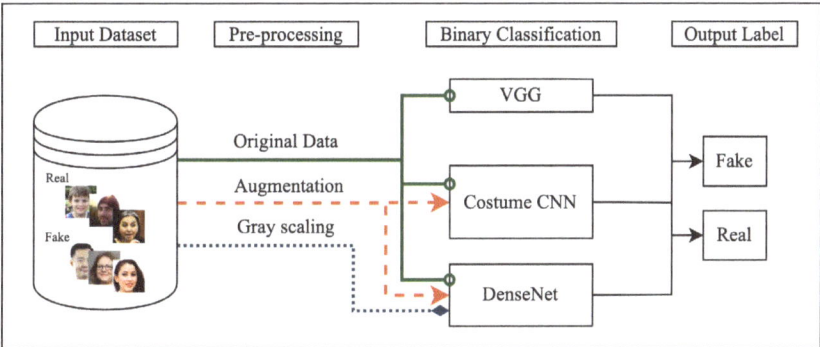

Figure 1. General overview of our proposed approach to detect deepfake media in a digital forensics scenario.

DenseNet has shown significant promise in the field of facial recognition. DenseNet as an extension of Residual CNN (ResNet) architecture has addressed the low-supervision problem of all its counterparts by initiating a between-layer connection using dense blocks. The dense blocks in the DenseNet architecture improve the learning process by leveraging a transition layer (essentially convolution, average pooling, and batch normalization between each dense block) that concatenates feature maps. As such, gradients from the initial input and loss function are shared by all the layers. The described implementation reduces the number of required parameters and feature maps, and consequently provides a less computationally expensive model. Therefore, we have decided to test DenseNet's capabilities and compare it with other neural network architectures.

VGG-19, as an algorithm that has been widely used to extract the features of the detected face frames [19], was chosen to be compared with the DenseNet architecture. VGG-19's architecture eases the face-annotation process by forming a large training dataset with the use of online knowledge sources that are then used to implement deep CNNs to perform the task of face recognition. The formed model is then evaluated on face recognition benchmarks to analyze model efficiency regarding the generation of facial features. During this process, VGG-19 is trained on classifiers with sigmoid activation function in the output layer which produces a vector representation of facial features (face embedding) to fine-tune the model. The fine-tuning process differentiates class similarities using Euclidean distance that is achieved using a triplet loss function that aims at comparing Euclidean spaces of similar and different faces using learning score vectors. The CNN architecture implemented in VGG-19 implements fully connected classifiers that include kernels and ReLU activation followed by maxpooling layers.

Finally, we have implemented a Custom CNN architecture to evaluate the performance of previously described algorithms and analyze the effectiveness of dropout, padding, augmentation and grayscale analysis on model performance.

This study aims to provide an in-depth analysis on the described algorithms, structures and mechanisms that could be leveraged in the implementation of an ensembled multi-attentional network to identify deepfake media. The result of this work contributes to the nascent literature on deepfakery by providing a comparative study on effective algorithms for deepfake detection on facial images within the possible use of digital forensics in criminal investigations.

The rest of this paper is organized as follows. Section 2 provides a literature review of the algorithms and datasets that are widely used for deepfake detection. Section 3 provides details on the analysis methods and configurations of the compared algorithms as well as with the details on the tested dataset. Section 4 provides the results of the comparative analysis. Finally, Section 5 concludes with implications, limitations, and suggestions for future research.

2. Literature Review

Anti-deepfake technology can be divided into three categories: (1) detection of the deepfake; (2) authentication of the published content; and (3) prevention of the spread of contents that can be used for deepfake production. Technology towards detection and authentication of deepfakery is growing fast; however, the capacity to generate deepfakes is proceeding much faster than the ability to detect them. Twitter has reported attempts to publish misinformation and fake media by 8 million accounts per week [20]. There has been a wide variety of deepfake media, and the detection techniques that have been used to identify them is shown in Figure 2. This has created a massive challenge for researchers to provide a solution that can promptly analyze all the posted material on the Internet and social media platforms to identify deepfakes. Previous research has mostly aimed at improving previously developed technologies to train a new detection system.

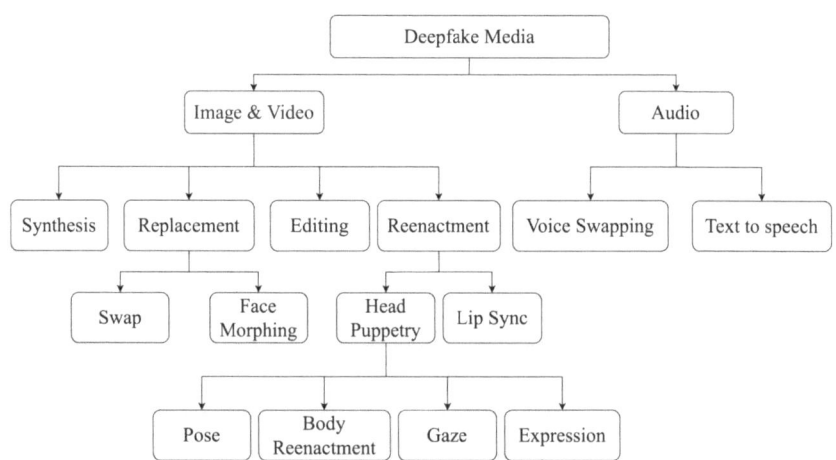

Figure 2. Current deepfake media types and detection techniques.

2.1. Deepfake Detection Datasets

Deepfake detection systems typically leverage binary classifiers to cluster information into real and fake classes. This method requires a great quantity of good-quality authentic and tampered data to train classification models. The first known datasets that had a great impact on the growth and improvement of deepfake detection technologies were UADFV [21] and DFTIMIT [22]. FaceForensics++ dataset includes 977 downloaded videos from YouTube, provides 1000 sequences of original unobstructed faces, as well as their manipulated versions. The manipulated versions were generated by four methods: Deepfakes, Face2Face, FaceSwap and NeuralTextures [23]. The DeepFakeDetection dataset (DFD) released by Google in collaboration with Jigsaw contains over 363 original sequences from 28 paid actors in 16 different scenes as well as over 3000 manipulated videos using deepfakes [23]. The Deepfake Detection Challenge (DFDC) dataset [24] published by Facebook is another publicly available large dataset that includes over 100,000 total clips from 3426 actors, produced with deepfake, GAN-based and unsupervised models. Celeb-DF (v2) [25] dataset published by [25] is an extension to Celeb-DF (v1) that contains real and fake videos that are generated via deepfake algorithm by providing images with the same quality as the synthesized videos circulating online. This dataset provides 5639 videos with subjects of different ages, ethnic groups and genders, and their corresponding deepfake videos. The DeeperForensics-1.0 dataset is a large-scale benchmark for face forgery detection that represents the largest face forgery detection dataset by far. This benchmark includes 60,000 videos forming a total of 17.6 million frames generated by an end-to-end face-swapping framework. Furthermore, extensive real-world perturbations are applied to obtain a more challenging benchmark of larger scale and higher diversity [26].

For our research and analysis, we took the "Real and Fake Face-Detection" dataset from Yonsei University [27] that contains expert-generated high-quality PhotoShopped face images. The dataset includes 960 fake and 1081 real images that are composites of different faces, separated by eyes, nose, mouth, or whole face. The second dataset that has been used in this work is the "140K Real and Fake Faces" that consists of 70K real faces from the Flickr dataset collected by Nvidia, as well as 70K fake faces sampled from the 1 million fake faces (generated by StyleGAN) that were published by Bojan [28]. These two datasets were used to include both GAN-generated images along with expert/human-generated images to provide many good-quality data. All the above-mentioned datasets can be used for image and video classification, segmentation, generation and augmentation of new data. Table 2 represents a cumulative comparison of the mentioned datasets; please note that the rows with a "*" sign include images only (not videos). Deepfake datasets have been categorized into two generations based on several factors and elements. Considering release time and synthesis algorithms involved in the generation of the data, UADFV and DF-TIMIT are categorized as the first generation. Considering the quality and quantity of the generated data, DFD, DeeperForensics, DFDC, and the Celeb-DF datasets are categorized as the second generation [25].

Table 2. Comparison of publicly available deepfake datasets.

Dataset	Real		Fake		Generation Method	Release Date	Generation Group
	Video	Frame	Video	Frame			
UADFV	49	17.3K	49	17.3K	FakeAPP	11/2018	1st
DF-TIMIT	320	34K	320	34K	Faceswap-GAN	12/2018	1st
*Real & Fake Face Detection	1081	405.2K	960	399.8K	Expert-generated high-quality photoshopped	01/2019	2st
FaceForensics++	1000	509.9k	1000	509.9K	DeepFakes, Face2Face, FaceSwap, NeuralTextures	01/2019	2nd
DeepFakeDetection	363	315.4K	3068	2242.7K	Similar to FaceForensics++	09/2019	2nd
DFDC	1131	488.4K	4113	1783.3K	Deepfake, GAN-based, and non-learned methods	10/2019	2nd
Celeb-DF	590	225.4K	5639	2116.8K	Improved DeepFake synthesis algorithm	11/2019	2nd
*140K Real & Fake Faces	70K	15.8M	70K	15.8M	StyleGAN	12/2019	2nd
DeeperForensics	50,000	12.6M	10,000	2.3M	Newly proposed end-to-end face swapping framework	06/2020	2nd

2.2. Deepfake Detection Algorithms

Deepfake detection techniques aim to conceal revealing traces of deepfakes by extracting semantic and contextual understanding of the content. Research in the field of media forensics provides a wide range of imperfections as indicators of fake media: face wobble, shimmer and distortion; waviness in a person's movements; inconsistencies with speech and mouth movements; abnormal movements of fixed objects such as a microphone stand; inconsistencies in lighting, reflections and shadows; blurred edges; angles and blurring of facial features; lack of breathing; unnatural eye direction; missing facial features such as a known mole on a cheek; softness and weight of clothing and hair; overly smooth skin; missing hair and teeth details; misalignment in face symmetry; inconsistencies in pixel levels; and strange behavior of an individual doing something implausible are all the indicators and features used by deepfake detection algorithms [13]. The use of deep-learning techniques and algorithms such as CNN and GAN has made deepfake detection more challenging for forensics models because deepfakes can preserve pose, facial expression and lighting of the photographs [29]. Frequency domain, JPEG Ghost and Error Level Analysis (ELA) are among the first methods that were used to identify manipulation traces on images. However, they are not successful in identifying manipulated images that are generated with deep-learning and GAN algorithms. Neural networks are one of the most widely used methods for deepfake detection. There are some proposals on the usage of X-rays [18], and spectrograms [30] to identify traces of blending and noise in deepfake media. However, such methods cannot detect random noise and suffer from a performance drop when encountering low-resolution images. Deepfakes are implemented mainly using a CNN that generates deepfake images and an encoder–decoder network structure (ED), or GAN [4] that synthesizes fake videos. Deepfake detection techniques focused on anomalies in the face region only can be categorized into holistic and feature-based matching techniques [31]. The holistic techniques, which are mostly used to identify deepfake face images and include Principal Component Analysis (PCA), Support Vector Machines (SVM), and CNN, mainly analyze the face as a whole. These techniques aim at reducing data dimensionality by forming a smaller set of linear combinations of the image pixels that are then fed to a binary classifier to identify authentic and fake images. Feature-based or attention-based matching techniques, however, are used for both deepfake video and image identification, and split the whole face into different regions of focus such as eye, nose, lips, skin, head position, color mismatches, etc. [32]. Holistic techniques are successful in detecting localized deepfake characteristics (i.e., anomalies in the face and jaw region) and can be leveraged to identify specific feature characteristics (eyes, nose, mouth) that could be significant in detection [12]. Convolutional Neural Network (CNN)-based image classification and recognition models have been proven to be trainable to classify manipulated images from authentic ones [33]. Luca et al. [34] aimed to extract and detect fingerprints that represent convolution traces left in the process of generating GAN images using the Expectation-Maximization algorithm. Wang et al. [35] demonstrated that with careful pre- and post-processing and data augmentation, a standard classifier trained on ProGAN, an unconditional CNN generator can be generalized surprisingly well to unseen architectures, datasets, and training methods. CNN have also been trained to detect manipulation techniques such as lack of eye-blinking [36], missing details in eyes from an image [37], and facial wrapping artifacts. Furthermore, CNNs have been shown to be able to capture distinctive traces of generation methods that have worked on further wrapping the faces with high-resolution sources [17].

VGG19 and VGG16 has significantly improved large-scale fake image recognition by increasing the layer depth (23/26 layers) of CNN-based models [38]. Chang et al. [39] presented an improved VGG network, namely NA-VGG, based on image augmentation and noise-level analysis to detect a deepfake face image. The experimental results using the Celeb-DF dataset shows that NA-VGG improved accuracy over other state-of-the-art fake image detectors. Kim et al. [40] demonstrated that VGG-16 has a better performance than the ShallowNet architecture to classify genuine facial images from disguised face images.

Furthermore, DenseNet architecture has also been demonstrated to be computationally more efficient with its feed-forward design network, which connects each layer to every other layer [41]. In DenseNet architecture, feature maps of all former layers are used as the input for each layer. DenseNet requires significantly fewer parameters and computation to achieve state-of-the-art performance [33]. Hsu, Chih-Chung, Yi-Xiu Zhuang, and Chia-Yen

Lee [42] in their work proposed a fake face-image detector based on the novel CFFN, consisting of an improved DenseNet backbone network and Siamese network architecture. Their comprehensive analysis demonstrated that deep features-based deepfake-detection systems such as DenseNet obtain significant accuracy when trained and tested on the same kind of manipulation technique.

Feature-based techniques have started identifying the deficiencies of deepfake generation methods such as unnatural eye-blinking patterns and temporal flickering, which gave rise to a more improved generation of deepfake models that were trained on datasets that have addressed the identified deficiencies. Yang et al. [43] demonstrated that facial landmarks could be used to provide an estimate of head posture direction. The work of [44,45] illustrated that eye pupils' inconsistencies are one of the indicators of fake media. Some studies [46] including audio into the training process have illustrated that the difference between lip movements and voice matching distinguishes real and fake media. There have been some efforts on domain-specific deepfake detection such as [47] that leveraged forensic techniques to model political leaders' facial expressions and speaking patterns; however, it would be a more difficult task to train and generalize such approach for the whole world. Even though feature-based techniques are more robust to deformations, they have been mainly designed to have the best performance on domain-specific datasets. Holistic techniques are competent in learning human faces and extracting higher-dimensional semantic features for classification.

Other techniques that leverage spatial features and spatio-temporal anomalies in the supervised domain such as Xception [48] and EfficientNet [49] have been shown to be more efficient than CNNs. Xception architecture claims to gain a more efficient use of model parameters due to depthwise separable convolutions that can understand as an inception module. Kumar and Bhavsar [16] demonstrated that Xception combined with metric learning can enhance the classification in high-compression scenarios. They were able to achieve an AUC score of 99.2% and accuracy of 90.71% for deepfake video identification on the Celeb-DF dataset. Ismail et al. [14] in their experimental analysis demonstrated that XceptionNet combined with an additional Bi-LSTM and LSTM layer can achieve a 79% ROC-AUC score. Li et al. [50] demonstrated that Xception does not have a good performance on face-image datasets (AUC of 73.2) and, furthermore, it has a high true-negative rate while having the lowest true-positive rate. To summarize, Xception may provide better performance for fake video detection; however, it does not address the generalizability issue across different datasets and does not perform well when fed with images only. EfficientNET proposes a new scaling method that uniformly scales all dimensions of depth/width/resolution using compound coefficient. Coccomini et al. [15] were able to achieve an AUC of 0.95% and F1-score of 88% on the DFDC dataset. Pokroy and Egorov [51] demonstrated that an increased scale in all dimensions may not always lead to higher accuracy due to the fact that CNNs will have to deal with more complex patterns that are difficult to transfer to a different task. Mitra et al. [52] were able to achieve a 96% accuracy on the FaseForensics++ dataset by making the complexity of detecting forged videos low using the depthwise separable convulsion of EfficientNet. In conclusion, Xception and EfficientNet, by uniformly scaling all dimensions, can gain a more efficient use of model parameters. Furthermore, they can extract spatial features and spatio-temporal anomalies by aggregating the inferred output both in time and across multiple faces due to their depthwise separable convolutions. These methods have illustrated that they can draw an improved conclusion on the whole video; however, they have not demonstrated any improvements to deepfake classification on a single image (i.e., deepfake image-detection).

Recent scholarly work has been focused on implementing an ensemble of holistic and feature-based detection networks by addressing the drawbacks of both methods. Dolescki et al. [53], in their work implementing a classification method, which involves a collection of classifiers with a certain utility function regarded as an aggregation operator, were able to achieve accuracy of 87%. Silva et al. [12] were able to achieve a 92% accuracy on the DFDC dataset by implementing a hierarchical explainable forensics algorithm that incorporates humans in the detection loop. Hanqing et al. [10] proposed a multi-attentional deepfake detection network that can achieve a 97% accuracy by implementing multiple spatial attention heads, textural feature enhancement blocks and aggregating low-level textural features and high-level semantic features. Bonettini et al. [11] were able to achieve AUC of 87% on DFDC by assembling different trained Convolutional Neural Network (CNN) models that combined EfficientNetB4 with attention layers and Siamese training. Du et al. [54] demonstrated that a good balance between accuracy and efficiency can be achieved with two separated EfficientNet architectures that simultaneously analyze raw content and its frequency-domain representation.

Given that the most successful approaches to identifying and preventing deepfakes are deep-learning methods that rely on CNNs as the backbone for a binary classification task [12], and a large 2D CNN model can prove to be better than EfficientNet model if deepfake classification is the only desired result [55], we have evaluated the most common backbone architecture of existing developed frameworks (CNN, VGG-19 and DenseNet) that are demonstrated to have the best performance on the task of deepfake image classification.

3. Approach

Our proposed method for deepfake detection on images is shown in Figure 1. We have taken two different classification procedures in this work. As shown in both Figures 1 and 3, input data goes through the same procedure with the same architecture; however, Figure 3 demonstrates a second round of analysis with an additional post-processing classification step that has been added to the last output layer of the analyzed models. The second round of analysis with additional post-processing was performed to analyze the effects of principal component analysis on the task of deepfake classification. Further details about the post-processing step are described in the final paragraphs of the evaluation subsection of this section.

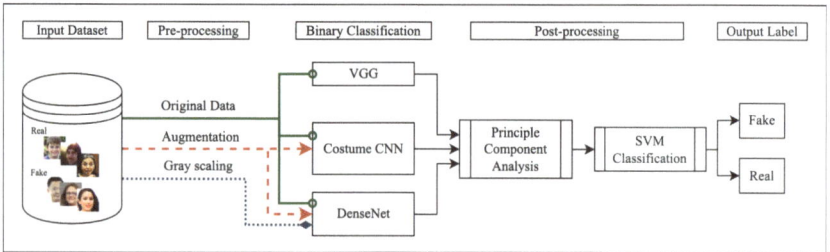

Figure 3. Detailed steps of post-processing in our proposed approach for deepfake detection.

3.1. Implementation

Input data are a dataset that is labeled and clustered into two categories of real and fake. They are augmented for training purposes using the following specifications:

- Rotation range of 20 for DenseNET and no rotation on Custom CNN
- Scaling factor of 1/255 was used for coefficient reduction
- Shear range of 0.2 to randomly apply shearing transformations
- Zoom range of 0.2 to randomly zoom inside pictures
- Randomized images using horizontal and vertical flipping

After augmentation, the face images are classified as either fake or real using three different models: Custom CNN, VGG, and DenseNET. We defined two classes for our binary classification task: 0 to denote the real (e.g., normal, validation, and disguised face images) and 1 to denote fake (e.g., impersonator face images) groups, respectively.

The "Real and Fake Face-Detection" dataset was used to train the three models at a learning rate of 0.001 and for 10 epochs. The test accuracy was then calculated using the test set. We applied data augmentation to flip all original images horizontally and vertically, hence a three-fold increase of the dataset size (original image + horizontally flipped image + vertically flipped image).

The Custom CNN architecture included six convolution layers (Conv2D) each paired with batch normalization, max pooling and dropout layers. Rectified Linear Unit (ReLU) and sigmoid activation functions were applied for the input and output layers respectively. Dropout was applied to each layer to minimize over-fitting and padding was also applied to the kernel to allow for a more accurate analysis of images. The Custom CNN architectures have been trained and validated on the original and augmented datasets with a 1/255 scaling factor. Data augmentation was performed to observe effects of data aggregation on model performance and promote the generalizability of the findings. Details on augmentation process includes horizontal flip along with a 0.2 zoom range, shear range of 0.2 along with rescaling factor to avoid image quality to factor in model behavior during classification since not all the images had the same pixel-level quality.

Following a similar approach to [56], **the VGG-19** model that was used is a 16-layer CNN architecture paired with three fully connected layers, five maxpooling layers and one SoftMax layer that is modeled from architectures in [56]. VGG-19 has been pretrained on a wide variety of object categories, which leads to its ability to learn rich feature representations. VGG-19 has demonstrated that it can provide a high accuracy level when classifying partial faces. This architecture demonstrated that its highest accuracy is accessible when its size is increased [57]; therefore, we have applied a high-end configuration to it by adding a dense layer after the last layer block that provides the facial features and added a dense layer as the output layer with sigmoid activation function to fine-tune the model for the task of deepfake detection.

The DenseNET architecture used in this work is Keras's DenseNet-264 architecture with an additional dense layer as the last output layer. This architecture starts with a 7×7 stride 2 convolutional layer followed by a 3×3 stride-2 MaxPooling layer. It also includes four dense blocks paired with batch normalization and ReLU activation function for the input layers and sigmoid activation function for the output layer. Furthermore, there are transition layers between each denseblock that include a 2 by 2 average pooling layer along with a 1 by 1 convolutional layer. The last dense block is followed by a classification layer that leverages the feature maps of all layers of the network for the task of classification which we have coupled with a denseblock with the sigmoid activation function as the output layer. This model was trained on 100,000 images and validated on 20,000 images. This model has been trained and validated on the original, grayscale and augmented datasets with a 1/255 scaling factor too. We aimed to add to the diversity of the training data by performing **augmentation to the DenseNet architecture** by applying a horizontal flip, a 20 range rotation along with the same rescaling procedure that was applied in the Custom CNN architecture. Because pixel-level resolution of grayscale and color images are different, we have also measured the importance of color on model behavior towards classifying data into the fake and real categories by training the DenseNet architecture on grayscale only data too. The VGG architecture, however, was only trained and tested on the original dataset. All the analyzed models in this work are used as they were designed with an additional custom dense layer with sigmoid activation function. The rationale behind adding this layer to all models was to add a useful rectifier activation function layer for the task of binary classification to produce a probability output in the range of 0 to 1 that can easily and automatically be converted to crisp class values.

3.2. Evaluation

The performance of the described models is assessed with accuracy, precision, recall, F1-score, average precision (AP) and area under the ROC curve.

Accuracy, simply put, indicates how close the model prediction is to the target or actual value (fake vs. real), meaning how many times the model was able to make a correct predication among all the predictions it has made. Equation (1) indicates the overall formula used to calculate prediction, where *TPR* stands for true prediction and *TOPR* stands for total predictions made by the model.

$$Accuracy = \frac{TPR}{TOPR} \tag{1}$$

Precision, on the other hand, refers to how consistent results are regardless of how close to the true value they are using the target label. Equation (2) demonstrates the ratio that indicates the proportion of positive identifications by model that were actually correct. *TP* in Equation (2) stands for the number of true positives and *FP* stands for the number of false positives.

$$Percision = \frac{TP}{TP + FP} \tag{2}$$

The recall is the proportion of actual positives that were identified by the model that were correct. Equation (3) demonstrates this ratio where *TP* is the number of true positives and *FN* the number of false negatives. The recall is intuitively the ability of the classifier to find all the positive samples.

$$Recall = \frac{TP}{TP + FN} \tag{3}$$

The F1-score, by taking into account both precision and recall, balances the precision and recall and indicates model ability to accurately predict both true-positive and true-negative classes. The F1 score can be interpreted as a harmonic mean of the precision and recall. For the task of deepfake classification, F1-score is a better measure to assess model performance, since both classes are of importance and the relative contribution of precision and recall to the F1 score are better than equal. Equation (4) demonstrates how F1-score is calculated.

$$F1 = \frac{2 * (Percision * Recall)}{Percision + Recall} \tag{4}$$

Average Precision (AP) was used as an aggregation function for the task of object detection to summarize the precision–recall curve as the weighted mean of precision achieved at each threshold, with the increase in recall from the previous threshold used as the weight based on Equation (5), where R_n and P_n are the precision and recall at the nth threshold [58].

$$AP = \sum_n (R_n - R_{n-1}) P_n \tag{5}$$

Finally, as shown in Figure 3, the output vectors of the final hidden layer of the analyzed architectures were extracted and treated as a representation of the images. Dimensions of the vectors for the Custom CNN architecture, VGG-19 and DenseNet architectures were 512, 2048 and 1024, respectively. Principal Component Analysis (PCA) was performed to keep the most dominant variable vector points and preserved 50 principal components. The resulting vectors from the PCA were fed into a support vector machine (SVM) to classify them into the two classes of real and fake.

4. Preliminary Results

This section provides the results obtained from the three different neural network architectures that have been tested in this work. The dataset section provides an overview of the advantages, drawbacks, and improvements of the datasets described in the literature review.

4.1. Dataset

Deepfake datasets should have careful consideration of quality, scale, and diversity. UADF and DFTMIT provide a baseline dataset for preliminary analysis in deepfake detection; however, they lack the quantity and diversity elements. The DeepFakeDetection dataset extends the preliminary FaceForensics dataset; however, it contains relatively few videos with few subjects and limited size and number of methods that are represented. The DFDC dataset addresses the drawbacks of the previously published datasets by providing a large number of clips, of varying quality, and with a good representation of the current state-of-the-art face-swap methods. However, it still has various visual artifacts that make them easily distinguishable from the real videos. The DFDC dataset resolves the limited availability of source footage, few videos and fewer subjects; however, the Celeb-DF dataset provides more relevant data to evaluate and support the future development of deepfake detection methods by fixing color mismatch, inaccurate face masks, and temporal flickering of previously discussed datasets. Finally, deeper forensics, by addressing the drawbacks of all mentioned datasets, provides a benchmark of larger scale and higher diversity that can be leveraged to achieve the best performance of deepfake detection algorithms. Table 3 summarizes the drawbacks and improvements of the described datasets.

Table 3. Dataset analysis summary.

Dataset	Drawbacks	Improvements
UADF DFTMIT	Lack of quantity and Diversity	Suitable baseline
DFD	Limited size and methods	Extension to FaceForensics dataset
DFDC	Distinguishable visual artifacts	Large number of clips of varying quality
Celeb-DF	Low realness score Biased: impractical for face Forgery detection	Fixed color mismatch Accurate face masks
Deeper Forensics-1.0	Challenging as a test database	High realness score

The mentioned datasets include videos that could be used for face detection in images; however, the "Real and Fake Face-Detection" dataset combined with the "140K Real and Fake Faces" includes both GAN-generated images as well as expert/human-generated images, and is considered by far one of the largest available face-image datasets. The two described datasets together include 70,960 fake and 71,081 real images. As shown in Table 4, 70K of the fake images are GAN-generated and 960 of them are human expert-generated. Similarly for the real images, 70K of them are GAN-generated and 1081 of them are human expert-generated. The distribution of the human-generated fake images is not balanced with the GAN-generated photos, but this is the largest human-generated image dataset available currently.

Table 4. Distribution of the used datasets.

Generation Method	Fake	Real
GAN	70K	70K
Human Expert	960	1081

4.2. Algorithms

The accuracy, precision and recall rates of analyzed models demonstrated in Table 5, the ROC curve demonstrated in Figure 4, the area under the ROC curve (AUC), F1-scores and AP results demonstrated in Table 6 were used to evaluate model performance in terms of separability and their ability to differentiate between classes. The algorithm comparison results revealed that the VGG-19 model had the best performance among all 3 other algorithms, with an accuracy level of 95%.

The results of this study demonstrate that VGG-19 can be a suitable choice not only for partial face images, but also for full-face images confirming the findings of [57]. The better performance of VGG-19 is because it is pretrained on a wide variety of objects. AP was used as an aggregation function to summarize the precision–recall curve into a single value that represents the average of all precisions. VGG-19, even though it had the highest accuracy, had the lowest AP of 95% in comparison to all other analyzed models. The DenseNet architecture on the original dataset and grayscale dataset had a closer performance to VGG-19, with 94% accuracy. Results from DenseNET architecture demonstrates that gray channel-based analysis does not have a huge impact on model accuracy level in classifying images into the two categories of real and fake. The DenseNet architecture, even though was second best in terms of performance, achieved an AP of 99% on both augmented and grayscale datasets, which is slightly in contrast to the results found in [59] in terms of precision rate; however, it aligns with claims regarding detection time. Custom CNN architecture had the lowest accuracy level (89%). The second-highest AP score after DenseNet was the Custom CNN model. Augmented input reduced model performance and accuracy level on both DenseNET and Custom CNN by 5–22%. However, the Custom CNN had a better performance on augmented data in comparison to the DenseNet architecture. Precision and recall rates from DenseNet architecture trained on augmented data suggest that the final dense block that we have coupled with the DenseNet classification layer did not have a positive impact on model behavior. The issue with reduced performance on augmented data might be resolved by training the model for a larger number of epochs, since augmentation results in harder training samples. VGG-19, even though it was great in terms of performance, aligns with results from [60]; it was computationally very expensive, especially if fed with augmented data. DenseNET was computationally more efficient in comparison to VGG-19 and Custom CNN, which aligns with the results from [40]. The F1-score of the DenseNet architecture on grayscale was the highest, reaching 97% suggesting it could be a suitable backbone when dealing with unbalanced class distribution in their dataset. The second-highest F1-score was achieved by VGG-19, as it achieved a 95% F1-score. The lowest F1-score was achieved by the Custom CNN on augmented data, as the F1-score was only 85%. Taking F1-score as a measurement to balance precision and recall, DenseNet on grayscale data might seem to be a better solution, however, since the dataset used for training in this analysis had a balanced class distribution accuracy level and is a better judge in this analysis. The results from the PCA-SVM classification demonstrated that VGG-19 was able to form a distinctive cluster of fake and real images using the PCA vectors as a representation of the image (demonstrated in Figure 5). Custom CNN architectures and DenseNet trained on the original and augmented datasets showed decent classification. However, DenseNet trained on grayscale images presented very poor performance (Table 5).

Table 5. Algorithm comparison results. OD stands for Original Dataset, AD stands for Augmented Dataset and GS stands for Grayscale Dataset.

	Model Performance			PCA-SVM Performance		
Architecture	Accuracy	Precision	Recall	Accuracy	Precision	Recall
VGG-19	95	93	97	99	99	99
DenseNet OD	94	92	96	98	98	98
DenseNet AD	73	66	95	86	86	86
DenseNet GS	94	91	99	50	50	47
Custom CNN OD	89	91	87	97	97	97
Custom CNN AD	84	87	79	91	90	91

Overall analysis of the results reveal that all the architectures had a higher efficiency in detection and classification of GAN-generated images due to the traces that GAN generators left on the generated media. Considering VGG-19's performance and behavior, even though it may not be the most computationally efficient model, it had a competitively better performance than the other analyzed model and it showed a promising improvement when coupled with PCA-SVM classification layers. This suggests that VGG-19 could be a more suitable backbone architecture for the task of deepfake detection related to the essential technical and legal requirements that determine evidence admissibility. Deepfakes are a threat to the admissibility of digital evidence in courts. Quick and effective detection of authentic media is critical in any criminal investigations. VGG-19 could be a fast solution for detecting deepfakes in courts. We must test more datasets from digital evidence and conduct further experiments.

Table 6. F-1, ROC-AUC, and AP scores.

Architecture	F-1	ROC-AUC	AP
VGG-19	95	96	93
DenseNet OD	92	99	99
DenseNet AD	92	97	97
DenseNet GS	97	99	99
Custom CNN OD	91	98	98
Custom CNN AD	85	95	95

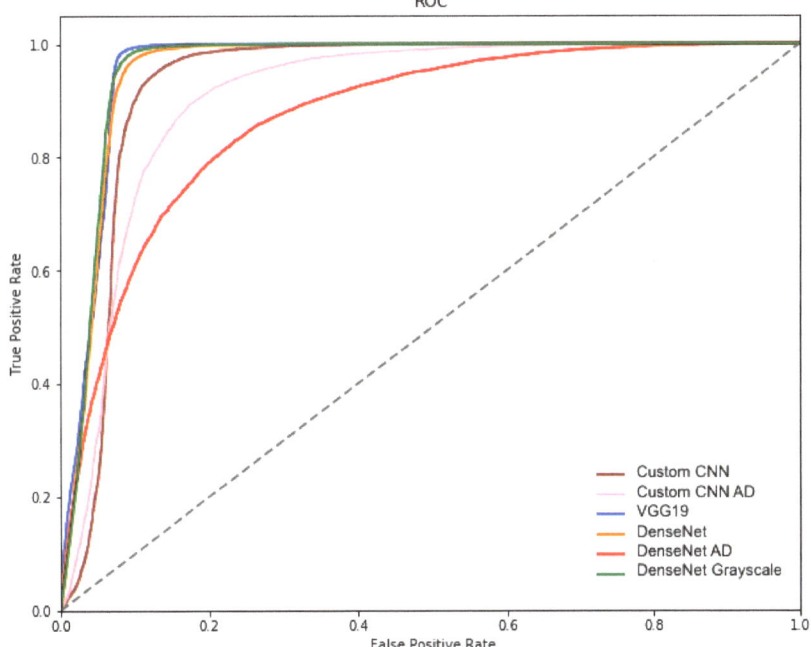

Figure 4. ROC curve representation.

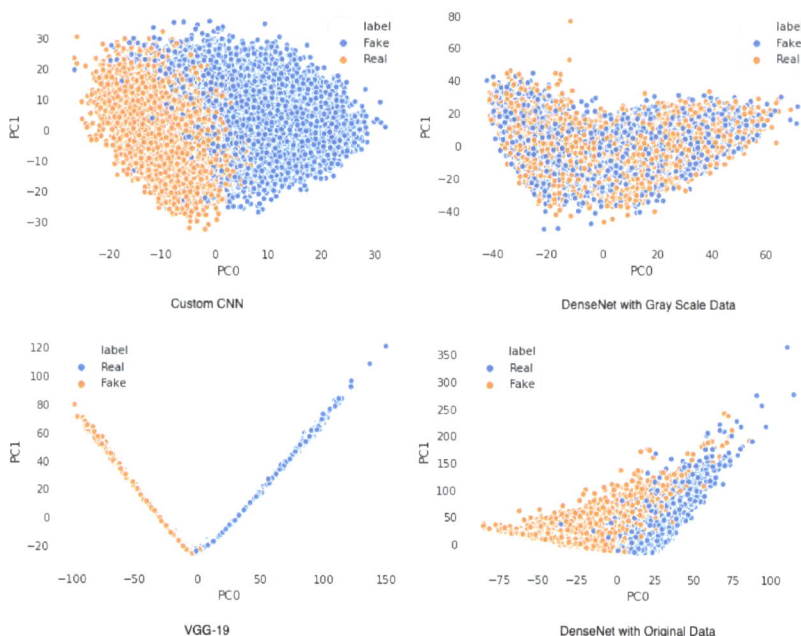

Figure 5. PCA-SVM clustering comparison.

5. Conclusions and Future Work

The results of our work demonstrated that deep-learning architectures are reliable and accurate at distinguishing fake vs. real images; however, detection of the minimal inaccuracies and misclassifications remain a critical area of research. Recent efforts have focused on improving the algorithms that create deepfakes by adding especially designed noise to digital photographs or videos that are not visible to human eyes and can fool the face-detection algorithms [61]. The results of our work indicate that VGG-19 performed best, taking accuracy, F1-score, precision, AUC-ROC and PCA-SVM measures into the account. DenseNet had a slightly better performance in terms of AP, and the results from the Custom CNN trained on original data were satisfactory too. This suggests that aggregation of the results from multiple models, i.e., ensemble or multi-attention approaches, can be more robust in distinguishing deepfake media.

Future work could also leverage unsupervised clustering methods such as auto-encoders to analyze its effectiveness on the task of deepfake classification and provide a better interpretation of the CNN algorithms designed in this work. There could be classification methods developed that would examine and flag social media users who uploaded images/videos before being posted on the Internet to avoid the spread of misinformation [62]. We plan to further improve performance with deep-learning algorithms as well as exploring the application of stenography, steganalysis and cryptography in the identification and classification of the genuine and disguised face images [63]. Future work not only has to include collecting and experimenting with different disguised classifiers, but also must work on the development of training data that can improve the performance of implemented architectures as suggested by [33]. The authors of the paper plan to discover the use of information pellets on the development of an ensemble framework. As suggested in [64] using a patch-based fuzzy rough set feature-selection strategy can preserve the discrimination ability of original patches. Such implementation can assist in anomaly detection for the task of deepfake detection. By integrating the local-to-global feature-learning method with multi-attention and ensemble-modeling (holistic, feature-based, noise-level, steganographic) approach, we believe we can achieve a superior performance than the current state-of-the-art methods. Considering the limitations of Eff-YNet network developed by [55], which has an advantage in examining visual differences within individual frames, analyzing EfficientNet performance on deepfake image datasets used in this work can be another direction for future work, as it may identify another suitable baseline model for ensembled approaches.

Author Contributions: Conceptualization, M.T. and H.C.; methodology, M.T.; software, M.T.; validation, M.T. and H.C.; formal analysis, M.T.; developed the theory and performed the computations, M.T.; resources, M.T.; data curation, M.T.; writing—original draft preparation, M.T.; writing—review and editing, H.C.; funding acquisition, H.C. All authors have read and agreed to the published version of the manuscript.

Funding: This research was partly funded by the National Centers of Academic Excellence in Cybersecurity Grant (H98230-21-1-0326), which is part of the National Security Agency. Research was partly sponsored by the Army Research Office and was accomplished under Grant Number W911NF-21-1-0264. The views and conclusions contained in this document are those of the authors and should not be interpreted as representing the official policies, either expressed or implied, of the Army Research Office or the U.S. Government. The U.S. Government is authorized to reproduce and distribute reprints for Government purposes notwithstanding any copyright notation herein.

Institutional Review Board Statement: Not applicable.

Informed Consent Statement: Not applicable.

Data Availability Statement: The datasets that have been leveraged in this work are publicly available on Kaggle for both challenges of "140K Real and Fake Faces" and "Real and Fake Face Detection". The "140K Real and Fake Faces" dataset available at https://www.kaggle.com/xhlulu/140k-real-and-fake-faces published on February 2020, accessed on October 2021, includes 70K real faces collected from Flickr and 70K fake faces that are generated by GANs. The "Real and Fake Face-Detection" dataset available at https://www.kaggle.com/ciplab/real-and-fake-face-detection published on January 2019, accessed on October 2021 includes 960 fake and 1081 real face images that are generated by human expert in high-quality via Photoshop.

Acknowledgments: The authors would like to show their gratitude to Shonda Bernadin and the MDPI journal reviewers. This paper and the research behind it would not have been possible without the exceptional support of them. Their insight and expertise and exacting attention to detail has greatly assisted this research

Conflicts of Interest: The authors declare no conflict of interest.

References

1. Ferreira, S.; Antunes, M.; Correia, M.E. Exposing Manipulated Photos and Videos in Digital Forensics Analysis. *J. Imaging* **2021**, *7*, 102. [CrossRef]
2. Harwell, D. Fake-Porn Videos are Being Weaponized to Harass and Humiliate Women: 'Everybody is a Potential Target'. 2018. Available online: https://www.defenseone.com/technology/2019/03/next-phase-ai-deep-faking-whole-world-and-china-ahead/155944/ (accessed on 28 November 2021).
3. Tucker, P. The Newest AI-Enabled Weapon: 'Deep-Faking' Photos of the Earth. 2021. Available online: https://www.washingtonpost.com/technology/2018/12/30/fake-porn-videos-are-being-weaponized-harass-humiliate-women-everybody-is-potential-target/ (accessed on 28 November 2021).
4. Goodfellow, I.; Pouget-Abadie, J.; Mirza, M.; Xu, B.; Warde-Farley, D.; Ozair, S.; Courville, A.; Bengio, Y. Generative adversarial nets. *Adv. Neural Inf. Process. Syst.* **2014**, *2*. Available online: https://proceedings.neurips.cc/paper/2014/hash/5ca3e9b122f61f8f06494c97b1afccf3-Abstract.html (accessed on 28 November 2021).
5. Sajjadi, M.S.; Scholkopf, B.; Hirsch, M. Enhancenet: Single image super-resolution through automated texture synthesis. In Proceedings of the IEEE International Conference on Computer Vision, Venice, Italy, 22–29 October 2017; pp. 4491–4500.
6. Yu, P.; Xia, Z.; Fei, J.; Lu, Y. A Survey on Deepfake Video Detection. *IET Biom.* **2021**, *10*, 607–624. [CrossRef]
7. Ferreira, S.; Antunes, M.; Correia, M.E. A Dataset of Photos and Videos for Digital Forensics Analysis Using Machine Learning Processing. *Data* **2021** , *6*, 87. [CrossRef]
8. Durall, R.; Keuper, M.; Pfreundt, F.J.; Keuper, J. Unmasking deepfakes with simple features. *arXiv* **2019**, arXiv:1911.00686 .
9. De keersmaecker, J.; Roets, A. 'Fake news': Incorrect, but hard to correct. The role of cognitive ability on the impact of false information on social impressions. *Intelligence* **2017**, *65*, 107–110. [CrossRef]

10. Zhao, H.; Zhou, W.; Chen, D.; Wei, T.; Zhang, W.; Yu, N. Multi-attentional deepfake detection. In Proceedings of the IEEE/CVF Conference on Computer Vision and Pattern Recognition, Nashville, TN, USA, 20–25 June 2021; pp. 2185–2194.

11. Bonettini, N.; Cannas, E.D.; Mandelli, S.; Bondi, L.; Bestagini, P.; Tubaro, S. Video face manipulation detection through ensemble of cnns. In Proceedings of the 2020 25th International Conference on Pattern Recognition (ICPR), Milan, Italy, 10–15 January 2021; IEEE: Piscataway, NJ, USA, 2021; pp. 5012–5019.

12. Silva, S.H.; Bethany, M.; Votto, A.M.; Scarff, I.H.; Beebe, N.; Najafirad, P. Deepfake forensics analysis: An explainable hierarchical ensemble of weakly supervised models. *Forensic. Sci. Int. Synerg.* **2022**, *4*, 100217. [CrossRef]

13. Westerlund, M. The emergence of deepfake technology: A review. *Technol. Innov. Manag. Rev.* **2019**, *9*, 40–45. [CrossRef]

14. Ismail, A.; Elpeltagy, M.; Zaki, M.; ElDahshan, K.A. Deepfake video detection: YOLO-Face convolution recurrent approach. *Peerj Comput. Sci.* **2021**, *7*, e730. [CrossRef]

15. Coccomini, D.; Messina, N.; Gennaro, C.; Falchi, F. Combining efficientnet and vision transformers for video deepfake detection. *arXiv* **2021**, arXiv:2107.02612.

16. Kumar, A.; Bhavsar, A.; Verma, R. Detecting deepfakes with metric learning. In Proceedings of the 2020 8th International Workshop on Biometrics and Forensics (IWBF), Porto, Portugal, 29–30 April 2020; IEEE: Piscataway, NJ, USA, 2020; pp. 1–6.

17. Li, Y.; Lyu, S. Exposing deepfake videos by detecting face warping artifacts. *arXiv* **2018**, arXiv:1811.00656.

18. Li, L.; Bao, J.; Zhang, T.; Yang, H.; Chen, D.; Wen, F.; Guo, B. Face X-ray for more general face forgery detection. In Proceedings of the 2020 IEEE/CVF Conference on Computer Vision and Pattern Recognition (CVPR), Seattle, WA, USA, 13–19 June 2020. [CrossRef]

19. Nguyen, H.H.; Yamagishi, J.; Echizen, I. Capsule-forensics: Using capsule networks to detect forged images and videos. In Proceedings of the ICASSP 2019–2019 IEEE International Conference on Acoustics, Speech and Signal Processing (ICASSP), Brighton, UK, 12–17 May 2019; IEEE: Piscataway, NJ, USA, 2019; pp. 2307–2311.

20. Albanesius, C. Deepfake Videos Are Here, and We're Not Ready. 2019. Available online: https://www.pcmag.com/news/deepfake-videos-are-here-and-were-not-ready (accessed on 5 December 2021).

21. Yang, X.; Li, Y.; Lyu, S. Exposing deep fakes using inconsistent head poses. In Proceedings of the ICASSP 2019–2019 IEEE International Conference on Acoustics, Speech and Signal Processing (ICASSP), Brighton, UK, 12–17 May 2019; IEEE: Piscataway, NJ, USA, 2019; pp. 8261–8265.

22. Korshunov, P.; Marcel, S. Deepfakes: A new threat to face recognition? assessment and detection. *arXiv* **2018**, arXiv:1812.08685.

23. Rössler, A.; Cozzolino, D.; Verdoliva, L.; Riess, C.; Thies, J.; Nießner, M. FaceForensics++: Learning to Detect Manipulated Facial Images. In Proceedings of the International Conference on Computer Vision (ICCV), Seoul, Korea, 27 October–2 November 2019.

24. Dolhansky, B.; Bitton, J.; Pflaum, B.; Lu, J.; Howes, R.; Wang, M.; Ferrer, C.C. The DeepFake Detection Challenge Dataset. *arXiv* **2020**, arXiv:2006.07397.

25. Li, Y.; Sun, P.; Qi, H.; Lyu, S. Celeb-DF: A Large-scale Challenging Dataset for DeepFake Forensics. In Proceedings of the IEEE Conference on Computer Vision and Patten Recognition (CVPR), Seattle, WA, USA, 14–19 June 2020; pp. 3207–3216.

26. Jiang, L.; Li, R.; Wu, W.; Qian, C.; Loy, C.C. Deeperforensics-1.0: A large-scale dataset for real-world face forgery detection. In Proceedings of the IEEE/CVF Conference on Computer Vision and Pattern Recognition (CVPR), Seattle, WA, USA, 14–19 June 2020; pp. 2889–2898.

27. Yonsei University. Real and Fake Face Detection. 2019. Available online: https://archive.org/details/real-and-fake-face-detection (accessed on 30 August 2021).

28. NVlabs. NVlabs/ffhq-Dataset: Flickr-Faces-HQ Dataset (FFHQ). 2019. Available online: https://archive.org/details/ffhq-dataset (accessed on 29 August 2021).

29. Nguyen, T.T.; Nguyen, C.M.; Nguyen, D.T.; Nguyen, D.T.; Nahavandi, S. Deep learning for deepfakes creation and detection: A survey. *arXiv* **2019**, arXiv:1909.11573.

30. Huang, Y.; Juefei-Xu, F.; Guo, Q.; Xie, X.; Ma, L.; Miao, W.; Liu, Y.; Pu, G. FakeRetouch: Evading deepfakes detection via the guidance of deliberate noise. *arXiv* **2020**, arXiv:2009.09213.

31. Zhao, W.; Chellappa, R.; Phillips, P.J.; Rosenfeld, A. Face recognition: A literature survey. *Acm Comput. Surv. (CSUR)* **2003**, *35*, 399–458. [CrossRef]

32. Maksutov, A.A.; Morozov, V.O.; Lavrenov, A.A.; Smirnov, A.S. Methods of deepfake detection based on machine learning. In Proceedings of the 2020 IEEE Conference of Russian Young Researchers in Electrical and Electronic Engineering (EIConRus), St. Petersburg, Russia, 27–30 January 2020; IEEE: Piscataway, NJ, USA, 2020; pp. 408–411.

33. Tariq, S.; Lee, S.; Kim, H.; Shin, Y.; Woo, S.S. Gan is a friend or foe? a framework to detect various fake face images. In Proceedings of the 34th ACM/SIGAPP Symposium on Applied Computing, Limassol, Cyprus, 8–12 April 2019; pp. 1296–1303.

34. Cozzolino, D.; Thies, J.; Rössler, A.; Riess, C.; Nießner, M.; Verdoliva, L. Forensictransfer: Weakly-supervised domain adaptation for forgery detection. *arXiv* **2018** arXiv:1812.02510.

35. Wang, S.Y.; Wang, O.; Zhang, R.; Owens, A.; Efros, A.A. CNN-generated images are surprisingly easy to spot ... for now. In Proceedings of the IEEE/CVF Conference on Computer Vision and Pattern Recognition, Seattle, WA, USA, 14–19 June 2020; pp. 8695–8704.

36. Li, Y.; Chang, M.; Lyu, S. Exposing AI Created Fake Videos by Detecting Eye Blinking. In Proceedings of the 2018 IEEE InterG National Workshop on Information Forensics and Security (WIFS), Hong Kong, China, 11–13 December 2018.

37. Afchar, D.; Nozick, V.; Yamagishi, J.; Echizen, I. Mesonet: A compact facial video forgery detection network. In Proceedings of the 2018 IEEE International Workshop on Information Forensics and Security (WIFS 2018), Hong Kong, China, 11–13 December 2018; IEEE: Piscataway, NJ, USA, 2018; pp. 1–7.
38. Simonyan, K.; Zisserman, A. Very deep convolutional networks for large-scale image recognition. *arXiv* **2014**, arXiv:1409.1556.
39. Chang, X.; Wu, J.; Yang, T.; Feng, G. Deepfake face image detection based on improved VGG convolutional neural network. In Proceedings of the 2020 39th Chinese Control Conference (CCC), Shenyang, China, 27–30 July 2020; IEEE: Piscataway, NJ, USA, 2020; pp. 7252–7256.
40. Kim, J.; Han, S.; Woo, S.S. Classifying Genuine Face images from Disguised Face Images. In Proceedings of the 2019 IEEE International Conference on Big Data (Big Data), Los Angelas, CA, USA, 9–12 December 2019; IEEE: Piscataway, NJ, USA, 2019; pp. 6248–6250.
41. Huang, G.; Liu, Z.; Van Der Maaten, L.; Weinberger, K.Q. Densely connected convolutional networks. In Proceedings of the IEEE Conference on Computer Vision and Pattern recognition (CVPR), Honolulu, HI, USA, 21–26 July 2017; IEEE: Piscataway, NJ, USA, 2017; pp. 4700–4708.
42. Hsu, C.C.; Zhuang, Y.X.; Lee, C.Y. Deep fake image detection based on pairwise learning. *Appl. Sci.* **2020**, *10*, 370. [CrossRef]
43. Matern, F.; Riess, C.; Stamminger, M. Exploiting visual artifacts to expose deepfakes and face manipulations. In Proceedings of the 2019 IEEE Winter Applications of Computer Vision Workshops (WACVW), Waikoloa Village, HI, USA, 1–7 January 2019. [CrossRef]
44. Jung, T.; Kim, S.; Kim, K. DeepVision: Deepfakes detection using human eye blinking pattern. *IEEE Access* **2020**, *8*, 83144–83154. [CrossRef]
45. Li, Y.; Chang, M.C.; Lyu, S. In ictu oculi: Exposing ai created fake videos by detecting eye blinking. In Proceedings of the 2018 IEEE International Workshop on Information Forensics and Security (WIFS 2018), Hong Kong, China, 11–13 December 2018; IEEE: Piscataway, NJ, USA, 2018; pp. 1–7.
46. Korshunov, P.; Marcel, S. Speaker inconsistency detection in tampered video. In Proceedings of the 2018 26th European Signal Processing Conference (EUSIPCO), Rome, Italy, 3–7 September 2018; IEEE: Piscataway, NJ, USA, 2018; pp. 2375–2379.
47. Agarwal, S.; Farid, H.; Gu, Y.; He, M.; Nagano, K.; Li, H. Protecting World Leaders Against Deep Fakes. In Proceedings of the CVPR Workshops, Long Beach, CA, USA, 16–20 June 2019; Volume 1.
48. Chollet, F. Xception: Deep learning with depthwise separable convolutions. In Proceedings of the IEEE Conference on Computer Vision and Pattern Recognition, (CVPR), Honolulu, HI, USA, 21–26 July 2017; pp. 1251–1258.
49. Tan, M.; Le, Q. Efficientnet: Rethinking model scaling for convolutional neural networks. In Proceedings of the International Conference on Machine Learning, PMLR, Long Beach, CA, USA, 9–15 June 2019; pp. 6105–6114.
50. Li, X.; Yu, K.; Ji, S.; Wang, Y.; Wu, C.; Xue, H. Fighting against deepfake: Patch&pair convolutional neural networks (PPCNN). In Proceedings of the Companion Proceedings of the Web Conference, Taipei, Taiwan, 20–24 April 2020; pp. 88–89.
51. Pokroy, A.A.; Egorov, A.D. EfficientNets for deepfake detection: Comparison of pretrained models. In Proceedings of the 2021 IEEE Conference of Russian Young Researchers in Electrical and Electronic Engineering (EIConRus), St. Petersburg, Russia, 26–29 January 2021; IEEE: Piscataway, NJ, USA, 2021; pp. 598–600.
52. Mitra, A.; Mohanty, S.P.; Corcoran, P.; Kougianos, E. A novel machine learning based method for deepfake video detection in social media. In Proceedings of the 2020 IEEE International Symposium on Smart Electronic Systems (iSES) (Formerly iNiS), Chennai, India, 14–16 December 2020; IEEE: Piscataway, NJ, USA, 2020; pp. 91–96.
53. Dolecki, M.; Karczmarek, P.; Kiersztyn, A.; Pedrycz, W. Utility functions as aggregation functions in face recognition. In Proceedings of the 2016 IEEE Symposium Series on Computational Intelligence (SSCI), Athens, Greece, 6–9 December 2016. [CrossRef]
54. Du, C.X.T.; Duong, L.H.; Trung, H.T.; Tam, P.M.; Hung, N.Q.V.; Jo, J.; Efficient-frequency: A hybrid visual forensic framework for facial forgery detection. In Proceedings of the 2020 IEEE Symposium Series on Computational Intelligence (IEEE SSCI), Canberra, Australia, 1–4 December 2020; IEEE: Piscataway, NJ, USA, 2020; pp. 707–712.
55. Tjon, E.; Moh, M.; Moh, T.S. Eff-YNet: A Dual Task Network for DeepFake Detection and Segmentation. In Proceedings of the 2021 15th International Conference on Ubiquitous Information Management and Communication (IMCOM), Seoul, Korea, 4–6 January 2021; IEEE: Piscataway, NJ, USA, 2021; pp. 1–8.
56. Do, N.T.; Na, I.S.; Kim, S.H. Forensics face detection from GANs using convolutional neural network. In Proceedings of the 2018 International Symposium on Information Technology Convergence (ISITC 2018), Jeonju, Korea, 24–27 October 2018.
57. Goel, R.; Mehmood, I.; Ugail, H. A Study of Deep Learning-Based Face Recognition Models for Sibling Identification. *Sensors* **2021**, *21*, 5068. [CrossRef]
58. Varoquaux, G.; Buitinck, L.; Louppe, G.; Grisel, O.; Pedregosa, F.; Mueller, A. Scikit-learn: Machine learning without learning the machinery. *Getmobile: Mob. Comput. Commun.* **2015**, *19*, 29–33. [CrossRef]
59. Son, S.B.; Park, S.H.; Lee, Y.K. A Measurement Study on Gray Channel-based Deepfake Detection. In Proceedings of the 2021 International Conference on Information and Communication Technology Convergence (ICTC), Jeju Island, Korea, 20–22 October 2021; IEEE: Piscataway, NJ, USA, 2021; pp. 428–430.
60. Amerini, I.; Galteri, L.; Caldelli, R.; Del Bimbo, A. Deepfake video detection through optical flow based cnn. In Proceedings of the IEEE/CVF International Conference on Computer Vision Workshops, Montreal, BC, Canada, 11–17 October 2021; p. 2.

61. Li, Y.; Yang, X.; Wu, B.; Lyu, S. Hiding faces in plain sight: Disrupting ai face synthesis with adversarial perturbations. *arXiv* **2019**, arXiv:1906.09288.
62. Tolosana, R.; Romero-Tapiador, S.; Fierrez, J.; Vera-Rodriguez, R. Deepfakes evolution: Analysis of facial regions and fake detection performance. In Proceedings of the International Conference on Pattern Recognition (ICPR), Virtual Event, 10–15 January 2021; Springer: Berlin/Heidelberg, Germany, 2021; pp. 442–456.
63. Corcoran, K.; Ressler, J.; Zhu, Y. Countermeasure against Deepfake Using Steganography and Facial Detection. *J. Comput. Commun.* **2021**, *9*, 120–131. [CrossRef]
64. Guo, Y.; Jiao, L.; Wang, S.; Wang, S.; Liu, F. Fuzzy sparse autoencoder framework for single image per person face recognition. *IEEE Trans. Cybern.* **2017**, *48*, 2402–2415. [CrossRef]

Journal of
*Cybersecurity
and Privacy*

MDPI

Article

CyBERT: Cybersecurity Claim Classification by Fine-Tuning the BERT Language Model

Kimia Ameri [1], Michael Hempel [1], Hamid Sharif [1,*], Juan Lopez Jr. [2] and Kalyan Perumalla [2]

[1] Department of Electrical & Computer Engineering, University of Nebraska-Lincoln, Lincoln, NE 68182 , USA; kameri2@unl.edu (K.A.); mhempel@unl.edu (M.H.)
[2] Oak Ridge National Laboratory, Oak Ridge, TN 37831, USA; lopezj@ornl.gov (J.L.J.); perumallaks@ornl.gov (K.P.)
* Correspondence: hsharif@unl.edu

Abstract: We introduce CyBERT, a cybersecurity feature claims classifier based on bidirectional encoder representations from transformers and a key component in our semi-automated cybersecurity vetting for industrial control systems (ICS). To train CyBERT, we created a corpus of labeled sequences from ICS device documentation collected across a wide range of vendors and devices. This corpus provides the foundation for fine-tuning BERT's language model, including a prediction-guided relabeling process. We propose an approach to obtain optimal hyperparameters, including the learning rate, the number of dense layers, and their configuration, to increase the accuracy of our classifier. Fine-tuning all hyperparameters of the resulting model led to an increase in classification accuracy from 76% obtained with BertForSequenceClassification's original architecture to 94.4% obtained with CyBERT. Furthermore, we evaluated CyBERT for the impact of randomness in the initialization, training, and data-sampling phases. CyBERT demonstrated a standard deviation of ±0.6% during validation across 100 random seed values. Finally, we also compared the performance of CyBERT to other well-established language models including GPT2, ULMFiT, and ELMo, as well as neural network models such as CNN, LSTM, and BiLSTM. The results showed that CyBERT outperforms these models on the validation accuracy and the F1 score, validating CyBERT's robustness and accuracy as a cybersecurity feature claims classifier.

Keywords: natural language processing; BERT; transfer learning; classification; cybersecurity; CYVET

Citation: Ameri, K.; Hempel, M.; Sharif, H.; Lopez Jr., J.; Perumalla, K. CyBERT: Cybersecurity Claim Classification by Fine-Tuning the BERT Language Model. *J. Cybersecur. Priv.* **2021**, *1*, 615–637. https://doi.org/10.3390/jcp1040031

Academic Editors: Giorgio Giacinto and Phil Legg

Received: 30 August 2021
Accepted: 28 October 2021
Published: 4 November 2021

1. Introduction

1.1. Motivating Context

The role of cybersecurity audits in operational technology (OT) is a purposeful and vital mechanism to identify the presence of cybersecurity controls. Cybersecurity assessments, on the other hand, test the effectiveness of controls. Many critical infrastructure segments, including the energy sector, heavily rely on OT and industrial control systems (ICS) for automation, centralized monitoring, and operational efficiency. ICS vendors continually offer new features in their devices in order to attract their customers to buy new or upgraded products, but consumers often do not readily realize how these features affect their cybersecurity posture and regulatory compliance [1].

As identified in our earlier work [2], different vendor-supplied features (VSF) can satisfy and match the corresponding cybersecurity requirements (CR), or enhance the features and go beyond the related requirements, or unintentionally violate or contradict some of these requirements defined by international standards and industry organizations. To address this issue of mismatches between vendor-supplied features and cybersecurity requirements, an effective vetting system is required to match, reconcile, and tally these feature claims against the relevant requirements. However, both features and requirements are typically provided in the form of documents in human-readable format. This severely complicates any automated vetting processes.

To resolve this problem, we are developing a semi-automated vetting engine for cyber-physical security assurance (CYVET) [2]. The overarching goal for CYVET is to enhance the current industry capabilities to verify and validate OT infrastructure cybersecurity claims, at both pre-deployment and post-deployment periods.

Our vetting approach to cybersecurity assurance focuses on two major components: Tally-Vet and Test-Vet. Tally-Vet represents that portion of the vetting approach that is designed to match, reconcile, and tally the claimed features against the relevant requirements. The Tally-Vet stage requires extensive application of natural language processing (NLP) throughout the entire verification operation. For Test-Vet, specific features need to be systematically tested and validated against actual software and hardware through hardware agents. By automating the vetting of vendor claims extracted from device documentation, the vetting approach is designed to provide an unbiased, objective, and semi-supervised approach to vetting the cybersecurity implications of an ICS device. ICS compliance analysis and reporting is simplified by using this framework, implemented in our CYVET system, which provides insights into ICS systems and matches capabilities to requirements [2].

An overall flow for the Tally-Vet aspect of CYVET is shown in Figure 1. In our previous study [1], we discussed our semi-supervised framework to build the ICS device information repository that underpins CYVET and its NLP processes. This data repository contains ICS device documents including manuals, brochures, and catalogs. One of the main challenges in the vetting approach is to analyze this data repository and identify sequences from vendor-supplied documents that represent the vendor's *stated claims* on product features. These sequences will then be used in the tally process by comparing them to the industry cybersecurity requirements. In the rest of the article, we use the term "Claim" to refer to any sequence in the text of vendor-supplied documents thus extracted that represent some cybersecurity-related claims about features of the product being evaluated.

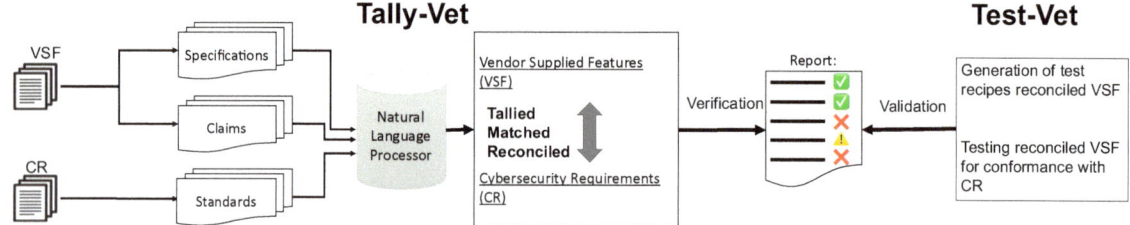

Figure 1. Overall workflow of the CYVET cybersecurity vetting approach.

Recent studies have demonstrated the achievable performance for unsupervised language models that are pre-trained on a large corpus and fine-tuned on downstream tasks such as sequence classification and sentiment analysis. Examples include the universal language model with fine-tuning (ULMFiT) [3], embeddings from language models (ElMo) [4], bidirectional encoder representations from transformers (BERT) [5], and the generative pre-training (GPT) model [6], which are some of the most well-established pre-trained language models.

1.2. Goals and Contributions

This article presents our research into establishing a novel classifier of *cybersecurity feature claims* by fine-tuning a pre-trained BERT language model. Specifically, any natural language sequence that specifically makes a claim towards the availability of a cybersecurity feature related to a product is defined as a claim in this article. All other claims, or sequences that do not make any claims, are subsequently labeled as not containing a cybersecurity claim.

CyBERT is intended to be used as a cybersecurity-specific classification model for detecting cybersecurity claims. This NLP model enables us to identify claims from a large pool of sequences in ICS device documents. Claim sequences are important for identifying the claimed set of cybersecurity device features. Being able to identify this set of claimed features subsequently enables us to compare feature claims against cybersecurity requirements, which is key to our Tally-Vet operation for OT infrastructure vetting.

The contributions of this work are summarized in the following items:

1. We introduce CyBERT, a BERT-based model that is trained on sequences gathered from ICS device documents. This new model is designed to identify cybersecurity claim-related sequences.
2. We present our extensive experiments conducted to optimize hyperparameters and model architecture selection.
3. We show and discuss our results of a comparative evaluation of CyBERT against other language models. The results suggest that a fine-tuned BERT configuration with two hidden dense layers and a classification layer achieves the highest accuracy.

An important part of NLP tasks is word embedding. Embedding represents each word as a multidimensional vector. Traditional neural network models use the traditional word-level embedding methods, including GloVe and Word2vec. These models are only trained based on a specific task to capture features and remove the contextual meaning of each word.

Newer language models, on the other hand, use contextualized embedding methods. These methods are designed to capture the semantics of words by including information about its surrounding context. The BERT-Base model is one such model that uses a contextualized embedding method and utilizes 768-dimensional tokens to represent its vocabulary entries. More details on these embedding methods are provided in Section 3.1 further below.

In this article, we compare the results and performance of our model with other well-known transformer-based models, such as GPT, as well as more traditional models, such as ULMFiT and neural network (NN) models. The results are discussed in detail in Section 5. Because of the above-mentioned limitations of word-level embedding methods such as GloVe, and the benefits of contextualized embedding methods, we used the BERT tokenizer for our language models.

The remainder of this article is organized as follows. In Section 2, we briefly review related works. We present background information related to NLP in Section 3. In Section 4, we describe the overall system framework and our proposed architecture including preparation of the domain-specific dataset, hyperparameter selection, and the fine-tuning strategy. We present and discuss our findings by comparing CyBERT's results with those of other NLP and neural network models in Section 5, and in Section 6 our conclusions are presented.

2. Related Works

Adapting a pre-trained language model for specifically targeted tasks can dramatically improve performance. In recent years, language models have demonstrated significant advances in downstream tasks including classification and sentiment analysis. In the following paragraphs, we discuss recent studies in language model improvements. These improvements are divided into pre-training language models and fine-tuning language models.

BERT [5] has gained popularity among researchers in a wide variety of fields. Lee et al. used a large biomedical corpus to build BioBERT, a pre-trained biomedical language representation model for biomedical text mining [7]. BioBERT is trained on the original corpora of BERT and expanded with additional biomedical corpora. The resulting BioBERT improves biomedical name entity recognition (NER), biomedical relation extraction (RE), and biomedical question answering (QA) tasks. Naseem et al. [8] used the same corpus as BioBERT to pre-train a new domain-specific language model based on the ALBERT [9] architecture, including its initial weights. The new pre-trained language model is then fine-tuned on four different biomedical NER datasets.

A pre-trained language model for scientific text (SciBERT) was introduced by Beltagy, I., Lo, K., and Cohan, A. [10]. This model was pre-trained on a large corpus of biomedical and computer science studies and a specific in-domain vocabulary (SCIVOCAB). SciBERT outperforms BERT and BioBERT on all downstream tasks in the scientific domain.

All of these studies demonstrate the benefits of pre-training a language model using a domain-specific corpus. However, although pre-training shows great improvements on the downstream tasks, the process is very computationally expensive and typically requires large additional corpora [7,11]. For those reasons, we focused on the fine-tuning process for our CyBERT language model.

Many NLP studies investigate the use of language models on specific downstream tasks, such as [12–16]. Several studies have shown that fine-tuning language models such as BERT for a downstream task on a domain-specific dataset may improve the performance of the model. Some examples of these models are patent classification with fine-tuning a pre-trained BERT Model (PatentBERT) [17], financial sentiment analysis with pre-trained language models (FinBERT) [18], or a pre-trained financial language representation model for financial text mining [19]. These research works have shown that fine-tuning can substantially improve the performance of BERT for a specific task. Sun et al. [15] showed that fine-tuning a pre-trained language model for a specific downstream task can be trained on a small dataset with only a few training shots and thus does not require a large additional corpus.

Language Models in Cybersecurity

The use of language models such as BERT specifically for applications in the cybersecurity domain is rather limited so far. One of the few studies from this domain is [20], which describes the use of BERT for classifying vulnerabilities. Some other examples are fine-tuning BERT for NER for the cybersecurity domain in English [21–23], Russian [24], and Chinese [25]. Another example is ExBERT [26], a fine-tuned BERT with sentence-level sentiment analysis for vulnerability exploitability prediction.

From our review, we could not find any language model tuned for cybersecurity text classification tasks. In this study, we thus developed a claim sequence database specifically for the cybersecurity domain. This database was then used to generate CyBERT, a fine-tuned BERT classifier on cybersecurity sequences to identify feature claims. These claim sequences will then be used in our cybersecurity vetting engine to verify those features against the published industry requirements for cybersecurity.

3. Background Knowledge

3.1. Word Embedding

Word embedding is a critical part of any sequence-related NLP task. With embedding, each word is represented in a multidimensional vector space. These vectorized words, or tokens, are subsequently used as an input for neural networks. Embedding techniques are mainly divided into word-level and contextualised techniques:

3.1.1. Word-Level Embedding

Traditional vector representations of words, such as word2vec [27], fastText [28], or GloVe [29] are generally used to provide subword features in conjunction with an embedded conventional word. A recurrent neural network (RNN) or convolutional neural network (CNN) encoder produces the word-level embedding of a word from the input word set [30,31]. A disadvantage of word-level representations is that they strictly compile all the different possible meanings of a word into a single representation, thus not taking the surrounding context into consideration. Therefore, these methods cannot disambiguate word meanings based on the context in which a word is used.

3.1.2. Contextualized Embedding

A contextualized embedding is designed to capture word semantics in a context based on their surrounding text [32]. ELMo [4], GPT [6], and BERT [5] are well-developed contextualized embedding tools for language models and downstream tasks.

ELMo can produce context-sensitive embeddings for each word within a sentence, which can then be supplied to downstream tasks. BERT, and GPT, on the other hand, utilizes a fine-tuning approach that can adapt the entire language model to a downstream task, resulting in a task-specific architecture.

BERT uses a masked language model (MLM) technique to train a deep bidirectional representation of a sentence by randomly masking an input token and then predicting it. It also utilizes next-sentence prediction (NSP) to characterize and learn sentence relationships. With the help of these two unsupervised tasks, BERT is combining the strengths of GPT and ELMo [21].

BERT uses the WordPiece embedding technique [33] with a 30,000-token vocabulary [5]. The WordPiece method divides each word into a limited set of common sub-words and eliminates the need to deal with unknown words. This technique is very flexible for single characters and highly efficient for full-word decoding [33].

3.2. Pre-Trained Models

A pre-trained language model mainly refers to an NLP model that was trained on a large text corpus using an unsupervised training approach and that represents a general language domain. These models can be used for next-word prediction, for example. Some pre-trained language models such as BERT and GPT architecture contain multiple transformers stacked on top of each other to extract features from inputs with an attention mechanism. Each transformer element itself utilizes an encoder–decoder architecture, with both the encoder and decoder comprised of six layers, each with a multi-head self attention and a fully connected feed-forward network [34].

Leveraging a pretrained architecture and its associated pretraining weights enables us to more easily transfer the learning to our specific problems. Broadly, pretrained models can be divided into two main categories, in terms of their application:

1. Multi-purpose language models such as ULMFiT [3], Google BERT [5], and OpenAI GPT [6].
2. Word-embedding language models such as ELMo [4].

Out of all reviewed models, including GPT, UlMFiT, and ElMo, we determined that BERT embodies our target domain the closest. It requires the least amount of training and adaptation. BERT is an open-source model with a very strong tokenizer and word-embedding matrix. Based on these advantages, it was therefore chosen as the basis for our work.

BERT has two versions: BERT-Base, with 12 encoder layers, an embedding size of 768 dimensions, 12 multi-head attentions, and 110M parameters in total as well as BERT-Large, with 24 encoder layers, an embedding size of 1024 dimensions, 16 multi-head attentions, and 340M parameters. Both of these models have been trained on the BookCorpus and the collection of pages from the English Wikipedia, which have more than 3.5 billion words in total [5].

Although adapting a pre-trained language model such as BERT for a specific task improves performance dramatically, there is an inherent risk of catastrophic forgetting during training when unlocking all layer weights. Furthermore, it also can suffer from randomness effects as a result of training with smaller datasets. Our efforts to avoid these two potential risks to CyBERT's successful model training included the approaches described in Sections 4.2.1.1 and 4.3.1 related to catastrophic forgetting and randomness effects, respectively.

4. Proposed Architecture

In this section, we introduce CyBERT and detail its fine-tuning strategy for BERT hyperparameters. Recall that CyBERT is a cybersecurity claim classifier to detect sequences related to device features. These claims then will be used to vet against relevant cybersecurity requirements.

There are two main steps in our framework: claim sequence database curation and fine-tuning BERT. Figure 2 shows an overview of CyBERT workflow. To the best of our knowledge, there currently is no readily available dataset representing a corpus specific to cybersecurity that we could use for training CyBERT. Hence, we created a new labeled dataset that contains claim-related sequences. For fine-tuning, CyBERT is first initialized with BERT's initial weights, adding dense layers and dropouts and subsequently tuning all layers and parameters using our labeled database and architecture.

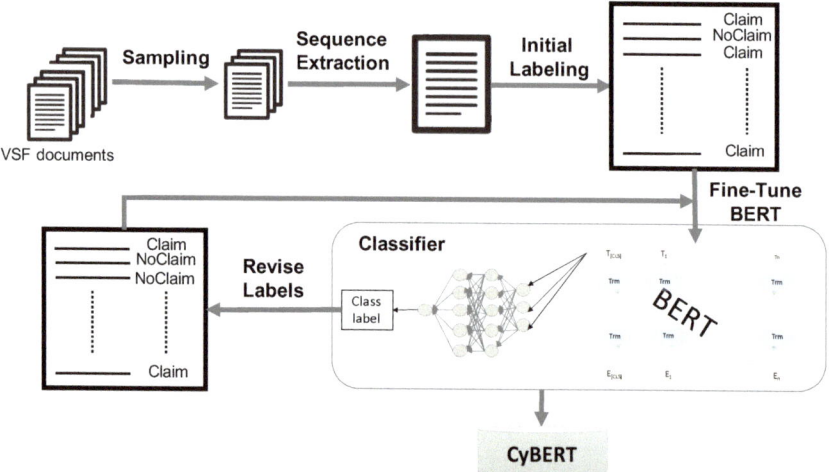

Figure 2. Overview of CyBERT workflow.

4.1. Dataset

As previously stated, there was no available dataset specific to the cybersecurity literature for NLP tasks, in particular with an emphasis on industrial control systems (ICS). Therefore, in our previous work [1] we proposed a framework to curate a large repository of ICS device information. This framework was designed to perform web scraping, data analytics, and natural language processing (NLP) techniques to identify ICS vendor websites, automate the collection of website-accessible documents, and automatically derive metadata from them for identification of documents relevant to this dataset.

All of the ICS device information documents that our framework curates were downloaded from vendor websites in PDF format.

Out of 19,793 documents, we scraped across the identified vendor websites; 3% were unreadable, and 5% were scanned documents. ICS product-related documents accounted for 63% of the downloaded documents. From those 12,581 product-related documents, 25% were classified as "manual," 69% were classified as "brochure," and 6% were "catalogs". On average, each of the product-related documents contained 31.2 pages. Some statistics from this repository are presented in Table 1.

The PyMuPDF python package was used to extract text from readable documents, and the Pytesseract python package was employed for optical character recognition (OCR) from any scanned PDF. These documents contain regular paragraphs, tables, lists, and images. Our system aimed to extract sequences from all of those document entities. Across the collection of ICS-related documents in our dataset, we extracted 216,0517 sequences with 41,073,376 words.

Table 1. ICS vendor and documents statistics in repository.

		Manual	Brochure	Catalog
Number of entities		2844	7832	666
Number of documents per vendor	Mean	19.77	47.75	4.06
	Max	164	839	111
	Min	0	0	0
Number of pages per vendor	Mean	19.77	3.37	83.84
	Max	164	12	2155
	Min	0	0	0
Number of pages per document	Mean	29.51	3.12	164.67
	Max	292	14	2155
	Min	3	1	10

Bias in machine learning often is the result of bias present in the training data set and is a known problem for any language model [35], including when training CyBERT. Language models such as BERT and GPT are well known to exhibit an exploitable biases, including for unethical AI behavior [36], the irresponsible use of AI [37], perpetuating stereotypes [38], and negative sentiments towards specific groups [39].

According to these articles, these issues are due to the characteristics of the training data. We therefore tried, as much as possible, during the curation of our dataset to remove any sequences that contained obvious bias towards or against vendors, devices, capabilities, etc., but we nevertheless do not presume that there is no bias present in our dataset. Hence, we are committed in our ongoing efforts to further evaluate and mitigate the bias within CyBERT's training data set, as well as from CyBERT's operation.

4.2. Fine-Tuning BERT

An appropriate fine-tuning strategy is needed to adapt BERT to a given downstream task in a target domain. Howard and Ruder have discussed the benefits of fine-tuning a language model on a specific dataset to improve the classification performance [3]. An illustration of the architecture for CyBERT is in Figure 3, where the model starts with initial weights from a general corpus and is subsequently fine-tuned based on target task-specific supervised data for text classification.

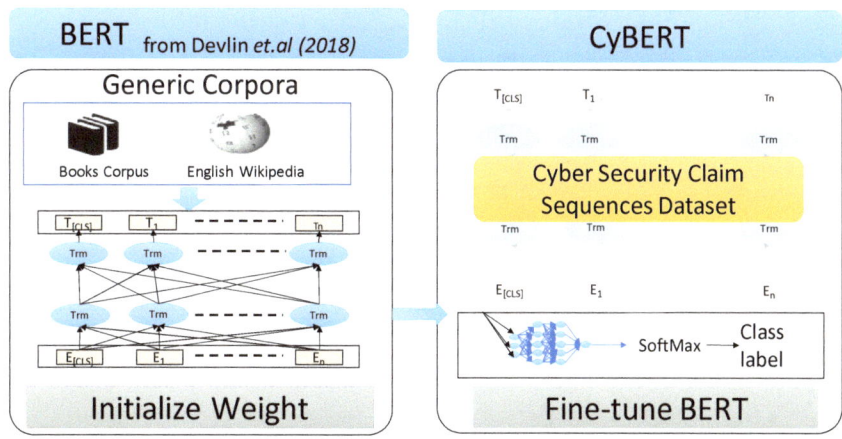

Figure 3. Overview of fine-tuning BERT for CyBERT.

A critical issue that must be considered when fine-tuning BERT for a target task is the problem of overfitting. It is necessary to develop a better optimization method with a suitable learning rate. In the following subsections, we describe in detail our strategies for learning rate (LR) and epoch limit selection to avoid catastrophic forgetting and overfitting, respectively. A third consideration for fine-tuning a BERT classifier is determining the most informative layer of BERT to connect to the classifier layer. The final fine-tuning step is finding best number of dense layers and dropout rate for the classifier based on the hyperparameters and the dataset.

4.2.1. Hyperparameters

4.2.1.1. Catastrophic Forgetting

During the process of learning new knowledge by unlocking weights already established from prior training, there is a risk that the pre-trained knowledge is erased. McCloskey et al. referred to this as the catastrophic forgetting effect in transfer learning [40]. Sun et al. showed that BERT is prone to the catastrophic forgetting problem [15]. We fine-tuned BERT with different learning rates (ranging from 1×10^{-4} to 1×10^{-7}) in order to investigate the catastrophic forgetting effects. Figure 4 shows the learning curves of error rates in our training and validation sets. The validation set is a portion of the overall data set and was used to determine whether the learned patterns are extendable to unseen data.

As demonstrated by Sun et al.'s [15] method, unfreezing all transformer layers and concatenating the layer weights would reduce the error rate. Therefore, we unfroze all layers in the BERT model during CyBERT's fine-tuning process. This allows all weights to be updated in all the layers during the training process. We conducted the training repeatedly, in order to allow us to fine-tune the selection of our starting learning rate, and then we carefully monitored the training progress, specifically to avoid the risk of catastrophic interference for the model.

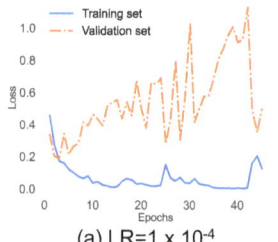 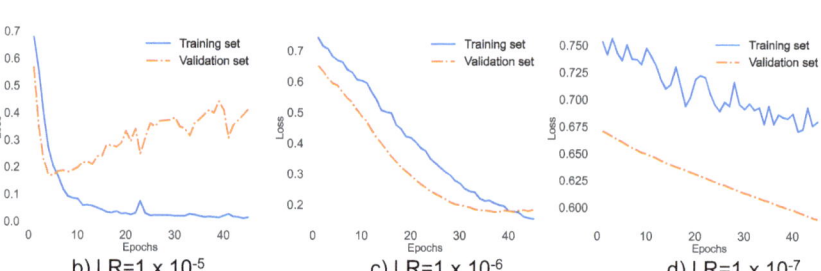

Figure 4. Learning rate effect on model convergence.

Figure 4 shows that a lower learning rate, such as 1×10^{-6}, is necessary for our fine-tuned BERT model in order to overcome the catastrophic forgetting effect. Furthermore, the figure also shows that fine-tuning BERT using a higher learning rate, such as 1×10^{-5} or 1×10^{-4}, results in convergence failure.

We utilized the cyclic method explained by Smith to determine the optimal learning rate range for our model [41]. In this method, the learning rate is initially low, and then it is increased exponentially for each batch. To find the best learning rate, we plotted training loss results for each batch. The best initial value of the learning rate was somewhere around the middle of the sharpest descending loss curve (left plot) or the lowest value in the loss derivatives with respect to the learning rate (red arrow in the right plot in Figure 5).

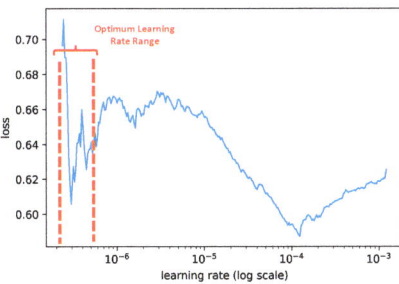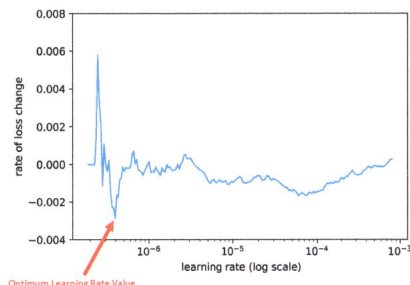

Figure 5. Impact of learning rates when fine-tuning our model.

We analyzed different values within the optimal range shown in Figure 5 to determine the best initial learning rate for our model. In our model, the loss function started to decrease very rapidly when the learning rate was between 1×10^{-7} and 1×10^{-6} (see Figure 5). By choosing a value in this range, we still were able to further decrease the LR using ReduceLROnPlateau. ReduceLROnPlateau reduces learning rate by a factor of 0.5 if the validation loss does not improve after two iterations (epochs).

4.2.1.2. Overfitting

Choosing the exact number of training epochs to use is a common problem in training neural networks. Overfitting of the training dataset can be caused by too many epochs, whereas underfitting may result from too few iterations. By selecting an appropriate early-stopping method we can start with a large number of epochs and stop the training process if the monitored metric does not show any improvement. This alleviates the needs to manually select the number of epochs and instead utilize a data-driven automation approach. In our model, we monitor the validation loss value and will stop training after four epochs if it does not show any improvement.

4.2.2. Selecting Optimal Classification Layer

The BERT-base model consists of an embedding layer, a stack of 12 encoders for the base model, and a pooling layer. The input embedding layer operates on the sum of the token embeddings, the segmentation embeddings, and the position embeddings. The final hidden state from encoders is corresponding to the special classification token (CLS). For the text classification task, this token is used as the aggregate sequence representation.

The first layer after the encoders is the next sentence prediction (NSP) layer. The NSP layer is utilized to understand sentence relationships [5]. This layer transforms the last encoder layer output (CLS token) into two vectors, each representing IsNext and Not-Next, respectively. The NSP layer then is connected to a fully connected neural network for classification.

We did not freeze any of the layers during the fine-tuning process. In this way, the model will adjust BERT's pre-trained weights based on our dataset, hyperparameters, and our given downstream task.

4.2.3. Selecting the Optimal Number of Dense Layers

Different layers of a neural network can capture different levels of syntactic information for text classification [3]. We studied the impact of different numbers of fully connected dense layers on top of the stacked encoders in BERT, in order to determine the best model based on our given dataset. The hyperparameters we adapted here are the different dropouts and the number of neurons for each dense layer. We achieved the best results for two dense layers with 64 and 16 neurons and dropout rates of 0.5 and 0.3, respectively. Table 2 shows the highest accuracy and learning rate based on the different number of dense layers.

Table 2. Comparing different number of dense layers in fine-tuning CyBERT.

Model Architecture	LR	Accuracy	F1 Score
BERT base + 1 dense	2×10^{-5}	0.92	0.91
BERT base + 2 dense	2×10^{-6}	0.92	0.92
BERT base + 3 dense	4×10^{-6}	**0.948**	**0.932**
BERT base + 4 dense	1×10^{-5}	0.93	0.93

4.2.4. Labeling Process

We designed and implemented a mobile application to aid in the manual labeling of extracted sequences. A snapshot of the application is provided in Figure 6. This mobile app was written as a `Xamarin.Forms app` [42], an open-source mobile app development framework for building Android and iOS apps with .NET and C#. This application supports initial labeling and relabeling and also supports labeling using multiple people, by associating designated labels with the person providing that label. This can subsequently be used for outlier removal, computation of majority decisions on final labels, and more.

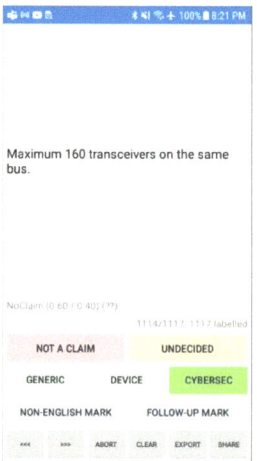

Figure 6. A snapshot of the manual labeling mobile app.

4.2.4.1. Initial Labelling

We manually labeled sequences extracted from a sample of ICS device documents. Claim sequences were initially categorized into three types, including generic claims, device claims, and cybersecurity claims. Having these individual claim types will help future investigation regarding claim type detection. For the purpose of this study, we grouped all these types of claims as claim labels and also removed the sequences with the "Not Sure" label from the classification dataset.

4.2.4.2. Prediction-Guided Relabeling Process

After obtaining our initial labeled dataset, we used it to train CyBERT. We followed the fine-tuning process we detailed earlier in this article. The trained model was then used to predict the class labels for each sequence, and we compared the results with the manual labels. From that comparison, we could find that there were a number of sequences whose class prediction probability was in the vicinity of 0.5, indicating a large uncertainty in some instances. We carefully reviewed each of those cases and adjusted the labels where necessary. The final class count and their distribution are reported in Table 3.

Table 3. Number of sequence labels and label distribution in each class.

Class Label	Final Label Counts	Final Label Distribution
NotClaim	4544	67.189%
ClaimDevice	848	12.53%
ClaimGeneric	807	11.93%
ClaimCybersec	335	4.95%
NotSure	226	3.34%

After this label review process, we repeated the fine-tuning process to obtain new model parameter values. A comparison of the obtained results pre- and post-label review demonstrate the improvement to CyBERT from this iterative refinement process. The obtained probabilities were sorted and plotted in the Figure 7, showing that we could successfully reduce the model uncertainty.

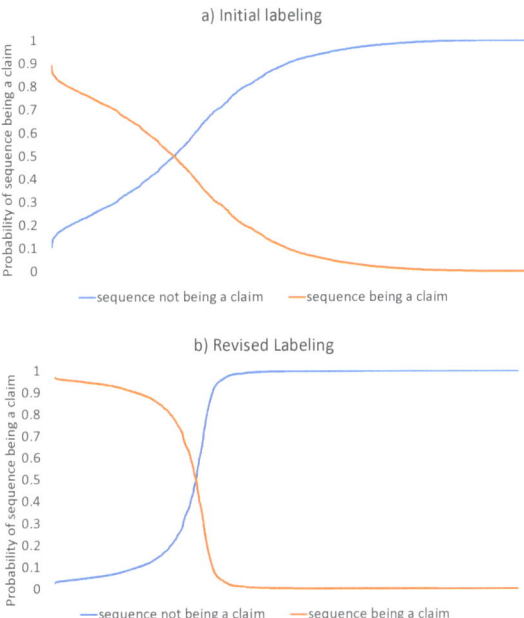

Figure 7. Sorted probabilities with (**a**) initial labeling and (**b**) revised labeling.

4.3. Classifier Training

One of the benefits of the pre-trained model is being able to train a model for downstream tasks by utilizing relatively small training data sets [15]. We manually labeled 6763 sequences from a set of documents then fine-tuned BERT on the resulting dataset. For training the classifier, we evaluated the impact of selecting different number of dense layers and learning rate values.

We subsequently tested the model on our dataset and adjusted labels for sentences causing uncertainty within the model. This iterative process helped us to reduce the uncertainty of our tuned model (Figure 7). We fine-tuned BERT on the revised database and tuned the associated hyperparameters to improve the claim classifier. The final model accuracy we achieved with CyBERT was 94.4%. We set the sequence length and batch size to 128 and 32, respectively.

4.3.1. Impact of Randomness

Fine-tuning BERT on a small dataset can be unstable [5]. Randomness in machine learning models can happen because of randomly initialized weights and biases, dropout regularization, and optimization techniques [43]. To investigate their effects and impact on our model, we performed the training stage 100 times, using the same model hyperparameters and only varying the random seeds, in order to achieve a statistically reliable result for our model accuracy.

The distributions of the training accuracy, validation accuracy, and testing accuracy are plotted in Figure 8. Table 4 reports the standard deviation, mean, and confidence interval (CI), as well as the margin of error for 100 training runs each for validation, training, and testing. These plots and the associated table show that CyBERT's true accuracy was within the 0.943 and 0.945 interval with a 95% CI.

These results suggest that the accuracy of our model can be impacted by the random seed value selection. Therefore, based on the recommendation published in the literature [5], we chose the random seed that leads to the highest validation accuracy for CyBERT.

Table 4. Standard deviation and mean for training, validation, and testing accuracy.

Dataset	SD	Mean	CI (95%)	Margin of Error
Training	0.012	0.959	0.957 to 0.961	0.00235
Validation	0.006	0.944	0.943 to 0.945	0.00118
Testing	0.007	0.935	0.934 to 0.936	0.00137

The results from Table 4 and Figure 7 confirms that even though our labeling set was small, the resulting CyBERT classifier can successfully identify cybersecurity feature claims within sequences with a high level of confidence.

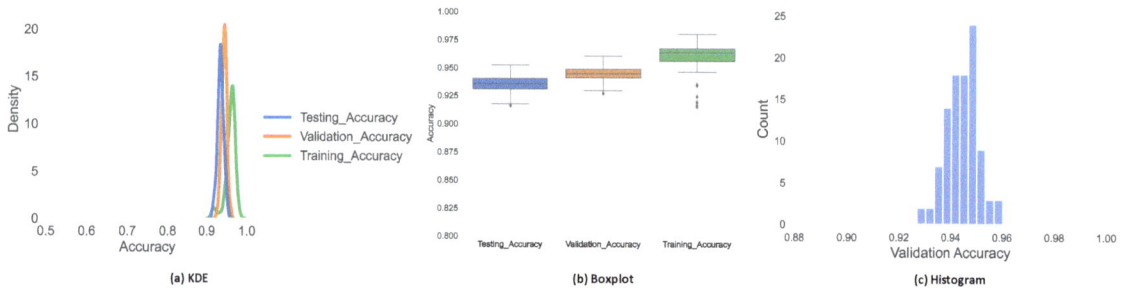

Figure 8. Kernel density estimation (**a**); box plot (**b**) for training, validation, and testing accuracy; validation accuracy histogram (**c**).

5. Results and Discussion

All the models in this study were executed on our university's supercomputing infrastructure, HCC Crane [44] with NVIDIA Tesla V100 GPUs with 16 GB of RAM per GPU. To obtain an unbiased estimate of out-of-sample accuracy, we divided the sequence dataset into training, validation, and test samples, utilizing 70%, 10%, and 20% or our total dataset, respectively.

For the comparison of the models, we used accuracy and macro-weighted F1 for all models. All accuracies reported in this article were based on predictions for the test set. Macro-weighted F1 is a measure of a model's accuracy on a dataset, which returns the average F1 score considering the proportion for each label in the dataset.

5.1. Comparing CyBERT with Pre-Trained BERT for Sequence Classification

In order to evaluate our strategy for fine-tuning BERT, we compared the results with BertForSequenceClassification. BertForSequenceClassification is a pre-trained BERT transformer model released by the Google research group in [5] with a dropout layer followed by a softmax classification/regression layer on top of the stacked decoder output. The predicted probability of each label is calculated as:

$$P(c|h) = \text{softmax}(Wh) \tag{1}$$

where h is the final hidden state of the first token in the BERT token embedding matrix (CLS), and W is the matrix for task-specific parameters.

To evaluate the impact of the architecture and the training approach, we conducted two separate experiments. In both, we started with the BertForSequenceClassification model. This model is comprised of 12 stacked encoders, a dropout layer, and a classifier layer. This model was initialized from pre-trained BERT.

In the first experiment, all transformer layers remained frozen. During training of the classifier it can therefore only tune the last layer, which is the classification layer. The resulting accuracy of this model on our dataset was 76%.

In the second experiment, for the purpose of comparison and to show the effect of fine-tuning, we employed the same model architecture as in the first experiment but enabled full fine-tuning by unfreezing all its layers. The fine-tuning process also involved finding the optimum LR based on this model architecture and dataset.

Table 5 shows the best accuracy among all the learning rates we studied for both approaches using BertForSequenceClassification, from among the tested range of 1×10^{-2} to 5×10^{-7}. The results show that unfreezing all encoders during fine-tuning of the model, training the classifier, and optimizing hyperparameters improved the model accuracy by 16 percentage points, from 76% to 92%.

As we have shown in the previous section, by further optimizing the architecture itself and introducing additional layers, we could further improve CyBERT's accuracy to 94.4%.

Table 5. Fine-tuning effect on BERT with one classification layer.

	LR	Accuracy	F1 Score
BertForSequenceClassification	1×10^{-7}	0.76	0.72
Fine-tune BERT-base uncased	2×10^{-5}	0.92	0.91

5.2. Comparing CyBERT with Other Language Models

5.2.1. Generative Pre-Trained Transformer (GPT)

GPT models are unsupervised transformer language models that are trained on a very large corpus of text. GPT-2 [6] was trained on a diverse corpus of unlabeled text (40 GB of Internet text). The GPT-2's main training objective is to be able to predict the next word while all of the previous words are given. Although BERT and GPT are both very strong language models, trained on a large corpus of data, and based on the transformer architecture using masked self attention, they are fundamentally different. GPT-2 uses decoder blocks from the transformers, while BERT utilizes encoder-only transformers. The other main difference between these two models is the word embedding. GPT-2 takes word vectors as input and produces the probability estimation of the next word as outputs (one token word at a time), while BERT uses the entire surrounding context together. GPT-2-small contains a 12-layer decoder-only transformer with 12 attention heads. Fine-tuning pre-trained GPT-2 is a two-stage semi-supervised approach. This process starts with using the pre-trained GPT model weights to set the initial parameters (unsupervised). Fine-tuning is then the supervised discrimination technique to adjust parameters to the target task. In this study, we fine-tuned GPT-2 (small and medium) with our dataset after unfreezing all layers in the transformer blocks. We also tried different learning rates and reported the values in Table 6. Due to model limitations, we were not able to perform GPT-2 large and GPT-2 extra large. We also requested OpenAI GPT-3 API services, but as of the time of writing this article, we were still awaiting approval for resource access.

Table 6. Fine-tuning GPT-2 small and medium.

	LR	Accuracy	F1 Score
GPT-2 Small	1×10^{-2}	0.86	0.84
	2×10^{-4}	0.89	0.87
	2×10^{-3}	0.88	0.85
	2×10^{-5}	**0.91**	**0.89**
	2×10^{-6}	0.85	0.81
	2×10^{-7}	0.70	0.52
GPT-2 Medium	2×10^{-2}	0.87	0.85
	2×10^{-3}	0.90	0.87
	2×10^{-4}	0.90	0.86
	2×10^{-5}	0.91	0.89
	2×10^{-6}	**0.92**	**0.91**
	2×10^{-7}	0.75	0.63

Table 6 indicates that the highest accuracy was 91%, which was achieved by the GPT-2 medium model with an LR of 2×10^{-6}. We observe from Figure 9 that the GPT-2 classifier model will not converge if the learning rate is higher than 2×10^{-6} (blue lines) for GPT-2 small, or 2×10^{-7} (orange lines) for GPT-2 medium, respectively. This phenomenon indicates the catastrophic forgetting effect present in the GPT-2 models. These plots indicate that the acceptable hyperparameters for these models for training small and medium GPT-2 models are in the vicinity of 2×10^{-6} and 2×10^{-7}, respectively.

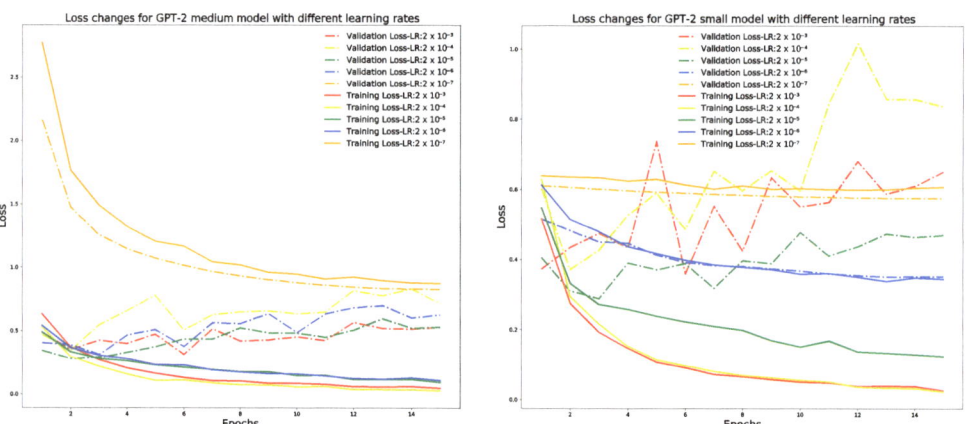

Figure 9. Loss changes for GPT-2 models with different learning rates: GPT-2 medium (**left**) and GPT-2 small (**right**) for 15 epochs.

5.2.2. ULMFiT

Universal language model fine-tuning (ULMFiT) [3] is a transfer learning method for NLP tasks including text classification. The ULMFiT architecture includes a three-layer weight-dropped LSTM (AWD-LSTM). The averaged stochastic gradient method (ASGD) AWD-LSTM [45] uses the DropConnect method to regulate weights in the recurrent networks. The ULMFiT training starts with a general language model pre-trained on a large Wikipedia text corpus (103 million words). For any domain-specific task, ULMFiT provides a discriminative fine-tuning process for the desired domain. The discriminative fine-tuning refers to using different learning rates to tune each layer. The final step is fine-tuning the updated language model on the target downstream task (such as text classification). In order to compare our CyBERT model with ULMFiT, we used the gradual unfreezing method to fine-tune ULMFiT. This process starts by only unfreezing the final layer while keeping all others frozen. The process then fine-tunes the model for several epochs and determines a new optimal learning rate for the tuned model up to this point before repeating this process while gradually unfreezing all other layers. The accuracy for each step is presented in Table 7.

Table 7. Fine-tuning ULMFiT.

Fine-tuning ULMFiT	Accuracy	F1 Score
Unfreeze last layer	0.83	0.83
Unfreeze last two layers	0.87	0.85
Unfreeze all layers	**0.91**	**0.91**

The best accuracy we achieved by fine-tuning ULMFiT on our dataset was 91% with unfreezing all three-layer AWD-LSTM weights. Unfreezing all layers will update all weights during the training process.

5.2.3. ELMo

Embeddings from language models (ELMo) [4] is a context-based word embedding method. This model learns contextualized word representations using two layers of BiLSTMs and a character-based encoding layer. Using a character-based layer, characters are encoded into a word's representation for the following two BiLSTM layers that enable hidden states to enhance a word's final embedding.

Classification using ELMo starts with tokenizing each sequence with ELMo, with the resulting embedding vectors subsequently used as input to different NN models. In our experiments using ELMo, we utilized a fully connected neural network, CNN, BiLSTM, and LSTM in order to compare the results with our model. For each model, based on the defined architecture, we first determined the best learning rate based on the method explained in [41]. Table 8 summarizes the best results for each type of neural network.

Table 8. Classification using ELMo.

	Architecture	LR	Accuracy	F1-Score
ELMo + NN	2 Dense	9×10^{-5}	0.91	0.9
ELMo + CNN	3 Convolution	4×10^{-7}	0.91	0.89
	2 Convolution	1×10^{-4}	0.91	0.89
	1 Convolution	6×10^{-5}	**0.92**	**0.9**
ELMo + BiLSTM	3 BiLSTM	2×10^{-4}	0.87	0.85
	2 BiLSTM	4×10^{-6}	0.88	0.86
	1 BiLSTM	1×10^{-4}	0.91	0.89
ELMo + LSTM	3 LSTM	9×10^{-4}	0.89	0.86
	2 LSTM	2×10^{-4}	0.89	0.87
	1 LSTM	2×10^{-5}	0.90	0.88

Table 8 shows that the highest accuracy was achieved by using the ELMo tokenizer and one convolutional layer with a filter size of 128, connected to two dense layers with 256 and 128 neurons, respectively, each followed by dropout layers with rates 0.3 and 0.2, respectively.

5.3. Comparing CyBERT with Neural Networks

Traditionally, text classification with NN models utilized word-level embedding methods such as GloVe. The problem with these embedding methods is that it removes the contextual meaning of these words.

Throughout all of the different evaluations shown in the following sections for the different NN models, in each case we first obtained the 768-dimensional BERT-Base uncased tokenizer embeddings for each WordPiece token in the input sequences. By utilizing the same tokenizer for all these models, we can exclude the effect of the tokenizer embedding on a model's performance.

5.3.1. Convolutional Neural Network

A convolutional neural network (CNN) is a class of artificial neural network models that is capable of extracting abstract features from complex data. Through many iterations, the model learns to map inputs to their class labels. CNNs are composed of two main components: (1) the first component consists of several filters and pooling layers that are applied to multi-dimensional arrays in order to create a feature space. These features are abstractions of the most significant characteristics contained within the input data; (2) the second component of CNNs contains a fully connected network that maps the extracted features to their target. In classification problems, this target is a group of data that shares a common property. In CNNs, the multi-dimensional output of the convolution component is flattened and passed to the fully connected network.

We studied the impact of different values for the CNN hyperparameters, including the number of convolutions, different dropout rates for each layer, and the number of dense layers after the convolutions. For each architecture, the best learning rate was determined using the LrFinder function [41]. The best accuracies for all architectures are reported in Table 9.

Table 9. Comparing CNN-based classifier results using the BERT tokenizer.

Architecture		LR	Accuracy	F1 Score
1 Convolution	**1 Dense**	4×10^{-4}	**0.88**	**0.87**
	2 Dense	5×10^{-4}	0.87	0.87
	3 Dense	1×10^{-4}	0.87	0.86
2 Convolution	1 Dense	5×10^{-5}	0.87	0.86
	2 Dense	5×10^{-5}	0.87	0.86
	3 Dense	2×10^{-3}	0.87	0.86
3 Convolution	1 Dense	4×10^{-4}	0.86	0.85
	2 Dense	4×10^{-4}	0.86	0.85
	3 Dense	1×10^{-4}	0.86	0.86

Table 9 shows that the best results were achieved using a network with one convolution (128 filters) connected to a dense layer with 256 neurons followed by a dropout layer with a 0.3 dropout rate.

5.3.2. LSTM

It has been shown in [46] that neural network models can be applied to learn distributed sentence representations and achieve good results in tasks related to sentiment classification and text categorization with little external domain knowledge. In long short-term memory (LSTM) neural networks, features are learned at the phrase-level by using a convolutional layer. This convolutional layer then feeds sequences of such higher-layer representations into LSTMs to learn their relationships to long-term features.

The LSTM model for NLP tasks requires an embedding matrix. We once again utilized the BERT-based uncased tokenizer for embedding each token into its vector for initializing the model. We evaluated different options for the number of LSTM and dense layers, in order to determine the best hyperparameters and the resulting architecture. The best learning rate for each architecture was determined again using the LrFinder function. We achieved the best accuracy with an architecture comprised of a single LSTM with 150 hidden units and a 0.1 dropout rate, combined with two dense layers with 150 and 124 neurons, respectively, coupled with the BERT tokenizer. The achieved accuracies for different configurations are reported in Table 10.

Table 10. Comparing LSTM-based classifier results using the BERT tokenizer.

Architecture		LR	Accuracy	F1 Score
1 LSTM	1 Dense	1×10^{-4}	0.873	0.864
	2 Dense	4×10^{-5}	**0.867**	**0.830**
	3 Dense	5×10^{-5}	0.871	0.859
2 LSTM	1 Dense	2×10^{-4}	0.871	0.860
	2 Dense	5×10^{-5}	0.872	0.862
	3 Dense	4×10^{-5}	0.866	0.855
3 LSTM	1 Dense	2×10^{-4}	0.871	0.862
	2 Dense	2×10^{-3}	0.865	0.853
	3 Dense	5×10^{-3}	0.861	0.851

5.3.3. BiLSTM

Bidirectional LSTM models are especially suited for sequential modelling and can be used to extract additional contextual information from the feature sequences provided by the convolutional layer [47]. The bidirectional LSTM actually concatenates two one-way actions to obtain the embeddings from the networks [48].

The BiLSTM recurrent network is once again utilizing the BERT-Base uncased tokenizer. In this model, we studied the impact of the number of BiLSTM layers, the number of hidden LSTM dimensions, the dropout rates for each layer, and the number of dense layers on top of the concatenated BiLSTMs. For each architecture, we determined the best learning rate using the LrFinder function. Table 11 shows the achieved accuracies and F1 scores for each architecture configuration we tested.

Table 11. Comparing BiLSTM-based classifier results using the BERT tokenizer.

Architecture		LR	Accuracy	F1 Score
1 BiLSTM	**1 Dense**	1×10^{-5}	**0.88**	**0.87**
	2 Dense	5×10^{-5}	0.87	0.86
	3 Dense	1×10^{-4}	0.88	0.87
2 BiLSTM	1 Dense	5×10^{-4}	0.87	0.86
	2 Dense	4×10^{-5}	0.87	0.86
	3 Dense	2×10^{-5}	0.87	0.85
3 BiLSTM	1 Dense	2×10^{-5}	0.87	0.86
	2 Dense	4×10^{-6}	0.86	0.85
	3 Dense	4×10^{-5}	0.87	0.86

Table 11 shows that the best result was achieved using a network with one BiLSTM with 150 hidden units and a 0.1 dropout rate, which was connected to one dense layer with 150 neurons followed by a 0.1 dropout rate.

5.4. Performance Comparison for All Models

As shown in Figure 10, we presented the training and validation accuracy and the loss values for all models during the training phase. The best validation accuracy was achieved by CyBERT, proposed by our NLP model, with a 95.4% accuracy. The loss plots indicate the effectiveness of the learning rate function we used for initializing all models. Additionally, the loss plots show the effectiveness of the early-stopping method to avoid overfitting in cases where the validation loss increases during the training phase.

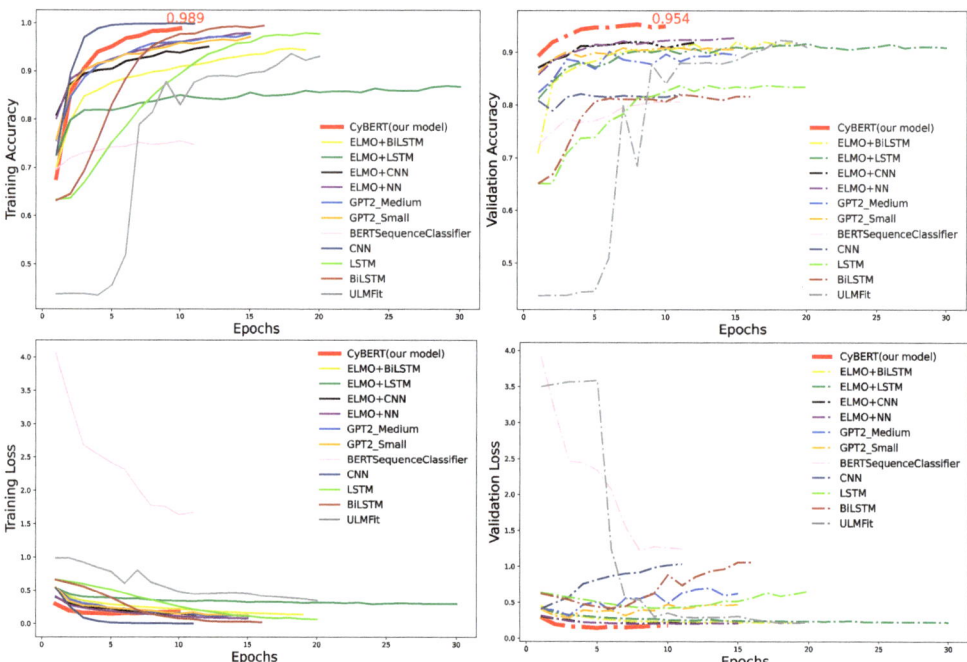

Figure 10. Comparing training accuracy (**left top**), validation accuracy (**right top**), training Loss (**bottom left**), and validation loss (**bottom right**) for all models.

Table 12 compares the accuracy for each model from our test set. The learning rates we report in this table indicate the best LR we found for each model based on the architecture and dataset we provided earlier. The learning rate was found via the LrFinder method and fine-tuned during the training phase.

Binary classification algorithms are often evaluated using receiver operating characteristic (ROC) curves. Instead of a single value, it provides a two-dimensional illustration of classifier performance. ROC plots the false-positive rates against the true-positive rates in classification. For the ideal classifier scenario, we want to observe a high true-positive rate and a low false-positive rate [49]. Figure 11 compares the ROC curve for all the models we tested in this study. The classifier was desired to be closer the upper-left corner of the ROC curve plot. Figure 11 illustrates that our CyBERT classifier performed better in all areas compared to all other models.

Table 12. Comparison across all tested models.

Model	Architecture	Accuracy	Macro Weighted F1	AUC	Training [*] Time	Testing [*] Time	Trainable Parameters
CyBERT (Our Model)	**12 Encoder 3 Dense**	**0.954**	**0.93**	**0.948**	32,970	97	108,647,026
BERT Classifier	12 Encoder 1 Dense	0.76	0.72	0.773	7832	77	109,482,240
CNN with BERT Tokenizer	1 Convolution 1 Dense	0.88	0.87	0.862	1470	75	11,330,286
LSTM with BERT Tokenizer	1 LSTM 2 Dense	0.86	0.83	0.852	1190	58	10,884,324
BiLSTM with BERT Tokenizer	1 BiLSTM 3 Dense	0.88	0.87	0.871	2412	61	12,604,804
GPT2-Small	12 Decoder 1 Dense	0.9	0.87	0.908	37,640	134	125,444,134
GPT2-Medium	24 Decoder 1 Dense	0.92	0.91	0.857	61,340	175	354,825,216
ELMo + NN	2 Dense	0.91	0.9	0.910	3950	88	295,554
ELMo + CNN	1 Convolution 2 Dense	0.92	0.9	0.912	4128	105	16,778,242
ELMo + LSTM	1 LSTM 2 Dense	0.90	0.88	0.916	15,603	74	19,785,410
ELMo + BiLSTM	1 BiLSTM 2 Dense	0.91	0.89	0.897	18,216	58	15,854,274
ULMFiT	3 AWD-LSTM	0.91	0.91	0.902	1873	42	62,652

[*] Times are in seconds.

The other important parameter for a classifier is the "area under the ROC curve" (AUC). Generally, the higher the AUC score, the better a classifier performs for the given task [49]. The AUC is reported for all models in Table 12 and Figure 11, which indicate that CyBERT had the highest AUC value among all tested models.

Figure 10 shows that the best value for AUC belongs to CyBERT, whichwasis 0.948. This indicates that CyBERT is better at distinguishing classes than any other models we compared it against in this study. The next-highest AUC values belonged to the ELMo models, which were all at least three percentage points lower than CyBERT's AUC.

The training time reported in Table 12 was only for the training phase after determining the optimum learning rate for each model. Language models such as BERT, GPT-2, and ELMo typically require more time for the training phase because of the higher number of trainable parameters. Among all these models, GPT-2 required the most time to complete training, for both medium and small models, followed by our proposed model, CyBERT. This result was expected based on the number of trainable parameters in these models. Once trained, we do not need to repeat training for these models. They are ready to be used for classification, unless the dataset needs to be updated.

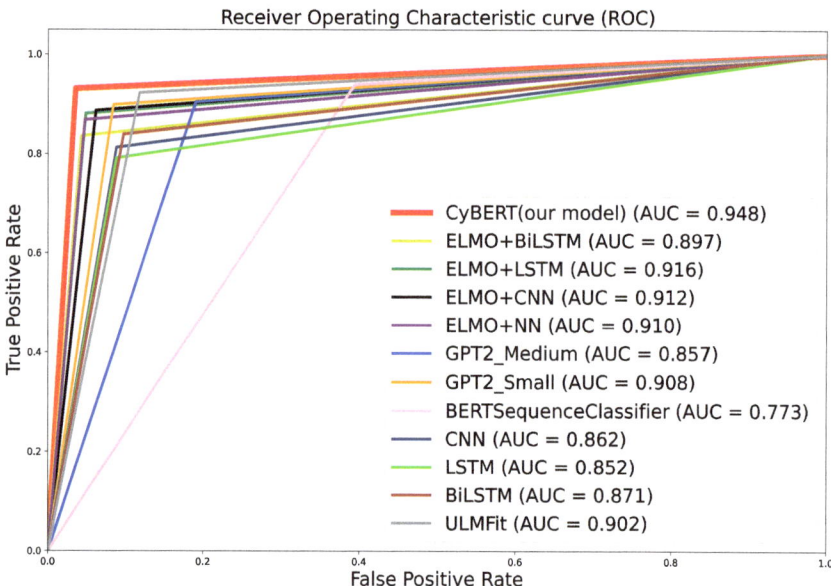

Figure 11. ROC comparison for all models.

5.5. Summary of Results

Our CyBERT as well as the original BertForSequenceClassification employ 12 encoders. CyBERT employs two additional dense layers. The resulting F1 and accuracy for CyBERT were 19 and 21 percentage points higher, respectively, than the performance for BertForSequenceClassification, which indicates the fine-tuning effect on the model performance. ULMFiT had the lowest number of trainable parameters and was the fastest model in training and testing. However, it had a 4, 2, and 5 percentage point lower accuracy, respectively, for accuracy, F1, and AUC, compared to CyBERT.

A comparison of the training and testing loss and accuracy results for all models is also provided in Figure 10, with the red curve indicating CyBERT's performance. The macro-weighted F1 for CyBERT was 0.93, whereas, for GPT2-small, it was 0.87, which represents a 6 percentage point improvement. Moreover, although CyBERT's training time was higher than the training times for the ELMo and ULMFiT language models, its accuracy was 3 and 4 percentage points higher, respectively, which is a significant improvement.

6. Conclusions

We introduced CyBERT, a classification model obtained through fine-tuning the BERT-base language model, utilizing our curated cybersecurity domain NLP dataset. This classification model is motivated by our ongoing research in developing an unbiased, objective, and semi-supervised approach, named CYVET, for vetting ICS device cybersecurity implications through a process of automatically vetting vendor claims extracted from device documentation via natural language processing against industry requirements. This article details one of the core building blocks of the overall CYVET approach for vetting cybersecurity claims.

We first generated a dataset comprised of a large number of ICS device documentations. We subsequently extracted and labeled sequences from these documents for the purpose of this study. The resulting dataset was used to train a CyBERT that can be used to detect claims about device features from within these documents. Our new CyBERT model increased the accuracy of this classification task by 19 percentage points compared to the original BERT text classifier.

We also provided an in-depth comparative analysis of BERT and CyBERT to show the necessity of our fine-tuning strategies. In addition to CyBERT, we implemented other pre-trained language models such as GPT-2, ELMo, ULMFiT, and various neural-network-based models, including a convolution neural network (CNN), LSTM, and BiLSTM, for comparison against our presented model. The extensive experimental results showed the effectiveness and robustness of CyBERT. The results demonstrate that the performance of our CyBERT is better than that of all other models we tested as part of this study.

Author Contributions: Investigation, K.A., M.H. and H.S.; writing—original draft preparation, K.A. and M.H.; writing—review and editing, K.A., M.H., H.S., K.P. and J.L.J.; supervision, H.S., M.H., K.P. and J.L.J.; project administration, K.P. and J.L.J.; funding acquisition, H.S., M.H., K.P. and J.L.J. All authors have read and agreed to the published version of the manuscript.

Funding: This research was funded by the US. Department of Energy through a subcontract from Oak Ridge National Laboratory, project No. 4000175929 (project CYVET).

Institutional Review Board Statement: Not applicable.

Informed Consent Statement: Not applicable.

Data Availability Statement: Not applicable.

Acknowledgments: This research has been supported in part by the Department of Energy Cybersecurity for Energy Delivery Systems program and the Oak Ridge National Laboratory.

Conflicts of Interest: The authors declare no conflict of interest.

Abbreviations

The following abbreviations are used in this manuscript:

CYVET	Cyber-physical security assurance
BERT	Bidirectional encoder representations from transformers
CyBERT	Cybersecurity BERT
ICS	Industrial control systems
CR	Cybersecurity requirements
VSF	Vendor-supplied features
OT	Operational technology
OCR	Optical character recognition
NLP	Natural language processing
ULMFiT	Universal language model with fine-tuning
ELMo	Embeddings from language models
GPT	Generative pre-training
NER	Name entity recognition
RE	Relation extraction
QA	Question answering
MLM	Masked language model
NSP	Next sentence prediction
LR	Learning rate
CI	Confidence interval
ASGD	Averaged stochastic gradient
RNN	Recurrent neural network
CNN	Convolutional neural network
NN	Neural network
LSTM	Long short-term memory
BiLSTM	Bidirectional LSTM
ROC	Receiver operating characteristic
AUC	Area under the ROC curve

References

1. Ameri, K.; Hempel, M.; Sharif, H.; Lopez, J., Jr.; Perumalla, K. Smart Semi-Supervised Accumulation of Large Repositories for Industrial Control Systems Device Information. In Proceedings of the ICCWS 2021 16th International Conference on Cyber Warfare and Security, Nashville, TN, USA, 25–26 Februray 2021; pp. 1–11.
2. Perumalla, K.; Lopez, J.; Alam, M.; Kotevska, O.; Hempel, M.; Sharif, H. A Novel Vetting Approach to Cybersecurity Verification in Energy Grid Systems. In Proceedings of the 2020 IEEE Kansas Power and Energy Conference (KPEC), Manhattan, KS, USA, 13–14 July 2020; pp. 1–6.
3. Howard, J.; Ruder, S. Universal language model fine-tuning for text classification. *arXiv* **2018**, arXiv:1801.06146.
4. Peters, M.E.; Neumann, M.; Iyyer, M.; Gardner, M.; Clark, C.; Lee, K.; Zettlemoyer, L. Deep contextualized word representations. *arXiv* **2018**, arXiv:1802.05365.
5. Devlin, J.; Chang, M.W.; Lee, K.; Toutanova, K. Bert: Pre-training of deep bidirectional transformers for language understanding. *arXiv* **2018**, arXiv:1810.04805.
6. Radford, A.; Wu, J.; Child, R.; Luan, D.; Amodei, D.; Sutskever, I. Language models are unsupervised multitask learners. *OpenAI Blog* **2019**, *1*, 9.
7. Lee, J.; Yoon, W.; Kim, S.; Kim, D.; Kim, S.; So, C.H.; Kang, J. BioBERT: A pre-trained biomedical language representation model for biomedical text mining. *Bioinformatics* **2020**, *36*, 1234–1240. [CrossRef] [PubMed]
8. Naseem, U.; Khushi, M.; Reddy, V.; Rajendran, S.; Razzak, I.; Kim, J. BioALBERT: A Simple and Effective Pre-trained Language Model for Biomedical Named Entity Recognition. *arXiv* **2020**, arXiv:2009.09223.
9. Lan, Z.; Chen, M.; Goodman, S.; Gimpel, K.; Sharma, P.; Soricut, R. Albert: A lite bert for self-supervised learning of language representations. *arXiv* **2019**, arXiv:1909.11942.
10. Beltagy, I.; Lo, K.; Cohan, A. SciBERT: A pretrained language model for scientific text. *arXiv* **2019**, arXiv:1903.10676.
11. Edwards, A.; Camacho-Collados, J.; De Ribaupierre, H.; Preece, A. Go simple and pre-train on domain-specific corpora: On the role of training data for text classification. In Proceedings of the 28th International Conference on Computational Linguistics, Barcelona, Spain, 8–13 December 2020; pp. 5522–5529.
12. Jwa, H.; Oh, D.; Park, K.; Kang, J.M.; Lim, H. exbake: Automatic fake news detection model based on bidirectional encoder representations from transformers (bert). *Appl. Sci.* **2019**, *9*, 4062. [CrossRef]
13. Vogel, I.; Meghana, M. Detecting Fake News Spreaders on Twitter from a Multilingual Perspective. In Proceedings of the 2020 IEEE 7th International Conference on Data Science and Advanced Analytics (DSAA), Sydney, Australia, 6–9 October 2020; pp. 599–606.
14. Liu, C.; Wu, X.; Yu, M.; Li, G.; Jiang, J.; Huang, W.; Lu, X. A two-stage model based on BERT for short fake news detection. In *Lecture Notes in Computer Science, Proceedings of the International Conference on Knowledge Science, Engineering and Management, Athens, Greece, 28–30 August 2019*; Springer: Cham, Switzerland, 2019; pp. 172–183.
15. Sun, C.; Qiu, X.; Xu, Y.; Huang, X. How to fine-tune bert for text classification? In *Lecture Notes in Computer Science, Proceedings of theChina National Conference on Chinese Computational Linguistics, Kunming, China, 18–20 October 2019*; Springer: Cham, Switzerland, 2019; pp. 194–206.
16. Khetan, V.; Ramnani, R.; Anand, M.; Sengupta, S.; Fano, A.E. Causal BERT: Language models for causality detection between events expressed in text. *arXiv* **2020**, arXiv:2012.05453.
17. Lee, J.S.; Hsiang, J. Patentbert: Patent classification with fine-tuning a pre-trained bert model. *arXiv* **2019**, arXiv:1906.02124.
18. Araci, D. Finbert: Financial sentiment analysis with pre-trained language models. *arXiv* **2019**, arXiv:1908.10063.
19. Liu, Z.; Huang, D.; Huang, K.; Li, Z.; Zhao, J. Finbert: A pre-trained financial language representation model for financial text mining. In Proceedings of the Twenty-Ninth International Joint Conference on Artificial Intelligence, IJCAI, Yokohama, Japan, 16–18 January 2021; pp. 5–10.
20. Das, S.S.; Serra, E.; Halappanavar, M.; Pothen, A.; Al-Shaer, E. V2W-BERT: A Framework for Effective Hierarchical Multiclass Classification of Software Vulnerabilities. *arXiv* **2021**, arXiv:2102.11498.
21. Zhou, S.; Liu, J.; Zhong, X.; Zhao, W. Named Entity Recognition Using BERT with Whole World Masking in Cybersecurity Domain. In Proceedings of the 2021 IEEE 6th International Conference on Big Data Analytics (ICBDA), Xiamen, China, 5–8 March 2021; pp. 316–320.
22. Chen, Y.; Ding, J.; Li, D.; Chen, Z. Joint BERT Model based Cybersecurity Named Entity Recognition. In Proceedings of the 2021 The 4th International Conference on Software Engineering and Information Management, Yokohama, Japan, 16–18 January 2021; pp. 236–242.
23. Gao, C.; Zhang, X.; Liu, H. Data and knowledge-driven named entity recognition for cyber security. *Cybersecurity* **2021**, *4*, 1–13. [CrossRef]
24. Tikhomirov, M.; Loukachevitch, N.; Sirotina, A.; Dobrov, B. Using bert and augmentation in named entity recognition for cybersecurity domain. In *Lecture Notes in Computer Science, Proceedings of the International Conference on Applications of Natural Language to Information Systems, Saarbrücken, Germany, 24–26 June 2020*; Springer: Cham, Switzerland, 2020; pp. 16–24.
25. Xie, B.; Shen, G.; Guo, C.; Cui, Y. The Named Entity Recognition of Chinese Cybersecurity Using an Active Learning Strategy. *Wirel. Commun. Mob. Comput.* **2021**, *2021*, 6629591. [CrossRef]
26. Yin, J.; Tang, M.; Cao, J.; Wang, H. Apply transfer learning to cybersecurity: Predicting exploitability of vulnerabilities by description. *Knowl.-Based Syst.* **2020**, *210*, 106529. [CrossRef]

27. Mikolov, T.; Sutskever, I.; Chen, K.; Corrado, G.S.; Dean, J. Distributed representations of words and phrases and their compositionality. In Proceedings of the Advances in Neural Information Processing Systems, Carson City, NV, USA, 5–10 December 2013; pp. 3111–3119.
28. Bojanowski, P.; Grave, E.; Joulin, A.; Mikolov, T. Enriching word vectors with subword information. *Trans. Assoc. Comput. Linguist.* **2017**, *5*, 135–146. [CrossRef]
29. Pennington, J.; Socher, R.; Manning, C.D. Glove: Global vectors for word representation. In Proceedings of the 2014 conference on empirical methods in natural language processing (EMNLP), Doha, Qatar, 25–29 October 2014; pp. 1532–1543.
30. Lample, G.; Ballesteros, M.; Subramanian, S.; Kawakami, K.; Dyer, C. Neural architectures for named entity recognition. *arXiv* **2016**, arXiv:1603.01360.
31. Zhang, X.; Zhao, J.; LeCun, Y. Character-level convolutional networks for text classification. *Adv. Neural Inf. Process. Syst.* **2015**, *28*, 649–657.
32. Akbik, A.; Blythe, D.; Vollgraf, R. Contextual string embeddings for sequence labeling. In Proceedings of the 27th international conference on computational linguistics, Santa Fe, NM, USA, 20–26 August 2018; pp. 1638–1649.
33. Wu, Y.; Schuster, M.; Chen, Z.; Le, Q.V.; Norouzi, M.; Macherey, W.; Krikun, M.; Cao, Y.; Gao, Q.; Macherey, K.; et al. Google's neural machine translation system: Bridging the gap between human and machine translation. *arXiv* **2016**, arXiv:1609.08144.
34. Vaswani, A.; Shazeer, N.; Parmar, N.; Uszkoreit, J.; Jones, L.; Gomez, A.N.; Kaiser, Ł.; Polosukhin, I. Attention is all you need. In Proceedings of the Advances in Neural Information Processing Systems, Long Beach, CA, USA, 4–9 December, 2017; pp. 5998–6008.
35. Bender, E.M.; Gebru, T.; McMillan-Major, A.; Shmitchell, S. On the Dangers of Stochastic Parrots: Can Language Models Be Too Big? In Proceedings of the 2021 ACM Conference on Fairness, Accountability, and Transparency, Virtual Event Canada, New York, NY, USA, 3–10 March 2021; pp. 610–623.
36. Leib, M.; Köbis, N.C.; Rilke, R.M.; Hagens, M.; Irlenbusch, B. The corruptive force of AI-generated advice. *arXiv* **2021**, arXiv:2102.07536.
37. McGuffie, K.; Newhouse, A. The radicalization risks of GPT-3 and advanced neural language models. *arXiv* **2020**, arXiv:2009.06807.
38. Basta, C.; Costa-Jussà, M.R.; Casas, N. Evaluating the underlying gender bias in contextualized word embeddings. *arXiv* **2019**, arXiv:1904.08783.
39. Hutchinson, B.; Prabhakaran, V.; Denton, E.; Webster, K.; Zhong, Y.; Denuyl, S. Social biases in NLP models as barriers for persons with disabilities. *arXiv* **2020**, arXiv:2005.00813.
40. McCloskey, M.; Cohen, N.J. Catastrophic interference in connectionist networks: The sequential learning problem. In *Psychology of Learning and Motivation*; Elsevier: Amsterdam, The Netherlands, 1989; Volume 24, pp. 109–165.
41. Smith, L.N. Cyclical learning rates for training neural networks. In Proceedings of the 2017 IEEE winter conference on applications of computer vision (WACV), Santa Rosa, CA, USA, 24–31 March 2017; pp. 464–472.
42. Hermes, D. *Xamarin Mobile Application Development: Cross-Platform c# and Xamarin. Forms Fundamentals*; Apress: Berkeley, CA, USA, 2015.
43. Dodge, J.; Ilharco, G.; Schwartz, R.; Farhadi, A.; Hajishirzi, H.; Smith, N. Fine-tuning pretrained language models: Weight initializations, data orders, and early stopping. *arXiv* **2020**, arXiv:2002.06305.
44. Holland Computing Center (HCC) at University of Nebraska-Lincoln. Available online: https://hcc.unl.edu/ (accessed on 1 January 2021).
45. Merity, S.; Keskar, N.S.; Socher, R. Regularizing and optimizing LSTM language models. *arXiv* **2017**, arXiv:1708.02182.
46. Zhou, C.; Sun, C.; Liu, Z.; Lau, F. A C-LSTM neural network for text classification. *arXiv* **2015**, arXiv:1511.08630.
47. Liu, G.; Guo, J. Bidirectional LSTM with attention mechanism and convolutional layer for text classification. *Neurocomputing* **2019**, *337*, 325–338. [CrossRef]
48. Liu, P.; Qiu, X.; Huang, X. Recurrent neural network for text classification with multi-task learning. *arXiv* **2016**, arXiv:1605.05101.
49. Fawcett, T. An introduction to ROC analysis. *Pattern Recognit. Lett.* **2006**, *27*, 861–874. [CrossRef]

Journal of *Cybersecurity and Privacy*

MDPI

Article

RSSI-Based MAC-Layer Spoofing Detection: Deep Learning Approach [†]

Pooria Madani * and Natalija Vlajic

Electrical Engineering and Computer Science, York University, Toronto, ON M3J 1P3, Canada; vlajic@eecs.yorku.ca
* Correspondence: madani@eecs.yorku.ca
† This paper is an extension version of the conference paper: Madani, P.; Vlajic, N.; Sadeghpour, S. MAC-Layer Spoofing Detection and Prevention in IoT Systems: Randomized Moving Target Approach. In Proceedings of the 2020 Joint Workshop on CPS & IoT Security and Privacy, Virtual Event, USA, 9 November 2020.

Abstract: In some wireless networks Received Signal Strength Indicator (RSSI) based device profiling may be the only viable approach to combating MAC-layer spoofing attacks, while in others it can be used as a valuable complement to the existing defenses. Unfortunately, the previous research works on the use of RSSI-based profiling as a means of detecting MAC-layer spoofing attacks are largely theoretical and thus fall short of providing insights and result that could be applied in the real world. Our work aims to fill this gap and examine the use of RSSI-based device profiling in dynamic real-world environments/networks with moving objects. The main contributions of our work and this paper are two-fold. First, we demonstrate that in dynamic real-world networks with moving objects, RSSI readings corresponding to one fixed transmitting node are neither stationary nor i.i.d., as generally has been assumed in the previous literature. This implies that in such networks, building an RSSI-based profile of a wireless device using a single statistical/ML model is likely to yield inaccurate results and, consequently, suboptimal detection performance against adversaries. Second, we propose a novel approach to MAC-layer spoofing detection based on RSSI profiling using multi-model Long Short-Term Memory (LSTM) autoencoder—a form of deep recurrent neural network. Through real-world experimentation we prove the performance superiority of this approach over some other solutions previously proposed in the literature. Furthermore, we demonstrate that a real-world defense system using our approach has a built-in ability to self-adjust (i.e., to deal with unpredictable changes in the environment) in an automated and adaptive manner.

Keywords: IoT security; spoofing; MAC authentication; intrusion detection system; LSTM autoencoders

Citation: Madani, P.; Vlajic, N. RSSI-Based MAC-Layer Spoofing Detection: Deep Learning Approach. *J. Cybersecur. Priv.* **2021**, *1*, 453–469. https://doi.org/10.3390/jcp1030023

Academic Editors: Phil Legg and Giorgio Giacinto

Received: 20 May 2021
Accepted: 29 July 2021
Published: 12 August 2021

Publisher's Note: MDPI stays neutral with regard to jurisdictional claims in published maps and institutional affiliations.

1. Introduction

The proliferation of the Internet of Things (IoT) and Wireless Sensor Network (WSN) networks has revived an old yet serious form of attack—*MAC-layer Spoofing* or also referred to as *Identity Spoofing*. In MAC address spoofing attack, as the name suggests, a rouge wireless node masquerades as another legitimate device by cloning the legitimate device's MAC address. Identity spoofing, in general, is a precursor for packet injection (another well-known type of attack) and thus requires careful consideration as part of any sound defense plan.

The most common way of defending against this form of attack is through the use of cryptographic techniques for MAC-address authentication [1]. Unfortunately, due to the resource limitations that are inherently present in many IoT and WSN devices (e.g., low processing power, low memory capacity, and limited battery life), many of these devices operate with very scaled-down (if any) versions of encryption and authentication protocols. For example, it is discovered that due to ease-of-installation by non-technical consumers, Philips IoT Smart Bulbs do not employ any form of encryption and authentication as specified by 802.15.5 protocol standard [2]. Or, in the case of a multihop WSN, the intermediate relaying nodes generally do not engage in the verification of the authenticity of the *relayed data frames*—authenticity verification of these frames takes place only at the final (i.e., destination) node. Authentication by intermediate nodes is typically omitted in order to reduce the nodes' energy consumption as well as minimize the possibility of a *battery exhaustion* attack [3] (readers should review seminal work by Nguyen et al. [4] for a complete survey of energy depletion attacks against low power wireless networks).

It should be noted that in a number of standardized wireless protocols that are still in use today, cryptographic authentication is simply not intended for all stages/frames of a communication process. For example, in all variants of IEEE 802.11 preceding 802.11 w, only data frames are protected, while control and management frames are used without any protection [5]. Thus, one should make provisions for extra security measures when cryptographic authentication is not supported by protocols deployed within certain application domains.

Clearly, in wireless systems with limited cryptographic and authentication protection, other alternative measures against MAC address spoofing are required. One such measure—which can also be used as an added layer of security even in wireless systems with extensive cryptographic and authentication protection—is the utilization of physical layer (i.e., signal-level) parameters. *Received Signal Strength Indicator* (RSSI) is a wireless communication variable that is directly influenced by the transmission power and the location of the transmitter as well as different environmental variables such as obstacles. As suggested in a number of earlier research works (e.g., [6–8]), RSSI values can be used to create the *fingerprint profile* of each device in a wireless network and then deploy these profiles to do a preliminary authenticity check against MAC spoofing attacks. Another point that makes RSSI profiling an attractive ally against MAC spoofing attacks is that the use of this single real-valued physical-layer variable is easy to implement, requires no modifications to existing higher layer protocols and applications, and has a very small processing and memory footprint.

There have been many research works in the past investigating the use of RSSI profiling for the purpose of MAC spoofing detection (some of which are surveyed in Section 2). Most of these works implicitly assume that: (1) RSSI samples received from a non-moving transmitting device form a stationary time-series with normally distributed variance, and (2) RSSI values are *independent and identically distributed* (i.i.d.) samples from an unknown normal distribution. Moreover, in the given works, the act of profiling a wireless device based on its RSSI values strongly relies on these two very assumptions. However, in our recently conducted study, the two assumptions (RSSI samples are stationary and i.i.d.) have come under scrutiny. Namely, through our extensive real-world experimentation, we have observed that RSSI values measured by a receiving node are highly affected by changes (e.g., moving objects) in their operating environments. In particular, we have observed that moving human bodies (and their absence) have a noticeable effect on RSSI values of IoT devices deployed in a residential environment, and as a result the variance of the RSSI time-series changes significantly when occupants are present and move around the property—we call this effect *time-series clustering* [9] (refer to Figure 1 where there are two different clusters, one with lower volatility than the other). Furthermore, it is clear from the depicted figure that there is a correlation between neighboring RSSI values; therefore, it would be hard to justify the claim that neighboring RSSI values are independent (as presumed by previous works [6–8]).

Except in a few usage cases where there are no moving objects in the environment (e.g., farmland monitoring), most real-world IoT networks deploy computing/sensing nodes in environments with some number of movable objects. Thus, in order to account for changes in RSSI values due to the above described clustering effect, it is necessary to have an adaptive and/or multi-model RSSI-based profiling scheme that will be able to improve/reduce the rates of false positives (in our previous work [10], we demonstrated how i.i.d. assumption pertaining to RSSI values can lead to probable evasion of detection systems that rely on RSSI-based profiling). In this work, we have proposed and studied a multi-classifier system to profile IoT devices based on their RSSI values under two moving object conditions (presence vs. absence of objects in the surrounding environment). Also, our profiling approach takes into consideration the relationship between neighboring RSSI values in the time-series to further improve the accuracy and robustness of IoT node profiles.

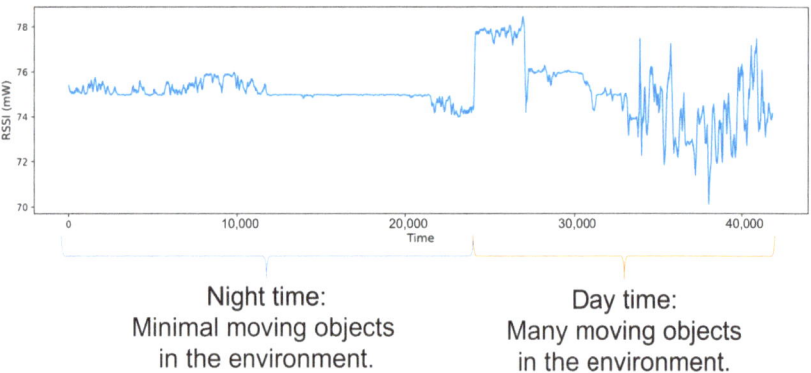

Figure 1. RSSI values of an IoT device deployed in a residential property with routine movements of occupants in a 24 h period.

The content of this paper is organized as follows: In Section 2, we discuss some of the notable previous works in RSSI-based MAC address spoofing detection. In Section 3, we present the threat model and the main assumptions about the adversary's capabilities as pertaining to our work. In Section 4, we propose our LSTM-based (Long Short-Term Memory) profiling scheme that has been devised to detect and classify MAC-spoofing traffics. In Section 5, we discuss adversarial traffic generation used to test the robustness of our approach and compare the effectiveness of our approach with the state-of-the-art RSSI based approaches previously proposed to deal with adversarial attacks.

2. Related Works

Wireless MAC Address Spoofing Detection is a well-studied topic in the literature on Wi-Fi and Wireless Sensor Networks. In the seminal paper [11], Faria and Cheriton were among the first ones to propose the use of RSSI values as a fingerprinting variable to detect MAC spoofing attacks in a WLAN environment. As part of their detection model, it is assumed that there are multiple access points (APs) capable of receiving the wireless signals from all clients in the network, so the RSSI values measured at each AP's antenna and for each transmitter are ultimately aggregated into a single profile. Consequently, a masquerading attack is detected by comparing the aggregated RSSI values of two consecutive data frames with the same MAC identifier. Also, they have demonstrated that using multi-sensing APs, and assuming constant transmitting power, a physical node can be triangulated with an accuracy of 5 to 10 m. Unfortunately, the practical merit of these findings is rather limited since the use of multiple overlapping APs in many WSN and IoT networks is not always possible.

Chen et al. [12] and Wu et al. [6] have both independently proposed the use of *k-means* clustering algorithm to detect signal/frame spoofing by a rogue access point (AP). Their work is grounded on the assumption that the sequence of last *n* RSSI values received from an AP would have minimum fluctuations around the mean in the absence of another rogue AP (i.e., an 'Evil Twin'). Thus, when clustering the elements of a received RSSI sequence into two clusters using k-means algorithm in the absence of an Evil Twin, the distance between two formed centroids would be small (i.e., smaller than a threshold value). At the same time, a large distance between the centroids of the two formed clusters would be indicative of the existence of an Evil Twin AP with its unique RSSI distribution. However, since this approach does not involve any offline learning (i.e., a previously trained model of what should be considered a legitimate distribution), the MAC address spoofer and the legitimate node must transmit in relatively close time intervals for the detection to actually work.

Sheng et al. [13] studied the effect of antenna diversity in 802.11 access points and their effect on RSSI device fingerprinting as well as spoofing detection. They demonstrated that RSSI values from a stationary receiver collected at a stationary transmitter form a mixture of two Gaussian distributions due to antenna diversity permitted under 802.11 protocol. As a result, they have trained a Gaussian mixture model for each wireless node and access point pair in the network and used a log-likelihood ratio test on the sequence of latest received RSSI at each access point from a given MAC address. A transmitting node is ruled spoofed if the ratio test fails by more than n Gaussian mixture models—where n is smaller than the number of available access points in the network and needs to be set empirically. However, using available off-the-shelf hacking tools an adversary can easily manipulate its transmission power to evade detection by this model, as discussed in later sections.

Gonzales et al. [14] have developed a novel technique known as context-leashing for the detection of public Evil Twin access points. They have argued that publicly available access points such as the ones available at franchise coffee shops (e.g., Starbucks) share service set identifiers (SSID) across different locations and oftentimes lack any authentication. This provides an opportunity for adversaries to spoof such SSIDs and trick clients into associating with a rogue access point (e.g., after performing a dissociation attack). The defense against the Evil Twin APs proposed in [8] assumes the use of a so-called context-leashing engine. Upon association with a publicly available access point, the context-leashing engine would collect a list of context $C_i = \{(c_1, r_1), \ldots, (c_n, r_n)\}$, which contains the list of all visible SSIDs (denoted by c_j, $j = 1, \ldots, n$) and their corresponding average RSSI values (denoted by r_j, $j = 1, \ldots, n$) that is reachable at the time of association with a particular SSID in the environment. For any future reassociation with a given SSID, a new context list is constructed and compared to the previously stored one. If the context-list of available neighboring SSIDs and their average RSSI values does not have a significant (empirically defined) overlap with the historical context-list, then the associated SSID is deemed an Evil Twin and the connection should be terminated. The main drawback of their method is the assumption that the list of SSIDs in a given geolocation remains relatively unchanged over time. However, with today's tethering capabilities of cellphones, this assumption is far from the truth.

3. Threat Model and Assumptions

In this section, we introduce the main annotation and assumptions of our work, which are also illustrated in Figure 2. First, consider a simple setup where there are a legitimate transmitting node (e.g., a temperature sensor) denoted by s and a legitimate receiving node (e.g., an IoT hub) denoted by r communicating over a wireless channel. Also, we assume that r utilizes an arbitrary approach (including what we propose in this work) to profile s based on RSSI samples, it has received in a period absent of any adversary, and then uses this profile at runtime to differentiate between received *data frames* that carry s' MAC address (legitimate vs. spoofed ones). Finally, let α denote the adversary with the following characteristics:

- The adversary is situated at a location from which it can observe/receive signals transmitted by all legitimate senders (when sending data frames) and receivers (when sending acknowledgment frames back) in the given network.
- The adversary is aware of the transmission power setting (P_{Tx}) of the legitimate sender(s), which is not a substantial assumption as system information about most IoT/WSN devices is publicly accessible on the Internet.

- The adversary has no prior knowledge of the actual physical/geographic locations of other (legitimate) nodes in the network.
- Network participants, including the adversary, are equipped with regular/common omnidirectional antennas, and are not capable of detecting the positional angle of the transmitting nodes. However, the adversary can move about in order to triangulate other nodes' locations based on the strength of the signal received from those nodes [10].
- The adversary itself is an *active* node capable of adjusting its transmission power.
- The adversary is also capable of altering (i.e., spoofing) its MAC address value—i.e., it can generate data frames that carry MAC addresses of other legitimate nodes from this particular network.

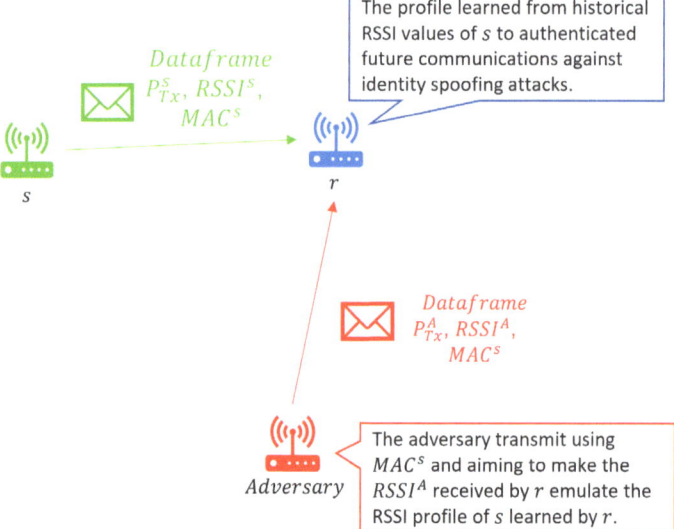

Figure 2. Overview of the threat model: the goal of the receiving node is to use historical (clean) RSSI values from the legitimate sender to learn a robust profile to use in future against identity attacks; while the goal of the adversary is to get past the established profile by taking over s identity.

The ultimate goal of adversary α is to impersonate a particular s by transmitting frames with s' spoofed MAC address. The spoofed frames are specifically intended for a particular r. Since, according to the assumptions of our work, the transmitter's RSSI values are registered and used by r for the purposes of MAC-spoofing detection, the adversary first needs to discover/adjust its transmission power (P_{Tx}) such that its spoofed frames (when received by r) get accepted as genuine with a high probability—i.e., some desired probability of evasion is achieved by the adversary. This particular problem—of how to discover/adjust the transmission power so as to achieve a certain evasion probability—is closely related to the optimal adversarial evasion problem introduced by Nelson et al. [15] and further extended by Madani and Vlajic [10] to the IoT realm.

4. Detection Approach: Deep Authentication

As demonstrated in Figure 1 (and argued in Section 1), given that RSSI time-series values of a wireless IoT device are not i.i.d., one could incorporate dependencies among neighboring RSSI values to build more robust and accurate predictive models for the purpose of device authentication. Deep autoencoders are deep generative neural networks that have demonstrated a strong capability of modeling latent variables in anomaly detection and authentication datasets [16]. LSTM autoencoders [17], in particular, are known for their generative modeling capabilities on time-series data. In this section we present our novel technique for authentication of legitimate IoT nodes using RSSI-based anomaly detectors deploying LSTM autoencoders. In addition, expanding on our argument from Section 1 with respect to the *time-series clustering-effect* of RSSI values in dynamic environments, we also discuss how our novel multi LSTM autoencoder architecture is able to switch between multiple trained LSTM models at runtime. Such a multi-LSTM autoencoder architecture would help with addressing the clustering effect of RSSI time-series.

4.1. LSTM Autoencoder Anomaly Detector

In the context of our work, let $X = <x_1, x_2, \ldots, x_n>$ denote an ordered sequence of n RSSI values received by node s. Then, the LSTM autoencoder is trained to learn two functions, namely, encoder $E(.)$ and decoder $D(.)$ such that $X \approx D(E(X))$. In other words, as depicted in Figure 3, the LSTM autoencoder learns an encoding state that best describes the structure of the training/input data and a decoding function that reconstruct the input sequence given the encoding state with minimal error. In general, large reconstruction errors occur when the input does not conform to the structure previously learned by the LSTM autoencoder. As such, a large reconstruction error can be used as a measure of input anomaly [16,18–20].

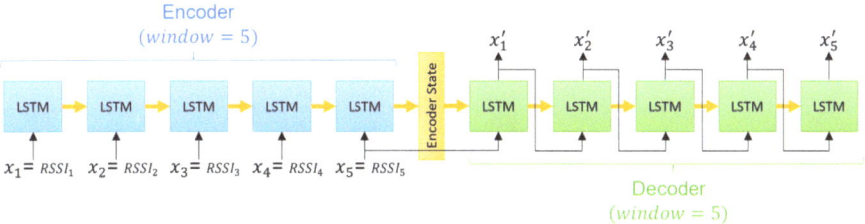

Figure 3. Anatomy of the LSTM autoencoder.

In order to build an RSSI profile of s (through the use of LSTM autoencoder), the receiving node r begins the process of collecting and assembling a time-series of RSSI values extracted from the data frames transmitted by s. Then, using a *rolling* window of size n, the time-series is segmented into m different overlapping sequences (where the extent of the overlap is controlled by the shift constant of the rolling window), which are further used to train the LSTM autoencoder. Since the LSTM autoencoder is supposed to learn the reconstruction of the input sequences, the m training inputs are also supplied as the expected outputs to the training algorithm with the *mean squared error* (MSE) as the loss function.

At runtime (i.e., during the actual use of the trained LSTM autoencoder for the purpose of attack/anomaly detection), n most recently observed RSSI samples are supplied into the trained LSTM autoencoder and then the MSE of the reconstructed sequence (relative to the provided input) is computed. Our experimental investigations (as described in Section 5) have demonstrated that the MSEs of the training data, in the absence of attack/spoofed instances, form a normal distribution. Therefore, our system uses Z-score to measure deviation from the expected MSE as the decision function to differentiate between the spoofed and the normal traffic. Specifically, for a Z-score $\geq l$ the system declares the inspected RSSI window as malicious, where l can be computed experimentally and set for the desired *false positive rate*.

4.2. Multiclassifer and Model Switching

As discussed in Section 1, in IoT environments with moving objects (e.g., residential or commercial premises), the RSSI time-series of a transmitting node can be divided into two significantly different time-series with substantially different volatility (i.e., time-series with clustering effect). Using the entirety of such a time-series (refer to Figure 1) for the training of our system's LSTM autoencoder would result in a less sensitive anomaly detection model. Thus, we propose to deploy/train two independent LSTM autoencoders—one for the volatile period of the observed time-series when moving objects are present, and one for the relatively calm period when the relative volatility is at its minimum.

Now, one obvious issue that would have to be adequately addressed in an anomaly detection system with two LSTM autoencoders is the issue of their scheduling. As one possible approach, the system operator could manually set the exact time when each of the trained LSTM autoencoders is to be deployed according to his/her knowledge of the environment. However, in such a system with manually determined 'switch times', a number of potential problems could arise. For example, an employee of a factory showing up earlier than usual could significantly affect the RSSI time-series of the nearby sensors/transmitters, which as a result could trigger a false positive alert (provided the detection model corresponding to the non-volatile conditions is still active).

One way to resolve the above challenges is by simultaneously monitoring MSE Z-scores output by the two models at runtime, and looking for the point in time when the Z-score of one of the models crosses another. For example, as shown in our experimentation and depicted in Figure 4, at night where there are fewer moving objects in the environment, the night's LSTM autoencoder model is reconstructing the RSSI time-series perfectly as reflected by its low Z-score, while at the same time the day's LSTM autoencoder does a poor job in reconstructing the same RSSI time-series. However, during the transition period when moving objects start to appear in the environment, the night's LSTM autoencoder performance starts to decline, while the performance of the day's LSTM autoencoder (which is trained to cope with daytime volatility) starts to exhibit noticeable improvement with respect to the reconstruction MSE. Thus, the moment when the two Z-score time-series cross over each other would be the optimal point in time when the system should switch from using the nighttime to using the day-time LSTM autoencoder model. This suggests that by simply monitoring the output of both trained LSTM autoencoder models, it is possible to determine the optimal 'switch time' in an adaptable and automated manner.

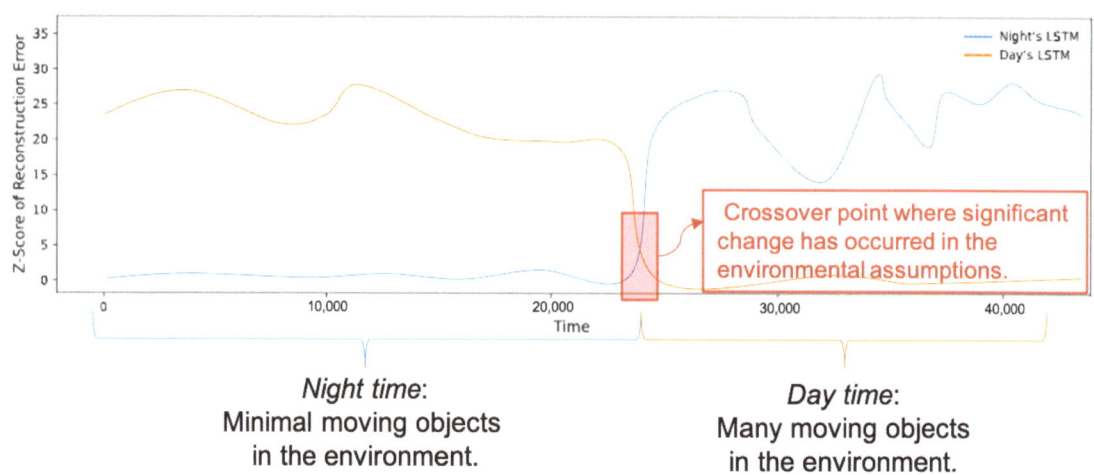

Figure 4. Starting at midnight, the Z-scores of reconstructed RSSI values corresponding to the transmitting node *s* using the two trained models (for day and night) are tracked. At about dawn, when occupants started to wake up and move about, the error rate of the night model significantly increases while the day model's error rate drops significantly.

5. Experiments and Results

5.1. Environment Setup

We have designed two experiments involving different forms of obstacles and moving objects to best collect the noise and other disturbances that IoT devices may face when attempting to profile their neighboring nodes using RSSI observations. In our experiments we have used three Digi XBee 3 Series programmable modules implementing IEEE 802.15.4. [21] (as depicted in Figures 5 and 6), where one device acts as the legitimate temperature reading sensor (denoted by s) transmitting its reading to the legitimate receiver (denoted by r) and the adversary (denoted by a) who spoofs the s' MAC address in the hope of providing false temperature readings to r.

In the first experiment (refer to Figures 6 and 7), s is situated in a waterproof container on the lawn outside the house, while r is situated in the second-floor bedroom. Aside from 5 occupants living on the property that move about the house during the day, outside pedestrians and moving vehicles affect s' RSSI values observed by r. The adversary is free to move about, both inside the property and outside, to carry out its spoofing attack (this is a very generous assumption to highlight a worst case scenario and superiority of our approach. In most settings, there is some degree of physical security that constrains adversaries in their physical positioning). This is an ideal experiment for resembling scenarios where IoT devices are separated by exterior walls and experience some degree of moving objects during the course of their daily operations.

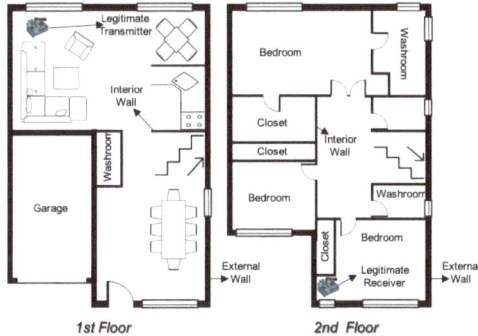

Figure 5. The legitimate transmitter is situated in the first floor family room while the legitimate receiver is situated in the second floor's bedroom separated by interior walls and an interior floor. The 5 occupants in the property are considered to be the influencing moving objects.

Figure 6. The legitimate transmitter is situated outdoors on the lawn transmitting temperature readings and the receiver is situated in the bedroom of the second floor separated by exterior building walls. The pedestrians and motor vehicles in the nearby residential area as well as the 5 occupants in the property are considered to be the influencing moving objects.

In the second experiment both r and s are situated in the property separated by a floor/ceiling and interior walls (depicted in Figure 6) while the adversary is allowed to move about inside and outside of the property. Similar to the first experiment the house occupants have their routine daily schedule of moving around the property during the day and resting (i.e., minimal movement) at night.

In the second experiment both r and s are situated in the property separated by a floor/ceiling and interior walls (depicted in Figure 5) while the adversary is allowed to move about inside and outside of the property. Similar to the first experiment, the house occupants have their routine daily schedule of moving around the property during the day and resting (i.e., minimal movement) at night.

Figure 7. Digi XBee 3 Series programmable module implementing IEEE 802.15.4. in a weatherproof secure enclosure protecting the devices from the elements when deployed.

In both experimental setups, r starts its training phase by collecting RSSI samples from s (refer to Figures 8 and 9) both during hours of minimal and significant movements (24 h of capture of RSSI at the sample rate of 1 frame/s)—where these hours are assumed to be empty of any adversarial presence to perturb the training dataset. Once the training stage is completed, r starts using its two trained LSTM autoencoder models to authenticate received signals and detect MAC-spoofed frames (each LSTM autoencoder has 2 LSTM layers with 20 nodes each and a final dense lake of size 1 and using Adam [22] optimizer for training).

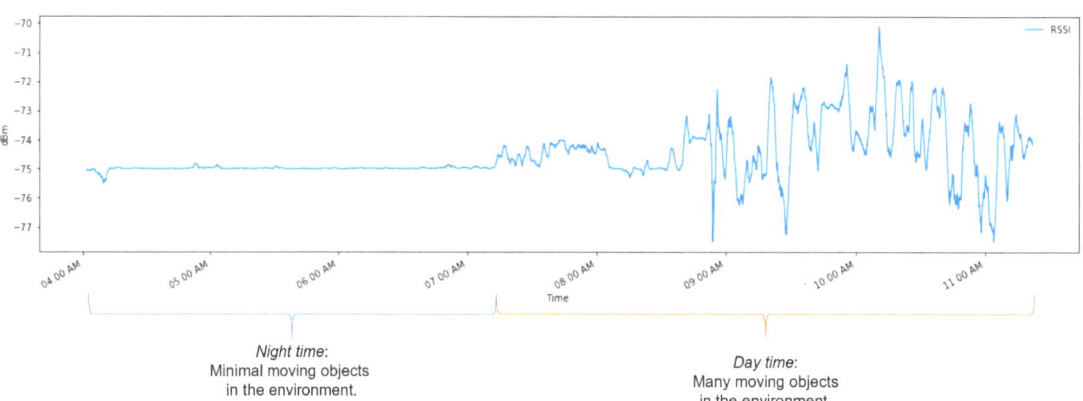

Figure 8. s' RSSI stream received by r during s' deployment outside of the property.

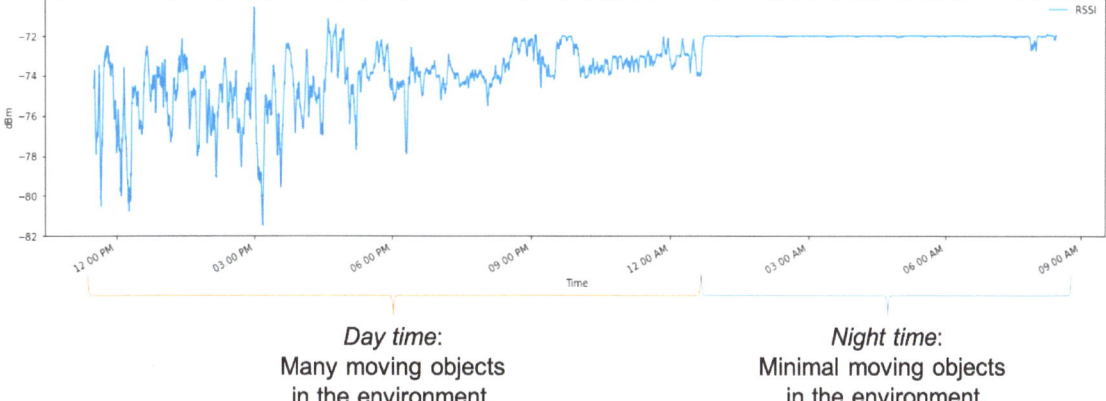

Day time:
Many moving objects
in the environment.

Night time:
Minimal moving objects
in the environment.

Figure 9. *s′* RSSI stream as received by *r* during *s′* deployment inside of the property.

5.2. Note on Special Spoofed Traffic Mix

All the surveyed works in Section 2 that use a rolling window on collected RSSI stream(s) for the purposes of signal classification (i.e., authentication) have implicitly assumed that each window of length n may fully consist of RSSI values from either an attacker or a legitimate device. However, this is not a realistic assumption given the unknown motivation and capabilities of adversaries. Moreover, many modern-day IoT devices (e.g., especially those used in home automation) are not battery operated and/or are not much concerned with energy preservation and as a result may be in frequent communication with other nearby devices. Consequently, in any given window of length n (used by the classification engine) there may exist some mix of the legitimate node's and the adversary's RSSI values as depicted in Figure 10.

(a)   (b)

Figure 10. (a) Case where the adversary starts transmitting right after the legitimate node terminated its transmission; **(b)** The adversary gains access to the channel while the legitimate node has not finished transmitting all of its frames.

5.3. Model Classification Performance

We have evaluated our novel spoofing detection approach against the Support Vector Machine (SVM) one-class anomaly detection technique described in [23] (as a baseline detection model) and the state-of-the-art Log-likelihood ratio test approach proposed in [13]. We have evaluated all three approaches against two real-world datasets (refer to Section 5.1) using 10-fold cross validation. The average classification/detection performance is reported in Table 2.

We have trained two classifiers for our autoencoder as well as each of the other two approaches (SVM [23] and Log-likelihood [13]): one for the period of high volatility (e.g., environmental moving objects—daytime) and another for the period of low volatility (e.g., minimal environmental moving objects—nighttime) as reported in Table 1. All three classifiers perform relatively better during the low volatility period (i.e., nighttime) than the high volatility period—with our approach performing the best in both categories significantly.

Table 1. Summary of Related Works.

	Methodology	Shortcomings
Faria and Cheriton [11]	Using multiple access point recording RSSI values of individual nodes in the network and compare them with historical records and vote on authenticity of the given transmission.	The assumption of the existence of multiple APs is not realistic in many IoT and WSN applications. Using their approach a single AP can be easily evaded as discussed in Madani and Valjic [10]. Also, they did not entertain the existence of variable noises as a result of moving objects in the environment during different time periods.
Chen et al. [12]	Using k-means clustering and comparing cluster centroids distance to find existence of anomalies in RSSI values.	Treating a sequence of RSSI as identically distributed and independent observations. In Sections 1 and 5.2 we have discussed in detail why such assumptions are wrong and can be advantageous to the adversary.
Wu et al. [6]	Using k-means clustering and comparing cluster centroids distance to find existence of anomalies in RSSI values.	Treating a sequence of RSSI as identically distributed and independent observations. In Sections 1 and 5.2 we have discussed in detail why such assumptions are wrong and can be advantageous to the adversary.
Sheng et al. [13]	Uses Gaussian mixture models to model observed RSSI from a given node and create a normal/expected RSSI profile.	Capturing diversity caused by antenna diversity implemented by wireless nodes. Although did not entertain the existence of variable noises as a result of moving objects in the environment during different time periods.
Gonzales et al. [14]	Uses available/neighboring SSIDs and their average RSSI values as observed by a given wireless node to establish expected/normal environment for initiating connection with a given access point.	A valid approach for verifying the validity of an SSID before connecting a mobile wireless node to it. However, this approach cannot guarantee the absence of spoofing once the connection is established and is not useful in settings where no other SSID is available in the environment.

We have also evaluated the classification performance of the three models against an adversarial traffic mix (as explained in Section 5.2). We can observe in Table 2 (also refer to Figures 11 and 12, that our approach slightly loses classification accuracy (by 1%) when 20% of RSSI values in a given window is generated by an adversary while the performance of the other two classifiers deteriorates significantly. This can partly be explained by the fact that our LSTM (Long Short-Term Memory) autoencoder approach takes into consideration the order in which RSSI samples appear (i.e., are collected), while the other two approaches treat RSSI values in a window as independent data points. It is clear from the obtained results that our approach is well equipped to deal with an active adversary that transmits during the transmission period of the legitimate node while such overlap of traffic is not well protected using existing approaches.

Table 2. Passive Adversary, who assumes a single spot in the environment and does not adjust its transmission power.

Model		0% Mixed Window Content						20% Mixed Window Content						50% Mixed Window Content					
		Day Classifier			Night Classifier			Day Classifier			Night Classifier			Day Classifier			Night Classifier		
		Precision	Recall	F1-Score	Precision	Recall	F1-Score	Precision	Recall	F1-Score	Precision	Recall	F1-Score	Precision	Recall	F1-Score	Precision	Recall	F1-Score
Multi Model	Normal	1.0	0.95	0.97	1.0	0.99	0.99	1.0	0.93	0.97	1.0	0.99	0.99	1.0	0.93	0.97	1.0	0.99	0.99
LSTM Autoencoder*	Spoofed	0.97	1.0	0.98	0.99	1.0	0.99	0.93	1.0	0.96	0.98	1.0	0.99	0.93	1.0	0.96	0.98	1.0	0.99
One-Class	Normal	0.66	0.52	0.58	0.73	0.42	0.53	0.56	0.52	0.54	0.60	0.48	0.53	0.58	0.52	0.55	0.59	0.48	0.53
SVM [23] (baseline)	Spoofed	0.69	0.80	0.74	0.50	0.79	0.61	0.48	0.52	0.50	0.37	0.49	0.42	0.50	0.56	0.53	0.36	0.47	0.41
Log-likelihood	Normal	0.85	0.92	0.88	0.83	0.89	0.86	0.75	0.89	0.81	0.73	0.78	0.75	0.77	0.91	0.83	0.81	0.89	0.85
ratio [13]	Spoofed	0.87	0.90	0.88	0.92	0.95	0.93	0.76	0.81	0.78	0.84	0.83	0.83	0.80	0.83	0.81	0.85	0.92	0.88

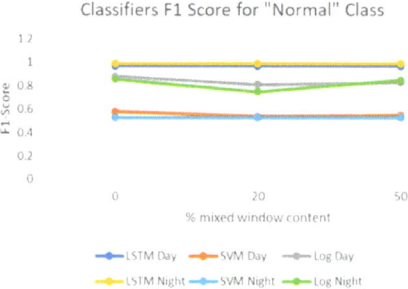

Figure 11. Comparison of 'Normal Classification' of our novel detection method with two other [13,23] state-of-the-art approaches proposed in the literature.

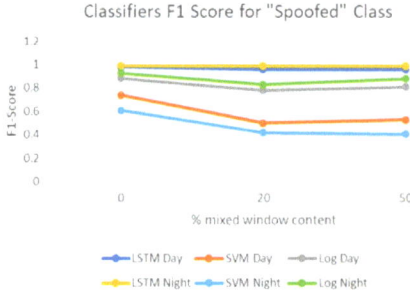

Figure 12. Comparison of 'Spoofed Classification' of our novel detection method with two other [13,23] state-of-the-art approaches proposed in the literature.

5.4. Model Switching at Runtime

In Section 4.2 we have explained the need for a bi-modal LSTM autoencoder classifier, and we have proposed a fully automated and adaptive approach to switching between the two train models/classifiers at runtime. Using the collected real-world datasets we have put this idea to test by continuously monitoring the reconstruction error of the two train models at runtime. As depicted in Figure 13, at night when the RSSI stream had relatively lower volatility, the night model (the blue line) resulted in low reconstruction error while the day model (the orange line) resulted in high reconstruction error—as to be expected. However, at the point in time when the volatility was about to pick up, we can observe a sudden jump in the night model's reconstruction error accompanied by significant improvement in the day model's reconstruction error, ultimately resulting in a crossover between the two error lines (orange and blue). This is a clear indication that the night model could be retired, and the day model could be activated for detection. Clearly, this demonstrates the viability of the crossover indicator to facilitate an automated and adaptive switching schedule between the two trained LSTM autoencoder models.

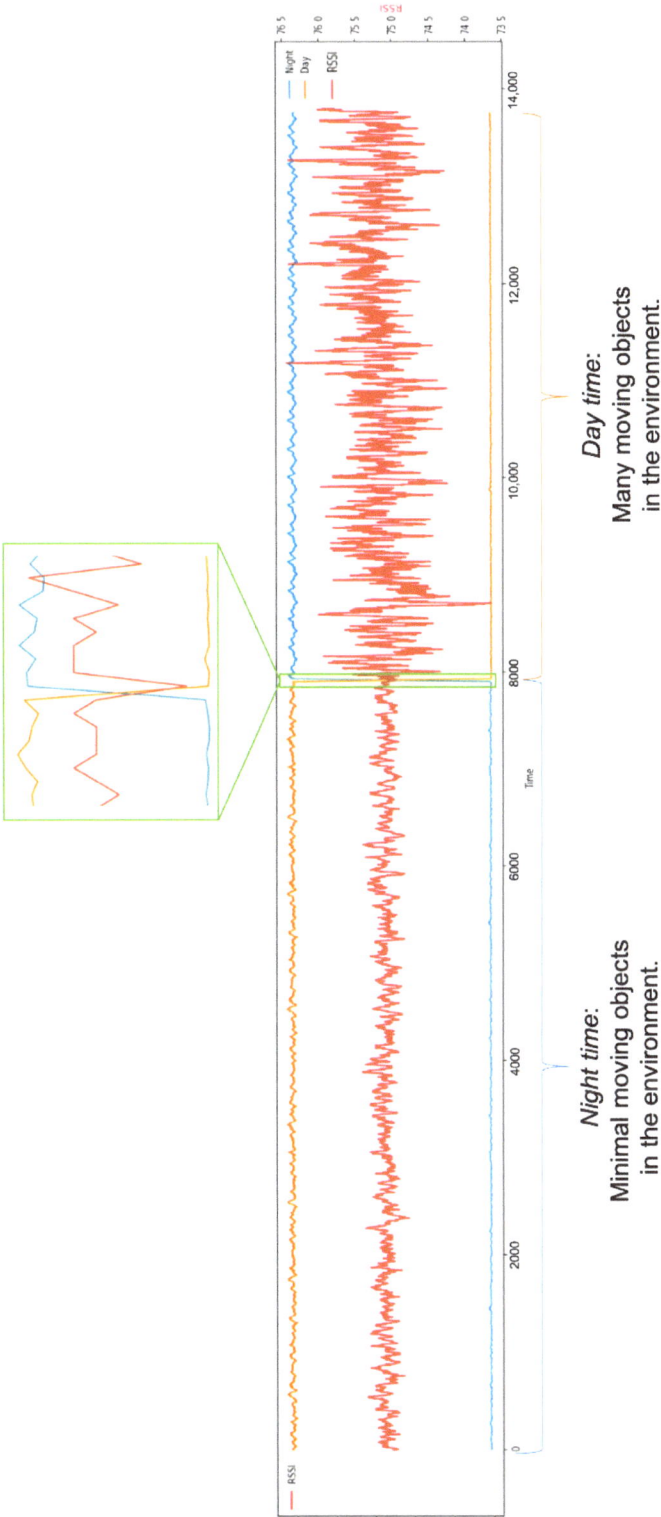

Figure 13. Tracking reconstruction error of two trained models during an entire day. The crossover point between the two reconstruction error lines (orange and blue) coincide with increase in volatility of RSSI stream (the red line)—a clear indicator to be used to switch between trained models.

6. Discussions and Conclusions

In this work we have proposed a novel RSSI-based MAC spoofing detection approach using a multi model LSTM autoencoder classifier. The advantages of our approach over earlier works in this field are twofold. First, our approach is capable of coping with periodic environmental (i.e., signal) disturbances caused by moving objects. Second, our approach can tolerate and detect presence of an adversary that transmits in close time intervals to legitimate network devices.

As part of this research, we have also studied the variability of RSSI streams in a real-world residential area, and (from the collected measurements) we have confirmed the existence of two very distinct periods in the observed RSSI streams (i.e., day vs night). These observations provide real-world justification for the use of a bi-modal LSTM autoencoder, with one autoencoder being trained for each variability period. In addition, we have proposed an automated and adaptive technique for determining the optimal point in time to switch between the two train models.

It may be worth clarifying that one of the key assumptions of our work is that the IoT network utilizing our solution is composed of a large number of sensing nodes (which are in charge of collecting and transmitting sensory readings from their immediate environment) and one or a few sink nodes (which are in charge of receiving and/or aggregating the sensory readings received from multiple sensor nodes). Furthermore, we assume that the sink nodes are generally more powerful (e.g., have better energy and processing capacity) compared to the sensing nodes.

Now, given the inherently 'one-way' nature of the assumed application and the respective communication patterns (i.e., sensors transmit while sinks receive), the most likely targets of an adversary existing in this environment (i.e., most likely recipients of spoofed packets) would be the sink nodes, and very rarely the 'ordinary' sensing nodes. Consequently, it is reasonable to assume that the proposed solution would have to be primarily, if not exclusively, implemented on the sink nodes in order help verify the authenticity of received sensor readings. As previously clarified, sink nodes are generally assumed to have reasonable energy and processing capabilities.

It is also worth pointing out that our proposed LSTM autoencoder approach is utilizing one-dimensional data (i.e., RSSI readings) as inputs, which makes the training of our model(s) extremely energy-inexpensive and fast, even for Zigbee IoT nodes as used in our experiments. Furthermore, using the trained LSTM autoencoders at runtime relies on very simple matrix multiplications, which are of similar complexity to SVM, linear regressions, or Gaussian models previously proposed in the literature, and which are well within the capabilities, even of IoT nodes, with limited energy and computational characteristics.

Given that most IoT networks have multiple participants, it is natural to wonder how our proposed method could be further expanded should participating nodes be capable and/or willing to cooperate with each other in order to detect an ongoing MAC spoofing attack. Although such an idea could likely enhance the overall detection and network performance, it also requires careful consideration and engineering in order to ensure robustness against (e.g.) potential byzantine nodes. We are planning an in-depth investigation of such a cooperative multi-node approach as one of the future research directions of our work.

In our previous work [10], we proposed an RSSI-based randomization technique for protection against an active adversary capable of modifying its transmission power and its location in the target/victim environment. Of course, such randomization could positively affect our novel proposed method but the classification performance might change drastically under a randomized schema. Finally, in this work we have assumed that the system operator is in charge of detecting low vs high volatility periods in the training RSSI time-series and divided the training set into two subsets for training the proposed bi-modal LSTM autoencoders. However, one could argue that due to variability in RSSI during the presence vs absence of moving objects, it is possible to detect two periods (for separating the training datasets for building the multi-model classifiers) using unsupervised clustering approaches such as k-means instead of relying on the judgment of a system operator for creating such separation. This is certainly an interesting future work that can further enhance our proposed *crossover model switching indicator*.

Author Contributions: Conceptualization, P.M. and N.V.; methodology, P.M.; software, P.M.; validation, P.M. and N.V.; data curation, P.M.; writing—original draft preparation, P.M.; writing—review and editing, P.M. and N.V.; supervision, N.V.; project administration, N.V. Both authors have read and agreed to the published version of the manuscript.

Funding: This research received no external funding.

Institutional Review Board Statement: Not applicable.

Informed Consent Statement: Not applicable.

Data Availability Statement: Not applicable.

Conflicts of Interest: The authors declare no conflict of interest.

References

1. Lashkari, A.H.; Danesh, M.M.S.; Samadi, B. A survey on wireless security protocols (WEP, WPA and WPA2/802.11 i). In Proceedings of the 2009 2nd IEEE International Conference on Computer Science and Information Technology, Beijing, China, 8–11 August 2009; pp. 48–52.
2. The Independent IT Security Institute AX Test. 2017. Available online: https://www.iot-tests.org/2017/06/hue-let-there-be-light/ (accessed on 1 September 2020).
3. Wood, A.D.; Stankovic, J.A. Denial of service in sensor networks. *Computer* **2002**, *35*, 54–62. [CrossRef]
4. Nguyen, V.L.; Lin, P.C.; Hwang, R.H. Energy depletion attacks in low power wireless networks. *IEEE Access* **2019**, *7*, 51915–51932. [CrossRef]
5. Ahmad, M.S.; Tadakamadla, S. Short paper: Security evaluation of IEEE 802.11 w specification. In Proceedings of the Fourth ACM Conference on Wireless Network Security, Hamburg, Germany, 14–17 June 2011; pp. 53–58.
6. Wu, W.; Gu, X.; Dong, K.; Shi, X.; Yang, M. PRAPD: A novel received signal strength-based approach for practical rogue access point detection. *Int. J. Distrib. Sens. Netw.* **2018**, *14*, 1550147718795838. [CrossRef]
7. Moosavirad, S.M.; Kabiri, P.; Mahini, H. RSSAT: A Wireless Intrusion Detection System Based on Received Signal Strength Acceptance Test. *J. Adv. Comput. Res.* **2013**, *4*, 65–80.
8. Demirbas, M.; Song, Y. An RSSI-based scheme for sybil attack detection in wireless sensor networks. In Proceedings of the 2006 International Symposium on a World of Wireless, Mobile and Multimedia Networks (WoWMoM'06), Buffalo-Niagara Falls, NY, USA , 26–29 June 2006; p. 5.
9. Aghabozorgi, S.; Shirkhorshidi, A.S.; Wah, T.Y. Time-series clustering—A decade review. *Inf. Syst.* **2015**, *53*, 16–38. [CrossRef]
10. Madani, P.; Vlajic, N.; Sadeghpour, S. MAC-Layer Spoofing Detection and Prevention in IoT Systems: Randomized Moving Target Approach. In Proceedings of the 2020 Joint Workshop on CPS & IoT Security and Privacy, Lisbon, Portugal, 15 September 2020; pp. 71–80.
11. Faria, D.B.; Cheriton, D.R. Detecting identity-based attacks in wireless networks using signalprints. In *Proceedings of the 5th ACM Workshop on Wireless Security*; ACM: New York, NY, USA, 2006; pp. 43–52.
12. Chen, Y.; Trappe, W.; Martin, R.P. Detecting and localizing wireless spoofing attacks. In Proceedings of the 2007 4th Annual IEEE Communications Society Conference on Sensor, Mesh and Ad Hoc Communications and Networks, San Diego, CA, USA, 18–21 June 2007; pp. 193–202.
13. Sheng, Y.; Tan, K.; Chen, G.; Kotz, D.; Campbell, A. Detecting 802.11 MAC layer spoofing using received signal strength. In Proceedings of the IEEE INFOCOM 2008—The 27th Conference on Computer Communications, Phoenix, AZ, USA, 13–18 April 2008; pp. 1768–1776.
14. Gonzales, H.; Bauer, K.; Lindqvist, J.; McCoy, D.; Sicker, D. Practical defenses for evil twin attacks in 802.11. In Proceedings of the 2010 IEEE Global Telecommunications Conference (GLOBECOM 2010), Miami, FL, USA, 6–10 December 2010; pp. 1–6.
15. Nelson, B.; Rubinstein, B.I.; Huang, L.; Joseph, A.D.; Lee, S.J.; Rao, S.; Tygar, J. Query Strategies for Evading Convex-Inducing Classifiers. *J. Mach. Learn. Res.* **2012**, *13*, 13–23.
16. Madani, P.; Vlajic, N. Robustness of deep autoencoder in intrusion detection under adversarial contamination. In Proceedings of the 5th Annual Symposium and Bootcamp on Hot Topics in the Science of Security, Raleigh, NC, USA, 10–11 April 2018; pp. 1–8.
17. Goodfellow, I.; Bengio, Y.; Courville, A.; Bengio, Y. *Deep Learning*; MIT press: Cambridge, UK, 2016; Volume 1.
18. Kim, J.; Kim, J.; Thu, H.L.T.; Kim, H. Long short term memory recurrent neural network classifier for intrusion detection. In Proceedings of the 2016 International Conference on Platform Technology and Service (PlatCon), Jeju, Korea, 15–17 February 2016; pp. 1–5.
19. Luo, W.; Liu, W.; Gao, S. Remembering history with convolutional lstm for anomaly detection. In Proceedings of the 2017 IEEE International Conference on Multimedia and Expo (ICME), Hong Kong, China, 10–14 July 2017; pp. 439–444.

20. Malhotra, P.; Ramakrishnan, A.; Anand, G.; Vig, L.; Agarwal, P.; Shroff, G. LSTM-based encoder-decoder for multi-sensor anomaly detection. *arXiv* **2016**, arXiv:1607.00148.
21. Safaric, S.; Malaric, K. ZigBee wireless standard. In Proceedings of the ELMAR 2006, Zadar, Croatia, 7–9 June 2006; pp. 259–262.
22. Zhang, Z. Improved adam optimizer for deep neural networks. In Proceedings of the 2018 IEEE/ACM 26th International Symposium on Quality of Service (IWQoS), Banff, AB, Canada, 4–6 June 2018; pp. 1–2.
23. Laxhammar, R. Conformal Anomaly Detection: Detecting Abnormal Trajectories in Surveillance Applications. Ph.D. Thesis, University of Skövde, Skövde, Sweden, 2014.

Journal of
Cybersecurity and Privacy

MDPI

Article
Model for Quantifying the Quality of Secure Service

Paul M. Simon *, Scott Graham *, Christopher Talbot and Micah Hayden

Air Force Institute of Technology, 2950 Hobson Way, Wright-Patterson AFB, OH 45433, USA;
christopher.talbot@afit.edu (C.T.); micah.hayden@afit.edu (M.H.)
* Correspondence: paul.simon.ctr@afit.edu (P.M.S.); scott.graham@afit.edu (S.G.)

Abstract: Although not common today, communications networks could adjust security postures based on changing mission security requirements, environmental conditions, or adversarial capability, through the coordinated use of multiple channels. This will require the ability to measure the security of communications networks in a meaningful way. To address this need, in this paper, we introduce the Quality of Secure Service (QoSS) model, a methodology to evaluate how well a system meets its security requirements. This construct enables a repeatable and quantifiable measure of security in a single- or multi-channel network under static configurations. In this approach, the quantification of security is based upon the probabilities that adversarial listeners and disruptors may gain access to or manipulate transmitted data. The initial model development, albeit a snap-shot of the network security, provides insights into what may affect end-to-end security and to what degree. The model was compared against the performance and expected security of several point-to-point networks, and three simplified architectures are presented as examples. Message fragmentation and duplication across the available channels provides a security performance trade-space, with an accompanying comprehensive measurement of the QoSS. The results indicate that security may be improved with message fragmentation across multiple channels when compared to the number of adversarial listeners or disruptors. This, in turn, points to the need, in future work, to build a full simulation environment with specific protocols and networks to validate the initial modeled results.

Keywords: communication model; security; metrics; probability; confidentiality; integrity

Citation: Simon, P.M.; Graham, S.; Talbot, C.; Hayden, M. Model for Quantifying the Quality of Secure Service. *J. Cybersecur. Priv.* **2021**, *1*, 289–301. https://doi.org/10.3390/jcp1020016

Academic Editor: Thaier Hayajneh

Received: 27 February 2021
Accepted: 29 April 2021
Published: 7 May 2021

Publisher's Note: MDPI stays neutral with regard to jurisdictional claims in published maps and institutional affiliations.

1. Introduction

Communication networks rely on a series of wired or wireless channels between intermediate nodes. In addition to noise, these channels may be affected by any combination of three malicious attack vectors: Denial of Service (DoS), data injection, or eavesdropping. A DoS attack may involve cutting a wire or overpowering a particular frequency (jamming). A data injection, or spoofing attack, involves the adversary sending fabricated data that takes the place of actual data. Finally, and the most difficult to discover, is an eavesdropping attack, which involves an adversary intercepting and extracting useful information from the channel. Managing those threats requires an ability to accurately gauge the likelihood or severity of the threat, and adapt the security features available in the system to meet it.

This paper describes a mathematical model for quantifying the Quality of Secure Service (QoSS) deployed in static communications networks. Just as Quality of Service (QoS) metrics describe measurable aspects of the available network, QoSS describes, in measurable and repeatable terms, the security available to an end-user, facilitating meaningful comparisons.

Even when security is momentarily adequate in a communication system, security mechanisms tend to be static, implemented at installation or while running [1], and cannot be adjusted dynamically based on changing environmental conditions or adversarial capability. This document illustrates the mathematical framework and analysis to define the design requirements for networks and provides a foundation for subsequent work analyzing dynamic network security performance in the presence of varied environmental characteristics[1]. The final model demonstrates the probability of data surviving intact against multiple forms of adversarial actions.

2. Goals and Approach

The current literature suggests three primary characteristics that define the security of traditional Information Technology (IT) systems. These are confidentiality, integrity, and availability, i.e., the CIA triad [2,3]. To quantify an overall level of security, we must have objective metrics to represent each of these individual characteristics. While objective metrics for availability are well established as QoS metrics, confidentiality and integrity [4] remain rather subjective and without commonly accepted quantifiable definitions. In addition, the user requirements for security may change based on changing operational conditions. Then, what are the appropriate measures for communication security?

To address the need, we propose a model to quantify the security characteristics of point-to-point communication between two devices[2]. The model is patterned after existing quantification models [5,6], and helps to define security requirements that, in the presence of adversarial actions, would enable communications to be successful. By comparison, this model does not rely on the application of security controls [7], but rather the analysis of the system architecture and probabilistic aspects of the network.

3. Components of a Security Model

According to Lundin [1], an equation to describe the tunable security for a communication system could be

$$TS : T \times Env \to R \tag{1}$$

where TS is the tunable security, which may be dynamically adjusted based on the user security requirements. The transmitter capabilities[3] are represented by T, the environmental descriptions are represented by Env, and the overall system security requirements are represented by R. The goal is to map the tunable security services to the system security requirements. To achieve this, the tunable security services must first be decomposed into the constituent parts, such as the available number of channels, the use or disuse of encryption, and the amount of fragmentation across the network. In many cases, the environmental descriptions are directly reflected in the traditional QoS measurements available from the service provider.

This initial version of the QoSS model is a static snap-shot, reflecting the system security at one point in time. The multiplication operator in Equation (1) does not adequately address the numerous non-linear relationships between system capability and environmental aspects. Instead, QoSS captures those factors as an array of features or values and then relates the transmitter capabilities and the environmental description to the CIA triad, where confidentiality, C, and integrity, I, replace the transmitter capabilities, and availability, A, replaces the environmental descriptors.

Security measures are typically subjective. To achieve objectivity, we substitute measurements of confidentiality and integrity with the probability of each, designated as $P(C)$ and $P(I)$, respectively, as discussed in subsequent sections. Although it is unconventional to consider a DoS attack as impacting data integrity (described in subsequent sections), doing so has the added benefit of collecting all adversarial influences into the metrics for confidentiality and integrity, leaving only the system and network capabilities to be considered as availability. Availability is a specific set of objective performance metrics, or QoS, provided by the transmitter, e.g., data or bit rate, jitter, bandwidth, transmission frequency, or power. The resulting QoSS equation is

$$QoSS : [P(C), P(I), A] \to Security\ Requirements \tag{2}$$

representing a snapshot of QoSS metrics mapped to the security requirements. If the array of metrics does not directly map to the security requirements, then the QoSS for that network is inadequate, and the system must be redesigned. The array of metrics also provides a foundation to perform one-to-one comparisons between two networks.

3.1. Probability of Confidentiality

Numerous researchers have attempted to quantify confidentiality with varying success [8,9]. Confidentiality is the aspect of a network that protects against unauthorized message receipt, i.e., preventing an eavesdropper from either receiving or decoding messages. One approach to quantifying confidentiality is to redefine it as a probability so that

$$P(C) = 1 - P(l) \qquad (3)$$

where $P(C)$ is the probability of confidentiality and $P(l)$ is the probability of leakage. Leakage refers to an untrusted listener having access to an "information flow from secret inputs to public outputs" [10]. Inspired by Perfectly Secure Message Tranmission (PSMT) [11], the set of all adversarial listeners, A_L, maps to a set of wires (channels), σ, that the listeners have access to; if one of the members of A_L has access to the information, then the probability of leakage exists.

For leakage to occur, a listener must intercept the message, decrypt it (if applicable), and then decode the data contained in the message. The probability of interception, $P(int)$, quantifies the probability that a listener with channel access will receive the message. The probability of decryption, $P(dcr)$, quantifies the probability that the adversary will decrypt it[4]. Finally, the probability of decoding, $P(dco)$, quantifies the probability that an adversary will decode the message[5].

Consider the relationship between the probabilities of interception, decryption, and decoding. For data leakage to occur, an adversary must be able to achieve all three actions, i.e., decryption is irrelevant if the adversary is unable to receive any messages. Conversely, receiving every transmission ever sent is irrelevant if an adversary is unable to decrypt or decode the messages. The logical binary relationship of how $P(l)$ relates to $P(int)$, $P(dcr)$, and $P(dco)$ is captured in Table 1. The proposed equation to describe $P(l)$ in terms of $P(int)$, $P(dcr)$, and $P(dco)$ is

$$P(l) = P(int) \times P(dcr) \times P(dco). \qquad (4)$$

Table 1. Logical binary relationship for the probability of leakage.

P(int)	P(dcr)	P(dco)	P(l)
0	0	0	0
0	0	1	0
0	1	0	0
0	1	1	0
1	0	0	0
1	0	1	0
1	1	0	0
1	1	1	1

3.2. Probability of Integrity

Quantifying integrity is equally challenging. Integrity is a measure of the consistency, accuracy, and trustworthiness of data. Integrity implies that data has not been changed by unauthorized users in transit. One method of quantifying integrity is the "prevention of unauthorized modification of information" [10]. Under this assumption, unauthorized modification is *corruption*, resulting in

$$P(I) = 1 - P(c) \qquad (5)$$

where $P(I)$ is the probability of integrity and $P(c)$ is the probability of corruption. Corruption here captures any damage to integrity yielding "two notions of corruption" where the "first leads us to a measure that we call *contamination*" and the "second leads us to ... *suppression*" [10]. Contamination may arise from adversarial action, *injection*, or non-adversarial input, *noise*. Further, an adversary may carefully inject portions of false data (a spoofing attack), inject massive amounts of false data to disable communications (the traditional DoS attack), or overtly jam a message with a false signal (traditional RF jamming).

Therefore, we choose to classify DoS attacks as being an attack on the integrity of the data or message, not as an attack on the availability of the network. Again, inspired by PSMT [11], the set of all adversarial disruptors, A_D, maps to a number of wires, ρ, that the disruptors have access to; if one of the members of A_D has access to the information, then the probability of corruption exists.

We, therefore, posit that corruption has three components: noise, data suppression, and data injection. The probability of noise occurring in a message, $P(n)$, is the probability that a message will be adversely affected by noise. Noise is a natural phenomenon that happens regardless of the transmitter's capability. The probability of suppression, $P(s)$, quantifies the probability that an adversary will suppress or jam the message, thus, preventing the receiver from obtaining the message[6]. Finally, the probability of injection, $P(inj)$, quantifies the probability that an adversary will inject false data into the message. $P(inj)$ requires the ability to insert malicious data into a data stream, a much more sophisticated activity than that of jamming[7]. Since noise is a natural phenomenon, it is consistently present and may influence $P(s)$ and $P(inj)$. Noise works cooperatively with $P(s)$ since both cause the receiver to incorrectly receive the intended message. Based on these probabilities, the logical binary relationship for $P(c)$ is shown in Table 2 and reflected as

$$1 - P(c) = \big(1 - P(n)\big) \times \big(1 - P(s)\big) \times \big(1 - P(inj)\big). \tag{6}$$

Equation (6) does not adequately capture the behavior of the system. Noise may be detrimental to data injection, making the injected data unusable. Due to the interaction between $P(n)$ and $P(inj)$, namely that noise affects both intended and malicious transmissions, a more comprehensive equation is

$$P(c) = \Big(\big(1 - P(n)\big) \times P(inj)\Big) + \big(P(n) + P(s)\big) - \big(P(n) \times P(s)\big)$$
$$- \Big(\big(1 - P(n)\big) \times P(inj) \times \big(P(n) + P(s)\big)\Big). \tag{7}$$

While less elegant than Equation (6), Equation (7) provides realistic results that account for all probabilities between 0 and 1 for each of the factors.

Table 2. Logical binary relationship for the probability of corruption.

P(n)	P(s)	P(inj)	P(c)
0	0	0	0
0	0	1	1
0	1	0	1
0	1	1	1
1	0	0	1
1	0	1	1
1	1	0	1
1	1	1	1

3.3. Availability

Methods exist for assessing and improving the performance of a system based on QoS measures [12]. For the QoSS model, the metrics used to describe availability are already conveyed in the QoS metrics. This is reflected as $A = QoS$, where QoS is the set of metrics that include cost, jitter, latency, bandwidth, and bit rate, which already provide a repeatable method of measuring availability.

3.4. Multiple Channels

Using multiple channels can improve the performance of data-in-transit in diverse ways. A straightforward example is directly increasing the data rate, such that additional channels provide more bandwidth, e.g., channel bonding within IEEE 802.11 [13–16]. Another example is frequency hopping through multiple channels, which is one of several techniques known as the spread spectrum and which provides protection from noise or jamming as the signal is "spread across a channel greater than that necessary to transmit the information" [17]. This technique is currently used in Bluetooth, and such transmission diversity is also a key element of 5G wireless [18,19].

An example of data-at-rest performance improvement through multiple channels is found in the Redundant Array of Inexpensive Disks (RAID) architecture. Developed in 1987, RAID demonstrated that by utilizing redundancy, an array could be more reliable than any one disk drive while allowing greater data throughput (In a RAID array, data is split across various disks so that if one disk should fail, the data may be fully recovered despite not having all the original blocks of data. Various combinations of nested RAID levels may be used to reduce the vulnerabilities of simultaneous disk failures [20]. The data may also be encrypted before or after splitting, or both, as a manner of increasing confidentiality.). Despite significant overhead, the ability to survive disk failures has made it very attractive in critical server environments.

Many applications in control systems maintain separate channels for data and control. For example, in SS7[8], the signaling path is separate and distinct from the voice channels that carry the telephone conversation. Having different channels, at different frequencies and differing bandwidths, allows for greater flexibility and higher-speed communications between network assets without the need to rely upon the availability or limitations of analog voice channels (In reality, these two channels are not entirely separated. The dual-tone, multi-frequency (DTMF) digits dialed by a caller begin within the voice channel, but are recognized by the control channel and are an example of the signaling messages, including dialing a phone number, entering control functions like call-forwarding, or advanced billing information [21,22]).

An abstract form of multi-channel communication is two-factor authentication (2FA), a subset of multi-factor authentication. This is an authentication methodology that requires a user to present two or more pieces of evidence to confirm the user's identity via separate delivery paths[9] [23]. By using multiple authentication factors sent via divergent paths, the likelihood that both messages are intercepted decreases. Even if a malicious actor intercepts one factor, full authentication by the malicious actor cannot occur without intercepting the other. Numerous other forms of 2FA also exist [24].

Central to the theme of this paper, *multiple channel* architecture may also be used to improve security through data fragmentation across heterogeneous channels [25–28]. This security focused capability, in concert with the performance advantages of multi-channel communications, is the motivation for creating a tunable multi-channel communication protocol and associated analysis techniques to determine the appropriate trade-offs under varying security and performance requirements.

4. The Quality of Secure Service Model

Although a communication network typically uses only one network channel between two given nodes, the possibility exists to utilize multiple paths between nodes, as shown in Figure 1. This figure shows an arbitrary network with eight individual channels, any of which may be used to transport data. A message sent through the network in Figure 1 may travel across one of the channels influenced by the set of adversarial listeners, A_L, or the set of adversarial disruptors, A_D.

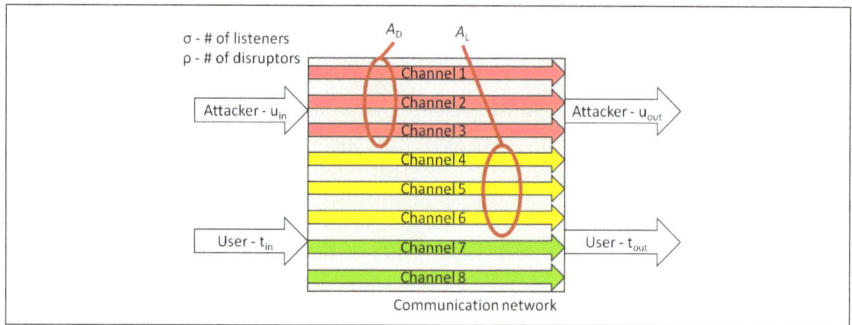

Figure 1. A network configuration with multiple possible channels.

The relationship between listeners, disruptors, and the total number of needed channels is described by PSMT, which "abstract[s] away the network entirely and concentrate[s] on solving the Secure Message Transmission Problem" for a single transmitter and receiver pair [11]. Additional articles explore multi-channel architectures [29,30], while others strive to prove the general case and optimize the statistical reliability and secrecy [31,32].

In our model, σ represents the number of wires (channels) between the transmitter and receiver available to the adversarial listener set, A_L, and ρ is the number of channels between the transmitter and receiver available to the adversarial disruptor set, A_D[10]. Communication is two-way between the transmitter and receiver and, following PSMT, the number of channels that must exist between transmitter and receiver is given by

$$n \geq max\{\sigma + \rho + 1;\ 2\rho + 1\}. \tag{8}$$

With this equation, we know how many channels must be used to maintain secure and reliable communication. If a channel is unavailable, then it must not be counted as part of n. If we assume the number of channels accessible to a listener or disruptor, then we can arrive at a specific quantification of n. For example, when $n = 8$ and $\sigma = 3$, the probability that any one channel of the eight could be listened to is 0.375. The probability of leakage for each channel within a multi-channel architecture becomes

$$P(l) = \frac{P(int) \cdot P(dcr) \cdot P(dco) \cdot \sigma}{n}. \tag{9}$$

Similarly, the probability of corruption for each channel within multi-channel architecture becomes

$$P(c) = \frac{\left(\begin{matrix}(1-P(n))P(inj) + (P(n)+P(s)) - (P(n)P(s)) \\ -(1-P(n))(P(n)+P(s))P(inj)\end{matrix}\right)\rho}{n}. \tag{10}$$

Therefore, the more channels there are in a network, the lower the probability of adversarial interference of the data[11]. This, then, follows the premise of PSMT: to have more channels than the combined set of listeners and disruptors $A_L \cup A_D$.

In the same manner that multiple channels may thwart adversarial interference, message fragmentation may also thwart eavesdropping. Message fragmentation is the splitting of data across the available channels, effectively parallelizing the data. Fragmentation describes how many portions the original message is divided into. Various methods of fragmentation are possible, including uniform or non-uniform fragmentation from 1-bit to the total m-bits in message M. Research has been published on particular approaches to fragmentation [28,33]; however, in this paper,we focus on the security effects and apply the assumption that fragments are of equal size across the network. If C_n is the set of n channels, and F_M is the set of k fragments of $1 \leq |f_i| \leq m$-bits of the message M, then

$$F_M = \{f_{(M,1)}, f_{(M,2)}, f_{(M,3)}, \ldots, f_{(M,k)}\} \tag{11}$$

$$f_{(M,i)} \subseteq M \text{ for } 1 \leq i \leq k \tag{12}$$

where each fragment is unique. The channel load, L, is the percentage of M on a particular channel j, such that

$$L_{(j,M)} = \frac{\sum_{i=1}^{n} |f_i| \text{ for } f_i \in C_{(j,M)}}{|M|} \tag{13}$$

and the Average Loading (AL) for the set of channels is

$$AL_M = \frac{\sum_{i=1}^{n} L_{(j,M)}}{n}. \tag{14}$$

For example, $F_M = \{f_1, f_2, f_3, f_4, f_5, f_6, f_7, f_8\}$ is the set of eight fragments of message M on a network that has $n = 8$ channels, and each channel transmits two fragments. Therefore, $AL = 0.25$. Message fragmentation also allows for duplicating data across channels. The Duplication Factor (DF) measures the average number of times a given fragment is transmitted, indicating the network redundancy. The DF may increase as compensatory tuning for known adversarial interactions. For the previous example, $DF = 2$, since each fragment is sent across two channels and, thus, duplicated twice. For these calculations of DF and AL, the fragment sizes are uniform.

The AL and DF directly affect $P(C)$ and $P(I)$. Of the constituent parts of $P(C)$, $P(int)$ is only affected by DF in aggregation across all channels because the probability of interception of a single channel is not necessarily improved by duplication or fragmentation. However, $P(int)$ may be increased by the message M being duplicated across multiple channels, offering an adversary more opportunities to intercept portions of the message.

Therefore, DF is only multiplied by $P(int)$ when averaging all the channels into a composite probability of leakage. For the constituent parts of $P(I)$, duplication directly affects $P(s)$ because sending fragments multiple times decreases the probability of lost data through suppression. $P(n)$ and $P(inj)$ are not directly influenced by duplication. Thus, $P(s)$ is divided by DF for each channel, giving

$$P(c) = \frac{\left((1-P(n))P(inj) + \left(P(n) + \frac{P(s)}{DF}\right) - \left(P(n)\frac{P(s)}{DF}\right) - (1-P(n))\left(P(n) + \frac{P(s)}{DF}\right)P(inj) \right)\rho}{n}. \tag{15}$$

Fragmentation does not necessarily increase or decrease $P(s)$ except that it allows for duplication. However, fragmentation does directly affect $P(inj)$ since each fragment sent needs to be modified by the adversary in order to have malicious data accepted at the receiver. Thus, $P(inj)$ is multiplied by AL for each channel, giving

$$P(c) = \frac{\left((1-P(n))P(inj)AL + \left(P(n) + \frac{P(s)}{DF}\right) - \left(P(n)\frac{P(s)}{DF}\right) - (1-P(n))\left(P(n) + \frac{P(s)}{DF}\right)P(inj)AL \right)\rho}{n}. \tag{16}$$

Applying the PSMT and decomposing the network into constituent channels yields

$$QoSS : \begin{bmatrix} P_1(C), & P_1(I), & QoS_1 \\ P_2(C), & P_2(I), & QoS_2 \\ \vdots & \vdots & \vdots \\ P_n(C), & P_n(I), & QoS_n \end{bmatrix} \rightarrow Sec\ Reqs, \tag{17}$$

which highlights that each channel has its own characteristics. From the end-user perspective, only the aggregated QoSS for the entire network is apparent. With insight into each channel's QoSS, an analyst may suggest a different quantity of channels, different fragmentation or duplication, or a different encoding or encryption algorithm if adversarial actors attempt to influence communications.

5. Case Studies of Multi-Channel QoSS

The three example networks presented here are used to highlight the initial estimates and are intended to be refined as the network understanding is increased. For simplicity, the probabilities used in the following examples are discrete values; however, any value between 0 and 1 is possible. In developing the QoSS model, estimating the intermediate values is a challenge. As a starting point, 0 may be used for a network that has absolutely no encryption, 0.5 may be used for a system that has minimal or sub-standard encryption, and 1 may be used for a system that employs strong encryption.

Incremental changes may be employed as desired or as needed after a baseline understanding is developed, much like understanding the incremental difference between AES-128 and AES-256, or the difference between DES, triple-DES, and AES. The primary goal of the initial model development is to apply estimates for each of the constituent elements as implied by [34]. Further refinement of those estimates may be applied after more thorough system analyses.

During the early stages of analysis, the difference between a probability of 0.76 and 0.77 remains undefined and the numbers tend to be more arbitrary. This serves to assign a starting point for analysis, thus, establishing a baseline. Given the three example networks that follow and some initial probabilistic estimates for the various characteristics, the QoSS model is applied. Each case has a realistic configuration that allows for one-to-one comparison.

5.1. Single-Channel Network

The first example is a network that utilizes a single wireless channel to provide a realistic baseline. With $n = 1$, there is $\sigma = 1$ listener, and $\rho = 1$ disruptor. $AL = 1$ because the message cannot be split, and $DF = 1$ since, for this architecture, the message is only sent once. Table 3 shows notional probabilities for a network that has no encryption, standard data encoding, and a moderate probability of interception because it uses a standard broadcast frequency and a moderately strong broadcast signal, which also results in a low probability of noise.

We assign a high probability of suppression under the assumption of an omnidirectional receiver, susceptible to jamming. The probability for injection is moderately high, though not as high as the probability of suppression, because injection is more challenging than suppression. These values serve as a baseline to demonstrate the effects of multiple channels in the subsequent examples.

Table 3. Input and output values for a single-channel network.

Channel	$P(int)$	$P(dcr)$	$P(dco)$	$P(l)$	$P(C)$	$P(n)$	$P(s)$	$P(inj)$	$P(c)$	$P(I)$
1	0.5	1	1	0.5	0.5	0.25	1	0.33	0.9381	0.0619

Based on these constraints, the single-channel network has a high probability of leakage, with a corresponding probability of confidentiality. The probability of corruption is also very high, with a correspondingly low probability of integrity. These probabilities may be improved by using encryption and by using directional receivers or a wired connection.

5.2. Three-Channel Network

The second example applies PSMT to the communication architecture, and demonstrates the initial application of multiple channels. In this example, the communication network uses three discrete, heterogeneous channels to communicate between the transmitter and the receiver. For this example, $n = 3$, $\sigma = 1$ listener, and $\rho = 1$ disruptor. One difference between the single channel case and the three-channel case is the AL. The original message is fragmented into three equal portions, f_1, f_2, and f_3, which are each transmitted twice as follows: $\{f_1, f_2\}$ on Channel 1, $\{f_2, f_3\}$ on Channel 2, and $\{f_3, f_1\}$ on Channel 3. For this case $AL = 0.66$, and $DF = 2$ (because each fragment is sent twice).

Table 4 shows the theorized characteristics for a network with various probability of interception and fixed values for probability of decryption and decoding. Additionally, Table 4 shows that the network has various probabilities of injection with fixed values for probability of noise and suppression.

Channel 1 has identical input factors to the single-channel network as demonstrated in Table 3; however, the message is fragmented across multiple channels, which causes the probability of confidentiality and probability of integrity to increase, not only for Channel 1, but for each channel in the network[12]. The average probability of confidentiality is 0.83 even without encryption, indicating that fracturing data across the multiple channels improves the probability of confidentiality and over-all QoSS, partially mitigating the lack of encryption.

Table 4. Input and output values for a three-channel network.

Channel (n)	$P_n(int)$	$P_n(dcr)$	$P_n(dco)$	$P_n(l)$	$P_n(C)$	$P_n(n)$	$P_n(s)$	$P_n(inj)$	$P_n(c)$	$P_n(I)$
1	0.5	1	1	0.1667	0.8333	0.25	1	0.33	0.2219	0.7781
2	0.75	1	1	0.2500	0.7500	0.25	1	0.4	0.2248	0.7752
3	0.25	1	1	0.0833	0.9167	0.25	1	0.26	0.2191	0.7809
Avg	0.5	1	1	0.1667	0.8333	0.25	1	0.33	0.2219	0.7781

5.3. Eight-Channel Network

The third example presents a communication network with eight discrete, heterogeneous channels. In this example, $n = 8$, $\sigma = 3$ listeners, and $\rho = 3$ disruptors. The original message is fragmented into eight equal portions, $\{f_1, f_2, ..., f_8\}$, of which $\{f_1, f_2\}$ are transmitted on Channel 1, $\{f_2, f_3\}$ on Channel 2, $\{f_3, f_4\}$ on Channel 3, and so on. Here, $AL = 0.25$, and $DF = 2$ because each fragment is sent twice. Table 5 shows the theorized input for the eight-channel network.

Of particular note, Table 5 has the same input as Table 4 for Channels 1–3, and other values for Channels 4–8, although with different results[13]. The only difference from the three-channel case is that, with eight channels, the message is fragmented across more channels, causing the confidentiality and integrity to increase. The average values for $P(int)$, $P(dcr)$, and $P(dco)$ are the same for the single-channel, three-channel, and eight-channel networks, although the average $P(l)$ and $P(C)$ are notably different.

Table 5. Input and output values for an eight-channel network.

Channel (n)	$P_n(int)$	$P_n(dcr)$	$P_n(dco)$	$P_n(l)$	$P_n(C)$	$P_n(n)$	$P_n(s)$	$P_n(inj)$	$P_n(c)$	$P_n(I)$
1	0.5	1	1	0.1875	0.8125	0.25	1	0.33	0.2402	0.7598
2	0.75	1	1	0.2813	0.7188	0.25	1	0.4	0.2414	0.7586
3	0.25	1	1	0.0938	0.9063	0.25	1	0.26	0.2389	0.7611
4	0.2	1	1	0.0750	0.9250	0.25	1	0.05	0.2353	0.7647
5	0.35	1	1	0.1313	0.8688	0.25	1	0.1	0.2361	0.7639
6	0.4	1	1	0.1500	0.8500	0.25	1	0.2	0.2379	0.7621
7	0.7	1	1	0.2625	0.7375	0.25	1	0.6	0.2449	0.7551
8	0.85	1	1	0.3188	0.6813	0.25	1	0.7	0.2467	0.7533
Avg	0.5	1	1	0.1875	0.8125	0.25	1	0.33	0.2402	0.7598

As expected, the single-channel network has the lowest theorized QoSS values. With a slightly higher percentage of listeners, the eight-channel network has a slightly higher $P(l)$ and correspondingly lower $P(C)$ than the three-channel network[14]. Similarly, the average values for $P(n)$, $P(s)$, and $P(inj)$ are the same for the single-channel, three-channel, and eight-channel networks, yet the $P(c)$ and $P(I)$ are significantly different.

5.4. Implications of Results

The most difficult aspect of developing the QoSS metrics is making assumptions about the network characteristics. For these examples, we began with an assumption that $P(dcr) = 1$ was a baseline value that an adversary would be able to access all critical data. What does this mean for $P(dcr) = 1$? Perhaps the assumption implies that no encryption is used, despite the fact that the use of encryption is strongly encouraged for all communications systems.

Similarly, is this possible for $P(dcr) = 0$? This assumption implies that the encryption is unbreakable at this time and under these communication and environmental conditions. The fact that we do not know the adversary's fullest capabilities, nor do we know the adversary's intentions, are considerations that must be included, within a range, in the estimate for the probabilistic aspect of our metrics. More accurately, we estimate what is possible within the current state-of-the-art and under a set of operational characteristics.

Adversarial intention is much more difficult to estimate; intentions may change rapidly or may vary on a case-by-case basis. In light of that, we have attempted to reflect all the adversarial intentions, whether it is jamming, spoofing, or eavesdropping, within the generalized probability of confidentiality and probability of integrity. With these estimations, both adversarial capability and intention are difficult to concretely quantify in the initial pass, and they are, thus, cast in probabilistic terms.

This version of the QoSS model is a single snap-shot in time; a time-varying QoSS model is in development in which the model estimations may be updated based on new research, information, or changing environmental and systemic conditions. As the QoSS model becomes more mature and broadly adopted, future iterations will benefit from increased understanding of these probabilistic approaches and an initial coarse estimate for design requirements may converge to refined security requirements if applied in an iterative manner.

These iterations point directly to the eventual need for a simulation environment and all the supporting protocols that allow for the verification and validation of the security metrics. To achieve that end, the network performance will need to be influenced by a simulated adversarial actor, and the amount of data leakage or corruption will be directly quantified based on the amount of transmitted data. Only with that final step of validation will we be certain that the model portrays a realistic version of a communication network.

6. Conclusions and Future Work

This manuscript represents an initial model intended to be used in developing an understanding of how real-world networks function in the presence of adversarial influence. The current analysis does not address the nuances of specific communication scenarios, and there is no existing network to validate our model. Quantifying security in real-world communication networks is difficult and mostly subjective. Without a metric for confidentiality and integrity, it is nearly impossible to state how secure one network is compared to another.

Using a probabilistic model that considers data leakage and data corruption in place of confidentiality and integrity, a set of metrics may be used to quantify the QoSS. This model allows the direct and repeatable quantification of the security available in a single- or multi-channel network under static configurations. The quantification of security is based directly upon the probabilities that adversarial listeners and disruptors are able to gain access to or change the original message.

Traditional measurements of QoS provide a foundation, and message fragmentation and duplication across the available channels provide demonstrably improved theoretical performance. A fully developed simulation would be useful in validating the modeled results. However, at this time, there is no existing network or simulation of a real network to validate the theoretical QoSS model. A simulation environment is in the process of development in order to include the ability to estimate an adversary's influence, as are the experiments and the network prototype that will be used to test the theoretical QoSS model.

Two additional manuscripts are nearing completion that will address two of the many thorny issues contained within real networks—in particular, multi-hop networks and the changes to the QoSS metrics that occur over time. This future work may require building specific data-handling protocols, and would monitor how the network end-points respond. With the simulation environment developed, the modeled results may be verified and the QoSS model may be validated or improved with additional data and insight.

Author Contributions: Conceptualization, P.M.S., S.G. and C.T.; refinement, P.M.S., S.G. and M.H.; methodology, P.M.S. and S.G.; software, P.M.S.; validation, P.M.S.; investigation, P.M.S.; resources, P.M.S.; writing—original draft preparation, P.M.S.; writing—review and editing, P.M.S., S.G. and M.H.; All authors have read and agreed to the published version of the manuscript.

Funding: This research was funded in part by the Air Force Institute of Technology, Center for Cyberspace Research (CCR).

Institutional Review Board Statement: This article does not contain any studies with human participants or animals performed by any of the authors.

Informed Consent Statement: Not applicable.

Acknowledgments: The views expressed in this paper are those of the authors, and do not reflect the official policy or position of the United States Air Force, Department of Defense, or the U.S. Government. This document has been approved for public release.

Conflicts of Interest: All authors declare that they have no conflict of interest.

Notes

1.   Analysis of the dynamic aspects of mobile networks or tunable security mechanisms is left for a subsequent paper, as are changing environmental conditions and temporal adversarial intrusions.
2.   Multi-hop architectures are outside the scope of this paper but are a straightforward extension of the model that will be addressed in a subsequent paper.
3.   Wired and wireless networks have different characteristic values based on the specific technologies and protocols used.
4.   This value reflects the quality of the encryption used, be it no encryption, a simple ROT13 algorithm, or a sophisticated encryption algorithm.
5.   This value highlights the differences in binary strings, and if the adversary has the ability to recognize those differences. For example, an adversary with a .mp3 file who mistakenly believes it is a .txt file, will not be able to derive useful information from that particular file.
6.   To clarify, $P(s)$ is the active jamming by an adversary as quantified at the receiver, whereas availability is quantified by the transmitter's capabilities.
7.   As the adversarial intent of suppression is counter to that of injection, it is unlikely, although not impossible, to have high $P(s)$ and high $P(inj)$. This would be akin to an adversary steering a receiving channel to a compromised channel by jamming the intended channel. Neither of these speaks directly to the intent of an adversary but rather to the requirements and built-in capabilities of the transmitter and receiver.
8.   Signaling System Number 7 (SS7) was developed in 1975 as a set of protocols used to set up and tear down public switched telephone network (PSTN) communication connections.
9.   The user's identity is verified by using a combination of two or more factors: something they know, something they have, or something they are.
10.   In the general case, A_L or A_D may be subsets of or intersect with each other; i.e., $A_L \subseteq A_D$, or $A_D \subseteq A_L$ or $A_L \cap A_D$.
11.   One potential implication is that each channel may carry both a portion of the data and be used as a method to check for errors on the others channels
12.   In a real communication architecture, all three channels would likely have more similar characteristics.
13.   As in the Three-Channel example, a real communication system would likely have channels with similar characteristics.
14.   Note the number of channels with respect to Equation (8) for this multi-channel space. For the eight-channel network, $n = 8$ even though seven channels would be sufficient based on $\sigma = 3$ listeners, $\rho = 3$ disruptors, and Equation (8).

References

1. Reine, L.; Lindskog, S.; Brunstrom, A. A Model-based Analysis of Tunability in Privacy Services. In *IFIP International Summer School on the Future of Identity in the Information Society*; Springer: Boston, MA, USA, 2007.
2. Hughes, J.; Cybenko, G. Quantitative metrics and risk assessment: The three tenets model of cybersecurity. *Technol. Innov. Manag. Rev.* **2013**, *3*, 15–24. [CrossRef]
3. Jabbour, K.; Poisson, J. Cyber risk assessment in distributed information systems. *Cyber Def. Rev.* **2016**, *1*, 91–112.
4. Wang, J.A.; Xia, M.; Zhang, F. Metrics for information security vulnerabilities. *J. Appl. Glob. Res.* **2008**, *1*, 48–58.
5. Duan, Q. Modeling and analysis of end-to-end quality of service provisioning in virtualization-based future Internet. In Proceedings of the 2010 Proceedings of 19th International Conference on Computer Communications and Networks, Zurich, Switzerland, 2–5 August 2010.
6. Firoiu, V.; Le Boudec, J.Y.; Towsley, D.; Zhang, Z.L. Theories and models for internet quality of service. *Proc. IEEE* **2002**, *90*, 1565–1591. [CrossRef]
7. Leon, P.G.; Saxena, A. An approach to quantitatively measure information security. In Proceedings of the 3rd India Software Engineering Conference, Mysore, India, 25–27 February 2010.
8. Clarkson, M. Quantification and Formalization of Security. Ph.D. Dissertation, Cornell University, Ithaca, NY, USA, 2010. Available online: https://ecommons.cornell.edu/handle/1813/14744 (accessed on 15 March 2021).
9. Nikhat, P.; Beg, M.R.; Khan, M.H. Model to quantify confidentiality at requirement phase. In Proceedings of the 2015 International Conference on Advanced Research in Computer Science Engineering & Technology (ICARCSET 2015), Unnao, India, 6–7 March 2015.
10. Clarkson, M.R.; Schneider, F.B. Quantification of integrity. *Math. Struct. Comput. Sci.* **2015**, *25*, 207–258. [CrossRef]
11. Dolev, D.; Dwork, C.; Waarts, O.; Yung, M. Perfectly secure message transmission. *J. ACM (JACM)* **1993**, *40*, 17–47. [CrossRef]
12. Almerhag, I.A.; Almarimi, A.A.; Goweder, A.M.; Elbekai, A.A. Network security for QoS routing metrics. In Proceedings of the International Conference on Computer and Communication Engineering (ICCCE'10), Kuala Lumpur, Malaysia, 11–12 May 2010.
13. Faridi, A.; Bellalta, B.; Checco, A. Analysis of dynamic channel bonding in dense networks of WLANs. *IEEE Trans. Mob. Comput.* **2016**, *16*, 2118–2131. [CrossRef]
14. Han, M.; Khairy, S.; Cai, L.X.; Cheng, Y. Performance analysis of opportunistic channel bonding in multi-channel WLANs. In Proceedings of the 2016 IEEE Global Communications Conference (GLOBECOM), Washington, DC, USA, 4–8 December 2016.
15. Lee, S.; Kim, T.; Lee, S.; Kim, K.; Kim, Y.H.; Golmie, N. Dynamic Channel Bonding Algorithm for Densely Deployed 802.11 ac Networks. *IEEE Trans. Commun.* **2019**, *67*, 8517–8531. [CrossRef]
16. Bukhari, S.H.R.; Rehmani, M.H.; Siraj, S. A survey of channel bonding for wireless networks and guidelines of channel bonding for futuristic cognitive radio sensor networks. *IEEE Commun. Surv. Tutor.* **2015**, *18*, 924–948.
17. Cook, C.; Marsh, H. An introduction to spread spectrum. *IEEE Commun. Mag.* **1983**, *21*, 8–16. [CrossRef]
18. Gao, J.; Zhang, Y.; Liu, Y. A novel diversity receiver design for cooperative transmission system. *IEEE Access* **2018**, *6*, 27176–27182. [CrossRef]
19. Moulika, V.; Bhagyalakshmi, L. Performance Investigation of Cooperative Diversity Techniques for 5G Wireless Networks. In Proceedings of the 2019 IEEE 1st International Conference on Energy, Systems and Information Processing (ICESIP), Chennai, India, 4–6 July 2019.
20. Hennessy, L.J.; Patterson, D.A. *Computer Architecture: A Quantitative Approach*; Elsevier: Amsterdam, The Netherlands, 2011.
21. Russell, T. *Signaling System # 7*; McGraw-Hill: New York, NY, USA, 2002; Volume 2.
22. Modarressi, A.R.; Ronald, A.S. Signaling system no. 7: A tutorial. *IEEE Commun. Mag.* **1990**, *28*, 19–20. [CrossRef]
23. Shankar, K.S. Special feature the total computer security problem: An oveview. *Computer* **1977**, *10*, 50–73. [CrossRef]
24. Archana, B.S.; Chandrashekar, A.; Bangi, A.G.; Sanjana, B.M.; Akram, S. Survey on usable and secure two-factor authentication. In Proceedings of the 2017 2nd IEEE International Conference on Recent Trends in Electronics, Information & Communication Technology (RTEICT), Bangalore, India, 19–20 May 2017.
25. Ciriani, V.; Vimercati, S.D.C.; Foresti, S.; Jajodia, S.; Paraboschi, S.; Samarati, P. Combining fragmentation and encryption to protect privacy in data storage. *ACM Trans. Inf. Syst. Secur. (TISSEC)* **2010**, *13*, 1–33. [CrossRef]
26. Feng, L.; Zhang, Y.; Li, H. Large file transmission using self-adaptive data fragmentation in opportunistic networks. In Proceedings of the 2015 Fifth International Conference on Communication Systems and Network Technologies, Gwalior, India, 4–6 April 2015.
27. Mikko, P.; Keranen, A.; Ott, J. Message fragmentation in opportunistic DTNs. In Proceedings of the 2008 International Symposium on a World of Wireless, Mobile and Multimedia Networks, Newport Beach, CA, USA, 23–26 June 2008.
28. Wampler, J.A.; Chien, H.; Andrew, T. Efficient distribution of fragmented sensor data for obfuscation. In Proceedings of the MILCOM 2017—2017 IEEE Military Communications Conference (MILCOM), Baltimore, MD, USA, 23–25 October 2017.
29. Abdel-Rahman, M.J.; Shankar, H.K.; Krunz, M. QoS-aware parallel sensing/probing architecture and adaptive cross-layer protocol design for opportunistic networks. *IEEE Trans. Veh. Technol.* **2015**, *65*, 2231–2242. [CrossRef]
30. Pohly, D.J.; Patrick, M. Modeling Privacy and Tradeoffs in Multichannel Secret Sharing Protocols. In Proceedings of the 2016 46th Annual IEEE/IFIP International Conference on Dependable Systems and Networks (DSN), Toulouse, France, 28 June–1 July 2016.
31. Desmedt, Y.; Wang, Y. Perfectly secure message transmission revisited. In *International Conference on the Theory and Applications of Cryptographic Techniques*; Springer: Berlin/Heidelberg, Germany, 2002.

32. Srinathan, K.; Arvind, N.; Pandu, C.R. Optimal perfectly secure message transmission. In *Annual International Cryptology Conference*; Springer: Berlin/Heidelberg, Germany, 2004.
33. Hudic, A.; Islam, S.; Kieseberg, P.; Rennert, S.; Weippl, E.R. Data confidentiality using fragmentation in cloud computing. *Int. J. Commun. Netw. Distrib. Syst.* **2012**, *1*, 1. [CrossRef]
34. Sweet, I.; Trilla, J.M.C.; Scherrer, C.; Hicks, M.; Magill, S. What's the Over/Under? Probabilistic Bounds on Information Leakage. In *International Conference on Principles of Security and Trust*; Springer: Cham, Switzerland, 2018.

MDPI AG
Grosspeteranlage 5
4052 Basel
Switzerland
Tel.: +41 61 683 77 34

Journal of Cybersecurity and Privacy Editorial Office
E-mail: jcp@mdpi.com
www.mdpi.com/journal/jcp